SOVIET RUSSIA IN WORLD POLITICS

SOVIET RUSSIA
IN WORLD POLITICS

by Robert D. Warth

Twayne Publishers, Inc.
New York 3

Copyright © 1963 by Twayne Publishers, Inc.

Library of Congress Catalog Card Number: 62–19358

TO TERRY

Printed and Bound by The Book Press, Brattleboro, Vermont

AUTHOR'S NOTE

This book claims no "inside information" and presents no certain answers to the "riddle of the Kremlin." But it does attempt to provide an accurate, objective, and reasonably complete historical account of Soviet foreign relations within the confines of a single volume. I am well aware that no subject could be more controversial and emotionally charged, and I am under no delusion that my efforts will receive unanimous approbation. Soviet publicists will undoubtedly consign the work to the Marxist purgatory of "bourgeois-imperialist historiography." On the other hand, to many cold war crusaders in the West who feel that Communism is an evil that must be crushed instead of examined, a history rather than an indictment of Soviet policy is in itself a suspect enterprise. Whether the record has been set forth with detachment and intellectual honesty the reader must, of course, decide for himself.

So much by way of apologia. The final product is my responsibility, but it is a pleasant duty to thank those who have made the task easier. My wife, to whom the book is dedicated, smoothed the routine impedimenta of authorship, including the onerous chore of typing the manuscript. Jacob Freid was a patient and discerning critic whose advice, while not invariably accepted, was always welcome. Staige Blackford was most diligent in helping to eliminate stylistic infelicities. Joseph Freeman took a keen interest in the project and supplied first-hand impressions of the Chicherin-Litvinov era. Louis Fischer, Philip Jaffe, Edward R. Tannenbaum, Fritz T. Epstein, William E. Stokes, and Monica Kelly also read and commented on various portions of the manuscript. Duke University Press kindly permitted me to use material previously published in my THE ALLIES AND THE RUSSIAN REVOLUTION (1954).

CONTENTS

SOVIET RUSSIA IN WORLD POLITICS

CHAPTER ONE

THE TSARIST LEGACY

On the eve of World War I, Tsar Nicholas II, the last and one of the weakest of Russia's hereditary monarchs, ruled an empire of approximately 175,000,000 people and 8,660,000 square miles. By far the largest country in the world, this immense land mass sprawling across the northern hemisphere of two continents excited both fear and envy in Russia's smaller neighbors. But their attitude was not unmixed with contempt, for this "giant with feet of clay" had for centuries lagged behind the advanced nations of Europe. Russia seemed bound to the archaic traditions of Oriental despotism: the parliamentary, industrialized society of the West was still an alien civilization. With a half-literate and overwhelmingly agricultural population, an antiquated social and economic system designed for the benefit of the landed gentry, and a political leadership devoid of initiative and ideas, the Tsar's "absolute" authority rested on a fragile base soon to crumble beneath the punishing blows of the Imperial German Army.

That so backward a nation could be ranked as a "great power" in 1914 was proof that Russia's leadership in the jungle of international politics had not always been inept. It was through victory over powerful neighbors—Sweden, Poland, and Turkey—that Russia in modern times won her place as a ranking power. Prior to her clash with these formidable rivals, the impact of the Muscovite state upon European civilization had been slight indeed. Isolated from the forces that were gradually removing the stamp of "medievalism" from the features of Western society, the Russian people experienced no equivalent economic and cultural resurgence. Even their semblance of national unity had been lost under two-and-a-half centuries of Tartar domination; and it was not until the fifteenth century that it was regained in a measure through the expansion of the once tiny principality of Moscow.

Under a succession of able sovereigns, Muscovy parried the Tartar threat. Simultaneously the lengthy process began of "gathering in the

Russian land"—of absorbing the territory which had once belonged to the old Kiev State. So successfully was this accomplished—albeit at the cost of almost continual warfare—that by the reign of Ivan IV ("the Terrible," 1533–1584) Muscovy had become strong enough to challenge the powerful Polish-Lithuanian state for the control of the Baltic littoral. Though the effort failed, less strategic areas were carved from the receding Tartar domain. These conquests were endangered, as were the painfully acquired lands of Ivan's predecessors, by the incompetence of his heir and the final extinction of the old Rurik dynasty in 1598. That Russia survived at all during the ensuing "Time of Troubles"—a period of civil war, peasant revolt, and foreign intervention—is a tribute to the national feeling of the Russian people and a commentary on the blunders of her enemies.

Michael Romanov, the founder of a new dynasty, was chosen Tsar in 1613. Under his rule and that of his son Alexis (1645–1676), Russia slowly regained her internal strength. It was also a period when absolutism was re-established as a firm principle of government with the bonds of serfdom securely fastened upon the peasant. In external affairs the old feuds with Sweden and Poland were resumed, and in 1667 the latter ceded the eastern half of the Ukraine to Russia after years of exhausting warfare. Despite this impressive revival after the misfortunes at the beginning of the century, the Russian state remained virtually landlocked. Only through the ice-bound port of Archangel did it possess a precarious water route to the West. The Baltic coast, the prize which had so long eluded Russia's grasp, was not to be obtained until the country had been shaken to its foundations by the strongest and most illustrious of its Tsars—Peter the Great (1682–1725). His reign was an epic struggle against sloth and ignorance at home and the "natural" enemies of Russia abroad. In neither sphere was his victory complete, but he bequeathed to his successors a nation which, for good or ill, has ever since been transfused into the bloodstream of Western civilization.

It was war, especially the Northern War (1700–1721), which drained the energies of Petrine Russia and brought her close to disaster on more than one occasion. The Tsar's famed antagonist, Charles XII of Sweden, like Napoleon at a later day, chafed at the restraint of only partial success and eventually lost all. Beaten in the heart of the Ukraine at Poltava (1709), Charles refused to admit defeat. But three years after his death in 1718, Sweden succumbed to the strain of two decades of incessant warfare against a shifting coalition of enemies, and by the Treaty of Nystadt surrendered the Baltic provinces to Russia. The conquest of this "window on the West" was a fitting climax to Peter's life and compensated to some extent for the hardships and brutalities of his reign. Left to the future was the problem of the Ottoman Empire, a declining but powerful state blocking the warm-water approaches to the Black Sea and the Mediterranean. Peter had gained a foothold in the Azov area only to lose it as he became embroiled in the Swedish war.

The assets which the great Tsar had so conscientiously assembled were freely dissipated during the "Epoch of Palace Revolutions" (1725–1762) that followed. Foreign policy was a secondary concern as the throne became the plaything of contending factions of the upper nobility. Of the half dozen sovereigns who nominally ruled in the next thirty-seven years, only one—Elizabeth (1741–1762)—could be said to have attained some degree of competency. During her reign Russia was drawn into a major conflict involving the Western powers for the first time. This was the Seven Years' War (1756–1763), in which England wrested a great colonial empire from France and an exhausted Prussia outlasted the armies of Austria, France, Russia, and Sweden. More than any other single event, it was Elizabeth's death that saved Prussia from defeat and probable dismemberment. The new Tsar, Peter III, abruptly withdrew his troops, cancelling a considerable investment in blood and treasure, although it had been made in a war that was scarcely in the national interest.

By bizarre and offensive conduct Peter annulled his small stock of good will in record time: in six months he was overthrown in a *coup d'etat* engineered by his wife, the future Catherine II (1762–1796). Catherine's personality, native ability, and veneer of Western culture long overshadowed her unprogressive domestic record and won for her the accolade of "Catherine the Great." Her foreign policy, if little else, was perhaps astute enough to justify the use of that term. She succeeded where Peter the Great had failed in obtaining for Russia permanent access to the northern shore of the Black Sea. The area was won by two wars with the Turks which, though decisive, merely set the stage for the "Eastern question"—one of the perpetual international tangles of the nineteenth century.

Catherine's second major triumph, the partitions of Poland, represents the pinnacle of Machiavellian diplomacy in a century noted for the amorality of its dynastic and political rivalries. The odium which later and less callous generations have attached to the deed is partially mitigated by the unexampled selfishness with which the Polish magnates allowed their country to become a virtually defenseless "geographical expression" and a standing invitation to aggression. It seemed to Catherine, as it did to Frederick the Great of Prussia and

Maria Theresa of Austria, that the dismemberment of Poland was the lesser of several alternative evils, among which a major European war seemed the most likely. The first partition (1772) deprived that hapless state of over a fourth of its territory and almost a third of its population. Russia, though she received by far the largest slice, was the only power with a legitimate claim to the newly annexed territory on ethnic and religious grounds. Most of this area today is included in the Byelo-Russian Republic of the U.S.S.R.

A belated political and cultural regeneration in Poland was cut short by a second partition in 1793. Catherine found a pretext for intervention when a group of dissident Polish nobles requested Russian aid. Except for a portion of the spoils donated to Prussia to assure a benign attitude toward the proceedings, the remainder of Poland was divided into two parts: one, the western Ukraine and most of Lithuania, which was incorporated into the Russian empire; the other, a rump state centered to the northeast of Warsaw, which retained its "independent" status. In 1794 a patriotic rising led by Thaddeus Kosciusko was crushed by Russian and Prussian troops, and a third and final partition by Russia, Prussia, and Austria obliterated Poland from the map of Europe. But the end of Poland was by no means the end of the Polish problem. At the close of the First World War the defeat of all three partitioning powers allowed the restoration of a sovereign Poland with boundaries which fell short of those of 1772.[1]

Catherine did not live to enjoy her final triumph over Russia's ancient enemy. Nor were her last years entirely serene and filled with a proud sense of accomplishment, for the specter of the French Revolution haunted her—as it did the other monarchs of Europe. Preoccupied with Polish affairs, Catherine failed to carry out her fanciful project of extirpating the Jacobin heresy with a counter-revolutionary army. Her son and successor, Paul I (1796–1801), in seeking to reverse his mother's policies wherever possible, abandoned the idea of aggressive action against France. However, the amazing victories of a young French general by the name of Napoleon Bonaparte eventually induced Paul to revise his pacific attitude in the light of the altered balance of power in Europe and the Near East. While Bonaparte was engaged in his Egyptian campaign Russia joined England and Austria in an alliance against France. Her most famous general, Alexander Suvorov, was recalled from retirement to command an expeditionary force which, in collaboration with the Austrians, was to drive the French from northern Italy. Despite some early victories in the spring of 1799, Austria's sabotage of Suvorov's strategy and the defeat of a combined Anglo-Russian army in a campaign against the French in the Netherlands resulted in Russia's decision to withdraw from the war. In a complete reversal of his foreign policy, the erratic Tsar then sought friendly relations with France and had devised a bizarre scheme to strike at Britain through an attack upon India when he was murdered in a palace revolution reminiscent of the dethronement of his father in 1762.

Paul's eldest son, a somewhat hesitant party to the plot, assumed power as Alexander I (1801–1825). The new ruler, while young and inexperienced, was determined to pursue his own course, and the first years of his reign were a welcome contrast to Paul's despotic regime. Alexander, like Catherine, had absorbed an ill-digested dose of Western liberalism, and in pursuit of a vaguely defined policy of "enlightenment" he introduced a few measures of reform without in any way disturbing the traditional Russian pattern of autocracy and serfdom.

In foreign policy ventures Russia was granted a moratorium. The expedition to India was recalled, and a period of cautious neutrality followed—unbroken until 1805 when Napoleon's European designs provoked a third coalition against France. Austria was soon detached from the alliance by Napoleon's brilliant victory at Austerlitz in which the Russian army was also severely mauled. Prussia, supplanting vanquished Austria, fared little better. By 1807 Russia was the sole land power on the continent capable of disputing French hegemony. At Friedland that summer the French veterans proved superior to Alexander's troops, but Napoleon was wary of prolonging the duel on Russian soil. Both rulers were anxious for a truce; and at a famous meeting on a raft moored between the banks of the Niemen River— the boundary between Prussia and Russia—the Peace of Tilsit was hammered out at the expense of the lesser powers.

Tilsit only postponed an inevitable clash and an invasion of Russia as fatal to Napoleon's fortunes as it had been to those of Charles XII. The dramatic events of 1812, immortalized in Leo Tolstoy's epic novel *War and Peace*, need no repetition here. Even after the catastrophic retreat of the Grand Army, the Napoleonic empire did not collapse until 1814. The dramatic epilogue which interrupted the Congress of Vienna—Napoleon's escape from Elba and the battle of Waterloo— was ended when the great conqueror was dispatched to a petulant martyrdom on the island of St. Helena in the South Atlantic.

Perhaps the thorniest problem of the peace conference was the disposition of the Duchy of Warsaw, Napoleon's artificial creation wrested from the Polish territory of Prussia and Austria. Russia received as the largest share of the disputed area the land which became the semiautonomous Kingdom of Poland under a liberal constitution. The peace settlement was guaranteed by the terms of the Quadruple Alliance, a pact which called for periodic consultation on European problems and led to armed intervention in Spain and Italy to suppress revolutionary outbursts. The liberals of that day and since have often confused the secret Quadruple Alliance—after 1818 the Quintuple Alliance—with the innocuous but highly publicized Holy Alliance. The latter was Alexander's inspiration, a meaningless document pledging the rulers of Europe to follow the Christian precepts of peace, justice, and charity. It had no real importance except as a misunderstood symbol of extreme political reaction.

By 1815 the Tsar's domestic policies had become increasingly conservative—in sharp contrast to his reputation abroad as an eccentric and even dangerous liberal. Prince Metternich, the Austrian chancellor, regarded him with unconcealed suspicion until Alexander proved amenable in the later years of his reign to the "Metternichean system" of suppressing liberal and revolutionary movements wherever they might occur. In matters of ideology, Nicholas I, who became emperor following his brother's death in 1825, was closer to the Austrian chancellor's ideal of the instinctive reactionary. But his willingness to aid the Greek rebels against their Turkish overlords—for reasons of state rather than sympathy with revolution—was the first major breach in the wall of reaction that Metternich had so tirelessly erected in Europe. Soundly beaten once more by Russia, Turkey was forced to acknowledge the independence of Greece and to make other concessions in her Balkan domain which left the door ajar for Russian intervention at some future date.

Although Nicholas was willing to countenance rebellion when it served Russian interests, the merest hint of disaffection at home was rigorously suppressed. This was the fate of the Decembrists, the ringleaders of a badly managed conspiracy of liberal army officers, at the beginning of his reign. Such, too, was the fate of the Polish rising of 1830–1831. As punishment "Congress Poland" lost its constitution and was subjected to stern measures of Russification. The regime was so stifling that the conservative rule of Catherine II seemed to the intelligentsia a veritable golden age of political and intellectual freedom. As the "gendarme of Europe," Russia stood ready to extinguish the noxious weed of popular rebellion wherever it might occur.

In 1848–1849 a revolutionary outburst threatened the very existence of absolute monarchy on the European continent. The Tsar's timely offer to assist the beleaguered sovereigns of Prussia and Austria—due as much to fear of another Polish revolt as to his natural hatred of liberalism—was gratefully accepted by the young Austrian emperor,

Francis Joseph. A Russian army of 150,000 men poured into Hungary from Congress Poland, and Austrian troops moved in from the west. The Magyar rebels, riddled with dissension and short of supplies, bowed to overwhelming force. The Hapsburg empire was restored, politically and territorially. In the German states the frightened monarchs who had granted liberal constitutions hastened to repair these lapses from conservatism. Once again it seemed to Nicholas that the world had been made safe for autocracy.

II

At mid-century the power of Russia never seemed greater; and if she was the *bête noire* of liberal Europe, it was a matter of pride to her ruler, who had staked his faith and reputation on the superiority of unrelieved reaction as the first and best principle of government. There were many in Russia as in the West who failed to share the Tsar's premises; only a few were bold enough to contend that the Russian colossus was a sham and a fraud, rotten within and feeble without. Yet within a few years, war, the ultimate proving ground for any regime, shattered the myth of Russian invincibility and exposed the weakness of her archaic social system.

The Crimean War, the only major European conflict in the century of comparative peace between the Congress of Vienna and the First World War, was an outgrowth of Russia's continuing designs in the Balkans and her interference in the affairs of Turkey, the chronic "Sick Man of Europe." With misplaced confidence in British neutrality and Austro-Prussian benevolence, Russia blundered too far down the path of aggression, and the Turks declared war in the fall of 1853. The annihilation of the Turkish navy by Russia's Black Sea fleet precipitated Anglo-French intervention to preserve the sagging Ottoman Empire from further deterioration. Even Austria made belligerent moves, fulfilling the astute prediction made at the time of the Hungarian rising by her foreign minister, Prince Schwarzenberg, that Austria would some day "astonish the world by her ingratitude."

After some difficulty and considerable delay in locating a suitable arena for military operations, the Crimean Peninsula became the focal point of hostilities. Sevastopol, the chief fortress and naval base on the peninsula, was besieged for nearly a year by Allied troops. A courageous defense was effectively sabotaged by the incompetence of the Tsar's vaunted bureaucracy. Similar mismanagement plagued the besiegers, who finally seized the stronghold in September 1855 and ended the military phase of what has been called the most inexcusable war in modern history. Though Russia was checked in her steady encroachment upon the Ottoman Empire, the setback was merely temporary: within fifteen years the peace settlement—the Treaty of Paris (1856) —had become a dead letter. As has happened more than once in Russian history, defeat was a spur to domestic reform. Nicholas died during the course of the war, the bankruptcy of his system evident even to himself. His eldest son and heir, Alexander II (1855–1881), to all appearances an equally devoted champion of reaction, won the accolade of "Tsar Liberator" for his emancipation of the serfs in 1861. Yet impersonal necessity, not the reforming instinct, dictated the great emancipation and the reforms that followed. As Alexander put it so succinctly in his memorable statement to the Moscow nobility in 1856: "It is better to begin to abolish bondage from above than to wait for the time when it will begin to abolish itself spontaneously from below."

Although Alexander's Russia was scarcely a working model of enlightened despotism, the glaring weaknesses revealed by the Crimean War were sufficiently overcome to allow her an ambitious role in the European power struggle. The steady Russian expansion eastward, though of special concern to the British Foreign Office, was relatively unnoticed by the European public. By the turn of the century hapless China became the terminus of rival imperialisms. Russian explorers and colonizers had long before stretched the Tsar's domain to the Pacific Ocean—and beyond—but for the most part it remained an unpopulated wilderness whose value was dimly perceived. A later acquisition—Central Asia—was an ill-defined territory under the hazy sovereignty of Moslem potentates. The final absorption of this area in the early 1880's placed Russia squarely on the flank of British interests in India and the Middle East.

Russia reasserted its supremacy in the Black Sea, and bolstered by the Three Emperors' League (an alliance of Russia, Austria-Hungary, and Germany signed in 1873), made tentative moves to regain its prerogatives in the Balkans. The fierce nationalism of the southern Slavs and the blundering of their senile Turkish masters continued to operate in Russia's favor. The upshot was another in that long chain of Russo-Turkish wars dating from the seventeenth century—a conflict between "the one-eyed and the blind," as the chief of the German general staff appropriately labeled it. Turkey—the "blind" in this case —sued for peace early in 1878 as Russian troops threatened Constantinople.

Ample retribution for the Crimean defeat had hardly been extracted from the Turks before the major powers intervened to demand a revision of the peace terms. At the Berlin Conference in the summer of 1878 Russia was forced to accept a repartition of the Balkan territories to insure Austria-Hungary a larger role in the future affairs of the peninsula. Russian patriots, outraged but impotent, witnessed the second humiliation of their country within a single generation. The Berlin settlement was fatal to the Three Emperors' League. An attempt to revive the alliance in 1881 was doomed by traditional Balkan rivalries. Not until the early nineties did Russia find in republican France a reliable diplomatic partner and thus the illusion, if seldom the reality, of increased security. The Franco-Russian combination—ideologically uncomfortable to both sides—remained a stable prop in the European alliance system through the outbreak of war in 1914.

The cementing of close and friendly relations with France coincided with heightened Russian ambitions in the Far East. Geographical propinquity and astute diplomacy—among other reasons—enabled Russia to embrace Manchuria as a sphere of influence while the other powers sought to acquire choice portions of the Chinese melon. Russia's hold was tightened by the construction of the Chinese Eastern Railroad across northern Manchuria, a strategic link between the Trans-Siberian line and the port of Vladivostok on the Pacific. In 1898 southern Manchuria was likewise "integrated" when the Russian government was granted a twenty-five year lease on the tip of the Liaotung Peninsula for the purpose of building a naval base, maintaining a commercial port, and constructing a railroad northward to connect with the Chinese Eastern. One of the ironies of great power diplomacy was that Japan, victorious in her war with China in 1894–1895, had been forced to abandon her newly won position on the same peninsula because of the "advice" emanating from St. Petersburg, Berlin, and Paris.

A resentful Japan was not likely to be the best of neighbors, especially to a power as insatiable as Russia was becoming under Nicholas II (1894–1917) and his inner clique of Far Eastern "experts." Not content with Manchuria, these adventurers urged expansion into Korea and northern China. The Japanese had considered Korea ("a dagger pointed at the heart of Japan") their special preserve since the Sino-Japanese War and were unwilling to countenance flagrant Russian interference. Tokyo proved conciliatory up to a point, but when St. Petersburg declined to compromise, war was the result. On February 8, 1904, the Japanese fleet struck without warning and with devastating effect at Port Arthur, Russia's new naval base on the Liaotung Peninsula.

Few Europeans entertained the improbable notion that the tiny island nation of Japan was a match for the mighty empire of the

Tsars. The series of military and naval defeats that Russia suffered was therefore all the more shocking to Western sensibilities, for the easy stereotype of Oriental inferiority was by now engrained in the white man's ethos. "A little victorious war to stem the tide of revolution"—a phrase ascribed to the Russian minister of the interior—was not forthcoming. Neither little nor victorious, the war also failed to forestall revolution. Rather it hastened the onset of a popular upheaval which in the summer and fall of 1905 almost overthrew the Romanov dynasty along with the established social order. That revolution failed —or to be more precise, was postponed for twelve years—did small credit to the health of the state since the war was terminated before the political structure had been drastically weakened.

The peace conference was held in the late summer of 1905 at Portsmouth, New Hampshire, under the good offices of President Theodore Roosevelt. Having approached financial and military exhaustion, Japan was unable to achieve at the conference table a status equal to her position on the battlefield. The Japanese delegates accordingly found it necessary to modify their demands and grudgingly accepted the southern half of the island of Sakhalin, a free hand in Korea, and the former Russian sphere in southern Manchuria in lieu of more favorable terms. Not until 1945 did a radically different and far more powerful Russia lay claim to the Tsarist legacy in the Far East.

Chastened by defeat abroad and revolution at home, Russia entered an era which her middle class liberals hoped would witness the remodeling of the nation along the lines of Western parliamentary democracy. In a moment of desperation the Tsar had conceded a representative assembly—the Duma—to end an unbroken tradition of dynastic absolutism. Unfortunately for advocates of bourgeois constitutionalism as the answer to Russia's ills, the Duma never became more than a façade for the cumbersome bureaucratic despotism so often found wanting in past crises and destined to collapse ignominiously in the greater crisis to come. On the surface, however, all was serene, and to nostalgic Russian *émigrés* of a later day the decade following the war with Japan would seem in comparison an age of peace and material progress.

Without defaulting from established foreign policy objectives, Russian diplomacy became considerably less venturesome. This was of necessity true in the Far East, where a partition of Manchuria into a northern (Russian) and a southern (Japanese) sphere of influence was arranged in 1907 and confirmed by later treaties. Europe replaced Asia as the center of Russia's immediate aspirations. The prevailing alliance system presented a hard choice between the budding Anglo-

French entente and the traditional Austro-German partnership. Largely because of the explosive Balkan situation, St. Petersburg viewed Austrian maneuvers with customary misgivings and sought a *rapprochement* with England. The growth of Germany as an industrial and military power had done much to lessen British fear of the Russian menace, and in 1907 an Anglo-Russian convention concerning their respective spheres in the Middle East marked the beginning of the Triple Entente of Britain, France, and Russia.

But a strengthened diplomatic front could not compensate for military weakness. In 1908 Austria's annexation of Bosnia and Herzegovina —nominally Turkish provinces—precipitated a crisis which a more powerful Russia might have resolved by means of war. Serbia, Russia's "little Slav brother," was infuriated by the transaction since she considered the two provinces ethnically if not legally hers. Serbo-Austrian relations were so embittered that the Bosnian question may be regarded as one of the major political causes of World War I.

Russia's diplomats, determined never again to lose face should a similar occasion arise, played an ever more perilous role in the labyrinth of Balkan politics. As the architect of the Balkan League (Serbia, Greece, Bulgaria, and Montenegro), Russia fought a veiled war by proxy with Turkey in 1912 when her protégés attacked and all but drove the Turks from Europe. Although the practical benefits which a truncated Ottoman Empire would confer upon Russia were partially squandered by a war among the victors, by the summer of 1914 St. Petersburg could view the diplomatic scene in the Middle East and elsewhere with more equanimity than at any time since the Port Arthur disaster.

Historians have long concluded that no one power or combination of powers was responsible for the "Great War" (as the war of 1914–1918 was called in a less hardened age). Yet the major powers, as well as some of the smaller ones, engaged in such reckless pursuit of the "national interest" that the end result could only be an armed clash. The share of "war guilt" which should properly be assigned to Russia has never been settled satisfactorily, nor is it likely to be. There can be no question, however, that her contribution to the ultimate disaster was very great. That the assassination of the Austrian heir apparent, Archduke Francis Ferdinand, on June 28, 1914, in the Bosnian capital of Sarajevo, should have been the incident which unleashed upon the world a new era of mass destruction was of course a wholly fortuitous event impossible to foretell. Indeed, for more than three weeks after the most fateful political murder in modern times there was no visible threat to peace. Only when Austria dispatched a forty-eight hour ultimatum to Serbia on July 23 did the signs of a new international crisis become apparent. With assurances of diplomatic support from St. Petersburg, the Serbian reply fell short of giving complete satisfaction to the severe Austrian demands. Every subsequent effort to localize the impending conflict proved futile.

On July 28 Austria declared war on Serbia. Too late Germany discovered that the "blank check" she had presented her ally was being filled in for an exorbitant amount. On the 30th the Tsar yielded to the importunities of his advisers and consented to general mobilization. One of the military axioms of the day was that "mobilization means war," and Russia became the first of the powers to place her armed forces on a full war footing. Austria mobilized the next day; France and Germany on August 1. Formal declarations of war came quickly, with England the last to declare herself. As one historian has put it: "The inexorable logic of interlocking measures of military preparedness . . . actually precipitated the unwanted conflagration."[2]

III

Russia had one great asset to contribute to victory in a general European war: manpower. If it had not proved sufficient in the Crimean or the Japanese wars, neither did Russia then have powerful allies as military, industrial, and financial bulwarks. But there was no time to philosophize on the chances of victory or defeat: war was an accomplished fact permitting no second guesses. The lumbering Russian "steamroller" gained momentum with unaccustomed speed and smashed into East Prussia against token opposition. The bulk of German strength was deployed on the western front, where the French, together with the British expeditionary force, were being prepared for a knockout blow. But the French rallied to win the critical battle of the Marne: Paris was saved. Had the German high command chosen to ignore a plea for reinforcements in East Prussia the decision might have been reversed. As it was, the two army corps sent to relieve the eastern front arrived after the Russians had suffered overwhelming defeat at Tannenberg. Thereafter, except for the less forbidding Austrian sector, the Russian army was powerless to maintain a sustained offensive.

The first months of the conflict revealed grave deficiencies which in two years would bring the Russian war effort to a standstill. The economy was handicapped from the outset by a policy of calling up recruits regardless of skills and occupations. Lacking proper training facilities, munitions, equipment, and clothing—of every resource by which modern wars are fought—the army's reliance upon unlimited quantities of flesh and blood was an inadequate but unavoidable substitute. With Allied help, some of the pressing needs of both the military and civilian economy were gradually overcome. In other spheres Russia's partners were helpless, for the regime seemed bent upon political suicide. The early days of the war had witnessed an apparent surge of patriotic fervor vastly reassuring to those who feared that the wave of strikes and political demonstrations in the early summer of 1914 heralded a return to the stormy days of 1905. But when military defeat took its toll of morale, as it did of dead and wounded, the reservoir of good will left to the dynasty emptied rapidly. The Tsar himself had neither the ability to lead nor the wisdom to follow. The Empress, though of stronger moral fiber, was innocent of political judgment and lost in her own neurotic world of superstitious piety. Irresistibly attracted to religious charlatans, she clung for advice to Gregory Rasputin, the unsavory "holy man" whose hidden political power—exaggerated but substantial—rested upon his presumed ability to curb the hemophilic bleeding of their son Alexis, the heir to the throne.

If Nicholas showed little disposition to "be Peter the Great," to "crush them all under you" (as his wife urged upon one occasion),[3] he did have that quality of stubborn and indiscriminate "firmness" which often conceals a weak-willed nature. His decision in 1915 to assume direct command of the armed forces; his uncanny knack of dismissing ministers of integrity for blundering incompetents; and his studied insults to the Duma all revealed, if not stupidity, at least a dangerous isolation from reality. Nothing can be more feeble than an autocracy without an autocrat—and the Russian Revolution was to prove once again the validity of that ancient political maxim.

Diplomacy, often a neglected art during wartime, flourished as an adjunct to the military and ideological aims of the belligerents. In 1915, in gross contradiction to pretensions of exclusive virtue, the Allied powers began to negotiate the notorious secret treaties outlining the future disposition of enemy territory. Since the participation of Turkey in the war on the side of the Central Powers was an open invitation to dismemberment, she was partitioned in a series of agreements which left Russia—on paper—in possession of Constantinople, the Straits of the Bosphorus and Dardanelles, and certain portions of Asiatic Turkey. Russia's "historic mission" at long last seemed close to realization. England and France were conceded much of the remainder of the Ottoman Empire in addition to spheres of influence in other areas of the Middle East. Italy, too, was granted a slice of the Sultan's realm for entering the war in 1915, although the promise of Austrian territory along the Adriatic and the Alps was the real inducement to desert her partners in the Triple Alliance. Rumania, bribed with Transylvania and other parts of the Austrian empire, joined the Allies in 1916. Shortly before the fall of the monarchy a final agreement was concluded allowing Russia freedom to determine her western frontier in return for supporting French ambitions along the Rhine. The bargain was kept secret from Britain, whose diplomats were apparently uninformed until the Bolsheviks published the details late in 1917.

By the fall of 1916, despite a successful offensive against Austria during the summer months, an alarming rate of desertion—some estimates ran as high as a million in November—furnished a revealing clue to the state of morale in the army. Chronic food shortages in the cities, coupled with a 300 per cent rise in prices from the pre-war level, prepared the ground for defeatist propaganda among factory workers and troops on garrison duty. Even the conservative and patriotic members of the Duma grew restive and dared to attack the "dark forces" around the throne. On December 2, in an effort to combat war weariness, the nation was informed of the secret agreement concerning Constantinople and the Straits. Except for a few tired phrases in the chauvinist press, the news was received with complete apathy.

Reports of separate peace negotiations and of pro-Germanism in high places, while almost wholly unfounded, occasionally agitated London and Paris. The Entente ambassadors in Petrograd (as the capital was now called in patriotic deference to the Slavic rather than the German spelling) faithfully reported the surface phenomena of Russian life, of which the Rasputin scandal was the most colorful. It became an article of faith among the upper classes that his baneful influence, once removed, would somehow purify the dynasty and restore the throne to its pristine glory. But the malady went far deeper, as the assassination of Rasputin on December 30 soon revealed. The royal couple retreated farther into their own private world and refused every measure by which the monarchy might yet be salvaged. Neither the candid warnings of the British ambassador nor those of the Duma president persuaded the Tsar that the fate of his dynasty was at hand.

The Duma met on February 27, 1917, as striking factory workers, orderly but sullen, crowded the streets of the capital. Ill-founded rumors of military *coups* and palace revolutions circulated among the deputies. It seemed only a question of time before a sham revolution from above—to save the monarchy in spite of itself—or a genuine revolution from below would remove the uncertainty of who or what would fill the political vacuum.

NOTES

1. See below, p. 85.
2. Michael T. Florinsky, *Russia* (New York, 1953), II, 1319.
3. *Letters of the Tsaritsa to the Tsar, 1914–1916* (London, 1923), p. 455.

CHAPTER TWO

REVOLUTIONARY DIPLOMACY: BOURGEOIS AND BOLSHEVIK

When in the second week of March 1917 the eagerly-awaited and long-predicted Revolution made its initial appearance, few recognized the symptoms of genuine revolt. Boisterous crowds milling in the streets were an uncommon occurrence in Russia, but such demonstrations do not ordinarily decide the fate of a nation. Yet with almost ridiculous ease the anonymous masses of Petrograd toppled the three-hundred-year-old House of Romanov from the throne of the Tsars.

By March 12 the defection of the garrison had dissolved any lingering doubts about the success of the Revolution. A committee of prominent Duma deputies tentatively assumed the functions of authority, more anxious to salvage the monarchy than to govern in the name of the unruly workers and soldiers of the capital. Following the Tsar's abdication and the prudent refusal of his brother, Grand Duke Michael, to acept the risky position of constitutional sovereign, the Provisional Government, chosen by the Duma committee, was faced with the self-appointed task of guiding the primitive forces of the Revolution into patriotic and "respectable" channels. The objectives of the new regime could hardly have been otherwise, for it was dominated by Constitutional Democrats ("Kadets"), members of the liberal bourgeois party. Their leader, the distinguished historian Paul Milyukov, accepted the post of minister of foreign affairs but was clearly the strongest figure in the government. His power was nominally secondary to that of the premier, Prince Georgi Lvov, who had achieved a reputation for his social welfare work during the war as head of the Union of Zemstvos.

Until its demise in November, the Provisional Government seldom exercised more than a show of power. Real authority lay within the Petrograd Soviet of Workers' and Soldiers' Deputies, a unique forum of revolutionary democracy which had first appeared during the turmoil of 1905. Soviets (councils) quickly spread to other parts of the country, and as the chosen representatives of the proletariat and peasantry these bodies more nearly reflected the actual state of popular opinion than the "legal" government. Only the moderate political complexion of the Petrograd Soviet's Executive Committee, respectfully deferential toward middle class leadership, prevented power from being thrust upon it. As the mood of the masses swung to the Left during the ensuing months, the composition of the Soviet likewise changed and the Provisional Government became as isolated from political reality as the Tsarist regime had been on the eve of its downfall.

The February Revolution[1] was followed with fascinated interest throughout the world. The Allied countries, of course, received the news with gratified surprise, for the upheaval was innocently regarded as a kind of anti-German uprising brought about by the Duma as a patriotic duty. Russia's allies could see only a revitalized and democratic nation purged of Tsarist tyranny and thus capable of renewed sacrifices in the common cause. The war weariness which had sparked the Revolution in the first place was misunderstood or conveniently ignored. The collapse of the Russian autocracy conferred at least one tangible benefit upon the Entente: Anglo-French war propaganda, crippled by the embarrassing presence of Tsarist Russia on the "democratic" side, was free to indulge in even more extravagant claims about the purity of the Allies and the wickedness of the enemy. In the case of the United States, then preparing to join the Allied coalition as an "associated" power, the Revolution was especially timely. President Woodrow Wilson, whose rationale for American intervention was couched in rather apocalyptic terms, noted in his war message (April 2) the "heartening things which have been happening within the last few weeks in Russia." He hailed with enthusiasm this new partner which had joined forces in "fighting for freedom in the world, for justice, and for peace."

The leaders of the Provisional Government, though they should have known better, behaved as if the Allied interpretation of the Revolution was eminently correct. They contemplated no departure from the foreign policy of the old regime. A manifesto on March 20 proclaimed Russia's determination to bring the war to a "victorious conclusion" and faithfully to observe "all alliances uniting us to other powers and all agreements made in the past." In private conversations with the British and French ambassadors Milyukov was more explicit: the war would be prosecuted with unrelenting vigor and the secret treaties would remain in force. As the president of the Duma complacently informed the British military attaché, "Russia is a big country and can wage a war and manage a revolution at the same time."[2]

That the Provisional Government was incapable of gauging the full depths of anti-war sentiment is understandable; but the failure of the Petrograd Soviet to do more than temporize revealed that it too lagged well behind public opinion. The Soviet dilemma was exposed during the first All-Russian Conference of Soviets which met in Petrograd on April 11. It passed a resolution by an overwhelming vote in support of a defensive war. One clause called for "preserving the capacity of the army for active operations"—a policy that few soldiers would have been willing to implement by practical deeds. Yet the Soviet continued to agitate for a democratic peace "without annexation or indemnities" based upon the "free development of all peoples." Only the Bolsheviks, the dissident Left wing of the Social Democratic movement, held aloof from "defensism," though their militant leader, Vladimir Ilyich Ulyanov (Lenin), did not return from his Swiss exile until April.

The growing cleavage between the government and the Soviet could have been concealed much longer had Milyukov been willing to mask his imperialist aims behind a smokescreen of florid rhetoric. Bluntly forthright, but with appalling tactlessness, he asserted Russia's right to the Straits, and then compounded his folly by referring to the possibility of annexing Rumania and establishing a protectorate over Armenia at the end of the war. Criticism of Milyukov in the socialist press erupted into open hostility. The Soviet insisted that the government's declaration of April 7, which had incorporated some of the catch phrases of the flourishing debate on war aims, should be dispatched as a formal note to the Allies. Backed into a corner, Milyukov was obliged to agree with his colleagues that the Soviet demand was reasonable provided an "explanation" accompanied the original declaration. On the morning of May 1 a carefully edited statement, collectively composed by the cabinet, though signed by the foreign minister, was transmitted to the Western capitals. Its sonorous prose spread only a perfunctory gloss of idealism over the candid language of great power diplomacy. It was seriously maintained that the "aspiration of the entire nation to carry the world war to a decisive victory has grown more powerful," and Russia's duty to "observe the obligations assumed toward our Allies" was reiterated. The note concluded by saying that "the leading democracies, inspired by identical desires, will find the means to obtain those guarantees and sanctions [annexations and indemnities?] which are indispensable for the prevention of sanguinary conflicts in the future."

After the message had been sent abroad, it was released for domestic consumption. Without exception the attitude of the Left wing press was one of seething resentment. The Bolshevik Central Committee called for the assumption of power by the Soviet and denounced the "imperialist" government for being "tied hand and foot by Franco-British and Russian capitalism." The Soviet Executive Committee met in a special session lasting until the early morning hours of May 3 in a futile attempt to decide upon a course of action. It recessed until the forenoon when it reconvened, but the working-class districts, inclined to regard the note as a deliberate provocation, were in no mood for further compromise. In the afternoon the Finland Regiment marched to the Marinsky Palace, the site of the Provisional Government, carrying banners with a variety of anti-government slogans and demanding Milyukov's resignation. Joined by factory workers, sailors, and additional regiments of the garrison, the number of armed demonstrators approached thirty thousand. Soviet leaders arrived on the scene and quickly persuaded the soldiers to disperse. Most of them returned peaceably to their barracks; others mingled with civilians to argue and agitate on street corners. Bolshevik orators sought to enlarge the scope of the protest by turning it against the government as a whole, while Kadet partisans directed a counter-attack against Lenin, whom they charged was a German agent trying to defame the patriotic Milyukov. In reality Lenin did his best to restrain the more zealous party workers, for the Bolsheviks were still entirely too weak for such precipitate and premature tactics.

In the evening a plenary session of the Soviet convened. The prevailing mood was one of extreme bitterness toward the government, and it was all that the moderate leaders could do to placate the members and answer the popular suggestion of a Bolshevik speaker that the Soviet seize power immediately. Directly after the meeting the Executive Committee assembled in the Marinsky Palace, where the government's ministers had gathered in nervous haste to ponder their troubles. They portrayed the country as verging upon imminent disaster and intimated that it behooved every man of good will to ignore petty quarrels, such as the wording of notes and declarations, and to rally to the defense of the Fatherland and the Revolution. Prince Lvov made a half-hearted threat to resign in favor of the Soviet, knowing full well that its leaders wanted nothing so much as to avoid the responsibilities of power. On the question of a proper foreign policy the Executive Committee made a show of firmness. But Milyukov would neither consent to a new note or to being shifted to a less controversial post in the cabinet. A solution was finally worked out whereby the government agreed to "explain" certain ambiguous points in the original note.

The disturbances of May 3 were only a prologue to those of the 4th. The soldiers and workers, hearing of the pro-government demonstration arranged by the Kadets the night before, gathered for a march to the center of the city and could not be dissuaded even by the exhortations of a special Soviet delegation. Clashes with Milyukov's partisans brought firearms into play, and mysterious shots from nearby buildings, for which each side blamed the other, resulted in a number of casualties. Order was not restored until the Soviet Executive Committee decreed that no military detachments could appear in the streets without the permission of at least two of its members.

In the evening the Executive Committee voted 34 to 19 to accept the government's interpretation of the so-called Milyukov note. The Bolsheviks and Menshevik Internationalists (the anti-war Left wing of that party) voted with the minority against the resolution, a conciliatory statement to the effect that the Provisional Government, now that it had been properly chastised by the "revolutionary democracy," had indeed abandoned the deceitful foreign policy of the Tsars.

Whether or not the government actually did what was claimed for it, the explanation, which was made public the next day, avoided the equivocation of previous communications. The most questionable phrase in the Milyukov note, that concerning "guarantees and sanctions," really meant, it was asserted, "the limitation of armaments, an international tribunal, etc." Another doubtful point, the "decisive victory" over the enemy, was clarified by the expedient of quoting the declaration of April 9 as evidence of the government's purity of motive in its desire for victory. The statement was to be "handed to the diplomatic representatives of the Allies by the minister of foreign affairs," but there is no evidence that it was actually done. Rather than send another note to the Allies, "a step which would menace the country with very serious consequences," Lvov protested that the whole cabinet was prepared to resign; and he was confirmed in his stand by Milyukov. Rather prematurely, the latter declared to an American correspondent: "The government has won a great victory. Our policy remains unchanged. We have conceded nothing."

Despite the prevailing distrust of the government, the members of the Soviet upheld the recommendation of their leaders by a large majority. Outwardly the crisis was resolved; inwardly the pressure was still building. Only when the threat of violence had passed did the ministers seem to realize that they were dangerously isolated from the popular mood and that concessions were necessary if the Provisional Government was to survive on a firmer basis than the disdainful tolerance of the Soviet. The obvious answer was to bring some of the better-known Soviet leaders into the cabinet. Minister of Justice Alexander Kerensky strongly favored the idea, for his prestige as the only Soviet deputy and "socialist" member of the government had suffered because of the foreign policy crisis. His pretense that the embarrassing pronouncements of the foreign minister were only his "personal opinion" was no longer tenable. Milyukov and War Minister Alexander Guchkov vehemently opposed bringing socialists into the government, and to force the issue Kerensky himself offered his resignation—under no misapprehension, however, that it would be accepted. After several days of bickering and unseemly squabbling, Kerensky had his way. Lvov announced on May 8 the government's intention to extend its basis, for, as he put it, "the frightful specter of civil war and anarchy hovers over Russia, threatening its freedom."

On May 9 the Soviet was formally invited to appoint representatives to join the cabinet. The Executive Committee balked unexpectedly, but faced with the choice of coalition or military and economic chaos, which Kerensky painted for them in the blackest of colors, the Soviet leaders were induced to reverse their stand. Their foremost demand was that Milyukov be replaced. His successor should introduce a "vigorous" foreign policy aimed at "the speediest possible attainment of a general peace on the principle of the self-determination of nationalities without annexation or indemnities; and in particular the preparation of negotiations with the Allies with the object of securing a revision of treaties on the basis of the Provisional Government's declaration of April 9." In a world-wide appeal to socialists published the next day the Soviet denounced the war as "a monstrous crime on the part of the imperialists" while rather inconsistently condemning a separate peace as a "betrayal of the cause of the workers' democracy of all countries."

The idea of shifting Milyukov to the Ministry of Education was seized upon as the best means of easing him out of a key position without the gracelessness of demanding his resignation. Seven cabinet ministers and the Executive Committee of the Kadet party unsuccessfully urged this course upon him. He resigned on May 16, convinced that the new policy was "harmful and dangerous" to Russia's best interests. The "voluntary" nature of his departure did not prevent him from declaring before a private gathering of Duma members, "I did not withdraw but was put out." There could be no artificial distinction between the "Tsar's diplomacy" and the "Provisional Government's diplomacy," he maintained in a lengthy defense of his conduct. "We agreed with our allies that if our common efforts were crowned by a common victory we should receive a common reward for our vital needs." Without apology but not without regret, Milyukov's public career came to an end.

The reorganized cabinet included nine "capitalist" and six socialist ministers. Guchkov, who had resigned on the 13th, was replaced by Kerensky; and Mikhail Tereshchenko, a wealthy young sugar manufacturer and former minister of finance, took the foreign affairs portfolio. Lvov stayed on as premier, more a figurehead than ever. Kerensky, Tereshchenko, and Nikolai Nekrasov, a Left Kadet and the minister of communications, formed an unofficial triumvirate which largely determined policy.

Milyukov's departure removed the stigma of imperialism from the government's foreign policy, but a more positive contribution was needed. The new cabinet opposed as "absolutely inacceptable" the Soviet proposition that pressure be put on the Allies for a revision of war aims. The phrase "without acquisitive policy or punitive indemnities" was offered as a substitute for the Soviet's clear-cut formula. It was also proposed that the Soviet help restore discipline in the army, presumably for future offensive action. Ultimately a compromise was reached which each faction interpreted in its own way, just as the government's previous declarations resorted to murky prose to "solve" a fundamental difference of opinion. Such a statement was issued on May 18, in which the first point, dealing with foreign policy, rejected a separate peace while promising to work for a general peace by taking "the preliminary steps towards effecting an understanding with the Allies on the basis of the declaration made by the Provisional Government on April 9." But the second point, calling for a strengthening of the army's fighting capacity "for both defensive and offensive operations" as the most important task which the government faced, demonstrated that a general peace was considered a remote and theoretical possibility, not to be taken too seriously.

The Allied governments, concerned largely with Russia's military efficiency, carefully refrained from any hint of displeasure at this public airing of a delicate matter. The possibility of an offensive was of course a pleasing prospect, and if one ignored the Provisional Government's talk of a general peace as a mere sop to Soviet opinion— which indeed it undoubtedly was—the outlook for inter-Allied cooperation seemed distinctly favorable. But to the Soviet the possibility of a just and democratic peace was not to be lightly dismissed. It took a practical step to implement its proclamations by calling for a conference of socialists from all countries to explore the chances for a general settlement. The groundwork had already been laid by Dutch and Scandinavian socialists, who had suggested Stockholm as the meeting place; and in May the Soviet extended invitations to numerous socialist factions in Europe and the United States to send delegates to Petrograd for an informal conference. Allied officials were suspicious of peace talk, especially from a source as suspect as a committee of neutral socialists. By refusing passports to its socialists, the United States became the first country to register an official objection to the Stockholm Conference. Secretary of State Robert Lansing fatuously termed the proposed meeting a "cleverly directed German war move," and the refrain of a "Stockholm plot" quickly gained currency in the West. France and Italy soon followed the American lead, and eventually Britain also adopted the passport weapon after overriding the pro-Stockholm sentiment of the Labor party.

The Provisional Government, without notable success, tried to convey the impression at home that it was wholly sympathetic to the meeting, abroad that it was hostile. The Soviet continued to be the unfaltering champion of the conference, and it was fortunate for the government that the Bolshevik opposition to Stockholm (as a gathering of "social-chauvinists") had weakened the issue in the minds of the most militant workers and soldiers; a repetition of the May demonstration might otherwise have been a distinct possibility. The lingering death of the Stockholm project nevertheless offered an unflattering view of Allied war aims: it was another link in the chain of circumstances which lowered the prestige of the Provisional Government and the moderates in the Soviet, lending credence to the Bolshevik thesis that the war was a conflict of predatory capitalist states for colonies, markets, and raw materials.

The Soviet's conspicuous failure to obtain so much as a respectful hearing beyond the borders of Russia did not prevent its leaders, particularly those with government posts, from pursuing the notion that a victorious military offensive would rehabilitate their country's prestige and hasten that just and honorable peace for which the Allies were presumably fighting. The idea of an offensive made a special appeal to the middle class, for patriotic endeavor was accepted as an infallible antidote to the radical virus which was unaccountably infecting the masses. The Allies anticipated renewed military activity on the eastern front with enthusiasm but refrained from active pressure save through the ineffectual medium of "good will" missions, whose members strove energetically during the summer months to rekindle the war spirit among the Russian people. "The combined impression of these Anglo-French delegations on the war and on the Russian Socialists," a British observer has remarked, "can be compared to a drop of water in the saltiest of seas."[3]

Kerensky was the most vociferous of these self-appointed spokesmen for military resurgence as a means of attaining the ideals of the "revolutionary democracy." Upon assuming his new duties as war minister, he devoted his full energies and seemingly inexhaustible eloquence to the task of generating a warlike mood where none existed. Yet the army was more akin to a gigantic debating society than an effective fighting machine. As he toured the front trying to convince the troops that Germany constituted the main threat to their Revolution, he earned the jeering title of "persuader-in-chief" from his political enemies of both Left and Right but little real support for his anti-German crusade. His grandiloquent speeches, often verging on the hysterical, assured an attentive hearing and some fleeting success. Unfortunately for his cause, this shallow radicalism of the revolutionary phrase did not long convince the unsophisticated peasant soldier that a war which the Soviet denounced on the one hand as imperialist, and on the other praised as a defense of the Revolution, was a war to be expedited at the risk of one's life.

On July 1, 1917, Kerensky announced that the "Russian revolutionary army has assumed the offensive with colossal enthusiasm." A more sober appraisal would have pointed out that the attack—limited to the southwestern front—began so inauspiciously that the officers were uncertain whether the men would obey orders. Only a few units could be relied upon without question; others were openly mutinous. The advantage of surprise and the low morale of the opposing Austrian troops made possible some local gains which official communiqués claimed as major victories. The German general staff, chafing so long under a political checkrein, gladly poured in reinforcements for a counterattack. The result was a catastrophic rout. A comparative handful remained to fight; the rest fled in disorder as pillaging and outrages of all kinds testified to the collapse of all semblance of discipline.

The complete breakdown at the front had its counterpart in the rear, where a semi-revolution in Petrograd—the "July Days"—threatened the further existence of the Provisional Government. The radical temper of the workers and soldiers in the capital had so far outstripped the population elsewhere that the Bolsheviks were finding it increasingly difficult to restrain their more hot-headed partisans from overt action. Always a political realist, Lenin cautioned against revolutionary adventurism. The first days of the offensive had brought ominous signs of unrest. The resignation of four Kadet ministers on July 15 was partially responsible for bringing the crisis to a head. On the following day the smoldering discontent exploded in a fashion reminiscent of the troubles in early May, but on this occasion the armed demonstration against the government was far more serious. Had a concerted attempt been made, the key ministers and official buildings could have been captured with ease. By the 18th the tide had begun to run in the government's favor, due in great part to the release by the Ministry of Justice of some questionable documents purporting to prove that Lenin and his associates were German agents. The Bolsheviks, blamed for the insurrection, were temporarily forced underground.

An aftermath of the July Days was the formation of the second coalition government. The major change was Lvov's resignation in favor of Kerensky, thus legalizing a situation already existing in fact. Tereshchenko remained as foreign minister and sought to calm the misgivings of Russia's allies about the latest crisis with a note of explanation. "The criminal propaganda of irresponsible elements was used by enemy agents and provoked mutiny in Perograd," he reported to the foreign offices of the West. "At the same time part of the troops on the front, seduced by the same propaganda, forgot their duty to the country and facilitated the enemy's penetration of our front." He tried to avoid ending the communication on a note of pessimism, however slight, by repeating in endless variation the determination of the Russian people to fight on against its internal and external foes.[4] Since the spectacle of enemy agents armed with subversive propaganda undermining the social structure of a whole nation had a certain appeal to minds unwilling or unable to deal with the realities of a revolutionary crisis, Tereshchenko's simple explanation of his country's troubles was accepted as beyond cavil in London, Paris, and Washington.

But agreement as to the causes of Russia's plight did not assuage the feeling of exasperated irritation which the Allies made increasingly plain in their attitude toward the Provisional Government. The conservative press spoke openly of the need for a "strong man" who would, in the words of the London *Saturday Review*, "save Russia with a whiff of shrapnel." Although Kerensky had been called the "mathematical center of Russian Bonapartism," the delusion that he was the new man of destiny lasted only until a more promising candidate appeared in the person of General Lavr Kornilov, whose comparative success in the July offensive had secured for him the supreme command of the army. He was not an outspoken reactionary, for his political views were entirely too primitive; yet it was with a sure instinct that the extreme Right—industrialists, landowners, officers, Kadets, and Allied military and diplomatic personnel—sighted the banner of counter-revolution long before the object of their attentions had done so himself. His declared aim was simply to "bring the people to victory and to a just and honorable peace" by restoring discipline to the front and suppressing "anarchy" in the rear.

By late August 1917 the shadowy outlines of the conspiracy were more sharply focused. Several cavalry divisions composed of Caucasian and Cossack troops were shifted to a vantage point near Petrograd in the guise of reserves for the Finnish front. It was hoped that a Bolshevik uprising would furnish an excuse to march on the capital; failing this, "patriotic" societies within the city were prepared to fake a demonstration in order to "save" the government from Bolshevism. Kerensky's actions during this period were not above suspicion, and his critics on the Left scented treachery. The Allied governments had a more compromising record than Kerensky's in dealing with the Kornilov movement. Officially they maintained an attitude of strict neutrality; unofficially the conduct of their representatives in Russia and the tone of their most influential organs of opinion left no doubt where the sympathies of the ruling groups in Britain and France lay. In their espousal of counter-revolution can be detected the faint pattern of future Allied intervention in the Russian civil war, though in this instance it was directed against the democratic government of a friendly ally more than two months before the Bolsheviks took power.

On September 9 Kerensky ordered Kornilov to relinquish his command. In refusing, the general issued a quaint manifesto of pious generalities—an echo from a bygone era—designed to rally sentiment for his cause. An attack on Petrograd was launched as the Soviet and the Left wing parties collaborated to defend the hapless government. But the threat evaporated almost as soon as it had begun. The secret Kornilovite societies in the city were smashed before they could act, and the morale of the advancing troops was sapped by Soviet propagandists. Insubordination became rife; among the few loyal units was a British armored car squadron which had fought in the July offensive. Kornilov and his chief aides were arrested, almost apologetically, by the Provisional Government. Escaping their token confinement after the October Revolution, they fled to South Russia and organized the first "White" army of the civil war.

The Kornilov insurrection was the turning point of the Revolution. Popular reaction against "bourgeois" leadership left the Bolsheviks

—the only proponents of an immediate peace and a division of the landed estates—as the residuary legatees of a new political climate. The Indian summer of the Provisional Government was spent with Kerensky grappling in a vacuum for some basis of support. The new cabinet announced on October 8 was a makeshift affair, and it was promptly denounced by the Petrograd Soviet—now Bolshevik dominated—as a "government of civil war." In a proclamation pleading for confidence in his regime, Kerensky made a belated gesture toward the Soviet's conception of a proper foreign policy by promising that the Russian representative at the forthcoming Allied conference would work for an agreement on war aims based upon "principles announced by the Russian Revolution."

During the summer Kerensky and Tereshchenko had tried to convince the Entente powers that a conference on war aims should be held at once. After the disastrous ending of the Stockholm affair, a substitute of some kind, no matter how inadequate, seemed imperative if Russia was to be salvaged for the common cause. But the only effective weapon at the Provisional Government's disposal, a threat to make a separate peace unless the Allies complied with its demand, was never invoked; indeed it was never considered. When a grudging consent to a conference had been obtained—and then without assurance that war aims would be discussed—it suffered repeated postponements. The meeting was finally set for Paris at the end of November 1917. Tereshchenko, as foreign minister, became Russia's official representative. On the unwarranted assumption that a Soviet delegate would be admitted to the proceedings, Mikhail Skobelev, who had recently resigned as minister of labor, was chosen by the Soviet Executive Committee to spread the gospel of "peace without annexations or indemnities" in the French capital. An elaborate set of instructions was drawn up recalling President Woodrow Wilson's later and more celebrated "fourteen points." But such recommendations as the neutralization of the Panama and Suez canals, the return of Germany's colonies, and a sweeping ban on reparations, were not likely to be received favorably at Paris—or even to be heard.

Russia was quickly informed that Skobelev was unwelcome; and at the end of October British and French spokesmen stated that the conference would concern itself with the prosecution of the war and disregard the subject of war aims. This crowning blow to Soviet aspirations exposed the moderate socialists to further ridicule from Bolsheviks and Kadets alike. Another nail had been driven into the coffin of the "revolutionary democracy." During the seven-and-a-half months of the Revolution the Allies had, without malice aforethought, done more to undermine the Provisional Government than an army of Bolshevik agitators.

Kerensky clung grimly to the notion that Russia's regeneration would come in time if only the Allies would be patient. While he was busily engaged on the eve of his fall in furnishing assurances of the government's fidelity to the Western alliance, the Bolsheviks were preparing the seizure of power. That decision had been reached at a stormy secret meeting of the party's Central Committee on October 23. The practical details of the insurrection were left to the newly created Military Revolutionary Committee, which had as the core of its striking force a Red Guard of some twenty thousand armed factory workers. In training since the Kornilov rebellion, this impromptu army would probably have fared poorly against a disciplined body of troops. It was a measure of the Provisional Government's strength and prestige that no such military assistance was available.

II

Late in the evening of November 6, 1917, and in the early morning hours of the 7th the Bolsheviks struck. The strategic buildings in Petrograd were occupied virtually without bloodshed, for no more than token resistance was offered—when it was offered at all. By daylight the capital was almost entirely in the hands of the Bolsheviks. The Winter Palace, where Kerensky and his colleagues had spent an anxious and sleepless night, was the last to be taken. Elsewhere the transition to Bolshevik rule was slower but usually orderly. The notable exception was Moscow, where a week of sanguinary fighting took place before the government's resistance was broken.

For the first time in history a government avowedly based on the principles of Marxian socialism had come into being. As was to be expected, the outside world greeted the Bolshevik Revolution with loathing and dismay while exhibiting little comprehension of the magnitude of the upheaval. The Central Powers, encouraged by the prospect of a separate peace, were the only dissenters from the prevalent view. The initial shock was tempered, however, by the widespread opinion that the Bolshevik triumph was but a freakish happenstance which would soon be remedied when "reason" and "sanity" reasserted their rightful position in the affairs of mankind.

At a historic session of the second All-Russian Congress of Soviets on November 8 Lenin asked for the adoption of two decrees, one on peace and the other on the distribution of the land. The former proposed that "all warring peoples and their governments begin immediately negotiations for a just and democratic peace." In its emphasis on a just peace the language was reminiscent of that used in previous Soviet and governmental pronouncements. But in the promise to begin publication of the secret treaties to which Russia had been a party—and the declaration that they were now annulled—a fundamental change in foreign policy was evident. New, too, was the distinction implied between peoples and governments: "While addressing this proposal of peace to all the governments and peoples of all the warring countries, the provisional workers' and peasants' government of Russia appeals also in particular to the class conscious workers of the three most forward nations of the world—England, France, and Germany." Despite the hostility to capitalism and capitalist governments apparent in the proclamation, the over-all tone was moderate and even conciliatory, probably in the hope that the belligerents would reply in a friendly spirit. If such was the reason, the Bolsheviks were doomed to disappointment, for neither the Allied nor the Central Powers deigned to reply.

The peace resolution was given overwhelming approval, as was the decree abolishing private ownership of land and transferring the estates of the landlords and the Church to local land committees for distribution to the peasants. The new governing body, the Soviet of People's Commissars, of which Lenin was president and Leon Trotsky commissar for foreign affairs, was also approved. Trotsky, so he later claimed, did not at first bother to distinguish between diplomacy and revolutionary agitation. When asked what kind of diplomatic work might arise, his reply, "I will issue a few revolutionary proclamations to the peoples of the world and then shut up shop,"[5] suggests the exultant mood of the Soviet leaders, impatient of custom and routine in the face of what they believed to be the opening stage of the world revolution.

The difficulties Trotsky encountered in assuming his new duties resembled those of his colleagues; the old bureaucracy was bitterly hostile to its new masters. When he entered the Foreign Office and ordered the peace decree translated into other languages, six hundred employees walked out. The secret treaties were secured from the archives over the strenuous opposition of the custodians, and Trotsky promptly reported that the documents were "more cynical in their provisions than we had supposed." The first installment appeared on November 23 in *Izvestia*, which had become the official government newspaper. In an introductory statement Trotsky declared secret diplomacy a "necessary weapon in the hands of the propertied minority . . . compelled to deceive the majority in order to make the latter serve its interests." Its abolition was the "first essential of an honorable, popular, and really democratic foreign policy." Publication continued in *Izvestia* and *Pravda* (the party organ) for several months, but except for short summaries and exerpts in the big city dailies only the *Manchester Guardian* and the *New York Evening Post* of the Allied press printed these significant documents in full.

Meanwhile the Bolshevik peace decree had not been allowed to lapse by default. On November 21 the Soviet government authorized fraternization with the enemy on all fronts and ordered the commander-in-chief, General Nikolai Dukhonin, to offer the enemy an armistice. On the same day Trotsky officially notified the Allied ambassadors of the existence of the new government and called attention to the peace decree. The ambassadors decided to ignore the note and to ask their governments to make no reply because the "pretended government," they complained, had been "established by force" and was "not recognized by the Russian people."

At Russian military headquarters in Mogilev near the front General Dukhonin ignored instructions to make overtures to the enemy. When reached by direct wire on November 22, he replied evasively and finally admitted his unwillingness to obey orders. Only a government "supported by the army and the country can have sufficient weight to impress the enemy," he remonstrated. The general was promptly dismissed and told to remain at his post until relieved by the new commander-in-chief, Ensign Nikolai Krylenko, a veteran Bolshevik propagandist. A proclamation to the troops explained the circumstances of the change and authorized the regiments at the front to elect representatives for the purpose of obtaining an armistice.

Krylenko set out for headquarters at a leisurely pace, removing untrustworthy officers and consolidating the Bolshevik regime in the area. Dukhonin breathed defiance with a counter-proclamation, but aside from the undisguised support of the Allied military and diplomatic representatives, his position was isolated and precarious. The chiefs of the Allied military missions accredited to headquarters (excluding the United States) sent him a formal note on November 23 protesting the proposed armistice and referring to the treaty of September 5, 1914, whereby the coalition had agreed never to make a separate peace. The message warned in conclusion that any violation of the treaty would "entail the gravest consequences." A rhetorical appeal over the heads of the *de facto* authorities was, if not ill-advised, certainly futile; to append a gratuitous threat, which the Soviet leaders took to mean a Japanese attack in the rear, was both clumsy and mistaken. Dukhonin saw that the note was printed in leaflet form and distributed among the troops.

Trotsky countered with a fiery manifesto to all army units and local Soviets denouncing the Allies for their "flagrant interference in the domestic affairs of our country with the object of bringing about civil war." "Let us all know," he proclaimed, "that the soldiers, workers, and peasants of Russia did not overthrow the governments of the Tsar and Kerensky just to become cannon fodder for the Allied imperialists." Although it fanned to a white heat the burning resentment of the soldiers against Dukhonin, Trotsky's rejoinder had no appreciable effect upon the Allies. Their representatives, joined by those of the United States—still technically an "associated" power—continued to flood headquarters with protests, ostensibly addressed to Dukhonin but actually intended for mass consumption.

These mutual recriminations in no way deterred the conclusion of an armistice which, without benefit of formal agreement, had been in existence for some time. Contact with the Germans at the front was established on November 26, and two days later the cease-fire order was given. In separate notes to the ambassadors and military attachés Trotsky again invited the Allies to take part in the preliminary negotiations scheduled to begin on December 2. Aside from these invitations sent in his capacity as commissar for foreign affairs, Trotsky aimed a manifesto at the peoples of the belligerent countries in his capacity as revolutionary agitator. The armistice negotiations had been postponed for five days, he declared, in order to give the Allies another opportunity to join the discussions. So far their only reply had been a refusal to recognize the Soviet regime. "The government of the victorious revolution stands in no need of recognition from the technicians of capitalist diplomacy, but we do ask the people: Does reactionary diplomacy express their thoughts and aspirations? Will they allow such diplomacy to pass by the great opportunity for peace offered by the Russian Revolution? . . . We want a general peace, but if the bourgeoisie of the Allied countries force us to conclude a separate peace, the responsibility will be theirs."[6]

The Allied governments could afford to remain silent, for the peoples of Europe, even if they had been as ripe for revolution as the Bolsheviks asserted, knew little or nothing of these hortatory proclamations. Powerless to stop the armistice with Germany and yet gravely worried by the prospective loss of a second front, the Allies floundered aimlessly in a sea of conflicting testimony as to the best course to pursue in dealing with this perplexing semi-ally, whose rulers were regarded by men of substance, both in and out of government, as more dangerous to the traditional values of Western civilization than the German autocrats against whom the war was supposedly being waged. There was agreement on one point alone: Bolshevism was a pernicious doctrine, and disapproval and non-recognition of a Bolshevik government was morally if not politically correct. As long as the separate peace did not become a reality, however, there remained doubt, disagreement, and confusion as to the practical wisdom of this policy.

For a time the Allies appeared to think that General Dukhonin was a force to be relied upon in resisting the Bolshevik peace plans. His usefulness in this capacity had come to an abrupt end when he was deposed as supreme commander, though his pleas for support continued. Prominent members of the Socialist Revolutionary party had gathered at Mogilev, sensing a possible center of resistance to Bolshevism, but they soon returned to Petrograd in a state of disillusion. The Allied military missions joined the exodus, leaving on December 1 for Kiev, where a separatist government gave promise of weaning the Ukrainians from Soviet rule. Two days later Krylenko arrived and found that the local garrison had already mutinied. Feeling ran high against Dukhonin since the news of the escape of Kornilov and his fellow officers had just been received; and Krylenko's half-hearted attempt to save the deposed commander failed to prevent his being killed by a frenzied mob of soldiers.

The first session of the Russo-German armistice talks began on the very day that the yearning for peace among the common soldiers had taken the unusual form of lynching their former commander-in-chief. The Russian delegation was probably the most unusual to appear at a peace conference in modern times. It was headed by Adolf Yoffe, an ascetic-looking intellectual who was to become the first Soviet ambassador to Berlin. One of his colleagues was Anastasia Bitsenko, famous for her assassination of a Tsarist official twelve years before. Besides representing the Left Socialist Revolutionaries, who were in a temporary alliance with the Bolsheviks, she served the added purpose of illustrating Marxist ideas on sex equality. By far the most curious delegates were the four representatives of the masses: a sailor, a soldier, a worker, and a peasant. Added for decorative purposes—they lent an air of revolutionary earnestness to the proceedings—they appeared to enjoy themselves even if they were seldom sure of what was going on. The peasant had been fortuitously acquired on the way to the railroad station when it was suddenly realized that a man of the soil was lacking to round out the party.

The German armistice proposals contained no punitive or otherwise humiliating terms, and it was hoped that the matter could be disposed of within a few hours, the formal peace conference to follow shortly. The German high command was interested above all in an immediate cessation of hostilities which would not delay the transfer to the western front of the bulk of its forces facing Russia. A spring offensive was planned, a gigantic thrust which would destroy the Allied armies before the immense resources of the United States in men and matériel could be effective. Already the arrival of American troops belied the German boast that her policy of unrestricted submarine warfare would prevent the arrival of a single soldier from across the Atlantic. Victory for the Central Powers would have to come soon—or never. Austria, Bulgaria, and Turkey were close to exhaustion, and their troops could no longer be considered reliable military auxiliaries; everything depended on the German army, still a formidable fighting machine and for the first time since 1914 potentially able to concentrate an equal or superior force in the west. But the morale of the civilian population, subjected to increasing privation by the Allied blockade, left much to be desired. Though organized peace sentiment was negligible, the workers showed signs of restlessness which erupted into serious industrial strikes in January 1918.

Such was the condition of Russia's opponents as the parley opened at the Polish town of Brest-Litovsk. A Russian request for complete freedom of publicity was accepted at the outset, a tactical victory which to Germany's later regret opened the way to long orations with an unduly large propaganda content. Yoffe outlined the Bolshevik view of peace terms based on the familiar formula of no annexations or indemnities and the right of all nationalities to self-determination. He proposed that it be a general and not a separate peace, but when pressed by Major General Max Hoffmann, the head of the German delegation, as to whether Russia was empowered to speak for her allies, Yoffe had to admit that the invitations already extended had not been answered. The Russian armistice proposals called for a six months' truce, the prompt cessation of German troop movements on the eastern front, and the evacuation of German forces from the Gulf of Riga. Germany preferred a much shorter armistice and refused to consider withdrawing from the Baltic area. Only the second point was accepted without objection: the units to be shifted to the western front were already in transit or had received orders to go.

The conference was recessed on December 5 to enable the Russian delegates to consult their superiors and to allow the other belligerents a further opportunity to join the negotiations. Trotsky gave the ambassadors a progress report and urged them to define their governments' attitude toward the peace conference. This communication, like the preceding ones, was ignored.

The period of intermittent talks at Brest-Litovsk, which did not bring peace to Russia until March 1918, was a time of anxiety, frustration, and uncertainty for the horde of official and unofficial Allied representatives in Petrograd. The former lived in self-imposed isolation, disdainful of the Soviet government and forbidden even that slight contact which routine diplomatic business required. This awkward and unnatural situation was improved to some extent by the use of unofficial agents who linked Bolshevik headquarters with the embassies and who could be repudiated whenever the exigencies of statecraft demanded. The chief emissaries in this *sub rosa* contact were Raymond Robins, head of the nominally non-political American Red Cross mission to Russia, R. H. Bruce Lockhart, Prime Minister David Lloyd George's special agent, and Captain Jacques Sadoul of the French military mission. These men possessed initiative and open-mindedness, qualities which the ambassadors so obviously lacked, and if not uncritical of the Soviet regime, they were willing to accept the Bolshevik Revolution as an accomplished fact and to judge its progress with detachment and good humor. Through frequent meetings with Lenin and Trotsky they came to admire the idealism and tenacity of purpose of the two leaders, however harsh and dogmatic their policies, and all three rejected the facile refrain that the Bolsheviks were in German pay or otherwise subservient to German policy.

Russia's new rulers, world revolutionists first and Russian revolutionists second, attempted by every means in their power and with a fine sense of impartiality to undermine the capitalist order wherever it existed; and though their sanguine hopes were not to be fulfilled, Germany rather than the Allies was the immediate enemy and was to experience a stealthy invasion of Bolshevik ideology which played a significant if largely unpublicized role in her subsequent collapse. It was in the week of grace before the resumption of the armistice talks that the Soviet propaganda offensive was mounted. The delegates had hardly returned from Brest-Litovsk before the first issue of *Die Fackel*, a propaganda organ designed for German consumption, was on its way to the front in editions sometimes reaching half a million copies in a single day.

Prisoners of war were subjected to a more systematic "educational" program. So saturated with revolutionary ideology were these troops that before being allowed to re-enter Germany they were confined for thirty-day periods in political "quarantine" camps to be purged of dangerous thoughts and recharged with patriotic values. The Allies, of course, heartily approved Bolshevik ideas when they were directed against the Central Powers. Edgar Sisson, working in Russia on behalf of the United States Committee on Public Information, shared the printing presses of the Soviet government, and while his antipathy to the Bolsheviks was extreme, he made a generous contribution to their propaganda funds. Regardless of incontrovertible evidence that the Germans and Bolsheviks were not working together—evidence which grew more impressive as the peace negotiations progressed and sharp disagreements arose—the legend of German-Bolshevik collusion persisted. The crowning folly of this delusion came when Sisson himself purchased some forged documents which were later dignified in a publication sponsored by the United States government and garishly entitled *The German-Bolshevik Conspiracy.*

The Russians signed the armistice agreement on December 15, 1917, with little change from the previous German terms. It was to last until January 14 and to be automatically prolonged unless a week's notice of termination was given by either party. Only in the "fraternization clause" did the Germans blunder, for in the article specifying "organized intercourse between the troops" a Pandora's box of revolutionary propaganda was opened. With only a week's interval, the formal peace conference convened at Brest-Litovsk. The Russian proposals closely adhered to the idealism of the peace decree of November 8 and were still based upon the notion of a general rather than a separate peace: no forceful expropriation of territories taken during the war, no war indemnities, and political freedom for all nationalities.

The Russians joyfully received the declaration read on Christmas Day by Count Ottokar Czernin, the Austrian foreign minister, that the Central Powers agreed in principle to their formula. They naïvely seemed to believe that Germany would actually disgorge her Polish and Baltic conquests. Hoffmann proceeded to disabuse them at luncheon the next day when he told Yoffe that his government did not consider it forcible annexation if portions of the former Russian empire broke off and decided "of their own free will" to unite with some other state. Yoffe, "looking as if he had received a blow on the head," arranged at once for an informal meeting to discuss this astonishing interpretation of Germany's "no annexation" policy. The Russians, angry and bitterly disappointed, could not budge the German position and threatened to disrupt the negotiations by departing for Petrograd.

Czernin desperately sought a compromise, for the Dual Monarchy needed peace and needed it badly. Yoffe had previously confided his hope that "we may yet be able to raise the revolution in your country too," and the Austrian minister had commented in his diary: "We shall hardly need any assistance from the good Joffe, I fancy, in bringing about a revolution among ourselves; the people will manage that, if the Entente persist in refusing to come to terms."[7] When the frantic Czernin received no backing from Baron Richard von Kühlmann, the German secretary of state for foreign affairs, he threatened to make a separate peace with the Russians and sent word to Hoffmann of his intention. The latter, cynically appraising Russia's military position, saw no reason for Czernin's agitation and coolly replied that he thought the idea a brilliant one since it would release for duty elsewhere twenty-five German divisions that were currently supporting the Austrian army on the eastern front.

Austria's bluff was thus called with scant ceremony, and Czernin withdrew into baffled silence. The conference was interrupted on December 28 to enable the Russians to proceed with the hopeless ritual of inviting their "allies" to participate. Dismayed and chagrined, Yoffe and his colleagues arrived in Petrograd as Trotsky's expected proclamation to the "peoples and governments of the Allied countries" —part invitation and part revolutionary manifesto—was released to the press. While admitting that the program of the Central Powers was "highly inconsistent" and a plan of "unprincipled compromise between the aims of imperialism and the resistance of the labor democracy," the very fact that it was proposed at all was pronounced "a great step forward" and in sharp contrast to the Allied policy of mouthing "general phrases about the necessity of carrying on the war to a finish." "If the Allied governments, in the blind stubbornness which characterizes decadent and perishing classes, once more refuses to participate in the negotiations," warned Trotsky, "then the working class will be confronted by the iron necessity of taking power out of the hands of those who cannot or will not give the people peace."

Wilson, Lloyd George, and Georges Clemenceau were in too stable a position to take seriously Trotsky's warning of the wrath to come if they persisted in their contemptuous silence. But the Allies could no longer with any assurance of success pose before world opinion as the champion of freedom and democracy and still maintain a stubborn taciturnity about their war aims. To be sure, there had been no lack of public declarations, pervaded with a tone of moral superiority, in which the just and pacific nature of Allied aims was paraded once again. Yet nothing specific had been said, and the course of the Russian Revolution—the vain pleas of the Petrograd Soviet, the abortive Stockholm Conference, the triumph of the Bolsheviks, the publication of the secret treaties, and the Brest-Litovsk Conference—demonstrated to the ever-increasing embarrassment of liberals, socialists, and idealists the vast distance between promise and performance.

The burden of placating dissenters in the West and undercutting the Central Powers on the ideological front could properly have been assumed only by President Wilson, unfettered as he was by secret commitments and convinced that the cause of the democracies was the cause of world civilization. It was admirably performed by the American president in his Fourteen Points address of January 8, 1918, before a joint session of Congress, which one of his biographers, extravagantly but not inaptly, has described as "the most effective piece of propaganda ever designed by any human brain in the history of mankind." The message was momentous and startling, a powerful if silent weapon in the assault which led to the German collapse some ten months later. Though brought forth by the impending resumption of the Brest-Litovsk deliberations, it had had a gestation period of several weeks while Wilson was being urged by a number of individuals to make some such statement.

The President spoke with genuine warmth of the sincerity and earnestness of the Russian delegates and their resistance to the German proposals of "conquest and domination," though he mistakenly declared that the negotiations had been broken off. "Their conception of what is right . . . has been stated with a frankness, a largeness of view, a generosity of spirit, and a universal human sympathy which must challenge the admiration of every friend of mankind." "They call to us," Wilson continued, "to say what it is that we desire, in what, if in anything, our purpose and our spirit differ from theirs; and I believe that the people of the United States would wish me to respond, with utter simplicity and frankness." Then, after a few additional remarks, the fourteen principles of the Wilsonian peace were stated. The sixth, relating to Russia, called for the evacuation of her territory, assistance of every kind "that she may need and may herself desire," the settlement of all questions affecting her in a manner to obtain "an unhampered and unembarrassed opportunity for the independent determination of her own political development and national policy," and the assurance of a "sincere welcome into the society of free nations under institutions of her own choosing."

Although future Allied policy was to make a mockery of the sixth point, as of so many others, the Bolshevik leaders were not so hostile toward the Allies that they failed to recognize its sympathetic tone and its value as anti-German propaganda. *Pravda* published most of the speech with a few skeptical remarks of its own; *Izvestia* printed it in full with a prominent display and commented favorably in an editorial. The anti-government press—censorship had not yet developed—was careful to omit the sections friendly to Russia because it reflected also to the credit of the Bolsheviks. In the form of posters, handbills, and pamphlets Sisson and his staff printed nearly two and a half million copies of the speech in Russian and another million in German. Huge quantities were circulated by other means, and the Bolshevik propaganda service distributed copies to prisoner-of-war camps and among German troops at the front.

III

Notwithstanding Yoffe's brave words about breaking off negotiations, there was never any doubt that the Russian delegation would reappear at Brest-Litovsk. Bolshevik strategy called for delaying tactics in the absence of military strength. A revolution in Germany, it was fondly believed, was an immediate possibility; and with Allied help the nucleus of a revolutionary army might be formed if all else failed. But "in order to delay the proceedings," Lenin declared, "there must be someone to do the delaying." Yoffe, while competent, was already beyond his depth. Only Trotsky, unrivalled as a dialectician, was equal to the demanding task, and at Lenin's urgent request he accepted the leadership of the peace delegation. Before his departure he tried to secure from Robins and Sadoul—Lockhart did not arrive in Russia until late January—some assurance of Allied assistance in the event of a rupture with Germany. Sadoul had been active for some time in campaigning for a statement promising military support to the Russians. The response he received was typical: the Bolsheviks were German agents, and in any case their days were numbered. Robins had temporarily better results with the vacillating American ambassador and obtained his signature to a document promising aid from his government in the event of a Russo-German break.

Thus feebly fortified, Trotsky left for Brest-Litovsk. This time the four ornaments to proletarian democracy remained in Petrograd. Besides Trotsky, another newcomer to the delegation was Karl Radek, a Polish Jew of Austrian nationality, who signaled his arrival by throwing propaganda leaflets from his train window to the German troops at the station.

At the first plenary session on January 9, 1918, it became apparent that in Trotsky, Kühlmann had found a worthy opponent. For days the two men faced each other across the conference table, one delivering semi-revolutionary harangues brimming with vituperation and biting sarcasm, the other, never forgetful for a moment that Germany was the master and Russia the slave, shrewdly manipulating his superior position to political advantage. To Kühlmann, Trotsky's malevolent expression indicated a desire to bring the parley "to a sudden and thorough end by throwing a few hand grenades over the green table."[8] Hoffmann, aroused by the inflammatory Bolshevik appeals to the German troops and impatient to "give the Russians another touch of the whip," finally obtained the consent of his colleagues "to bring the negotiations back to a basis of facts" away from the "theoretical discussions" into which they had degenerated. He bluntly reminded the Bolsheviks that even though they talked as if they could dictate terms, the German army stood victoriously on Russian soil. He charged, moreover, that the Soviet regime was based purely on power and "ruthlessly suppresses by force all who think otherwise."

While the outburst came as no surprise to Kühlmann, Czernin, accustomed to more finesse in such matters, was alarmed by the crudity of Hoffmann's mailed-fist approach. Germany's designs on Russia were already under fire in the liberal and socialist press at home, and the general's intemperate outburst provided fresh ammunition for these critics. In the Allied countries, where public opinion had been fed throughout the war on the horrors of German militarism and aggression, the incident was treated as a characteristic example of the Prussian military mind in action. In his rebuttal Trotsky gave the delegates a beginners' course in Marxist principles, stressing the moral that in a class society every government is based on force.

The German foreign minister did not push the pace of the discussions after Hoffmann's tirade, and the ensuing sessions fell back into the routine pattern of theory and polemics. Trotsky again seized the initiative and pilloried the Central Powers before world opinion as ruthless practitioners of power politics. With no adequate conception of the Allied fear of Bolshevism, Kühlmann missed a splendid opportunity to portray his country as the champion of civilization—the remaining barrier between the engulfing Red menace and the West. On January 18 the Germans agreed to a recess while Trotsky consulted his colleagues in Petrograd. The Germans had made their annexationist demands quite clear, and he left with a map upon which Hoffmann had drawn a blue line showing the future boundary of a badly truncated Russia.

Trotsky had already conceived a daring plan to end the war by a unilateral declaration and a refusal to sign the peace terms. The unprecedented doctrine of "neither war nor peace" was designed as a "pedagogical demonstration" to the European proletariat—proof of the deadly enmity existing between Imperial Germany and Bolshevik Russia. Lenin thought the scheme too risky. "If it were necessary for us to go under to assure the success of the German revolution, we should have to do it," he conceded. "But when will it come? No one knows. And at the moment, there is nothing so important as our revolution. It must be safeguarded against danger at any price."[9]

Nikolai Bukharin, Radek, and other "Left Communists" went beyond Trotsky's position to advocate a "holy war" against the German invaders. With indifferent success Lenin warned against this "intoxication with the revolutionary phrase." "A revolutionary war at this time," he argued, "would place us in the position of agents of Anglo-French imperialism insofar as we should be aiding the cause of the latter." The Allies would make no firm commitment to aid the Bolsheviks, and their reluctance confirmed Trotsky's suspicion that they were making secret overtures to Germany at Russia's expense. "The peace terms which Germany offers us are also the terms of America, France, and England," he charged in a speech before the third Congress of Soviets on January 26. "They are the account which the imperialists of the world are making with the Russian Revolution."

The Bolshevik Central Committee, by a vote of nine to seven, had decided on January 22 to accept Trotsky's formula of "no war—no peace" if it became necessary but to delay the negotiations as long as possible. Trotsky promised Lenin that if the Germans advanced he would favor accepting the peace terms. Some Russian territory would be overrun, but Lenin was now willing to try the experiment as a lesser peril than the proposed revolutionary war. "For the sake of a good peace with Trotsky," he said with a chuckle, "Latvia and Estonia are worth losing."

Bolshevik propaganda continued unabated through January, and toward the end of the month an epidemic of strikes and workers' demonstrations in Berlin, Vienna, Hamburg, and other cities did indeed seem to presage the great awakening of the Central European proletariat. Gregory Zinoviev, as president of the Petrograd Soviet, greeted the strikers as "brothers" and hailed their "glorious fight against German and universal imperialism." "You have shown," he declared, "that the Austro-German working class will not allow the hangmen and spoilers to impose a peace of violation and annexations on the Socialist Republic of the Soviets." Unhappily for this idyll of revolutionary solidarity, the authorities dealt harshly with the strikers, and by February 3 the movement was in a state of collapse. Incendiary Bolshevik proclamations by radio to the German troops so incensed Berlin that Kühlmann was ordered to present a twenty-four-hour ultimatum to the Russians—now back at Brest-Litovsk—requiring the cession of additional territory in the Baltic region. The foreign minister,

believing himself on the verge of an agreement with Trotsky, coura-
geously stood his ground and threatened to resign unless the order
was rescinded.

Kühlmann emerged victorious from this test of will only to find that
he had risked his position in vain. On February 10 Trotsky astounded
the opposing delegation by announcing Russia's withdrawal from the
war and her refusal to sign the peace terms. Until his concluding
remarks the Germans and Austrians had listened with confident satisfaction, assured that his customary denunciation of imperialism was
only a rhetorical gesture of defiance before bowing to the inevitable.
But when he finished and placed a signed declaration of the Russian
position on the conference table, the enemy representatives could only
stare in dumbfounded amazement.

The Russian delegation departed for home that same evening in a
mood of exhilaration—as if they had scored a diplomatic triumph.
Kühlmann and Czernin, puzzled as to the proper procedure in a situation seemingly without parallel in recorded history, were nevertheless
relieved that they had not been forced to deliver an ultimatum, for
they were fully aware of the moral damage their cause had already
suffered at Brest-Litovsk. The two diplomats were content to accept
a *de facto* peace, but the high command bestirred itself and secured
the approval of the chancellor and the Kaiser for a denunciation of
the armistice and a resumption of hostilities.

In Petrograd most of the Bolshevik luminaries remained incurably
optimistic. Even those who conceded the possibility of a German
advance permitted themselves the luxury of believing that the morale
of the enemy troops had been undermined by propaganda and that
the working masses would rise in their rear. These illusions were dis-
pelled on February 18 when the Germans pushed forward without a
show of active resistance; the few Russians at the front either surrendered or fled. An offer to accept the old peace terms elicited no
response since the German authorities were not yet glutted with territory that was theirs for the taking. The Bolsheviks made preparations to
fight a revolutionary war against the "hordes of bourgeois-imperialistic
Germany." The Allies were also sharply attacked for sabotaging Soviet
peace efforts by aiding counter-revolutionary generals in South Russia.
"All of us, including Lenin," Trotsky later commented, "were of the
impression that the Germans had come to an agreement with the
Allies about crushing the Soviets and that a peace on the western
front was to be built on the bones of the Russian Revolution."

However tainted the source, aid was still eagerly sought from the
Allies: even a defensive war for the most just of all causes could not

be fought with enthusiasm alone. Despite the silence in London, Paris, and Washington, the ambassadors agreed in principle to render assistance. On February 22 the party Central Committee met to consider the offer. Trotsky was favorable on condition that the Bolsheviks be left completely free in matters of foreign policy. Bukharin, though still a strong advocate of the revolutionary war, spoke against making such arrangements with imperialist governments. Lenin was not present but scribbled a note "in favor of taking potatoes and arms from the bandits of Anglo-French imperialism." The decision to accept was carried by a single vote. After the meeting Bukharin flung his arms around Trotsky and sobbed, "We are turning the party into a dung-heap."

As the Germans drew closer to Petrograd the ambassadors fled to Vologda several hundred miles to the northeast. Since the enemy forces eventually stopped some eighty miles short of the capital, their hurried departure proved unnecessary. The Bolshevik peace offer had at last been answered with an ultimatum beside which the previous terms seemed almost lenient. The message was not received until February 23, and a notice of acceptance was to be forwarded within forty-eight hours. Lenin had lost patience with the patriotic delusions of the Bukharin clique. "It is time to put an end to revolutionary phrases and get down to real work," he told the Central Committee on the same day. "If this is not done, I resign from the government. To carry on a revolutionary war, an army, which we do not have, is needed. Under the circumstances there is nothing to do but to accept the terms." When the vote was taken, six sided with Lenin, four abstained (including Trotsky), and four voted for war. The latter group then resigned from the party. Lenin went through an exhausting ordeal late in the evening before the Soviet Executive Committee. After an all-night session, his inexorable arguments won a clear majority for submission to the German ultimatum. There were howls of "Traitors . . . Judases . . . German spies!" from the Socialist Revolutionaries of the Left as the Bolsheviks prepared to leave.

The Russian delegation, now headed by Gregory Sokolnikov, left for the familiar scene at Brest-Litovsk on February 24. Delayed by transportation difficulties caused by the demolition activities of the Red Guard in opposing the Germans, the journey took four days. To dramatize the undeniable fact that it was a dictated peace, the Russians assumed an air of martyrdom and refused to discuss the terms. The treaty was signed on March 3 as Sokolnikov declared in a prepared statement that it was a peace "which Russia, grinding its teeth, is compelled to accept . . . a peace which gives back the land to the landlords and again drives the workers into the serfdom of the factory owners." Over 1,265,000 square miles was torn from Russia (chiefly the Ukraine, the Baltic region, and Poland) containing a third of her population, a third of her cultivated land, and half of her industry. It was a lesson and a warning to the Allies that no amount of synthetic anti-German propaganda manufactured for home consumption could equal. As Philip Scheidemann, the German Social Democrat, later remarked in his memoirs, "Cats cannot leave off mousing."[10]

The treaty was signed but not ratified. The Left Communist faction, in whose militant "revolutionary" patriotism the most ardent nationalist of the old regime could have found little to criticize, raged against Lenin's "obscene" policy in the *Kommunist,* their newly founded organ, and prepared for a suicidal stand against what they conceived to be a traitorous surrender to Germany. The trio of Allied diplomatic agents also tried to thwart ratification by promising ample support from their governments. In reality their influence on Allied policy was severely limited. Lockhart alone had direct contact with his government, and it was subject to the vagaries of imperfect telegraphic communication and considerable animosity toward his conduct within the Foreign Office. Robins and Sadoul lacked even the dubious advantage which the Englishman enjoyed, for neither had the confidence of his ambassador. The only positive action the Allies took was the landing of three hundred British and French marines at the port of Murmansk in North Russia on March 9. Designed to counter any German moves in that direction and accomplished with the tacit consent of the Soviet government, the operation was the unintentional but initial step in a war of intervention that was to bring further suffering and bloodshed to the exhausted nation.

Because of the proximity of German troops, the Bolsheviks had begun to shift the government from Petrograd to the Kremlin in Moscow, the historic site of Russia's capital before the reign of Peter the Great. The fourth All-Russian Congress of Soviets was scheduled to meet in the transplanted capital on March 12 to decide for war or peace by its vote to reject or ratify the Brest-Litovsk treaty. Lockhart's failure to secure a guarantee or even a vague promise of help for Russia had not discouraged his confreres from their persistent efforts toward the same end. Sadoul had found the American ambassador more cooperative than his own, and Robins hastened to obtain from Lenin and Trotsky an oral pledge to oppose ratification of the treaty if Washington would respond with something other than generalities. Unknown to Robins, the message failed to reach Washington before the Soviet meeting. The Congress had been postponed for two days, possibly to allow sufficient time for a reply from the United States.

After a preliminary session on the evening of the 15th, debate on the treaty began the next morning, continued all day, and resumed on the 16th. Most of the speakers opposed ratification, but from the applause which greeted the proponents of both views it was difficult to judge which side would win. Lenin rose to speak late in the evening of the final session. For an hour and twenty minutes his quiet, compelling voice demonstrated with remorseless logic the futility of further resistance. He called the treaty a "Tilsit peace" in reference to the humiliating terms which Prussia had been forced to accept from Napoleonic France in 1807. Just as the German people had secured vengeance, so the Russian people, he implied, would be able to overthrow the settlement. He was the last speaker. The vote was taken: for ratification, 784; against, 261; abstentions, 115.

On March 22, 1918, the German Reichstag added its seal of approval to the new "Tilsit," confident that Russia's erstwhile allies would soon falter before the spring offensive which was already mounting in fury on the western front.

NOTES

1. February according to the Julian calendar, then used in Russia, which was thirteen days behind the Western calendar. Except to designate the "February" and "October" Revolutions, the Western calendar has been used for all dates.

2. Major-General Sir Alfred Knox, *With the Russian Army, 1914–1917* (London, 1921), II, 569.

3. R. H. Bruce Lockhart, *Two Revolutions* (London, 1957), p. 91.

4. Text in *Papers Relating to the Foreign Relations of the United States: Russia, 1918* (Washington, 1931–32), I, 172–73.

5. Leon Trotsky, *My Life* (New York, 1930), p. 341.

6. James Bunyan and H. H. Fisher, *The Bolshevik Revolution, 1917–1918: Documents and Materials* (Stanford, Calif., 1934), pp. 258–59.

7. Count Ottokar Czernin, *In the World War* (New York, 1920), p. 246.

8. Richard von Kühlmann, *Erinnerungen* (Heidelberg, 1948), p. 530.

9. Trotsky, *My Life*, p. 382.

10. Philip Scheidemann, *The Making of New Germany* (New York, 1929), II, 115.

CHAPTER THREE

A TIME OF TROUBLES

The *peredishka*—breathing space—that Bolshevik Russia gained at Brest-Litovsk was unexpectedly brief. Peace with Germany was the prelude to a new war, a savage conflict between the new Soviet power and a diverse group of counter-revolutionaries supported by Russia's former allies. A three year period of civil war, foreign intervention, famine, and social chaos ensued. It was an agonizing experience reminiscent of the "Time of Troubles" that Russia had endured early in the seventeenth century.

That the Bolsheviks should be under internal attack so soon after their revolution in November, and under external attack so soon after their dearly bought peace in March, seems, at first glance, to be a historical paradox defying the rules of probability. Yet the seeds of the conflict were sprouting as far back as the *Kornilovshchina* of September 1917.[1] Initially, only the generals of a beaten and disintegrating army represented a threat to the New Soviet order; and after the murder of their commander-in-chief, they appeared to be powerless relics of a vanishing past. But southeast of Moscow, in the Cossack territory of the lower Don, they found a less hostile environment and began to recruit an anti-Bolshevik army. Representatives of the Allied military missions, willing to back "patriots" of any description if they displayed anti-German credentials, quickly established contact and made arrangements for material aid.

Perhaps the first step in the chain of events preceding armed intervention was the secret Anglo-French convention of December 23, 1917, in which South Russia was divided into tentative spheres of influence. Negotiated in Paris without the knowledge of the United States, the agreement was essentially aimed at defining the respective areas of anti-Bolshevik activity near the Black Sea rather than outlining a course of military action. It did, however, indicate the economic and political desires of the two countries and the future pattern of intervention. Probably because of her interest in oil and the approaches to India, Britain was allotted the Cossack territories, the Caucasus, Armenia, Georgia, and Kurdistan. The French zone encompassed Bessarabia, the Ukraine, and the Crimea.

At the time of the secret agreement no definite Russian policy had been formulated. The Allied diplomats, even when they had become convinced of the usefulness of direct as well as indirect intervention, were baffled by the difficulties of exerting pressure on the Soviet regime. Japan, whose presence in the Allied coalition was a dubious blessing, had easier access to Russian territory than her partners and thus became the logical mandatory power. As early as January 1917 it had been suggested that Tokyo send troops to bolster the eastern front, but neither Russia nor Japan had been responsive. Now the situation had altered so radically within a year's time that a number of Japanese military leaders began to display an abnormal interest in the problem of "upholding order" in Siberia. Britain, with some reluctance, and France, more enthusiastically, proposed to the United States that Japan be permitted to intervene in the Russian Far East, ostensibly as part of the grand strategy designed to hasten the enemy's capitulation. It was never adequately explained how a Japanese army in Siberia, at least 5,000 railroad miles from the nearest enemy troops, was to contribute in any substantial measure to ultimate victory. The most rational presentation of the scheme was contained in a note sent to Secretary of State Lansing early in January 1918 by the French ambassador to Washington urging assent to the "desirability of some joint action" in Siberia. The purpose, said the ambassador, would be to "protect" Siberia from Bolshevik "contagion," to secure the use of the Trans-Siberian and other railroads for "the advantage of the Allies," and to safeguard the vast amount of war matériel stored at Vladivostok.[2]

President Wilson was cool toward intervention from the beginning. He recognized that such a move represented a flagrant departure from the idealism professed in his Fourteen Points address. But motives of idealism, however strongly they may have appealed to Wilson's Presbyterian conscience, fail to explain American opposition to a Japanese venture in Siberia. The need to maintain a semblance of unity against the common foe concealed for the time being Washington's growing concern with the rapid shift in the balance of power on the Asiatic mainland. An apparently tractable David to Russia's Goliath in 1905, Japan had emerged in little more than a decade as the heir to both German and Russian interests in China and the pretender to much more. During the previous November Lansing had secretly placated Tokyo by conceding Nippon's "special interests" in China in return for the harmless ritual of another endorsement of the cherished Open Door principle. The State Department was uneasily aware that it might be charged with a "sellout" of China if Lansing's concession became known. But it was unwilling to expand the formula to include Siberia despite the facile excuses by which Japan, encouraged by her European allies, sought to establish a bridgehead upon Russian soil.

In a memorandum to the State Department late in January 1918 the British tried to overcome American objections to intervention by pointing out the propitious changes on the Russian scene. Whereas "the whole country presented a spectacle of unredeemed chaos" only a few weeks ago, now "local organisations appear to have sprung up in south and southeast Russia which, with encouragement and assistance, might do something to prevent Russia from falling immediately and completely under the control of Germany." Turning to the argument that "Russian susceptibility would be deeply wounded by such a project," it was solemnly avowed that the Russians would "welcome some form of foreign intervention in their affairs" and that they would find Japan, on a mandate from the other Allied powers, "with no thought of annexation or future control" preferable to the Germans, "who would make Russia orderly only by making it German."[3]

Wilson remained unconvinced; and though his stand prevented large-scale intervention for the time being, Japan's interest in Siberia was becoming too strong to be ignored indefinitely. Press dispatches reporting an imminent Japanese landing at Vladivostok had been widespread since early December. An official spokesman in Tokyo finally branded them "absurd and nonsensical," although it seems likely that they were semi-official feelers put out by the Japanese government to gauge world reaction before embarking on a Siberian expedition. Because of the attitude of the United States, the Japanese ambassador in Washington assured Lansing in late December that his government had no intention of sending troops to Vladivostok, even though London and Paris had been the first to endorse the undertaking.

On January 12, 1918, a Japanese cruiser entered the harbor at Vladivostok for the usual reasons assigned in such cases—that of protecting Japanese citizens and property. The early arrival of another Japanese vessel and a British warship concentrated an impressive array of naval strength in the harbor. The American ambassador in Tokyo was instructed to protest. As Lansing delicately phrased it, "the presence of more than one Japanese war vessel at Vladivostok at present is likely to be misconstrued and create a feeling of mistrust as to the purposes of the Allied Governments which Japan does not desire any more than the United States." Had Wilson consented, a Japanese landing might have followed soon afterward. The military clique in Tokyo, powerful but not yet dominant, awaited an appropriate moment. Increasing Anglo-French pressure, as well as the strongly favorable recommendations of American representatives around the globe, anti-Bolshevik and pro-interventionist almost to a man, did much to weaken the President's determined opposition.

For a time late in February Wilson temporized. But on March 5, in identical notes to the Allied capitals, the United States questioned the wisdom of intervention while conceding the "extreme danger of anarchy to which the Siberian provinces are exposed and the imminent risk also of German invasion and domination." Tokyo's pride was soothed by assurances that Washington had the "utmost confidence in the Japanese Government and would be entirely willing . . . to entrust the enterprise to it." Certain objectionable features interfered, such as the "hot resentment [which] would be generated in Russia" and the fact that the Central Powers "could and would make it appear that Japan was doing in the East exactly what Germany is doing in the West." In reply Tokyo promised to refrain from unilateral action—with the customary proviso that "should hostile activities in Siberia develop to such a degree as to jeopardize the national security or vital interests of Japan she may be compelled to resort to prompt and efficient measures of self-protection."

A pretext for Japanese intervention could not be long delayed under the conditions then developing in eastern Siberia and northern Manchuria. In the absence of effective control from Moscow, the political void was filled by an assortment of military adventurers who ravaged the local population in the name of patriotism and anti-Bolshevism. These freebooters contributed substantially to the "anarchy" which so exercised the Entente, yet their diplomatic and military representatives in the Far East offered them aid and friendship. Japan was especially generous in subsidizing those disposed to serve her interests.

In Vladivostok lawless acts were by no means rare under a condition of latent civil war; and on April 4, 1918, unidentified bandits—presumably Russians—killed a Japanese citizen and wounded two others. Several hundred armed sailors were landed the next morning from the two Japanese cruisers in the harbor and began to patrol the city. Fifty British marines were also disembarked, officially to guard their consulate but actually to "ensure that any move made would be an Allied one, not an independent Japanese venture."[4]

The spoliation of Siberia thus began in the classic pattern which the great powers had developed in China and other "backward" areas over the previous century. Many among the Japanese ruling hierarchy expected a more ambitious military enterprise to follow the original foothold. But it was delayed for several months as Tokyo hesitated and her allies refused to regard the landing as more than a police operation similar to those which American marines had conducted in the "banana republics" of Central America. The Bolshevik authorities, taking a grave view of the incident, lost no time in denouncing "the imperialist attack from the East" and calling upon the other Allied powers to make known their attitude. The landing at Vladivostok did much to undermine the efforts of Robins, Lockhart, and Sadoul to bring the Soviet regime into the Allied camp by the back door. The tenuous collaboration leading to the Murmansk expedition[5] might have been repeated at Archangel and Vladivostok had Japan's motives been less suspicious. Amid conflicting counsel and a welter of cross purposes, vacillation continued to substitute for policy in London and Paris.

Partly as a result of Trotsky's conciliatory attitude, the British temporarily swung over to Lockhart's repeated pleas for intervention with Moscow's consent. On April 25 Foreign Secretary Arthur Balfour proposed that the United States, instead of accepting Japan as a mandatory power, contribute to a combined Allied force after proper arrangements had been made with the Soviet government. Opinion in Washington, skeptical of Bolshevik willingness to cooperate, remained unfavorable to any form of intervention; and there matters rested until startling developments along the Trans-Siberian Railway triggered the active stage of the civil war.

II

At Chelyabinsk, a railway junction in western Siberia, a minor clash occurred on May 14 between Hungarian war prisoners returning to their homeland and Czechoslovak troops en route to Vladivostok. Czechoslovakia was as yet, of course, a theoretical entity whose future existence hinged upon the dissolution of the Austro-Hungarian empire; and to hasten the process, the nucleus of a Czech army had been formed on Russian soil shortly after the beginning of the war. Recruiting from the prisoner of war camps proceeded more swiftly following the February Revolution, but the Czechs were only an embarrassment to the Soviet authorities. After Brest-Litovsk they were allowed to leave the country along the Trans-Siberian to the Pacific, where Allied vessels were to transport them to the western front.

When news of the Chelyabinsk incident reached Moscow, the local Soviets were ordered to disarm the Czechs and to prevent their further progress to the east. Those found armed along the railroad were, in Trotsky's words, "to be shot on the spot." Unfortunately for the Soviet regime, the power to enforce its decrees was sorely lacking. The infant Red Army was then in the process of conversion from a volunteer worker's militia to a conscript army based upon compulsory military and labor service for the entire population. The Czechs resisted every hostile move, and against feeble or nonexistent opposition they took over the towns and cities along the right of way. By the end of June some 35,000 Czech legionnaires, in collaboration with various White detachments, had commandeered most of the Trans-Siberian from the Volga city of Samara (now Kuibyshev) in the west to Vladivostok in the east.

Notwithstanding the interpretation of these events by Soviet historians—that the Czech uprising was a prearranged conspiracy of the Allied powers to justify intervention in Siberia—the news was a genuine surprise to Western statesmen. But it did not prevent their perceiving the advantages to be gained by "rescuing" the Czechs from their predicament. Coupled with reports that the Bolsheviks were arming thousands of German and Austrian war prisoners to fight the Czechs and their White allies, the interventionists had new and persuasive arguments with which to confront the American president. The war prisoner bugaboo, though even then it had been exposed as a fraud—perhaps a deliberate one—retained its place in the growing folklore of anti-Bolshevism. Pressure mounted for a decision from Washington, for intervention was now almost a certainty with or without American consent. Still Wilson hesitated. "I have been sweating blood over the question what it is right and feasible to do in Russia," he wrote on July 8. "It goes to pieces like quicksilver under my touch."[6]

Within a week Wilson had made his decision. He personally drafted a formal statement of American policy, and copies were circulated to the Allied ambassadors. Known as the *aide-mémoire* and dated July 17, 1918, this peculiar document began by repeating the arguments against intervention that American officials had so often used in the past: it would "add to the present sad confusion in Russia rather than cure it," and it would be of "no advantage in the prosecution of our main design, to win the war against Germany." Therefore, the United States could not take part in it "or sanction it in principle." As a forecast of the consequences of intervention it was to prove amazingly accurate. The balance of the statement, however, ignored the logic of the beginning. "Military action" in Russia—apparently somehow distinguishable from "military intervention"—was declared admissible "only to help the Czecho-Slovaks consolidate their forces," to assist "any efforts at self-government or self-defense" by the Russian population, and to "guard military stores." A small American force was obliquely promised for the enterprise, and the other powers were served notice that they would be asked to assure the Russian people "in the most public and solemn manner" that they contemplated no interference with Russia's internal affairs, political sovereignty, or territorial integrity. A paraphrase of the document, released to the public on August 3, was the first acknowledgment that the United States was joining the Siberian expedition.

The situation in North Russia had meanwhile altered almost as radically as it had in Siberia. After the Czech rising, the Bolsheviks called for the dissolution of the Murmansk venture. For the first time openly defying the Soviet regime, these forces—still predominantly British—extended their control beyond the city itself, and by midsummer they occupied the Murmansk coast and the northernmost sections of the railway to Petrograd. To no avail, Georgi Chicherin, Trotsky's replacement as commissar for foreign affairs, bitterly assailed this "unprovoked British attack" in a note to Lockhart.

Though Allied troops dominated the area until the fall of 1919, the Murmansk front was an isolated and comparatively insignificant theater of operations. The major Allied effort in North Russia shifted to Archangel, the largest port on the White Sea, where an Anglo-French force of about 1,500 landed early in August 1918. The local government was controlled by Socialist Revolutionaries, a short-lived but refreshing departure from the pattern of military dictatorship which flourished elsewhere under White auspices. On September 6 a *coup* engineered by Georgi Chaplin, a former Russian naval commander who had obtained the support of Allied officers, ousted the "radicals." Socialism, whatever the party label attached, was to a certain type of military mind simply a less offensive variety of Bolshevism. The Allied authorities collaborated closely with Chaplin and his successors, notably General Eugene Miller, until the final evacuation. Difficulties of climate and terrain, coupled with a lack of reinforcements, prevented a strike southward to join the Czechs on the Volga. Aside from minor clashes with Red forces, North Russia was insulated from the major centers of the civil war.

The disintegration of the outlying portions of the Russian empire under the abrasion of civil disorder and foreign invasion left to the Soviet regime only a fast shrinking area centered around Moscow and Petrograd. Geographical dismemberment at least gave the Bolsheviks the advantage of a central defensive position from which to confront a far-flung circle of enemies. Military weakness was but one of the problems facing Lenin and his associates. Men less sure of themselves and of the historic role their doctrine was destined to play might have been overwhelmed by the enormity of the burden. The armed forces necessarily received priority in a struggle which the orthodox regarded as a "holy war" to save the citadel of Marxism from the mercenaries of aggressive capitalism.

To supplement the sacrifices of the Red Army on the battlefield, the hidden foes on the home front were summarily dealt with by a revitalized Cheka—the All-Russian Extraordinary Commission to Combat Counter-Revolution and Sabotage. Founded in December 1917, the original Cheka was a model of comportment compared to the instrument of terror it was to become. Only in the summer of 1918, when the danger to the regime first became acute, did its repressive activities reach major proportions. It is doubtful, however, that the Red terror at its most ferocious equalled the savagery and senseless brutality of the White terror.

On July 6 an attempted *coup* in Moscow by the Left Socialist Revolutionaries, sparked by the assassination of the German ambassador, precipitated the transition from moderation to violence in curbing the anti-Bolshevik opposition. The plot failed to incite a renewed Russo-German conflict, and the clumsy attempt to seize the capital was frustrated. On the same day an unrelated but temporarily more successful *coup* took place in the city of Yaroslavl on the upper Volga. It was masterminded by Boris Savinkov, a notorious Socialist Revolutionary terrorist in Tsarist times, and financed by French diplomatic and military representatives. The conspirators were eventually driven from Yaroslavl and repulsed in their attacks upon nearby towns. The Allied descent upon Archangel came too late to combine forces with the insurgents, most of whom were executed. Savinkov escaped to resume his fantastic career, though it was conducted on a less spectacular scale thereafter.

The economic system hastily fashioned to bolster the military needs of the state was appropriately labeled "War Communism," for it was an awkward blend of Marxist dogma and makeshift emergency measures. Even in an advanced capitalist country operating under a normal peacetime economy, the difficulties of giving practical substance to socialist theory would have been formidable. Considering the conditions under which socialism was introduced to Russia, the wonder is not that it worked badly but that it worked at all. The Bolsheviks nationalized key sectors of the economy and introduced various egalitarian reforms. Private enterprise and the profit motive were to be gradually stifled to make way for the socialist millenium. The civil war rudely interrupted this utopian vision, but instead of giving way to orthodox capitalist nostrums, more, not less, socialism was prescribed. On June 28, 1918, the major industries were nationalized by decree, and by the end of 1920 all but the smallest industrial firms had been expropriated. The state likewise established a near monopoly over domestic trade and maintained an elaborate system of rationing and wage controls. Payment in kind eventually replaced wages, and barter was substitued as a medium of exchange.

What foreign trade could circumvent the Allied economic blockade was also a function of the state. The peasants, their land hunger satiated, were cool to the idea of collective and state farms, a few of which were organized on an experimental basis. Agricultural production declined sharply, chiefly because of inflation and a shortage of manufactured goods. Even compulsory grain seizures failed to insure a regular food supply for the urban population and the Red Army. Mass migration to the countryside began, while the black market and other illegal means of obtaining food saved thousands of city dwellers from slow starvation. Hunger and disease, added to the rigors of the winter climate, took millions of lives otherwise untroubled by the carnage of civil strife. Such, in brief, was Russia's economic plight during her new Time of Troubles.

But the summer of 1918, the climax to four years of war and revolution, furnished only an inkling of the hardships in the years ahead. On August 2 the initial landing at Archangel was made by Russia's onetime allies. Fearful of a drive on Moscow, the Bolsheviks broached the subject of possible military aid from Germany to forestall the expected Allied attack. The proposal was stillborn, however, because of the German army's critical position on the western front. In any event, it was soon evident that Siberia would be the scene of the major Allied penetration. On August 3 a British battalion landed at Vladivostok. American, Japanese, and French troops followed and were supplemented late in October by small Canadian and Italian detachments. By mid-November approximately 9,000 American soldiers were in Siberia, a force more than twice the size of the token armies contributed by the European powers.

Dwarfing the American contingent and in total disregard of Washington's original suggestion that 7,000 men be the maximum contribution of any one nation to the Siberian venture, Japan seized the opportunity to pour an estimated 73,000 into the Russian Far East. Additional troops—perhaps 30,000—occupied northern Manchuria along the Chinese Eastern Railway. Because of secret agreements signed with Tokyo in May 1918, China's "legal" government in Peking was perilously close to becoming a Japanese puppet. In formal obeisance to world opinion, Tokyo promised to respect Russia's territorial integrity and to refrain from interference in her domestic politics. The element of hypocrisy—a phenomenon of international diplomacy in no way peculiar to Japan—was so blatant in this instance that it should be pointed out in partial mitigation that Tokyo's diplomats were seldom in a position to curb the military oligarchy which determined policy in Siberia.

Unable to fend off the invaders, the Soviet government retaliated by indirect but wholly inadequate means. On August 5 some two hundred British and French subjects in Moscow were jailed as hostages. The British and French consulates were also raided and members of both staffs temporarily imprisoned. The American consulate enjoyed immunity; and press attacks upon the Allies, including atrocities allegedly committed in North Russia, invariably excluded the United States in apparent tribute to the relatively neutral position that American spokesmen took toward Russia's internal affairs. While the hostage policy was relaxed in the face of vigorous protests, the position of the remaining Allied diplomatic and military personnel had become untenable. Virtually prisoners within the capital, they were forbidden to join the ambassadors, who had journeyed from Vologda to Archangel late in July.

On August 30, 1918, two unrelated acts of violence—the head of the Petrograd Cheka was assassinated and Lenin was wounded—precipitated a fresh outburst of terror and another roundup of Allied officials. During a raid on the British embassy in Petrograd the naval attaché was killed in a gun battle with agents of the Cheka. Lockhart was charged with conspiring to overthrow the regime, and the newspapers exposed what they called "a net of bloody intrigue and monstrous crime."[7] Originally an outspoken opponent of intervention without Moscow's consent, Lockhart had come around to the official British view and was giving financial aid to several anti-Bolshevik groups. Culpable as his activities were, evidence of a "Lockhart plot" was sketchy and unconvincing. He was released several weeks later, and with other officials he was allowed to leave the country in exchange for a group of Bolsheviks interned in England. One of the latter was Maxim Litvinov, the unofficial Soviet envoy to Britain and the future commissar for foreign affairs.

Events soon exposed the pretense that the Siberian expedition had been sent to extricate the Czechs from their predicament. These supposedly hapless victims of Soviet treachery sought to consolidate their hold on the Volga region in obedience to Allied orders; and Czech forces already in Vladivostok returned along the Trans-Siberian to spearhead the Allied offensive. On September 2 Moscow placed the country under martial law. Three days later, coinciding with the proclamation of the Red terror, Soviet troops launched an assault upon the Czech stronghold of Kazan on the upper Volga. The Bolsheviks seized the city, their first major victory of the civil war; and the Czechs, together with their White allies, were pushed back to the Urals before the Russian winter temporarily suspended active operations. The performance of the Red Army represented a personal triumph for the new commissar for war, Leon Trotsky, whose genius as a revolutionary leader had been well established but whose talents as a military organizer were yet to be demonstrated.

In Siberia the Allies were already pursuing divergent aims. Disagreements and misunderstandings were rife, particularly in the field, but the frosty civility of Japanese-American relations was not typical of the enterprise as a whole. To the Japanese commanders eastern Siberia was a conquered province, though no more than a few skirmishes sufficed for the "conquest." The Cossack chieftains Ivan Kalmykov and Gregory Semyenov, beholden to Tokyo for ready funds, added to the rigors of the Siberian occupation. Kalmykov and his brigands operated from Khabarovsk, a city about 400 miles north of Vladivostok. Semyenov, with a larger force at his disposal, had originally received support from the Entente powers. By October of 1918 he had become solely a Japanese agent, and from their headquarters in Chita his bands terrorized the region from the Manchurian border to Lake Baikal. The number of his victims is unknown, but an estimate of over 30,000 peasants killed in a single year does not seem excessive.[8] Both men eventually died by violence: Kalmykov was shot in 1920 by the Chinese, and Semyenov was executed by the Russians in 1946 following the Red Army's victorious Manchurian campaign at the close of World War II.

The Anglo-French military authorities, with no thought of a permanent hold on Siberia, took a benign attitude toward Japanese aims until the barbarities of Semyenov, Kalmykov, and a host of imitators began to endanger the interventionists and the White movement alike. In contrast to the Japanese generals, who used anti-Bolshevism as a convenient cloak for empire-building at Russian expense, soldiers like General Alfred Knox, the chief British military representative in Siberia, and General Maurice Janin, commander of the French forces, regarded the extermination of Bolshevism as a moral and political crusade to uphold the principles of Western civilization. The American commander, General William S. Graves, took a literal view of his original instructions from President Wilson and scandalized his Allied colleagues by refusing to be drawn into the anti-Bolshevik campaign. His forces were used to guard Allied supplies at Vladivostok and portions of the Trans-Siberian Railway east of Lake Baikal. Despite Graves' suggestion in October that a few detachments be sent to aid the hard-pressed Czechs on the Volga, Wilson adamantly opposed further involvement in Russian affairs. Because the decision was unpublicized, Graves was harshly criticized by American diplomats for his neutral stand.

III

On November 11, 1918, the guns fell silent on the western front. With unexpected swiftness Allied might had prevailed. The Kaiser had abdicated, and a republic was proclaimed in Berlin. In Moscow hope welled anew that the German proletariat would prove worthy of its Marxist heritage and seize power in its own right. Though the German revolution was to prove an elusive phantom, forever dissolving in the cold light of reality, the immediate advantages of the Allied victory for Russia's traditional national interests were apparent. On November 13 a Soviet decree formally annulled the Brest-Litovsk treaty and quixotically gave the credit for the overthrow of this "peace of violence and plunder" to the "simultaneous blows dealt by the German and Russian revolutionary proletariat" rather than to the military superiority of the Allied armies.

The Armistice terms included a clause directing German troops to remain temporarily in position on the eastern front in those areas that had once belonged to Tsarist Russia, a patent effort to check the spread of Bolshevism in Poland and the Baltic area. In the Ukraine the German collapse left a vacuum which the Red Army and its various rivals endeavored to fill. The puppet regime of General Paul Skoropadsky, hetman of the Ukraine, withered away, and the general found it advisable to flee Kiev in December. A successor government, the infirm "Directory" headed by Simon Petlyura, was ousted from the city early in February 1919 by Red forces. General Peter Krasnov, the Don Cossack leader, was also seriously affected by the German withdrawal. His troops, relying upon German assistance, had won some local engagements along the lower Don and were now exposed to Red infiltration on their Ukrainian flank.

The strongest of the White governments in South Russia clung to a pro-Allied and anti-German orientation. Based upon the "Volunteer Army" formed by ex-Tsarist generals shortly after the Bolshevik Revolution,[9] it had led a precarious existence during the first part of 1918.

Under a new commander, General Anton Denikin, the army began to revive; and by the close of the year the resistance of strong Red partisan units in the northern Caucasus was broken. Reinforcements came from the Don Cossacks, who placed their military forces under Denikin's control in exchange for autonomy. Krasnov, unreconciled to a subordinate capacity, resigned shortly afterward and later joined the Whites in the Baltic region. By the early months of 1919 the Volunteer Army was at last in a position to expand its conquests—just as the Red Army became strong enough to extend its operations into the Ukraine.

Denikin's prospects were greatly enhanced by the defeat of the Central Powers and the opening of the Straits to Allied shipping. Already in receipt of some financial aid, he now expected more substantial largess in the form of munitions, supplies, and possibly troops. Two Allied cruisers arrived at the Black Sea port of Novorossiisk on November 23, 1918, and four days later a military mission reached the Volunteer Army's headquarters at Ekaterinodar (now Krasnodar), about sixty miles northeast. Britain supplied Denikin's army, and France furnished most of the manpower sent into the Black Sea area.

Allied intervention in South Russia proceeded along the lines of the 1917 Anglo-French convention,[10] whose terms were reaffirmed after the Armistice. British troops based in Persia occupied Batum, Tiflis, and Baku in the Caucasus and a number of cities in the Trans-Caspian area. French troops were delayed until December 18 when the first contingent of 1,800 arrived at Odessa. The major Black Sea and Crimean ports were gradually occupied by a force estimated at its peak to be over 60,000.

As in North Russia and Siberia, the interventionists were uncertain of their goal. The French commander in Odessa had been told to "make common cause with the patriotic Russians," and in the absence of a clearer directive as to which brand of Russian patriotism was the more desirable, gave his initial support to representatives of the Volunteer Army. The choice caused friction from the first, for the Ukrainian nationalist troops of Petlyura dominated most of the city, and circumstances eventually forced the French to come to terms with him. The morale of the invaders was, understandably, very poor. As one of their officers put it, "No French soldier who saved his life after the Marne and Verdun would want to lose it on the fields of Russia."[11] Luckily for their military reputation, the French encountered no hostile force as their lines were extended northward. In Odessa clandestine Bolshevik propaganda made considerable headway in the garrison and among units of the fleet. In the spring, with the resurgence of Red partisans in the area, the French authorities were faced with a bitter choice: fight or evacuate.

In Siberia the Whites had achieved at least superficial unity under a new leader—Admiral Alexander Kolchak, the former commander of the Black Sea fleet. He had left Russia for an official trip to the United States during the summer of 1917 and arrived in Japan on the return journey shortly after the Bolshevik Revolution. Beyond a brief appearance in the late spring of 1918 as the commander of the White Russian troops guarding the Chinese Eastern Railway zone, he played no conspicuous role in the developing civil war until his arrival at Omsk the following October. A moderate coalition government—the so-called Directorate—had recently been established at this central Siberian city. Supported by the Czechs and most of the White forces west of Lake Baikal, the leaders looked upon their regime as the legitimate heir to the Provisional Government. Kolchak was persuaded to accept the vacant post of war minister instead of going on to South Russia as he had originally intended. Although a man of honesty, courage, and personal integrity, the admiral had no military experience, his administrative ability was limited, and he was almost totally devoid of those personal qualities of which popular leaders are made. Yet it was all but inevitable under the conditions then existing in Siberia that politically illiterate but patriotic conservatives of Kolchak's type would rise to the fore of the anti-Bolshevik movement.

On November 17, 1918, in a *Putsch* reminiscent of that which had overthrown the Socialist Revolutionary regime in Archangel the previous September, the Directorate was purged of its socialist members. A clique of former Tsarist officers was at the root of the affair; the British representative, General Knox, if not a party to the plot, gave his enthusiastic approval. Kolchak was chosen "supreme ruler" and given the additional position of "commander-in-chief of all the land and naval forces of Russia." With few exceptions, the Western press hailed Kolchak as Russia's new savior, a "democratic patriot" to whom all elements of the population but a rabid minority of discredited Bolsheviks would soon rally. Such a distorted version of Russian events was not, of course, confined solely to Kolchak and his regime. Throughout the period of revolution and civil war public opinion in the West was molded by journalism as irresponsible as the twentieth century has yet produced.

Through General Knox, Britain provided for the material needs of the Omsk regime. It was no simple task: Semyenov and Kalmykov dominated the Trans-Siberian east of Lake Baikal and frequently delayed or confiscated goods bound for Omsk. Kolchak's political and military position was more vulnerable than it appeared. His army was top-heavy with officers but thin in the ranks; the peasants, fearing a return of the landlord regime, resisted conscription and swelled the partisan bands. Worst of all, the Czechs had become disenchanted with Kolchak and his unsavory following. Pending evacuation, they served as railway guards and refrained from further interference in the tortured affairs of Siberia. Since Denikin's forces seemed likely to reach Moscow first, Kolchak launched an offensive in the face of the approaching winter and made some superficially impressive gains before the campaign ground to a halt during the frigid months of January and February 1919.

During the period of relative inactivity that characterized the civil war during the winter of 1918–1919, Allied officials began to have doubts about their Russian policy. The collapse of the Central Powers had left untenable the specious argument that intervention was necessary to restore the eastern front which the Bolsheviks had so treacherously abandoned. Critical voices now raised the inevitable query: why were Allied troops still on Russian soil? A bloodletting of unparalleled ferocity having just ceased, it was only natural that public opinion was nowhere thirsting for a crusade against Bolshevism at the price of still more casualties. The politicians understood this better than the generals and diplomats. Of the major Allied statesmen, Premier Georges Clemenceau of France was the most outspoken in favor of more rather than less intervention. His opinion was shared by his military advisers—emphatically so by his chief of staff, Marshal Ferdinand Foch. As Russia's chief creditor, France had suffered the most heavily from the Bolshevik repudiation of the Tsarist debt and had felt the serpent's sting of the Brest-Litovsk "betrayal" the more acutely for being a faithful partner in the long-standing Franco-Russian alliance.

Great Britain was less resolute, perhaps because of Lloyd George's premonition that Bolshevism, while as "dangerous to civilization as German militarism," could not be crushed with the bayonet. His most redoubtable opponent, War Minister Winston Churchill, was an eloquent and untiring champion of any and all measures to dispatch the Communist state in its infancy; and his views often carried more weight in the war cabinet than those of the vacillating prime minister. It was Britain, however, not France, which bore the brunt of interventionist expense in its manifold forms.

The United States, reflecting the qualms of Wilson and his closest advisers, was the most reluctant of the powers to back further interference in Russian affairs. The President would have preferred to liquidate the whole sorry enterprise, for the conditions that had induced him to act no longer existed. But he felt duty-bound to work harmoniously with his allies, the most obstreperous of which—Japan —was now mired so deeply in Siberia that a unilateral renunciation of intervention might aggravate rather than alleviate a confused and abnormal situation.

The Bolsheviks were fully aware of these differences among the Allies and were especially gratified by the latent American-Japanese hostility in the Far East. Anxious for peace—even another Brest-Litovsk if need be—they looked upon Wilson with misgivings but as more approachable than his European partners because of his not unfriendly pronouncements on Russia from the time of his Fourteen Points address. Accordingly, a series of notes was sent to Washington to sound out the President on possible peace terms. The first, dated October 24, 1918, was less an offer to negotiate than a rhetorical indictment of Allied policy. Its insinuation that the Atlantic powers— naturally predatory because of their capitalist social order—could be bought off with concessions and territory was deliberately insulting; and the insolent tone of scornful sarcasm was well calculated to irritate Wilson, whose sense of humor—never robust—was altogether lacking on matters relating to Bolshevism and Soviet Russia. It is hardly surprising that no reply was forthcoming. Yet a straightforward offer to negotiate in a second note to Lansing on November 5 was likewise ignored.

The Soviet peace offensive nevertheless continued with several statements and proclamations indicating a desire for a settlement. Early in December Maxim Litvinov, who had become Chicherin's assistant in the Foreign Affairs Commissariat, was sent to Sweden to publicize Moscow's conciliatory attitude and to lay the groundwork for a *rapprochement* with the Allies through neutral channels. Litvinov's activities yielded no apparent results until the dispatch of his masterly Christmas Eve message to Wilson, then in Paris for the coming peace conference. The provocative outburst of two months before had now given way to a frank appeal to the President's "sense of justice and impartiality." Whatever he might think of Russia's "new social system," there was surely "no justification for sending foreign troops to fight against it, or for arming and supporting classes interested in the restoration of the old system of exploitation of man by man." The play to Wilson's idealism sounded the right psychological note and produced immediate results. Lloyd George was also favorably impressed by Litvinov's overture, and with the concurrence of the cabinet a British memorandum was circulated to the other Allied governments on January 3, 1919, suggesting both a temporary truce in Russia and an invitation to all factions, including the Bolsheviks, to send representatives to the Paris Peace Conference.

Although the proposal was abortive because of French objections ("the French government . . . will make no contract with crime"), Wilson sent William H. Buckler, an attaché at the American embassy in London, to sound out Litvinov in Stockholm. After conversations in mid-January, Buckler telegraphed that the Bolsheviks were prepared to make economic and territorial concessions, to protect foreign business firms, and to negotiate a debt settlement. He concluded that the "Soviet Government's conciliatory attitude is unquestionable."[12]

While the Buckler mission was offering the first sign that Moscow's campaign of amiability was being heeded in the West, the peace conference convened in Paris. It was a notable assembly, the most important diplomatic gathering since the Congress of Vienna more than a hundred years before. As can be seen more clearly in retrospect, the circumstances under which the conference met made it unlikely that another *pax Britannica* would follow the settlement at Paris. Allied public opinion demanded not only vengeance but a dictated peace. The wars of nationalism had reached their logical culmination: for the first time in modern history the vanquished powers were allowed no part in the negotiations. Despite his impressive knowledge of history and politics, Wilson was unprepared to fulfill his promise of a "peace of reconciliation." The "war to end war" had torn the fabric of Western civilization more deeply than he knew. His reliance upon mass idealism to thwart the vested political and economic interests that bred new wars was misplaced. The crowds who greeted him as the prophet of a new and better world were substantially the same as those who hailed the vacuous slogans of the day: "Hang the Kaiser!" and "Make the Germans Pay!" For a canny opportunist like Lloyd George and a cynical realist like Clemenceau the path of least resistance was the ultimate in political wisdom.

Among the unsolved—possibly insoluble—problems confronting the peacemakers, none was more complicated or perplexing than the "Russian question." Tangible difficulties—intervention, civil war, political boundaries, economic rehabilitation—were at least realities capable of being met with specific measures. But what was to be done about the survival of capitalist civilization itself in the face of an insidious threat which neither money, nor guns, nor economic blockade seemed able to stifle? As Karl Marx and Frederick Engels had put it in the opening passage of the *Communist Manifesto:* "A specter is haunting Europe—the specter of Communism." The apparition so easily exorcised in 1848 appeared to be of more durable stuff in 1919. By one of history's supreme ironies, Russia—the citadel of European reaction just two short years before—became the symbol of radicalism run amuck. Wherever in the coming weeks the "Red menace" could be discerned in Europe, Moscow, rightly or wrongly, was regarded as the focus of infection. The Bolsheviks were only too eager to take credit for the least indication of popular discontent, for it was a source of doctrinal satisfaction as well as a matter of pride that their regime, weak as it was, had the power of counterattacking beyond its circle of enemies. But so feebly developed was the spirit of nationalism among these revolutionary zealots that few would have balked at conceding Russia to the Whites in exchange for a German "October."

Russia was the unseen presence at Paris. None of the individuals and groups presuming to speak in the name of that troubled land were officially recognized at the conference. The Bolsheviks were automatically excluded; the Whites, vehemently protesting their lack of representation, confined their activities to propaganda and lobbying. The most elaborate of the *émigré* organizations was the Russian Political Conference, composed largely of former Tsarist diplomats and organized in Paris not long after the Bolshevik Revolution. For the most part it succeeded in bestowing an appearance of unity upon the White movement abroad, though dissatisfaction found expression in some quarters, and such prominent Russian expatriates as Kerensky and Milyukov were excluded altogether.

The first sessions of the Council of Ten (a body representing the executive and foreign minister of each of the five major Allies) revealed a fundamental but predictable disagreement between Anglo-American and Franco-Italian policy toward Russia. Both Wilson and Lloyd George eloquently portrayed the difficulties of combatting Bolshevism with armed force, particularly when none was available save the limited and uncertain strength represented by the White armies. Unpersuaded, Clemenceau and his foreign minister insisted that the last French ambassador to Russia, Joseph Noulens, be heard. On January 20, 1919, the well-coached envoy made his appearance. A fanatical anti-Bolshevik, he stressed the extreme debility of the Soviet government and the ease with which a token Allied force could topple it. Noulens was so blatantly a propagandist and so patently misinformed that he made a poor impression. Lloyd George dismissed him as a "pompous . . . shallow and unintelligent partisan."[13]

The next morning the former Danish minister to Petrograd, Harald de Scavenius, presented a more objective report while also urging further intervention. He envisaged a four-pronged attack converging upon Moscow: the Allies from the north, the Czechs and Kolchak from the east, Denikin from the south, and the Poles from the west. One hundred and fifty thousand volunteers, he estimated, would bring victory. When Lloyd George canvassed his colleagues as to the troops they could muster for such a force, the answers were revealingly unanimous: none.

After Scavenius had withdrawn, Wilson countered by reading Buckler's telegram from Stockholm. In the afternoon he offered a revised version of the plan recently broached by Lloyd George (that Bolshevik representatives be called to Paris "somewhat in the way that the Roman Empire summoned chiefs of outlying tributary states to render an account of their actions"). To assuage French pride and to insure that Paris would be undefiled by Bolshevik propaganda, it was proposed that a conference meet in the Greek city of Salonika. At length Clemenceau grudgingly agreed, not because he was convinced but because he wished to preserve a spirit of unity. Charged with drafting a suitable proclamation, Wilson personally typed a statement and presented it to the Council on the afternoon of January 22. Except for minor alterations and a change in the meeting place to the Turkish island of Prinkipo near Constantinople, the text was accepted unanimously. The Prinkipo proposal bore the distinctive imprint of its author's fervid idealism. The bulk of the document was, in fact, no more than a recitation of the good intentions allegedly motivating the Allies in their attitude toward Russia: "They [the powers] recognize the absolute right of the Russian people to direct their own affairs. . . . They do not wish to exploit or make use of Russia in any way. They recognize the revolution without reservation, and will in no way and in no circumstances aid or give countenance to any attempt at a counter-revolution." That Allied policy neither then nor later resembled in the slightest degree these stated aspirations was apparently accepted with equanimity by the signatories. The statement concluded with a blanket invitation to "every organized group" in Russia "now exercising, or attempting to exercise, political authority or military control," to send representatives to confer with the Allies on February 15 provided "there is a truce of arms amongst the parties involved."

The message was released to the press on the same day, only to meet a storm of editorial criticism in the Entente press and shrill outcries from the White *émigrés*. It was not officially transmitted to any of the contending factions, and the Soviet authorities first heard of the proposed meeting through a news item picked up by the Moscow radio. Though the Bolsheviks were piqued at this supposed slight, Chicherin was instructed to accept the invitation. In a radio message to the Allied governments, he offered major concessions along the lines of Litvinov's proposals to Buckler. At the time, both Wilson and Lloyd George were publicly silent about the Soviet response. Only several weeks later, after the Prinkipo Conference had been doomed by the refusal of the Whites to attend, did Wilson reveal that he and Lloyd George had judged the reply "studiously insulting" because of its implication that the Allies could be bought off with economic and territorial concessions. If that were truly the case, it is puzzling that they were not similarly displeased with the results of the Litvinov-Buckler parley. Undoubtedly the "insult" would have been more easily swallowed had the Whites proved cooperative. The anti-Bolshevik groups, both in Russia and in France, assumed a tone of outraged dignity at the notion of dealing with "red-handed murderers and assassins." Among the leading *émigrés,* only Kerensky had a kind word in public for Prinkipo—and that more than four months after the original proposal.

In point of fact, a conference to end the Russian civil war could have been convened without undue difficulty by February 15 or at any time within the next year had the Allies simply threatened to curtail further aid to the Whites. But the possibility was so remote that it was never considered; indeed, Kolchak and Denikin continued to receive war matériel and assurances of additional support while the Prinkipo plan was still under consideration. Although it is unnecessary to question the good faith of Wilson and Lloyd George, it is clear that the conference failed because the Russian Whites were encouraged by the Allies, especially the French, to boycott the proceedings.

The burial of the Prinkipo scheme coincided with Lloyd George's return to London on February 9, 1919, and Wilson's departure for the United States six days later. The only glimmer of hope for an armistice in Russia now centered on a confidential American mission to Moscow sent on the initiative of Lansing and Edward M. House, presumably with the President's knowledge and consent. It was headed by William C. Bullitt, then a State Department aide with the peace delegation and later the first American ambassador to the Soviet Union. He brought tentative and unofficial peace terms formulated chiefly by House and Philip Kerr, the prime minister's confidential secretary. He arrived in Russia early in March and remained in Moscow approximately a week while Chicherin and Litvinov, under Lenin's general supervision, met him daily in an attempt to draft an armistice agreement. Bullitt returned to Paris toward the end of the month with a document promising a cease fire by April 10, provided the Allies accepted the other

Soviet proposals. These included recognition by Moscow of the territorial conquests of the White regimes, withdrawal of Allied troops
and a lifting of the blockade, a political amnesty, and Soviet responsibility for Russia's foreign debts. Bullitt was impressed with the stability of Bolshevik rule, and in his formal report he boldly maintained
that "no government save a socialist government can be set up in
Russia to-day except by foreign bayonets."[14]

Unfortunately, the auguries for a new peace effort were not as
propitious as they had been a month or two earlier. Wilson, back in
Paris, was concerned with German problems and because of his admitted "one track mind" refused even to see Bullitt. Lloyd George
preferred to temporize, fearful of the power of the London press and
the Conservative opposition; and he went on record with a public
denial that a Soviet peace overture had ever been made. Furthermore,
Bolshevism had for the first time leaped the Russian frontier. On
March 21 a Soviet republic was proclaimed in Hungary, and two
weeks later Bavaria succumbed to the engulfing Red tide.[15] Though
both regimes were to prove ephemeral, most Western diplomats would
have agreed with House that they were "sitting upon an open powder
magazine which some day a spark may ignite." There were those in
Moscow who thought the conflagration at hand. In the Western capitals, where uneasiness but not panic reigned, advocates of negotiation
and advocates of intervention still argued as to the best means of
halting the Bolshevik menace. By mid-April of 1919 Kolchak's spring
offensive toward the Volga showed such promise that the interventionists were definitely in the ascendancy. In the last analysis, as Bullitt correctly surmised, this shift of fortune on the battlefield was
responsible for the quiet scuttling of his project.

Before the April 10 deadline set by Moscow automatically cancelled
the proposal, an unwitting but potentially useful mediator appeared
from an unexpected quarter: Fridtjof Nansen, the internationally
known Norwegian explorer, statesman, and humanitarian, was persuaded by Herbert Hoover, chairman of the American Relief Administration, to head a commission for Russian relief. Together they
drafted identical letters to the "Big Four" (Wilson, Lloyd George,
Clemenceau, and Premier Vittorio Orlando of Italy) in Nansen's name
asking for approval and support of the enterprise. Bullitt was asked to
outline a suitable reply, for House conceived the notion that peace
might be forthcoming more easily via a backdoor approach ("under
the guise of a purely humanitarian plan") than a frontal—and dis-
tressingly public—assault. After Bullitt had fused the twin problems
of peace and food to his own satisfaction, the text was virtually emas-

culated by other State Department officials to include terms, recommended by Hoover, which the Soviet government could hardly have accepted. Bullitt, under protest, was permitted to make only stylistic changes, and it was substantially this version that Nansen received on April 17 as an answer from the Big Four. The letter expressed qualified approval of the proposed commission and referred to the "cessation of all hostilities" as an "obvious" precondition of relief measures. But nothing, not even an offer to withdraw Allied troops, was said about how an armistice might be attained. Nor was the vague proviso that food distribution was to be "solely under the control of the people of Russia" reassuring to the suspicious Bolsheviks.

When the letters were made public, the Russian Whites broke forth in a torrent of abuse. The plan was designed, they complained, to give moral and material aid to the Bolsheviks on the very eve of their overthrow. Since the United States was expected to finance the scheme, the conservative French press pointed to American economic imperialism as the motivating factor behind it—a charge that would have come more appropriately from Soviet Russia. As innocuous as the exchange of letters was, Nansen experienced considerable difficulty in transmitting the text to Moscow. The government radio stations in Western Europe refused him their facilities, and he decided to go to Russia himself. In Berlin en route he was able to get a message through, and a reply from Chicherin awaited him in Norway. Dated May 7, 1919, it thanked Nansen warmly for his generous offer but was openly skeptical of Allied motives. To insure that the relief program was really humanitarian and non-political, the Soviet government again suggested peace negotiations. The Allies were wholly indifferent to this fresh overture. No reply was considered and none was sent. Nansen abandoned his journey to Moscow as hopeless, and Bullitt resigned from government service with a scorching letter to the President concerning the iniquities of a peace that would "make new international conflicts certain."

Wilson's apathy toward Russian affairs after the failure of the Prinkipo meeting settled the fate of the lethargic peace efforts that followed. In effect, he gave the initiative to Clemenceau, whose policy of stoking the fires of civil war was pursued unwaveringly throughout the Paris Peace Conference. Lloyd George lacked the excuse of apathy. His dubious stock of political courage wilted under the steady drumfire of his Right wing critics. His considered opinion in January was that conciliation rather than force would solve the Russian problem; by April he had shifted to the view that the Allies owed a moral obligation to Kolchak and Denikin. To send them munitions, he told the

House of Commons on April 16, was "not in the least regard . . . a departure from the fundamental policy of Great Britain not to interfere in the internal affairs of any land." The fleeting Anglo-American entente on Russian affairs had thus reverted to the original Anglo-French policy—never really abandoned—of subsidizing the anti-Bolshevik movement.

As if to compensate that relatively powerless segment of Allied opinion outspokenly in favor of a "hands off Russia" policy from the beginning, the extreme advocates of direct intervention, such as Churchill and Foch, suffered a defeat that no further alarms about the Red peril could effectively counteract. The setback occurred in South Russia, where the French forces occupying the northern shore of the Black Sea[16] were obliged to withdraw. French censorship allowed few details to filter through, but it became evident that if the Russian conflict was to be prolonged it could not be accomplished with Allied manpower. The primary reason for the failure of French intervention was the deteriorating morale of the expeditionary force, leading in the end to disaffection and mutiny. In their only sizable engagement on Russian soil, the French suffered perhaps 400 casualties in a futile defense of Kherson on March 10, 1919, against pro-Soviet Ukrainian partisans. The bulk of their troops were withdrawn to Odessa, where the military situation would not have been unfavorable had the will to fight remained. On April 2 orders from Paris for an immediate evacuation relieved the mounting anxiety of the local commander. Within four days the last French vessels cleared the harbor with 30,000 civilians and 10,000 soldiers of the Volunteer Army in addition to the interventionist forces. Less than two weeks later the French units in the Crimea were withdrawn as mutiny broke out in the fleet at Sevastopol. Among the ringleaders of the revolt was Andre Marty, a petty officer who was to become one of the leaders of the French Communist party. A living legend in international Communist circles in the 1930's, his role in the Black Sea mutiny was considerably more modest than either his friends or his enemies were later to portray it.

The disaster in South Russia—scantily reported in the West—was overshadowed by the news from Kolchak's headquarters, where false optimism and distorted information combined to produce daily bulletins heralding the imminent fall of the Red capital. The admiral's fortunes reached a peak in the spring of 1919. With his failure to capture Kazan and Samara, the key cities on the upper Volga, his power began to seep away. A Red offensive in May rolled the Whites back in a steady retreat to the Urals. Kolchak's sole victory was diplomatic, and it availed him nothing in the end. The Allied Supreme Council in

Paris, attempting to establish formal relations with his regime, sent a message to Omsk on May 26. In the usual litany of self-justification, the note denied any intention of interfering in Russia's internal affairs; and for good measure, the reasons for the collapse of the Prinkipo Conference were flagrantly misrepresented. The body of the message asked Kolchak's agreement to a number of propositions: the summoning of a constituent assembly upon his reaching Moscow; free elections; responsibility for Russia's foreign debts; independence for Poland and Finland; and an autonomous status, pending a final settlement, for the Baltic states, the Caucasus, and the Trans-Caspian territories. However galling to his pride, the admiral could but accept in substance the Allied conditions. They were, after all, mainly "for the record" to forestall liberal criticism of the Allies for backing a reactionary dictator. Nonetheless, an "escape clause" was left open in Kolchak's answer by reserving to the future constituent assembly "the final sanction of the decisions which may be taken in the name of Russia." Perhaps as a reflection of the changing military complexion in Siberia, the Supreme Council in its acknowledgment on June 12 withheld formal recognition from the Omsk government but expressed satisfaction with the terms of the reply and promised further support.

Most of this additional assistance came from the United States, where funds advanced to the Provisional Government in 1917 were used to pay for the war matériel rushed across the Pacific to Vladivostok. East of Lake Baikal the greater portion of Kolchak's lifeline—the Trans-Siberian—was still safeguarded by American troops and its operating efficiency maintained by a corps of American railway experts. The importance of keeping open this vital transportation artery justified the continued presence of American soldiers in Siberia, Wilson contended, in his reply to a Senate resolution of June 27, 1919, seeking information on conditions there. Yet the abstention of these troops from active participation in the anti-Bolshevik struggle so infuriated Kolchak that he was moved upon one occasion to fulminate against the expeditionary force as "a factor of disintegration and disorders" whose recruits were composed of the "refuse of the American army" and "Jewish emigrants with a corresponding commanding staff."[17] Graves himself absorbed much abuse as a Bolshevik sympathizer from Allied commanders as well as from the Whites.

The disintegration of the Kolchak army was delayed by the resurgence of Denikin's forces in the south and Trotsky's consequent hesitancy in ordering a further advance. But Lenin sided with the proponents of a "hot pursuit," and by late summer it was clear except to devotees of the highly colored accounts in the Western press that the Omsk regime was on the point of collapse. Superiority on the battlefield was only part of the story. That the peasants usually welcomed the Reds as liberators attested to the popularity of the Kolchak forces. Indifference, desertion, and mutiny in White ranks were additional symptoms of inner decay. By October the semblance of an orderly retreat had been abandoned. As tens of thousands of soldiers and refugees swarmed into Omsk, the government fled to Irkutsk, 1,300 miles to the east. It was soon followed by Allied military and diplomatic personnel, including the Czech legionnaires, whose insistence upon priority in the evacuation was bitterly resented by the Whites. The overburdened railroad could accommodate only a fraction of its potential passengers. Possibly a million persons perished from hunger, disease, and cold in the exodus—far more than the victims claimed on Siberian battlefields. Of more than 200,000 men who had once been under Kolchak's command, less than 20,000 were in organized units after reaching the relative safety of eastern Siberia.

The Red Army entered Omsk on November 14, 1919, and pushed on in an almost bloodless mopping up operation. The admiral himself, slow to comprehend the extent of the disaster, finally abdicated as "supreme ruler" in favor of Denikin early in the new year. Semyenov was appointed commander of all White forces east of Lake Baikal. Kolchak sought sanctuary with the Czechs, but upon reaching Irkutsk he was handed over to the city authorities. A pro-Soviet committee assumed power a short time later, and to avoid a rescue attempt by a nearby White detachment he was shot by a firing squad on February 7, 1920.

The Kolchak debacle did not end the civil war, but the back of the White movement was broken, and the Allies were at last thoroughly disenchanted with the notion that proxy armies could accomplish what their own were unwilling to do. The North Russian venture under British auspices[18] had already been liquidated in the fall of 1919—a fiasco from start to finish. What had begun in Murmansk as an anti-German move had gradually assumed an outright anti-Soviet complexion. After the Armistice with Germany, it was too late to remove the troops before the ports froze over for the winter; and the Entente powers did not, in any case, object in principle to a prolongation of the expedition if it was decided later to enlarge the scope of the intervention in the spring. Washington made it plain, however, that the American contingent would be withdrawn as soon as weather conditions permitted.

The terrible cold of the Arctic winter and the purposelessness of the campaign combined to produce a state of morale that at times bordered on mutiny. News of open insubordination in the ranks caused such perturbation in London and Paris that serious consideration was given toward evacuation. The officers sought to revive the flagging spirits of their men with anti-Bolshevik propaganda, including harrowing tales of Red atrocities. Largely for this reason, the expedition was further disfigured by the shooting of Soviet prisoners of war.

In the summer of 1919 the Americans—about 5,600 in all—departed for home, leaving 244 of their dead behind. A portion of the British troops and the single French unit assigned to Archangel were also removed. The transports brought British reinforcements in even greater numbers than those who left, but the psychological blow to the anti-Bolshevik cause in North Russia was irreparable. More destructive in the long run was the continuation of a regime of repression, which in the name of stamping out Bolshevism alienated the civilian population by arbitrary arrests and unwarranted executions. The Russian recruits—many of them conscripts—proved unreliable, and frequent instances of disaffection culminated on July 7 in a mutinous outburst in which a number of British and Russian officers were killed in their quarters. Two weeks later a regiment holding the front southwest of Archangel abandoned it to the Red Army, thereby severing communications with Murmansk until reinforcements were able to repair the gap.

Already disillusioned by the strength of the Reds and the impossibility of linking his army with that of Kolchak, the Allied commander, General Sir William Ironside, despaired of salvaging a forlorn enterprise. He advised London to undertake evacuation as soon as possible. To the consternation of the White government, the forthcoming departure of the British units was announced at the end of July. Offensive operations nevertheless took place during the summer, and it was late in September before the expeditionary force and some 6,500 civilians left Archangel. The last of the troops in Murmansk were withdrawn a few weeks later. The British spent approximately $500,000,000 on the North Russian campaign; and of their total commitment of over 18,000 men, nearly a thousand casualties were suffered, including 327 fatalities. While these losses were trivial compared to the human and financial cost of the World War, the utter futility of the venture, either as a counter-revolutionary movement or as a military measure against Germany, serves to underscore the folly of this minor sideshow in the total drama of Allied intervention.

Refusing every opportunity to evacuate his forces, the Russian commander, General Miller, resolved to fight on against hopeless odds with the uncertain support of some 25,000 White troops. Engaged on other fronts, the Reds made no concerted drive against the northern territory until February 1920. Aided by further mutinous outbreaks, they entered Archangel on the 21st and Murmansk several days later. Miller, his staff, and members of the government fled to Norway on an icebreaker, and the core of his army—about 1,500 anti-Bolsheviks— escaped to Finland. So ended the White movement in North Russia— an ineffectual appendage to Britain's anti-Soviet policy.

IV

The year 1919 brought an upsurge of counter-revolutionary strength from a wholly new direction—the Baltic region. This fresh addition to the cause of anti-Bolshevism was the Northwest Army under the command of General Nikolai Yudenich, a Russian officer who had won distinction for his campaigns against the Turks in the World War. This force was an outgrowth of the confused struggle over the Baltic provinces following the German withdrawal. Moscow recognized the three Baltic states as "Soviet Republics" on December 23, 1918, but was unable to enforce its authority. A brief Soviet occupation of Latvia and part of Lithuania was ended in the spring of 1919 by a Latvian-German force of volunteers financed by secret funds from the German high command. The Red Army had been unable to penetrate Estonia. A small corps of Russian Whites had joined the defense; and this contingent, augmented by Red deserters and Estonian troops, launched a spring offensive capped in mid-June by the capture of Krasnaya Gorka, a Baltic fortress less than fifty miles from Petrograd.

Shortly thereafter Kolchak appointed Yudenich commander of all White forces in the Baltic region—in effect, the unit which became known as the Northwest Army. Civilians and soldiers in the occupied area were fed by the American Relief Administration; the British promised munitions and equipment; and Kolchak's government advanced $500,000 from funds furnished by England. A Soviet counterattack, backed by reinforcements recalled from the pursuit of Kolchak's retreating army, regained most of the lost ground in July and August. The reconquest was aided by the temporary defection of Estonia in protest over Yudenich's unsympathetic attitude toward her national aspirations. Denikin's forces threatening Moscow from the south prevented a more vigorous Red offensive. Early in August the anticipated supplies from England began to arrive in quantity for Yudenich's army. The British military representative was thus in a position to demand that the Whites set up a "democratic government"—he gave them a forty-minute ultimatum on August 10—which would recognize the independence of Estonia, whose passive support was vital to any undertaking against Soviet Russia. The necessary measures were adopted forthwith, and at the behest of the British plans were made for another march on Petrograd.

On the eve of the projected campaign—both sides were reinforced during the course of the battle—Yudenich commanded an army of over 18,000 as opposed to 25,000 soldiers of rather inferior quality constituting the Seventh Red Army. The superior armament of the Northwest Army, especially in heavy artillery and British-manned tanks, tended to equalize the manpower differential. The British navy blockaded Petrograd, and a torpedo boat action against the Russian fleet at Kronstadt was reported to have sunk two capital ships. On the diplomatic front, British pressure on Finland to join the attack was unsuccessful.

In late September of 1919, just as Denikin's push toward Moscow was gaining momentum, Yudenich hurled his army against Petrograd. The Soviet regime was again in grave peril; and the Western press, nettled by Kolchak's failure, hailed anew the imminent downfall of the Bolshevik edifice with anticipatory delight. Lenin proposed the abandonment of Petrograd to strengthen the defenses of Moscow. Even a retreat to the Urals was considered. As the symbol of the Revolution, Petrograd was of immense psychological significance despite its limited strategic value, and Trotsky's insistence that it could be saved without impairing the southern front won over the skeptics. Placed in command, the Red commissar reached the stricken city on October 16 and with characteristic *élan* galvanized the dispirited defenders into a supreme effort. On the 21st the Whites were halted within sight of their goal and never regained the initiative. The retreat soon began, and within three weeks the shattered remnants of the Northwest Army passed on to Estonian soil, where the local authorities, anxious to avoid a Soviet attack, disarmed the survivors.

The Bolshevik triumph at Petrograd was duplicated on the more critical front south of Moscow. The now formidable Volunteer Army[19] —since renamed the Armed Forces of South Russia—had prospered in the spring of 1919, less from its own inner resources than from the difficulties of the Soviet regime. In the Ukraine these troubles included widespread peasant disturbances and the rebellion of Red partisan units, one of which had driven the French from Kherson in March. The way was thus prepared for a vigorous White offensive in late May and early June; and it brought Denikin the accolade of Russia's foremost anti-Bolshevik crusader to replace the tarnished figure of Kolchak. The moral and material assistance lavished upon the Siberian Whites by the Allies was as generously forthcoming in the case of

South Russia, though it was almost exclusively a British prerogative. Besides several hundred military advisers and technicians, including a few aviators, Britain sent through the Black Sea port of Novorossiisk arms, equipment, and supplies for nearly a quarter of a million men.

Stretching over a 700 mile front from Tsaritsyn (later Stalingrad) in the east to Kiev in the west, Denikin's lines became dangerously overextended by late summer. His peak strength of 150,000 men was constantly drained by combat hardships and disaffection in the rear, while the Red Army, with manpower reserves to draw upon, grew steadily stronger until it outnumbered the enemy by perhaps 75,000. At Orel, 240 miles south of Moscow, the climactic struggle of the campaign took place in mid-October. The Whites were driven from the city; and within three weeks the familiar signs of disintegration, so fatal to the armies of Kolchak and Yudenich, reduced Denikin's forces to disorder and impotence.

By the beginning of 1920 the Soviet regime was firmly entrenched. The Whites were scattered and disorganized, and the Allied troops in Siberia were content to play a passive role. The real threat to Bolshevik rule was economic dislocation and the gaunt specter of famine and disease. Hunger was an adversary before whom the army was helpless, and the party leaders hastened to shore up the battered economy as soon as the exigencies of war permitted. Since War Communism was still their frame of reference, it was extended rather than modified. For a time it was hoped that the militarization of labor might provide a solution to the problems of production; and Trotsky's panacea of converting idle units of the Red Army into labor battalions was given a trial, only to prove, in the words of one observer, "an empty bureaucratic fantasy."[20]

The prospects for one sector of the economy—foreign trade—were enhanced by the lifting of the Allied economic blockade on January 16, 1920. The move was a portent of lessened hostility toward the Bolsheviks, but in no sense was their regime regarded as worthy of the normal amenities between civilized states. As Lloyd George informed the House of Commons on February 10, "Commerce has a sobering influence"; and trade "will bring an end to the ferocity, the rapine, and the crudities of Bolshevism surer than any other method." Force, he acknowledged, had "failed to restore Russia to sanity."

In Siberia the application of force had indeed failed, but the expedition had not yet run its course. The last of the Entente troops had been withdrawn two months before. The Czechs, however, were still in the process of evacuation, a cumbersome procedure not completed until September 1920. Japan was disturbed by the departure of her allies, and her leaders had sought to delay it. As participants in a collective enterprise, they were safer from the censure of world opinion and the scrutiny of the Japanese people; alone, of course, Soviet weakness enabled them to exploit Siberia almost at will. The Americans did not leave until February and March of 1920. As the last transport cleared the harbor at Vladivostok on April 1, a Japanese band on the quay played "Hard Times Come Again No More."

Within a few days of the American evacuation, Japanese troops seized Vladivostok and most of the cities of the Maritime Province from the local Russian authorities. The occupation was carried out with calculated brutality: in Khabarovsk, for example, the townspeople were machine-gunned in the streets in a two-day reign of terror. Japanese spokesmen managed to confuse the outside world with their own version of events. Nonetheless, unfavorable world publicity might have sobered Tokyo's expansionists had not the Nikolayevsk incident of May 25 provided a ready-made excuse for further saber-rattling in eastern Siberia.

Nikolayevsk, strategically located near the mouth of the Amur River and across the straits from the northern part of Sakhalin Island, had been taken by Red partisans in February 1920. The approach of Japanese troops led to a frenzied orgy of destruction in which the city was burned and several hundred Japanese soldiers and civilians were killed. In Tokyo an elaborate government-sponsored propaganda campaign, including public meetings and parades, sought with limited success to whip up a spirit of chauvinism. On July 3 it was announced that in retaliation for the massacre northern Sakhalin and the entire Siberian coast from Nikolayevsk southward to the Korean border would be placed under Japanese occupation pending a satisfactory settlement and the establishment of a responsible Russian government.

Soviet authority extended no farther east than Lake Baikal, for Moscow curbed the Red Army commanders lest Tokyo be provoked to a full-scale invasion. In Russia's enfeebled condition Japan was too powerful to oppose by armed force. The Kremlin parried instead with diplomacy. Its most artful stratagem was the creation of a separate state in Siberia known as the Far Eastern Republic. This artificial entity was largely the handiwork of Alexander Krasnoshchekov, a political exile who had returned to Russia from the United States in 1917. A convinced Bolshevik, he had played a role of some importance in Siberian politics prior to the intervention. Kolchak's rout enabled him to revive his dormant plan for a non-Communist buffer state between Japan in the east and Soviet Russia in the west. With Moscow's secret consent, his ambition was realized on April 6, 1920, when a congress of workers and partisans founded the Provisional Government of the Far Eastern Republic at Verkhne-Udinsk near the eastern shore of Lake Baikal. Its jurisdiction—necessarily somewhat hypothetical—included the southern portion of eastern Siberia and northern Sakhalin.

The Republic was eventually to acquire all the outward accouterment of a progressive capitalist democracy while remaining a camouflaged stalking horse for Moscow's diplomatic aims. The Soviet government conferred official recognition upon its own appendage on May 14; and though the precedent was not followed by any other country, the supposedly independent status of the Republic was given general credence abroad. At first distinctly nonplussed by the appearance of this hybrid regime within her sphere of influence, Japan in due course made overtures with a view toward dominating the new state and using it as a tool against Moscow. By mid-summer Red partisans menaced Nippon's position; and with mounting criticism of intervention at home and growing displeasure in Washington, Japanese and F.E.R. representatives agreed that Tokyo would withdraw its troops from the Trans-Baikal region in return for the "neutrality" of Moscow's satellite republic.

Among the varied causes of Japan's more conciliatory policy was the impressive performance of the Red Army against the Poles, a struggle that might be called the last of the wars of intervention against revolutionary Russia. The rebirth of Poland had come with the collapse of the Central Powers. As an Allied protégé the new republic had fared well at the Paris Peace Conference by regaining as her western and southern border essentially the pre-partition frontiers of 1772. Poland was in fact the eastern anchor of the Versailles settlement. Her boundary facing Russia was left undefined at Paris; indeed the Poles had been engaged in seizing eastern Galicia from the Ukrainian forces of Petlyura and a portion of Lithuania from Soviet and Lithuanian troops while the peace conference was still in progress. By the summer of 1919 the *fait accompli* was tacitly accepted by the West, a miscalculation that only encouraged the "greater Poland" fantasies of her leaders —notably the Polish "strong man," Marshal Joseph Pilsudski. For the rest of the year Polish troops were poised on the *de facto* Russian frontier, well to the east of a fair ethnic line but unwilling to launch an all-out attack that would surely install Kolchak, Denikin, or Yudenich in power. As hostile to Red Russia as the Poles were, a White Russia was infinitely worse, for to the Whites an independent Poland was anathema—and especially so in the case of Pilsudski's dream of a federation to include the Ukraine, Lithuania, and Byelo-Russia.

Beholden to France for diplomatic and military assistance, the Poles maneuvered with masterful finesse in displaying the proper degree of bellicosity toward the Bolsheviks while offering clandestine assurances that their intentions were honorable and, for the moment, pacific. With the White movement broken by late fall, the Soviet leaders strove to perpetuate the informal truce by offering Warsaw generous territorial concessions. The almost supplicating tone of these communications failed to sway Pilsudski—only one was even acknowledged. The Polish public was not informed of the Soviet overtures, though in any case there is no reason to suppose that a sizable body of opinion objected to a provocative policy toward Russia, whatever reservations might exist about an unprovoked attack. Finally, in answer to a Soviet note of March 27, 1920, the Polish foreign minister suggested peace talks at Borisov, close behind the Polish lines, but without proper safeguards to insure an effective truce. The terms were made intentionally humiliating so as to be unacceptable. Moscow's counter-offer of a general armistice and a neutral country as more appropriate for the negotiations met a negative response.

Pilsudski was determined to force the issue on the field of battle, and after months of border incidents the Poles struck suddenly on April 27 in the direction of the Ukraine. Petlyura's diminished forces also joined the assault. Resistance was haphazard, and by May 7 Kiev was taken. What seemed a brilliant stroke of military strategy concealed a costly political blunder. Conservative Russians to whom Bolshevism was an execration rallied to defend the fatherland against the invader; and opinion in the West, while far from pro-Soviet, was inclined to be critical of such bare-faced aggression. The Red leaders were gratified by the ground-swell of patriotic sentiment but deliberately chose to fight the war as a class conflict in accordance with their Marxist presuppositions. Soviet propaganda was therefore respectful of Poland's right to independence, and sympathy was invariably expressed for the workers and peasants under the yoke of a "capitalist-landlord regime."

The Poles had little opportunity to enjoy their triumph. The Ukrainian peasants were quick to resent the excesses of the Polish troops and the pro-landlord policy that marked their occupation. The appearance toward the end of the month of Semyon Budyenny's cavalry corps, already renowned for its exploits against Denikin, was welcomed with enthusiasm. With the additional help of several infantry units, the Poles were driven beyond their original base in a retreat that verged upon a rout. To the north, an offensive under the command of the youthful Soviet general Mikhail Tukhachevsky forced the enemy to abandon Byelo-Russia and Lithuania in July and to fall back upon the approaches to Warsaw.

With mounting despair, the Poles implored the Entente to intervene and save them from the consequences of their own folly. British policy, in contrast with that of France, had never been more than lukewarm toward Poland, but the prospect of a victorious Red Army in Central Europe moved her statesmen to prompt action. Lord Curzon, the foreign secretary, warned Moscow in a note on July 11, 1920, to conclude a truce on a provisional ethnographic frontier—the final boundary to be determined later at a conference in London—or to face the consequences of all-out Entente support to Poland. Chicherin's reply on the 17th rebuffed outside mediation in favor of direct negotiations with Warsaw. The still reluctant Poles, heeding London's advice, asked for a parley five days later. Moscow's reply was positive but unenthusiastic. Nothing came of the proposed talks, for the Russians were now the reluctant party to the dispute. Lenin and his colleagues, with Trotsky and Radek the chief dissenters, were lured on by the mirage of a Soviet Poland and yielded to the temptation of exporting Bolshevism by force—to "probe Europe with the bayonets of the Red Army," as Lenin is said to have put it.[21]

Late in July Soviet troops crossed the projected "Curzon line." Moscow formed a committee of Polish Communists to serve as the political authority in the occupied area—the nucleus of Poland's future Soviet government. The committee busied itself with appeals to the "toiling masses" and similar propaganda activity, only to demonstrate the profound miscalculation of the Bolsheviks in believing that the Red soldiers would be greeted as liberators rather than the invading army of a hereditary enemy.

The Poles asked for definite peace terms, and the Soviet government complied on August 10 with a series of demands indicating greater interest in a Red Poland than in territorial gain. The proposed boundary was actually considerably to the east of the Curzon line. Lloyd George, incorrectly informed as to the Russian terms, urged Warsaw to accept. Pilsudski braced his troops for a last stand before the capital. War matériel was now in better supply thanks to the generosity of the Entente, whose support was advertised by the presence of a military and political mission. The French chief of staff, General Maxime Weygand, became the leading military adviser to the Poles and was credited by many Western observers with saving Warsaw. Aid to Poland was achieved against the vehement opposition of many organized groups of European workers. In the most publicized instance of proletarian militance, London dockworkers refused to load munitions for Poland upon the *Jolly George,* an English vessel bound for Danzig.

As defenders of their homeland, the Polish troops were better equipped psychologically than when they had fought on alien soil. The Red Army, in turn, encountered the difficulties of sustaining an offensive far from its base of operations amidst a hostile population. Its main strength was centered north of Warsaw, and between these troops and the southern army, where Budyenny's cavalry was still the major component, a dangerous gap appeared. On August 16, as the Russians pressed into the suburbs of the city, the Poles launched a well-prepared counter-thrust that startled even the most optimistic by the ease of its success. The "miracle of the Vistula" had been wrought against apparently impossible odds. Poland had thrown back the Asiatic hordes of Bolshevism on the very threshold of Western civilization—or so it seemed to conservative Europeans.

Once the Red Army was in full retreat the Kremlin made no attempt to retrieve its blunder. Loss of territory was distinctly secondary to ideological defeat, and the Poles reconquered their lost provinces against an apathetic defense. Both sides had known the exaltation of victory and the despondency of defeat. In a chastened mood, they began peace negotiations at Riga on September 21, 1920. The Russians, seeking a quick agreement in order to deal with the last of the White generals, offered generous terms considering the position of the two armies. On October 12 an armistice was concluded with the boundary running between the Curzon line and the frontier of 1772. More than 6,000,000 Ukrainians and Byelo-Russians were thus placed under Polish rule. The formal Treaty of Riga, signed on March 18, 1921, remained in force until the outbreak of World War II began a new chapter in Russo-Polish relations.

V

The war with Poland had permitted a temporary revival of the Whites under Baron Peter Wrangel, one of Denikin's prominent generals. Denikin himself had been expelled from the Caucasus with the vestiges of his once proud army in March 1920.[22] Some of his troops had been evacuated on British ships to the Crimean Peninsula. Still the commander of more than 35,000 men, he chose to resign in Wrangel's favor because of the loss of confidence in his leadership. But prospects for a new offensive seemed dismal indeed when it was learned that the British had wearied of the long struggle and were threatening to curtail further aid.

The Polish attack offered the first hope of effective action against the Bolsheviks, and Wrangel gladly accepted the French suggestion that the two forces coordinate their military effort. Since the Polish retreat from Kiev made this impossible, the basis of cooperation was the purely fortuitous one of a joint endeavor against a common enemy. The increasing agitation of British labor against subsidizing the civil war induced Downing Street to strive for an armistice, although the flow of supplies to the Crimea discreetly continued. French assistance, less inhibited and in greater quantity, enabled Wrangel to enjoy the distinction of being the only outstanding White commander who was not in the final analysis a British puppet. The French also encouraged Wrangel by recognizing his regime as the *de facto* government of Russia.

Early in the summer of 1920 the Whites broke out of the Crimean bottleneck but were unable to exploit their position in the southern Ukraine. A descent upon the Cossack territory of the Kuban on the eastern shore of the Sea of Azov failed dismally, and in the fall an offensive toward the lower Dnieper also collapsed. The end of hostilities with Poland allowed the full force of the Red Army to fall upon Wrangel—in Trotsky's biting phrase, the "German hireling of the French loan-sharks."[23] The outcome was a foregone conclusion. The Whites were driven back to their peninsular base, and after a vain attempt early in November to hold their fortified positions at the Isthmus of Perekop, the connecting link between the Crimea and the mainland, the remaining troops fled to the nearest ports. Some 100,000 soldiers and 50,000 civilians escaped on board Russian and Allied vessels. At Constantinople an attempt was made to keep the army intact in order to pursue the struggle against Bolshevism at a later date. But eventually the units dispersed to the Balkans—and beyond— where tens of thousands of other *émigrés* were already painfully adjusting to a new way of life.

Except for the groups still under Japanese protection, Wrangel's Crimean campaign represented the dying gasp of the White movement in Russia. Left to their own devices the Whites could never have become a serious threat to the Soviet regime. With foreign backing they had come close to victory; without it the possibility of recovering their homeland, a fantasy nourished by a generation of expatriates, was to prove delusive.

The exhausted Russia that emerged from more than six years of intermittent foreign and domestic strife was considerably diminished geographically. Aside from the areas yet to be reclaimed to Soviet rule, the lost territory was exclusively in European Russia; and from the standpoint of power politics almost all of it constituted a part of the *cordon sanitaire,* a belt of small anti-Soviet, Western-oriented states which from Finland in the north to Bulgaria in the south was intended to seal off Russia—and the Bolshevik bacillus—from the rest of Europe.

The tiny Baltic republics achieved formal independence in 1920 when Moscow, seeking a *rapprochement* with the Entente, negotiated separate agreements with each. Estonia because the first to sign on February 2. Lithuania, fearful of Polish aggression, followed on July 12, and Latvia completed the pacts on August 11. All three received an equitable boundary settlement and a generous monetary indemnity as a share of the gold reserves of the Tsarist regime. Careful to maintain officially "correct" diplomatic relations with their powerful Slavic neighbor, they were too small to exert the full liberty of action to which their sovereignty entitled them and became the center of much anti-Soviet intrigue.

Finland was the last of the Russian succession states to come to terms with Moscow. Finnish independence had been recognized in the waning moments of the year 1917, but civil war broke out soon afterward, with the Reds requesting Soviet help and the Whites appealing similarly to Germany and Sweden. Since the Bolsheviks were unable to furnish armed assistance—only 1,000 volunteers remained after the Brest-Litovsk peace—German intervention with troops and matériel was decisive in achieving a White victory in May 1918. After several abortive attempts to arrive at a territorial settlement, the Treaty of Dorpat (Tartu) was signed on October 14, 1920. Finland relinquished her demands for eastern Karelia but received a part of the Karelian Isthmus near Petrograd and the district of Petsamo in the far north, giving her a narrow corridor to the Arctic Ocean.

Other Soviet territorial losses were minor but not inconsequential. In January 1918 Rumania had taken advantage of Soviet weakness by occupying Bessarabia, an area originally ceded to Russia by the Turks in 1812. Moscow naturally regarded it as a Soviet irredenta—an "Alsace-Lorraine on the Dniester"—until the upheaval of World War II brought its return.

The Ottoman Empire had been awarded the districts of Kars, Ardahan, and Batum along the Caucasian frontier by the Treaty of Brest-Litovsk. But the establishment of Georgia as an independent state under a Menshevik government and British occupation of the area until the summer of 1920 prevented effective negotiations with Turkey after the defeat of the Central Powers. Soviet aid to the revolutionary Turkish government of Mustapha Kemal in its war with the Greeks and the conquest of Georgia by the Red Army in February and March of 1921 facilitated an amicable settlement on March 16 in which Batum was returned to Soviet rule and Kars and Ardahan were ceded to Turkey.

Following the defeat of various separatist movements in Soviet Central Asia in 1920 and early 1921, the Japanese remained the only organized force on Russian soil hostile to Muscovite authority. In accordance with the agreement with the Far Eastern Republic,[24] Japanese troops were gradually withdrawn from the Trans-Baikal region along with various White units. Semyenov's were among them, and with the evacuation of his forces from Chita, it became the new capital of the Republic late in October 1920. Yet two more years were to elapse before Japan abandoned her hold on the Maritime Province. During the intervening period Tokyo fought a diplomatic delaying action with Moscow and Washington while constantly improvising new means of disguising her aggressive role in eastern Siberia. Her course took the familiar form of aiding and abetting a number of White Russian political adventurers still flourishing in the region.

Perhaps the most ambitious—certainly the most bizarre—was Baron Roman von Ungern-Sternberg, one of Semyenov's former officers. A Russian of Baltic German descent who claimed the famous Mongol conqueror Genghis Khan as an ancestor, the baron preached a mystic Pan-Mongolism interlarded with a political ideology which, save for its fervent monarchism, bore a striking resemblance to the Nazi creed of a later time and place. He was a worthy disciple of Semyenov in the techniques of pillage and murder, and, like the latter, he found the Trans-Baikal region unhealthy for further depredations after the fall of 1920. With a cavalry force of approximately a thousand men, he marched south toward Outer Mongolia and eventually seized Urga (now Ulan Bator), the capital, on February 2, 1921. A massacre of Jews, Chinese, and "Reds" inaugurated Ungern's dictatorship, and with Japanese encouragement and material support he prepared his augmented forces for an attack on Trans-Baikalia. Late in May he crossed the Mongolian border heading in the general direction of Lake Baikal, only to be repulsed by Red troops and driven into western Mongolia. Here his renewed offensive was shattered, and he himself was captured and executed.

It was this campaign—no more than a minor epilogue to the annals of the civil war—which furnished the initial impetus for the assertion of Soviet hegemony over Outer Mongolia. The occupation of Urga in July 1921 by Red Army units led to the installation of a regime friendly to Soviet Russia and correspondingly cool toward China. That the pre-war position of Tsarist Russia in Outer Mongolia was thus revived was a barometer of the growing strength of the Soviet state and the first indication that the Bolsheviks were not immune to the imperialistic temptations for which they so freely excoriated the capitalist powers.

Vladivostok was now the last redoubt for the Japanese and their hirelings on the Russian mainland. Red partisans operating in the name of the Far Eastern Republic infiltrated the area, and in November 1921 Japan sponsored a White offensive north of Vladivostok. Beyond Khabarovsk they met Red reinforcements under the command of General Vasily Blücher, and in the early months of 1922 they were pushed back over the route of their previous advance. Only the intervention of Japanese troops saved them from annihilation. Moscow still preferred a diplomatic to a military solution and refrained from ordering a drive on Vladivostok to force the issue.

Negotiations had begun the previous August between Japanese and Far Eastern Republic representatives at Dairen on the southern tip of the Liaotung Peninsula. Japan's willingness to begin discussions was motivated by her wish to avoid an open review of her Siberian policy at the forthcoming conference on disarmament and Far Eastern problems in Washington. The parley at Dairen dragged on through the fall of 1921 with no prospect of a settlement despite tempting economic concessions offered by the Republic. Tokyo's exorbitant demands included the establishment of a permanent buffer state in eastern Siberia, a leasehold over northern Sakhalin, and the elimination of Russian military and naval power in the Pacific—all without setting a definite date for the departure of her troops.

Although her representatives were not invited, the opening of the Washington Conference in November 1921 presented Moscow with an indirect but welcome opportunity to raise the Siberian question before an assembly of the great powers. Soviet Russia registered vigorous protests with the participating governments about her exclusion and vowed that she would not be bound by the decisions reached. Yet her envoys managed to get a foot in the door as a "trade delegation" from the Far Eastern Republic. They competed as such with representatives of several White Russian groups, including the pro-Japanese government at Vladivostok, but made a greater and generally favorable impact upon Western opinion by speeches and publications attacking Japan's Siberian venture. Even the Russian division of the State Department received them informally and learned the details of the secret Japanese demands made at Dairen.

That the American and Soviet governments were both impatient to pry the Japanese off Siberian soil in no way interrupted the frosty relationship between Moscow and Washington. Until 1933, and frequently beyond, the State Department gave its anti-Soviet policy precedence over a common sense arrangement that would have permitted joint pressure against Japan's encroachment upon China. Only briefly were the Japanese delegates embarrassed at the conference by consideration of the Russian problem. At a committee meeting on January 23, 1922, when the Siberian situation appeared on the agenda, Baron Kijuro Shidehara read a prepared statement promising withdrawal as soon as an agreement could be reached at Dairen. He concluded his remarks with the conventional formula regarding the "fixed and settled policy of Japan to respect the territorial integrity of Russia, and to observe the principle of non-intervention in the internal affairs of that country." These were substantially the phrases that Tokyo had presented in answer to two previous notes from Washington. This time Secretary of State Charles Evans Hughes pressed the issue. The next day he reviewed the circumstances of Allied intervention and made some pointed remarks regarding Japan's policy while expressing the hope that she "does not seek, through her military operations in Siberia, to impair the rights of the Russian people in any respect, or to obtain any unfair commercial advantages, or to absorb for her own use the Siberian fisheries, or to set up an exclusive exploitation either of the resources of Sakhalin or of the Maritime Province."[25]

For a formal diplomatic conclave this language was blunt indeed. Judging by immediate results, it failed to impress Tokyo's policy-makers. The talks at Dairen, recessed during the Washington Conference, remained deadlocked and were finally abandoned in mid-April of 1922. Japan's military clique was reluctant to sacrifice its costly bridgehead at Vladivostok; but unless more troops were landed —at the risk of a serious conflict with the Soviet government and the open hostility of the United States—the chances of reviving the White Russians as a military threat after the failure of their winter offensive was hopeless.

In June 1922 the political winds shifted in Tokyo and Baron Tomosaburo Kato, who had headed the Japanese delegation at the Washington Conference, was elevated to the premiership. A professional naval officer, Kato opposed the Siberian adventure and found ready support in the Diet and from a public still burdened by press censorship and other restrictions on free speech. On June 24 Washington was informed of Japan's intention to evacuate the Maritime Province by the end of October. Hughes expressed gratification but complained of the omission of northern Sakhalin from the order, a matter which Tokyo explained would have to await a settlement of the Nikolayevsk affair.

A conference on the Sakhalin question convened at Changchun, Manchuria, on September 5, 1922, as Japan began to fulfill her pledge. In contrast to the meeting at Dairen, Russia was officially represented by one of its top diplomats—Adolf Yoffe. But the outcome was the same: Moscow refused to pay the high price in economic concessions demanded by Tokyo.

Red troops were meanwhile overpowering the last White resistance outside Vladivostok, and on October 25 they entered the city on the heels of the departing Nipponese forces. After four-and-a-half years the Russian mainland was at last free of foreign occupation. The Whites who had not already found sanctuary in Manchuria were evacuated on Japanese and other vessels. The final step in the restoration of Russian sovereignty was the dissolution of the Far Eastern Republic on November 15 and its formal absorption in the Russian Soviet Federated Republic. Because of the poor state of Soviet-American relations, neither the Kremlin nor the State Department acknowledged the importance of Washington's contribution in maneuvering Japan out of Siberia.

Moscow's victory was tarnished only by Japanese occupation of northern Sakhalin. Two years and more elapsed before a satisfactory accord was reached. In the spring of 1923 Yoffe, after completing his mission in China,[26] accepted an invitation to Tokyo and exchanged views with an unofficial Japanese spokesman. Unable to come to a tentative agreement, formal negotiations took place during the summer with no better results. By the following year Moscow was in a stronger diplomatic position, and sentiment in Japan had grown more favorable toward extracting what advantage was still to be gained from a situation that had become a financial and political liability. In Peking a long series of meetings began in June between Leo Karakhan, the Soviet ambassador to China, and the Japanese minister. A comprehensive treaty was at last signed on January 20, 1925, in which Soviet Russia was given *de jure* recognition and Japan was granted the right to exploit coal, oil, and timber resources in northern Sakhalin for periods up to fifty years. The Japanese garrison was removed in the spring and early summer in fulfillment of the terms of the pact.

The termination of Japan's empire-building in the Russian Far East marked an anti-climactic finish to the undeclared war of aggression which the Allied powers had waged in a halting and perfunctory manner, but with such catastrophic effects upon the fabric of Russian society. In material damage alone the destruction wrought by intervention and its indirect form—subsidized civil war—was staggering. The human losses are even more difficult to calculate; but ten million dead, the majority from famine and disease rather than through the exactions of the battlefield and the terror so freely practiced by both sides, would seem to be a conservative estimate. Nor can statistics adequately portray the mental and physical suffering of millions of others whose lives were uprooted by the ravages of war.

The perspective of history offers but one precedent of note—the war of intervention against Jacobin France in 1792, an equally futile attempt to stamp out revolution by armed force. But the hostilities begun in 1792 were the prologue to an ordeal ending with the defeat of Napoleonic France in 1815; the war against Bolshevik Russia begun in 1918 was the backwash of the great world conflict preceding it and represented the lowest common denominator of the soiled idealism and witless patriotism which—among less sordid emotions—had for four years helped to sustain the combatants. The exhaustion and disillusionment attending the Great War was perhaps the essential deterrent to a full assault by the capitalist powers upon the one of their number that had succumbed to the Marxist heresy. Yet the notion of a united capitalist conspiracy to crush Bolshevism—naturally popular among Soviet theorists—falters for many reasons. Most obviously, it fails to account for the hesitant and ambiguous role of the United States, where a domestic "Red scare" of alarming proportions developed in 1919–1920, and for the aggressive role of Japan, where anti-Bolshevism was used only as a transparent disguise for old-fashioned imperialism. Whatever the motives involved, the squalid episode poisoned the international atmosphere and added incentive to the avowed aim of the Soviet leaders to end their isolation by the destruction of world capitalism.

The other legacies of intervention are less tangible. The extent to which the autocratic features of Soviet society were stamped upon it by the bitter struggle for survival defies a satisfactory answer. Surely, many a humble peasant, innocent of any political sophistication, must have looked to the central government at Moscow—Bolshevik or no—for succor from the invading hordes who would "save" Russia as a locust plague spares the farmer the labor of harvesting his crop. For all the ill-effects of the preposterous enterprise, there are those would-be disciples of *Realpolitik* who profess to find at least one positive result—namely, that it prevented Bolshevism from spreading beyond the Soviet frontier. The proposition is at best debatable, even for the period between the wars, and it lost whatever validity it may have had with the reversal of the *cordon sanitaire* in Russia's favor in the 1940's.

No more appropriate epitaph upon the prolonged blunder of intervention has been written than that with which General Graves closed his account of the Siberian adventure a decade after the events described: "The various Governments taking part in the intervention take very little pride in this venture. Who can blame them?"[27]

NOTES

1. See above, p. 36.
2. *Papers Relating to the Foreign Relations of the United States, 1918: Russia,* II, 21.
3. *Ibid.,* pp. 35–36.
4. David Lloyd George, *War Memoirs* (Boston, 1933–37), VI, 167.
5. See above, p. 53.
6. Ray S. Baker, *Woodrow Wilson: Life and Letters* (New York, 1927–39), VIII, 266.
7. James Bunyan, *Intervention, Civil War, and Communism in Russia, April–December 1918: Documents and Materials* (Baltimore, 1936), p. 147.
8. U.S. Senate, 67th Congress, 2nd Session, *Deportation of Gregorie Semenoff: Hearings Before the Committee on Education and Labor* (Washington, 1922), p. 52.
9. See above, p. 36.
10. See above, p. 55.
11. Quoted in William Henry Chamberlin, *The Russian Revolution* (New York, 1935), II, 166.
12. *Papers Relating to the Foreign Relations of the United States, 1919: The Paris Peace Conference* (Washington, 1942–47), III, 644.
13. David Lloyd George, *The Truth About the Peace Treaties* (London, 1938), I, 338.
14. *The Bullitt Mission to Russia* (New York, 1919), p. 54.
15. See below, pp. 101–102.
16. See above, p. 67.
17. I. Subbotovsky, *Soyuzniki, russkie reaktsionery i interventsia* [The Allies, the Russian Reactionaries, and Intervention] (Leningrad, 1926), p. 102.
18. See above, p. 61.
19. See above, pp. 66–67.
20. F. Dan, *Dva goda skitany* [Two Years of Wanderings] (Berlin, 1922), p. 46.
21. Isaac Deutscher, *Stalin* (New York, 1949), p. 215; Chamberlin, *The Russian Revolution,* II, 306.
22. See above, p. 83.
23. Leon Trotsky, *Kak vooruzhalas revolyutsia* [How the Revolution Armed Itself] (Moscow, 1923–25), Vol. II, Bk. 2, p. 200.
24. See above, p. 85.
25. *Conference on the Limitation of Armament* (Washington, 1922), p. 348.
26. See below, pp. 139–40.
27. William S. Graves, *America's Siberian Adventure* (New York, 1931), p. 356.

CHAPTER FOUR

COMINTERN VS. NARKOMINDEL

Soviet policy has always presented two faces to the capitalist world; and this disturbing dualism was never more clear-cut than in the earlier—though not the earliest—years of Bolshevik rule. The one, dedicated to the original Marxist proposition that socialism is destined to emerge triumphant from the bankruptcy of industrial capitalism, was represented in theory and sometimes in practice by the Communist International (Comintern), founded in Moscow in March 1919, and presided over by Gregory Zinoviev; the other, based on the reality of competing nation-states with whom Soviet Russia—as Tsarist Russia before it—perforce had to accommodate itself, was represented in theory and sometimes in practice by the People's Commissariat for Foreign Affairs (Narkomindel) headed by Georgi Chicherin. Since both organizations were in reality controlled by an inner core within the Communist party (as the Bolsheviks officially called themselves after March 1918), the dualism inherent in the aims of the Comintern and those of the Narkomindel was confined to permissible limits. For a time after the October Revolution it was the messianic message of proletarian revolt that subordinated conventional diplomatic practice; then, as the months and years rolled on and the underpinnings of bourgeois society failed to collapse, the program of world revolution became a definite adjunct to the foreign policy of the Soviet state.

It was a bitter blow to the Bolsheviks that their revolution remained isolated in a backward agrarian country without the industrial base, the educational level, and the skilled labor to make socialism an immediate reality. The tempting vista of industrial Germany lay just beyond the horizon—before the war the vanguard of international socialism, with the largest social democratic party in Europe, a militant and self-confident working class, and in Karl Kautsky, August Bebel, Rudolf Hilferding, and a host of others the accepted oracles of European Marxism. As elsewhere, the call to arms in 1914 had destroyed the illusion that proletarian solidarity could transcend national boundaries. The emotional release of patriotism proved more potent than the austere doctrines of Marx.

Until defeat loosened the habit of discipline and obedience, the German masses remained insusceptible to the Bolshevik propaganda offensive. But Soviet efforts to foment rebellion were nonetheless unceasing. Yoffe, appointed ambassador to Berlin after the peace of Brest-Litovsk, was less a diplomatic emissary than a revolutionary agent. The Russian embassy served as staff headquarters for the expected German revolution. Tons of anti-government and anti-war literature were dispensed, and Soviet funds provided arms for the revolutionaries, subsidized socialist newspapers, and obtained government secrets with which the socialists could undermine public confidence in the Kaiser's regime. Yoffe's activities became so notorious that on the eve of its fall the government arranged for the police to plant subversive leaflets in a box of Soviet diplomatic papers, and they were conveniently discovered when the container was "accidentally" dropped at a Berlin railway station. He and his staff were deported on November 6, 1918, only two days after the incident. The Kaiser's abdication on the 9th induced Yoffe to linger at the frontier in momentary expectation that the new revolutionary regime would recall him to Berlin.

Yoffe waited in vain, for the "socialist" government that now held the reins of power, while theoretically committed to Marxism by ties of tradition and sentiment, had no more intention of overthrowing the capitalist order than the avowedly bourgeois parties of the Center and Right. As Friedrich Ebert, the Social Democratic chancellor of the provisional government confessed, "I hate revolution like mortal sin."[1] Only the Spartacus League, a Left wing faction within the Independent Social Democratic party, was morally prepared for a German "October," though its leaders, Karl Liebknecht and Rosa Luxemburg, were by no means auxiliaries of Moscow.

In spite of the inauspicious beginning of the German revolution, a wave of anticipatory excitement swept the Kremlin. Each new development was hailed as a portent of the inevitable triumph of the European proletariat. The Soviet press and radio flooded its German "comrades" with greetings and exhortations, and the government graciously offered two trainloads of grain to meet the pressing food shortage. A polite refusal from Berlin revealed that the Allies had promised more generous assistance. As a symptom of the Western orientation of the new German republic, the incident did not noticeably dampen Russian enthusiasm, though it was a slap in the face which rankled. Moscow's wounded pride was partially assuaged when the Russians were invited to participate in the forthcoming All-German Congress of Workers' and Soldiers' Councils which had been organized on the Soviet model. An imposing delegation of party leaders was appointed, including Yoffe, Radek, and Bukharin, but it was barred from crossing the frontier by the German government. The resourceful Radek, disguised as an Austrian prisoner of war, slipped across illegally and arrived in Berlin too late to attend the final session of the Congress on December 21, 1918. He contacted the leading Spartacists, however, and spoke at their convention at the end of the year when they seceded from the Independent Social Democratic party to become—with the accession of a few other groups—the German Communist party.

Moscow naturally hailed the development as a decisive break with the "social-chauvinists," who were betraying the German working class, and as another harbinger of the revolution-to-be. Yet a realistic view of the inherent weaknesses of the new party—which, for the moment at least, the Bolsheviks were constitutionally incapable of taking—would have posed grave doubts as to its immediate prospects. The German party was far removed from the tightly disciplined organization that Lenin had molded in Russia; worse still, it was composed in the main of intellectuals whose roots in the aims and aspirations of the urban masses were of the most tenuous sort. With all its limitations, the party drank deeply of the intoxicating atmosphere of revolutionary Berlin and blundered into a test of strength with Chancellor Ebert's Social Democratic regime.

During "Spartacus Week" (January 5–12, 1919) Berlin erupted into civil war, and less serious disorders occurred in Bremen and the Ruhr valley. Poorly armed workers seized a number of strategic buildings in the capital, and for a time this grotesque counterfeit of the Bolshevik Revolution appeared to have some chance of success. But the government was not isolated, as Kerensky's had been, and it mortgaged its own future by calling upon regular army units and volunteer bands of professional soldiers known as the Free Corps—Nazi storm troopers in embryo. Efficiently and brutally, the insurrection was quelled. Among the victims were Liebknecht and Luxemburg, who were arrested in hiding on the 15th, clubbed with rifle butts, and shot to death. In the ensuing roundup of Communist suspects, Radek was imprisoned, and his cell eventually became a kind of political *salon* for distinguished visitors, their ticket of admission a pass from the War Ministry.

While Germany lay in the grip of a bloody counter-revolution, the Bolsheviks sought to certify the demise of the socialist Second International by calling for the creation of a "new revolutionary International." The appeal was drafted by Trotsky and broadcast from Moscow on January 24. Representatives from thirty-nine organizations were invited to attend a conference for the purpose of founding a "common fighting organ" for "the permanent co-ordination and systematic leadership of the [Communist] movement" which would subordinate the interests of the party "in each country to the common interests of the international revolution."[2]

Few outsiders were able to reach Moscow by the time the first "preparatory" session convened on March 2, 1919. Nineteen countries were officially represented by the device of appointing foreign sympathizers already in Russia as delegates, most of whom spoke for nonexistent Communist parties. Since the German party was the only Communist movement worthy of the name outside Russia, the role of its lone delegate, Hugo Eberlein (a colleague had been arrested at the German border), assumed special importance. His instructions were to oppose the founding of a new International as premature, and he steadfastly clung to his position until he was persuaded on March 4 to abstain from voting so as not to disrupt the unanimity of the occasion. A resolution then transformed the gathering into the first congress of the Communist International without a dissenting voice.

The proceedings that followed could only be anti-climactic. Speeches, resolutions, manifestoes, and the drafting of a platform crowded the remaining sessions and furnished a unique opportunity for an ideological girding of the loins for the struggles that lay ahead. An executive committee was elected with Zinoviev as president and Radek —still a prisoner in Berlin—as secretary. The choice of Zinoviev was not entirely a happy one. As Trotsky later observed, he "lacked that little thing called character." Yet his unprincipled opportunism and taste for duplicity found compensation in an exceptional talent for oratory and a gift for literary polemics. In the long run, while his soaring flights of fancy in assessing the prospects for world revolution did a distinct disservice to the cause he faithfully served during his seven year tenure, his day-to-day enthusiasm and diligence set an example that his more phlegmatic comrades might well have envied.

By force of circumstances the Comintern was born in Moscow— and there it stayed. Originally, the Bolsheviks had no intention of subordinating its destinies to the power of the Soviet state; indeed, such a thought could not have occurred to them in the extravagant optimism that characterized their appraisal of the revolutionary potential of the European masses. But since the first duty of all Communists was the preservation of Soviet Russia as a Marxist oasis in the capitalist desert, the reality of a Muscovite Comintern was not concealed by the theoretical equality of the partnership. And as long as the Narko-mindel's diplomacy was directed to the same end, there could be no possibility of a nascent cleavage in the aims of the two organizations. The Comintern's prestige was enormous in its first years—even its enemies overrated its potentialities. Zinoviev reveled in a world of secret missions, clandestine funds, and propagandist literature. "Expensive agencies with numerous personnel were established overnight," recalled Angelica Balabanov, Radek's interim replacement. "The International became a bureaucratic apparatus before a real Communist movement was born."[3]

Scarcely two weeks after the closing session of the initial Comintern congress, revolution unexpectedly broke out in what would have seemed one of the most unlikely of all European countries—Hungary. Neither a spontaneous popular upheaval nor a *coup d'état*, the upheaval which brought the Hungarian Soviet regime into being was the hybrid product of pressure from below and involuntary decision from above. Hungary had emerged from the war independent of Austria and provisionally a democratic republic resting upon a semi-feudal agrarian base. A small but militant Communist party had been organized by war prisoners returning from Russia, among whom Bela Kun, formerly an obscure journalist from Transylvania, quickly won distinction. In February 1919 Kun and some of his associates were arrested in the wake of a Communist clash with the police. It was thus from a prison cell that the future Hungarian dictator was summoned on March 21 to assume the mantle of supreme power.

The immediate occasion for this drastic shift in the political complexion of the country was the receipt of another ultimatum from the Allied military representative in Budapest demanding additional territorial concessions. Unwilling to endure a further assault upon the dignity of his nation and beset by insurmountable economic difficulties, the government of Count Michael Karolyi simply resigned in favor of a Social Democratic-Communist coalition—an early-day "Popular Front"—which as a political movement already possessed mass appeal in Budapest and a near monopoly of the available armed force. Kun was the dominating figure in the new government from the first; and but for his lack of political discrimination in at once pushing through a series of radical social reforms, the Hungarian Soviet Republic might have had a fighting chance for survival.

The formation of a Soviet republic in Bavaria on April 7, 1919, appeared to add substance to Moscow's prognosis of a German revolution. Yet the regime was even less substantial than Kun's, for it was founded on a wave of utopian sentiment among radical intellectuals and "coffee house anarchists" in Munich—spurred on by the news from Budapest and an expected rising of Viennese workers. So farcical did it seem to serious revolutionaries that the Communists dismissed it as sheer adventurism. Within the week their foresight was confirmed by the government's disintegration, whereupon they compounded the initial folly by stepping into the vacuum with a cabinet of their own. The step was taken with misgivings and under the delusion that the revolutionary honor of the party demanded solidarity with the Munich workers, who were making preparations to defend the city against Free Corps units sent from Berlin and other parts of Germany. The end could be delayed only temporarily. On May 1 counter-revolutionary troops stormed into Munich and exacted a bloody toll from hundreds of suspects of varying political persuasion. Reaction reigned supreme in Bavaria, and Munich became the stronghold of all manner of nationalist fanatics bent upon the destruction of the German Republic as a façade for Marxists and Jews.

The Hungarian Soviet Republic did not long outlast the gory climax to the Bavarian experiment. It became obvious by the early summer of 1919 that the Kun regime, surrounded by small but greedy neighbors in Czechoslovakia, Rumania, and Yugoslavia, subjected to a food blockade by the Allied governments, and deprived of Russian support by the circumstances of the civil war, was gradually succumbing to the pressure of political and economic realities. Kun hoped for a reprieve through a revolution in Austria and had done his best to foment one by sending agents under the leadership of Ernst Bettelheim, a former Budapest lawyer. They organized an abortive *Putsch* in Vienna on June 15 that managed only to discredit the already weak Austrian Communist movement. Like many another ruler groping desperately for a political miracle, Kun sought to rally patriotic support with a foreign adventure. Rumania, already gorged with Hungarian territory, was an appropriate target for revenge but an inappropriate choice as a victim. The infant Hungarian Red army was by then honeycombed with dissension, and the troops loyal to the government made a sorry showing. Kun resigned on August 1 as the Rumanians approached Budapest, and together with most of his colleagues he fled to Vienna. Reaching Moscow a year later, they were welcomed with all the deference due seasoned veterans of a "successful"—albeit temporary—Communist experiment beyond the Russian border. Hungary was given over to a White terror beside which the well publicized excesses of the Reds paled into insignificance.

By the fall of 1919, except for sporadic strikes and working class unrest in several European cities, only a wave of factory seizures and agrarian disturbances in Italy sustained Bolshevik morale, now considerably chastened from the confident mood of the previous spring. Here, too, their hopes of Communist victory were to be dashed, at first by the lack of militant revolutionary leadership and in the end by the rise of an essentially new phenomenon in European history—fascism. Their knowledge of such external events was meager, however, and had to be pieced together from individual accounts, radio reports, and printed matter smuggled across the blockaded Russian frontier. Domestically, at any rate, the critical military situation had eased enormously with the defeat of Kolchak, Denikin, and Yudenich. The failure of the White movement and the consequent re-examination of Allied policy led to the first halting steps toward admitting Soviet Russia into the comity of nations.

Moscow, in like manner, was able to make more effective use of conventional diplomatic procedures. For the first time Chicherin came to play a role of some independent importance. While his desire for world revolution was scarcely less keen than Zinoviev's, he was better fitted by training and temperament to supervise the functions of the Narkomindel. This remarkable man, who was to preside over his department until the late twenties—and nominally until 1930—was of noble birth and a former archivist in the Tsarist Foreign Office. A Menshevik prior to his admission to Bolshevik ranks early in 1918, he was a man of retiring personality and aesthetic tastes whose eccentric ways were not those of a "typical" revolutionary. But his gift for diplomacy and his intellectual brilliance won him an enviable reputation at home and abroad. Yet for all his talent, he was never admitted to the inner councils of authority. As if to emphasize his anomalous position, his deputy, Maxim Litvinov, and a number of other well known Soviet diplomats stood higher in the party than their titular chief. Nor was the Narkomindel a sovereign entity even within its own sphere. Foreign affairs, like other business of state, was a party prerogative; and the party was in turn increasingly dominated by the Political Bureau (Politburo), the top echelon in the Communist hierarchy.

Moscow's first success in arranging a modus vivendi with the West was a meager achievement but one which Lenin described as opening "a window on Europe." It pertained to an Anglo-Soviet agreement on the repatriation of war prisoners and was signed on February 12, 1920, after protracted negotiations in Copenhagen between Litvinov and James O'Grady, a Labor member of Parliament. Similar pacts were then concluded with most of the other European countries.

A more tangible straw in the wind came as a result of the lifting of

the Allied blockade against Russia.[4] A Soviet trade delegation headed
by Leonid Krasin, commissar for trade and industry, left for Stockholm
and Copenhagen in March. After signing a trade agreement with a
group of Swedish firms, Krasin was invited to come to London. There
he saw Lloyd George at the end of May 1920, and later talks between
the two men covered a wide range of Anglo-Soviet differences. A
tentative understanding had been achieved by mid-summer when the
Soviet counter-offensive against Poland disrupted the promising negotiations, and relations reverted to the troubled state of the previous
year. Once again diplomacy was forced to make way for revolutionary
agitation.

The Comintern, now a year older, was a better organized and more
effective medium of propaganda; and Communist movements, however feeble, did at least exist in most Western countries by 1920. Even
in Asia Moscow's influence was felt, not so much because Communist
doctrine struck a responsive chord as because the national aspirations
of the more politically conscious layer of the population had begun to
stir beneath the weight of colonial domination. Little did the Bolsheviks suspect that Marxism, designed for the working masses of
advanced capitalist societies, was eventually to find a more secure
haven in agrarian China than in industrial Germany.

It was nevertheless to Germany that the Bolsheviks still looked as
the revolutionary tinderbox of Europe. Official contact between the
two governments had been resumed early in 1920 when Radek was
allowed to return to Russia and Victor Kopp, one of Chicherin's promising assistants, was recognized by Berlin as the Soviet representative
for the repatriation of war prisoners. His counterpart in Moscow was
Gustav Hilger, who had worked there in 1918 evacuating German
prisoners. In time both men attained a quasi-ambassadorial status until
the appointment of diplomatic envoys in the autumn of 1921. Mindful
of the difficulties of Yoffe and Radek, Kopp was discreet in his associations, and contact between Moscow and the German Communists was
therefore limited to the mails, irregular courier service, and an occasional telegraphic communication. The party had split in October
1919 at a secret congress in Heidelberg, and the expelled faction,
which insisted upon a boycott of the labor unions, created the Communist Labor party and carried with it nearly half of the 50,000 Communist party members.

Their political fortunes at a low ebb, the German Communist leaders did little to inspire confidence in their judgment during the Kapp
Putsch of March 1920. This attempt by a group of reactionary army
officers to overthrow the Republic was narrowly averted by a nation-

wide general strike. Workers of Communist persuasion were among the most active participants in the struggle against counter-revolution; and only when the party rank and file had definitely committed themselves did their leaders grudgingly assent to a policy which they regarded with misgivings, choosing as it did between warring factions of the "bourgeois" enemy. More than a decade later the party leadership was to fail in similar circumstances but with more disastrous results. Moscow diagnosed the abortive *Putsch* with confident ease: it was the "German Kornilov affair"; and the analogy between the Russian and German revolutions, which as apostles of "scientific" socialism the Bolsheviks were unable to resist, was further strained to demonstrate the approach of Germany's "October."

That fabulous event appeared on the verge of realization with the Red Army's drive on Warsaw several months later.[5] By coincidence the second congress of the Comintern opened while the news from the front was overwhelmingly favorable to the Soviet cause and lent the proceedings an intoxicating air of revolutionary accomplishment which the founding congress had lacked. With over two hundred delegates from thirty-five countries, the International was now a thriving concern, though the preponderance of Bolsheviks and foreigners-in-residence again made it inevitably a Russian-directed affair. Particularly noteworthy was the representation of China, Japan, India, and other Asiatic countries. Although the credentials committee had been generous in inviting and seating delegates whose doctrinal purity was questionable, the major business of the congress centered upon the formulation of a set of rules to determine the admission of parties to the Comintern. At length a statement of principles was agreed upon —the famous "twenty-one conditions"—with but two negative votes. A number of prominent Marxists were branded "notorious opportunists" whose exclusion was automatic—Kautsky, Hilferding, and Ramsay MacDonald were among them—but no organizations were specifically excommunicated or denied entrance. The document was ideally designed for its purpose—that of splitting the Left wing of the socialist movement abroad; and it marked the formal occasion of the Comintern's adaptation of Bolshevik orthodoxy as a policy guide in furthering the world revolution.

Just as Lenin had split the Russian Social Democratic party after 1903 with his uncompromising tactics and had been historically justified by the October Revolution, so the Comintern was now justified, he and his followers reasoned, in applying a tested formula to the wider scene. In their dogmatic certainty the Bolsheviks unconsciously abandoned the internationalism of Marxism by projecting their own

Russian experiences upon a totally different set of conditions in Western and Central Europe. And when in later years hopes for world revolution had receded and the party line had hardened even more, it was the path of least resistance to charge dissenters with heresy in place of re-examining the premises of a lifetime. But for the time being Moscow willingly countenanced the recruiting of "opportunist" elements in practice—though denying it in theory—because pliability was regarded as a greater revolutionary virtue than independent judgment.

When the second congress closed on August 7, 1920, the Red Army was at the gates of the Polish capital. The denouement was a double blow—a setback for Soviet foreign policy and a defeat for the aims of the Comintern. United in the flush of expectant victory, their paths now diverged once more, never to coincide with such precision again. A new *rapprochement* was sought with the West, while the Comintern, robbed of immediate satisfaction, pursued its goals with the relentless assurance of ultimate triumph.

Germany was still the linchpin of the European revolution. In October 1920 Zinoviev acknowledged its crucial role by personally attending a special congress of the Independent Socialist party at Halle that was to accept or reject the twenty-one conditions. The ten day permit granted for his visit was mute evidence that relations between Berlin and Moscow had improved somewhat over the past year. Zinoviev's four hour speech—a remarkable tour de force in a foreign tongue—was instrumental in swinging a substantial majority toward affiliation with the Comintern. In December the party split was confirmed: a large proportion of the Independent Socialists joined the Communists, making a combined membership of perhaps 350,000; a smaller group wandered in the political wilderness until it reunited with the Social Democrats in the fall of 1922.

In France representatives of the Socialist party met in the last days of 1920 at Tours, where an even more decisive verdict was rendered for the Comintern. The majority constituted itself the Communist party, and the minority retained the traditional label.

The decision in Italy was of greater moment because of the active revolutionary currents among the workers. At the Socialist party convention at Leghorn in January 1921 the delegates split three ways. A large majority balked at the rigidity of the twenty-one conditions and remained temporarily in the party; about one-third accepted them unreservedly and formed a Communist party; and a tiny Right wing maintained its staunch anti-Communism. The splintering of the Italian socialist movement was among the factors that led to the Fascist victory less than two years later.

Aside from the mass party in Germany and possibly the modest parties in France and Italy, Western Communism was not a serious political issue save as a bogey with which to frighten the timid. That millions were uneasy, if not actually frightened, by the Communist menace was largely responsible for the reluctance of the powers to accept Soviet Russia into the society of respectable nations. When it became evident that Poland had been safely delivered from the Red Army, tension relaxed noticeably, and Western statesmen began to appraise the Russians with less emotional revulsion. Lloyd George again seized the initiative, for Britain's lifeline was still based on trade, and the Russian market could not be lightly disregarded.

His talks with Krasin were resumed in late November 1920, even though the latter's colleague, Leo Kamenev, one of the five members of the Politburo, was ordered to leave the country for alleged misdeeds involving interference in domestic affairs. Negotiations continued through the winter, and on March 16, 1921, a trade agreement was signed "pending the conclusion of a formal general peace treaty." Political considerations were also involved in the bargain because of London's concern over Communist propaganda in the Middle East. Moscow had already made disturbing diplomatic inroads in Britain's sphere of influence in Persia and Afghanistan, and the unrest in India was partly ascribed to the machinations of the Kremlin. Consequently both countries agreed to refrain from "hostile action" and "official propaganda." The Soviet government specifically promised to include "the British Empire, especially in India and in the independent state of Afghanistan" in its guarantee. Since Moscow invariably denied any jurisdiction over Comintern activities, the pledge was less than airtight and was to furnish the occasion for chronic complaints from London.

The first diplomatic bridge between the Communist and capitalist worlds, the Anglo-Soviet commercial treaty was more important as a symbol than a tangible achievement. Before the year was out Moscow concluded similar agreements with most of the other European countries with one significant exception—France. The treaty was therefore a milestone in the evolution of Soviet foreign policy; and it coincided with a fundamental change on the domestic scene. The emergency that had called War Communism into being ended with Wrangel's defeat, and the critical state of the economy called for drastic measures of rehabilitation. The government's grain seizures led to widespread disturbances in the countryside; and popular dissatisfaction, which also found expression in a wave of strikes, was climaxed by the Kronstadt revolt of March 1921 when the sailors at the famous fortress and naval base near Petrograd openly rebelled against the Soviet regime. As a threat to Bolshevik rule it had no prospect of success and was crushed after a difficult campaign across the frozen Bay of Finland; but as a psychological shock to the complacency of the party elite its effect was immediate and profound.

At the tenth party congress, which met in Moscow while the Kronstadters were still under siege, the "New Economic Policy" (as it came to be called) was accepted as a temporary compromise between Marxist theory and the needs of production. A strategic retreat from the original goals of Communism, it permitted a partial restoration of capitalism, though the state retained the "commanding heights" of heavy industry, foreign trade, and finance. The peasants were appeased by the introduction of a tax in kind—a percentage of their produce—to replace the onerous system of confiscation. The consensus abroad was that the Bolsheviks had been forced to abandon their utopian nostrums as impractical and that the eternal verities of capitalism had been convincingly demonstrated in the very camp of its enemies. While it cannot be said that such a notion of N.E.P. was directly responsible for the subsequent improvement in Soviet relations with the European powers, the lessened emotional hostility toward Bolshevism allowed the Western governments more freedom of action in seeking an accommodation.

The Comintern's voice was not muted in 1921, but for the first time a note of discouragement was evident, particularly after the failure of the "March Action" in central Germany. The defeat of this rising, centered among the coal miners of Mansfeld, was especially galling to Zinoviev, for he had dispatched Bela Kun to lead the German Communists along a more militant revolutionary path—apparently without consulting the Politburo in any formal manner. The March fiasco produced a crisis in the German party: almost half the members resigned or drifted away during the next three months; and the expulsion of Paul Levi, the torchbearer of the Spartacus tradition who had denounced the adventure in a stinging pamphlet, marked another step in the party's growing subservience to Moscow.

An "N.E.P." in Comintern affairs was set in motion when the third congress convened in June. A post-mortem on the March Action dominated the first stage of the proceedings. The Comintern leadership—Zinoviev in effect—was absolved of responsibility and the German Communists were made to shoulder the burden. Yet a resolution, unanimously carried, blandly pronounced the experience a "step forward." For all the pageantry of the congress, which as a spectacle far outshone the previous gatherings, it was clear that the triumphant mood of 1920 was sorely lacking. Both Lenin and Trotsky conceded, somewhat obliquely, that the original revolutionary timetable was in need of revision. What the latter afterward referred to as the "strategy of temporary retreat" was never openly avowed at the congress, but a drastic shift in tactics from the sterile sectarianism of "splitting" to that of building mass parties was the major policy decision. In fact, if not in name, *Putschism* was now condemned as a grave doctrinal error. The new dispensation did not yet embrace the notion of a "united front" with the socialists, for collaboration with "social patriots" continued to exude the rank odor of heresy to most Communists. Only in later years, when the Comintern had lost all independent import-ance, did Moscow acquire the habit of reversing the party line with callous indifference to the sensibilities of its acolytes abroad.

The German party, still the bellwether of the Communist move-ment in the West, was the obvious choice to inaugurate the Comin-tern's "revisionist" policy. Radek, as Moscow's "German expert," was sent to consult the party leaders and to smooth over the obstacles pre-venting a favorable reception of the Comintern line at the forthcoming congress at Jena. When it met in August 1921 the delegates proved so tractable that their formal proclamation demanded little that the Social Democrats could not have subscribed to. They went to even greater lengths than the Comintern delegates had dared by calling for a "united workers' front," thereby serving as a sounding board for the next logical step in Moscow's reassessment of Communist tactics. The "victory" was gained at the cost of Right wing domination of the German party, a development that only a year earlier the Bolsheviks would have viewed with dismay.

In December 1921 the Comintern Executive Committee announced the new formula in a detailed pronouncement exhorting the member parties to "support the slogan of a united workers' front." But there were definite limits to the concessions the Communists were supposed to make. They were not to abandon their organizational identity nor the essentials of their creed. Common action would be possible on a strictly utilitarian basis to which all parties had agreed beforehand. Moreover, the Bolshevik notion of a united front, while not specifically indicated in the Comintern's instructions, was directed less toward genuine cooperation than to gaining the confidence of the non-Com-munist workers who might later be induced to desert their leaders. This policy of the "united front from below" was epitomized by Lenin's famous remark apropos of the British Labor party leadership: Com-munists should support them "as the rope supports the man who is being hanged." The ambiguities that lay concealed in the language of the document and in Moscow's intentions remained to be spelled out in practice. The French and Italian Communists were unexpectedly obstreperous and followed a course of passive resistance which the Comintern, reluctant to use the weapon of excommunication, was obliged to endure for the time being in the knowledge that further schisms (and in the name of a united front!) would reduce the Communist movement to a farce.

The policy of conciliation reached a peak in April 1922 when a Comintern delegation, including Radek and Bukharin, attended a conference in Berlin with representatives of the despised Second International. The sponsor of the affair was the "Vienna Union," an organization of "centrists" derisively and more popularly known as the "Two-and-a-Half International" for its advocacy of unity between the two hostile Internationals. That anything was accomplished beyond vitriolic exchanges was due to the Communists' determination to avoid an open break. They assumed responsibility for several compromises involving Russian internal matters—which Moscow later repudiated in part. A committee was organized in Berlin to explore the possibility of further cooperation but was dissolved after its first session late in May. Neither International wished to maintain the pretense of harmony, and in the spring of the next year the "Two-and-a-Half" joined the Second, though the merger added little to the strength of organized socialism.

II

The diplomatic counterpart of the Comintern's moderate line was yielding a more substantial profit. Soviet Russia's improved status in European affairs was publicly acknowledged for the first time when an invitation was tendered to a conference on economic problems at Genoa in April 1922. Nor was the invitation made gratuitously. The powers had come to realize that the economic reconstruction of Europe was impossible without Soviet participation and that the enormous reparations burden imposed on Germany could not be redeemed without utilizing her unfilled industrial capacity. The Russian market, unexplored but alluring, was the obvious outlet for manufactured goods. Moscow had already taken the initiative in calling for an international conference to restore normal commercial relations as part of a "final peace treaty" with the West. As an added inducement and a token of good faith, Soviet responsibility for the Tsarist debt was acknowledged in principle for the first time. The Genoa meeting thus involved mutual recognition of Europe's interdependence and the necessity for some kind of working arrangement among the powers.

Chicherin headed the impressive delegation sent to mark the occasion of Russia's emergence into the European diplomatic arena after four-and-a-half years of involuntary hibernation. Lenin's dictum —"we go to Genoa not as Communists but as merchants"—was observed in the main, so much so that the courteous and businesslike attitude of the Russians was rather disconcerting to those journalists and diplomats whose mental image of a Bolshevik had been molded by cartoon caricatures in the Western press. Lloyd George attended personally in an attempt to heighten the significance of the affair. As the foremost proponent of the Genoa meeting, his political prestige was heavily invested in a successful outcome. The United States, the only non-European country invited, declined to send a representative because of the strong popular mood of isolationism and because of the conspicuous role assigned to Soviet Russia.

On April 10, after the usual opening round of ceremonial remarks, Chicherin roused the delegates from their accustomed lethargy by a frank and daring speech. After a discursive review of Soviet policy, he conjured up an enticing panorama of Russia's limitless natural resources which would—for a price, presumably—be thrown open to exploitation by Western capitalists. Shifting to the world scene, he pointed out the difficulties of economic rehabilitation while the "threat of new wars" hovered near and raised the issue of a "general limitation of armaments," a proposition which goaded the French spokesman into a bombastic protest on the ground that the disarmament question was not on the agenda. Lloyd George exerted his persuasive charm to smooth over the incident, and Chicherin waived his proposal, satisfied with a moral victory.

The next day commissions were organized to deal with technical matters, while the really meaningful negotiations were conducted privately at Lloyd George's villa. A settlement with Moscow became the cardinal issue, and the major barrier to an understanding was the twin problem of debts and nationalized foreign property. As for the first, Chicherin willingly conceded that "if my neighbor has lent me money, I must pay him back." But, he added, "if this neighbor has broken into my house, killed my children, destroyed my furniture and burnt my house, he must at least begin by restoring to me what he has destroyed."[6] Opposed to total Allied claims of $13,000,000,000 in loans and confiscated property, the Soviet government advanced the staggering sum of $60,000,000,000 for damages resulting from intervention. Chicherin as much as admitted that the figure was solely for bargaining purposes by offering in the end to scale it down to $25,000,000 and to accept a token payment in return for reconstruction credits. The proposal was flatly refused, and the best counter-offer—cancellation of the Russian war debt against the intervention claim—fell far short of Moscow's insistence that the pre-war debt should be offset by loans and that property claims should be paid in the form of concessions on Soviet soil.

The deliberations had progressed only a week when the Western plenipotentiaries were stunned by the news that a Soviet-German pact had just been signed at the nearby town of Rapallo. The origins of this startling development can be traced as far back as the prison cell where Radek had sojourned as a "guest" of the German government in 1919. The contacts he made there were resumed and broadened on his subsequent visits to Germany, and in 1921 the haphazard Moscow-Berlin nexus had become a well-worn, if still clandestine, trunk line accommodating negotiators in separate political, military, and economic channels. It was all but inevitable that two of the erstwhile great powers in world politics, who had for different reasons become temporary pariahs in the international community, would in time be able to surmount doctrinal incompatibility for the mutual benefits to be derived from closer collaboration against a common oppressor. The Bismarckian tradition of a Russian alliance, dormant for thirty years, remained vibrantly alive in the same circles that anathematized the Bolshevik creed. In like manner, the tardiness of the German revolution encouraged the Russians to loosen their ideological blinkers and to do business at the old stand of *Realpolitik*.

Germany's diplomats, still hopeful of eroding the Versailles system with good manners, had consistently lagged behind her generals and industrialists in adopting an Eastern orientation. Only in the first months of 1922 did Moscow's emissaries successfully penetrate to the top level of German officialdom. The ground had accordingly been well prepared when the Soviet delegation to Genoa stopped over in Berlin en route. A draft treaty soon emerged from the discussions, and the Russians were eager to sign on the spot. The Germans probably would have acceded had not Foreign Minister Walther Rathenau interposed his veto. A prudent desire to avoid antagonizing Britain and France by confronting them with a *fait accompli* on the eve of the Genoa Conference—an almost certain guarantee of its failure— was the kernel of his objection. The Germans, Rathenau among them, were not admitted to the inner sanctum at Genoa and grew fearful of a Soviet bargain with the Entente in which the Bolsheviks would be encouraged to extract reparations from Germany under Article 116 of the Versailles treaty. It was therefore with perfect timing that the Soviet representatives, who had never entertained such a scheme, contacted the despairing German delegates. Rathenau's reluctance was overcome, the details were ironed out on the afternoon of April 16—Easter Sunday—and on the same evening the historic agreement was signed.

For both powers Rapallo represented an emancipation proclamation, not by reason of anything in the treaty, the provisions of which were politically harmless, but because it cut short an unnatural situation whereby the destinies of Europe were arbitrated exclusively from London and Paris. With the leverage of Rapallo the two outcasts could now bargain on more equal terms. Specifically, the treaty provided for the full restoration of diplomatic relations and the mutual cancellation of all financial claims on condition that the Soviet government "shall not satisfy similar claims made by any third state."[7] This phrase set up an effective roadblock against any future financial settlement with the Western powers. The commercial article was of greater significance: both countries approved the "most favored nation" principle, and the German government promised to assist private firms in trading with the Russians, thereby implying that it would refuse to participate in any international consortium for the development of Soviet resources.

The Anglo-French reaction was a mixture of anger and dismay. Germany was accused of violating the terms under which she had been invited to the conference. But for Lloyd George's dogged determination to achieve some tangible results, further negotiations might have been abandoned forthwith. For more than a month the discussions dragged on in mounting futility until in the end the crippling blow of Rapallo proved fatal. As a face-saving gesture, an innocuous non-aggression pact was orally approved by the delegates. In the same spirit the agenda was referred to a conference of experts who met that summer at The Hague and were no more able to resolve the difficulties than their superiors had been.

In Soviet Russia the Rapallo agreement was, as a matter of course, acclaimed a diplomatic triumph despite its disturbing implication that the German workers had been abandoned as less desirable partners than their bourgeois rulers. No one dared pose the problem as baldly as this, though the inherent contradiction in Soviet policy was recognized and found justifiable by the necessity of breaking through the encirclement of capitalist states. The German revolution, appearances to the contrary, remained the life's blood of the Comintern. Nevertheless the seeds of "socialism in one country" were liberally

sown at Rapallo; and if the Trotskyists were later to accuse the Stalinists of sabotaging "permanent revolution," their indignation was the
less convincing for their willingness to applaud the measures that
helped to render it a utopian doctrine in a world of competing nation-
states.

German opinion was less unanimous in praising Rapallo. Rathenau
and Ebert—to name only two—feared reprisals, particularly from
France. The independent Left attacked the treaty as a cynical betrayal of socialism, and the Communists handled the issue so gingerly
as to betray considerable embarrassment. Ratification and an exchange
of ambassadors came later in the year, by which time German-Soviet
trade had spurted gratifyingly and concessions had been granted a
number of German firms. Military collaboration also progressed satisfactorily. By 1924 German aviators were in training at an airport in
Lipetsk, several hundred miles northeast of Moscow, the vanguard
of a sizable influx of Reichswehr officers and technicians. The Germans were of inestimable value in increasing the efficiency of the Red
Army while at the same time furthering their own country's national
interest in circumventing the military restrictions of the Versailles
treaty. A modest rearmament program was likewise begun on Russian
soil with German financial and technical assistance. No word of the
Reichswehr-Red Army collaboration leaked into the public domain
until December 1926, although unfounded reports had continued to
circulate in the West that Rapallo concealed a secret military alliance,
and French and Polish intelligence was privy to some of the details of
the clandestine relationship.

Moscow's new-found assurance in the arena of global politics was
revealed in a tentative move to nullify the Entente's *cordon sanitaire*
in Eastern Europe, already outflanked by the pact with Germany and
weakened by Britain's gradual disengagement from continental affairs.
This Soviet bid for leadership among the states on her western border
involved nothing more spectacular than calling a disarmament conference. After much delay, representatives of Poland, Finland, and the
three Baltic republics—Rumania spurned the invitation because of the
Soviet refusal to recognize the annexation of Bessarabia—gathered in
Moscow early in December 1922. Litvinov, the leading Russian spokesman, proposed a drastic reduction of land forces; but he was unable
to strike a responsive chord among the other diplomats, due largely
to the intransigence of the Poles, who had pretensions of their own in
Eastern Europe. The failure of the conference did not discourage later
ostentatious endeavors to interest the powers, both great and small, in
disarmament measures; indeed it was to be a favorite Soviet refrain

throughout the twenties. As proof of its sincerity Moscow announced late in December an immediate 25 per cent cut in the size of the Red Army to a total of 600,000 men.

As Litvinov vainly labored in Moscow, Chicherin was achieving no more productive results in Lausanne, Switzerland, where the powers were arranging peace with the Turkish Republic after its victory over the Entente-backed Greek government. The Russians had been invited at the last minute after strongly protesting their exclusion and declaring that they would not be bound by the terms of the settlement. Their participation was restricted to a consideration of the perennial Straits question. Here the traditional attitude of the powers was reversed because of Soviet naval weakness. Britain and France sought continued free access to the Black Sea for their warships, while the Soviet government, more Turkish than the Turks on this issue, urged that the Straits be closed to naval vessels and placed under complete Turkish control. A draft agreement, embodying the viewpoint of the Western powers in all essentials, was accepted on February 1, 1923. Shortly thereafter the conference broke up in discord over an unrelated dispute involving peace terms with Turkey and did not reconvene until late in April.

The Russians were unrepresented at these later negotiations since the agenda did not include the Straits question. However, their envoy in Rome, Vaslav Vorovsky, was sent as an observer, only to be killed two weeks later by a Russian *émigré*. The assassin was hailed as a hero in anti-Soviet quarters and acquitted by a Swiss court. The Straits convention was signed by Turkey and the European powers on July 24 and by Vorovsky's successor on August 14. In failing to ratify the document, Moscow expressed its disapproval while making the best of a bad bargain by cooperating with the international commission set up to enforce the terms of the convention.

The Anglo-Russian rivalry at Lausanne was a familiar echo of the nineteenth century feud over their respective interests in the Middle East. Appropriately, both countries were represented at the conference by a symbol of past imperial ambitions: Chicherin, the Bolshevik of noble lineage, and Curzon, the former viceroy of India. The latter, of course, was more than a symbol of Britain's imperial greatness. As foreign secretary in a Conservative cabinet—Lloyd George's government had been overthrown in October 1922—he was perhaps its foremost living embodiment. In Curzon's view Communist subversion presented a more deadly challenge to the integrity of the British Empire than the undisguised expansionism of the Tsars. First-hand exposure to Chicherin's barbed comments and acid wit only confirmed his opinion that Soviet Russia constituted a most dangerous adversary and that a firm hand in dealing with this precocious upstart would be the wisest course. Curzon's freedom of action had been restricted with Lloyd George on the scene; the new prime minister, Andrew Bonar Law, allowed his foreign secretary a free rein. As Kamenev wryly remarked to a British correspondent in Moscow, Lloyd George "realized he was living in the twentieth century, though he had not always the courage to make the necessary deductions and act on them," while Curzon "is determined that if this is not the nineteenth century world he will behave as if it were."[8]

During the break in the conference Moscow gave London an excellent pretext for a diplomatic showdown. In reply to a plea requesting clemency for a Russian Catholic priest condemned to death for espionage, a deliberately impertinent note was dispatched signed by a subordinate official in the Narkomindel citing the iniquity of British policy in Ireland, India, and Egypt. The British chargé d'affaires in Moscow refused to accept it, whereupon a less offensive rejoinder was sent expressing the wish that Britain would in the future refrain from interfering in Soviet domestic affairs. An anti-Soviet campaign, which had never ceased in some sections of the British press since 1917, mounted in fury and prepared public opinion for a stern and explicit note to the Soviet government on May 8, 1923. Popularly known as the "Curzon ultimatum," it dwelt at length upon Russia's "pernicious activities" in the Middle East and referred also to "outrages inflicted upon British subjects" and the seizure of British fishing trawlers. Satisfaction was demanded on all points within ten days under penalty of a cancellation of the trade agreement, a step that would have meant a complete rupture of relations.

Moscow was taken aback by the censorious and threatening tone of the communication, and visions of a new intervention—a refrain immediately adopted by the Soviet press—began to haunt the leaders in the Kremlin. Vorovsky's assassination on May 10 and the current state visit of Marshal Foch to Poland furnished alarmists with other disconcerting bits of evidence that "international capital" was preparing some new aggression. Curzon's diplomatic offensive did not envisage military action, but to avoid his "clumsy trap"—as Trotsky later called it—a soft answer was promptly returned. Written by Trotsky and signed by Litvinov, it undertook to rebut the charges in a document almost as long as the original complaint. The Soviet case notwithstanding, the minor causes of friction were removed by Moscow's willingness to accept the British demands. As to propaganda and subversion, the familiar argument regarding the Comintern's supposedly independent status was repeated, and the "dubious data" upon which London's representations had been made was cited in some detail. In short, the note failed to give complete satisfaction, but it so mollified British opinion that Curzon's aim of a diplomatic break had to be temporarily abandoned. The time limit on the ultimatum was extended to allow further negotiation on the "all-important question of hostile propaganda." Eventually the two governments worked out a statement on that troublesome issue which was more explicit than that contained in the trade agreement. Curzon was well pleased with his work. "I think that I may claim to have won a considerable victory over the Soviet Government," he wrote to a friend. "I expect them to behave with more circumspection for some time to come."[9]

While Moscow was engaged in pacifying Britain, the situation in Germany had altered substantially because of the French occupation of the Ruhr beginning in January 1923. This armed attempt to extract reparations in kind met the passive resistance of the Ruhr workers and the Berlin authorities but at the cost of an enormous acceleration of the already severe monetary inflation. The ensuing economic chaos once more encouraged the votaries of the German revolution. Yet Communist zeal both in Russia and in Germany to strike a blow at France, the deadly enemy of both countries, disclosed latent nationalist tendencies; and the result was a schizoid policy dedicated to the support of the bourgeois German government in foreign affairs and its simultaneous overthrow on the domestic scene.

Radek, still pursuing his double role of Comintern agent and Rapallo salesman while shuttling between Moscow and Berlin, was largely responsible for the hesitancy of the German party as it groped for a consistent formula during the spring and summer of 1923. His flirtation with the notion of "national Boleshevism" as an anti-French maneuver found concrete expression in a speech delivered to a meeting of the Comintern Executive Committee in June. He extolled the heroism of one Albert Leo Schlageter, a young German fanatic of the extreme Right recently executed by a French firing squad for sabotaging a Ruhr railroad bridge. The implied suggestion that Moscow's united front was broad enough to include those counter-revolutionaries already beginning to bear the fascist label was deceptive: these "activists," it was hoped, would be lured into Communist ranks for a common struggle against French imperialism. Fascism as such was denounced in a resolution which bore no indication that the Executive Committee considered it a contradiction to what Radek had said. He was acting as a weather vane for his political superiors, of whom Zinoviev and Bukharin were probably the most directly concerned.

Lenin played no part in the decision. He had been isolated from affairs of state since March because of a paralytic stroke, his third in less than two years.

The "Schlageter line," as it came to be known, was not regarded at the time as a sensational revision of established Comintern policy. But for two months the German Communists were thrown into a ferment from which no clear directive emerged, although the unpopularity of the new formulation, especially among the rank and file, led to bizarre incongruities. Street fights between Communists and extreme nationalists were a common occurrence while the leaders of both causes addressed joint meetings and debated the possibility of tactical cooperation in their respective journals. In mid-August the National Socialists (Nazis) called a halt to further fraternization, an event that signalized the abandonment of the Schlageter line.

The simultaneous economic crisis, attended by a wave of strikes and the fall of Chancellor Wilhelm Cuno's government, presented the best opportunity for a proletarian insurrection since the winter of 1918–1919. Hindsight was to reveal that the moment for decisive action—if it ever existed at all—passed just as the leading Bolsheviks hastily gathered to examine the situation. Trotsky alone preserved his pristine faith in the German revolution. Previous false alarms had dampened but not entirely quenched his colleagues' will to believe. The collective judgment was that conditions were ripening and that preliminary arrangements should begin forthwith, a resolute decision belied by the leisurely pace of the preparations and the almost academic appraisal of the task at hand. Trotsky, for example, could not resist the symbolism of the Bolshevik Revolution and proposed November 7 for the projected seizure of power. The date was eventually left open in deference to Heinrich Brandler, the German Communist chief, who had been called to Moscow for consultation along with several of his comrades. His misgivings about the enterprise were silenced by the infinitely greater authority and prestige of the Bolshevik leaders, and he left the Russian capital in October thoroughly committed to prompt and forceful action.

It had been hoped that a successful rising in Bulgaria would furnish inspirational guidance to the German Communists. The flourishing Bulgarian Communist party had held aloof while the peasant-oriented government of Alexander Stambulisky had been overthrown during the previous June by a coalition of the Right. To redeem the error— for which the Comintern bore no direct responsibility—the now severely persecuted party was authorized by Moscow to strike back at its oppressor. Before workable plans could be made, the government arrested the most prominent conspirators on September 12, 1923. Goaded into desperate but premature measures, the devitalized party attempted a *coup* ten days later and suffered a disastrous defeat. The White terror which followed compared in its savagery to that in Hungary after the rout of Bela Kun's regime: liberalism and Communism alike were stamped out.

In the face of this melancholy precedent the organization of the German revolution began to pick up momentum. Moscow sent civilian and military specialists to supervise, train, and equip the "Red hundreds"—a workers' militia designed to serve as the battering ram of the insurrection. Top level Comintern agents, of whom Radek was the best known, were also dispatched in October to action stations in Germany. By way of diplomatic preparation, Victor Kopp, the former Soviet representative to Berlin, journeyed to Latvia, Lithuania, and Poland in October seeking assurance that these states would not interfere in Germany's internal affairs should a Communist regime be established. The Baltic governments readily agreed in principle, and even the Poles were surprisingly cordial, for events in Germany had shorn the issue of immediate relevance by the time Kopp reached Warsaw.

The new German government, with Gustav Stresemann as chancellor, stood in greater peril from the Right than from the Left. The decision late in September to call off the anti-French resistance infuriated the nationalists and stiffened their determination to overthrow the Republic under the guise of saving it from the Communists. Yet in characteristic fashion the authorities were chiefly concerned with the Communist threat and chose to throw down the gauntlet in Saxony, where Brandler and two other party leaders had accepted posts in a Social Democratic cabinet. Berlin ordered the dissolution of the "Red hundreds" in Saxony and sent in troops when the expected refusal came. Effective resistance depended upon the cooperation of the non-Communist Left, and on October 21, 1923, Brandler pleaded for a general strike at a conference of factory councils and labor organizations in Chemnitz. The proposition was received so coldly that he quickly abandoned the idea of an insurrection. Couriers waiting to spread the signal for the uprising to the rest of Germany were shocked by the sudden change in plans but obediently carried out Brandler's order. By some mischance, two couriers had already left for Hamburg under the impression that the time for action had arrived.

Early in the morning of October 23 the Hamburg police stations

were attacked by armed Communist detachments, their morale fired
by the illusion that all Germany was in revolt and that Russian military intervention was imminent. After several days of fighting, regular
troops put an abrupt end to the affair. Moscow had lost touch with the
situation and was still predicting ultimate victory in Germany as late
as the 25th. The Saxon government was deposed, and the Communist
party was outlawed until March of the following year.

As Berlin turned to deal with the much more serious Hitler-Luden-
dorff *Putsch* in Munich, a prolonged autopsy on the German disaster
began in Moscow. Brandler inevitably became the scapegoat, though
his fall from grace less deeply concerned the Russian than the German
party, which now fell under the domination of its Left wing. Recriminations among the Bolsheviks were complicated by the veiled struggle
for power during Lenin's last illness. Zinoviev's loss of prestige as president of the Comintern was a foregone conclusion. But his status
as a key figure in the Politburo made him less vulnerable to attack,
and Radek was chosen as the sacrificial offering to atone for the collective sins of the party hierarchy. An unwilling victim, he was nevertheless censured by the Politburo, the Central Committee, and the
eighteenth party conference and barred from future participation in
German affairs. The rebuke also represented a veiled move against
Trotsky by the "Old Bolsheviks," for Radek was considered one of his
disciples.

Apart from the immediate political jockeying, the failure of the
German revolution to materialize after six years of false starts was
a fatal blow to the Comintern's dwindling pretensions of playing an
independent role in the formation of Soviet foreign policy. Never again
was the chimera of world revolution allowed to jeopardize the national
interest of the Soviet state. Only the weakness of Germany's international position preserved the spirit of Rapallo. Her leaders felt
obliged to observe the polite fantasy that the Soviet government was
entirely divorced from the operations of the Comintern. Unlike the
British, who seldom missed an opportunity to raise the Comintern
issue regardless of the comparative absence of provocation, the Germans retained their policy of discretion to the end of the Weimar era.
A symbolic demonstration of the expediency of the arrangement was
furnished on the occasion of the anniversary celebration of the Bolshevik Revolution at the Soviet embassy in Berlin on November 7,
1923. German Communists, diplomats, industrialists, and bankers
mixed together with perfect outward aplomb while avoiding reference
to the recent events in Hamburg and Saxony.

III

On January 21, 1924, Lenin died. It was a surprise to the outside world and a profound shock to the Russian people, few of whom were aware of the critical nature of his condition. The spontaneous expression of grief that swept the nation was an instinctive tribute to the unique character of his leadership and to the dedicated idealism of a lifetime of service in what he genuinely believed was the cause of oppressed humanity. While their estimate may have been mistaken —idealism in one society is fanaticism to another—no other figure of the twentieth century has had a greater impact on the course of world history.

It was universally assumed that Trotsky, the obvious heir apparent, would step in to fill the political void. That Lenin's successor would be the enigmatic and colorless Georgian Bolshevik, Joseph Stalin, no one could have foreseen. Little known outside the party, he was still far from the nonentity often portrayed in Western accounts of his rise to power. He had been an important government figure from the time of the October Revolution, a member of the Bolshevik Central Committee since 1912, and one of the original members of the Politburo. But not until the spring of 1922 when he became general secretary of the party, a drab but vital bureaucratic post that his better known associates did not begrudge him, was Stalin presented an opportunity to scale the political heights. Since he was not an intellectual in any of the various connotations which that elusive term implies, he was regarded as something of a philistine, particularly by Trotsky, and the story of the intraparty struggle for power is in large part a record of the continual underestimation of Stalin as a serious contender for Lenin's mantle.

Stalin's forte was organization, administration, and political intrigue. His single-minded devotion to Russian Bolshevism and his indifference to the legacy of Western Marxism were perhaps his greatest assets at a time when harsh reality was writ large: socialism, if it was to survive in Soviet Russia, would have to depend upon the human and material resources within her borders, not upon the uncertain mood of the European proletariat. If it was no whim of fate that brought such a man to the fore at the historically correct moment, neither was it through coincidence alone that Trotsky, the unquenchable firebrand of world revolution, began to feel the first quivers of a political earthquake in 1923, the year of the abortive German revolution, and to be buried in the ruins of the ensuing cataclysm in 1927, the year of the abortive Chinese revolution.

Stalin had seldom concerned himself with Comintern or Narkomin-del affairs—and then usually to echo Lenin's opinion or to venture a noncommital pronouncement. As the "troika" (Stalin, Zinoviev, and Kamenev) emerged more distinctly in 1924 as a combination to halt Trotsky, foreign policy remained a major issue, largely because the latter clung to his thesis that Russian socialism hinged upon the success or failure of European socialism and that only faulty tactics and poor leadership had nullified the German revolution. The now predominant motif of Soviet foreign policy—diplomacy—was not directly involved in the internal quarrel, although a number of Trotsky's most influential supporters were given assignments abroad.

The year 1924 marked the formal emergence of the Soviet Union into international respectability through the establishment of diplomatic relations with the European powers. Recognition by Germany—also an outcast—and by such minor states as Poland and Turkey had not offset the insult of a diplomatic boycott by the major powers. The dam burst when Great Britain notified the Soviet government on February 1 that full recognition had been granted and that Russian representatives would be welcomed in London to negotiate a treaty for the settlement of all outstanding differences.

So sudden a reversal of British policy after the Curzon ultimatum was a direct result of the Conservative defeat in the general election of December 1923. A Labor government, with Ramsay MacDonald as prime minister, had assumed power in January; and though it required Liberal support for a Parliamentary majority, it was the Labor party's first venture into national office. The moderately friendly state of Anglo-Soviet relations during Labor's brief ministry was marred only by British reluctance to exchange ambassadors and the undisguised contempt of the Bolshevik leaders for socialists of the Mac-Donald stripe. Trotsky disdainfully referred to him in public as a "Christian Menshevik," and the Soviet press pilloried him unmercifully. Such tactless behavior undoubtedly had much to do with the prime minister's disinclination to override King George V in his stubborn refusal to receive an ambassador from the government which he blamed for the murder of his cousin, the former Tsar, Nicholas II. Chargés d'affaires performed the necessary diplomatic functions, an anomalous situation that ended only in 1929.

British recognition barely preceded that of Fascist Italy, a matter of some regret to her recently installed dictator, Benito Mussolini, who had sought special economic advantages as a reward for Italy's priority in establishing formal relations. The treaty, signed on February 7, granted some commercial concessions but not as many as the Duce would have obtained had he acted more swiftly. Austria, Greece, Norway, and Sweden soon followed the Anglo-Italian lead. Thereafter many of the smaller states looked to the example of France, still the bulwark of anti-Sovietism in Europe. As in Britain, however, a general election in May 1924 revealed that the sentiment of the French voters had shifted to the Left. The new government of Premier Edouard Herriot promptly announced its intention of restoring normal relations, an act that was consummated on October 28 in a note to Moscow. Ambassadors were exchanged, but the subsequent failure to settle the question of the Tsarist debt—an especially sore issue in France—put a continuing chill on the Kremlin's hopes of reaching an accommodation with the French government.

The restoration of *de jure* relations with China on May 31, 1924,[10] and with Japan on January 20, 1925,[11] left the United States the only major power still refusing to recognize Moscow. Washington's attitude was unaltered by the cessation of the "Red scare" in 1920 and the Republican victory at the polls in November of the same year. The operations of the nominally unofficial American Relief Administration in relieving Russian famine distress in 1921–1923 had generated much good will and furnished an excellent starting point for a diplomatic understanding. But the hostility and indifference toward Soviet Russia that prevailed in the United States prevented the small "recognition lobby," which included several liberal senators, from making inroads upon official policy. On several occasions Moscow made friendly overtures, only to be rebuffed by silence or by didactic strictures regarding Soviet conduct and the reprehensible nature of her institutions.

Washington's position ostensibly rested upon high-minded legal and moral principles. With varying emphasis, these were frequently declared to be the sanctity of private property (American business concerns had been nationalized), the validity of international obligations (the "Kerensky debt"), and the principle of non-interference in the internal affairs of other states (Comintern propaganda and subversion). Moscow's declared willingness to meet these objections made no headway because the fundamental reasons for non-recognition lay in the wide disparity between Soviet Communism and American capitalism. That the economic differences as such were not an insuperable obstacle was made clear by the policy of the other capitalist powers. The difficulty was inherently an ideological one, for nowhere else were government officials and the arbiters of opinion more rigidly bound to the fetish of "free enterprise" as the preordained way of life for all peoples aspiring to higher civilization. This *Weltanschauung* was supported by the intuitive conviction that moral indignation and the subtle pressure of non-recognition would contribute to the inexorable workings of economic law and help to bring about the inevitable collapse of the Soviet regime.

In their more candid utterances, American spokesmen did not mince words in getting to the root of the matter. Secretary of Commerce Herbert Hoover declared in March 1921, for example, that there could be no restoration of real production in Russia without the "abandonment of their present economic system"; and Secretary of State Hughes stated shortly afterward in a note to Litvinov that not even trade relations could be considered until there was "convincing evidence" of "fundamental changes" in the structure of the Soviet economy.[12] The Russians were, of course, no less positive about the final collapse of capitalism, but after the German disaster they seldom indulged in the luxury of molding their foreign policy along the lines of their acquired prejudices. American policy lost none of its wish-fulfillment fantasies until the Great Depression and the shadow of World War II brought the sobering shock of reality to bear upon an abnormal situation.

Moscow's diplomatic gains in 1924 fell considerably short of equal treatment in the international community. The Soviet Union was still excluded from the League of Nations—though she was hardly disposed to join such a "holy alliance" of capitalist states—unrecognized by a majority of the countries of the world, and unable to obtain a satisfactory resolution of her disagreements with Britain and France after the promising beginning that recognition had brought. For a time it seemed that even Germany, Russia's only friend in Europe, would be lost as the result of a minor diplomatic incident. On May 3 Berlin police invaded the quarters of the Soviet trade delegation in search of an escaped German Communist who had taken refuge there. Their conduct in ransacking files and inspecting documents demonstrated that the loss of the prisoner was perhaps incidental to a thorough examination of the premises for evidence of subversion.

The German Foreign Office was caught off guard but rallied to defend a policy it did not approve and for which it bore no responsibility. The Soviet ambassador departed for Moscow in protest and trade relations were suspended. After an acrimonious exchange of correspondence, negotiations in Moscow with the German ambassador finally achieved the substance of the Soviet demands in a protocol signed on July 29: an apology, payment for damages, punishment of the offending police officials, and partial extraterritorial rights for the trade delegation. Full extrality was conferred upon all Russian trade offices in Germany in October 1925. Though the estrangement was temporary, Germany's willingness to deal with the West—soon to bear fruit in the Dawes Plan and the Locarno Pact—was to give the Russians more serious cause for concern.

The British equivalent of the Berlin raid came some three years later as a dramatic climax to an anti-Soviet diplomatic offensive conducted by the Conservatives, who had abruptly terminated the brief honeymoon with Moscow instituted by the Labor government.[13] MacDonald's ouster after only nine months in office was directly linked to Labor's conciliatory policy toward the U.S.S.R. During the spring and summer of 1924 the newly appointed Soviet chargé d'affaires, Christian Rakovsky, had labored at the head of his delegation to come to an agreement on the problem which had proved insoluble at Genoa and The Hague—debts and property claims. By placing the subject of war debts and counter-claims in "cold storage," the British tacitly accepted the Soviet position on this point. On other questions satisfactory progress was likewise made until on August 5, after a continuous twenty-hour session lasting through the night, the issue of confiscated property caused a rupture in the negotiations. The intervention of prominent Laborites brought a reconciliation; and on August 8 two treaties were signed, one relating to commerce and navigation and superseding the existing trade agreement, the other to a variety of issues in which the disputed matter of property claims was to be settled by separate negotiation between Moscow and the expropriated owners. Still another treaty was to iron out the details, and in return the British government made a vague promise to guarantee a Russian loan.

The ink was scarcely dry on the signatures before anguished cries of protest arose from the business community and the supporting London press. Influential public opinion was not prepared to concede that half a loaf was better than none. As the criticism mounted, Lloyd George, who had long been a proponent of a settlement on similar terms, perceived the shift in the political wind and joined the outcry. In the face of Liberal defection, Parliamentary sanction for the treaties appeared most improbable. To add to MacDonald's political woes, the largest and most irresponsible section of the press, representing the emotional reaction of the Tory die-hards to all things smacking of Bolshevism and Soviet Russia, began a heavy-handed but not unsuccessful "Red scare" campaign based upon the ridiculous premise that the Labor party was an adjunct of the world Communist movement.

On October 8, 1924, the government suffered a loss of prestige in the House of Commons when a Conservative-Liberal majority voted to investigate the withdrawal of an indictment for sedition against John R. Campbell, editor of a Communist weekly. The case was trivial in itself, but MacDonald chose to interpret the resolution as a vote of censure and to "go to the country" for a fresh mandate from the people. On October 25, just four days before the general election, the press published the text of the notorious "Zinoviev letter." The message purported to be a set of instructions from the Comintern president to the British Communist party containing inflammatory remarks of a subversive nature and emphasizing the importance of undermining the military establishment. The Foreign Office had released it, together with a copy of a note of protest to Rakovsky, and so lent an air of authenticity to a document that might otherwise have been regarded with more skepticism. The Conservative dailies surpassed their previous fantasies on the "Red menace" in pointing up the moral that the Labor government had now been thoroughly discredited. Zinoviev labeled the letter a "gross fabrication" in a message to the British Trades Union Congress, and Rakovsky referred to the signature as a "clumsy forgery" in a note to the Foreign Office. MacDonald, who several years later was to declare it a "fraud perhaps unmatched in its cold calculation and preparation in our political history," was less certain at the time and left his supporters in a state of bewilderment by his fumbling attempt to explain his role in the affair.

A significant percentage of the voters appear to have gone to the polls with the notion that only the Conservatives could save the country from Moscow. In any case, Labor was soundly beaten, and Stanley Baldwin's new government interpreted its victory as a mandate to ignore the treaties and to pursue an intransigent policy toward Soviet Russia. As for the curious document credited with stampeding the electorate, the overwhelming weight of the evidence points to forgery. Its apparent success as an election-eve stunt was probably due more to the auspicious timing of its release than to the skill of the unknown author or authors. Since the summer of 1917, when the Provisional Government had discovered the political profit to be derived from the use of questionable documents against the Bolsheviks,[14] the supply of such material had outrun the demand, and the demand had been far from negligible. As one observer has acidly commented, for years there had been "enough 'red letters' fluttering around Whitehall . . . to paper the walls of the Foreign Office."[15] The Conservative government stoutly upheld the genuiness of the letter and refused an official investigation as late as March 1928 after further evidence tended to cast doubt on the official verdict. In the absence of testimony by the perpetrators of the deed, the intriguing mystery of the "Zinoviev letter" was never solved with finality, and the ill will engendered by the incident led to an estrangement between the two powers that lasted nearly five years.

The prospect of a Franco-Russian *détente* also proved illusory. But Parisian policy-makers were less blatantly anti-Soviet than before recognition and no diplomatic misadventure marred the even tenor of outwardly correct diplomatic relations. The new British foreign secretary, Austen Chamberlain, visited Paris early in December 1924 and obtained Herriot's agreement to a common Russian policy. The meeting marked the transfer of European leadership from France to Britain in the effort to quarantine Moscow. Whereas the French had pursued an anti-Soviet and anti-German foreign policy at the same time—with results that could have been predicted—Britain followed a more astute course in attempting to separate the Rapallo partners by conciliating Germany. Since Berlin had never considered Rapallo more than a marriage of convenience, a flirtation with the West was an inviting prospect. The scaling down of Germany's reparation payments through the Dawes Plan, and an international loan, which enabled her economy to recover from its ruinous condition at the time of the Ruhr occupation, prepared the way for a more ambitious settlement along political lines.

Before the end of 1924 Moscow was already apprehensive that Germany had lost her freedom of action by becoming a "colony of Western European capitalism." In March 1925 Germany's application for admission to the League of Nations was rejected, but the disclosure of plans for a Franco-German security pact guaranteed by the British seemed to justify Moscow's worst fears. Negotiations to extend the political and economic implications of Rapallo—underway since the previous year—reached a hopeless impasse. The German ambassador to Russia, Count Ulrich von Brockdorff-Rantzau, vigorously opposed Foreign Minister Stresemann's dalliance with the West and went to Berlin to argue the matter in person. Unsuccessful, he was with difficulty persuaded to withdraw his resignation, and he returned to his post late in June after an absence of three months.

The ambassador's arrival was badly timed, for the atmosphere in Moscow, already laden with mistrust of Germany's intentions, had reached the saturation point with the trial of two German students for an alleged plot to assassinate Stalin and Trotsky. The Kremlin secretly considered them political hostages rather than potential murderers, and they were eventually exchanged for Peter Skoblevsky, a Comintern agent condemned to death for his activities during the ill-fated Communist rising in Germany in 1923. Small wonder that Rantzau found the Russians unresponsive to the innocuous formula for an understanding that he brought back from Berlin.

Moscow attempted to parry the impending blow from Locarno by raising the bogey of a Russo-Polish pact. Chicherin arrived in Warsaw toward the end of September 1925 midst a fanfare of publicity. Polish officials gave him a cordial reception, and it was announced in a joint communiqué that the discussions had centered on a commercial treaty and the need for closer political relations. Chicherin moved on to Berlin for talks with Stresemann while engaged in a running fire of comment to the press to the effect that Germany had become a pawn in Britain's anti-Soviet policy. If he had hoped that his pause in Warsaw and his intended visit to Paris would serve as a deterrent to the forthcoming Western security pact, he was badly mistaken. Stresemann refused to be bluffed but did everything in his power to convince the Soviet commissar that Rapallo would remain intact both in letter and in spirit. As a more tangible gesture of good will, he gave his consent to a commercial and consular treaty with Moscow, a document hanging fire since July chiefly because it had been regarded as a lever to gain Soviet assent to Germany's arrangement with the West.

The treaty was signed in Moscow on October 12, 1925, four days before the delegates assembled at Locarno, Switzerland, accepted the historic guarantee of the Franco-Belgian-German frontier and to a number of subsidiary agreements reinforcing the Versailles settlement. The anti-Soviet flavor that Moscow claimed to discern in the bargain was virtually ignored elsewhere as Europe relaxed after seven years of post-war tension and allowed the soothing balm of the "Locarno spirit" to take hold. The aftermath did not justify this wave of optimism; nor were the British, who had undeniably emerged from the conference at the helm of European diplomacy, able to capitalize on their position by driving a wedge between Berlin and Moscow. Germany's goal was now the establishment of a proper balance between Locarno and Rapallo. To regenerate the latter the dormant negotiations for a political treaty were revived. The kind of agreement Moscow had in mind was incorporated in an iron-clad neutrality pact with Turkey signed in Paris on December 12, 1925, by Chicherin and the Turkish ambassador. The Germans preferred a less stringent neutrality pledge—one that would not tie their hands in case of Soviet aggression. When a suitable compromise had been found, the formal signature was delayed so as not to prejudice Germany's acceptability as a League member.

In March 1926 Germany was rebuffed by the League for the second time in what had been considered a mere formality. The resentment aroused in Germany by the episode induced Stresemann to go ahead with the treaty, and it was signed in Berlin on April 24. A five year agreement, it specifically reaffirmed Rapallo as the basis of Russo-German relations. The heart of the document affirmed the neutrality of either country should an attack be launched upon one of them by another power or combination of powers. As an additional gesture of good faith, Stresemann and the Soviet ambassador exchanged formal notes on the same day in which Germany promised that her future participation in the League would in no way jeopardize Russian interests or the Rapallo collaboration. Within the limits of a paper guarantee, Moscow was thereby assured that Berlin was reasonably secure from Anglo-French seduction.

IV

Although the Comintern had not fallen upon evil days in the middle years of the decade—the Chinese venture was still a thriving concern[16] —the flames of revolution in Europe were flickering and the power struggle in the Soviet Union was inevitably molding a different organization from the messianic enterprise of the first years. The era of revolutionary romanticism had come to an end in 1923, and if the mystique of "October" and the impending struggle against "international capital" retained its place in the liturgy of Communism, it was not because objective conditions warranted optimism.

The fifth Comintern congress met in the summer of 1924—the last until 1928—and it inevitably bore the brand of the German failure. The un-Marxian notion that tactics, not the times, were somehow to blame dominated the proceedings. "Brandlerism" was now an all-embracing epithet for opportunism, reformism, and every variety of "social-patriotic" deviation. The united front policy was severely restricted in its application to the European scene, though it did not affect the unique situation in China. Leftist militancy was the keynote, and the way to achieve it, according to the new line, was to "Bolshevize" the national parties: to tighten the reins of discipline, to restrict freedom of discussion, and to oust the waverers.

The mid-twenties, a period of capitalist stabilization, was precisely the wrong time to introduce the rigidities of the Russian party in the name of the revolution. To the independent-minded who had not already fallen by the wayside, the "Stalinization" of the Comintern was too much. Some, clutching at straws, saw Trotsky as the standard-bearer of revolutionary democracy—or at least the stalwart defender of the Leninist heritage. The purges and splits that had disabled the

European parties after the second Comintern congress were resumed on a smaller scale and then expanded as the Trotskyist opposition, foundering in the Soviet Union, clung more tenaciously to its sources of strength abroad. That the havoc wrought in Communist ranks was no greater may be ascribed to the circumstance that those who had survived the rigors of party work ordinarily came to accept, as a matter of routine, first the leadership and then the dictation of Moscow —a process of natural selection which operated to the advantage of whoever dominated the Politburo but was of doubtful value to the cause of world revolution.

The French party was the most deeply affected by the new policy. In July 1925 Boris Souvarine, its leading theoretician, was expelled, and within another year few of the founding fathers of French Communism remained. For almost a decade, until the party revived in the Popular Front atmosphere of the middle thirties, the Socialists were a much more vital force in the political and intellectual life of France.

The German party, still the largest and most influential outside Russia, showed a drastic membership decline as a result of the autumn fiasco of 1923, and its polling strength dropped off sharply after a surprising resurgence in the Reichstag elections of May 1924. The recently installed Left wing leadership of Arkady Maslow and Ruth Fischer was soon embroiled in the Russian party struggle, which early in 1925 entered a new stage with Trotsky's resignation as commissar of war and a realignment within the Politburo. Now arrayed against his erstwhile allies, Stalin sent out a feeler to the German leaders, who spurned it in the conviction that the Russification of the Comintern would proceed more swiftly under his jurisdiction. Maslow and Fischer openly declared for Trotsky in 1926 and were soon drummed out of the German party upon Stalin's instructions.

Even with the bleeding ulcer of internal political strife, the Comintern presented a bold face to the capitalist enemy. Its activities, mainly propagandist and agitational in these years, were a constant source of embarrassment to Chicherin and the Narkomindel. Despite the lack of revolutionary opportunity in Europe, the Comintern had an indirect hand in two minor diversions—one in Estonia, the other in Bulgaria. The Estonian adventure was in retaliation for the wholesale arrest of Estonian Communists in November 1924. Zinoviev organized an armed insurrection, which broke out in Reval, the Estonian capital, on December 1 with the aid of several score Red Army officers who had crossed the frontier. The rising was quickly put down, and within twenty-four hours 150 Estonian Communists were executed for their part in the conspiracy. Instead of the triumph Zinoviev had expected, the incident was scored up as a personal blunder and helped to ease him into the political abyss.

Zinoviev's prestige was less seriously involved in the Bulgarian affair of the following year when a bomb explosion in a Sofia cathedral on April 16 killed many important government officials. Widely regarded in the West as a Comintern exploit, the details of the plot are still in doubt notwithstanding savage reprisals involving hundreds of alleged conspirators. The Communists were among the chief victims, and that leading members of the Bulgarian party were implicated is well authenticated. Their relationship to the Comintern—or to the Russian secret police as some would have it—is more conjectural; yet the virtual elimination of Communism in Bulgaria was a defeat that could not but reflect upon the Comintern and its president. After the fourteenth party congress in December 1925, at which Stalin's victory over his former partners was decisively recorded, Zinoviev's control over the Comintern apparatus was purely nominal. Bukharin, one of Stalin's leading supporters in the Politburo and the chief theoretician for the recently proclaimed dogma of "socialism in one country," assumed the organizational reins and became president upon Zinoviev's dismissal in October 1926.

The expulsion of Trotsky, Zinoviev, and Kamenev from the Politburo in the latter half of 1926 completed Stalin's political triumph. But the consolidation of his power was unfinished. In both internal and external affairs Stalin had assumed a cautious "middle of the road" position. The Comintern was even more clearly subordinated to the national interest, a status that by no means indicated an abandonment of the revolutionary struggle.

The ambiguity of Soviet policy was brought to a focus in the British general strike in May 1926. A year before an Anglo-Russian Trades-Union Unity Committee had been formed in an awkward attempt to bridge the gap between the so-called Amsterdam International of the Western labor unions and the faltering Profintern (Red International of Labor Unions) founded in Moscow in 1921. The entente was partially the result of the widespread pro-Soviet propensities of British labor, something of a contradiction in a country whose working class was regarded as more conservative than any outside the United States. Moscow hoped for double dividends: an improvement in Anglo-Soviet relations and a link with the labor movement which the weak British Communist party had been unable to forge. The first was to be accomplished by Labor party and trade union pressure on the Conservative government. The second envisaged an alliance with the British unions to split the Amsterdam International and the creation of a "united front from below" to discredit the very leaders with whom Moscow was collaborating. A policy with such conflicting aims could not be assured of a harmonious future.

The general strike broke out as an expression of labor solidarity with the coal miners, whose grievances were of long-standing duration. It was government, not labor, that raised the specter of class warfare once the strike began. The union leaders, divided and uncertain, were aghast at their own audacity and disconcerted by the unfriendly reaction of public opinion. The unexpected militancy of the British workers caught Moscow by surprise, and for a brief moment the Soviet press caught the scent of proletarian revolt. After nine days the general council of the Trades Union Congress made an abject surrender to the government, a decision which the three representatives of the Soviet labor unions then in London were obliged to endorse as a means of maintaining the Anglo-Russian committee.

The miners continued their increasingly hopeless struggle for another nine months. Their plight aroused widespread sympathy in the Soviet Union, and an estimated £1,250,000 was raised to aid them. While the assistance of party agitators was of no little importance in securing contributions, the essentially voluntary nature of the enterprise did not prevent charges in Britain that the funds were actually those of the Soviet government. Nor was there a lack of more fanciful commentators to assert that the general strike, as well as the coal strike preceding it, had been organized and financed by Moscow. It was to prevent just such publicity that the Trades Union leaders had spurned Soviet help. The miners, less squeamish, accepted £383,898 up to the middle of June, according to the British home secretary. A British note of protest on June 14 confined itself to the accusation that the Soviet government had allowed the "remittance to England of sums intended to support the general strike." The Soviet reply declared that the government had nothing to do with the money and could not in any case forbid the unions from sending funds abroad to help other workers if they so wished.

On June 24, 1926, the British Home Office released a "blue book" of documents seized in raids made during the previous October on the headquarters of the British Communist party and other places. Evidence of the Kremlin's machinations in England was hardly alarming, and "this miserable abortion of a book," as Lloyd George termed it, was bitingly satirized in the House of Commons the next day. The debate over "Russian gold" grew so heated that the speaker, unable to restore order, was obliged to suspend the session. On the 27th Moscow issued a formal statement on Anglo-Soviet relations. The tone was conciliatory but did not entirely conceal some sharp barbs for British policy and a complaint about the "hostile, frivolously tendentious, and grossly unbecoming sallies" of certain officials, of whom only Churchill, then chancellor of the exchequer, was singled out for special comment.

The collapse of the general strike, for which the British union leaders were blamed, reflected unfavorably upon Stalin's opportunism in promoting Anglo-Russian labor cooperation. Trotsky had warned of the sterility of such tactics. Since Stalin thought the arrangement would prove a useful device in exposing the predatory schemes of the British government—a judgment that proved incorrect—the committee functioned after a fashion until the British labor leaders finally dissolved it in September 1927. A rupture of diplomatic relations had been narrowly averted. Baldwin and Chamberlain wished to avoid an increase in international tension and resisted the demands of the Conservative die-hards for a complete break. The mounting pressure for action at length dictated a propitiatory offering in the form of another official protest in the endless series of notes "exposing" Communist propaganda and subversion. The remonstrance, dated February 23, 1927, was buttressed by eleven enclosures documenting the charge that the 1923 agreement had been repeatedly violated, and it closed by threatening the severance of diplomatic and commercial relations. The language lacked the peremptory tone of the "Curzon ultimatum" and encouraged a detailed reply, signed by Litvinov, conceding nothing to the British case and quoting a number of anti-Soviet pronouncements made by Conservative leaders. The rebuff undoubtedly strengthened the proponents of a bellicose policy toward Moscow, although it is likely that Soviet activity in China, which was blamed for the revolutionary disturbances endangering the British sphere of influence there, had more to do with the sensational denouement to Anglo-Soviet friction in the spring of 1927.

On May 12 London police and agents from Scotland Yard raided a building jointly occupied by the Soviet trade delegation and the All-Russian Cooperative Society (Arcos Ltd.), a firm organized to facilitate Anglo-Soviet trade. A systematic search of the premises took more than three days and was enlivened by the use of safe-cracking equipment, pneumatic drills, and oxyacetylene torches. The purpose of the raid, it was eventually disclosed by the home secretary, was to recover a missing War Office document. Soviet officialdom in both London and Moscow was caught off guard despite the example of the raid on the Soviet embassy in Peking on April 6[17]—possibly a result of British pressure—and warnings by friendly British businessmen of some similar move in London.

The Soviet government considered the raid a deliberate provocation, and its chargé in London lodged an immediate protest which was supplemented by a lengthy note from Moscow on May 17. The Baldwin government was determined upon a break and announced the termination of the trade agreement and the suspension of diplomatic relations on May 26. To justify its stand that the trade delegation had been a center of "espionage and intrigues" under the "guise of peaceful trading," a "white paper" was released on the same day distilled mainly from the tons of correspondence and other papers carted away from the Arcos building. The publication revealed only routine Communist activity and served to conceal the embarrassing fact that the all-important War Office document had not been found. The leader of the Labor opposition in the House of Commons called the white paper a "bright, diverting, comic publication, for which I did not think any government in the world would have become responsible"; and a generous segment of the Liberal and Labor press expressed dissatisfaction with the flimsy pretext for the rupture.

The news was greeted in the Soviet Union with mass meetings of protest, countless anti-British speeches by local party leaders, and street demonstrations in the larger cities. The press made a concerted attempt to play up the danger of war, which was to be the major theme of Soviet commentary on the international scene during the coming weeks and months. Bolshevik psychology, nursed on constant fears of "capitalist encirclement," was prone to exaggerate the threat. Yet the party's top leaders were surely not seriously worried about the imminence of hostilities. Certainly Chicherin and Litvinov were not. The press campaign seems to have been in part an attempt to discredit the already badly weakened Trotskyist opposition for its refusal to close ranks and stop attacking the party majority in the face of possible war.

On June 7, 1927, the assassination in Warsaw of the Soviet minister to Poland by a Russian *émigré* generated a new period of tension in Soviet-Polish relations and furnished fresh ammunition for the proponents of the "British plot" theory. The incident also touched off a spy scare of no mean proportions in which melodramatic charges of British espionage figured prominently.

In England and other Western countries the Soviet war psychosis was accepted as a temporary Communist aberration. Germany showed no disposition to disturb her delicately balanced position between East and West. In France the anti-Soviet forces rallied under the stimulus of the British example but fell short of achieving the same result. As in London, a number of Parisian dailies regaled their readers with material on the domestic Red menace as a means of arousing public opinion. Rakovsky, the Soviet ambassador to France and former chargé in London, became their chief target during his visit to Moscow in August. An ardent Trotskyist, he signed a public declaration with other members of the opposition protesting their loyalty to the party in case of war and promising to do everything in their power to subvert the soldiers of the capitalist armies should such a conflict occur. The French government chose to make an issue of the incident and protested to Moscow. Foreign Minister Aristide Briand expressed satisfaction with the explanation offered, which in effect disavowed the ambassador's act, and but for the furious press campaign demanding Rakovsky's recall the incident might have ended there. To avoid further deterioration of Franco-Soviet relations, Moscow unexpectedly conceded several points in the intermittent debt negotiations first begun in April 1925. After Rakovsky had released this presumably welcome news, Premier Raymond Poincare and his anti-Soviet colleagues accused him of trying to influence public opinion in France and requested his recall. In a note to Moscow on October 7 his "subversive" August statement was reintroduced in an attempt to bolster the French case. The Russians countered by pointing out France's willingness at the time to consider the August incident closed, but to avoid additional controversy Rakovsky was withdrawn.

Thus at the end of 1927, a moment of unchallenged supremacy for Stalin on the domestic scene, Trotsky and his sympathizers gained a measure of vindication through the successive defeats of Soviet foreign policy. In Europe the Russians were thrown back to a status approximating that of 1921. And in Asia the collapse of Moscow's laboriously erected enterprise in China, the subject of a particularly bitter controversy between Stalin and Trotsky, appeared to demolish almost a decade of patient effort. Yet the roots of Communism were not completely torn out, and more than twenty years later, to the Kremlin's surprise, the Chinese Communists achieved virtually unaided what the Soviet Union had failed to accomplish with its elaborate preparations in the twenties.

NOTES

1. Paul Frölich, *Rosa Luxemburg* (London, 1940), p. 288.
2. Jane Degras (ed.), *The Communist International, 1919–1943: Documents* (New York, 1956–), I, 5.
3. Angelica Balabanov, *My Life as a Rebel* (New York, 1938), p. 223.
4. See above, p. 63.
5. See above, p. 87.
6. J. Saxon Mills, *The Genoa Conference* (London, 1922?), pp. 284–85.

7. Leonard Shapiro (comp. and ed.), *Soviet Treaty Series* (Washington, 1950–55), I, 169.

8. *Manchester Guardian*, February 19, 1923.

9. Earl of Ronaldshay, *The Life of Lord Curzon* (London, 1928), III, 356.

10. See below, p. 141.

11. See below, p. 94.

12. *New York Times*, March 22, 1921; *Current History*, XIV (May, 1921), p. 190.

13. See above, p. 122.

14. See above, p. 35.

15. Macneill Weir, *The Tragedy of Ramsay MacDonald* (London, n.d.), p. 190.

16. See below, Chapter 5.

17. See below, p. 150.

CHAPTER FIVE

REVOLUTIONARY ADVENTURISM IN CHINA

China became the crux of Soviet policy in the Far East, an almost inevitable result of historical continuity and geographical proximity. The mutual hostility of the Allied powers and the new Bolshevik state precluded cooperation on Chinese problems and made it doubly certain that China—the classic semi-colonial victim of capitalist imperialism—would enlist Moscow's sympathetic attention. But until the end of intervention and civil war Sino-Soviet relations did not exist in any ordinary sense of the word; and it was the rivalry of the great powers, notably that between Japan and the United States, which preserved China as a legal if not entirely sovereign territorial entity.

At the time of the Bolshevik Revolution, China had been a republic for nearly six years. The collapse of the Manchu dynasty and the introduction of parliamentary democracy had not been the easy road to progress and stability that many Chinese intellectuals expected. On the contrary, governmental chaos was the chief result of this improvised and misguided experiment in the unfamiliar political customs of the West. A host of war lords, avaricious and unconscionable, split the nation into a number of semi-independent satrapies, and the legal government became the plaything of the faction controlling Peking, China's ancient capital.

During the summer of 1918, in an exalted mood of revolutionary idealism, Moscow renounced the rights and privileges procured from China by the Tsarist regime. The declaration, made by Chicherin in the course of a speech before the fifth Congress of Soviets, was stated more explicitly on July 25 of the next year in a formal proclamation signed by Leo Karakhan, deputy commissar for foreign affairs, in the name of the Soviet government. The "Karakhan manifesto," as the document was henceforth labeled, was unequivocal in its language: the Chinese Eastern Railway was being returned "to the Chinese people without compensation of any kind." Since Moscow had no control over the railroad—it was patrolled by Japanese troops nominally under the authority of an Allied railway commission—the generosity of the gift was not overwhelming. Yet the glaring contrast between the Bolshevik action and the privileged position of the other powers could not fail to create a favorable impression of the Soviet regime when the text of the manifesto finally reached Peking in March 1920. Sober second thoughts in Moscow, dictated by the Red Army's advance in Siberia, led to the repudiation of the sentence concerning the Chinese Eastern Railway, and hard bargaining over the disputed line followed when contact between the two governments was re-established.

As in Europe, the dual approach of overt diplomacy and covert revolutionary agitation characterized Soviet policy in the Far East. While no Asiatic country was so isolated that it did not feel in some degree the after-effects of the Bolshevik upheaval, the colonial status of India and the states of Southeast Asia, coupled with the traditional conservatism of Japan, forestalled all but the most modest of revolutionary gains. In China the prospects were much better, though Lenin and his associates were firmly attached to the orthodox Marxist dictum that colonial and semi-colonial countries still in a pre-capitalist stage of economic development would achieve their emancipation in a bourgeois nationalist revolution. The Bolsheviks were therefore prepared on ideological grounds to collaborate with leaders striving to remove the shackles of Western and Japanese imperialism.

Sun Yat-sen was the most eminent revolutionary in China of this general description. A figure of extraordinary prestige as the "father" of the Chinese revolution of 1911–1912, his position had become more honorable than politically significant. He was still the leader of the impotent Kuomintang (National People's party), and in the summer of 1917 he had installed himself and the remnants of his once considerable following in Canton, the largest city of southern China. As the figurehead of the Canton government, he had become embroiled in local war lord politics while vainly seeking a means of revitalizing the Kuomintang and fulfilling his dream of an armed expedition to subdue the militarists of the north.

Long before Lenin himself had become famous he had paid his respects to Sun as a "revolutionary democrat, full of nobility and heroism," in spite of the "virginal naïveté" of some of his ideas;[1] and the Bolsheviks observed Sun's activities with more than casual interest during the early years of their rule. Gregory Voitinsky, a Comintern agent sent to help organize a Chinese Communist party, was the first Soviet representative to contact Sun. The meeting took place in Shanghai in the autumn of 1920, and the Kuomintang leader was reported to have expressed regret at the absence of communication between Canton and Moscow. Voitinsky was unable to bring the various Marxist groups into a united party, a task only partially completed in July 1921 when delegates to the first congress of the Chinese Communist party met secretly in Shanghai.

Earlier in 1921 another Soviet representative, Hendrik Sneevliet, a Dutch Communist from Indonesia who used the name "G. Maring," had been sent to China upon a diplomatic mission—that of consulting Sun and Wu Pei-fu, then the dominant war lord of North China, about the possibility of an understanding with Moscow. While the meeting with Wu had no important aftermath—he later broke an agreement to protect Communists in his area—the conversations with Sun led to direct overtures from Moscow for a Soviet-Kuomintang alliance. Largely upon Sneevliet's insistence, the Chinese Communists accepted the idea of collaboration with the Kuomintang in August 1922. According to the tentative agreement with Sun, they were to enter the Kuomintang as individuals and to refrain from forming separate Communist cells. The Comintern cautiously acknowledged the arrangement as a means of achieving a mass base in China. Moscow continued to regard the Chinese Communists somewhat dubiously as a miscellaneous collection of intellectual dilettantes; and Radek's biting remark that they had "shut themselves up in their rooms and studied Marx and Lenin as they had once studied Confucius"[2] must have been regarded in some quarters as singularly appropriate.

Adolf Yoffe arrived in Peking late in the summer of 1922, and the two strands of Soviet policy in China merged in his person. He was authorized to reach a diplomatic settlement with the Peking government and to seek out Sun with more definite proposals for a partnership than Maring's instructions had warranted. On two previous occasions Moscow had sent emissaries to Peking to no purpose. The first, Ignatius Yurin, was technically a representative of the Far Eastern Republic, and his prolonged stay in the Chinese capital in 1920–1921 had been without issue chiefly because of Soviet interference in Outer Mongolia at the time of Ungern-Sternberg's defeat.[3] In December 1921 a direct envoy from Moscow, Alexander Paikes, had arrived with glib assurances regarding the status of Mongolia and the Chinese Eastern Railway. He, too, found it advisable to leave when the ground was cut from under him by the publication in April 1922 of a secret Soviet-Mongolian treaty, signed five months before, recognizing Outer Mongolia as part of the Soviet orbit.

The assignment of a diplomat of Yoffe's reputation to the Far East indicated that the priority habitually assigned to European affairs by the Kremlin had ceased to be automatic. Chinese intellectuals acknowledged the honor, even if the Peking government did not, by receiving Yoffe with enthusiasm. He was no novice in the art of creating favorable publicity: press interviews and propaganda handouts were a constant feature of his mission. The negotiations had not progressed beyond some preliminary fencing before Yoffe departed for the Changchun Conference,[4] leaving the Peking authorities to worry about a possible Soviet-Japanese combination at China's expense. His return to Peking empty-handed early in October 1922 made his task all the more difficult. Again the troublesome Mongolian and railroad issues proved the major barriers to a settlement, and Yoffe's public statements on the matter, adroit though they were, lost him a good deal of his initial popularity. Like his predecessors, Yoffe had to admit failure, and he began his journey to the south in January 1923 to pursue the other half of his Chinese mission.

Sun was now a political refugee in the French concession at Shanghai, where he had settled after his unceremonious ouster from Canton the summer before by the local war lord. He was eager to recoup his political fortunes, and if Yoffe was disappointed by the low state to which the Kuomintang had fallen, he gave no hint of it in his respectful treatment of the venerable nationalist leader. On January 26 a subsequently famous joint communiqué was released to the press outlining the conditions of a Soviet-Kuomintang accord. The two agreed that China was not ready for Communism and that national unification and independence from foreign control should be the Kuomintang's primary goal. Soviet support was promised to help achieve both aims. The previous pronouncements from Moscow renouncing Tsarist imperialism were reaffirmed, including a definite statement that Outer Mongolia would not be forcibly separated from China and that future negotiations would determine the disposition of the Chinese Eastern Railway. Both Sun and Yoffe were well pleased with their bargain, and the latter went on to Tokyo. There, in addition to his negotiations with the Japanese,[5] he conferred at some length with Liao Chung-kai, one of Sun's oldest and most trusted colleagues. Shortly after Yoffe's departure, the complexion of southern Chinese politics shifted once more and allowed Sun to return to his Cantonese base.

Neither the Sun-Yoffe agreement nor the successive failures to reach an understanding with Peking dissuaded the Soviet government from pursuing its basically contradictory policy. While Moscow began to implement its promises to Sun, a fourth Soviet mission arrived in Peking early in September 1923 to woo Canton's rival—the legal government of China. It was headed by Leo Karakhan, whose association with the manifesto of July 25, 1919, and with a more qualified declaration of Soviet views on China (September 27, 1920) had made his name better known than Yoffe's to politically conscious Chinese. His journey through Manchuria, where he had paused to confer with the Japanese-backed ruler of the territory, Chang Tso-lin, had been almost a triumphal procession. Karakhan handled his public relations more skillfully than Yoffe but found the Peking negotiators no less tenacious. They immediately rejected his demand that *de jure* recognition of the Soviet government should precede a discussion of the questions at issue.

No discernible progress was made until February of the next year when Britain's breach of the diplomatic boycott of Soviet Russia by the great powers[6] acted as a spur upon the Chinese diplomats, and they began to demonstrate a more conciliatory spirit. On March 14, 1924, a preliminary agreement on general principles was initiated, automatically restoring normal relations between the two governments. Moscow conceded that Outer Mongolia was an "integral part" of China and promised to withdraw the few hundred Russian troops still there; but the Soviet-Mongol pact was not disavowed. Chang Tso-lin's control of the Chinese Eastern Railway failed to prevent a tentative settlement in which China was eventually to redeem the railroad. Most important to Peking, the Soviet government formally renounced the privileged position of the Tsars, including extraterritorial rights and the Russian share of the indemnity payable to the foreign powers as a result of the Boxer uprising of 1900.

Although Moscow's largess fell considerably short of its earlier unilateral pronouncements, no other power was prepared to offer an equivalent measure of self-denial. French, American, and Japanese pressure upon Peking, combined with cabinet criticism of the vague provisions about Mongolia, caused the government to refuse ratification. At this point Karakhan lost his temper and threatened a complete break. The Chinese public, however, strongly favored the agreement, and the government renewed negotiations—this time in secret to avoid the unwelcome interference of foreign diplomats. On May 31 the treaty was signed without essential change. Because of the chaotic political conditions in Peking in later years the specific details of the pact were never clarified, but to the Chinese people it represented an important first step in their long struggle to throw off the yoke of nineteenth century imperialism. Moscow's subsequent treaty with Chang Tso-lin (September 24, 1924), though protested by Peking, carried through the May arrangement for joint Sino-Soviet management of the vital Manchurian rail artery. In essence it meant Russian control in practice and Chinese sovereignty in theory.

While the extended Moscow-Peking deliberations were under way, relations between Moscow and Canton had grown steadily closer. In August 1923 Sun sent Chiang Kai-shek, his leading military adviser and confidential agent, to Moscow to consult the Soviet leaders and to study the Red Army's methods. Despite his comparative youth, Chiang was a seasoned military strategist and a veteran of war lord politics. His four-month sojourn in Russia made no lasting impression upon his political philosophy, which was chiefly that of an ambitious opportunist, but he was seemingly impressed with Communist discipline and technique and assumed a fashionably "radical" pose upon his return.

As its top agent in Canton the Soviet government secretly appointed Mikhail Borodin, a Comintern agent of some reputation who had been entrusted with previous missions to Mexico, Scotland, and Turkey. He was gifted with tact, poise, and intelligence, and from the time of his arrival in Canton on October 6, 1923, with a letter of introduction from Karakhan, he was the motivating force behind a thorough reorganization of the Kuomintang along the lines of the Russian Communist party. Sun had always been inclined to overemphasize the purely military aspects of the problem of unifying China, and Borodin was able to convince him that the development of a trained party cadre and the building of a solid foundation among the masses by propaganda and agitation should precede military action. Conservative members who refused to abide by the "Moscow orientation" and the new tactics resigned or were expelled. With the Chinese Communists forming a kind of Left wing vanguard within the Kuomintang, but excluded by Sun from a dominating role in the leadership, a non-Marxian program of social reform found a widening response from the land-starved peasants of southern China and the exploited workers of Canton, Hongkong, Shanghai, and the Wuhan cities (Hankow, Wuchang, and Hanyang). Promising young party workers—chiefly non-Communists—were sent to Russia to further their revolutionary education. Beginning in the fall of 1925 they were trained at the newly founded Sun Yat-sen University in Moscow.

The military program, though it came later, was not neglected. General Vasily Blücher, the Red Army's most famous commander in the Siberian phase of the civil war, became Borodin's counterpart as a military adviser under the name "Galen." The task of training a Kuomintang army was begun by scores of other Red Army specialists, most of whom were appointed instructors at the Whampoa Military Academy established near Canton in May 1924 with Chiang Kai-shek as commandant. By October arms and equipment began to reach Canton by the sea route from Vladivostok. Russian funds, limited but welcome, provided the means for these activities.

Quite apart from the elaborate plans of the Kuomintang leadership, the party's actual status in Canton was still precarious. In the last analysis, Sun's "government" depended upon the avowed or tacit support of the local war lords, and until the summer of 1924 the Kuomintang had no reliable armed force of its own. In August the Merchants' Volunteer Corps, a military organization financed by the British and backed by the wealthy compradores of Canton and Hongkong, became alarmed by the leftward trend of the Kuomintang and conspired with the very militarists against whose depredations the Corps had originally been founded as a protective barrier. On the 26th the British consul general in Canton intervened in the impending conflict and threatened naval action in favor of the militarists. Sun was infuriated by this manifestation of British "gunboat diplomacy" and protested vigorously to Prime Minister Ramsay MacDonald and to the League of Nations. Though the protests themselves were probably unavailing, the British were neutral during the decisive test in mid-October when a motley Kuomintang army, led by Whampoa cadets, defeated the mercenaries of the Corps.

The Kuomintang's future in Canton now more secure, Sun set out for Peking via Japan for a conference with the northern war lords. Already incurably ill with cancer, he arrived too late to influence the new political coalition in northern China. His death on March 12, 1925, elevated Sun to the stature of a revolutionary saint—a vulnerable figure in his lifetime, but as a legend impervious to critical judgment. From the standpoint of political martyrology his demise could not have been more timely, for his career was cut short at a fateful moment in the history of China. His name thereafter was associated with revolutionary success, not with the blunders that inevitably disfigure every great political and social upheaval. The loss of the leader whom all factions of the Kuomintang had willingly obeyed was the catalyst that produced the long-disguised struggle between the Left and Right wings of the party. For the balance of the year the former held sway. The party machinery was still in its hands, and in the late winter and spring of 1925 the defeat of most of the remaining militarists of the south, representing the landlord and merchant classes, deprived the Kuomintang Right of potential allies.

On May 30, 1925, an incident occurred in Shanghai that temporarily concealed the growing party split. A Chinese mob, demonstrating in the International Settlement as an aftermath of labor disputes in Japanese-owned cotton mills, was fired upon by police under the command of a British officer. The "Shanghai massacre"—at least a score were killed and a larger number wounded—triggered a wave of anti-foreign outbreaks unequalled in China since the Boxer episode. One of many protest demonstrations led to an even graver incident on June 23 when more than fifty Chinese were killed by British and French marines near the foreign concession in Canton. A general strike in Hongkong and Canton, followed by a boycott of British goods, bit deeply into the profits and prestige of the most bitterly hated of the Western powers. Since Kuomintang propaganda laid particular stress on the struggle against imperialism, the party was a major beneficiary of the new mood of the masses—a mood that it had helped to create. Communists and other leftists in the party distinguished themselves in leading the strike and boycott movement, and the foreign powers, especially Great Britain, professed to see the sinister hand of Moscow behind the resurgence of Chinese nationalism.

The Right wing, theoretically as anti-imperialist as the "radicals," became seriously concerned at the dangerous forces unleashed, for the masses failed to show a fine sense of discrimination between foreign and domestic property interests. Designating their faction the "Sun Yat-senist Society," the most powerful group of conservatives worked to rid the party of Bolshevism—both real and fancied—and in so doing embraced the old combination of landlords, merchants, compradores, and militarists. In pursuing these general objectives, Liao Chung-kai, the acknowledged leader of the Kuomintang Left, was assassinated on August 20, 1925. The plot miscarried in the sense that leading conservatives were implicated and unable to bring their plans to fruition. Two were executed, two were arrested and later released, and others fled or were forced to leave Canton.

On the theory that the nationalist revolution was in danger, Borodin maneuvered the appointment of a dictatorial triumvirate at a special conference of party leaders. One was his protégé, Chiang Kai-shek, at the time the least known to the general public. Chiang's position was soon enhanced by the elimination through exile to Moscow of one of the two other triumvirs—Hsü Chung-chi—the commander of one of the Kuomintang armies and a member of the Right wing. His three divisions were disarmed with minimal bloodshed on September 19 by Whampoa cadets aided by Hongkong workers.

Aside from his mentor Borodin, whose position was untouchable as long as the *rapprochement* with Moscow lasted, Chiang's remaining rival was Wang Ching-wei, one of Sun's oldest followers and then a convinced adherent of the Left wing. Between the two the discomfited

Right unerringly chose Chiang as the lesser evil in a November conclave at Sun's grave in the Western Hills outside Peking. Their slogan, "Ally with Chiang to overthrow Wang," was politically premature, and Chiang hastened to dissociate himself from their embrace. The Western Hills conference marked the first open acknowledgment of the split by either side. Those in attendance no longer held positions of power in Canton or in Kwangtung province, but they boldly proclaimed themselves the new Kuomintang Executive Committee and decreed the expulsion of all Communists from the party. As far as surface indications went, the impotence of the Western Hills faction was demonstrated at the second congress of the Kuomintang which opened on January 4, 1926, at Canton. The party line was unaltered, and the expulsion of two Western Hills conferees and the disciplining of the rest exposed the empty threat of the Right.

Most of the Kuomintang leaders felt that Sun's goal of a northern expedition was now practicable. The decision to go ahead was made late in January 1926, and Chiang was placed in charge of the preparations as inspector-general of the armies. Early in February Borodin left Canton to consult Feng Yü-hsiang, the so-called "Christian general" of the northwest, then in control of the Peking government. Feng, already cultivated by Yoffe, Karakhan, and Borodin himself, was receiving arms and financial support from Moscow. Though Kuomintang-oriented, he had been reluctant fully to commit himself, and the Russian hoped to persuade him to cooperate with the northern expedition. Before a bargain could be sealed with the hesitant Feng, rival war lords forced him to retire from Peking in the game of musical chairs that had been going on in the northern capital for almost a decade. After conferring with Borodin early in April in Outer Mongolia, he went on to Moscow in pursuit of further Soviet aid and while there professed enthusiasm for the Communist system.

In Borodin's absence Chiang thought the time ripe to consolidate his own authority as the undisputed head of the party. In the early morning hours of March 20, on the pretext of a Communist conspiracy to seize power, his troops arrested the leading Communists in Canton and surrounded the residence of the Kuomintang's Russian advisers. Forceful measures were also taken against individuals and labor organizations associated with the party Left. Within a few hours Chiang's *coup* was complete. Yet he was careful not to push his success too far. Soviet assistance was still necessary, and his hold upon the armed forces was as yet too uncertain to permit an undisguised dictatorship. Within a few days the troops were withdrawn and most of the prisoners released. Wang Ching-wei, however, was safely eliminated from power by his prudent withdrawal to a European exile, and it was apparent that Chiang, even if he lacked Sun's prestige and moral authority, was the undisputed master of the Kuomintang and the Nationalist government.

Borodin returned to Canton via Siberia late in April and renewed his collaboration with Chiang in an outward show of friendship. Each was anxious to propitiate the other, although Chiang held the upper hand because of Moscow's wish to preserve the alliance with the Kuomintang at all costs. A number of Russian political and military advisers whom Chiang found objectionable were replaced, and he reciprocated by instituting a mild purge of some of his reactionary colleagues.

The events of March 20 suffered an almost total blackout in the Soviet Union; and references to it in the Communist organs of the West denied news reports of the affair as the work of the reactionary capitalist press. In view of the unusual effort to prevent the facts from becoming known, the plain implications of Chiang's action could not have escaped the Kremlin. But Stalin had thoroughly committed himself to the Kuomintang alliance and was loath to admit even by implication the justice of Trotsky's criticism of his policy by breaking off the relationship. Nor did he or Borodin feel that Chiang was capable of going his own way unaided. In effect, a tacit truce had been declared between Moscow and Canton to permit the Nationalist revolution to mature. Trotsky later claimed to have opposed the Communist-Kuomintang coalition "from the very beginning."[7] If so—and there is good reason to doubt it—his views were kept within the confines of top-level party discussion until well into 1927. His objection on the doctrinal grounds of "bourgeois opportunism" could be met in terms of Marxian orthodoxy by the theory that Lenin himself had vouchsafed: the first duty of Communists in backward colonial countries lay in achieving a bourgeois nationalist revolution. If Trotsky spurned the notion that socialism could be achieved unaided in the Soviet Union, his consistency left something to be desired in his implied argument that the Chinese Communists were capable of establishing what the Russian Communists, infinitely better situated in terms of mass support and economic resources, were presumably unable to accomplish. And on the score of foreign policy, Trotsky could find no reason to complain of expediency, for Soviet Russia's most formidable antagonist—Great Britain—was being directly challenged on the neutral soil of China.

II

The ambiguous status of the Communists within the Kuomintang was clarified on May 15, 1926, at a plenary session of the party's Central Committee. That their future role would be severely restricted was revealed not only by Chiang's original *coup* but also by the contrived atmosphere of tension: a Communist rising was widely rumored and martial law was declared on the eve of the meeting. The committee obediently passed a series of measures insuring the complete political subordination of the Communists, including a rigid limitation on their appointment to party and government posts and the submission of a formal membership list. Capitulation was vehemently opposed by many Communists, and Borodin had some difficulty in enforcing the Moscow line. "The present period is [one] in which the Communists should do . . . coolie service for the Kuomintang," he is reported to have told a doubting associate.[8]

The May 15 meeting also put a seal of approval upon Chiang's dictatorship and confirmed the plans for the military offensive drawn up by General Blücher and his Russian assistants. Stalin opposed the campaign as a foolhardy venture but did not block the Chinese Communists from participation. Before the expedition was formally launched on July 9 Chiang was appointed commander-in-chief; but his direct control was limited to about one-fifth of the 100,000-man army, which had been divided into six corps. As a professional military organization it was not a formidable force either in training or in equipment, and most of the soldiers, being products of the war lord system, were only superficially indoctrinated with Kuomintang ideals. Yet the inferiority of the mercenary troops the enemy generals were able to put in the field was soon demonstrated in so striking a fashion that even the Kuomintang leaders were surprised.

The purely military phase of the operation proceeded for the most part without the mass carnage that has generally characterized warfare in the twentieth century. The political transformation wrought by the victorious Kuomintang was of revolutionary significance. Party agitators supplied with propaganda materials preceded the troops, and so effective was their work in "softening up" the enemy and winning over the already sympathetic civilian population that the northern expedition was at times more a triumphant promenade than an orthodox military campaign. And when propaganda failed, lavish bribes to the opposing generals often succeeded. In the wake of the advancing armies the workers and peasants were organized into unions, many of which became strong centers of Communist ideology. But Moscow insisted that the revolutionary potential thus aroused should be kept firmly in check to avoid upsetting the delicate equilibrium within the Kuomintang.

By October 1926 Wu Pei-fu's troops were in full retreat and the Wuhan cities of the middle Yangtze had been seized. Wuhan became the new center of the Kuomintang Left as Chiang led the campaign farther to the east. In early November the eastern armies took Nanchang, the capital of Kiangsi province, and pressed on toward Shanghai and the lower Yangtze.

The expeditionary base at Canton and the Kwangtung province had meanwhile witnessed a resurgence of conservatism represented by the landlords, the business community, and British officialdom. Without interference from Kuomintang headquarters, which was controlled by Chiang's subordinates, the peasant associations were broken and their leaders often beaten or killed. A similar fate befell the labor unions in Canton, where the authorities intervened to suppress strikes and to decree the compulsory arbitration of labor disputes. The Hongkong strike and boycott was ended on October 10 without regard to the wishes of the Canton Strike Committee. In December the Nationalist capital was moved to Hankow, and Canton was placed under the brutal ministrations of Li Chi-shen, a Kwangsi militarist who virtually excluded the Communists and the Kuomintang Left from both party and official posts.

At the end of the year a new party crisis was brewing. Chiang's absence in the field and the unexpected progress of the campaign to the Yangtze had weakened his hold on the party. The transfer of Nationalist headquarters to Hankow against his wishes had been his first major setback since his climb to power. The Left wing, enboldened by the proletarian environment at Wuhan and the unopposed seizure of the British concessions at Hankow and Kiukiang, urged the return of Wang Ching-wei; and in a satiric imitation of the Western Hills slogan, they proclaimed their intention to "welcome Wang to overthrow Chiang." The latter was established at Nanchang, where the leading members of the Right wing had gathered. He sent out feelers to Japanese representatives, to commercial interests in Shanghai, and to Chang Tso-lin in Peking while at the same time trying to regain his hold on the party organization.

Early in January 1927 Chiang telegraphed the party leaders in Hankow requesting a session of the Central Committee in Nanchang. When this obvious move was spurned, he journeyed to Hankow to examine the situation in person. His reception was perceptibly chilly, and Borodin ventured a few incautious remarks about power-seeking militarists at a banquet that Chiang attended. He returned to Nanchang on January 18 determined to crush the Communists, barely disguising his intention even in his public speeches. The Hankow government replied in kind by excoriating Chiang as a war lord who was using the party to fasten his own brand of military despotism upon the Chinese people.

On March 10, 1927, the members of the Central Committee, about two-thirds of whom attended, met in Hankow and stripped Chiang of his party and government prerogatives. But they hesitated to declare open warfare by expelling him from the party; reports of a definite split were branded "pure fabrication." Chiang, too, played along with the masquerade. He had yet to consolidate his position in Shanghai, where an alliance with local and foreign business interests would insure financial independence from Moscow. Under Communist and radical Kuomintang leadership, a general strike broke out in Shanghai on March 21, and a workers' insurrection soon followed. It was an impressive but premature demonstration of the power of the Left. Chiang's troops marched into the city only after their "allies" within had weakened themselves by defeating the mercenaries of the local war lord.

On March 24 Kuomintang troops under Wuhan leadership seized Nanking and committed various outrages against foreign residents. The powers protested to Chiang and to the government at Hankow, and a year later the unified Nationalist government made a satisfactory settlement. It was widely accepted in the foreign press, both in China and abroad, that Wuhan had deliberately fomented the disorders in order to complicate Chiang's relationship with the powers. In reality such devious strategy was beyond the Left-wingers, who were still anxious to bring Chiang back into the fold.

On March 26 Chiang arrived in Shanghai after by-passing Nanking. Hailed in Communist circles throughout the world as a revolutionary hero, he began immediate preparations for an all-out attack upon the Shanghai workers and the Kuomintang Left under the banner of anti-Communism. He was confronted with a more socially conscious mass movement than he had expected, and until a larger body of reliable troops could be brought in, he followed the "Wuhan line" of repeated denials of an impending split. While Chiang was deliberately masking his plans with calculated prevarication, the Wuhan Nationalists genuinely desired reconciliation. Instead of dealing from strength by consolidating their position on the middle Yangtze, however, they decided, in an excess of overconfidence, to strike northward against Chang Tsolin's armies.

The re-emergence of Wang Ching-wei upon the scene after a year's absence in Europe seemed to offer some hope of healing the breach. He talked with Chiang in Shanghai during the first week in April and went on to Hankow with the idea of convening the full Central Committee in Nanking to restore party unity. Wang had not been overly impressed with Chiang's argument about the Communist menace but was lulled into the belief that a reasonable compromise was possible. Chiang even went through an elaborate farce in sending out a circular telegram announcing his submission to Wang's leadership. In obedience to Comintern directives, Chen Tu-hsiu, the leader of the Chinese Communists, hastened to assure Wang of his party's complete loyalty to the Kuomintang in a joint declaration on April 4. Moscow's policy was essentially unaltered against the accumulating evidence of Chiang's reactionary proclivities.

The Trotsky opposition was not yet openly advocating a decisive break with the Kuomintang and the formation of workers' and peasants' Soviets on the Russian model of 1917. Though Trotsky was always inclined to be overly enamored of the Russian analogy, such tactics could not have fared worse than Stalin's. Effectively muzzled as far as public pronouncements were concerned, the opposition suffered, too, from what has been called a "conspiracy of silence" about the ominous developments in China. All was sweetness and light in the Soviet and Comintern press, and even the foreign Comintern delegation touring China at the time cooperated to preserve the air of unreality. The official view, while somewhat more skeptical of Chiang, was still based on the assumption that the Kuomintang Right was being used to gain Communist ends. And at the proper time, Stalin told an audience of Moscow party members on April 5, the Right could be "squeezed out like a lemon, and then flung away."[9] These were precisely Chiang's tactics: he had finished squeezing the Communist lemon and was on the point of throwing it away.

On the day after Stalin's speech, troops and police in Peking, with the permission of the diplomatic corps, entered the embassy compound and searched various Soviet buildings. A huge mass of documents were seized in all stages of legibility—some were in ashes, others partially burned—and an undetermined number of Chinese and Russian citizens were arrested on the premises. Of the former, twenty were later executed by strangulation and ten others given varying prison terms. The Russians might have shared a similar fate but for the advice of the Dutch minister, the dean of the diplomatic corps, that such summary treatment of foreigners would not look well abroad. They were eventually released after several months in prison. The most sensational documents seized in the raid—those involving Moscow's role in the Chinese revolution—were widely quoted in the world press, and several English language editions of selected material were published in China. Although at least one of the compilations contained spurious documents, the bulk of the material bore every indication of authenticity despite reliance upon the forgery thesis in Soviet comment on the affair.

Chiang lost no time in condemning the raid: a message to the Soviet embassy pronounced it an "unprecented outrage." Moscow used the statement as evidence that Chiang represented no threat to the revolution. Yet his collusion with Chang Tso-lin is suggested by the "coincidence" that April 6 was also the day on which Chinese troops surrounded the Soviet consulate in Shanghai and searched all persons entering or leaving the building. The next day Soviet buildings in the French concession at Tientsin were ransacked, and on the 10th Moscow broke off relations with Chang's government because of the Peking and Tientsin raids.

Before dawn on April 12, 1927, Chiang put an end to his long campaign of feints, false alarms, and concealed provocation by launching his "purification movement" against the Kuomintang Left and the Communists. His troops had already quietly disarmed the Wuhan units in Nanking and arrested a number of Communist leaders in Shanghai. The reign of terror that now began was carried out by military detachments and armed bands of thugs from the Shanghai underworld especially recruited for the occasion. Foreign troops and police from the International Settlement also collaborated with Chiang's forces. The workers, taken by surprise, were poorly armed because of a previous Comintern directive to bury their weapons. Possibly five hundred, many of them important labor leaders, were killed in the fighting or executed during the day. The Communist-controlled General Labor Union, slow to grasp the fact that Chiang was behind the *coup,* finally called for a general strike the next day which was joined by 100,000 workers. In the afternoon a protest parade was ambushed, and over three hundred persons were killed. For days suspects were rounded up for the drumhead military courts and then passed on to firing squads. At length the bankers, merchants, and compradores of Shanghai, who had given generously to Chiang's war chest to save themselves from Communism, discovered that their "protectors" were a ruinous luxury. Forced "loans" and expropriations were collected on a huge scale under threat of arrest and execution. But in the long run most Shanghai businessmen probably felt that the excesses against their own class were a small price to pay for the elimination of the labor movement and the establishment of a stable and conservative government. Certainly the landlords, diplomats, foreign entrepreneurs, and missionaries had no doubts on that score.

The purge was hardly less severe in Canton and the other cities under Chiang's jurisdiction. Only in the central provinces of Hunan and Hupeh, where agrarian revolt had begun to flare up, did the Wuhan proletariat find potential allies. At Hankow on April 17 the Central Committee formally denounced Chiang and his associates for their crimes and expelled them from the party. The move amounted to harmless play-acting unless the Wuhan government was prepared to enforce its decrees by marching against Nanking, where Chiang had organized his own government. In such a military showdown the advantage still lay with Wuhan; nor was it too late to reverse the earlier plan for a drive toward Peking. But the strategy of undercutting Chiang's prestige by striking at Chang Tso-lin had greater appeal and became official policy.

In theory the military power of the Kuomintang Left had not been weakened by the recent events; but the revolutionary *élan* that had once sustained the Wuhan authorities was now sorely lacking. Inspired by the successful counter-revolution elsewhere, the local businessmen brought the commercial and industrial life of the tri-city area to a virtual standstill by a lockout of the workers and other measures of economic sabotage. If the regime had really been dominated by Communists, as the Kuomintang Right charged, more forceful measures might have been taken to end the paralysis. Counsels of moderation, of which Wang Ching-wei's was now the foremost, prevailed instead, and the workers were forced to beat a retreat. The Kuomintang "radicals" were in the last analysis as concerned with the sanctity of private property as Chiang and his followers.

III

The Kremlin's initial reaction to the Shanghai *coup* had been one of stunned silence. When the full import of the catastrophe had been absorbed, party spokesmen were understandably reluctant to confer credit upon Trotsky by implying that the official doctrine had been mistaken. It was intimated that Chiang's "treason" was no surprise, and Stalin himself formulated the authorized version on April 21 by maintaining that events had "fully and entirely proved the correctness" of the collaboration policy.[10] Now that the break was complete, he felt that the only realistic choice lay in a reaffirmation of the alliance with the Kuomintang Left. The press refused to publish Trotsky's rebuttal, a renewed plea for independent Communist action and a warning that new treacheries were brewing in Wuhan. "The bloody lesson of

Shanghai passed without leaving a trace," he lamented in 1930. "The Communists, as before, were being transformed into cattle herders for the party of the bourgeois executioners."[11]

Say what he might, Trotsky had some of the prestige but none of the power to determine basic decisions. His later charge that Stalin "betrayed" the Chinese revolution rests partly upon the assumption that his more revolutionary-sounding formula would have succeeded —rather a doubtful proposition considering the infinitely superior military position of the Kuomintang Left in comparison with the Communists. It must nevertheless be acknowledged that the Trotsky who was so inept in his forecasts and analyses of the German revolution had a somewhat surer touch with its Chinese counterpart. One suspects that the contrast lay not so much in his foresight (or lack of it) as in his temperament, for he discerned revolutionary currents whenever and wherever the masses stirred; and the historical paradox of Communism was that it took root in the agrarian East rather than in the industrial West.

Late in May the eighth plenum of the Comintern Executive Committee met semi-secretly in Moscow, and there Stalin and Trotsky confronted each other for the last time on the Chinese question while a massacre of peasants and workers in Hunan province organized by a Wuhan general offered confirmation of the opposition's diagnosis of the situation. As a matter of course, the final resolution backed the collaboration policy, though not without some "leftist" phrases about deepening the agrarian revolution and arming and mobilizing the masses. Since neither was to be done outside the Kuomintang, the practical application of this theoretical formulation amounted to a further check upon revolutionary activity.

In a telegram to the Comintern representatives, which reached Hankow on June 1, Stalin issued a confusing and contradictory directive calling for Communist action from within the Kuomintang to assure a more revolutionary course. The Chinese Communist leaders considered the plan unworkable and Borodin agreed. M. N. Roy, the Indian Comintern agent who had arrived from Moscow several weeks before, made the mistake of showing the message to Wang Ching-wei for his approval. Wang not only disapproved but professed to see in it a Communist bid for power and a violation of the Sun-Yoffe agreement. He was already gravitating toward the counter-revolutionary Wuhan generals and found a ready excuse in Stalin's telegram for a move to expel the Communists from the Kuomintang. The Wuhan government refused to follow the Communist plea for a punitive expedition to suppress the reactionary forces in Hunan and contented itself with an "investigation."

The military expedition north of the Yangtze had in the meantime pushed back Chang Tso-lin's armies in a series of hard-fought battles. It was climaxed by a bloody three-day engagement late in May that forced the enemy to retreat beyond the Yellow River. The flower of the Wuhan army—some 14,000 killed and wounded—fell in that decisive battle, most of them sympathetic to the Communist cause. With both sides exhausted, the balance of power in the area lay in the hands of Feng Yü-hsiang, who had returned from Moscow in September 1926 with the Kremlin's blessing and tangible support in the form of arms and money. On Chinese soil he reverted to his old war lord habits; pretending allegiance to Wuhan, he eagerly sought contact with Nanking.

During the second week in June the leading Wuhan politicians and generals conferred with Feng at Chengchow, a northern Honan city that his troops had occupied. There was general agreement that Communism should be eliminated, but a difference of opinion arose as to how it should be done. The militarists favored immediate and drastic measures against the workers and peasants in the name of anti-Communism; the civilians were inclined to support a gradual approach. As for the consolidation of North China under Wuhan leadership, Feng remained coy and made no promises about a march on Peking. He preferred to consolidate his holdings and wait to see what Nanking had to offer. On June 19 he met Chiang at Hsuchow in northwestern Kiangsu, and the two agreed to combine forces against Chang Tso-lin. Feng telegraphed the Wuhan leaders, offering them an opportunity to join the coalition in order to "unite the Nationalist faction in a fight against our common enemies." Borodin was to be dismissed, and those who disapproved of the new course would be allowed "to go abroad for a rest."

The Kuomintang Left, after a series of secret meetings at Wang's residence, had already decided to expel the Communists, and Feng was so informed. Since Wuhan regarded its claim to legitimacy as superior to Nanking's—it demanded the dissolution of the rival organization—Feng's role as a peacemaker came to nothing. Because of his setbacks in the north, made possible by Japanese intervention in Shantung, Chiang was obliged to postpone the projected hostilities with Wuhan and sent reinforcements to save his capital from a Wuhan counterattack.

An overwhelming majority of the Kuomintang generals, whether of Hankow or Nanking, were of one accord regarding political aims.

They constituted a powerful force for reconciliation at the expense of social and agrarian revolution. Wang and his associates were not anxious to abdicate in favor of a military clique and temporized by preparing public opinion for the break with the Communists. Moscow was still pressing its Chinese disciples to save the Kuomintang alliance at a time when even the usually optimistic Borodin considered the prospect hopeless. Chen Tu-hsiu saw no alternative to the complete defeat of the Communist movement than to withdraw the party from the Kuomintang. But without Moscow's consent, he hesitated to take the initiative himself.

On July 6, when it was too late to salvage anything from the debacle, the Kremlin's appeasement tactics were abruptly terminated by a proclamation from Bukharin advising the Chinese masses to arm themselves in self-defense. The new line became official eight days later when a resolution of the Comintern Executive Committee denounced the Wuhan government as a "counter-revolutionary force" and blamed the Central Committee of the Chinese Communist party for the "opportunist deviations" of which Stalin, Bukharin, and other members of the Politburo were actually guilty. The sanctity of Muscovite dogma had to be maintained to fortify the faithful and to safeguard them from the Trotskyist heresy. Chen was deposed as party chairman and expelled two years later with eighty other members who displayed Trotskyist tendencies.

On July 15, 1927, the anti-Communist purge in Wuhan formally began. Party members who had not fled in time were fair game for the execution squads. Borodin, his usefulness at an end, left Hankow toward the end of the month, his hosts bidding him farewell with ceremonial courtesy. He returned to Moscow through Feng's territory and was treated with deferential hospitality by the Honan war lord, who had not entirely abandoned hope of further Soviet aid.

Several prominent Wuhan officials made their way into European exile during the year, among them Madame Sun Yat-sen, a sister of Chiang's bride-to-be, and because of her name a figure of great prestige among Chinese intellectuals. She left China with a ringing denunciation of the betrayers of her husband's memory and became the only Kuomintang member of importance to hew to the "Russian orientation" through the years of Chiang's rule.

As the torture and murder of real and alleged Communists continued unabated in Wuhan territory and in Feng's domain in the northwest, Moscow strove to compensate for its errors by pushing "ultra-leftism" in China. Now that the mass base for revolutionary action had been "splattered into froth"—to use Trotsky's vivid phrase[12]—

the *Putschist* tactics that had fared so badly in Europe were applied. Besso Lominadze, a Georgian protégé of Stalin's, and Heinz Neumann, a young German party member, were dispatched to the scene to carry out the new strategy. On August 7 a dozen or more leading Communists gathered for a special meeting in the Japanese concession at Hankow to consider Moscow's instructions. Appropriate expressions of condemnation for the old leadership were heard, and a party reorganization, followed by many expulsions, assured a loyal reception for an adventurist policy.

A series of risings took place in China during the last five months of the year in a futile attempt to comply with the Soviet directives. The first was already in the process of dissolution by the time of the special party conference. Two Communist generals, joined by several thousand troops, had revolted on August 1 in the name of the Kuomintang Left and seized the city of Nanchang. Within a few days they were forced to retreat into Kwangtung, where their army was defeated in successive engagements and the remnants joined anti-Kuomintang guerrilla bands among the peasants.

Similar revolts, known collectively as the Autumn Harvest Uprisings, occurred on a smaller scale in central China. Most of them were isolated rural insurrections in which poorly armed peasants were decimated by regular troops in the classic pattern of abortive agrarian revolutions. Mao Tse-tung, the future leader of Red China, played the major role in the organizational work that underlay these risings. For his failure he was demoted by the Chinese Communist party, and he withdrew with the remnants of his peasant army to Chingkanshan, an old bandit stronghold in the mountains of western Kiangsi. From this lowly beginning a more durable Communist movement, with an agrarian base and without Soviet aid, eventually grew strong enough to challenge the Kuomintang dictatorship.

During the autumn outbreaks the Kuomintang achieved a precarious unity by forming a coalition government in Nanking. It was made possible by Chiang's unexpected resignation and his voluntary retirement from the political scene. His action, occasioned by further military reverses in the north and the disaffection of his commanders, was a histrionic gesture in the approved Chinese fashion: in no sense did it represent a permanent withdrawal from politics. He was simply offstage awaiting his cue. It was not long in coming, for the absence of a dominating figure, as he had foreseen, set off fresh currents of intrigue and resulted in a widespread demand for his return. In mid-November, when Chiang reached the Chinese mainland from Japan, his perennial rival, Wang Ching-wei, had been ensconced in Canton as nominal ruler for over a month. But Wang came to Shanghai for a conference, and in his absence fighting broke out among the Kwangtung generals, presenting the Communists with an opportunity to seize power in Canton.

Moscow's demand for action in one or more of the great urban centers of China had been growing ever more insistent. But proletarian apathy had prevented even a successful general strike. Canton, as the original revolutionary base of the northern expedition, had retained something of its reputation for radicalism through successive purges and became a rather insecure haven for refugee Communists. Upon Moscow's insistence and in consultation with Neumann and Lominadze, the local party leaders reluctantly decided on November 26 to exploit the existing situation and set the insurrection for December 16. That the date coincided with the fifteenth congress of the Russian Communist party, at which the Trotskyist opposition was to be expelled, was no accident: Stalin himself timed the rising so as to display a victory for his policy before the assembled delegates. The plans leaked out, and when the warring militarists declared a truce to settle with the Communists before resuming their own quarrel, the "zero hour" was pushed up to 3:30 A.M. on the 11th.

The attack was launched on schedule by several thousand Red Guards and a detachment of former Whampoa cadets. Without working class support and lacking adequate weapons, the rebels yet managed to occupy most of the city and to set up a government known later as the Canton Commune. There was scarcely time to do more than proclaim a revolutionary program of social reform before Kuomintang troops poured into the city to overwhelm the defenders. By the afternoon of the 13th the last pocket of resistance had been wiped out, and the soldiers exacted a bloody and indiscriminate vengeance from those suspected of Communist tendencies. Some 6,000 men and women were killed, of whom the "lucky" ones were shot or drowned without preliminary torture. For good measure, the Soviet consulate in Canton was invaded and its staff deported after harsh treatment and the murder of several Russians.

So ended the tragic affair of the Canton Commune—and with it Moscow's hopes for the Chinese revolution. Inept decisions, for which Stalin bore ultimate responsibility, combined with difficulties rooted in Chinese society and politics to produce a defeat for Soviet policy more far-reaching than the setback in Europe. Russia in 1928 entered a new era of "building socialism in a single country," which in turn engendered a Soviet brand of partriotism and an end to foreign adventures. In China the "Russian period" left a lasting and bitter imprint upon victors and vanquished alike. The Kuomintang terror in 1927 took the lives of perhaps 25,000 Communists and at least 200,000 non-Communists. It continued through the years of Chiang's rule at a more moderate pace. Political persecution, without stilling mass discontent through measures of reform, is normally a prescription for the failure of any regime. A willing prisoner of the vested interests he had cultivated in his ascent to power, Chiang never understood the dynamics of social revolution and substituted improvisation for statesmanship until the accumulated grievances of generations again found an outlet in Communism—but this time a far more indigenous variety unencumbered by the fetish of Moscow's infallibility.

NOTES

1. V. I. Lenin, *Sochinenia* [Works] (2nd ed.; Moscow, 1926–32), XVI, 27 and 29.

2. *Bericht über den IV. Kongress der Kommunistischen Internationale* (Hamburg, 1923), p. 141.

3. See above, p. 91.

4. See above, p. 94.

5. See above, p. 94.

6. See above, p. 122.

7. Leon Trotsky, *Problems of the Chinese Revolution* (New York, 1932), p. 19.

8. Tchen Du Hsiu [Chen Tsu-hsiu], "How Stalin-Bucharin Destroyed the Chinese Revolution," *The Militant* (New York), November 15, 1930.

9. An unpublished speech quoted in Harold R. Isaacs, *The Tragedy of the Chinese Revolution* (Stanford, Calif., 1951), p. 162; Trotsky, *Problems of the Chinese Revolution*, p. 390.

10. *International Press Correspondence*, April 28, 1927, p. 544.

11. Trotsky, *Problems of the Chinese Revolution*, pp. 285–86.

12. Isaacs, *Tragedy of the Chinese Revolution*, p. 261.

CHAPTER SIX

STALIN AND THE RISE
OF SOVIET NATIONALISM

The year 1928 marked the end of N.E.P. and the beginning of what has sometimes been called the "second Russian Revolution." It was an attempt unprecedented in world history to impose an industrial and agrarian revolution upon a country by political fiat. Not only was the industrial economy to be transformed within the space of a few years to challenge the productive facilities of the advanced capitalist nations; the individual—and inefficient—peasant farms were also to be collectivized in a unique experiment designed to "socialize" agriculture and to liquidate as a class the only real threat to the Communist regime—the *kulaks* or well-to-do peasants. These aims were by no means clear in 1928, for the pressure of internal events, chiefly the acute grain shortage, nagged at the Soviet leaders and forced decisions upon them. Only in 1930 did the pattern of the future emerge from the amorphous shadows of the N.E.P.

The inaugural program, known as the Five Year Plan, was launched on October 1, 1928, with all the fanfare that experienced propagandists could contrive but not without grave misgivings even within the Politburo itself. Stalin, who had been a "centrist" during the long struggle with Trotsky, now emerged as an "ultra-leftist" to humble Bukharin and his associates and to welcome back into the fold such penitents as Zinoviev, Kamenev, and Radek. The unrepentant Trotsky, expelled from the country early in 1929 after a year's exile in Soviet Central Asia, began his wanderings as the prophet of the ineffectual Fourth (Trotskyist) International.

Stalin's relatively lenient treatment of his political enemies in the late twenties, in contrast to the drastic measures of the mid-thirties, furnishes a rough index to the growth of his personal power in the intervening period. His position in 1928, while comparable to Lenin's after 1917, was not yet that of a despotic ruler, for he was hedged about by a variety of party rules and traditions, some of which were never wholly discarded as a matter of common sense expediency. There was also the Right opposition to be dealt with; and on this score, though the immediacy of the war danger was not stressed as it had been in the latter half of 1927, Stalin was able to point anew to the threat of "capitalist encirclement" as a compelling reason for rapid industrialization and as a rebuke to the peasant conciliators of the Bukharin school.

Bukharin was virtually stripped of his functions as Comintern president behind the scenes of the sixth world congress held in July 1928. He was not formally removed from office until April 1929, and only in November of the same year did he lose his seat in the Politburo. The Comintern presidency was left vacant and the routine business of the organization delegated to a group of Stalin's disciples, among whom Vyacheslav Molotov was the best known. In low repute during these years, the Comintern never regained even the moderate prestige it enjoyed in the mid-twenties. "One Soviet tractor is worth more than ten good foreign Communists" was the kind of remark heard in Stalin's entourage as the industrial program increased in tempo.[1]

Notwithstanding the cynicism with which the Communist movement abroad came to be regarded, the Kremlin always placed some value on Comintern activities as a weapon of international politics; and the Marxist theory of capitalism's inevitable demise retained its old-time vigor as the basic premise of Soviet ideology. Indeed, as if to compensate for the nationalist tendencies that many Old Bolsheviks viewed with uneasiness and distrust, Stalin hewed to the radical line handed down after the breakup of the Kuomintang-Communist bloc in China. True, *Putschism* was no longer encouraged, but it was officially proclaimed as early as December 1927 that the period of temporary capitalist stabilization had come to an end and that a new revolutionary era was at hand. Stalin was right on the first count and wrong on the second. In less than two years the stock market crash on Wall Street heralded a major world depression—a capitalist crisis more sudden and severe than any Marxist had dared predict. But its obvious corollary—revolutionary discontent—failed to materialize in a manner that the Comintern could exploit, and the years of the Great Depression, with leftist extremism as the keynote, was a period of disappointment and frustration for international Communism.

In forecasting new internal troubles for capitalism, Stalin claimed that the transition from "peaceful coexistence" in international relations to an era of "imperialist attacks" and "intervention against the U.S.S.R." was under way. Here, too, his prognosis was partially substantiated by the aggressive hostility of Japan and Nazi Germany in the 1930's, though of course his timing was faulty and the presumed anti-Soviet intervention—by now the stock-in-trade of every Russian commentator on foreign affairs—was nowhere in sight. Soviet isolation was nevertheless a stark reality and mitigated only by two circumstances: the somewhat diluted "spirit of Rapallo" that still held Moscow and Berlin together in a community of interest and Soviet participation in the League of Nations' Preparatory Disarmament Commission at Geneva. It was here that Litvinov, as the Soviet representative, made his sensational debut in great power diplomacy. Chicherin, in chronic ill health, had long been a persistent foe of the League as a kept creature of the Entente, and he regarded the Geneva meeting with suspicion. He was also anti-Stalinist and withdrew from active work in 1928, although he retained his title until Litvinov formally replaced him in 1930.

When Litvinov arrived in Geneva in November 1927, after German mediation had finally disposed of the Soviet-Swiss dispute growing out of the Vorovsky assassination in 1923,[2] three sessions of the Preparatory Commission—the first had begun almost two years before—had already met and accomplished precisely nothing. Neither Litvinov nor his superiors in the Politburo, who had carefully briefed him before his departure, expected the addition of a Soviet delegate to disturb the commission's unblemished record of prolonged futility. But Geneva was a sounding board of rare dimensions, and Moscow was fully prepared to take advantage of this exceptional opportunity to pillory the capitalist powers for their hypocritical gestures toward disarmament and to prove its desire for peace with something more tangible than urbane platitudes. Having done this much, Moscow hoped that world opinion would make any anti-Soviet moves by the West politically untenable. And there was always the possibility that some kind of agreement on arms reduction might really be achieved.

With these general motives in view, Litvinov proceeded to explode a verbal bombshell on November 30. He proposed nothing less than the abolition of all land, sea, and air forces, the destruction of all weapons, military supplies, and munitions plants, and a blanket prohibition upon defense budgets, war propaganda, and military preparedness of any kind—in short, disarmament to the level of sticks, stones, and bare knuckles. He tried—unsuccessfully—to forestall the inevitable charge of "Communist propaganda" with an ironical reference to the auspices under which he spoke: "If the Preparatory Commission for the Disarmament Conference is not a suitable place in which to make peace propaganda, then apparently we are here under a misunderstanding."[3] The other delegates, with few exceptions, regarded his famous speech as petulant nonsense, an annoying farce that hard-working diplomats were at liberty to ignore. Yet Litvinov's manifest sincerity caught the imagination of that larger audience he was seeking, and there can be no doubt that the Geneva meeting was an international public relations triumph for Moscow.

Consideration of the Soviet plan was postponed until March 1928 when Litvinov renewed his plea and called on the American delegation, whose government was then sponsoring a pact for the outlawry of war, to come to his aid. But only Germany and Turkey, countries which like the Soviet Union had little to lose by general disarmament, gave a sympathetic hearing in the detailed discussions that followed. As expected, the project was rejected as impracticable on March 23, and Litvinov was ready with a modified plan of gradual disarmament that likewise failed to win approval in the intermittent sessions of the Preparatory Commission lasting through November of 1930. The main disarmament conference, when it finally met in February 1932, was already foredoomed to failure by Japanese aggression in Manchuria; and it was made doubly certain by the Nazi victory in Germany the next year.

Widespread and influential peace sentiment—for the most part a reflection of growing disillusionment with the First World War—found expression in a less mundane sphere than armament reduction: an international agreement to prohibit war itself. The Kellogg-Briand Pact, as this unique instrument of pacification is commonly known, is often cited as the crowning monument to diplomatic naïveté in modern times—without, however, a respectful tribute to the unsophisticated sources of idealism from which it sprang or any indication of the skepticism with which the powers regarded the project. It was essentially an American idea as an answer to French Foreign Minister Aristide Briand's subtle proposal for a Franco-American entente.

After prolonged negotiations and with reservations on the part of Britain and France, the pact renouncing war "as an instrument of national policy" was signed by representatives of fifteen leading nations in Paris on August 27, 1928. The Soviet Union was not invited to the ceremony—a calculated display of discourtesy that Kremlin spokesmen were quick to resent. On the same day the French ambassador in Moscow asked Litvinov if the Soviet government wished to adhere. Litvinov's reply took the form of a note to Paris and Washington. It was bitingly critical of the pact, which was termed a "dead letter" because the vital subject of armament limitation had been ignored. The League of Nations had demonstrated its "total impotence" in rejecting his disarmament proposals at Geneva, but nevertheless Litvinov expressed his government's desire to sign the treaty. Chicherin and other prominent party members, especially those affiliated with the Comintern, opposed Moscow's participation and publicly criticized the document as a pious fraud and a means of outside interference in Soviet affairs. The Politburo decided to cooperate because, like the Geneva talks, it reduced Moscow's isolation and weakened the likelihood of aggressive anti-Soviet moves. The Russians became the first to adhere when, on September 27, the French embassy in Washington presented the State Department with formal credentials signifying the Soviet government's acceptance of the pact. International law experts cited the dictum that treaty relations automatically confer recognition, but Washington refused to acknowledge the traditional interpretation.

During the long hiatus between the signature and the ratification of the Kellogg Pact by the powers, Moscow took the initiative in negotiating a regional anti-war guarantee usually referred to as the "Litvinov protocol." On February 9, 1929, the Soviet Union, Poland, Rumania, Latvia, and Estonia signed the agreement in Moscow, and Lithuania, the free city of Danzig, Turkey, and Persia subsequently endorsed it. Only Finland held aloof among Russia's western neighbors. Moscow considered the protocol a diplomatic victory insofar as it weakened Poland's hold over the Baltic states by helping to allay their fear of Soviet aggression.

Not until July 24, 1929, following ratification by the fifteen original signatory powers and the adherence of thirty-one others, did the parent instrument attain the force of international law by President Herbert Hoover's proclamation at a White House ceremony. Even as Hoover spoke, a Sino-Soviet war crisis over control of the Chinese Eastern Railway was simmering in Manchuria. The dispute climaxed a long series of incidents beginning shortly after the 1924 agreements with the Peking and Mukden authorities.[4] After the assassination of Chang Tso-lin by Japanese agents in the summer of 1928, his son, Chang Hsüeh-liang (the "Young Marshal"), had inherited his father's Manchurian domain and declared his allegiance to the Kuomintang government of Nanking. Using as a pretext the "Communist activity" theme, Chinese police raided the Soviet consulates at Harbin and three other Manchurian cities on May 27–28, 1929. At Harbin thirty-nine Soviet citizens were arrested and a number of employees, including the consul-general, temporarily detained. Two truckloads of documents were confiscated, some of which were published later as evidence that Communist propaganda had been disseminated through the consulate.

A stiff Soviet protest to Nanking was ignored, and at a meeting in Peking, now under Nationalist control, Chiang Kai-shek and the Young Marshal decided to take over the Chinese Eastern Railway at once. On July 10 Chinese troops occupied the Soviet buildings in the railway zone, seized the telephone and telegraph system, and arrested most of the Russian personnel. Approximately a thousand persons were later imprisoned in a concentration camp near Harbin. The Soviet protest—sent to both Nanking and Mukden—assumed the form of a three-day ultimatum: the return of the railroad to its previous status, the release of all Soviet nationals, and an immediate conference on the railroad question. China's reply was judged "unsatisfactory in content and hypocritical in tone,"[5] and further diplomatic and commercial relations were suspended on July 17. By this time close to a thousand Chinese had been arrested in the Soviet Union as a retaliatory measure.

Nanking was clearly disconcerted by the adverse neutral reaction, for the great powers still held extraterritorial rights that would be jeopardized by unilateral action of this type. Nor did the danger of war just as the Kellogg Pact went into effect appear to reflect credit upon China's sense of international responsibility. The Chinese authorities therefore took pains to reassure the powers by repeated disclaimers of bellicose intentions. Moscow was likewise solicitous, if less ostentatious, about a peaceful resolution of the crisis, but it replied to a French offer of mediation with the polite intimation that outside interference was unwelcome and "pointless" in any case because of Nanking's adamant stand. Both sides began concentrating troops on the Siberian-Manchurian border, and local skirmishes by the end of July anticipated a solution by force rather than by negotiation.

In August and early September an exchange of communications between Moscow and Nanking took place through the good offices of the German government without result. The weak Red Army detachments in the Far East had been hastily reinforced, chiefly by Siberian recruits, and under the command of General Blücher they constituted a formidable military organization of over 100,000 men. Nanking, discomforted by Moscow's belligerent attitude, had apparently expected Russia's internal troubles to forestall an active fight for the railroad and was unable to send aid to Chang because of Feng Yü-hsiang's sudden revolt in October against the Nationalist government. Because of her sphere of influence in central and southern Manchuria, Japan was the most directly concerned of the neutral powers and tacitly consented to a limited Soviet offensive. Such a policy of strength was not without its domestic critics: although the Soviet case was legally sound, to many Communists it smacked of power politics in the imperialist tradition. In a partial sense, the Soviet government was now a victim of its own propagandists, who had stressed for years China's struggle against the unequal treaty system. It had long since become evident, however, that the national interest far outweighed revolutionary sentimentality in the concerns of the Kremlin, and it was pointed out to the "idealists" that China was too weak to hold the railroad even if it should be relinquished. The undeclared war with China represents nonetheless an important milestone in the rise of Soviet nationalism under Stalin.

On November 17, 1929, the period of local engagements ended with a well coordinated attack by the Red Army in the direction of Manchuli in the western portion of the railroad line. The force was small —probably not more than 3,000 men—but sufficient to scatter without appreciable bloodshed the larger Manchurian contingent, which looted and terrorized the civilian population as it fell back toward Harbin. Within a few days Mukden asked for terms, hoping for diplomatic intervention by the powers. In Washington, Secretary of State Henry L. Stimson sought and received the hesitant backing of London, Paris, and Rome—Berlin and Tokyo dissented—for an invocation of the Kellogg Pact; and on December 2 each of the four governments sent similar notes to Moscow and Nanking urging a peaceful solution of the dispute. The Chinese reply was conciliatory, but the Soviet government charged that the notes placed "totally unjustifiable pressure" on the bilateral negotiations then in progress and for that reason could not be considered a friendly act. Litvinov, who signed the virtually identical communications to the four powers, added a stinging sally in his note to Washington: his government could not help "expressing its astonishment" that the United States, "which at its own desire has no official relations with the Government of the Soviet Union, finds it possible to approach the Soviet Government with advice and 'instructions.'"[6]

Although Stimson tried to put a good face on this unprecedented rebuke by implying that the danger of war had been averted by his prompt action in mobilizing international public opinion, the Sino-Soviet talks progressed smoothly and resulted in Mukden's complete capitulation to Moscow's original demands. Nanking reluctantly acquiesced, and a provisional peace treaty was signed at Khabarovsk on December 22 restoring the *status quo ante bellum*. A conference in Moscow to iron out the remaining points of difference was delayed until October 1930 by Nanking's intransigence. China's refusal to resume normal relations and Moscow's anger at the activity of White Russian *émigrés* in Manchuria were perhaps the two major points of friction. Neither the October meeting nor subsequent attempts to reach an agreement were successful. The impasse continued until Japan's invasion of Manchuria in the fall of 1931 altered the complexion of Sino-Soviet relations—and of world politics in general.

II

In Europe the Soviet Union was able in 1929 to undo the damage to her diplomatic security wrought by the break with Great Britain in 1927. As in 1924, the course of British politics determined the resumption of official relations. The Conservative government was staunchly anti-Soviet, and while it had refrained from active provocation, Moscow was always prepared to believe the worst. Chamberlain was rumored to have proposed a Franco-British-German bloc against Russia at Geneva; and Lord Birkenhead, the secretary of state for India and an anti-Bolshevik of the most extreme persuasion, made a much publicized "golfing visit" to Berlin in the spring of 1928 without receiving any encouragement for the anti-Soviet project that he presumably outlined to Stresemann.

The Labor party's modest victory at the polls in May 1929 could hardly be interpreted as a mandate for improved Anglo-Soviet relations. Yet Labor had previously pledged the restoration of diplomatic harmony between the two powers, and after a short but to Moscow very irritating delay following the formation of MacDonald's government early in June, the Russians were invited to send a representative to discuss the problem of debts and propaganda. Valerian Dovgalevsky, borrowed from his post in Paris to fill the assignment, insisted that an exchange of ambassadors should precede a final settlement, and negotiations were broken off on August 1 amid a running fire of anti-British invective from Soviet publicists. Clearly perturbed by Moscow's reaction, MacDonald and his associates bent over backward to ease the tension by denying Trotsky's request for political asylum in England.

The British were the first to relent—a "humiliating surrender" that angered the Conservative opposition and much of the press. On October 3, 1929, a formal protocol was signed, and both parties agreed to the appointment of ambassadors and an agenda of issues to be resolved upon the restoration of normal relations. Supported by the

Liberals, the government obtained approval of the protocol by a vote of 324 to 199 in the House of Commons on November 5 following a turbulent debate reminiscent of past sessions on the "Russian question." Gregory Sokolnikov, the commissar of finance, was appointed ambassador, the first to fill the position since the death of the Tsar's emissary in January 1917. The King objected to receiving a Soviet ambassador, and so the Prince of Wales acted as his father's representative when Sokolnikov presented his credentials on December 20. The veteran career diplomatist Sir Esmond Ovey, a sound but undistinguished choice as the British ambassador, was received at the Kremlin two days later.

Considering the past furor about Soviet propaganda—the issue over which the diplomatic conflict ostensibly began—it is ironic that the problem was never satisfactorily settled: both parties merely reaffirmed the wholly ineffective pledge against propaganda contained in the unratified 1924 recognition agreement. The matter continued to agitate the Conservatives, but with the passage of time and the demonstrated stability of the Soviet regime fewer and fewer voices were raised in protest. The debt negotiations were resumed and made no progress. Better results attended the discussions concerning a new trade pact, and a temporary treaty, pending a more satisfactory agreement, was signed on April 16, 1930.

Anglo-Soviet cordiality remained distinctly absent in spite of the considerable improvement over the hostility of past years. The same was true in the case of France even though there had been no break in the continuity of diplomatic relations. Here the still unsettled debt question rankled more deeply than in Britain. Moscow saw no reason to revise its firmly rooted opinion that the Entente powers were still the major impediments to Soviet security. A further complication appeared in the early thirties as a result of the depression in the capitalist world and the accelerated pace of the Five Year Plan in the "land of socialism." To obtain foreign exchange for the importation of vitally needed industrial goods Moscow was obliged to sell wheat and various raw materials in the depressed world market. The export of these commodities brought irresponsible charges of "dumping," and the competition posed by Soviet trade was portrayed in alarming terms as a "world menace." As early as October 1930 France took "anti-dumping" measures, seconded by the United States and some of the smaller powers. Russian reprisals followed, but by 1932 the hobgoblin of a "trade war" had vanished completely after a sharp drop in Soviet exports because of the fulfillment of planned production quotas.

Germany continued to be Russia's only friend among the great powers—not that the Rapallo mood was sustained unbroken into the thirties. Indeed, Chicherin's semi-retirement in 1928 and the death of Ambassador Brockdorff-Rantzau in the same year symbolized the shift to a matter-of-fact relationship in which the romantic glow of the Rapallo tradition gradually faded from view. As the shackles of Versailles were further loosened by the Young Plan for reparations and the Allied evacuation of the Rhineland in 1930, both Moscow and Berlin became increasingly aware that the latter's new freedom to maneuver placed their friendship in jeopardy. This period of mutual uneasiness was soon smoothed over, for it was apparent that there was little to be gained and much to be lost by drifting apart. Moreover, Entente statesmen were reluctant to consider the Soviet Union a wholly respectable power, and the ingrained anti-German propensities of French policy prevented an overture to Berlin. Soviet-German trade flourished during the Five Year Plan, particularly in the products of heavy industry that Moscow needed, and furnished added incentive to good relations because of growing unemployment in Germany. The Soviet government also employed more than 5,000 German engineers and technicians among the foreigners who were recruited at high salaries for specialized tasks.

Perhaps the high tide of good will in the late Rapallo era was reached with the renewal of the Treaty of Berlin on June 24, 1931. Even so, the German authorities tried unsuccessfully to keep the news out of the press to avoid offending the French, and ratification by the Reichstag was delayed almost two years. By this time the treaty was politically meaningless, although the hollow shell of Rapallo remained to mark the divergent paths of the two countries.

Moscow had been seeking some kind of insurance against an independent German course even before the summer of 1931. In May of that year Dovgalevsky held confidential talks in Paris with a French Foreign Office spokesman, and in August a non-aggression pact was readied for signature. Negotiations for a commercial agreement also began during the summer and were accompanied by the removal of mutual trade restrictions begun during the "dumping" scare. A further sign of progress was the reappointment to Madrid of Jean Herbette, the belligerently anti-Soviet ambassador to Moscow.

More serious from Berlin's vantage point were the parallel Russo-Polish talks. As France's Eastern watchdog, Pilsudski's Poland had never enjoyed friendly relations with either Germany or the Soviet Union, and Berlin correctly interpreted the Moscow-Warsaw *rapprochment* as an indication of Soviet willingness to abandon the anti-Versailles orientation of the Rapallo policy. A Russo-Polish non-aggression treaty was concluded on July 25, 1932, and the only concession made to Germany's viewpoint was the omission of a guarantee of Poland's frontiers. A similar pledge had been made in the nonaggression pacts that Moscow signed with the Baltic states during the first half of the year. The negotiations with Rumania had been less successful—the Bessarabian question remained unsolved—but Moscow formally assured Paris that she would never resort to violence to gain her ends with Rumania. Now satisfied that her Eastern partner was secure, France, having dallied for more than a year, signed the original document on November 29, 1932.

To all outward appearances, Soviet Russia at the close of 1932 enjoyed greater security in Europe than at any previous time in her short and perilous history. Yet the first month of the new year brought Adolf Hitler and the Nazi party into power in Germany—an event that was not only a shattering blow to Soviet diplomacy but an ideological defeat for Communism far more serious than the fiasco in China. Stalin and his colleagues bore a share of the blame for the Nazi triumph. The precise extent of their "guilt" is still a matter of conjecture, for it involved not direct responsibility but a tragic miscalculation of the nature and strength of German fascism.

Before 1930 the phenomenon of fascism was familiar to the world chiefly as an Italian product; and though it had won the sympathy of influential statesmen and industrialists by supposedly saving Italy from Communism, it was not a movement that appeared to have a promising future. Soviet theorists, joined by many independent Marxists, were content to classify fascism as the decadent stage of monopoly capitalism and a certain harbinger of a collapsing bourgeois social order. This analysis had not prevented the maintenance of normal and largely uneventful relations between Moscow and Rome since 1924. German fascism, in the form of the National Socialist (Nazi) party, was catapulted to sudden prominence in the election of September 1930 by winning 105 seats in the Reichstag, thus becoming second to the Social Democratic party in the size of its parliamentary representation. Although the Nazis depended largely upon the lower middle class for electoral support, their immediate success was due to the onset of the Great Depression, in which many unemployed workers manifested an un-Marxian devotion to the new "radicalism of the Right."

The German Communists and Social Democrats shared the dangerous illusion that revolution was a monopoly of the Left. Both were fiercely anti-Nazi on doctrinal grounds, but the legacy of mutual animosity was unchecked by the presence of a common enemy. The Communists had been the only major beneficiary besides the Nazis in the 1930 election. With 77 deputies, they were the third largest party in Germany and could reasonably expect more gains as the depression deepened. Under the leadership of Ernst Thaelmann, Moscow's choice as party chief, the Comintern policy of leftist extremism, officially proclaimed at the sixth congress in 1928, was carried to fatuous and disastrous lengths. The Social Democrats, it was solemnly revealed, were "social fascists" whose treachery to the working class was concealed by gaudy phrases and calculated deceit. Unmasking their hypocrisy was seemingly the number one "revolutionary" task of German Communism, while the Nazis, even if they should obtain power by some political freak, were regarded as the pathological but harmless gravediggers of capitalism. Some of the Communist leaders, unable to stomach the new line, broke away to form the so-called Communist Party Opposition. The new organization favored a united front with the Social Democrats, but unfortunately for the "official" party it was fated to become a minor splinter group.

Only with Social Democratic backing was Chancellor Heinrich Brüning of the Catholic Center party able to hold together a fragile coalition cabinet; and only by using the dangerous precedent of legislation by emergency decree was he able to overcome the parliamentary paralysis brought about by the obstreperous tactics of the Nazis, Nationalists, and Communists in the Reichstag. The tacit cooperation between the extremes of Left and Right reached a peak when the latter attempted to oust the Social Democratic-Center government of Prussia. At first opposed to the plan, the Communists, upon Stalin's orders, lent their support during a referendum in the summer of 1931 in which nearly ten million votes—about 37 per cent of the total—were cast against the government. But many who normally voted Communist had refused to swallow the party mandate, and even in Moscow there were grumbles of discontent in the Politburo. But there was no basic shift in strategy. The next summer a Communist motion of no confidence in the Prussian parliament passed with the aid of Nazi votes, though a number of Communists had been beaten up in the same chamber by Nazi deputies just nine days before. The incident was a revealing demonstration in microcosm of German Communism's will to suicide in pursuit of a doctrinal ideal far removed from political reality.

In the presidential election of March 1932 Thaelmann ran a poor third against President Paul von Hindenburg and Hitler. In the runoff election the Communists stubbornly insisted on nominating their candidate again and lost more than a million votes as the moderate parties again combined to re-elect Hindenburg by a handsome margin. The aged military hero, a spokesman for Junker reaction, was a poor choice as guardian of the commonweal. At the end of May he dismissed Brüning—an "agrarian Bolshevik" to the Prussian landowners—and appointed Franz von Papen, a wealthy mediocrity in the extreme Right of the Center party. By this act Hindenburg could be said to have sealed the fate of German democracy.

A new wave of political violence broke out in which bloody clashes between Communists and Nazis in no way deterred Moscow from its conviction that Hitler was only preparing the way for a Communist victory. A number of Social Democratic leaders, alarmed at Papen's flirtation with the Nazis, made tentative and half-hearted overtures to the Communists for an anti-fascist front, but the offer foundered on the rocks of reciprocal ill-will and the rigidity of Moscow's "social fascist" line. On July 31 the Nazis reached the pinnacle of their electoral success by winning a smashing plurality in the Reichstag—230 seats out of 608. Since the Communists also gained heavily at the expense of the Social Democrats, the outcome merely confirmed their original view that the extinction of bourgeois democracy in Germany would inevitably redound to their benefit. The Nazis then demanded the chancellorship, and when it was refused Hitler declined to force the issue with a *Putsch*. He remembered keenly his ludicrous failure in 1923. Many of his followers despaired of achieving power as the Reichstag was dissolved for new elections, and Nazi strength ebbed perceptibly.

Early in November 1932 a Communist-led strike of Berlin transport workers broke out, and the Nazis unexpectedly gave their support. The authorities dealt with the subsequent disorders in their customary fashion: severity for the Communists and deference for the Nazis. Reichstag elections were held during the strike, registering the first Nazi setback in over two years. They lost 34 deputies, while the Communists, in winning 11 seats, increased their total to an even 100. For once Communist theory appeared in some degree to have been justified by events. Hitler declared that the masses were being driven toward Bolshevism, and he threatened a bolt in that direction should the chancellorship be denied him. But the specter of "Brown Bolshevism" was not taken seriously by those aware that the Nazis had been lavishly subsidized by leading German industrialists. There was, however, a drift toward the Communists by some of the Left wing elements in the Nazi party and by Social Democrats disgusted with the lethargy of their leaders.

On December 3, 1932, General Kurt von Schleicher became chancellor following another cabinet crisis. As minister of war he had been the dominant figure in Papen's government, and because of his close identification with the Reichswehr-Red Army collaboration Moscow correctly appraised him a friend of Rapallo. Nazi fortunes, at a low ebb, were revived by a political conspiracy of Schleicher's enemies, of whom Papen was the key figure. Isolated and rebuffed by Hindenburg, Schleicher resigned on January 28, 1933. Two days later the old president, now well on the road to senility, appointed Hitler to the chancellorship. Having waited for such a moment with equanimity, the Communists, as the avowed heirs of the revolutionary situation, could suggest only another general strike—the sixth in less than four years. Neither the workers nor the maligned leaders of "social fascism" gave heed. In Moscow the Comintern leaders solemnly intoned the Stalinist catechism: "The conquest of power by Hitler does not signify a defeat for the Communist Party and the working class. The revoltionary upsurge has been temporarily interrupted.[7]

On February 27 the Nazis took the decisive psychological step in the consolidation of their dictatorship by burning the Reichstag building and blaming the Communists for the deed. The Red peril, now officially proclaimed, heralded an open season on Communists. In the Reichstag elections of March 5 they polled nearly 5,000,000 votes—an impressive showing under the circumstances—but their 81 deputies were prevented from taking their seats. With most of the party leaders arrested, killed, or in flight, the German Comintern organ, transferred to Switzerland, still maintained on April 1 that the "open dictatorship of Fascism destroys all democratic illusions, frees the masses from the influence of the Social-democratic Party, and thus accelerates the speed of Germany's march towards the proletarian revolution."[8] Not all the German Communists were able to digest the party line against the evidence of their senses, and when a minority faction accused Thaelmann and the Central Committee of responsibility for the Nazi triumph, the same organ condemned their views as a "crass mixture of naked opportunism, insidious Trotskyism, and downright putschism."[9] Confidence in an ultimate Communist victory gradually faded in the coming months, but it was well into 1934 before the Comintern ventured a fundamental reinterpretation of the German disaster.

Soviet-German relations deteriorated rapidly after the advent of Hitler, though the change was neither abrupt nor dramatic. The initiative came from Berlin and was largely motivated by anti-Communist ideology. Moscow was prepared to pursue the Rapallo policy and to ignore the fate of German Communism—just as the Weimar

Republic had endured Communist activity in silence as a matter of political expediency. While Hitler's annexationist plans for Russia were openly revealed in his *Mein Kampf,* and the obsessive hatred of Communism that he and other Nazi leaders made a point of demonstrating on nearly every public occasion were not taken lightly in Moscow, it was hoped that the responsibilities of power would sober the new regime. As late as December 1933 Litvinov summed up the Kremlin's opportunistic outlook by expressing sympathy for the "sufferings of our German comrades" but pointing out that the U.S.S.R. managed to maintain "good relations with capitalist states of whatever regime, even if it is fascist."

Hitler seemed amenable to the idea of continued ties with Moscow, and save for an anti-Soviet outburst early in March 1933, his pronouncements during the spring were designed to reassure the Russians. Aside from the virtual extermination of the German Communist party, various incidents served to belie Hitler's words. Russian citizens, particularly Jews, were sometimes attacked or otherwise molested, and commercial relations were seriously impaired by police raids on Soviet trade delegations in Hamburg and Leipzig and by restrictions of a less violent nature. The German press was increasingly virulent in its anti-Soviet campaign, and individual leaders, of whom Litvinov was a prime target because of his Jewish origin, were subjected to scurrilous personal abuse. The tone of the Soviet press, by contrast, was still comparatively moderate and unprovocative. But anti-Nazi sentiment was crystallizing. A straw in the wind was the funeral service in Moscow on June 22, 1933, for Klara Zetkin, a veteran German Communist, which was transformed into a mass demonstration against the Nazi regime; and the presence of Stalin and other party notables lent added significance to the occasion.

Meanwhile, at the League of Nations Disarmament Conference in Geneva, Germany's demand for arms equality had received no support from Litvinov, the Soviet delegate, and the occasion foreshadowed Moscow's conversion from a rabid critic of Versailles to an antirevisionist power. During the summer recess Litvinov attended the World Economic Conference in London and approached representatives of the East European nations with a new proposal for a nonaggression pact. It was to be based on the airtight definition of aggression that he had first presented in a somewhat different version at Geneva in February 1933. The overture was accepted with unexpected cordiality, and by July 23, when Finland finally adhered, the treaty embraced the U.S.S.R., the Baltic states, Poland, Rumania, Czechoslovakia, Yugoslavia, Turkey, Persia, and Afghanistan. The Soviet press commented that Germany, too, was welcome as a signatory, but it began to display an increasingly critical attitude toward Nazi policy, especially after the German representatives at the London conference circulated a memorandum advocating the economic exploitation of the Ukraine in apparent confirmation of Hitler's blueprint in *Mein Kampf*. For the first time the Treaty of Versailles won some cautious words of praise, and even the League of Nations—that "alliance of world bandits" as Lenin had once called it—was no longer an object of suspicion and ridicule.

Early in August the German ambassador to Moscow, Herbert von Dirksen, was transferred to Tokyo. The last words of his final report from Moscow, "The Rapallo chapter is closed," seemed unduly pessimistic at the time, for his successor, Rudolf Nadolny, a veteran career diplomat, was even more favorably disposed toward close Soviet-German relations and was given a free hand.[10] But Nadolny's eager attempts to alter the growing estrangement were futile. Barely more than six months after his arrival, he resigned in protest over an anti-Soviet policy that the Nazi government no longer bothered to disguise. The mutually profitable Red Army-Reichswehr collaboration had broken down as early as the summer of 1933, ostensibly because Moscow chose to believe reports that Vice-Chancellor Papen had disclosed the details of the clandestine relationship to the French ambassador in Berlin. Papen denied it, but miltary cooperation was not renewed even though informal contacts continued until the purge of the Red Army in 1937. Nor were German technicians still welcome in the Soviet Union; many had already left before the Nazi triumph, since the pressing need for foreign skills had declined by 1932.

In October 1933 Germany announced her withdrawal from the League of Nations; and late in December Stalin officially sanctioned a pro-League policy by declaring, in his circumlocutious manner, that "notwithstanding its colossal defects" Soviet support for the League was "not impossible."[11] A month later at the seventeenth party congress his speech contained an unmistakable warning to Germany and Japan. "Those who try to attack our country," he concluded, "will receive a stunning rebuff to teach them not to poke their pig's snout into our Soviet garden again." He carefully refrained, nevertheless, from slamming the door against German friendship—an attitude that Hitler at least verbally reciprocated a few days later in a speech before the Reichstag. In retrospect, however, the beginning of the end had been reached on Janauary 26 by the signature of a German-Polish non-aggression pact. Poland, the perpetual weather vane of Russian-German relations, was now definitely in Berlin's diplomatic orbit. In

March, when Litvinov sought a Soviet-German pledge to respect the independence and integrity of the Baltic states, Berlin's refusal was uncompromising. During the next two months he achieved a measure of compensation by renewing the non-aggression treaties with Poland and the Baltic states which were not due to expire for another year.

Until well into 1934 the Kremlin retained some illusions about reversing the trend of Soviet-German relations. But that remote possibility was ended on June 30 during the "night of the long knives" —Hitler's liquidation of the "radical" Nazi leaders whose aspirations included a seizure of power and a return to the Rapallo tradition. Litvinov, long an advocate of *rapprochement* with the West, became the symbol *par excellence* of resistance to fascist aggression; and his slogans, "collective security" and the "indivisibility of peace," were to epitomize Soviet diplomacy in the mid-thirties.

III

Just as the rise of Nazi Germany seriously disturbed the balance of power in Europe, so the equilibrium of the Far East was upset by Japanese aggression in China. The invasion of Manchuria in September 1931 was in reality the opening campaign in the Pacific phase of the Second World War. Having emerged victoriously in a struggle less than two years before to retain their rights in the Chinese Eastern Railway, the Russians were confronted with a far graver menace than China had ever been. It was no longer a question of facing the Young Marshal's second-rate troops; memories of Tokyo's similar venture in Siberia were still fresh enough to discourage a test of military strength with the legions of Nippon. Determined to avoid war at any cost short of an attack on Soviet territory, Moscow adopted a policy of strict neutrality throughout the "Manchurian incident." The Soviet press was less circumspect in indicating that the Kremlin's sympathies lay with China—a viewpoint that was somewhat disguised by attacks on the cowardice and corruption of the Kuomintang government and by abuse of the League and the Western powers for their alleged complicity in encouraging Tokyo to proceed as she wished.

Japan embarked upon a new era of aggrandizement at a well chosen moment. Soviet energies were concentrated upon the completion of the first Five Year Plan, and the Kremlin's desire for a peaceful interlude of internal development was evident even to professional purveyors of the Communist menace. The United States, Japan's most formidable potential foe, had refrained from interference in Asian affairs except by moral suasion since the seizure of the Philippines during the Spanish-American War, and American public opinion was scarcely in an interventionist mood. Great Britain, the European power whose interests were most directly involved, was undergoing a severe financial crisis as a result of the world depression and was psychologically unprepared to oppose aggression in so distant a part of the globe. As for China, her extreme debility in the 1929 dispute with the Soviet Union was so patent that Tokyo's military experts perceived no problem on that score; and her diplomatic isolation, if not assured, was a calculated risk that could be borne with minimal danger.

The course of Soviet-Japanese relations since the settlement of 1925[12] had been remarkably harmonious in view of what had gone before. Tokyo's initial steps to localize the conflict included reassurances to Moscow that the railway zone would be kept inviolate and that she desired the friendly understanding between the two countries to continue. The Soviet leaders apparently accepted these comforting words in good faith, and their alarm was all the more genuine when the military commanders in the field failed to make good the promises emanating from the Japanese Foreign Office. The other powers experienced similar difficulties in their dealings with Tokyo. The Manchurian affair marked the reassertion of military over civilian control in the Japanese government after some years of relative quiescence on the part of the expansionists.

Following the seizure of Mukden in September, Japanese troops fanned out along the South Manchurian Railway network against resistance that was wholly ineffective when it was offered at all. Southern Manchuria was occupied within a few weeks, and by the end of November parts of the Chinese Eastern Railway were within the zone of military operations. Tokyo maintained a diplomatic smokescreen, which in the case of Moscow involved false charges that Chinese troops were receiving Soviet aid. The Kremlin was plainly worried by Japan's movements, and on December 31, 1931, Litvinov suggested a non-aggression pact. Outside observers surmised that the offer was an opening gambit for some sort of alliance or sphere of influence arrangement in Manchuria. Moscow's denial was categorical, but to the skeptics, unconvincing. Tokyo's formal refusal did not come for almost a year; nor did subsequent Soviet overtures receive a favorable response even though the Kremlin was undoubtedly prepared to make substantial concessions. Japan's reluctance to commit herself demonstrated uncertainty as to her future course of empire, and only after thorough testing of the Red Army in actual combat in the late thirties[13] did her military oligarchy choose the path of least resistance—Southeast Asia.

The occupation of Harbin, the administrative center of the Chinese

Eastern, in February 1932 posed the question of possible Soviet-Japanese hostilities more starkly yet. During the winter months Soviet armed forces in Siberia were strengthened, especially in the Maritime Province, while certain signs elsewhere in the country pointed to a war scare as genuine as that of 1927 had been artificial. But no hint of alarm was allowed in the press. On March 1 the "independent" state of Manchukuo was proclaimed in Mukden, though none of the powers responded with diplomatic recognition. Moscow decided to placate Tokyo by acceding to a new slate of collaborationist Chinese administrators on the railroad's governing board, and thereafter—with Soviet consent—the line was used to transport Japanese troops.

A further retreat came in April when the League of Nations Commission of Inquiry headed by Lord Lytton of Great Britain was rebuffed in an effort to obtain Soviet cooperation in its investigation. The League had already absorbed much criticism from Soviet propagandists for its handling of the dispute, and the Lytton Commission was likewise derided as hypocritical camouflage which was actually abetting the aggressor. Japan was also attacked for manufacturing "Red plots" for the commission's delectation. Completed early in September 1932, the report was submitted to the League Council later in the month. While forthright in arraigning Japan before the bar of justice, it did not recommend the complete restoration of Manchuria to China; and from Moscow's perspective the comment on Soviet-Japanese relations revealed an unwarranted acceptance of Tokyo's thesis that Communism was a serious threat to her interests in the Far East.

Indeed, a sizable body of influential Western opinion regarded Japanese expansion into Manchuria as a safeguard against the spread of Communism into northeastern Asia; and Anglo-American reluctance to apply diplomatic pressure upon Tokyo was conditioned in part by the kind of sentiment that motivated the Lytton Commission's misguided remarks on Japan's supposed fear of Communism.

China had already despaired of salvaging Manchuria through the intervention of the Western powers. The sudden improvement of Sino-Soviet relations in 1932 was a sign that Nanking was willing to overlook Moscow's ideological taint in favor of friendlier relations with a potential ally. Domestically, Chiang and his associates continued their repressive anti-Communist program, although the campaigns to exterminate "Red banditry" in the south had been a conspicuous failure.[14] An overture from Nanking came through Dr. W. W. Yen, the leader of the Chinese delegation at Geneva, who approached Litvinov during the summer session of the disarmament conference. The negotiations that followed were kept rigidly confidential. They were reported to include a Sino-Soviet offer to the American delegation of a tripartite pact directed against Japan, a scheme that Washington refused to consider. The two diplomats exchanged notes restoring normal relations on December 12, 1932. Litvinov's formal comment on the event made a bid for American recognition by ascribing some of the "present troubles in the Far East" to the fact that "not all of the States situated on the shores of the Pacific Ocean have been maintaining diplomatic relations with one another." Tokyo failed to react with its customary diplomatic aplomb. The news was "most unwelcome" an official spokesman declared the next day. "The elements most disturbing to the peace of the world have now joined hands"; and he added ominously: "Japan stands squarely against these forces."[15]

On the whole, Soviet-Japanese relations were somewhat improved during the latter half of 1932. Since the immediate danger of a Japanese attack had diminished, the Kremlin was inclined to be less deferential; and Tokyo implicitly acknowledged that the situation had altered by moderating its attacks in the government-inspired press and by the near-cessation of minor anti-Soviet provocations which had occasioned some lively diplomatic exchanges during the previous winter. A fisheries dispute was settled amicably on August 13, but it did not lead to conciliation on more fundamental matters. A few weeks later an incident following General Su Ping-wen's revolt against the Manchukuo regime highlighted Moscow's more confident attitude. The general and his troops eventually fled across the Soviet border and were interned. Tokyo's demand that these "bandits" be handed over was summarily rejected, and a diplomatic counterattack was developed over the perennial question of "White Guard" activities in Manchuria.

On the other hand, Moscow still showed no disposition to cooperate with the League of Nations. On February 24, 1933, the League Assembly approved a statement condemning Japan's position, and her delegates walked out, never to return. On March 27 Japan gave formal notice of her withdrawal from the League. Earlier that month Moscow had refused an invitation to join the Advisory Committee on the Sino-Japanese conflict. But it was done in such an uncommonly polite manner —and with the promise that the Soviet government would "always associate itself" with moves "aiming at the speediest and most equitable settlement" of the crisis—that a basic policy revision appeared in the making. Nazi Germany soon completed the Kremlin's re-education.

A belated aftermath of the Manchurian imbroglio was the sale of the Chinese Eastern Railway in 1935. The Soviet government made its first offer to sell the line on May 2, 1933, after repeated interference by Manchukuo authorities with the operation of the railroad. Since it was strategically untenable and no longer a commercial asset because of frequent traffic interruptions, Moscow hoped to cut the Gordian knot of Manchurian railway politics by withdrawing from the area altogether. To Nanking's vigorous protest that a sale would violate her rights in the line, Moscow offered the obvious retort—though it was phrased with diplomatic restraint—that China was not in a position to claim rights in a territory no longer under her control.

Negotiations began in Tokyo late in June 1933, with Japan supposedly the "mediator" between the Soviet Union and Manchukuo. The wide disparity between the asking and offering price deadlocked the conference from the beginning, and it was suspended early in October after mutual recriminations involving Soviet charges that the Japanese were plotting to seize the railway. The arrest of a number of Russian employees lent substance to Moscow's case. The talks were resumed in January 1934 and again proved abortive after eight months of futile bargaining. Bitter charges and counter-charges concerning further railway incidents seemed to place an agreement definitely out of reach, but early the following September the Japanese foreign minister sought out the Soviet ambassador and offered 130,000,000 yen for the line. The amount was only 30,000,000 below the previous Soviet request, and formal discussions began anew. This time progress was more rapid. A figure of 140,000,000 yen ($39,368,000), of which two-thirds was to be paid in goods, was agreed to within the month. An additional sum of about 30,000,000 yen was to cover the cost of pensions for the dismissed Soviet employees. The purchase price— a fraction of the original construction cost—reflected Moscow's anxiety to be rid of its dangerously exposed property. Relatively minor points of difference delayed the formal signature until March 23, 1935.

IV

The rise of an actual aggressor in the Far East and a potential aggressor in Europe had one incidental result that Moscow could count as a diplomatic victory of major importance: the end of the sixteen-year recognition boycott by the United States. As in Britain and France in the 1920's, an election furnished the immediate occasion for the shift in policy. When Franklin D. Roosevelt became president in March 1933, the Democratic party had been out of office for twelve years and the country was in the depths of the most severe depression in American history. Since economic problems naturally took precedence, it was some months before Roosevelt began seriously to concern himself with Soviet-American relations. By 1933 the "recognition lobby" which had survived through the years was no longer small and lacking in influence. The depression had done much to puncture American complacency about the superiority of its economic system, and the possibility of trade with Russia was a debating point that scored heavily with public opinion. Yet compared to the turmoil of international politics, trade was a negligible factor in the minds of the President and his advisers.

After an unofficial sounding to ascertain the Kremlin's attitude toward negotiating the issues, Roosevelt dispatched a message directly to Moscow on October 10, 1933, inviting the Russians to send a representative to Washington. The Soviet reply was cordial and obliquely referred to the absence of relations as an encouragement to Japanese aggression. Moscow was anxious to please, if somewhat concerned about the concessions that might be required to gain recognition, and sent Litvinov, who, as its top diplomatic official and a shrewd negotiator, was calculated to satisfy the American desire for a high-level figure and to safeguard Soviet interests at the same time. Appropriately enough, he arrived in Washington on November 7—the sixteenth anniversary of the Bolshevik Revolution. He exchanged amenities with the President, and the next day he talked with Secretary of State Cordell Hull and other State Department officials. Litvinov had hoped that recognition might precede negotiations. In this he was disappointed, and the ensuing parleys, devoted mainly to propaganda and debts, brought sharp differences of opinion which Roosevelt's affable charm did much to minimize.

In a series of letters dated November 16, 1933, but actually signed by Roosevelt and Litvinov in the early morning of the 17th, formal recognition was conferred upon the Soviet government, and both powers made certain promises that later seemed unduly rash. The propaganda and subversion agreement, which included a proscription of the Comintern's "un-American activities" without specially naming that organization, was altogether the most stringent guarantee that Moscow had yet made. Subsequent events demonstrated, of course, that the Kremlin was no more willing to assume responsibility for the Comintern than it had been in the past. The debt question followed the Anglo-French pattern and remained in abeyance, though Litvinov committed himself to a confidential "gentlemen's agreement" with Roosevelt. The sum of $75,000,000 was suggested as a minimum figure for a settlement provided that an American loan was forthcoming. The Soviet envoy publicly agreed to waive Moscow's claims regarding

American intervention in Siberia—a significant admission of the anti-Japanese character of the expedition that was not lost on Tokyo.

William C. Bullitt, who had favored a *rapprochement* with Moscow ever since his mission in 1919[16] and had been involved in the recognition negotiations, was named the first American ambassador to the Soviet Union. His appointment was accepted enthusiastically by the Kremlin as an augury of good relations, but in less than two years Bullitt became intensely disillusioned and was transferred to the ambassadorship in Paris, where his passionate anti-Soviet convictions found a receptive audience in diplomatic circles. Alexander Troyanovsky, the Soviet ambassador to Japan, was assigned to the Washington post in another move denoting Moscow's concern with the fate of Manchuria. The Western press, in fact, interpreted the shift in American policy as primarily an answer to Japanese aggression and a prelude to close collaboration on Far Eastern problems. Only the Japanese newspapers refrained from such comment, thereby betraying an uneasiness already manifest in official circles.

The future course of Soviet-American relations did little to justify these confident predictions. On the few occasions when Roosevelt dared to move ahead of public opinion on a matter of foreign policy, it never involved cooperation with Moscow to "quarantine" the aggressor states. Diplomatic action would have been particularly appropriate in the Far East, where both powers had a common interest in protecting China. Yet anti-Sovietism was less a restraining factor than a virulent isolationism blindly bent upon staying out of the next war by avoiding the mistakes that had led to intervention in the last one. Washington showed no disposition to surmount the petty annoyances that plagued its relations with Moscow and consistently took a legalistic view of the difficulties. The debt question was unsolved, commercial intercourse continued at a relatively low level, even after the completion of a trade agreement in July 1935, and Comintern activities aroused the State Department to an unusually bitter protest later in the same month. The malaise of American foreign policy in the 1930's was nowhere more evident than in its failure to act in conjunction with the Soviet Union when the vital interests of the United States were so transparently affected.

For its part, Moscow displayed an unconcealed eagerness for collective action with Washington and soon abandoned two of its major fixations about the United States. One had been a major ideological crutch for more than a decade: the inevitability of an Anglo-American war in an all-out struggle for capitalist commercial supremacy. It was a clear-cut case of the precedence that Marxist theory frequently enjoyed over the realities of international politics. The other—a passing phenomenon—involved an extension of the "ultra-leftism" which had brought nothing but grief to the Communist cause in Germany: the identification of Roosevelt's "New Deal" with fascism. The scuttling of both concepts reflected no great credit upon the acumen of Soviet policy-makers, but it was symptomatic of a late awakening to the fact that the capitalism of Britain, France, and the United States, though it might be subject to the postulates of Marxian economics, offered distinct political advantages—both to the Soviet Union and to the peoples concerned—over the capitalism of Germany, Italy, and Japan.

Within the short span of five years beginning in the fall of 1928 the Soviet Union had undergone a domestic revolution and was forced to begin a fundamental revision of its foreign policy. The economy, placed under forced draft, spurted sensationally, but Russia's "iron age" also inaugurated the political degeneration of Soviet Communism. The death agonies of world capitalism, so confidently anticipated by two generations of Marxist theoreticians, were again frustrated during the Great Depression. Instead, a new and more terrible form of political nihilism—fascism—rose from the crisis of bourgeois democracy to confound the expectations of Russian Communists and Western liberals alike. Stalin, never a profound ideologist, was slow to grasp the dynamic potentialities of the new doctrine, though his miscalculations were no greater than those of democratic politicians in the West. During the years of peril that followed, the problems of building a socialist society were subordinated to the problems attending the survival of the Russian state.

NOTES

1. Isaac Deutscher, *Stalin: A Political Biography* (New York, 1949), p. 405n.

2. See above, p. 115.

3. League of Nations, *Documents of the Preparatory Commission for the Disarmament Conference . . .* (Geneva, 1928), Section V, p. 12.

4. See above, p. 141.

5. Jane Degras (ed.), *Soviet Documents on Foreign Policy* (New York, 1951–53), II, 387.

6. *Ibid.*, p. 408; *Papers Relating to the Foreign Relations of the United States, 1929* (Washington, 1943–44), II, 406.

7. Ypsilon, *Pattern for World Revolution* (Chicago, 1947), p. 165.

8. *Rundschau,* No. 10, quoted in Franz Borkenau, *World Communism* (New York, 1939), p. 377.

9. No. 17, quoted *ibid.*, p. 379.

10. Gustav Hilger and Alfred G. Meyer, *The Incompatible Allies* (New York, 1953), pp. 260–63.

11. Degras, *Soviet Documents on Foreign Policy,* III, 45.

12. See above, p. 94.
13. See below, pp. 219 and 221–22.
14. See below, p. 215.
15. *Manchester Guardian,* December 14, 1932.
16. See above, pp. 74–75.

CHAPTER SEVEN

COLLECTIVE SECURITY
AND THE POPULAR FRONT

As the mid-point of the decade approached, the distinctive features of Soviet nationalism and of Stalin's personal dictatorship had unmistakably stamped themselves upon the regime. The expanding importance of the secret police mocked the vain hopes of a more liberal regime. The economic growth achieved during the first Five Year Plan was impressive, but it had not been accomplished without mass coercion and a deliberate reduction in the standard of living; nor had the cultural fabric of society escaped the dead hand of conformity. The success of the first Plan had encouraged the setting of even more ambitious goals for the second, which began on January 1, 1933. The emphasis on heavy industry was maintained, though the rate of increase dropped slightly and the manufacture of consumer goods assumed a higher priority.

A significant feature of the second Five Year Plan was the emphasis on industrial development beyond the Urals. The concentration of productive facilities in European Russia was a major military weakness that Soviet planners hoped to correct before war came. Along with the industrial revolution in Siberia, special measures were taken to bolster the defenses of the Soviet Far East. The double-tracking of the Trans-Siberian Railroad to the Manchurian border was completed; and in 1934 construction began on the Baikal-Amur Railroad, designed to furnish a more secure wartime route than the existing line near the Manchurian-Siberian frontier. The special Far Eastern "Red Banner" Army under General Blücher's command was continually augmented in numbers and equipment. A powerful air force was based in the area, and fortifications were erected along the Amur and Usuri rivers.

From 1932 onward the military budget grew year by year, an increase duplicated by the production of munitions and war-related goods. In 1934 the Red Army was expanded from 562,000 to 940,000 men (exclusive of frontier guards and special troops of the political police). In 1935 the reintroduction of ranks in the army and navy inaugurated a series of measures intended to raise the morale and professional status of the officer corps. The plan was but a variant of the concerted drive throughout the educational system—in schools, factories, collective farms, and cultural organizations—to reawaken a patriotic spirit in the Soviet citizenry. Great Russian chauvinism and Tsarist imperialism were still condemned, but the rewriting of Russian history to glorify military heroes and "progressive" rulers like Peter the Great represented the abandonment of the rigid Marxist interpretation previously followed by Soviet historians.

In literature and the arts the trend toward patriotic themes and what later came to be called "socialist realism" reinforced the Kremlin's drive to harness the intelligentsia for the practical needs of the state. If mediocrity flourished because of the cultural strait-jacket, so much the worse for culture. In short, Lenin's desire to "overtake and outstrip the advanced capitalist countries" had by 1935 become Stalin's major goal—a matter, as he saw it, of national survival; and in its achievement the Kremlin attempted to mobilize every individual either by persuasion or by compulsion.

By astute diplomacy the Soviet leaders hoped to avoid or to delay a catastrophe they had always predicted and which they now realized was hypothetical compared to the threat of a massive pincer movement by Germany in the west and Japan in the east. The old predators of capitalism—Britain and France—seemed toothless indeed beside the aggressive dynamism of the fascist powers. The radical revision of Soviet foreign policy within the next few years found its most dramatic expression in the entrance of the U.S.S.R. into the League of Nations on September 18, 1934. While Russia's policy can scarcely be attributed to altruism, her conduct as a member of the League was from that time until the eve of the Second World War more consistent with its aims and principles than that of the other major powers. Litvinov, who headed the Soviet delegation until his dismissal as commissar for foreign affairs in 1939, accepted such minor slights as his initial appointment to the Committee on Seaweeds with equanimity and set an example of courage and integrity which the other League representatives might well have emulated. Unfortunately, his influence on Soviet policy was more superficial than his admirers in the West were prepared to believe.

France acted as Russia's chief sponsor in the diplomatic maneuvers assuring a friendly welcome by the League members and a permanent seat on the Council. The friendship between the once implacable foes had advanced steadily from the time of their non-aggression pact in 1932.[1] But the unanimous ratification of that instrument by the French Chamber of Deputies on May 18, 1933, would have been inconceivable had not Hitler's rise to power in Germany intervened. Litvinov's visit to Paris in July 1933 and the return visit of former premier Edouard Herriot to Moscow, followed shortly by the arrival of a delegation led by the French air minister, denoted more than a normal exchange of felicitations.

After confidential preliminary soundings, Foreign Minister Joseph Paul-Boncour broached the subject of a mutual assistance treaty to Litvinov on October 31, 1933. Parallel trade negotiations resulted in the initialing of a provisional commercial agreement early the next year. The diplomatic *rapprochement* took a fresh turn in February 1934 with the formation of a new French government in which Louis Barthou, a conservative politically but an accomplished disciple of *Realpolitik*, accepted the post of foreign minister. His idea was to broaden the original proposal into a grand alliance against Germany. With this objective in mind, he saw Litvinov at Geneva on May 18, 1934, and consulted the Poles and France's Little Entente allies (Czechoslovakia, Rumania, and Yugoslavia). Britain favored an "Eastern Locarno" to include Germany. But Hitler had no wish to tie his hands with a security arrangement of this sort, and when Litvinov stopped over in Berlin on his way home from Geneva in June the Nazi foreign minister was deliberately vague and noncommittal.

On September 10, 1934, Germany formally declared her opposition to the scheme unless arms equality were granted. Poland followed suit in less uncompromising terms. Barthou was more pleased than not by Germany's public repudiation of an Eastern pact, for it enabled him to pursue his original plan. Before it could be explored, he was fatally wounded in the fusillade of bullets that killed King Alexander of Yugoslavia in Marseilles on October 9. Although it cannot be said that the assassination was the Sarajevo of World War II, Barthou's death can in retrospect be viewed as a fateful step in France's blundering path toward self-destruction. No able replacement was found prior to the final catastrophe.

Pierre Laval, whose ignominious career was to be crowned by his execution for treason in 1945, became the new foreign minister. He preferred to re-explore the possibility of an Eastern Locarno. To assuage Moscow's anxiety about his approaches to Berlin and Warsaw, Laval signed a joint declaration with Litvinov on December 5, 1934, promising that neither power would compromise an Eastern security pact by negotiating without the other's knowledge. Czechoslovakia adhered three days later. As Moscow waited patiently for further action from France, Laval journeyed to Rome in January 1935 and obtained a Franco-Italian accord which opened the door to the later conquest of Ethiopia. The Kremlin, with no direct interest in the bargain, was fully aware that France might prefer Fascist Italy to Communist Russia in her search for security. By his subsequent conduct Laval revealed that he had chosen Rome, though for the time being he was willing to bring Franco-Soviet collaboration to a head. Not until Hitler once more spurned the anxious inquiries from London and Paris for some indication that Germany would abide by the European *status quo* did the negotiations for a Franco-Soviet pact proceed.

Great Britain gave her tacit blessing to the arrangement and sought to dissipate Russia's well-grounded suspicion that she had regarded the Eastern orientation of her French partner with less than enthusiasm by sending Anthony Eden, the Lord Privy Seal, on to Moscow late in March 1935 after the British delegation had concluded its conversations in Berlin. As the first British statesman to set foot on Soviet soil since the Revolution, his visit naturally attracted more than normal attention. Eden's cordial reception and the friendly spirit attending his meetings with Stalin, Molotov, and Litvinov, marked a temporary plateau of good will amid the normal austerity of Anglo-Soviet relations. The lack of harmony between the two nations since the resumption of relations in 1929 was largely the choice of the British government. Moscow's sole provocation of any consequence had been the arrest in March 1933 of six British employees of Metropolitan-Vickers Ltd. on flimsy charges of espionage and sabotage. London retaliated by suspending negotiations for a new Anglo-Soviet trade agreement and threatening an embargo against Russian goods. The leniency of the sentences—one was acquitted, three deported, and two given short prison terms—undoubtedly reflected anxiety over the indignant tenor of the British reaction. The embargo was duly enforced on April 26, and Moscow promptly replied in kind by recalling the chiefs of its trade delegation. Sober reconsideration on both sides led to an agreement on July 1, 1933, in which the trade restrictions were withdrawn and the two prisoners released.

The conclusion of a new commercial treaty in February 1934 repaired the damage wrought by the Metro-Vickers affair, and the rise of the new barbarism in Germany brought a desire for closer relations with Moscow even among fervid anti-Communists. Others, however, continued to regard fascism as a bulwark against Communism and radical social reform, an opinion widely held among the industrial and political elite of the Western democracies. The non-Communist Left, too, by its inability to shed pacifist illusions and by guilt feelings about the injustices of Versailles, contributed in no small measure to the sorry record of both Britain and France in halting Axis aggression. The failure of Anglo-Soviet relations to attain the lukewarm level of the Franco-Soviet entente rested in great part upon Britain's traditional aloofness from continental affairs until her own vital interests were threatened.

For most Frenchmen the German menace transcended the ideological luxury of anti-Communism. Thus the announcement on April 9, 1935, of the anticipated signature of a Franco-Soviet mutual assistance pact was well received by the French public. Most of the details were worked out by Laval and Litvinov at Geneva, and on May 2 the treaty was signed in Paris. The decisive article obliged either power to go to the aid of the other in case of an "unprovoked attack on the part of a European state." By this formula France avoided the possibility of being drawn into a Soviet-Japanese war. Other provisions insured that the terms of the agreement were compatible with Locarno and the League covenant. The pact was to take effect upon the exchange of ratifications and to remain in force indefinitely, except at the end of five years it could be terminated upon a year's notice by either party. Two weeks later Czechoslovakia and the U.S.S.R. signed an almost identical treaty, with the added stipulation that France must come to the aid of the attacked country before the intervention of either signatory would be binding.

Laval visited Moscow in mid-May, and if his brief sojourn was primarily a courtesy call, it was not without significance. An official communiqué was issued on the 16th. Aside from registering conventional expressions of mutual congratulation, both governments went on record as still favoring an Eastern Locarno.[2] A reference to Stalin's "complete understanding and approval of the national defense policy pursued by France" was a subtle notice that the French Communists were to abandon "revolutionary defeatism"—a policy duly implemented by the sudden cessation of Communist opposition to the proposed lengthening of French military service to two years. Laval's failure to supplement the two treaties with military commitments was in basic contradiction to the motives that had presumably brought France and the Soviet Union together. Military talks later took place, but since no military convention was concluded, the agreements made at Paris and Prague were truly "scraps of paper" in essence if not in intent.

France wanted security but was reluctant to pay the price that her position demanded. The mirage of an understanding with Germany and Poland was a perpetual lure, for Hitler's fulminations against Bolshevism, particularly after the Franco-Soviet Pact, offered the possibility that the expansionist drive of the Nazis might be surfeited in the East while the Western democracies stood aside. This was Moscow's recurring nightmare, and the course of Franco-British diplomacy during the next four years fanned nascent suspicion into the white heat of resentment.

Laval's continued effort to maintain a diplomatic bridge to Berlin and Warsaw was deeply disturbing to Moscow. More suggestive of the Quay d'Orsay's dual policy was the calculated delay in the ratification of the treaty occasioned by Laval's request for parliamentary approval. Normal procedure for such a document would have been ratification by presidential decree. During the debate in the Chamber of Deputies the vehement opposition of the Right became manifest, and some proponents of the pact were curiously apologetic. The imprecautions of the German press were no asset to the opposition, however, and it was approved on February 27, 1936, by a vote of 353 to 164. The Senate likewise assented on March 12, 231 votes to 52.

II

Moscow reinforced its policy of collective security by an appropriate reversal of the Comintern line. In the turn toward a "Popular Front" against fascism, world Communism for once flowed with the current of opinion instead of against it. The annihilation of German Communism left the French party in the pivotal role of the Comintern's chief outpost in the West; and Moscow's new diplomatic responsibilities made France the logical site for a broader experiment in united front tactics. While the new dispensation was not officially proclaimed until the seventh congress of the Comintern in the summer of 1935, its gestation may be observed in the aftermath of the street rioting in Paris on February 6, 1934. A mob of fascists, royalists, and assorted anti-republicans—even a few Communists were involved—had attempted to storm the Chamber of Deputies; and though it was driven off in a hail of police bullets, the danger to the Republic seemed sufficiently alarming to arouse considerable soul-searching among French Communist leaders. The German lesson was too recent to ignore despite the intransigent radicalism still dominating Comintern ideology. Without consulting Moscow, the party allowed its rank-and-file members to participate in the twenty-four-hour general strike called on February 12 as an anti-fascist demonstration by the General Confederation of Labor and the Socialist party.

Beyond the immediate incident, the French Communists reverted to their usual anti-Socialist habits as far as official pronouncements were concerned. In practice the leadership encouraged—or at any rate did not oppose—the blossoming "united front from below" as Communists and Socialists collaborated in the numerous anti-fascist street demonstrations and brawls in provincial cities during the spring and summer. The Kremlin was not entirely satisfied with the leadership of the French party and tapped Jacques Doriot, the Communist deputy mayor of St. Denis and a premature "united fronter," to introduce the new Comintern line in France. But, unaccountably, he spurned Stalin's overtures, which included the promise of a greater measure of power than any Communist chief in the West had yet possessed. He was shortly expelled from the party and became one of the most fanatical proponents of fascism in France.

Stalin's second choice was Maurice Thorez, one of the younger members of the French Politburo. More amenable to party discipline than Doriot, he obeyed a summons from Moscow in April 1934 and was confronted there with a whole new set of instructions. The party leadership was thrust upon him, and he returned to spell out the new course to his colleagues. In June a party conference accepted the united front policy; and on July 27 a formal pact was signed with the Socialists—a joint program of resistance to German and Austrian fascism, the defense of democratic liberties, and the prevention of war preparations. The latter item—it was essentially a Socialist platform —mirrored the strong tradition of sentimental pacifism with which the Left was still very largely infected.

The new-found unity of the French Left was only the initial step in the Communist move to enlarge the common front into what Thorez on October 9, 1934, described for the first time as a "Popular Front of labor, liberty, and peace."[3] In November the Communists launched tentative feelers for an understanding with the Radical Socialists, the strongest of the bourgeois parties. The Socialists, who conceived of their alliance with the Communists as a Left bloc, dragged their feet. Not until an impressive Communist victory in the municipal elections in the early summer of 1935 and the resurgence of the Croix de Feu, the leading fascist organization, did the Socialists consent to a tripartite arrangement with the Radicals. The baptismal rites were performed on July 14—Bastille Day—at a monster demonstration in Paris in which the tricolor and the red flag flew side by side, though the "International" seemed more popular than the "Marseillaise." Encouraged by their progress, the Communists ventured beyond the Radicals in a search for potential allies. They were even prepared to sacrifice anticlericalism, the one staple in the diet of French intellectuals, but the Church hierarchy failed to respond.

When the long delayed seventh—and last—congress of the Comintern met in Moscow on July 25, 1935, to put its seal of approval on the Popular Front movement, the example of France more than outweighed the coolness of the Second International toward collaboration. According to the official count, 510 delegates representing sixty-five affiliated parties met in the Moscow House of Trade Unions. Georgi Dimitrov, the Bulgarian hero of the Reichstag fire trial in Leipzig, had already assumed the leading role in Comintern affairs and was formally elected to the post of general secretary. Following the opening report of Wilhelm Pieck, the German Communist leader, who reviewed the melancholy record of the Comintern since the last congress in 1928, Dimitrov handed down the new line. Such complete unanimity of opinion prevailed that the numerous speeches—the final session took place on August 25—only marked the cumulative intellectual sterility which had overtaken successive congresses.

France was held up before the delegates as the tactical model for a world-wide people's anti-fascist front; and Thorez and Marcel Cachin expounded at length upon the French experience. No longer was bourgeois democracy a fit subject for derision; the adjective "bourgeois" in fact temporarily disappeared from the Communist lexicon. Nor did the doctrine of class struggle enjoy continued favor. The downtrodden ceased to be regarded as the sole depositories of virtue, and nationalism, seemingly a fascist monopoly, was pressed into service. The Communists were to become more patriotic than the patriots to awaken the masses to the fascist danger and to avoid the stigma of a party beholden to an alien faith. In France they would claim the great revolutionary tradition of 1789 and 1848; in Britain the heritage of the Glorious Revolution and the Bill of Rights; in the United States the spirit of 1776 and the struggle against the "aggressive slavocracy." As Dimitrov told his audience, "Proletarian internationalism must, so to speak, 'acclimatize itself' in each country in order to sink deep roots in its native land."[4] There was something ludicrously incongruous in the notion of the Comintern, the organizational embodiment of international revolution, extolling the virtues of patriotic endeavor. But the State Department and the British Foreign Office, obtuse sticklers for the diplomatic proprieties, could see no irony or humor in the situation and solemnly dispatched protests to Moscow as if the Comintern still clung to its old subversive habits.

To the Kremlin, of course, the obligation of all Communists to defend the Soviet "fatherland," whether by revolution or by counter-revolution, was axiomatic, and the introduction of the new Comintern policy was a deadly serious business. Neither Anglo-American protest about too much revolution nor carping voices from Trotskyists and Left wing socialists about too little made the slightest impression upon Moscow's grim determination to mobilize all available resources in the struggle for survival. To Communists in the democratic countries the Popular Front was a spiritual oasis after years of wandering in the arid wastes of sectarianism. At last their cause had become intellectually respectable; and if they could not with impunity wallow in the ideological fleshpots of capitalist civilization, there were no insuperable barriers to a community of interest with the whole gamut of liberal and —upon occasion—conservative thought. In England their party was small; in the United States minuscule. But like a layer of concentric rings, the Communists were surrounded by a larger body of "fellow travelers," who were in turn dwarfed by an amorphous group of sympathizers. The latter shaded gradually into the area of more orthodox opinion, where the liberal intelligentsia, sometimes of definite anti-Communist persuasion, were willing to consort with the devil himself in a coalition against fascism; others, aghast at the unprecedented misery of the Great Depression, were attracted by the planned economy of the Soviet Union, where a chronic labor shortage seemed the chief bottleneck in attaining new production records under the second Five Year Plan.

While it is true that intellectuals did not, and cannot by the nature of their function, aspire to political or economic power, as opinion-molders they were far more influential than their numerical insignificance would indicate. Yet as a political force capable of determining national policy, the Popular Front movement can be said to have achieved real success—and that rather fleeting—in but three countries: France, Spain, and China. The second half of the year 1936 was the high-water mark of the movement, a period in which France, as the bastion of the Kremlin's security system, was governed by a Socialist-Radical cabinet with Communist support. Fascism as an internal danger was by this time largely impotent; externally the threat had multiplied so greatly that only a few pacifists and the extreme Right still tried to minimize it.

Italy's invasion of Ethiopia in October 1935 had been met with the farce of economic and financial sanctions by the League of Nations and was immediately followed by a secret Franco-British scheme to dismember the victim before it could be done by Mussolini's legions. Laval's ministry temporarily survived the disclosure of this sordid deal, but in January 1936 the government resigned and was replaced by a caretaker cabinet. It was confronted with the most dangerous crisis in France's post-war history—the German occupation of the demilitarized Rhineland on March 7. The French, by failing to call Hitler's bluff, snatched defeat from the very jaws of victory. The Locarno Pact was thus interred alongside the Versailles treaty. Moscow could find little reassurance in the impressive majority for the ratification of the Franco-Soviet alliance in the Senate five days later.[5]

The spring elections in France were fought exclusively on the issue of the Popular Front. The Right and Center parties had little to offer except the conviction that the Left was selling the country to Moscow. The Communists, Socialists, and Radicals all suscribed to a common statement of principles, but each party conducted its own election campaign. The Left emerged with a decisive majority in the Chamber, and the number of Communist deputies spurted sensationally from 10 to 72. As the largest party, with 146 deputies, the Socialists dominated the government, and their leader, Leon Blum, assumed the premiership on June 4, 1936. The Communists balked at sharing the responsibilities of government, demonstrating a predilection for an independent course that augured poorly for the future of the coalition. Blum gently warned the Communists that French fascism was not dead: "I am being spoken of as a Kerensky who is preparing the way for a Lenin. I can assure you that this is not going to be a Kerensky government; and it is equally certain that if we fail we shall not be succeeded by a Lenin."[6]

The first months of the Popular Front regime, while troubled by an epidemic of "sitdown" strikes, were occupied with the passage of a long overdue program of social reform. Although the Right reacted to the French "New Deal" with much the same aversion that characterized the conservative Republican opposition to Roosevelt's more renowned New Deal in the United States—"rather Hitler than Blum" was the slogan of the extremists—the average Frenchman appeared better pleased with his government than at any time since the war. In large part it was foreign policy that proved the undoing of the Blum coalition. More specifically, it was the malignant tumor of the Spanish civil war which ate out the body politic of France—a kind of external Dreyfus Affair arousing ideological passion to new heights of divisive bitterness. The conflict in Spain was another and even more alarming symptom of the paralyzing debility that had overtaken French (and Western) diplomacy. However wide the gulf between Laval and Blum on domestic issues, their differences on foreign policy were not as great as those which the aftermath of the Marseilles assassination had exposed between Barthou and Laval. Blum could not repeat Laval's blunder of an Italian *détente*—Mussolini had already shown his preference for Hitler—but he persisted in ignoring the potentialities of the Franco-Russian Pact for a single-minded pursuit of Britain's favor.

That a triple entente akin to the pre-1914 arrangement did not develop to meet the German challenge was primarily a failing of British policy, for France, after the Rhineland *coup*, displayed less and less initiative in pursuing an independent course of her own. The polarity of London's attitude toward Moscow and the somnambulistic character of Downing Street's diplomacy was neatly illustrated by the conference on the Straits question at Montreux, Switzerland, during the summer of 1936. The Ethiopian campaign had brought the Mediterranean into sharp focus, and the alteration of the European balance of power since the Lausanne Conference of 1923[7] insured a more favorable reception for the formal Turkish proposal to revise the Straits convention. Faced by the prospect of unilateral action, the efficacy of which Hitler and Mussolini had done much to popularize, the powers accepted the inevitability of revision with good grace.

The full-panoplied diplomatic conference opened on June 22. The Russo-Turkish "Straits entente" still held firm, and the only significant opposition to the draft convention presented by the Turks came from Britain. Turkey's right to restore her sovereignty in the Straits (*i.e.,* remilitarization) was conceded, but Britain strenuously objected to the clauses severely limiting access to the Black Sea in wartime without a corresponding curtailment of the right of egress into the Mediterranean by the ships of a riparian power. In other words, the Soviet fleet, virtually nonexistent in 1923, would acquire a new strategic importance through its unchallenged supremacy in the Black Sea and its ability to engage a hostile fleet in the Mediterranean without fear of effective pursuit through the Straits. The conference therefore developed into a duel between Britain and the U.S.S.R. in which the former was almost as isolated as the latter had been at Lausanne. Concerned with the sanctity of the Anglo-German naval agreement of June 1935, British policy at Montreux gave aid and comfort to the position of Germany and Italy, neither of which was represented at the negotiations. After verging on a breakdown several times, the discussions were satisfactorily concluded on July 20 by the signature of a convention embodying much of the Soviet-Turkish point of view. The complex arrangements were rendered somewhat academic by the restoration of Turkish military power in the Straits, but the dispute over the Soviet fleet was solved by providing that the warships of belligerent powers (assuming Turkish neutrality) would not pass through the Straits in either direction unless to aid a victim of aggression—as determined by the League covenant—or in fulfillment of a mutual assistance treaty to which Turkey was a signatory.

The Soviet government was, on the whole, pleased with the results of Montreux. Yet the expectation that Turkey would be drawn into the Franco-Soviet alliance system was not confirmed; and the friendship between Moscow and Ankara began to deteriorate despite Hitler's new *Drang nach Osten* and Mussolini's campaign to make the Mediterranean an Italian lake. Soviet relations with the other states of the Middle East remained outwardly cordial, but Communist infiltration was greatly feared by the rulers of this predominantly Moslem region and contributed to the success of Nazi propaganda in Iran. The contrast between the economic and cultural stagnation of Afghanistan and Iran and the corresponding progress in Soviet Central Asia was not so great a boon to Communist penetration of the area as might be expected. The severity of repressive counter-measures against Communism, while partially responsible, was perhaps less important than the unpredictable mixture of altruism and ruthlessness with which the Russian authorities "uplifted" the native population. The Moslem masses, whether Soviet or non-Soviet, clung by and large to their traditional habits and customs.

III

The German-Italian liaison that had flourished during the Ethiopian campaign reached the stage of a formal political accord in October 1936. The similarity of aims and methods which cemented the "Rome-Berlin Axis" also drew Japan into cooperation with the fascist dictators. On November 25 a "German-Japanese Agreement against the Communist International," colloquially known as the Anti-Comintern Pact, was signed in Berlin and sealed a political partnership in the guise of saving civilization from Bolshevism. The terms of the five-year pact were confined to a statement of the ways and means of dealing with the "subversive activities" of the Comintern. But a secret protocol obliged the signatories to consult one another and to "take no measures which would tend to ease the situation of the U.S.S.R." in case of an unprovoked Russian attack on either country.[8] The agreement was no surprise to Moscow, for the Soviet intelligence service had kept abreast of the prolonged negotiations. There was astonished chagrin in Berlin and Tokyo when Litvinov publicly revealed the substance of the protocol on November 28. Italy adhered to the pact on November 6, 1937, but was not informed of the secret agreement.

The anti-Communist theme of Axis propaganda had been enormously inflated by the outbreak of the Spanish civil war. The Nazi party rally at Nuremberg in September 1936 opened this new ideological offensive as speaker after speaker flayed the "international Jewish-Marxist conspiracy" emanating from Moscow. Hitler openly proclaimed Germany's ambitions in the East: "If I had the Ural Mountains with their incalculable store of treasures in raw materials, Siberia with its vast forests, and the Ukraine with its tremendous wheat fields, Germany and the National Socialist leadership would swim in plenty!"[9] Moscow rose to the challenge, most notably in a well-publicized speech delivered to units of the Red Army in Kiev by Marshal Kliment Voroshilov, who promised swift retribution for any "crazy attacks against Soviet territory." The premier of the Soviet Ukraine, Panas Lyubchenko, expressed a similar theme more picturesquely at the special meeting of the Congress of Soviets called late in November to adopt the new "Stalin constitution." "Our answer to the Nazi dream of invading the Ukraine," he declared, "is an old Ukrainian saying: Just as a pig can never look at the sky, so Hitler will never be able to see our cabbage patch."[10] Stalin himself described the new constitution as "an indictment of fascism inspiring all civilized people fighting for democracy against fascist barbarism." At the same congress Litvinov spoke at length on foreign affairs. Fascism, he maintained, was the result of contradictions within bourgeois society. It had ceased to be "an internal affair of the countries which preach it"; and he went on to examine the Spanish situation as the "first large-scale sortie of fascism beyond its borders."[11]

At the time of Litvinov's address, the war in Spain had been under way since July. Although its origins lay deeply imbedded in the structure of Spanish society, the conflict by its very nature quickly assumed an international character, and with the early intervention of the fascist powers it became the dress rehearsal for World War II. Before the outbreak of hostilities Soviet-Spanish relations hardly existed, for Madrid was one of the few remaining European governments that refused to recognize the Soviet regime. Moscow did have some negligible contact with Spanish politics through the Comintern. The Communist party in Spain was so insignificant, however, that before the establishment of the Republic in 1931 its membership was less than a thousand. Communist strength gradually increased during the next few years, yet compared to the other parties of the Left it remained a tiny minority.

The Spanish Communists, as was to be expected, had only scorn for the Republic until the change in the Comintern line associated with the events in France. In October 1934 the Socialists proclaimed a general strike against the conservative republican government, and it led to armed rebellion in Barcelona, Madrid, and the region of Asturias in northwestern Spain. The two urban risings were quickly crushed; but in Asturias the government called in Moorish troops and foreign legionnaires from Morocco to subdue the stubborn resistance of some 70,000 miners and iron-workers. A prologue to the civil war, the Asturias affair witnessed the beginning of the Spanish Popular Front: workers' committees of Socialists, Anarcho-Syndicalists, and Communists had joined in leading the revolt.

By the time of the elections to the Cortes (the national parliament) in mid-February of 1936 the Left coalition had broadened to include the liberal republican parties, and with a common program of moderate social reform the Popular Front won a decisive victory at the polls. The disastrous drop in the Center vote was symptomatic of the growing polarization of national sentiment into irreconcilable camps. On one side stood the workers, the poorer peasants, and some elements of the middle class; on the other stood the landlords, the upper strata of businessmen and industrialists, the Church hierarchy, and most of the army officers. Along such class positions the battle lines were drawn for the impending struggle.

Alarmed by the strength of the Left and unwilling to countenance even the slight alteration of the *status quo* contemplated by the new government, monarchists and other rightist groups began almost openly to plot against the Republic. Of these groups the Falange (Phalanx) movement, conceived as a Spanish prototype of Mussolini's Fascist party, rapidly expanded to become the most violent and uncompromising of the counter-revolutionary organizations. While emerging later as the strongest political force within the Nationalist coalition, the effective leadership of the developing conspiracy lay within the upper reaches of the officer corps. Only the Communists, whose influence and membership rolls had grown steadily since February, began to take a serious view of the situation. Relatively inconsequential as yet, they failed to shake the government's complacency. Although the party still condoned revolutionary slogans, its immediate aim of bolstering the Popular Front made it the most conservative of the "radical" parties. The good-natured Socialist jest during the elections—"Vote Communist to save Spain from Marxism"—was more apt than the Communists themselves were prepared to admit.

But the cream of the jest came with the military *coup* of July 17–18, 1936, under the pretext of rescuing Spain from an imminent Communist insurrection. Few Spaniards not already persuaded were deceived by this familiar tactic; yet many conservatives in the democratic countries, particularly Roman Catholics, chose to interpret the conflict as a Christian crusade against Red atheism and barbarism. General Francisco Franco, shortly to be invested with the leadership of Spanish fascism, lacked the demogogic *mystique* of a Hitler or a Mussolini but conscientiously sought to adapt himself to the requirements of his new position; and in gratefully accepting the intervention of Germany and Italy, the military *junta* that had furnished the driving power for the assault upon the Republic was inexorably pushed toward the unfamiliar territory of Falangist pseudo-radicalism.

With the bulk of the regular armed forces in revolt, the Nationalist blueprint for the seizure of power was seriously disrupted by spontaneous defensive action on the part of the workers. This hastily created Republican (or Loyalist) militia was beholden to the Left wing parties, particularly the Socialists, for political guidance; and through elected committees the essential functions of government were taken over from the feeble grasp of the legally constituted regime. The rebels were defeated in Madrid and Barcelona, and about half the country remained under Loyalist control. But the industrial north was cut off from the central and eastern portions under Madrid's authority. Supremacy in the air and on the sea enabled the Nationalists to reinforce their army with Moorish troops from Morocco; and in the autumn the first wave of Italian and German "volunteers" added to the superior strength of Franco's forces.

London and Paris reacted to the Spanish war with a policy of strict neutrality—an attitude quite at variance with strong popular sentiment for the Loyalist cause. Since Madrid was legally entitled to purchase arms to offset the aid received by the rebels from Rome and Berlin, the neutrality of the democratic powers was not only unnecessary from the standpoint of international law but politically and morally indefensible. Blum's Popular Front government, the ideological partner of Republican Spain, took the initiative in decreeing an arms embargo—thus in effect favoring the Nationalists by default. Blum and his supporters within the cabinet rationalized their folly with appropriate sentiments: the entente with Britain must be maintained at any price, and the conflict had to be isolated to preserve the peace of Europe. The sincerity of their action is not open to question; the absurdity of it—demonstrable at the time—became self-evident when France fell to the Nazis less than four years later. Spain, like Ethiopia, was intended as a propitiatory offering, but it merely whetted the insatiable Axis appetite for further easy conquest. The British cabinet of Prime Minister Stanley Baldwin had only to face down a mild groundswell of criticism compared with the fury of the outcry that nearly swamped Blum. Even his own party, whose members had been subjected to years of pacifist indoctrination, proved obstreperous.

The Anglo-French arms embargo, save for a few loopholes, became effective before the end of July 1936, and during the first week in August the other powers were solicited about a non-intervention agreement. Berlin and Rome deliberately procrastinated in hope of making their support to Franco decisive while London and Paris obligingly stood by. Late in August the U.S.S.R., Germany, Italy, and Portugal formally adhered to the "hands off" plan—as did the less vitally concerned European countries. A special committee sat intermittently in London for the next twenty-three months to enforce the embargo agreement; and while the *opéra bouffe* of "non-intervention" continued, Hitler and Mussolini converted Spain into a proving ground for their respective armies.

Moscow's proposal for a control system over Spanish and Portuguese ports was rejected, and on October 7 the Soviet representative warned the London committee that unless violations of the non-intervention agreement were "immediately discontinued," his government would "consider itself free of the obligations arising from that agreement."[12] Formal notice was given on October 23, although the Soviet delegate retained his seat on the Non-Intervention Committee and Moscow was silent about the extent—and even the fact—of its military aid to Republican Spain. Non-military support in the form of food, clothing, and money had already been granted through government-sponsored collections. These relief measures lagged after Moscow's temporary allegiance to the non-intervention pact and were resumed in mid-September. Communists were, of course, active in the democratic countries in raising funds for Spanish relief.

Soviet war matériel began to arrive in October. Except for a few pilots and tank commanders, the Russians sent to Spain were technical advisers who had been instructed to avoid combat. Compared to the lavishness of the Italo-German effort, Soviet aid was not extensive, but it saved the Republic in the critical first months of the war when defeat seemed inevitable. In 1937 Moscow's contribution was greatly diminished, particularly after the April control scheme of the Non-Intervention Committee began. Some supplies undoubtedly continued to reach Spain until the summer of 1938 when the Loyalist cause seemed hopeless and Soviet diplomacy was preoccupied elsewhere. And at no time did Moscow contemplate intervening on a scale that would frighten conservative opinion in England and France.

Although cautious about committing its own manpower, the Soviet government authorized the Comintern to establish International Brigades. Foreign volunteers had already furnished the nucleus for such an organization, and in the fall of 1936 recruiting proceeded on a systematic basis. While not necessarily either Communists or "fellow travelers"—somewhat over half were probably party members—the recruits were usually screened for their political reliability. The last thing Moscow desired in Spain were radicals bent upon fomenting revolution. Few, if any, Russians were permitted to volunteer. However, some 500 political refugees in the U.S.S.R., nearly all Communists, were encouraged to join the Brigades. The commanders and political commissars were almost invariably Communists, but the Soviet contingent of specialists was kept rigidly apart. Motivated by a sense of political idealism and consequently with a higher morale than regular units, the volunteers were often in the thick of the fighting, especially in the defense of Madrid, and suffered disproportionately heavy casualties. Though their combat effectiveness probably never exceeded 18,000 men at any one time, approximately 40,000 fought with the Brigades before their dissolution in 1938.

Because the Soviet Union was the only country—aside from Mexico —to take advantage of its legal right to sell arms to Spain's legitimate government, Russian prestige was naturally very high among all supporters of the Republic, and the Communist party's popularity correspondingly advanced to a record level. From an estimated membership of 50,000 at the beginning of the war, the party quadrupled, at the very least, within a single year, and its influence within the government increased even more impressively.

The moderate bourgeois regime which had come into power on July 19, 1936, gave way on September 4 to a cabinet headed by Francisco Largo Caballero, the leader of the Socialist party. Two Communists joined his ministry, the first occasion that party members participated in a Western government. Since the war emergency dictated a conservative course as well as an end to localism and the revolutionary excesses of some of the workers' committees, the Anarchists and many Left Socialists considered the government "counter-revolutionary." After Soviet intervention had given them an improved bargaining position, the Communists became more vocal in their insistence upon moderation in domestic reform and the subordination of every task to winning the war. In a letter of practical advice to Largo Caballero on September 21, 1936, Stalin emphasized the need for conciliating the peasants and the middle class and for winning the support and sympathy of the democratic powers.[13] The Communists were in fact the most conservative element within the Popular Front, and to insure rigid obedience to the party line Moscow dispatched its own agents to Spain to supplement—even to displace—the indigenous Communist leadership.

During the early part of 1937 the Communists became dissatisfied with Largo Caballero. He had refused to disavow some of the extremist demands of the Left Socialists and was reluctant to use forceful measures against Anarchists and members of the P.O.U.M. (Workers' Party of Marxist Unity), a group of dissident Left Communists accused of "Trotskyism." If there was one exhibit in the Comintern's chamber of horrors to match fascism, it was Trotskyism, for Moscow was still in the throes of the notorious treason trials. After the execution of sixteen Old Bolsheviks, including Zinoviev and Kamenev, in August 1936, thirteen others were condemned to death and four—Radek among them—were sentenced to long prison terms in January 1937. All were supposedly agents of a conspiracy hatched by Trotsky and supported by Nazi Germany for the overthrow of the Stalin regime and the restoration of capitalism. Seemingly the most sacrosanct of party heroes, the victims were obliged to wait a generation for an implied but still unsatisfactory measure of posthumous rehabilitation following the desanctification of Stalin in 1956.

Only by twisting the facts beyond recognition could the P.O.U.M. be considered the Spanish outpost of the Trotskyist heresy, though the membership undoubtedly sympathized with many of Trotsky's ideas. Together with the Anarchists, they stood for revolutionary action and reviled the Communists as traitors to the working class. When quasi-legal measures for suppressing both organizations proved inadequate, more violent means were employed, and the news aroused widespread indignation among independent leftists in Spain and abroad.

Early in May 1937 the latent civil war within the Republican camp erupted in Barcelona, headquarters for several groups of the revolutionary Left and the center of Catalonian separatism. In response to repeated provocations, the P.O.U.M., aided by extreme elements among the Anarchists, rose against the central government. The revolt was closer to an armed protest than a serious attempt to seize power. Nevertheless, there were several hundred fatal casualties in three days of fighting before the semi-insurrection was quelled. The Communists then demanded a purge of the active revolutionaries and the outlawing of the P.O.U.M. Their two representatives in the cabinet left the government when Largo Caballero refused to comply. He resigned on May 16 and was replaced by Juan Negrin, a moderate Socialist, who presided over a revised Popular Front regime.

Nominally with no more power than before, the Communists found Negrin more cooperative; and with a more firmly entrenched position in the military establishment and a tight grip on the secret police apparatus, their control over Republican policy was greater than it had been at any time in 1936. The P.O.U.M. was declared illegal, many of its members arrested, and the leaders tried for treason in October 1938. The Communist charge that they were agents of Franco did not stand up in court, but five were sentenced to long prison terms for their part in the Barcelona affair. Andres Nin, the P.O.U.M. chieftain, was shot while in custody.

In June 1937 the Communists intensified their campaign for a merger with the Socialists on the Catalonian model (the two provincial parties had united shortly after the beginning of the war on terms leading to Communist domination). The Socialists, wary of repeating their mistake on a larger scale, consented on August 17 to a working agreement intended as a preliminary step toward unification. In the fall, however, Negrin declined further negotiations, and the Communists accepted the rebuff with good grace. Their prestige had suffered because of the P.O.U.M. affair; and the new meeting of the Cortes on October 1, where the presence of sixteen Communist deputies out of some two hundred, testified to their weakness in the formal political structure of the Republic.

The propaganda campaign against the Anarchists had been suspended during the summer of 1937 even though the political police were still active in rounding up "uncontrollables." The Communists urged that the Anarchists be readmitted to the Popular Front, a suggestion the Socialists and Republicans received with marked coolness until the worsened military situation and a disclaimer of revolutionary intentions by the Anarchists permitted two of their number to be admitted to the cabinet in the spring of 1938.

The Communist vendetta against Trotskyism was, on the other hand, pursued with inquisitorial zeal. Yet the extermination of the P.O.U.M. had been so ruthless that after the summer of 1937 few fresh victims of consequence were to be found. The chief political malefactors continued to be Russian. In 1937 the Great Purge reached its peak in the Soviet Union—the imprisonment, exile, or execution of tens and possibly hundreds of thousands, most of whom held responsible party and government posts. Few were arrested on grounds other than mere suspicion, but guilt or innocence seemed to lose their accepted meanings as the hunt for real or fancied offenders proceeded with no restraints of justice or logic. More spectacular "traitors" were discovered in the Red Army. An estimated 6,000 officers of the rank of colonel or above were arrested and approximately 1,500 executed. The most famous victim, Marshal Tukhachevsky, was shot together with seven prominent generals after a secret court-martial. The last and most important of the public trials took place in March 1938: Bukharin and seventeen others were executed and three sentenced to long prison terms.

Whether by coincidence or by suspected ideological impurities acquired in Spain, most of the highly placed Russians who served the Republic were victims of the purge. Among diplomatic personnel, Ambassador Marcel Rosenberg disappeared after his recall to the Soviet Union early in 1937; and a similar fate befell his successor, Jacob Gaikis. The consul general in Barcelona, Vladimir Antonov-Ovseyenko, who had led the assault on the Winter Palace during the Bolshevik Revolution and had been identified with the Trotsky opposition during the twenties, was executed after acting as Stalin's chief political "cleanser" in Catalonia. The roster of the missing and presumably purged also included General Ian Berzin, the chief adviser to the Loyalist general staff, and his aide, General Arthur Stashevsky. General "Emil Kleber" (Lazar Stern), the enigmatic commander of the International Brigades during their heroic defense of Madrid in 1936, was thought to have been another victim, but he was later reported to have commanded troops during the Russo-Finnish war.[14]

Foreign Communists in Russia were scrutinized with special vigilance, and the Comintern apparatus in Moscow was decimated. Bela Kun and Heinz Neumann were perhaps the most notable expatriates of the hundreds who disappeared in the terror. The Polish Communist party was dissolved altogether after the execution of its leaders, and the German, Hungarian, and Yugoslav parties barely escaped extinction. Yet there were many foreigners—then virtually unknown—who retained Stalin's favor and survived the Great Purge to emerge as figures of world prominence after World War II. And there were others whom Stalin, for no apparent reason, entrusted with political tasks of the utmost delicacy. In Spain such a role was conferred upon Andre Marty of Black Sea mutiny fame,[15] previously in disgrace for his opposition to the Popular Front policy in France. Overseer of political orthodoxy and military discipline in the International Brigades, he later became Stalin's chief "hatchet-man" for the whole of Republican Spain.

As the political terror began to wane in the Soviet Union, so did its backlash in Spain. The docility of the Communists in the last few months of 1937 was remarkable considering their aggressive role during the first half of the year. For a time they even refrained from open attacks upon Defense Minister Indalecio Prieto, who made strenuous efforts to reduce Comunist influence in the military establishment. Nationalist victories in February and March of 1938 ended this unusual self-restraint toward Prieto, for his advocacy of a negotiated peace ran directly counter to Communist insistence upon war to the end. Dropped in a new cabinet reorganization in April, he remained a thorn in the government's side because of his denunciation of Negrin and his defeatist attitude.

Moscow's Spanish policy fluctuated with the eddies and tides of global politics. Litvinov consistently upheld the cause of the Spanish Republic at Geneva and strove to arouse the democratic powers from their lethargy. Yet the Kremlin continued to look upon them as prospective allies who might be alienated by precipitate action in Spain. Nor was Soviet security to be endangered by flaunting before the Axis powers a unilateral policy of all-out intervention. If Moscow's distrust of Western good faith in the "non-intervention" fiasco was justified, so was the concern in London and Paris for the morale and efficiency of an army whose leading generals had just been executed for treason. The resumption of the Japanese attack upon China in July 1937 renewed the threat to Russia's eastern flank and further narrowed her area of choice in Spain.

In August 1937 a more serious outbreak of "piracy" in the Mediterranean—neutral shipping was attacked by Nationalist aircraft and by Italian warships and submarines—inspired a Franco-British proposal for a conference at Nyon, Switzerland. On September 10, the day before the opening session, Germany and Italy declined an invitation to attend. The Soviet government was skeptical of Western intentions, especially since the British had begun a new courtship of the Axis powers during the summer. It was therefore an agreeable surprise when Britain, joined by France, resolved to call a halt to the illegal warfare against merchant vessels by systematic naval patrol action. Litvinov, the Soviet representative, criticized the scheme for excluding the ships of Loyalist Spain but signed the agreement on September 14 along with eight other nations. The Nyon Pact virtually eliminated the submarine menace. It also had the unique distinction of being the only effective measure against the aggressor nations that the three non-fascist powers performed in concert during the "appeasement era."

Spurred on by the success at Nyon, thirty-two member states of the League Assembly, with only Portugal and Albania dissenting, adopted a resolution on October 2 condemning Axis intervention in Spain—without, however, specifically naming either of the culprits involved. Moral censure alone was unfortunately not well suited to the situation. The promise of a stiffened attitude in London and Paris was not fulfilled, and the Non-Intervention Committee burlesque was allowed to proceed. Moscow's threat to cut off its share of the committee's expenses was never carried out, apparently because of apprehension over being diplomatically isolated and because of the lower priority that help for Spain had now assumed in the Kremlin's hierarchy of foreign policy aims. The U.S.S.R. was nevertheless the only power to support the plea of the Spanish government before the League Council in May 1938 that the non-intervention policy be abandoned. Britain and France lacked the grace to abstain and voted against the resolution. From this point on the crisis over Czechoslovakia overshadowed the Spanish question, and Soviet aid, somewhat more generous after Prieto's fall, trickled to a halt during the summer months.

With the complete cessation of Russian supplies, Communist influence began to decline. But when the Munich Pact[16] conclusively demonstrated that the Western powers would never interfere with a fascist victory in Spain, Negrin was forced to rely heavily upon the Communists in the government's determination to fight on in a hopeless cause. The Nationalists seized Barcelona in January 1939 and occupied the whole of Catalonia. Only southeastern Spain, with Madrid as its chief rampart, remained in Loyalist hands. Negrin began to replace advocates of a negotiated peace by Communist officers, a policy that precipitated a *coup* by a portion of the army command on March 4. When a Communist-led attack against the new regime failed to dislodge it, the government leaders flew to exile in France. An anti-Communist purge was well under way when Franco's victorious troops entered Madrid on March 28, 1939, and a more rigorous blood-bath was instituted without bothering to observe the niceties of political distinction in Republican ranks.

If Spain was the anvil, Munich was the hammer which forged the Nazi-Soviet Pact. Although there has been no shortage of commentators who have discerned perfidy in Moscow's every move during the "Litvinov era"—obviously Stalin and his cohorts could not be paragons of virtue abroad while maintaining a police state at home—the record of Western duplicity and weakness in comparison to that of the Soviet Union is hardly flattering to the cause of democratic statesmanship. Insofar as pro-Franco propaganda against "Red" Spain was taken seriously, the Atlantic powers need only have reverted to the normal procedures of international law in selling arms to the Spanish government and their influence would have far exceeded that of Russia and her Spanish admirers. Deprived of Soviet aid, the Loyalists could not have survived the first six months of the war; nor could they have staved off defeat during the next two years against such overwhelming odds without the disciplined militance that the Communists brought to bear on the Popular Front coalition. Many disgruntled *émigrés*, in a wide-ranging search for scapegoats, later singled out the Communists as the prime movers behind the Republican disaster. The proposition is completely untenable. Yet there can be little doubt that the disruption of the radical Left by transplanting the terroristic methods of the Russian secret police was damaging to the war effort, even when measured by the Kremlin's Machiavellian standards. To those Marxists like Trotsky who held firmly to a revolutionary interpretation of the master, Stalin's unforgivable sin in Spain was the calculated attempt to expunge any chance of a social upheaval—the very event that frightened conservatives thought they saw in every Soviet move in Spain.

Communism's counter-revolutionary role in Spain was a logical extension of the Popular Front strategem, and the failure of that policy to justify itself in terms of the Russian national interest was deemed a good and sufficient reason for a re-examination of its premises. In France signs of Moscow's disenchantment preceded the collapse in Spain. As early as September 1936 the Communist party had called a protest strike against the non-intervention policy. Not long afterward Thorez warned Blum in a speech at St. Etienne that the "fate of the Popular Front is not tied to the existence of one specific cabinet."[17] Early the following December, after a debate in the Chamber of Deputies on Spain, the Communists abstained from a vote of confidence in the government. Although a party statement temporarily healed the rift by promising support on all issues except Spain, it was apparent that mutual confidence was lacking. The Radicals, who at first welcomed the Communists as perverse but possibly genuine converts to the Jacobin tradition, were already estranged by the specter of class warfare attending the "sitdown" strikes and by a firm resolve to stay clear of the Spanish imbroglio.

The Blum cabinet fell in June 1937 when the Radicals in the Senate joined members of the Right wing parties in refusing the government special powers to deal with the financial crisis. Under the Radical premiership of Camille Chautemps the Senate was more obliging, and the Popular Front, though materially damaged, remained in working order. The Communists became more tractable, especially after the exposure of a new internal fascist threat in the fall. Their policy reflected Moscow's fear that a conservative government might seek a bargain with Hitler and repudiate the Franco-Soviet Pact. If the treaty's military significance was dubious, the Russians clung to it as a guarantee against political isolation. Blum had conferred in February 1937 with Soviet Ambassador Vladimir Potemkin about a military convention, but the French were reluctant to pressure Poland or Rumania into granting passage to the Red Army in case of war, and further conversations about military commitments were stifled.

In January 1938 Chautemps reformed his cabinet without the Socialists. Having already "returned to the Communists their liberty of decision," he had served notice that the Radicals were prepared to dissolve the Popular Front. A fresh cabinet crisis in March returned Blum as premier in an outward re-creation of the June 1936 government; but inwardly the new ministry was an emaciated substitute for the once robust coalition.

In the leaderless interval between Chautemps and Blum, Hitler struck once more: Austria was absorbed into the greater Reich. The *Anschluss* was no great surprise to the well informed—Britain had tacitly consented beforehand—but it had the added effect of placing Czechoslovakia squarely in the path of the Nazi juggernaut. French opinion nonetheless received a nasty shock; and even those whose complacency had not been jarred by the war in Spain grew alarmed at the disappearance of Austria from the map of Europe. Yet the parties of the Center and the non-fascist Right failed to rally to Blum's call for a "National Union." Political instinct correctly informed his opponents that the government's tenure would be brief. After less than a month in office, the Senate again rejected Blum, and the era of the Popular Front in France came to a definite close. Among the fallen was Foreign Minister Paul-Boncour, who had furnished a brief but lively interlude in the dismal record of French diplomacy by permitting the Spanish government to purchase arms.

The Quai d'Orsay's unexpected show of independence was not well received across the channel. It was intimated that Paul-Boncour would not be a good choice to succeed himself, and the new Radical-Right wing government of Premier Edouard Daladier included a "safe" foreign minister in Georges Bonnet, the ambassador to Washington during Blum's first ministry. Daladier and Bonnet departed for London late in April 1938 to cement the Anglo-French entente by acknowledging Downing Street's diplomatic pre-eminence.

Neville Chamberlain, who had succeeded Baldwin as prime minister in May 1937, and Lord Halifax, Eden's replacement as foreign secretary in February 1938, were the chief architects of British appeasement during its final disastrous phase. Eden's departure was interpreted as a danger signal in Moscow—not that he had been a consistent and unfaltering champion of collective security. But Chamberlain's record was not one to inspire confidence, and his remark that the "peace of Europe must depend on the attitude of . . . Germany, Italy, France, and ourselves" had a sinister ring to Soviet ears. The prime minister was regarded as a spokesman for the most reactionary strata of the British bourgeoisie, a class that Soviet publicists never tired of berating for its pro-fascist proclivities. He confessed privately to "the most profound distrust of Russia."[18] His abhorrence of Communism probably contributed at least as much to his feelings on the subject as the opinion of his military and diplomatic advisers that the Red Army, particularly after the purge, was not to be relied upon in a major conflict. Rather than open hostility, the Soviet government received the silent treatment from Britain in 1938.

Chamberlain and Halifax would undoubtedly have preferred a death struggle between the German and Soviet dictatorships as the ultimate solution to Britain's problems. At any rate, Moscow's ripening suspicions were to be confirmed in the Munich Pact. Until that time Stalin continued with increasing reluctance to side with the proponents of a collective security policy, over which Litvinov still presided at the diplomatic level. It seems likely that Molotov, Andrei Zhdanov, and possibly others in the Politburo grew disillusioned with the undignified and unrewarding courtship of the Western powers long before the Czech crisis. Anti-fascism was by no means an immutable principle to the pragmatic Stalin, and he must often have toyed with the notion of a deal with Hitler. But the curt rebuff attending the Kremlin's cautious soundings in the winter of 1936–1937 —through the Soviet trade representative in Berlin—did not encourage further overtures until 1939. That Litvinov survived the Great Purge when his aides were falling around him like tenpins is convincing evidence that Stalin valued his services as the interpreter of Soviet foreign policy to the democratic world and contemplated no immediate change in its anti-fascist complexion.

The Austrian *Anschluss* prompted a reaction from Moscow in the form of a press statement by Litvinov on March 15, 1938, that Czechoslovakia could count on Soviet aid in fulfillment of their mutual assistance treaty provided France likewise stood by her obligation. On the 17th Litvinov used the same medium to invite the powers, either within the League framework or outside it, to discuss the "practical measures which the circumstances demand"—that is, to take a "firm and unambiguous stand in regard to the problem of the collective salvation of peace." Notes were dispatched on the same day to London, Paris, Prague, and Washington calling attention to the Litvinov declaration.[19] Polite but discouraging answers were forthcoming. Halifax told the French ambassador that the proposal did not possess "any great value," and Chamberlain informed the House of Commons on March 24—the day of the British reply—that the Soviet invitation was unacceptable because the negotiation of "mutual undertakings in advance to resist aggression" would take away the government's freedom of action to choose war or peace in a specific situation.

Perceiving no obstacle to his plans for the conquest of Czechoslovakia, Hitler conferred with his generals on April 21 and set October 1, 1938, as the absolute deadline for an attack. The "softening up" process was begun three days later by Konrad Henlein, a Nazi agent and the leader of the Sudeten German minority, in a speech at Carlsbad virtually demanding the dissolution of Czechoslovakia as a sovereign entity. Chamberlain bowed to the increased pressure by openly suggesting the cession of Czech border territory to Germany in an informal press interview on May 7. Prague stood firm against this "friendly" counsel. Czech opinion was cheered by the forthright statement on the 8th of Mikhail Kalinin, the titular Soviet president, that his government would "fulfill all [its] obligations toward Czechoslovakia and France to the last letter."[20] Bonnet sought out Litvinov in Geneva the next day and was told substantially the same thing. But the Soviet commissar added the proviso that military support would not be attempted without the permission of either the Polish or Rumanian government. Since Poland would almost certainly refuse such a request, Bonnet consulted the Rumanian foreign minister and received a negative reply. The recently ratified constitution forbade the passage of foreign troops across Rumanian soil without special legislation. Subsequent feelers in Warsaw revealed that the Poles were adamant in refusing transit rights to the Red Army.

Later in the month the Czech government ordered a partial mobilization in anticipation of a possible German attack. London and Paris reprimanded Prague for acting too hastily, while Moscow, judging from the Soviet press, maintained a formally correct attitude toward its alliance commitments. The "May crisis" passed without incident, although Hitler was goaded by the taunts of the Western press into stepping up his military preparations. The German generals did not share his optimism that Czechoslovakia could be vanquished by political action and a localized war. They considered Russian intervention a likely eventuality, and many, anticipating a general war with grave apprehension, prepared to remove Hitler as a last extremity.

During the summer months Germany threw up a diplomatic smoke screen by pretending interest in a peaceful settlement of the Sudeten issue; and Henlein was told to go through the motions of conducting separate negotiations with the Prague authorities. London completely ignored Moscow, and Soviet commentators charged that Lord Runciman's mission to Prague in August to mediate between the Czech government and the Sudeten party (a bit of blackmail on Chamberlain's part which he had the effrontery to claim was in response to an official Czech request) was an attempt to isolate Czechoslovakia from her allies and to prepare her as a sacrifice to the "peace" of Europe.

Paris, though none too pleased with the Runciman mission, took no steps to counter the distinct drift toward a partition plan by seeking diplomatic support from Moscow. Late in August Bonnet approached the Soviet ambassador in Paris on the question of Russian aid for Czechoslovakia; and he instructed the French chargé in Moscow to obtain Litvinov's views in the event that Warsaw and Bucharest held to their previous course. Litvinov suggested an appeal to the League to overcome the problem of transit rights and received an evasive reply to his inquiry about France's intentions. He also brought up the matter of Russo-Czech-French staff conversations—once again to no avail—and reverted to his March 17 conference proposal, a scheme that might at least produce a collective declaration. The impasse continued as Bonnet and Litvinov returned to Geneva for the next session of the League Council on September 9. Bucharest had relented to the extent of withdrawing its objections to the passage of Soviet aircraft; but troops were in a different category, and the Rumanians refused to budge.

Anticipating Franco-British capitulation, Hitler gave orders on September 9 for "Operation Green" (the invasion of Czechoslovakia) to begin on the 30th of the month. Nazi propaganda against Prague as an adjunct of international Communism had already gone into high gear. "Moscow and the eternal grimacing Jewish-Bolshevist rabble" behind "these absurd pygmies" (the Czechs) had brought on the crisis, Herman Goering charged in a speech at the annual party rally in Nuremberg on the 10th. Hitler's belligerent address two days later signaled a rising of the Sudeten Germans which the Czechoslovak government met by prompt and generally effective measures. Henlein broke off his talks with Runciman and fled to Germany on the 14th. By this time Chamberlain had announced that he would fly to Germany to meet Hitler. At his mountain retreat near Berchtesgaden, the Nazi leader presented what amounted to an ultimatum: "self-determination" for the Sudeten Germans—*i.e.*, the annexation of the Sudetenland to the Third Reich. Returning to London, Chamberlain consulted his colleagues and saw Daladier and Bonnet. On the 19th the two democratic powers sent the Czech government a series of "proposals" incorporating Germany's demands on the Sudetenland. In truth, the document went Hitler one better by calling for the dissolution of the Czech alliance system in return for an "international guarantee" of Czechoslovakia's new boundaries.

Czech opinion, both official and popular, was staggered by this unprecedented betrayal. Such demands from Hitler were expected; from "allies" it was unthinkable. Only the Soviet government, which Chamberlain and Daladier had studiously ignored throughout the crisis, pledged itself anew to carry out its treaty obligations. The prospect of war, with Communist Russia as Czechoslovakia's sole partner, was more frightening to some of her statesmen than surrender to the Anglo-French terms. President Eduard Beneš was not among this company. He was assured by the Soviet minister in Prague on September 21 that regardless of what France did Russian support would be forthcoming whenever the League declared Germany the aggressor. When Beneš observed that a delay of this sort might prove disastrous in view of Czechoslovakia's isolated position, Moscow sent immediate word that Soviet assistance could be counted on as soon as the case was presented to the League.

Exhausted by his sleepless ordeal, Beneš was not prepared to withstand the overwhelming pressure from the West and the importunities of the cabinet simply on the strength of the Soviet pledge, however sincere it might be. The government acquiesced late in the afternoon of the 21st as the nation submitted to the decision in the sullen anger of bitter frustration. Chamberlain flew to meet Hitler the next day with every expectation that "peace in our time" was now assured. In his own words, he was "profoundly shocked" to learn that the Nazis had raised the ante in his absence. For a brief period it looked as if war might come after all. The Czechs mobilized on the 23rd, and a salutary air of confidence blew across the country. Moscow warned Warsaw that their non-aggression treaty would be denounced if Polish troops moved into Czechoslovakia. Rumania and Yugoslavia displayed a friendly attitude toward Prague, thus giving further pause to the jackal-like behavior of Poland and Hungary in their eagerness to share the prospective spoils. London, Paris, and Prague agreed that the new German conditions, which would have meant abandoning territory with an indisputably Czech population, were unacceptable.

On the evening of September 26 the British Foreign Office issued a statement declaring that if "a German attack is made upon Czechoslovakia the immediate result must be that France will be bound to come to her assistance, and Great Britain and Russia will certainly stand by France." This resolute pronouncement bore none of the ear-marks of a Chamberlain-Halifax creation, and for the first and last time during the crisis the U.S.S.R. was mentioned in an official British document. Yet the reference was not based upon direct and recent information from Moscow—simply the assumption that the Soviet government, which had unfailingly emphasized its fidelity to the Czech treaty, would be eager to respond when called upon. It was a symptom of Western obtuseness that the Soviet leaders could not fail to collate with other disturbing signs that their country was still regarded as a pariah—albeit more dangerous than the weak Com-munist state of the twenties—to be ignored and rebuffed unless the extremity of the danger warranted fighting fire with fire.

War now seemed inevitable despite everything Chamberlain had done to appease the Führer. "How horrible, fantastic, and incredible," he reported to the British people in an agony of disbelief, that "we should be digging trenches and trying on gas-masks here because of a quarrel in a far-away country between people of whom we know nothing." Rather than a considered statement of fact, his words re-flected an emotional unwillingness to face the reality that the fate of Czechoslovakia was indeed interlocked with the security of the British Empire. The miraculous respite for which he longed came on the 28th —an invitation from Hitler to a conference in Munich. Daladier and Mussolini were also invited. The latter's inclusion was pronounced "monstrous" by the Moscow *Izvestia*, particularly in view of the ab-sence of either a Soviet or a Czech representative. Chamberlain, in an access of exalted optimism, was determined that he should not be deprived of this last chance for peace. And he was not denied, for Daladier remained passive while a "compromise" was worked out granting practically all that Hitler had asked.

The Munich agreement was signed in the early morning of Septem-ber 30. Prague accepted the *Diktat* at noon before word again came from Moscow that the Czechs could depend upon Soviet military support in any eventuality. Just what measures the Russians would —or could—have taken the Western world was never to know. The rump state that survived was militarily indefensible and soon became a German vassal. Over 800,000 Czechs and 2,825,000 Sudeten Germans were included in the territory annexed by the Reich. By their cynical abandonment of Czechoslovakia, the two Western de-mocracies gained eleven months of crisis-ridden peace; in return they wrecked the once elaborate French security system and served notice upon the Soviet government that its counsel and assistance were of little moment in the affairs of Europe. Moreover, Hitler was in effect given a blank check to do as he wished in the East, although there is no convincing evidence that Chamberlain and Daladier, however dishonorable their actions at Munich, had been motivated by more than a frantic but mistaken desire for peace.

Only if the Soviet leaders had been afflicted with the blind staggers could they have avoided drawing from Munich the elementary conclusion that collective security was a bankrupt illusion. And whatever their deficiencies in other respects, Stalin and his underlings had a lively concern for the safety of the state and a correspondingly flexible disdain for the ideological superstructure of international Communism. Having stood by Czechoslovakia and Spain with unswerving loyalty, the Russians were at the peak of their moral influence; but in the absence of more substantial rewards, Moscow preferred the bulwark of political security to the purity of lofty motives. As Potemkin, then a deputy commissar for foreign affairs, so candidly put it in an interview with the French ambassador on October 4: "My poor friend, what have you done? For us I see no other way out than a fourth partition of Poland."[21]

IV

The Asiatic member of the fascist triplice—Japan—was no less a threat to the Soviet Union than her European partners during the perilous years from the Rhineland *coup* to Munich. Moscow's attempt to withdraw from Manchuria, the worst danger spot, by selling the Chinese Eastern Railway[22] had only temporarily alleviated the ever-present tension with Tokyo. Inner and Outer Mongolia became the new arena of conflict as Japan's creeping aggression sought with considerable success to wrest the northernmost provinces of China from Nanking's control without arousing the international repercussions attending the Manchurian invasion.

Outer Mongolia, a Soviet protectorate since 1921, lay athwart the path of conquest, and a never-ending series of border incidents became particularly serious by early 1935. During the second half of the year representatives of the Mongolian People's Republic and Manchukuo met in Manchouli in an attempt to reach agreement on the disputed issues. With Moscow's encouragement behind the scenes, the Manchukuo-Japanese demands for the "opening" of Mongolia were resisted, and the failure of the conference led to new border clashes in December.

The Soviet press assumed a more peremptory tone toward Tokyo's ambitions in the area. A Mongol delegation, including the prime minister of the Republic, visited Moscow during the winter to confer about the situation. Russia's determination to fight if challenged was proclaimed in February 1936 by Stalin himself during an interview with Roy Howard, an American newspaper publisher: "If Japan ventures to attack the Mongolian People's Republic, seeking to destroy its independence, we will have to assist the Mongolian People's Republic." On March 12 a "pact of mutual assistance" was signed in Ulan Bator, the Mongolian capital, promising Soviet aid in case of aggression. These measures, climaxed by the formal treaty, had a wholesome effect upon Soviet-Japanese relations. During the summer raids into Outer Mongolia ceased altogether, though Japanese provocations along the Siberian frontier were not infrequent.

The basis for a more amicable relationship was laid in the fall of the year: a new eight-year fisheries convention was tentatively agreed upon, negotiations at Manchouli on the border dispute were resumed, and the Japanese oil concession in northern Sakhalin was renewed. But following the conclusion of the Anti-Comintern Pact,[23] Moscow assumed a stiffer attitude. The Manchouli Conference was suspended, and the Soviet government refused to sign the draft agreement on the fisheries. Tokyo was kept dangling, however, by a one year extension of the convention just before it expired at the end of 1936.

Diplomatic incidents mounted during the next year. Official relations became so strained that the Russian embassy in Tokyo was virtually in a state of siege; and the closing of consulates, the retaliatory seizure of vessels, and innumerable other tokens of mutual displeasure amounted to a diplomatic—and occasionally even military —conflict of major proportions.

When the Japanese invasion of China began in July 1937 the Soviet government was assured, at least temporarily, that its territory and that of its Far Eastern satellite was safe from attack. Before that date relations between Moscow and Nanking had been none too cordial. The Chinese government had twice protested the Soviet-Mongol pact as an unwarranted infringement of its sovereignty in Outer Mongolia and had looked askance at Soviet penetration of Sinkiang. By accepting Japanese absorption of the northern provinces, Chiang hoped to reach an accommodation with Tokyo based on an anti-Communist and anti-Soviet platform. His paramount concern was the internal Communist threat, and in its elimination he had lavished a goodly portion of the military and financial resources of the state.

Even after the Canton Commune fiasco[24] the Comintern had been unable to comprehend the un-Marxian phenomena of rural Communism without "proletarian hegemony" and had authorized the

Moscow-trained Li Li-san to continue the policy of urban insurrection. The failure of the "Li Li-san line" led to his recall to the Soviet Union in March 1931, but not until 1933 did the Central Committee of the Chinese party move from Shanghai to the real center of Communist power—Juichin, the capital of Mao Tse-tung's "Chinese Soviet Republic" in Kiangsi. Three "bandit suppression" campaigns by the central government (December 1930–October 1931) had been repulsed by the Red guerrilla armies. Following the partial collapse of the prolonged fourth campaign (June 1932–February 1933), Chiang discarded the strategy of a frontal assault for one of blockade and encirclement. The Kuomintang army now had German military advisers, of whom the senior officer, General Hans von Seeckt, had once commanded the Reichswehr in the earlier years of its collaboration with the Red Army.

The fifth attempt finally dislodged the "bandits" from southeast China. To escape the enveloping Kuomintang trap, the main body of some 90,000 Communists from the Kiangsi area set out in October 1934 upon the famous "Long March," a tortuous 6,000 mile trek to the northwest. The armed exodus, led by Mao Tse-tung and Chu Teh, followed a westerly course into Yunnan, turned abruptly northward along the western border of Szechwan, and then shifted to a northeasterly direction until the haven of northern Shensi was reached. Pursued most of the way by Nationalist troops—the government periodically announced the enemy's destruction—the Chinese Red Army also overcame incredible hardships of climate and terrain in a feat without parallel in military history. No more than 20,000 of the original marchers completed the year-long journey. By propaganda and by a "Robin Hood" policy of expropriating from the rich to help the poor, the Communists acquired millions of sympathizers, some of whom joined the ranks to replace those who died or dropped out along the line of march.

From their new base of operations—the city of Yenan became the capital after its occupation in December 1936—the Chinese Reds were able to play a strategic role in the intricate Moscow-Nanking-Tokyo power struggle. In South China they could preach but not practice resistance to the Japanese invader; in Shensi it was possible to conduct large-scale partisan warfare against the forces of Nippon. Furthermore, the proximity of Russian territory theoretically placed the moral and material resources of a great power at their disposal. Contact between Moscow and the Chinese Communists had been limited and irregular during the early 1930's, and the ascendancy of the Maoist leadership in the party appears to have been accomplished without Soviet interference. But this relative autonomy did not signify a lack of orthodoxy, for despite its agrarian base and predominantly peasant composition, the party faithfully mirrored the Marxist-Leninist-Stalinist doctrines then prevailing in Moscow.

The conclusion of the Long March coincided with the Popular Front directives of the seventh Comintern congress. The Chinese Communists—quite possibly informed beforehand—anticipated the policy change, but they had no opportunity to go beyond a proclamation favoring an "anti-Japanese people's united front" before engaging in a battle for survival with their prospective allies. Because of the implacable hostility between the Communists and the Kuomintang since the 1927 split, meaningful cooperation, even against a common enemy, was not easily effected. Chiang certainly manifested no disposition for a truce. His political police seemed as eager as ever to equate anti-Japanese views with Communism.

Late in 1935 the National Salvation movement, beginning among university students, attracted popular support by its campaign for an end to the civil war and the appeasement of Japan. On November 1 Wang Ching-wei, Nanking's foreign minister and an advocate of more concessions to Tokyo, was wounded by an assassin. The attack was symptomatic of a growing feeling among Chinese patriots that the generalissimo (as Chiang preferred to be called) was pursuing a personal vendetta at the expense of national survival. Wang and his clique were ousted from the government not long afterwards as a gesture toward public opinion: "bad advice" could no longer excuse Chiang's conduct.

The government was not only unresponsive to popular sentiment during the course of the next year, but measures to suppress criticism were applied more ruthlessly than ever. Had Tokyo been content with Manchukuo and North China, it is probable that a common front against Communism—both the Chinese and Russian variety—could have been arranged with Nanking. Negotiations took place on a number of occasions, and on October 9 Chiang himself conferred with the Japanese ambassador without arriving at a definite understanding. He had spurned repeated overtures by the Communists, and even loyal supporters began to grow restless at his forbearance toward the Japanese. One of them, "Young Marshal" Chang Hsüeh-liang, who had been driven from Manchuria in 1932, was the commander of forces sent to blockade the Communists in their new Shensi homeland. At his headquarters in Sian, Chang, together with his *Tungpei* (northeastern, *i.e.*, Manchurian) troops, sampled the heady brew of National Salvationism and found it to their taste. He established such amiable relations with the Communists that in late October Chiang flew to Sian to investigate at first hand the causes of this mystifying insubordination. He became convinced that the *Tungpei* army was unreliable and should be withdrawn for more trustworthy troops. The extermination of Communism was still his *idée fixe,* and he refused to heed the Young Marshal's pleas for a united front against Japan.

Meanwhile popular indignation reached fever pitch when it was learned that seven leaders of the National Salvation Association had been arrested. At the same time, three crack divisions sent to inaugurate a new anti-Communist campaign were badly mauled by Red troops and beat a hasty retreat. The Young Marshal chose the occasion for a renewed appeal to the generalissimo to reconsider and allow the *Tungpei* army to fight with the Communists against the Japanese. Chiang replied evasively and furthered his preparations to exterminate the "Red bandits." On December 7, 1936, he and his staff arrived in Sian for another tour of inspection. He made it perfectly clear to Chang and the other generals that his opinion was utterly inflexible on the Communist issue. Too late, he sensed the explosive mood of resentment that his policy had aroused in Sian. Early in the morning of the 12th Chiang was "kidnapped"—that is, placed in protective custody—and all centers of Kuomintang authority in the city were seized by the Young Marshal's troops.

The incident became an immediate sensation abroad. It was widely believed that the affair was Communist-inspired and that the sinister hand of Moscow lay behind the plot. In reality the Russians were taken by surprise, though there is some evidence that the Chinese Communists knew and approved of Chang's plans. Chiang's detention was most inopportune for the Soviet government: the Nationalist leader headed the regime with which Moscow hoped to forge an anti-Japanese alliance. The elimination of Chiang, the arch-fiend of a few years back, would lead only, in the Kremlin's view, to civil war and an opportunity for further aggrandizement by the Tokyo militarists. The Soviet press therefore attacked the Sian insurrectionists and even went so far as to charge that Japanese agents (including Chang himself!) were implicated. The Chinese Communists had approved the *coup* and sent representatives headed by Chou En-lai to confer with the Young Marshal and his accomplices. Upon learning of Moscow's attitude—a peremptory message from Stalin to Mao Tse-tung reportedly ordered the Chinese Communists to use their influence to release Chiang[25]—they attempted to calm the *Tungpei* "radicals" and proposed a peace conference of all political factions to decide Chiang's fate and to organize national resistance to Japan.

In Nanking the censors were able for a time to suppress the rebel side of the story. Most foreign correspondents innocently accepted the government's propaganda handouts, which wove a fantastic mosaic of Red intrigue and conspiracy in Sian. Since few officials thought Chiang would emerge from his captivity alive, a muted struggle for the succession began without delay. Wang Ching-wei, hastily summoned from his German exile—he conferred with Hitler and other important Nazi leaders just before his departure for China—together with War Minister Ho Ying-chin, were the leading representatives of the pro-Japanese Kuomintang Right and the most likely candidates for supreme power. When word reached Chiang of these political maneuvers, he dropped his air of silent martyrdom and began to listen to the united front program of the "mutineers" that the Young Marshal and Chou En-lai respectfully submitted. By December 20 Chiang had agreed in principle to the demands of his captors but made no formal commitment to reverse his policy: he must return to Nanking with his prestige intact. Chang and the Communists were willing to accept his good faith as a pledge of their own sincerity. The junior *Tungpei* officers were less amenable to the arrangement. They were out for blood and found the Communist stand a puzzling contradiction to what they had previously understood of the Red position toward Chiang. In the end they allowed themselves to be persuaded, and the generalissimo flew back to the capital on Christmas Day accompanied by the "repentant" Young Marshal.

Assuming that Chiang had agreed to forego civil war for unity against Japan, the nation rejoiced at his deliverance. The immediate aftermath was not at all reassuring to popular opinion. The blockade of the Communist area was reimposed, and Sian was occupied by government troops. Chang was placed under house arrest, though his ten-year prison sentence was commuted. But in February 1937 the elaborate shadow boxing—a traditional ritual of Chinese politics—no longer concealed the *de facto* Kuomintang-Communist truce. In subsequent negotiations Yenan agreed to abandon its revolutionary role and to subordinate its army to Nanking's control. Chiang, for his part, promised reforms, particularly in the realm of civil liberties. By late spring an informal united front was achieved in essentials even if neither side could wholly overcome its long-standing distrust of the other.

Tokyo had foreseen the Nanking-Yenan alliance and was on its good behavior for a time in a futile effort to woo Chiang from the Communists. The Japanese were also fully aware that Sino-Soviet talks had been underway before the Sian affair and that its aftermath would probably serve to clinch an agreement between Moscow and Nanking that could only be anti-Japanese in intent. Soviet-Japanese relations were pitched at their usual state of controlled hostility. Neither power sought war, but Tokyo's "border probing" policy in Manchuria was revived on a somewhat larger scale late in June in order to test Russian defenses along the Amur River. Ostensibly the clash began over the possession of two islands in the river channel. Moscow did not force the issue, and Tokyo emerged the victor.

What might have provoked a serious international incident in normal times was quickly forgotten in the wake of a Sino-Japanese clash on July 7, 1937, at Marco Polo Bridge just outside Peking. Unlike the Mukden affair in 1931, the Japanese were not prepared for an immediate offensive. But when local attempts to settle the matter failed, the Imperial Army seized the opportunity to renew the conflict, dormant since the conquest of Manchuria. Within three months the Japanese occupied the populated centers of northern China against little organized resistance. Only the Eighth Route (Communist) Army under General Chu Teh, by the effective use of guerrilla tactics learned by painful experience against Kuomintang troops, withstood the Japanese assault. Shensi and western Shansi, the Communist domain, remained inviolate throughout the war.

Moscow had offered Nanking a mutual assistance pact in the spring of 1937, but it had been declined for fear of offending Tokyo. Now that Japanese sensibilities no longer mattered, China expressed an interest which the Soviet government failed in its turn to reciprocate. Russian opinion tallied with the general consensus that China's fighting capacity was too feeble to resist Japan for more than a few weeks. However, a long pending non-aggression pact was signed on August 21. In addition to the customary provisions of such treaties, Nanking accepted the Soviet position in Mongolia and Sinkiang. The agreement signified a new era of Sino-Soviet collaboration which, unlike the case with the Western democracies, was not seriously impaired by the Nazi-Soviet Pact of 1939. Until Russia was herself attacked, Soviet military aid and technical advice was one of the mainstays of Chinese resistance. Moscow granted at least $300,000,000 in credits during this period, and about half of the sum was actually spent before further deliveries were suspended in June 1941. Most of the Soviet military advisers and "volunteer" combat pilots were hastily withdrawn late in the summer of 1938 at the time of the Czech crisis. Supplies were sent exclusively to the Chinese Nationalist government, for Moscow was more anxious to curb Japan than to risk a recurrence of civil war by assisting the Chinese Communists.

The tacit united front between Yenan and Nanking, which had shown serious signs of disintegration prior to the Japanese attack, became official in September 1937; and for the first eighteen months relations were correct, if not entirely congenial. Friction on a local scale sometimes disturbed the prevailing harmony by late 1938; yet it was well into 1939 before the cessation of major Japanese military operations permitted a partial revival of political differences. The Nationalists, whose government was re-established in the remote Szechwan city of Chungking in 1938, deeply resented Communist expansion beyond their sector in the northwest. The Communist guerrilla armies behind the Japanese lines were obliged to maintain themselves without supplies from Chungking; and the trickle of matériel to Yenan disappeared entirely in 1939. The Kremlin's seeming disregard for the fate of Chinese Communism did not significantly weaken the bonds between Moscow and Yenan. If Mao and his colleagues had doubts about the wisdom of Stalin's policies, they gave no indication of it. Chinese "Trotskyists," for example, were pursued with unrelenting zeal because of their alleged pro-Japanese plottings, although their real crime involved resistance to party directives on collaboration with the Kuomintang.

As in the case of Spain and Czechoslovakia, Moscow's support of China also extended to the level of international diplomacy. Nanking's appeal to the League of Nations was considered at length in the autumn of 1937, and Litvinov missed no opportunity to prod its members into taking a bolder stand. On October 6 the Assembly accepted the report of the Far Eastern Advisory Commission naming Japan the aggressor. Litvinov regretted that the League offered only moral support for China, and the Soviet press took a sour view of the proposed meeting in Brussels of the Nine-Power (Washington Conference) treaty signatories as "empty chatter under cover of which the Japanese militarists will continue their criminal war against the Chinese peoples."[26] Moscow nevertheless agreed to participate, though she had not been a signatory, while Tokyo flatly refused to attend.

The conference opened on November 3, 1937, and confirmed the Kremlin's gloomy forecast. The United States failed to provide the leadership that some had been led to expect by President Roosevelt's notable "quarantine the aggressor" speech in Chicago on October 5. The British delegation was equally timid; and Litvinov departed in disgust before the meetings were adjourned on November 24. The conferees adopted a vapid final resolution expressing the hope that the Far Eastern conflict might somehow be peaceably resolved. Three days later Litvinov spoke in Leningrad with sarcastic and corrosive

bitterness of the Western powers, who were exerting "all their diplomacy to obtain confirmation and explanation" of the bellicose acts
and cynical declarations of Germany, Italy, and Japan. Perhaps, he
suggested, "they are groping for a deal with the aggressor."[27]

No further collective measures offered any impediment, moral or
material, to Japan's path of conquest in China. Chungking sought
assistance from the League Council on three subsequent occasions,
but each time Moscow's staunch support was unavailing. After the fall
of Canton and Hankow in October 1938, Tokyo was reluctant to commit more men and money to the Chinese quagmire. The Japanese
readily absorbed the lesson of Munich and preferred to turn southward toward the rich colonial empires of Britain, France, and the
Netherlands. Yet before the outbreak of the European war—an open
invitation for aggrandizement in Southeast Asia—Tokyo was still un-
decided about the best course to pursue. Through the sobering experience of actual military combat, the Japanese army learned that
war with the Soviet Union was not to be undertaken lightly. Despite
the purges, the high level of Soviet preparedness in the Far East by
1938 enabled Moscow to meet Tokyo's highhandedness with firmness
and resolution. As Zhdanov had advised the Narkomindel in a speech
on January 17 of the same year: "[It] should act more energetically in
regard to the insolent, hooligan, and provocative sallies of the agents
of Japan and Manchukuo."[28]

Japanese and Soviet arms clashed in a second trial of strength in
the summer of 1938 at Changkufeng Hill near Lake Khasan, a strategic location at the junction of the Manchurian-Korean-Siberian
frontier. Like the Amur River episode, which had been a relatively
minor affair, the fighting was preceded by border violations and
numerous other diplomatic complications. In the latter part of July,
Japanese patrols attempted to seize the strategic height and were
thrown back. Both sides gathered reinforcements estimated at over
50,000 troops apiece, and with the aid of artillery, tanks, and planes,
a major battle took place. The Japanese were soundly beaten. The
official casualty reports were contradictory, but the number of dead
and wounded must have totalled several thousand. A truce was arranged on August 11, and the Soviet forces retained *de facto* possession of the disputed area.

While an undeclared war had been averted by a mutual desire to
localize the conflict, relations between the two countries continued
to be extremely tense. Secret German-Japanese negotiations for a
military alliance against the Soviet Union were conducted in the last

half of 1938 and through most of the following year—until the signature of the Nazi-Soviet Pact dealt Tokyo a stunning blow.

In May 1939 another border dispute broke out near Lake Buir on the Mongolian-Manchurian frontier. At first the Kwantung Army (as the Japanese troops in Manchukuo were called) drove back the Soviet-Mongolian forces. But after heavy reinforcements, a Soviet counterattack in August inflicted severe losses on the Japanese and induced Tokyo to accept an armistice on September 16. With the Red Army in control of the region in dispute, a boundary commission later demarcated the frontier according to Moscow's claims. It was a costly lesson to the Japanese. They admitted 18,000 casualties and revealed with surprising candor that the Red Army had demonstrated its technical superiority. Since Moscow was by this time primarily concerned with European affairs and Tokyo with the South Pacific, an informal *modus vivendi* was attained that eventually received the official sanction of both powers.

V

The U.S.S.R.'s isolated position in post-Munich Europe gave rise to a bumper crop of rumors concerning her future intentions; but to outside observers the tangible portents of her policy were at first rather meager. The Soviet press assiduously contradicted Anglo-French statements designed to gloss over their neglectful treatment of Russia at Munich, and much space was devoted to establishing the proposition that the West was eager to push the Soviet Union and Germany into a war of extermination. The first major pronouncement on Soviet policy after Munich was Molotov's address on November 6, 1938, in connection with the anniversary celebration of the Bolshevik Revolution. He warned that "the second imperialist war has already begun on an immense field from Gibraltar to Shanghai," and he scoffed at the notion that weakness rather than fear of "a workers' movement" prevented the democracies from acting against the aggressor. While more contemptuous of the Western powers than any comparable public statement since 1935, the speech caught few overtones of the ferment in high party councils and aroused only perfunctory interest in London and Paris.

Soviet-German relations had not formally improved; yet to the discerning the less intemperate tone of the press and radio of both countries in commenting on the policy of the other—the result of an oral understanding in October between Litvinov and the German ambassador[29]—was an omen of no little significance. In December the two powers signed a routine trade agreement without the usual delays attending such transactions; and talks began on a broader basis, though they were confined entirely to commercial matters. At Hitler's diplomatic reception on January 12, 1939, it was widely observed that he spoke longer to the Soviet ambassador than to anyone else— a mark of deference that would have been scarcely credible six months before. Germany was no more willing to fight a two-front war than Russia was to face Germany alone; and it is a commentary on their deep-rooted antagonism that it took so long to reach an accommodation from which both parties expected to gain.

In March 1939 the eighteenth party congress met in Moscow—the last until 1952. As yet, neither the German nor the Soviet governments had made an overture to the other. Stalin, in presenting his report to the delegates on the 10th, contrived a difficult feat of verbal jugglery by issuing a warning and a rebuke to the Western powers—though still couched in the terminology of collective security—while delicately hinting to Berlin that he was open to suggestions. The speech drew upon the premises of Marxism to an extent that had become rare in Soviet declarations since the introduction of the Popular Front: "The new economic crisis must lead, and is actually leading, to a further sharpening of the imperialist struggle. It is no longer a question of competition in the markets, of a commercial war, of dumping. . . . It is now a question of a new redivision of the world, of spheres of influence and colonies, by military action." Stalin's analysis of the Anglo-French retreat before the aggressors was heavily edged with sarcasm, but it implied a willingness to join a genuine anti-fascist coalition. Nevertheless, one of the tasks of the party was "to be cautious and not allow our country to be drawn into conflicts by warmongers who are accustomed to have others pull the chestnuts out of the fire for them." If, on the other hand, there really were "lunatics in Germany" with designs on the Soviet Ukraine, "rest assured that we shall find enough strait-jackets for them." In one of his most striking passages, the Soviet dictator reminded the West that Russia too could be perfidious: "Far be it from me to moralize on the policy of non-intervention [*i.e.*, appeasement], to talk of betrayal, treachery and so on. It would be naïve to preach morals to people who recognize no human morality. Politics is politics, as the old, case-hardened bourgeois diplomats say. It must be remarked, however, that the big and dangerous political game started by the supporters of the policy of non-intervention may end in a serious fiasco for them."[30]

It was evident that Stalin had come to no definite conclusions about a course of action. To tread warily and to await developments was all that wisdom required for the moment. Five days after his address the

German army marched into Prague: Czechoslovakia had ceased to exist. Having flattered himself that he alone possessed an intuitive insight into the recesses of Hitler's mind, Chamberlain was at last aroused from his lethargy by this fresh outrage; for it was a personal affront as well as a cynical breach of a solemn international contract. But it required the combined pressure of press, Parliament, and public opinion before he reached the proper pitch of righteous indignation. London and Paris sent stiff notes of protest to Berlin; and Moscow, perhaps momentarily encouraged, permitted Litvinov to dispatch a scorching denunciation of the German move as "arbitrary, violent and aggressive."

The British were at first apprehensive that Rumania was to be Hitler's next victim. Halifax inquired of the Soviet ambassador on March 18 what his government would do if Rumania were attacked. Moscow's response was to propose a conference of the most vitally concerned powers at Bucharest. London rejected the idea as "premature." Warsaw, fearful of arousing Berlin's ire and ever suspicious of the Russians, had objected. Nor did the Poles welcome Soviet participation in a four-power declaration favoring consultation should Poland's integrity be threatened. Chamberlain found it ideologically comfortable and militarily feasible—since the Polish army was rated as good as if not better than the Red Army—to accept Warsaw's anti-Soviet phobia, and he declined to pursue the subject with Moscow. On March 31 he announced in Parliament an Anglo-French guarantee of Polish independence. The proceedings could hardly have bolstered the Kremlin's confidence—assuming that some residue remained—in the sincerity or wisdom of Downing Street's diplomacy.

Lacking a Soviet commitment, Chamberlain's coalition, enlarged to include Greece and Rumania on April 13, was a jerry-built structure; and he was frequently reminded of its precariousness by his political opponents. On April 15 the British ambassador in Moscow approached Litvinov with a proposition requiring Soviet intervention should the Western powers become involved in a war to protect Poland and Rumania against Nazi aggression. The Soviet counter-proposal suggested a triple alliance, a mutual guarantee of all states between the Baltic and the Black Sea, and a supplementary military convention. These features were too far-reaching for London and Paris. The Soviet government, quite understandably, demanded a binding military alliance, while Britain and France, sympathetic to the Eastern countries' fear of Soviet domination, wanted freedom to maneuver—to call upon the Russians only when needed and to avoid committing themselves to attack Germany should Hitler strike at Moscow.

On May 3, 1939, a Soviet communiqué announced the "resignation" of Litvinov and the appointment of Molotov to head the Narkomindel. Although the Moscow radio asserted that the change would not affect Soviet foreign policy—Stalin was not yet prepared to burn his bridges to the West—the significance of the event was fully recognized in informed quarters. Litvinov had always been identified as a "Westerner"; and as the showpiece of collective security, his departure from the diplomatic scene could not help but reflect the Politburo's decision to explore the possibilities of a bargain with Berlin. As a Jew, moreover, he was a favorite target of Nazi propagandists, and his replacement by the "Aryan" Molotov was calculated to smooth the path of negotiations.

The new foreign minister, a faithful henchman of Stalin's even before 1917, was farther up in the party hierarchy than either Chicherin or Litvinov had ever hoped to be, but he lacked their finesse and sophistication. Perhaps his methodical habits, rather dour demeanor, and lack of imagination were responsible for Lenin's reputed remark that he was the "best filing clerk in Russia"; and his dogged patience in outsitting all comers in matters of controversy had earned him the nickname "Stone Bottom" from the witty Radek.[31] Unquestionably an efficient administrator, he also possessed a tenacious memory and was to prove his mettle as a capable, if stodgy, diplomat within the bounds set by Stalin. He completed the Narkomindel's transformation—noticeably accelerated during the Great Purge—from a haven for relatively cosmopolitan Old Bolsheviks to a wholly subordinate bureaucratic instrument staffed with a new generation of professional civil servants.

Litvinov's dismissal was decisive in convincing Hitler and his advisers that Moscow's cautious feelers had been no false alarm. Berlin lost little time in making a formal approach, and from that point onward the thread of negotiations remained unbroken despite the lack of substantial initial progress. Yet it was apparently well into the summer before the Russians abandoned consideration of an anti-Nazi alliance. Whether they would have chosen partnership with the West in preference to a pact with Hitler cannot be ascertained, for the democracies failed to make the test on Soviet terms; but having offered an alliance in April and witnessed its rejection, the Soviet Union could not be reproached for acting in the interest of its own survival. The wisdom of that action, a germane question by the summer of 1941, was scarcely apropos in the summer of 1939.

The British attitude toward negotiating with the Russians was both languid and higgling when time was of the essence and details of little consequence. If, as Churchill told the House of Commons on May 19, he could not "understand all these refinements of diplomacy and delay," one need have no difficulty in guessing Stalin's state of mind. On May 27, five days after a German-Italian alliance ("the pact of steel") had been signed, London and Paris took a halting step in Moscow's direction by offering to discuss a tripartite pact. But the formula they submitted contained a number of significant reservations. Should the Baltic states, for example, serve as an invasion route for the Wehrmacht, the Western powers would not be obliged to go to Russia's aid.

Addressing the Supreme Soviet on the international situation at the end of May, Molotov made an informal answer to the most recent proposal by observing that it still fell short of complete reciprocity. Two days later Moscow presented a detailed critique demanding the elimination of all reservations preventing the automatic invocation of a mutual assistance pact in the event of German aggression virtually anywhere in Europe. On June 7 Chamberlain revealed that a representative was being sent to Moscow to supplement the efforts of the British ambassador. It became known the next day that the individual in question was William Strang, a junior official in the Foreign Office and unknown to the general public. Considering the delicacy of the task and the urgency of action, the choice of an envoy was unfortunate. Moscow had evidently expected Halifax or a figure of comparable stature. Chamberlain's critics were quick to condemn the appointment, recalling that he himself had flown to see Hitler upon three occasions. An invitation to Halifax through the Soviet ambassador on the 12th was turned aside with a noncommittal answer.

On June 15, 1939, the day after his arrival in Moscow, Strang and Molotov, together with the British and French ambassadors, were closeted for almost three hours. Frequent but shorter sessions followed. The West made some concessions, but with such seeming reluctance that the sincerity of its intentions was made to appear questionable. Molotov's manner was one of stubborn pertinacity, and the ungracious tone of the Soviet press was the clue to the Kremlin's irritation at what was regarded as quibbling procrastination on the part of the Anglo-French negotiators. The increasing exasperation of the Russians found an outlet in Zhdanov's candid article in *Pravda* on June 29. He reported that no substantial progress was discernible and concluded his critical analysis by declaring that the "English and French desire not a real treaty acceptable to the U.S.S.R., but only *talk* about a treaty in order to speculate before public opinion in their countries on the allegedly unyielding attitude of the U.S.S.R., and thus make easier for themselves the road to a deal with the aggressors." Zhdanov's insistence that the views expressed were his "personal opinion" which his "friends" did not share was strong circumstantial evidence that some members of the Politburo still preferred a Western orientation and that Stalin had not yet made up his mind.

In July, when London and Paris had at last met the Soviet requirement for a guarantee of the Baltic states, Moscow raised its price. The fresh difficulty arose over the question of defining "indirect aggression." The Russians' legitimate concern that an internal *coup* (*e.g.*, Austria and Czechoslovakia) would be grounds for invoking the reciprocal obligations of the treaty had to be squared with the Anglo-French fear —equally valid as it turned out—that Moscow desired to intervene in the internal affairs of her smaller neighbors to forestall the Germans. A mutually satisfactory formula was unfortunately never found.

The problem of linking the political and military aspects of the pact was less serious, but the Soviet government insisted that the two parts be signed simultaneously. As Strang cogently summed up the deadlocked parley on July 20: "We should perhaps have been wiser to pay the Soviet price for this agreement at an earlier stage, since we are not in a good position to bargain and since, as the international situation deteriorates, the Soviet price is likely to rise." The Russians are determined, he went on, "that any obligations which they undertake shall be clearly defined, with all the 'i's dotted and all the 't's crossed."[32]

At the end of the month it was announced that an Anglo-French military mission was being sent to Moscow. The members left London on August 5 by boat—a rather leisurely means of travel in an age of air transport. Two days later Strang flew home from Moscow with nothing to show for his efforts.

Military talks got under way on August 12, the day after the arrival of the mission. War Commissar Voroshilov headed the Soviet delegation. ("Thank God that that fellow [Molotov] will not participate in the military negotiations!" the French ambassador is reported to have exclaimed.)[33] He expressed his dissatisfaction that the British envoys lacked full plenipotentiary powers, but it was decided to proceed. The first sign of trouble came when Voroshilov asked for the Anglo-French plans in case of war. General Joseph Doumenc, the French representative, replied with prudent generalities that the Russian marshal pronounced meaningless. On the 14th a Soviet demand for the passage of her troops across Polish and Rumanian territory and for permission to occupy the islands and main ports of the Baltic states was received with consternation. Since Warsaw was expected to prove recalcitrant, the discussions were adjourned from the 17th to the 21st to allow sufficient time to win over the Poles. The secret German-Soviet *pourparlers* were now well advanced. On the 19th a commercial agreement between the two countries was signed, and rumors of an imminent diplomatic sensation began to circulate. On the authorization of his government, Doumenc informed Voroshilov on the 21st that the Poles had given their consent. In point of fact, Warsaw had not yet done so but had weakened under French pressure. Voroshilov seemed skeptical of Doumenc's assurances and insisted that Poland and Rumania, as sovereign states, should communicate directly with Moscow before resuming the conference.

On the same evening Berlin revealed that Joachim von Ribbentrop, the Nazi foreign minister, was flying to Moscow to sign a non-aggression pact. The Kremlin confirmed the report on the following day. Ribbentrop arrived about noon on the 23rd, and the agreement was concluded late that night. Although the forewarnings were plain enough in retrospect, the West was caught totally unprepared. As insurance against any complications with Berlin, Molotov hinted to the British and French ambassadors that the pact with Germany need not eliminate future collaboration in the "furtherance of peace." Already prepared to leave, the military mission lingered until Voroshilov stated bluntly on the 26th that a continuation of the conference would be fruitless. The mission departed on the same day. The death knell of collective security had finally been sounded.

NOTES

1. See above, p. 169.
2. Text in Degras, *Soviet Documents on Foreign Policy*, III, 131–32.
3. Maurice Thorez, *Son of the People* (London, 1938), p. 89.
4. *VII Congress of the Communist International: Abridged Stenographic Report of the Proceedings* (Moscow, 1939), p. 182.
5. See above, p. 189.
6. Alexander Werth, *Which Way France?* (New York, 1937), p. 288.
7. See above, p. 115.
8. *Documents on German Foreign Policy, 1918–1945* (Washington, 1949–), Series D, I, 734.
9. Adolf Hitler, *My New Order*, edited by R. de Roussy de Sales (New York, 1941), p. 400.
10. *New York Times*, November 27, 1936.
11. *Against Aggression: Speeches by Maxim Litvinov* (New York, 1939), p. 63.
12. Degras, *Soviet Documents on Foreign Policy*, III, 212.
13. Text in the *New York Times*, June 4, 1939.
14. Robert G. Colodny, *The Struggle for Madrid* (New York, 1958), p. 180.
15. See above, p. 77.
16. See below, p. 212.

17. *Populaire,* November 1, 1936, quoted in Franz Borkenau, *European Communism* (New York, 1953), p. 205.

18. Keith Feiling, *The Life of Neville Chamberlain* (London, 1946), p. 403.

19. Text in *Documents on British Foreign Policy, 1919–1939* (London, 1946–), Third Series, I, 62–64.

20. *Documents on German Foreign Policy,* Series D, II, 268.

21. Robert Coulondre, *De Staline à Hitler* (Paris, 1950), p. 165.

22. See above, pp. 178–79.

23. See above, p. 195.

24. See above, p. 157.

25. Edgar Snow, *Random Notes on Red China* (Cambridge, Mass., 1957), p. 2.

26. *Pravda,* October 28, 1937.

27. Degras, *Soviet Documents on Foreign Policy,* III, 266.

28. *Ibid.,* p. 270.

29. Hilger and Meyer, *Incompatible Allies,* p. 288.

30. Degras, *Soviet Documents on Foreign Policy,* III, 320–22.

31. Walter Duranty, *Stalin & Co.* (New York, 1949), p. 93; C. L. Sulzberger, *The Big Thaw* (New York, 1956), p. 89.

32. *Documents on British Foreign Policy,* Third Series, VI, 423.

33. *Nazi-Soviet Relations, 1939–1941* (Washington, 1948), p. 42.

CHAPTER EIGHT

THE NAZI-SOVIET MISALLIANCE

The secret negotiations leading to the uneasy bargain between Hitler and Stalin were neither as tortuous nor as protracted as the parallel discussions with the Western powers. Once Germany had resolved to secure Russian neutrality in the prospective war over Poland, she was able to outbid Britain and France with ease: as the aggressor, no moral or political scruples hindered her from making territorial concessions to Moscow in the East.

The thaw in German-Soviet relations had been slow in coming even after Stalin's speech of March 10, 1939. Berlin was properly alerted, but there was no immediate attempt to explore the implications of this new tack in the Kremlin's course. Early in April Georgi Astakhov, the Soviet chargé in Berlin, clearly indicated Moscow's interest in a possible agreement in his talks with German officials.

On April 17 Soviet Ambassador Alexei Merekalov had an interview with State Secretary Baron Ernst von Weizsäcker—the first since he had assumed the ambassadorship during the previous summer. Toward the end of the discussion, which concerned a commercial transaction, Merekalov seized an opening and turned the subject to politics. He pointed out that ideological differences had not greatly influenced Soviet-Italian relations and that there was nothing on the Russian side to prevent an improvement in relations with Germany. The ambassador returned to Moscow a few days later. Shortly afterward Potemkin left on a swing through the East European capitals to sound out the Poles, Turks, Bulgarians, and Rumanians on the prospects for halting Axis aggression. The results were not encouraging, and his prospective meeting with Halifax in Geneva was called off by the Soviet government.

Berlin began to take Moscow's hints more seriously after Litvinov's dismissal. The German press was told to avoid anti-Soviet comment, a development that Moscow only gradually reciprocated. Hitler asked for a briefing on Soviet policy, and Gustav Hilger, the counselor of the Moscow embassy, was recalled for the purpose. The upshot was a decision to make an overture to the Kremlin. Ribbentrop instructed the ambassador to Russia, Count Werner von der Schulenburg, to seek an interview with Molotov but to confine the conversation to economic questions. The meeting took place on May 20, 1939, and lasted more than an hour. Molotov was friendly but refused to be drawn out except for a reference to the necessity of constructing "political bases" before proceeding to economic negotiations. Schulenburg was told to "sit tight" and wait for Moscow to make the next move. Berlin grew alarmed, however, at the apparent progress of the Anglo-Russian parley, and Weizsächer saw Astakhov on May 30 in order to raise the topic of better political relations.

Although June brought an end to the "feeling out" period of Soviet-German contact, the two powers sparred cautiously, neither assured that the other was not using it as a pawn for some devious political finagle. Had the tenuous *pourparlers* been left to Hitler, Ribbentrop, and Weizsäcker, agreement might never have been reached. But in Schulenburg and Hilger the Bismarckian tradition remained alive. The latter conducted rather inconclusive talks—ostensibly on commercial matters—with Anastas Mikoyan, commissar for foreign trade; and Schulenburg, temporarily in Berlin, frankly told Astakhov that while his government desired a *rapprochment* a Soviet pact with Britain and France would be regarded as a hostile move. When the ambassador returned to Moscow late in June, he was received by Molotov, who failed to go beyond the theme that a normalization of relations would be desirable.

No discernible progress was made during the first half of July as the Politburo apparently debated whether to proceed with the trade negotiations. On July 22 the Soviet press tersely announced that economic discussions had been resumed. Five days later Dr. Karl Schnurre of the German Foreign Office outlined a prospective three-stage settlement of the differences between the two countries to Astakhov and Eugene Babarin, the Soviet trade representative in Berlin. Schnurre, still deliberately vague about political details, remarked that Germany, Italy, and the Soviet Union had at least one common ideological tie: opposition to the capitalist democracies. Ribbentrop contributed a veiled suggestion to Astakhov on August 2 that a partition of Poland might be arranged. When the Russian pressed him for more definite terms, the foreign minister promised to be more obliging as soon as the Soviet government evinced the desire for a new relationship.

Schulenburg, who had been instructed to extend the discussions to

Poland and the Baltic states if Molotov showed signs of abandoning his reserved attitude, was received by the Soviet foreign minister on August 3. The ambassador remained discreet since he found Molotov cordial enough but still reluctant to speak frankly. In reporting his impressions to Berlin, he acknowledged that the "old mistrust of Germany persists" and that Moscow seemed "determined to sign with England and France if they fulfill all Soviet wishes."[1] The Kremlin's strategy had been to spin out the negotiations with both sides and to await the best offer. The Anglo-French terms were by now well defined; no more concessions were to be expected. The German proposals were, on the other hand, just emerging from the shadows, and Molotov's reluctance to itemize Soviet demands was well calculated to flush out the real intentions of the Nazi regime.

On August 12, 1939, the German Foreign Office was notified through Astakhov that the Soviet government was prepared to take up "by degrees" the political questions previously raised and that the conference should be held in Moscow with either Schulenburg or a special envoy as the German representative. This was the signal Berlin had been waiting for. Ribbentrop sent a telegram that Schulenburg was to read to Molotov. Exuberantly optimistic about a mutually advantageous agreement, it requested a meeting with Stalin to allow the Nazi foreign minister to "set forth the Führer's views." Molotov was in a receptive mood when he saw the ambassador on the evening of the 15th, and for the first time he spoke of the possibility of a non-aggression pact. As for Ribbentrop's proposed visit, he deferred an answer but declared that such a journey required adequate preparation to insure something more than an exchange of opinion.

Schulenburg saw Molotov again on August 17 and read Ribbentrop's latest communication urging "a basic and rapid clarification of German-Russian relations" because of the "possibility of the occurrence any day of serious incidents" (an attack on Poland was set for August 26). Satisfaction was promised on all points raised by Molotov two days before: a non-aggression pact, a joint "guarantee" of the Baltic states, and Germany's good offices in settling Soviet-Japanese difficulties. Ribbentrop declared himself ready to fly to Moscow any time after August 18. The Kremlin was still excessively cautious, and Molotov read a friendly statement in reply, presumably reflecting Stalin's views, that failed to advance the pace of the discussions. The proposal to "dispatch such a distinguished public figure and statesman" was pronounced gratifying and in "noteworthy contrast" to Britain's action in sending "only an official of the second class to Moscow."[2]

A Soviet-German trade agreement was signed in Berlin on August 19. Credit was provided for Soviet purchases of industrial goods, particularly machine tools; and in exchange various raw materials were to be shipped to Germany. The immediate importance of the agreement was less economic than political, for it was quite likely the deciding argument in convincing the Russians of Germany's good faith. Schulenburg saw Molotov twice on the 19th. Ribbentrop was to arrive on August 27 or 28, and a draft non-aggression pact was furnished for transmittal to Berlin. On the 20th Hitler sent Stalin a personal message requesting that his foreign minister be received not later than the 23rd. Impressed, Stalin finally yielded and consented to Ribbentrop's arrival on that date. Hitler was beside himself with joy. "Now I have the world in my pocket!" he exclaimed as he drummed on the wall with both fists.[3]

The German delegation was greeted at the airport by Potemkin. With Stalin, Molotov, Ribbentrop, and Schulenburg the leading participants, a lengthy conference took place in the afternoon. Negotiations resumed in the evening and continued until a non-aggression pact was signed in the early hours of August 24. The utmost conviviality prevailed, and the event was celebrated with champagne. Stalin offered a toast to Hitler: "I know how much the German nation loves its Führer," he said,[4] perhaps unconsciously projecting an idealized image of his own relationship to the Russian people.

The portion of the treaty revealed to the public was not a novel diplomatic instrument. It contained the usual provisions regarding aggression, arbitration, and consultation; it was to run for ten years—fifteen unless denounced—and stipulated that neither party should join any combination of powers aligned against the other, thus forestalling the possibility of a Soviet move back in the direction of collective security. Yet it differed from previous Soviet non-aggression pacts in two respects: there was no clause providing for a denunciation of the agreement should one of the signatories commit an act of aggression against a third power; and the concluding article stated that the treaty "comes into force immediately after its signature" instead of the customary waiting period until ratification. The absence of the first item assured that there would be no hitch in the impending attack on Poland, while the inclusion of the second allowed Hitler to proceed with his plans at once and insured that neither partner would renege on the bargain.

The most significant part of the treaty was a secret protocol partitioning Eastern Europe into "spheres of influence." The Soviet portion included Finland, Estonia, Latvia, eastern Poland, and Bessarabia. The Germans, in addition, disclaimed political interest in south-eastern Europe. The absence of a more explicit Balkan settlement was an attempt to postpone controversy and thus to avoid delaying a general agreement. The pact with Germany must have seemed to the Kremlin a brilliant diplomatic *coup*. At one stroke the Soviet Union had secured a spectator's role in the impending European conflict; it had breached the *cordon sanitaire* to gain a political though not yet a territorial position in Eastern Europe approximating that of Tsarist Russia; and it had erected a buffer zone for insurance against Nazi duplicity. Moreover, the Soviet state had won precious time needed to complete its program of industrialization and military preparedness. The weakness of Britain, France, and Poland and the corresponding strength of Nazi Germany was as unexpected to Stalin as it was to Western observers.

The astounding news of the Nazi-Soviet Pact was released in a joint communiqué within hours of its signature. Stalin had objected to Ribbentrop's flowery and bombastic text on the grounds that it might unduly affront public opinion: "For many years now we have been pouring buckets of slop over each other's heads, and our propaganda boys could never do enough in that direction; and now all of a sudden are we to make our peoples believe that all is forgotten and forgiven?"[5] The Soviet dictator's brief lecture on diplomatic finesse was sufficient: the published text was sober and to the point. His concern about Russian opinion was certainly justified, for the population had been blanketed with anti-Nazi propaganda almost as thoroughly as the Germans had been with the anti-Communist variety. Yet the shock to Western opinion was hardly less great than that to the Russian public, and in this respect Stalin and his associates displayed complete indifference.

It was a measure of the Comintern's loss of influence and the growth of Soviet nationalism that the Communist parties abroad were kept in total ignorance of an event that was to inaugurate a 180-degree turn in the party line. If it had been possible before for non-Russian Communists to persuade themselves that the struggle for their ideals was something apart from Soviet foreign policy, now it was inconceivable save for the "hard core" of the most rigidly doctrinaire. After some days of floundering confusion and acute embarrassment, during which the party organs in the West attempted to deny the significance of the pact, the Popular Front balloon—already a somewhat leaky vessel—burst asunder. Unable to swallow the new line about a "second imperialist war," those who had been attracted to the party in the first place by its militant anti-fascist crusade defected in droves.

Even more serious to the Communist movement in Britain, France, and the United States was the now hostile milieu in which it was forced to operate. No longer did a large following among the liberal intelligentsia cushion the members from the shock of their own isolation. To the politically unsophisticated, Communism had always smacked of subversion and bloody revolution; and now that the party began to apologize for Nazi aggression, prejudice combined with fact to produce an impenetrable barrier of suspicion and aversion.

In government circles enough intelligence data on the Soviet-German negotiations had accumulated to blunt the impact of the shock. But it had gone largely unheeded, and most Western statesmen and diplomats were as incredulous as the general public. Some sections of the press tried at first to put a good face on this amazing diplomatic revolution. From Washington it was reported that persons "close to the State Department" believed that the agreement was "not very significant and that von Ribbentrop's trip to Moscow was only a bluff."[6] If there was similar naïveté at Downing Street and the Quai d'Orsay, it soon evaporated. The bitter truth was writ too large: Britain and France had been outmaneuvered. One could bemoan Moscow's perfidy, but it was the spectral phantom of the Munich betrayal which had returned to haunt the West.

None of the powers was more astonished and indignant than Japan, where the German move was correctly regarded as an act of bad faith and a breach of the Anti-Comintern Pact. Her diplomats had failed to take seriously several warnings of a possible Soviet-German accord, and even Ribbentrop's direct statement in June to the Japanese ambassador in Italy that a pact would be concluded had been considered an obvious bluff in Tokyo. The premier and his cabinet, unable to survive the humiliating diplomatic rebuff administered by Germany, resigned to make way for a caretaker regime. The ambassador to Berlin was instructed to lodge a formal protest with the German government, but Weizsäcker talked him into "postponing" it. For the time being, Japan's course was one of neutrality toward the European conflict and concentration on winding up the "China affair." On the question of Soviet-Japanese relations, her policy-makers were left to contemplate Stalin's remark to Ribbentrop which the latter passed on to Tokyo: "If the Japanese desire war, they can have war; if they desire an understanding, they can have that too."[7]

II

The German assault on Poland, put off from August 26, began at dawn on September 1, 1939. Berlin had half-expected an Anglo-French overture for a new Munich. Hitler professed indifference. His only fear, he told his generals a week before the opening of hostilities, was that "some *Schweinhund* [would] make a proposal for mediation."[8] But the declaration of war by Britain and France on September 3 laid to rest any lingering doubts about a new era of appeasement. The swift collapse of Polish resistance was a shock to Western opinion, nourished as it was on the illusion that Poland was entitled to great power status in European affairs. Without sharing this attitude, Moscow was likewise unprepared for the crushing victory of the Wehrmacht. Indeed, Molotov, Zhdanov, and probably Stalin himself, had anticipated a further retreat by the Western powers; and to balance the disparity of strength between Poland and Germany it had been strongly intimated that the Poles might expect Soviet aid in the form of supplies. Before Warsaw could obtain confirmation of this surprising offer, Moscow reversed its position. In a message to his government on September 8 the Polish ambassador quoted Molotov as saying that the "intervention of Great Britain and France [had] created an entirely new situation."[9]

The Kremlin was henceforth concerned with implementing the provisions of the secret protocol. As early as September 3 Ribbentrop wired Schulenburg to take up with Molotov the advisability of Soviet occupation of its allotted sphere. But Moscow preferred delaying tactics to see how the Poles fared and to avoid overt partisanship during the struggle. On September 7 a partial mobilization of the Red Army was ordered; and though it was conducted in secrecy as far as possible, a run on consumer goods and reports of hoarding signified considerable popular alarm. The press and other propaganda media had not yet clarified the new departure of Soviet policy, and the belief was widespread that Germany—no other enemy was conceivable to the masses after so many years of anti-Nazi indoctrination—was the object of these military measures. The speed of the Nazi advance obliged Moscow to make its move earlier than had been anticipated, for a march into eastern Poland after an armistice between Warsaw and Berlin would have clearly marked the Soviet Union an aggressor nation. Molotov explained to Schulenburg on the 10th that the government intended to announce its intervention in order to save the Ukrainian and Byelo-Russian population from the German "threat." Ribbentrop, no doubt after consultation with Hitler, registered his objection and attempted to needle Moscow into faster action by calling attention to the "political vacuum" and the "construction of new states" that might occur in the Soviet zone in case of further delay in fulfilling the secret partition plan.

On the morning of September 17 the Red Army crossed the Polish frontier. Warsaw's ambassador was formally notified of the invasion in a communication stressing the collapse and "internal bankruptcy" of the Polish state. The Soviet government avoided giving undue offense to Berlin by referring to the Ukrainian and Byelo-Russian population of Poland as its "blood brothers" who had been "left without protection." In conclusion Moscow declared its intention of taking "every step to deliver the Polish people from the disastrous war into which they have been plunged by their unwise leaders and to give them an opportunity to live a peaceful life."[10] Because of Moscow's later decision to avoid overrunning ethnic Poland, this final comment was omitted from the subsequently published versions of the statement. The next day a disingenuous joint Soviet-German communiqué was released explaining that the intervention of both powers was aimed at restoring "peace and order" and helping "the Polish population to reconstruct the conditions of its political existence."[11] The announcement had been drafted by Stalin, who objected to the original German formulation as unnecessarily frank. His suspicion that German troops would not stop at the line previously agreed upon—they had in fact already crossed it in some places—was allayed by Ribbentrop in a message sent on the 19th. Three days later Voroshilov and the German military attaché concluded formal arrangements for the occupation of the conquered territories.

Polish resistance to the Soviet troops was feeble. It was later declared that the Red Army's casualties were only 737 killed and 1,862 wounded. Informed Western observers had previously assumed the existence of secret provisions of the Nazi-Soviet Pact. The Soviet occupation of eastern Poland tended to confirm their judgment, but there was ample room for speculation as to the full meaning of Moscow's act. While few adjectives were spared in condemning the attack on moral grounds, even so skeptical a critic of Soviet policy as Neville Chamberlain warned against a premature verdict on the "motives or consequences of the Russian action"; and Lloyd George cautioned: "It would be an act of supreme folly to place the Russian advance in the same category as that of the Germans."[12] There remained a hope that Moscow might yet come into the Western camp, if only because, as the London *Daily Express* put it, "the two thieves may fall out over the division of the spoils."

Soviet public opinion was hardly less confused by the turn of events, though "spontaneous" meetings were held throughout the country to orient the masses on the oppressive policy of the Poles in dealing with their Ukrainian and Byelo-Russian minorities. In the lower ranks of the Red Army there was similar bewilderment; even the officers, on the assumption that they had come to fight the Germans, "liberated" Polish towns to the applause of the equally misinformed local population.

Stalin originally contemplated the existence of a residual Polish state, but by September 19, when Molotov told Schulenburg that the time was ripe for a definitive agreement on the future of Poland, he had changed his mind. Ribbentrop assented and prepared for a second trip to Moscow. Arriving on September 27, he received a more lavish reception than upon the occasion of his first visit. After an all night conference a "boundary and friendship treaty" was signed in the early morning of the 29th. The heart of the agreement was contained in one of the secret supplementary protocols: Poland was partitioned on a line to the east of the Pissa, Narev, Vistula, and San rivers (the boundary set in August). Moscow was thus provided with a more ethnically justifiable frontier, for it was close to the Curzon line in the center with westward bulges, totalling about 8,000 square miles, in the north and south. In return for this territorial concession to Germany, most of Lithuania was placed within the Soviet sphere. A further provision was made for a transfer of populations. Approximately 235,000 Germans were eventually repatriated from eastern Poland and the Baltic states, while some 56,000 Ukrainians, Byelo-Russians, and Jews left the German portion of Poland.

A joint declaration accompanied the treaty. It called upon Britain and France to end the war; otherwise, both Germany and the Soviet Union would undertake to "engage in mutual consultations with regard to necessary measures." This was the prelude to a far-ranging "peace offensive," soon to be echoed by the Communist movement abroad. In reality Soviet security rested precisely upon the continuation of the war. As long as Hitler's hands were tied in the West, he could have no thought of turning upon his "friends" in the East. But having thoroughly committed himself to the German partnership, Stalin spared no effort to prove his good intentions. There was one path, however, that did not tempt him: a military alliance. The Russians had gone to such lengths to avoid war that the notion of deliberately seeking it, even after the fall of France demonstrated the helplessness of the West, was entirely alien to their aspirations. Whatever may be said about the morality of the Kremlin's method of reclaiming its lost territory in the East, Soviet moves during the 1939–1941 period were basically defensive. Yet Nazi propaganda skillfully created the impression that a secret military pact had been concluded with Moscow; and in London and Paris there was intense concern that the Ribbentrop visit presaged an even more formidable coalition against the democratic powers.

Soon after the fourth partition of Poland, the Russians consolidated their position in the Baltic region. Their first move was made on September 18 when Tass, the Soviet news agency, released a statement complaining of Estonia's unneutral conduct in the case of an escaped Polish submarine. The Estonian foreign minister hastened to Moscow for "trade negotiations." Confronted with the threat of a Soviet attack and abandoned to her fate by Berlin, Estonia bowed to relentless pressure and signed a pact of mutual assistance on September 28, 1939, granting Moscow the right to maintain military, naval, and air bases.

Latvia was next, and her foreign minister conferred directly with Stalin and Molotov—a mark of deference denied the Estonian envoy —at the Kremlin early in October. He, too, surrendered to the Soviet ultimatum and signed an agreement on the 5th almost identical with that concluded by Estonia. Five days later Lithuania fell into line. The treaty included a few mitigating features which at least preserved the illusion of equality between two grossly unequal states. As an additional token of favor, Vilna, the medieval capital of Lithuania seized by Poland in 1920, was returned. The comparatively generous treatment of Lithuania was presumably a reward for her resistance to German demands (Latvia and Estonia had signed non-aggression pacts with Berlin the previous June) and for her confirmed enmity toward Russia's enemy—Poland.

Although the three Baltic republics now became Soviet protectorates, there was no interference in their domestic affairs. Content for the moment to strengthen its military hold on the Baltic littoral, Moscow made much of its forbearance in declining—unlike the rapacious capitalist countries—to gobble up its smaller neighbors. The Soviet press could not mention the fact that Germany represented the only potential threat to Russian security via the Baltic states. Britain thus took on the role of the power against whose menacing designs on northeastern Europe the Soviet Union had supposedly been obliged to intercede.

In the case of Finland, the Soviet government quickly discovered that the tactics so effective in bringing its three tiny Baltic neighbors into line were less persuasive. Even during the century of their sub-servience to Tsarist Russia, the Finns had enjoyed an autonomous status denied the other non-Russian nationalities. As an independent republic, Finland had maintained a parliamentary regime on the model of the other Scandinavian nations, though the strength of the Finnish Right—anti-Soviet and pro-German—had at times been a source of grave concern to her democratically minded citizens. But Finland's leaders had carefully avoided commitments that would jeopardize their country's neutrality in a European conflict. On October 5, 1939, Molotov suggested to the Finnish minister in Moscow that Helsinki send a representative to discuss a number of "concrete political questions" affecting Soviet-Finnish relations. He refused to elaborate, but there could be no mystery about the nature of the business to be transacted in view of the recent pacts with the other Baltic states. Yet Moscow's aims were entirely strategic and involved no desire to delimit Finnish sovereignty. The "Mannerheim Line," Finland's network of fortifications across the Karelian Isthmus, was at some points within artillery range of Leningrad; and the Gulf of Finland exposed the city to possible attack by water.

Moscow had initiated secret talks with Helsinki as early as April 1938 in an effort to seal off Finland as an avenue for German aggression. Neither then nor later did the Finns respond favorably to Soviet offers to lease or exchange for territory elsewhere some of their islands in the Gulf of Finland. But the Kremlin's mood was less tractable by the time of Molotov's renewed invitation. On October 8 Molotov expressed impatience at Helsinki's delay in sending an envoy for the negotiations. Juho Paasikivi, the Finnish minister to Sweden and a former prime minister, left for Moscow on the evening of the 9th, and the government ordered partial mobilization the following day as a precautionary measure. Stalin himself took charge of the discussions —eight in all. The Soviet proposal for a mutual assistance pact was soon abandoned in the face of Finnish opposition. The difficulty arose over Stalin's other demands: the frontier at the Karelian Isthmus to be moved about twenty-four miles farther north of Leningrad (compensation was offered by the cession of twice as much territory in a nonstrategic area); the lease of the port of Hangö at the head of the Gulf of Finland for use as a naval base; the cession of four islands in the Gulf; a boundary adjustment at Petsamo near the Arctic Ocean; and demilitarization of the Soviet-Finnish border.

On October 23, after the Finnish delegation returned to Helsinki for consultation, Paasikivi presented a formal reply offering to give up the islands and to push the isthmus frontier about eight miles northward. The other points were rejected. Moscow pronounced these concessions inadequate, and the parley was temporarily suspended. On the 31st Molotov spoke at length on Soviet foreign policy before the Supreme Soviet and devoted a good deal of attention to relations with Finland. Since the details of the negotiations had been kept confidential, the Finns considered publicity without prior notification a highly improper procedure. Now, they correctly surmised, Soviet prestige as a great power would permit no retreat.

When conversations were resumed on November 3, neither side was disposed to compromise on a major issue. Molotov bluntly told the Finns: "We civilians seem unable to accomplish anything more. Now it is up to the military to have their say."[13] But negotiations were not broken off until the 13th, and the Finns departed for home with the expressed wish that another conference might take place with more satisfactory results. The Soviet press and radio loosed verbal thunderbolts at Helsinki's "ruling clique" in which Marshal Carl Mannerheim, the aged "butcher" of the Finnish civil war in 1918, figured prominently. In the light of later events, the Finns would have been well advised to submit to the Russian terms. They were not unreasonable in the context of East European power politics, though admittedly Helsinki's case was impregnable from a moral and legal standpoint. Finland relied too heavily on the sympathy and support of the Western democracies and upon Soviet forbearance. The latter's good behavior over a period of two decades had lulled Finnish opinion into a complacent mood about the possibility of an attack, leaving the country psychologically unprepared for war even when the menacing tone of Soviet propaganda became unmistakable.

On November 26, 1939, Moscow complained to Helsinki that artillery shells had been fired across the frontier on the Karelian Isthmus resulting in a number of casualties to Russian soldiers. To all appearances, the alleged provocation was a deliberately contrived border incident—a *casus belli* for which the Finns were to be blamed. Two days later, after Helsinki had denied responsibility and refused Moscow's demand to withdraw its troops at least twelve miles from the isthmus boundary, the Soviet government denounced the non-aggression treaty between the two countries. Moscow severed diplomatic relations on the 29th, charging that attacks against Soviet forces "are known to be continuing" at several places along the frontier. The Finnish government made a last gesture of conciliation by offering a troop withdrawal and proposing a resumption of the Stalin-Paasikivi talks. The Kremlin ignored the appeal, for the Red Army had already been set in motion.

On the morning of November 30 Soviet troops violated the frontier in force, and bombers began a series of raids on Helsinki and other cities. Shortly thereafter a new Finnish "government" composed of Finnish political refugees was established at Terijöki, a border town. It was headed by Otto Kuusinen, a leading figure in the Comintern since its inception. On December 2 Moscow solemnly concluded a mutual assistance pact with this appendage which more than satisfied its previous claims. Rendered sluggish by their own propaganda, the Soviet leaders gave every indication of believing that the Finnish masses, exploited by their "capitalist" masters, would rally to the Kuusinen regime and welcome the Red Army with gratitude. Whatever possibilities existed along these lines—sympathy for Communist Russia had been far from negligible among Finnish workers—was nullified by the Kremlin's blunderbuss tactics. The nation was united as it had never been before in its determination to resist attack. The device of using a puppet government as a civilian front for a military operation was not a new Soviet technique. Used unsuccessfully in the Finnish civil war and in the Polish war of 1920,[14] it had brought more gratifying results in the Mongolian campaign of 1921.[15]

As the underdog fighting the Russian behemoth, Finland won worldwide sympathy. Much of it was anti-Communist reflex action. As Sir Stafford Cripps, soon to become the new ambassador to Moscow, wryly commented: "Now, naturally, all of Russia's enemies talk about the sacredness of Finnish democracy, not because they love democracy but because they hate Russia."[16] But moral approbation for Finland's cause brought too little of tangible value to fend off the invader. The League of Nations, already moribund after years of placating the Axis powers, was abruptly resurrected to chastise the Russians. On December 14, 1939, the U.S.S.R. was expelled from the organization with an appropriate resolution of censure. It was supremely ironic that Litvinov's Cassandra cries, fallen upon deaf ears for so long, had at last found a ready response when the aggressor state was Communist rather than fascist. Though the Soviet press, because of Berlin's sensibilities, was content to ridicule the League without moralizing, the action could only have strengthened Stalin's conviction that Anglo-French appeasement had been a calculated attempt to turn the German menace eastward.

Germany's policy was outwardly one of strict neutrality. Her leaders were well aware that the sudden Soviet concern for the sanctity of Leningrad and its approaches did not arise from the hypothetical threat presented by Britain. Yet as befitted the party to a business deal that had not yet begun to sour, Berlin, far from manifesting resentment at Moscow's action, gave encouragement to the Russian case through the medium of the press and secretly assisted Soviet submarines in the Gulf of Bothnia. Almost every other non-belligerent—even Fascist Italy—gave some sort of moral or material support to the Finns, with Britain and France providing most of the munitions. Opinion in the West was not only anti-Soviet on ideological grounds; it was widely believed even in official quarters that Russia and Germany were secret military allies and that helping Finland only furthered the struggle against the common foe. Popular pressure for a diplomatic rupture with Moscow was heavy. In February 1940 the French police raided the headquarters of the Soviet trade organization and the homes of its employees; and in March the Soviet ambassador was declared *persona non grata* by the French government and recalled to Moscow.

At a time when Soviet relations with the West had deteriorated to their lowest state since the days of intervention, Anglo-French military strategists conceived a dubious scheme to strike a double blow at Russia through the Scandinavian countries and the Middle East. Unwilling to carry the attack to the German army across the defensive fortifications of the Maginot Line, they were nevertheless prepared to deploy men and matériel in an expedition that could only have strengthened the bond between Hitler and Stalin. In retrospect the dangerous foolhardiness of the plan seems almost incredible. Its military rationale centered on the idea of cutting off Germany's source of iron ore in northern Sweden; yet it is impossible to avoid the suspicion that anti-Soviet political motivations underlay the project.

By early March 1940 an Allied force of perhaps 50,000 men was preparing for the expedition to Finland. Delayed by the refusal of the Swedish and Norwegian governments to grant transit rights, London and Paris were considering measures of coercion when reports of Russo-Finnish armistice negotiations caused the campaign to be abandoned. The notion of attacking the Soviet Union in the Caucasus involved a plan to bomb the oil fields of the Baku area. The Turks, bound by the provisions of a recent military pact with Britain and France, were to violate Soviet territory in a diversionary operation while Allied submarines disrupted Soviet shipping in the Black Sea. Set for late June or early July, the scheme was frustrated, not by the conclusion of peace between Moscow and Helsinki but by the smashing Nazi victory in France and the Low Countries.

The "Winter War" had meanwhile ended as most military experts had foreseen—in a decisive Russian victory. But it had lasted long enough to tarnish the Red Army's reputation and to confirm the impression of Western military experts that the purges had eliminated the Soviet Union as a first-rate military power for some time to come. Moscow had entered the conflict half-prepared, complacent in the belief that a few inferior divisions would perform the necessary military task while the Finnish masses made short work of their "reactionary" government. By the beginning of the new year, as the courage of Finland's gallant army aroused the surprised admiration of world opinion, the Russians perceived that a change in tactics was mandatory. In place of dissipating much of their strength in poorly coordinated assaults through the deep pine forests guarding the Finnish frontier from Lake Ladoga to the Arctic, they decided to concentrate an overwhelming force, with proper tank, artillery, and air support, in front of the Mannerheim Line.

The Red Army renewed its offensive on February 1, 1940. The fortifications were breached within two weeks, and in early March the exhausted Finns yielded to Moscow's terms. Helsinki had previously dispatched a steady barrage of peace feelers through various neutral channels, but not until late in January did the Soviet government jettison the Kuusinen government and indicate a readiness to negotiate. Since only military defeat could soften Helsinki's stand, nothing came of the ensuing exchange of communications via Sweden. Peace negotiations began on March 8 after a Finnish delegation arrived secretly in Moscow. Confronted with more onerous conditions than they had been led to expect, the Finns balked at first. The Finnish commander-in-chief, Marshal Mannerheim, advised that the military situation on the Karelian Isthmus was untenable, and Helsinki instructed its envoys on the 11th that the Soviet demands would have to be accepted. The peace treaty was signed during the evening of the next day. According to official totals, the Russians lost 48,745 dead and 158,863 wounded, the Finns 19,576 dead, 43,500 wounded, and 3,263 missing. Both sides may be suspected of minimizing their casualties.

The peace settlement, considered at the time a defeat for the Allied cause, did not impair Finnish independence and was more generous than Moscow could have exacted. But to the Finns the terms were unreasonable and unjust, for nearly a tenth of their pre-war area—much of it of great economic value—was lost. Territorial concessions included the Karelian Isthmus in its entirety, together with the northern and western shore of Lake Ladoga; minor territory near Kandalaksha and on the Rybachi and Sredni Peninsulas of the Arctic Ocean; a number of islands in the Gulf of Finland; and a thirty-year lease on the Hangö Peninsula. In addition, the Russians secured transit rights to Norway and Sweden, the demilitarization of Finland's Arctic coastline, and a non-aggression agreement.

Although Helsinki's fears of further Soviet aggression were probably unjustified, Moscow's hectoring attitude—particularly the Soviet veto (October 1940) of the proposed defensive alliance and political union between Finland and Sweden—was not helpful to the restoration of mutual respect. Nor did the Finnish leaders, by their drift toward a pro-German policy, exercise the discretion expected of a small power genuinely struggling to avoid the strangling embrace of either of her powerful neighbors.

III

The fate of Finland had loomed large in world affairs during the "phony war" in the West. It was all but forgotten, however, in the hectic period following the German invasion of Denmark and Norway on April 9, 1940. The Russians had not been forewarned of Germany's Scandinavian venture. The Soviet press dutifully attacked the Allies as "warmongers" who had forced the action on Berlin, but Moscow was disturbed by the news, notwithstanding the fact that any Anglo-French move against Russia, notably the contemplated descent upon Baku, would have to be abandoned. Nevertheless, as long as Sweden remained a neutral buffer, the Kremlin was not unduly alarmed; and the necessary reassurances to Molotov's inquiry about Germany's intentions were furnished by Ribbentrop on April 15 in a definite promise to respect Swedish neutrality.

Now heavily engaged in the West, Germany betrayed some anxiety about Russia's attitude. During the winter their positions had been reversed. Stalin had then gone out of his way to demonstrate Soviet benevolence toward Germany. "The friendship of the peoples of Germany and the Soviet Union, cemented by blood, has every reason to be lasting and firm," he assured Ribbentrop in answer to a message honoring his sixtieth birthday in December 1939.[17] As the initiative once more passed to the Russians, Stalin declined Hitler's invitation, broached late in March, for a state visit to Berlin. Nor would he permit Molotov to attend in his stead. When Hitler celebrated his birthday on April 20, a greeting from the Soviet dictator was conspicuously absent from the list of such messages announced in Berlin.

The Soviet government, satisfied that its Baltic flank was reasonably secure, looked to its political defenses in southeastern Europe. The most significant immediate development was the opening of secret talks in the Turkish capital between Soviet and Yugoslav representatives at the end of March. The absence of diplomatic relations between the two countries determined the choice of a neutral site for the parley. Belgrade's reorientation toward Moscow, late in coming, was conditioned wholly by the collapse of the Little Entente and the fear of an attack by one or both of the Axis partners. The discussions· were transferred to the Soviet capital after a Yugoslav delegation, officially described as a trade mission, arrived late in April and concluded a commercial agreement with political overtones on May 11,

1940. But to Belgrade's disappointment an outright guarantee of Soviet assistance in case of Italian aggression was not forthcoming, and the negotiations were suspended. Moscow was apparently deterred by the knowledge that such a pact might seriously impair its relations with Berlin, while the latter held a tight rein on her ally's Yugoslav ambitions so as not to offend the Russians. Despite Ribbentrop's best efforts, Italo-Soviet relations continued to be strained until a temporary improvement set in during the summer months.

The Russians had not yet collected their Bessarabian patrimony from Rumania; and Soviet press attacks and frontier incidents in the spring kept Bucharest in a state of nervous anticipation. At this juncture Germany launched her major assault in the West. The whole structure of Soviet foreign policy had been geared to the premise that Anglo-French military power would effectively checkmate the Nazi juggernaut. Moscow was staggered by the swift capitulation of the Dutch and Belgians and by the rout of the French army. Until the end of May the Soviet press and radio predicted that an Allied counterattack would yet save the situation. When it failed to materialize, the silence of *Pravda* and *Izvestia*—they failed to publish a leading article on the war during the month of June—was more eloquent of the Kremlin's alarm than a barrage of editorials. Outwardly Moscow was calm in the face of this shattering reversal of its strategic calculations; and Germany appeared satisfied that the Russians were maintaining a "positive attitude" toward her military triumphs. On June 17 Molotov warmly congratulated Schulenburg on the splendid success of the Wehrmacht—a lump of sugar to sweeten the news that Estonia, Latvia, and Lithuania were being "coordinated." Anglo-French intrigue in trying to sow discord between Germany and the Soviet Union in the Baltic states was responsible, the Russian foreign minister solemnly declared.

The occupation of the three Baltic countries by the Red Army had been surprisingly circumspect. Authoritarian and anti-Communist though they were, the regimes were allowed to remain politically intact. Only the knowledge that Russian forbearance might end at any moment obliged the Baltic leaders to trim their sails. Nearly all preferred German to Soviet occupation, for property relations were in no danger of alteration under the Nazi theory of society. Lithuania was the first to succumb to Soviet domination. On June 15, 1940, following an ultimatum from Moscow, the government resigned, and Red Army detachments entered the major cities of the Republic. The president and other top officials fled to Germany, and a new cabinet was formed under the guidance of Vladimir Dekanozov, a deputy commissar for foreign affairs sent from Moscow for the purpose. Political prisonners—chiefly Communist—were released as panic spread among the wealthier portion of the population. But no measures of socialization were immediately instituted.

On June 16 Molotov presented identical demands to the Estonian and Latvian ministers in Moscow. Both countries hastened to comply as Soviet reinforcements poured across the frontiers. The Lithuanian pattern was repeated: Zhdanov organized a pro-Soviet and non-Communist government in Estonia; Andrei Vyshinsky, the famed prosecutor at the Moscow trials, performed a similar service in Latvia. Communists and other pro-Soviet elements were so vociferous in their enthusiasm that a few disorders broke out and were suppressed at Moscow's behest. Concerned with measures of national defense, Stalin had no desire to be embarrassed by social disorganization on what was in effect a new German-Soviet frontier.

For the time being the Russians were content to develop "independent" regimes outside the Soviet system. The capitalist order was undisturbed. Elections—plebiscites in effect—were held in mid-July, and in each country more than 90 per cent of the ballots cast favored a single slate of candidates running under a "Union of Working People" label—a pro-Soviet party organized for the occasion. Thereafter the total absorption of the Baltic states was inevitable. The new parliaments requested admission into the U.S.S.R. and proceeded to carry through various measures of socialization. On August 1 the Supreme Soviet met in Moscow; on the 8th the three countries officially became the fourteenth, fifteenth, and sixteenth Soviet Socialist Republics. The means of legitimizing the annexation were crude, but Moscow was in no position to acknowledge the strategic rationale of the move; nor was it seemly to refer to the Tsarist title deeds to furnish a legal gloss to the transaction.

Bessarabia and northern Bukovina were also incorporated into the U.S.S.R. at the same session of the Supreme Soviet. Rumania, no longer able to object to the seizure, had come into Germany's political orbit after the fall of France. Attempting to strike before Berlin's control was complete, Molotov told Schulenburg on June 23 of the Soviet plan to annex Bessarabia—already within the assigned Soviet sphere—and Bukovina, which had never belonged to Russia but was partly inhabited by Ukrainians. Berlin raised no objections about Bessarabia, but its inscrutable attitude toward the acquisition of Bukovina induced the Soviet government to settle for the northern part of the region. Within forty-eight hours of an ultimatum to Bucharest on June 26 several divisions of the Red Army took possession of the "ceded" area. The Rumanian government was secretly advised that Germany regarded the Soviet occupation as a mere "temporary adjustment" and that Hitler "would settle things later."[18] As in Poland and the Baltic states, a population transfer took place. Some 300,000 persons, about one-third German, were evacuated to Rumania proper or to Germany, and over 150,000 refugees, chiefly Jews and Ukrainians, left Rumania for the Soviet-occupied territories.

The settlement of the Bessarabian question closed an era of surface cordiality in Soviet-German relations. A strained politeness was the best that could be managed by the autumn months. On the other hand, Moscow's relations with the West underwent a perceptible change for the better. London's attitude had become less hostile following Chamberlain's resignation on May 10, 1940, and the elevation of Churchill to the prime ministership. The latter's extreme views on Communism were a matter of public record, but as a lonely advocate of collective security with the Soviet Union in the 1930's he had not mixed ideological sentiment with political realism in the Chamberlain manner. On May 23 Moscow was informed that Ambassador Sir William Seeds, recalled after the outbreak of the Finnish war, would not be returning to his post, and an inquiry was made as to the acceptability of Sir Stafford Cripps as a special envoy in charge of trade negotiations. Long a Left wing socialist—he had a year before been expelled from the Labor party for publicly opposing its timid policy—Cripps was a recognized friend of Russia, and the choice was expected to please the Kremlin. The Soviet government declined to receive him on the condition proposed but hinted that he would be welcome as a replacement for Seeds. This solution was adopted, and Cripps arrived in Moscow on June 12 together with Erik Labonne, the newly appointed French ambassador.

Cripps was received by Stalin on July 1 in a manner that Churchill later described in exaggerated tones as "formal and frigid." He presented a friendly personal message from the prime minister which made a veiled bid for Anglo-Russian collaboration against Hitler: Britain was ready to "discuss fully any of the vast problems created by Germany's present attempt to pursue in Europe a methodical process by successive stages of conquest and absorption."[19] Stalin had no wish to compromise himself in Berlin's eyes and ignored the overture. Aware that Hitler might turn upon him at any moment, he was inclined to dismiss the danger and to abide by the Nazi-Soviet Pact as long as possible. Cripps was soon discouraged by the lack of response to his proposals but constantly persevered in his efforts to improve relations.

Berlin's attitude toward Moscow was increasingly wary, though there was no outward sign of friction. During the last part of July Hitler consulted his military advisers about a possible attack on the Soviet Union in the fall. Organizational difficulties were insurmountable upon such short notice, and it was decided in principle that an invasion would be lauched in the spring of 1941. While presumably subject to revision, the decision was based upon a cold-blooded estimate of Germany's political and military situation; it had nothing to do with the achievements or blunders of Soviet foreign policy. The immediate problem of the Nazi government still centered upon beating Britain to her knees—a project already viewed with considerable pessimism insofar as a cross-channel invasion was concerned—and as long as that task was unfinished Hitler could not countenance a strong Russia in Eastern Europe.

By the late summer of 1940 it appeared that the failure to define the respective German and Soviet spheres in the Balkans would be the major source of trouble between the two powers. Rumania, now an easy prey to the territorial demands of Bulgaria and Hungary, was the focal point of the hidden rivalry between Moscow and Berlin. On August 19, and again ten days later, Soviet notes to Bucharest protested various frontier incidents in a manner suggesting a desire to include Rumania in the Russian diplomatic orbit. On August 30 Germany and Italy guaranteed Rumania's boundaries, a move clearly aimed at Russia. When Schulenburg called on Molotov the next day to inform him of the guarantee and of the so-called Vienna Award—a territorial settlement in Hungary's favor that Berlin forced on Bucharest—the Soviet commissar was very reserved and claimed that Berlin had violated the consultation provision of the non-aggression pact. Ribbentrop took exception to the statement; and after an exchange of correspondence with Schulenburg, Molotov was presented with a memorandum explaining Germany's position. But the tough-minded Molotov persisted in maintaining that the cession of Rumanian territory to Hungary had not been made in good faith: Berlin could not have been in doubt about Moscow's interest in both countries.

Schulenburg returned to Berlin to report to his superiors on September 21. Molotov had given him a detailed reply to the German memorandum containing an offer to amend or delete the article specifying consultation. Ribbentrop returned a soft answer, promising a personal letter to Stalin reviewing the political situation. Molotov would be invited to Berlin for a general discussion. By this time Rumania had fallen completely under the Nazi sway. German troops poured into the country, ostensibly to train the Rumanian army.

Moscow was obliged to accept this diplomatic setback with no outward show of concern. Berlin, however, was fully aware of the resentment that had been aroused.

The Danubian Conference called by Berlin on September 12 was a further source of irritation to Moscow. The Russians were partially mollified when the existing international machinery for the settlement of Danubian questions was scrapped and a new commission was organized in Bucharest. The first session was held on October 28, with only representatives of the riparian states and Italy present. A public exchange of recriminations between Moscow and London on Soviet participation in the commission helped to conceal the real issue: a power struggle over the lower reaches of the river. The Russians proposed a joint commission with Rumania to administer the lower Danube; and since the Germans objected to what would in effect be Soviet control, the Bucharest Conference, deadlocked from the first, was finally adjourned on December 21.

Another point that irked the Kremlin was German aid to Finland, an arrangement begun in the late summer of 1940. Berlin successfully conveyed the idea that the Sovietization of Finland on the order of the Baltic states would be a dangerous undertaking. Yet Germany's support of the Finns was explained as an anti-British move—just as the Soviet government had publicly justified its measures against Finland on the same grounds. In answer to Molotov's inquiry on September 26 about German troops in Finland, Ribbentrop assured him that the matter involved only the transfer of certain units to the northern part of Norway. But Molotov's persistence in returning to the question denoted the Kremlin's anxiety. The Finnish government became increasingly pro-German, though the people were largely anti-Nazi as well as anti-Communist; and the likelihood of a second round in the Russo-Finnish war seemed a distinct possibility to neutral observers.

On September 26 Moscow received more unwelcome—though not unexpected—news: formal notice that Germany, Japan, and Italy were signing a mutual assistance treaty in Berlin the next day. The Tripartite Pact was primarily aimed at the United States, for it obligated the signatories to aid one another "with all political, economic, and military means" if attacked by a power not yet involved in the European or the Sino-Japanese war. (A separate article stated that the agreement in no way affected the relations of the three powers with Moscow.) The Russians made no overt expression of displeasure, but they could hardly avoid inferring that the Anti-Comintern Pact was perhaps being revived in a more sinister form. Ribbentrop ignored Molotov's request that he provide the full text of the treaty, including any secret protocols, before signature. He delayed a reply until October 2 and then maintained that in view of the nature of the treaty, which fully protected Russian interests, no consultation was necessary under the terms of the Nazi-Soviet treaty. He further asserted—quite falsely—that there were no secret provisions of the Tripartite Pact.

Schulenburg returned to Moscow in mid-October carrying a personal letter from Ribbentrop to Stalin. German policy since the Polish campaign was summarized at length, and an offer was made on behalf of the Axis powers to share with the Soviet Union the "historical mission" of dividing the world into spheres of influence. Molotov was invited to visit Berlin to discuss the matter in detail. Stalin's answer, brief and businesslike, accepted the invitation on Molotov's behalf but was otherwise non-committal.

The German capital was drab and damp under leaden skies as Molotov and his large entourage arrived on November 12, 1940. The pomp and glitter of the reception furnished a stark contrast to the inhospitable weather. Ribbentrop and his Russian guest were soon closeted for a briefing on the Nazi project. The Soviet Union's portion of this "territorial readjustment" would be in the Middle East, where it was suggested that the most advantageous access to the open sea might be found in the Persian Gulf and the Arabian Sea rather than through the Mediterranean.

In the afternoon Molotov and Hitler conferred together for some three hours. The Nazi leader was in an amiable mood, and with his customary verbosity he outlined a vague but grandiose scheme of global partition which Ribbentrop had already sketched. The tenor of Molotov's remarks made it clear that his instructions had been explicit on the point of resisting German attempts to lure Russia from the Balkans toward less strategic areas. He failed to obtain explicit answers regarding Soviet interests in Bulgaria, Rumania, and Turkey; nor did the Führer respond with directness to his queries about Finland's future status and the boundaries of Japan's "Greater East Asian Sphere."

Their conversation the next day was more specific, and the inherent difficulties of reaching an agreement became obvious. Hitler tried to assure Molotov that Germany was not politically concerned with Finland and that the country was still considered a part of the Soviet sphere. Promising a withdrawal of all troops should a general settlement be made, he persisted in farfetched speculation about British and American intervention in the Baltic area as a spurious reason for the "transit" of German units through Finland. As for the Balkans,

Hitler refused to abandon the Axis guarantee of Rumania, though Molotov bluntly stated that it was aimed at the Soviet Union. He likewise refused to accept a Russian guarantee of Bulgaria, pleading the necessity of first consulting Mussolini. His only concession was a promise of German support for a revision of the Montreux convention on the Straits. Since Moscow had in mind separate negotiations with Turkey, the offer was hardly generous.

In a final effort to arrive at an accommodation, Ribbentrop and the Soviet foreign minister met for a late evening session. The talk took place in the air raid shelter of the Wilhelmstrasse: British bombers had been sent over Berlin for the express purpose of interrupting the conference. When Ribbentrop spoke of England as "finished," Molotov reportedly replied, "If that is so why are we in this shelter and whose are these bombs which fall?"[20]

Ribbentrop submitted a draft treaty between the Soviet Union and the three Axis powers.[21] A ten year pact, it provided for political and economic cooperation, including respect for "each other's natural spheres of influence," consultation on problems arising from their mutual contact, and an agreement not to join or support any combination of powers directed against the four signatories. Two secret protocols were to supplement the public portions of the treaty. One defined in general terms their respective "territorial aspirations" outside Europe: Germany, Central Africa; Italy, North and Northeast Africa; Japan, the area south of Manchukuo and the Japanese home islands (the exact boundaries to be clarified through diplomatic channels); and the Soviet Union, southward "in the direction of the Indian Ocean." The other was a tentative agreement to exert pressure on Turkey to bring her into "political collaboration" with the four powers and a declaration that the Straits convention would be revised in Russia's favor. Ribbentrop also expressed Berlin's hope that a Soviet-Japanese non-aggression pact might result from the more cordial atmosphere induced by the prospective quadripartite treaty.

The stolid Molotov was not to be dazzled by the seductive mirage that his host so adroitly conjured and stubbornly returned to the Balkan question. Nor would Ribbentrop budge from the position that he and Hitler had previously stated. He simply reiterated the proposition that Germany had no territorial interests in the Balkans. Molotov promised to consult Stalin and left Berlin about noon of the following day—November 14. A joint communiqué pronounced the conference a success, but London correctly inferred that nothing substantial had been accomplished.

Moscow's formal answer was delivered to Schulenburg on November

25, 1940. The draft four-power agreement was declared acceptable subject to a number of conditions: German troops to be withdrawn from Finland, Bulgaria (including a military and naval base near the Straits) to be recognized as within the Soviet "security zone," the area "south of Batum and Baku in the general direction of the Persian Gulf" to be placed in the Soviet sphere, and Japan to renounce her oil and coal concessions in northern Sakhalin. These terms merely confirmed Hitler's opinion that Russia could not be induced to give up her European interests in favor of Germany—in other words, that Soviet foreign policy would remain independent and therefore potentially dangerous to the security of the Reich. Although Molotov solicited Berlin's comment, the courtesy of a reply—even "off the record"—was not extended to the Kremlin.

Hitler's war plans were now advancing rapidly, and on December 18 he released a personal memorandum to his commanders on "Operation Barbarossa"—the famous directive outlining his scheme to "crush Soviet Russia in a quick campaign." He placed special emphasis upon secrecy and set May 15, 1941, as the target date.

The Nazi leaders made haste to consolidate their hold on the Balkans once Russia's ambitions had been clarified. Only three days after Molotov's departure, King Boris of Bulgaria arrived in the German capital at Hitler's invitation. Bulgaria was expected to adhere to the Tripartite Pact, just as Hungary, Rumania, and Slovakia (the "independent" remnant of Czechoslovakia) did during the next few days. Berlin, however, agreed to allow Sofia a period of grace to soften the shock to Bulgarian opinion. The Russians vainly sought to keep the door from being slammed in their faces by frequent representations to Sofia; and the semi-legal Bulgarian Communist party carried on anti-Axis propaganda in a vain that was still forbidden, even by indirection, to the Western parties. Assured of Germany's protection, the Bulgarian government declined on November 30 the Soviet offer of a mutual assistance pact.

Early in the new year Moscow received information about German troop concentrations on the Bulgarian frontier. The Russian ministers in Sofia, Bucharest, Budapest, and Belgrade were recalled for consultation, and on January 13, 1941, Tass released a sharply worded statement denying foreign press reports that the Soviet government had been consulted or had consented to the troop movement. After this oblique warning failed to elicit an explanation from Berlin, Molotov protested to Schulenburg on January 17; and Dekanozov, the new Soviet ambassador to the Reich, told Weizsäcker that his government would "consider the appearance of any foreign armed forces on the territory of Bulgaria and of the Straits as a violation of the security interests of the U.S.S.R."[22] Ribbentrop instructed Weizsäcker and Schulenburg to justify the presence of German troops in the Balkans as necessary for the "sole purpose of preventing the British from gaining any foothold on Greek soil," where the Italian army had become bogged down after launching an attack the previous October. Moscow was hardly mollified by such a transparent explanation; but to prevent a serious breach the question was not reopened, though Soviet pressure on Bulgaria was unremitting in a final effort to prevent her from becoming a German satellite.

At length Berlin chose to consolidate its position without further hesitation. Schulenburg informed Molotov on February 28, 1941, of Bulgaria's adherence to the Tripartite Pact; and on March 1 the Kremlin was told that the Wehrmacht was crossing the frontier. The Soviet reaction was awaited with some apprehension. Since it was confined to words—Molotov protested to Schulenburg and the press published Moscow's stiff note to Sofia—Hitler was able to pursue his Balkan policy with less risk in the assurance that the Russians would not resist by armed force.

Soviet-German economic relations, which could reasonably have been expected to follow the downward plunge of their political association, were not seriously affected. The mutually advantageous arrangement between the two countries—German industrial products in exchange for Russian foodstuffs and raw materials—was undoubtedly responsible. Nevertheless, German deliveries had lagged behind schedule after the signature of the commercial treaty of February 11, 1940, and the Soviet government had threatened a response in kind. In October 1940 Berlin made an intense effort to fulfill its obligations. Further economic negotiations during the winter resulted in a new agreement on January 10, 1941, which at Soviet insistence provided that exports and imports between the two countries should be balanced quarterly. By March 1941 the Russians had become more anxious to please. They made a number of important economic concessions and scrupulously adhered to their promised deliveries. Vital rubber supplies, for example, were shipped from the Far East via the Trans-Siberian Railway to the very eve of the German attack.

IV

As Japan became more deeply committed to South Asia as its sphere of expansion, the political and military position of the Soviet Union in the Far East automatically improved. Yet the presence of the Nazi war machine, poised and intact, prevented the Kremlin from driving a hard bargain with Tokyo. Berlin continually urged a non-aggression pact with Moscow upon its Oriental partner: in a Japan free from worries about a Soviet threat the Reich saw the only means of neutralizing British sea power and preventing American involvement in the war. For this reason Hitler encouraged the Japanese occupation of French Indo-China and the Dutch East Indies, an Anglo-American strategic preserve after the fall of France and the Netherlands.

By the time of the Tripartite Pact (September 27, 1940) Japan was anxious to secure Soviet neutrality in the event of an extension of the war to the Pacific. Her leaders also hoped that Moscow's assistance to China might cease if the proper inducements were offered. Unable to reach a political settlement with Chiang and unwilling to sink more men and matériel into the Chinese quagmire, Tokyo arranged a peace treaty in November with a puppet regime in Nanking presided over by Wang Ching-wei.

As for the Nationalist government at Chungking, it somehow managed to survive despite war, inflation, and blatant corruption. It maintained only a semblance of military resistance while an alarming number of soldiers, ill-paid and poorly equipped, deserted to the Japanese-supplied Nanking army. Chiang's elite units were reserved for the renewed civil war, which entered a more serious phase in 1940 after frequent clashes between Communist and Kuomintang troops. Although the united front was in theory preserved until the defeat of Japan, after January 1941, when Nationalist forces annihilated the rear echelon of the Communist New Fourth Army near the Yangtze, relations between Chungking and Yenan were temporarily severed, and an armed truce was the best that could be subsequently arranged.

Moscow—and thus the international Communist press—occasionally ventured some mild criticism of Chiang, but its pro-Nationalist policy was sustained during the period of its quasi-alliance with Berlin. While this presented many doctrinal incongruities, the Chinese Communists did not swerve from the Comintern line: the Western democracies, "warmongers" in Europe, were implicitly accepted as friends and allies insofar as they helped China to resist Japanese aggression.

Rumors of a Soviet-Japanese partition of Asia at China's expense—a Far Eastern counterpart of the Nazi-Soviet Pact—gained momentum in the fall of 1940. On November 15 the Kremlin saw fit to deny that such an agreement had been reached. Tokyo had indeed initiated discussions for a settlement with Moscow as early as July 1940, and negotiations continued between Molotov and the new Japanese ambassador during the fall and winter months. The latter sought a non-aggression pact on the Soviet-German model and hinted at Tokyo's readiness to purchase northern Sakhalin. Moscow desired only a simple neutrality agreement and not only refused to entertain the idea of selling its half of the island but also proposed that Japan give up her concessions there.

In March 1941 Tokyo's foreign minister, Yosuke Matsuoka, the talkative and conceited "Japanese counterpart of Ribbentrop," accepted an invitation to visit Berlin. His real business lay in Moscow, but he did not wish to appear too eager for an agreement. Stalin and Molotov received him on the 24th when he stopped off at the Soviet capital. The visitor treated them to a theoretical discourse on Communism, asserting that while the Japanese were "moral Communists" they had no faith in its political and economic form. He made veiled references to a possible Soviet-Japanese sphere of influence agreement but deferred a more detailed discussion until his return from Berlin.

Matsuoka was received with ceremonial display in the Reich capital and made a side trip to Rome. He held lengthy conversations with Hitler and Ribbentrop, both of whom dropped hints about the possibility of a Russo-German conflict without divulging the closely guarded secret of "Operation Barbarossa." The Nazi leaders were so confident of victory that they valued Japan more as an ally against Britain (and potentially the United States) than against the Soviet Union. They consequently urged an immediate attack upon Singapore regardless of the outcome of the pending Soviet-Japanese negotiations.

Returning to Moscow on April 7, Matsuoka soon dropped the idea of a non-aggression pact. The price was too high: the restitution of southern Sakhalin. In reverting to Moscow's preference—a neutrality pact—the chief obstacle was Stalin's continued insistence that Japan surrender her concessions in North Sakhalin. Matsuoka apparently shrugged off the oblique references in Berlin to an impending showdown between Germany and the Soviet Union; otherwise he would have been more amenable about returning to Tokyo empty-handed. There is some evidence that he preyed on Stalin's fears of a German invasion, though it is more probable that the Wehrmacht's rapid advance in Yugoslavia and Greece, after an attack beginning on April 6, was a more persuasive reminder of Nazi striking power. In any event, Stalin suddenly lowered his demands: the Sakhalin concessions need not be surrendered immediately, on the written understanding that the issue would be settled in Moscow's favor in several months.

The Russo-Japanese treaty was signed on April 13, 1941, and on the whole it was a notable diplomatic victory for the Soviet Union. It was to remain valid ten years unless denounced at the end of five. The main provision stipulated neutrality "should one of the contracting parties become the object of hostilities on the part of one or several third powers." A supplementary declaration promised respect for each other's appendages—Manchukuo and the Mongolian People's Republic.[23] Chungking vainly protested to Moscow about this cavalier treatment of its territory, and for a time Chinese opinion registered indignation in spite of Russian assurances that her policy toward China would not be affected. In Tokyo the agreement was severely criticized in some quarters: it failed to mention the cessation of Soviet aid to Chiang and provided no tangible guarantees of the Kremlin's good faith.

The Japanese foreign minister began his homeward journey shortly after signing the pact. Stalin made an unprecendented appearance at the railway station to bid his guest farewell. Before the astonished gaze of the assembled diplomats and correspondents, he embraced Matsuoka; and after asking for Schulenburg, he threw his arms around the ambassador with the words: "We must remain friends and you must now do everything to that end!"[24] With a similar remark, he also embraced the startled German military attaché. The scene—in retrospect it has a certain macabre humor—was staged to impress Hitler with the sincerity of the Russian desire for peace.

It was, of course, far too late to change the pattern of Nazi war plans. But from the time of Stalin's well-publicized performance at the Moscow railway station until the actual invasion, Soviet policy toward Germany was as conciliatory as it had previously been obstinate. (Perhaps the "man of steel" recalled a proverb from his boyhood days in Georgia: "If you cannot cut your enemy's throat, clasp him in your arms.")

Yugoslavia furnished the key to this remarkable policy shift. On March 27, 1941, a swiftly executed *coup d'état* had displaced the existing pro-Axis regime in Belgrade (the Tripartite Pact had been signed two days before). The new government, while based on a resurgence of patriotic sentiment, was reluctant to commit suicide by defying Germany. But Hitler was fanatically bent on punishing the Yugoslavs and made immediate preparations for an invasion. The price was to prove costly—a five-week postponement of the Russian campaign. The Kremlin was pleased by developments in Belgrade but uncertain about a proper course of action. The Yugoslav Communists, sniffing the wind from Moscow with difficulty, demonstrated against Nazi Germany and "imperialist Britain" alike. Since a military alliance was considered too risky, the Russians offered encouragement in the form of a treaty of friendship and non-aggression, and arrangements were concluded after midnight on April 6. The ink had scarcely dried on the signatures before the German *blitzkrieg* was launched. Stalin believed that the mountainous terrain of Yugoslavia and Greece would present a formidable obstacle to the mechanized units that had advanced so rapidly on the asphalt roads of France. Again he underestimated Germany's military prowess. By the third week in April the Yugoslav and Greek armies had been crushed, and the Nazis were masters of the Balkan Peninsula.

As April passed into May rumors and predictions of a German attack on Russia were commonplace. Some of the information was amazingly accurate. That June 22 was the actual invasion date was an open secret in Berlin diplomatic circles at least five weeks beforehand. Soviet intelligence reports warned of the impending blow, and Washington and London passed on information about German troop movements toward the Russian frontier. German aircraft were spotted over Soviet territory with increasing frequency, and a protest to Berlin on April 22, in which eighty such instances were cited between March 27 and April 18, remained unanswered. Yet if Stalin took these warnings seriously, he apparently felt competent to avert the catastrophe. Soviet moves in the final weeks of peace suggest his confidence in achieving a fresh bargain with Hitler. German troop concentrations were dismissed simply as a transparent means of extorting major concessions. The Russian dictator strove in a variety of ways to make clear to Berlin that his country was no longer a competitor in the Balkans and that the Germans had *carte blanche* to deal with non-Russian Europe as they saw fit.

On April 15 Moscow abruptly gave way on a minor but doggedly contested boundary dispute between the two powers in the Baltic area. An attempt was also made to improve relations with Finland and Rumania. On May 3 Moscow officially recognized the pro-Nazi government of Iraq. To these concessions Stalin added a personal element on May 6 when he took over from Molotov the chairmanship of the Council of People's Commissars and thus became the prime minister of the U.S.S.R.—the first government office he had assumed during his career. The move was generally taken to mean that Stalin, having legalized his status as the Soviet ruler, was prepared to meet Hitler's terms for a new accord. The aftermath demonstrated the soundness of this interpretation. The most important gesture of appeasement came three days later when relations were severed with the governments-in-exile of Belgium, Norway, and Yugoslavia. Mindful of public opinion, the news was not released by the Soviet press.

Stalin's concerted effort to stave off attack by propitiatory measures made no impression whatever on the Führer except to strengthen his conviction of Russian weakness. The German public was kept in ignorance of these concessions, for the press was ordered to maintain silence. Schulenburg and his embassy colleagues, increasingly alarmed at their government's intentions, composed a memorandum warning of the dangers of war with the Soviet Union. It reached Hitler and was lying on his desk when he received the ambassador in Berlin on April 28. But it was unmentioned as Schulenburg tried to persuade Hitler that the Russians represented no threat to Germany. The ambassador returned to his post in Moscow convinced that the die had been cast for war, though the Führer's parting remark had been: "Oh, one more thing: I do not intend a war against Russia."[25]

On June 13 the Kremlin made a final attempt to draw out the Germans. In view of the imminence of hostilities it was to make Stalin look very foolish indeed. Sir Stafford Cripps had left Moscow three days before, disgusted with the Soviet government's continued dalliance with the Nazis. His abrupt departure served as a pretext for a message to Berlin disguised in the form of a Tass comminqué. Cripps was blamed for instigating "absurd" rumors about the "proximity of war between the Soviet Union and Germany"; and the Nazis were credited with "strictly observing" the non-aggression pact.[26] But Moscow did not deny that troop movements had taken place on both sides of the frontier—a subtle method of informing the Germans that the danger had been foreseen and that it had been met by appropriate defensive measures.

There was not the slightest reaction from Berlin, and the failure of the German press even to mention the statement signified Hitler's lack of interest in anything that the Russians might have to say. At length Moscow authorized a discrete inquiry by Dekanozov; and on June 18 he saw Weizsäcker but was unable to steer the conversation into the proper channel. Ribbentrop was "out of town" when Dekanozov tried to obtain an interview with him on the 21st. Molotov had meanwhile summoned Schulenburg to his office, where he bluntly referred to the deterioration of German-Soviet relations. He appeared genuinely bewildered by Berlin's attitude and asked almost plaintively if Schulenburg "could tell him what had brought about the present situation." Embarrassed, the ambassador declined to comment on the subject—he "lacked the pertinent information"—and gave the routine reply that he would pass on Molotov's remarks to his superiors.[27]

At three o'clock the following morning Schulenburg was told to present the Soviet government with a declaration of war in the form of a lengthy statement by Ribbentrop justifying Germany's action. Molotov, tired and haggard, received the ambassador for the last time shortly after 4 A.M. He listened quietly as the communication was read. "Is this supposed to be a declaration of war?" he asked, and as Schulenburg shrugged in ignorance, he answered his own question in the affirmative and spoke of the bombardment of Soviet cities by German aircraft. For a time he allowed his indignation free rein and denounced the betrayal as unprecedented in history. "Surely we have not deserved this?" he inquired. Schulenburg, obeying his instructions to the letter, refused to be drawn into conversation. His brief but significant role in the history of Soviet-German relations had ended. After a silent handshake, he left the Kremlin—still a faithful servant of the Reich but with gloomy forebodings for the future.

NOTES

1. *Nazi-Soviet Relations,* p. 41.
2. *Ibid.,* p. 60.
3. Hilger and Meyer, *Incompatible Allies,* p. 300; A. Rossi, *The Russo-German Alliance* (Boston, 1951), p. 37.
4. *Nazi-Soviet Relations,* p. 75.
5. Hilger and Meyer, *Incompatible Allies,* p. 304.
6. David J. Dallin, *Soviet Russia's Foreign Policy, 1939–1942* (New Haven, Conn., 1942), p. 63.
7. *Nazi-Soviet Relations,* p. 72.
8. *Nazi Conspiracy and Aggression* (Washington, 1946), I, 702.
9. *Polish White Book* (London, 1939), No. 172.
10. Degras, *Soviet Documents on Foreign Policy,* III, 374.
11. *Nazi-Soviet Relations,* p. 99.
12. Frederick L. Schuman, *Night Over Europe* (New York, 1941), p. 383.
13. John H. Wuorinen (ed.), *Finland and World War II* (New York, 1948), p. 59; Väinö Tanner, *The Winter War* (Stanford, Calif., 1957), pp. 66–67.
14. See above, p. 87.
15. See above, p. 91.
16. *The U.S.S.R. and Finland* (New York, 1939), p. 30.
17. *Pravda,* December 25, 1939.
18. Dallin, *Soviet Russia's Foreign Policy,* p. 236.
19. Winston S. Churchill, *Their Finest Hour* (Boston, 1949), p. 136.
20. *Ibid.,* p. 586.
21. Text in *Nazi-Soviet Relations,* p. 249.
22. *Ibid.,* p. 269.
23. Text in Degras, *Soviet Documents on Foreign Policy,* III, 486–87.
24. *Nazi-Soviet Relations,* p. 324; Grigore Gafencu, *Prelude to the Russian Campaign* (London, 1945), pp. 157–58.
25. Hilger and Meyer, *Incompatible Allies,* p. 328.
26. Degras, *Soviet Documents on Foreign Policy,* III, 489.
27. *Nazi-Soviet Relations,* pp. 355–56; Hilger and Meyer, *Incompatible Allies,* p. 335.

CHAPTER NINE

INTO THE MAELSTROM

Before daybreak on Sunday, June 22, 1941, the Nazi legions violated the Russian frontier. The invasion was a complete tactical surprise despite repeated Anglo-American warnings predicting the actual date of the attack. Stalin, a prisoner of his own logic, rejected the reliability of the early reports. Convinced that the assault was simply a provocation by several undisciplined German units, he ordered his commanders to withhold their fire. Unable at last to deny the full import of the evidence—and of his own prolonged gullibility in trusting Hitler—he withdrew into himself and allowed Molotov to inform the Russian people by radio of the German invasion. Stalin apparently failed to regain his equilibrium for several weeks, and his loss of nerve was such that after the initial disaster at the front he was ready to concede that all had been lost.

Public opinion in Britain, and to a lesser extent in the United States, soon became as strongly pro-Soviet as it had once been anti-Soviet. Yet, except for the small but highly vocal coterie of Communists in both countries (whose patriotism, of course, now knew no bounds), few were willing to concede that the Red Army was capable of halting the powerful Wehrmacht even for a limited period; and in the United States, where professional anti-Communism was to survive even the lean years of a common war effort, what seemed the impending doom of the Soviet state was savored with unconcealed relish in some quarters. A few hopefully saw it as a colossal blunder, as potentially fatal for Hitler as the invasion of the Grand Army had been for Napoleon.

At the official level the exigencies of war naturally created a close bond between Moscow and London. In ringing prose Churchill proclaimed his government's solidarity with the Russians, though he was candid enough to acknowledge that no one had been "a more consistent opponent of Communism than I have for the last twenty-five years." As he told his private secretary, "If Hitler invaded Hell I would make at least a favourable reference to the Devil in the House of Commons." Following his public declaration, Churchill sent a personal message to Stalin assuring him of Britain's desire to do "everything to help you that time, geography, and our growing resources allow."[1] Military missions were exchanged, and on July 12 a mutual assistance pact was signed in which both powers agreed to refrain from separate negotiations with the enemy.

Britain's limited ability to aid her ally—from a supply standpoint Soviet involvement was a hindrance rather than a help—meant that the United States, already a British arsenal through the "lend-lease" program, would be expected to assume most of the burden of assisting the Russians. Soviet-American relations had been frosty indeed before the German invasion, especially during the Finnish war. But Washington had been thoroughly aware of the danger to American interests in the Far East should Moscow and Tokyo compose their differences along the lines of the Hitler-Stalin Pact; and in some respects, therefore, its policy had been more conciliatory toward the Russians than London's. The outbreak of the Russo-German conflict did not, however, bring forth the kind of sentiment for unstinting support to the Soviet Union that it did in embattled Britain. Official policy lagged behind public opinion, and the first cautious steps that were taken countered the view of many of President Roosevelt's advisers that aid to Britain should be stepped up during this temporary respite, since Russian resistance could not be expected to last beyond the summer months.

Until the mission to Moscow of Harry Hopkins, American assistance to the Soviet Union was a limited and haphazard affair, to a great extent snarled in bureaucratic red tape. One of the President's closest intimates, Hopkins was authorized to undertake the trip while in London, and he arrived in the Soviet capital on July 30 after a tiring air journey. The Kremlin sensed the importance of the mission, and the Soviet press devoted unusual space to it for the duration of Hopkins' stay. He conveyed personal messages to Stalin from both Roosevelt and Churchill and emphasized the American government's desire to facilitate all possible aid. The Soviet dictator was extraordinarily frank in describing the military situation. Hopkins was, in fact, the first foreigner to obtain "inside" information on the Soviet war effort. Stalin's general demeanor and his confidence in the ability of the Red Army to stem the German advance ("moving mechanized forces through Russia was very different than moving them over the boulevards of Belgium and France") deeply impressed the American representative. His report to the President, while in great part a factual statement of Soviet military requirements, was flavored by this optimistic impression of Russia's chances and served—along with his cables and his personal influence—to counteract the still-prevalent opinion in Washington that the collapse of the U.S.S.R. was inevitable.

The concluding portion of the Hopkins report was highly secret, for it paraphrased Stalin's forthright plea for the intervention of the United States. The Soviet Union's desperate plight was revealed most starkly in the offer to welcome "American troops on any part of the Russian front under the complete command of the American Army."[2] Roosevelt felt it unnecessary to pursue the subject, and neither Stalin nor any other Soviet official reverted again to the suggestion about sending American troops. Hopkins himself stayed in Moscow only two days. He rejoined the President at the Atlantic Conference—the famous meeting at sea between Roosevelt and Churchill off the coast of Newfoundland.

By August 1941 the Soviet military position was critical, but the Germans had lost much of the momentum of their original breakthrough. The Red Army suffered grievous losses by attempting to halt the invasion near the frontier rather than by defense in depth and strategic retreat. The swift loss of the "buffer" territory acquired since the Nazi-Soviet Pact of 1939 could only confirm the original prognosis of Western military observers. Hitler diverted the Wehrmacht's promising drive toward Moscow in an attempt to crush Russian resistance in the Ukraine and to open the oil-coal-industrial complex of the south to German exploitation. The decision may be seen in hindsight as the first of his many military blunders. He ignored all protests by repeating one of his favorite maxims: "My generals know nothing about the economic aspects of war."

At the time, Hitler's strategy appeared a stroke of genius: 600,000 Russian troops were encircled and taken prisoner near Kiev in a gigantic battle occupying the whole month of September. The dread specter of "General Winter"—the historic nemesis of Charles XII in the eighteenth century and of Napoleon in the nineteenth—by then hovered over the landscape. An all-out offensive against Moscow brought further German victories: the Red Army lost another 600,000 prisoners, yet it managed an increasingly stubborn resistance as the battle lines were enveloped in a sea of mud. By late October the personnel of the embassies and the more important government offices were evacuated from the capital while looting and other disorders indicated the panicky mood of the population. But Stalin's refusal to leave the Kremlin set an example that gradually improved morale.

Fresh reserves from Siberia were flung into battle as the Wehrmacht, ill-equipped for a winter campaign, pressed on to the forests covering the western approaches to the city. There they could go no farther. The cold became so intense that on December 8 Hitler was forced to announce the suspension of operations for the winter.

The newly appointed commander of the Moscow front, Marshal Georgi Zhukov, quickly seized the initiative and launched a massive counterattack. Despite Hitler's rigid "no withdrawal" policy, which exposed his troops to unnecessary losses and hardships, the Germans were pushed back an average of one hundred fifty miles in the Moscow sector. Less impressive gains were achieved in other sections of the front. After an uninterrupted series of victories following the invasion of Poland in 1939, the Wehrmacht at last tasted the bitterness of defeat.

That the Red Army not only survived the furious German onslaught of the summer months but mounted an offensive of its own during the winter was a gloomy portent for the Nazi war machine. Hitler had counted upon a quick and decisive campaign in the East. "We have only to kick in the door," he had told one of his generals, "and the whole rotten structure will come crashing down."[3] When—incredibly—the Russians did not collapse, he was unprepared for a long war. Unable for political reasons to retreat, he could only plunge ahead into a deeper military morass. The Japanese attack on Pearl Harbor in December insured the Soviet Union against fighting a two-front war and brought the dread certainty that eventually Germany herself would be engaged on two fronts unless the Russians could be beaten first.

Soviet manpower losses in 1941 were grievous, but because of seemingly inexhaustible reserves they were not fatal. Germany's casualties, while not nearly as severe, were less easily replaced, and the strain increased as the war continued. In war matériel the Germans still enjoyed a wide margin of superiority which the United States did much to equalize by sharply stepping up the pace of its shipments.

During the Atlantic Conference Roosevelt and Churchill dispatched a message to Stalin promising maximum assistance and urging a meeting in Moscow to discuss long range plans. Stalin agreed, and on September 22 a joint Anglo-American mission left for Archangel on a British cruiser. W. Averell Harriman, lend-lease expediter in London, was the chief American representative, and Lord Beaverbrook, the minister of supply, headed the British delegation. Stalin received the two representatives hospitably; but the amenities over, his manner became brusque and pettish as Harriman and Beaverbrook painstakingly reviewed the list of supplies available to the Russians. Stalin had recovered his good humor by the final meeting on September 30. He was particularly enthusiastic about the prospect of American jeeps and trucks and expressed the opinion that the gasoline engine was the key to ultimate victory.

On October 1, 1941, Harriman, Beaverbrook, and Molotov signed a protocol containing more than one hundred fifty items—munitions, equipment, raw materials, and medical supplies—to be delivered to the Soviet Union. Colonel Philip R. Faymonville, the American military attaché during the late thirties, remained in Moscow as the lend-lease representative, a choice that was criticized in Washington on the grounds that he was too sympathetic to the Soviet regime. Roosevelt cabled his approval of the protocol to Stalin on October 30 and stated that one billion dollars in credit had been granted without interest to pay for the deliveries. The Russians were nevertheless expected to repay the loan—a condition that had not been exacted from the British. This discrimination was rectified during the next year. On November 7, 1941, it was publicly announced that the Soviet Union would be one of the recipients of lend-lease.

The Harriman-Beaverbrook mission had been incidentally concerned with a distinctly subsidiary matter but one that was to plague Soviet Russia's relations with her Western allies until June 1944: the question of a second front. As early as July 18, 1941, Stalin had raised the issue in a message to Churchill. He returned to it again on September 4, and on this occasion the Soviet ambassador, Ivan Maisky, reinforced Stalin's circumspect plea with an ardent appeal for an immediate landing on the coast of France or in the Low Countries. Churchill was obliged to turn aside these requests as militarily untenable, though he feared that Maisky's remarks ("language of vague import") about the gravity of the crisis on the Russian front might imply the Kremlin's desire for a separate peace.

Stalin tried a new tack on September 15 by proposing to Churchill that twenty-five or thirty British divisions be sent to the Soviet Union via Archangel or through Iran. Churchill considered the idea fantastic and avoided the subject in his reply. The most he would offer was to relieve the five Russian divisions in Iran, where the weak pro-Nazi government was then in the process of dissolution after a joint Anglo-Soviet occupation of the country. In Moscow Beaverbrook suggested that British forces might be moved into the Caucasus from Iran, but Stalin's biting comment that the fighting was in the Ukraine not in the Caucasus inhibited further discussion. Molotov later informed Cripps, who had returned to his ambassadorial post after the German invasion, that the proposal was not acceptable. The Soviet leaders undoubtedly had keen memories of British intervention in the Caucasus during the civil war, and only the direst emergency could have induced them to request the aid of foreign troops even for combat duty.

Upon his return to London, Beaverbrook became a vigorous advocate of an immediate second front and castigated the military men who would "have us wait until the last button has been sewn on the last gaiter before we launch an attack."[4] But Churchill was not to be budged. Nor did the prospect of dispatching a small force to aid the Red Army appeal to him. As he wrote Cripps on October 28, "It would be silly to send two or three British or British-Indian divisions into the heart of Russia to be surrounded and cut to pieces as a symbolic sacrifice."[5]

Relations between the two allies were further irritated by Britain's reluctance to declare war on Germany's satellites—Finland, Rumania, and Hungary. Churchill pointed out to Stalin that such a move would be only an empty gesture. Finland, moreover, had many friends in the United States; and a declaration of war on Rumania and Hungary might so freeze the political situation that it would be impossible for pro-Allied elements to regain control. Stalin expressed his displeasure in no uncertain terms. His reply on November 8 ranged over several issues and complained of a "lack of clarity" in Anglo-Soviet relations because there was no definite understanding on war and peace aims and no agreement on mutual military assistance. His rude and sarcastic tone was too much for Churchill, who remained expressively silent.

Stalin offered an indirect apology on November 20 when Maisky told Eden that Stalin had not intended to be offensive. The prime minister was sufficiently mollified to seek a common meeting ground once more. He proposed that Foreign Secretary Anthony Eden visit Moscow to discuss both the military and political aspects of the war and the future peace settlement. Stalin's answer consenting to Eden's mission was couched in a conciliatory spirit: the nadir of Anglo-Soviet relations appeared to have safely passed.

A number of circumstances converged to help repair the leaky vessel of wartime amity. The British offensive in North Africa began on November 18, 1941, and probably reassured the Soviet leaders that Britain was not contemplating the mutual extermination of Germany and the U.S.S.R. The tension was also enormously eased by the Wehrmacht's failure to take Moscow before the winter snows set in. Against Churchill's better judgment and solely to demonstrate Britain's loyalty to her ally, war was declared on Finland, Rumania, and Hungary on December 6. The next day's dramatic events—the Japanese strike at

Pearl Harbor—brought the United States into the war and altered the whole nature of the conflict. It also alleviated, temporarily at least, a fundamental cause of Anglo-Soviet friction—fear of a separate deal with Germany by the other power.

Eden secretly departed for Moscow within hours of the Pearl Harbor attack without waiting for further clarification of American policy. The United States had been apprehensive that the meeting in Moscow might compromise the principles of the Atlantic Charter, an idealistic document that Roosevelt and Churchill had signed on August 14, 1941, and to which the Russians adhered on September 24. As a practical matter, the future status of Poland and the Baltic countries was involved, for both London and Washington were aware that the Soviet Union would demand approximately her June 1941 boundary. In his first meeting with Eden, Stalin did indeed lay claim to the territory in question; and he subsequently made the conclusion of a formal Anglo-Soviet military alliance—one of Eden's primary objectives—contingent upon London's agreement. The most that Eden would promise was to press his government for a favorable consideration of the Soviet position. The mission returned to London without real results, but the talks had been amicable and both the British and Russian people were led to believe by the publication of an adroit communiqué that something tangible had been achieved.

In the end the Soviet political demands were met: the Western powers would otherwise have faced a *fait accompli*. But in the early winter of 1941–1942 there were few outside observers who, even if they conceded the Red Army a chance for ultimate victory, did not expect an exhausted and vastly weakened Russia to emerge in the postwar world. Whatever the outcome, it appeared certain that the Soviet Union's bargaining position would be feeble indeed. Yet as early as March 1942 Churchill was prepared to make concessions: only Soviet power stood against the Nazis on the European continent. Then, too, the Russians had come to terms with Hitler once; they might do so again. Such, at any rate, was the impression that Western diplomats gleaned from Stalin's order of the day of February 23, 1942, denouncing as a "stupid lie and a witless slander" the "prattle" of the foreign press in claiming that the aim of the Red Army was to "exterminate the German people and destroy the German state." On the contrary, said the Soviet dictator, German fascism was the enemy: "History shows that Hitlers come and go, but the German people and the German state remain."[6]

Hitler did not nibble at the bait—if in fact it was so intended. He was stubbornly bent upon resuming the offensive when good weather returned. The British placed little faith in Stalin's constancy, and visions of their inept diplomacy in 1939 culminating in the Nazi-Soviet Pact must have haunted Downing Street. Washington continued to be a major obstacle to a political settlement with the Russians, but Roosevelt was eventually won over to the idea that the Baltic states could be sacrificed provided their peoples were given an opportunity to emigrate.

Molotov arrived in London on May 20, 1942, to speed the stalled negotiations on the projected Anglo-Soviet treaty and to raise anew the question of a second front. Churchill refused Moscow's Polish demands as incompatible with Britain's pre-war guarantee of Poland's territorial integrity. The Polish question seemed likely to block an agreement of any kind, but Eden finally proposed a twenty-year military alliance without reference to future frontiers. Rather unexpectedly, Stalin gave his consent to the treaty on these terms, and it was signed on May 26.

Stalin's unusual forbearance in pursuing his political objectives in this instance was in no sense an abandonment of Soviet territorial claims. It derived instead from two other considerations: the State Department's last-minute opposition to a political treaty, expressed in a vehement message to London which Roosevelt had okayed; and, more important, the prospect of a second front in 1942, a prize that the United States ambassador to Britain, John G. Winant, dangled before Molotov. It was thus with some expectations on this score that the Soviet commissar accepted a prior invitation from the President and flew on to Washington.

Molotov held several lengthy conversations with Roosevelt, most of them in the presence of various American officials. The new Soviet ambassador to Washington, Maxim Litvinov, also attended. Relegated to semi-obscurity after 1939, he had been resurrected as a symbol of Allied unity. The discussions were far-reaching, but on the central issue of the second front the President, upon consultation with his chief of staff, General George Marshall, precipitously promised some kind of action before the end of the year. After Molotov's departure, a communiqué was released simultaneously in Washington and Moscow referring to the "full understanding" reached "with regard to the urgent tasks of creating a second front in Europe in 1942." London concurred in the wording, which had been formulated by Molotov and accepted by Roosevelt, only because it "might make the Germans apprehensive and consequently hold as many of their troops in the West as possible."[7]

Churchill had never pretended to favor a second front and was careful to dissociate his government from Washington's view by pre-

senting Molotov with an *aide-mémoire* when the latter stopped over
in London on his way back to Moscow. While the document stated
that preparations were going forward for an invasion of the Continent
in August or September 1942, it was made explicit that no commitment had been made. The Soviet leaders nevertheless proceeded on
the assumption that a landing in France by late fall was a foregone
conclusion, and the Soviet press enthusiastically spread the glad tid-
ings to the general public.

One can readily understand the Russians' will to believe. The Wehrmacht's summer offensive, with the oil of the Caucasus as the major
goal, was making sensational gains. A preliminary campaign to seal
off the Crimea had begun in May 1942 and was climaxed by the
storming of Sevastopol on July 1. After smashing a Russian offensive
in the Kharkov area and winning a number of local engagements, the
Germans had launched their main assault on June 28. Rostov, the
major Russian city on the lower Don, was taken within a month, and
the northern Caucasus were opened to the enemy. The middle Don
region was breached with equal success, and a drive began toward
Stalingrad, originally an objective of secondary importance. Hitler
insisted that the "city of Stalin" be captured whatever the cost—a
strategic error that denuded the German flank of reserves.

In August 1942, at a time when the Russian front was in a perilous
state, Churchill decided to inform Stalin in person that there could be
no second front in Europe that year. He flew via Cairo and Teheran
and pondered, as he wrote later, "my mission to this sullen, sinister
Bolshevik State I had once tried so hard to strangle at its birth, and
which, until Hitler appeared, I had regarded as the mortal foe of
civilised freedom."[8] The two war leaders, partners by circumstance
but adversaries by character and conviction, met for the first time at
the Kremlin on August 12. Churchill minced no words in imparting the
bad news, and Stalin responded with equal bluntness—at times he was
almost insulting in his implication that the Western powers were
afraid of meeting the Germans in open battle. Churchill did have an
emotional horror of a cross-channel invasion: his memory of the mass
slaughter of British youth during the First World War was still painfully vivid. But his arguments to Stalin were based on practical considerations alone. Having informed his Russian listeners of the worst
—Molotov and Voroshilov were also present—Churchill then unfolded
plans for an invasion of French North Africa ("Operation Torch") in
October. The substitute project relieved much of the accumulated
tension. Stalin's comment, "May God prosper this undertaking," was
the heartfelt but disconcerting benediction of an avowed atheist.

The note of cordiality that ended the discussion was not carried over to the next day. Stalin was extremely bitter in his reproaches, and his remarks on the reluctance of the British infantry to come to grips with the Germans amounted to a direct accusation of cowardice. Yet he was less animated than Churchill, who eloquently defended his position and appealed for a better working relationship. Stalin at last responded, and though he grumbled from time to time about the second front, he did not allow what must have been a grievous disappointment to mar the remainder of Churchill's visit. A basis for some intimacy was established shortly before the prime minister's departure when he was invited to Stalin's private apartment. There, from 8:30 P.M. to 2:30 A.M. amid a generous repast of food and drink, conviviality and small talk prevailed, with Molotov filling the role of straight man for Stalin's rather heavy-handed humor.

Churchill left at dawn on August 16, satisfied that he had handled an onerous assignment with minimum friction. He was somewhat reassured by Stalin's confidence that the Germans would not break through the barrier of the Caucasus to seize the Baku oil region. The British were even more concerned by the prospect of a German pincer movement in the Middle East should the Russians fail to hold. The German *Afrika Korps* was then threatening Egypt, and the danger was very real that these troops would shatter the British lines and eventually join their comrades from the Russian front in Iran or Turkey. Stalin also revealed a few details of a great counter-offensive in the Stalingrad area, already in the planning stage.

The battle for Stalingrad had not reached its climax at the time of Churchill's visit. The Germans inched forward with battering ram tactics, leaving themselves little room for maneuver. They reached the outskirts of the city early in September, but the Russians fought doggedly for every house and every street. Shellfire and air attacks systematically reduced the city to ruins. Assisted by armed factory workers, the Red Army clung to isolated positions along the Volga, although it seemed inevitable to the outside world that while Moscow and Leningrad had somehow resisted the German onslaught, Stalingrad must fall. By the end of October the Wehrmacht had cut the city in half and controlled the Volga. Russian reserves had meanwhile built up on the northern and southern flanks of Stalingrad. Stalin audaciously gambled on the accuracy of his intelligence data that Japan would remain immobile in the Far East, and crack divisions of the Red Army guarding the eastern frontier were transferred to the west.

The gigantic Soviet counter-thrust was launched on November 19 just before the heavy snows began. The plan was to pinion the

German forces between the converging arms of a double-pronged attack—one spearhead thrusting along the banks of the Don northwest of Stalingrad, the other directed westward from a position southeast of the city. The encirclement of the German Sixth Army—some 270,000 men—was completed in four days. But the trap was not firmly sealed, for the Russian line was still a thin one, and a fighting retreat might well have succeeded. But Hitler, whose "instinct" advised against a withdrawal from the Volga, vetoed the idea. In mid-December a relief force attempting to reach the beleaguered army was turned back, and no reserves were available for a second try. The Red Army had only to close the ring. Suffering severely from hunger and cold, the remnants of the Sixth Army surrendered on February 1-2, 1943. Over 90,000 prisoners were taken, including twenty-three generals and the recently promoted commander, Field Marshal Friedrich Paulus.

II

The battle of Stalingrad was the turning point of the Russian campaign—indeed, of the Second World War. Never again were the Germans capable of mounting a sustained offensive on any front. The proverbial Russian "steamroller," a myth in 1914, became a reality in 1943–1945. Soviet morale, which had shown signs of deterioration in the summer and fall of 1942, was lifted to new heights. The government took additional measures to bolster the patriotic mood—and to augment its own popularity—by a "return to tradition." In the Red Army alone the transformation was extraordinary. A series of decrees abolished the egalitarianism of the October Revolution: ranks were reorganized and officers given a privileged status unknown since Tsarist times; guard regiments and special Cossack units were revived; and new awards were created in the name of great heroes of the Russian past. Stalin himself assumed the rank of marshal after the battle of Stalingrad and was formally designated commander-in-chief of the Soviet armed forces.

Marxist principles were placed in cold storage for the duration. Atheism was no longer *de rigueur,* and the Church, which had so long existed on sufferance, was showered with concessions. In return, the Church hierarchy loyally supported the government and rallied the Orthodox faithful to the defense of the Fatherland.

In other respects besides religion, Marxist principles were temporarily discarded. The theory that war was a product of imperialist rivalry among capitalist powers was no longer heard, and a sharp distinction was drawn between democratic and fascist states. The doctrine of class struggle was symbolically repudiated when the "International," that colorful and rousing song of proletarian militancy, was replaced as the Soviet national anthem by a conventional homily to Russian patriotism. A more striking example of wartime opportunism was the decision in May 1943 to dissolve the Comintern. The move was intended primarily as a gesture of good will toward Britain and the United States, and as such it was greeted with appropriate remarks of gratitude. The status of the Western Communist parties was actually unchanged save in the most formal organizational sense; loyalty to Moscow as the citadel of international Communism was in no way affected by the disappearance of a bureaucracy that had long ceased to play any role of substance either in Soviet foreign affairs or in furthering the cause of world revolution.

In its unremitting efforts to arouse and sustain an exalted mood of patriotism and self-sacrifice, the Soviet government found its best and most faithful ally in Germany herself. National feeling is, of course, inevitably outraged by an invading army. But in this case other reasons were involved. Nazi theory numbered the Slavs among the inferior races, and instead of treading the path of political expediency, as Hitler's propagandists had done with the "inferior" Orientals of Japan (and with the Russians between 1939 and 1941), Berlin made no secret of its intention to exploit the U.S.S.R. as a conquered province in the new "thousand-year Reich." Millions of Soviet citizens, particularly the non-Russian nationalities in the Ukraine, the Caucasus, and the annexed border territories, were prepared to greet the invaders as liberators or at least to become passive spectators. Although many did collaborate, German occupation policy was disillusioning. The shooting of hostages for acts of sabotage; wanton destruction of property and cultural shrines; the drafting or recruitment of forced labor for German war industries; the practice of genocide against the Jewish population; and the inhumane and often brutal treatment of war prisoners fed the fires of the Kremlin's "hate propaganda." Stalin's onetime distinction between the German people and their Nazi masters was largely forgotten until the closing stages of the war; he himself invariably concluded his orders of the day with the refrain, "Death to the German invaders!"

Each side made an abortive effort to subvert the other by the use of captured generals. The Russians were the least successful. A National Committee for Free Germany was formed in Moscow in July 1943 and was eventually headed by Marshal Paulus. Its appeal was to conservative pre-Nazi German opinion. Rather ineffective, it was allowed to languish at the close of the war. The Germans encouraged the establishment in December 1942 of a Russian Committee of Liberation headed by General Andrei Vlasov, who had been captured during the summer. The so-called Russian Army of Liberation under his command was in reality no more than a name for scattered units of former war prisoners who had volunteered for service in the Wehrmacht. Not until late 1944, with the war nearly lost, did the Germans permit the formation of an independent army of approximately 50,000 men. Only one division saw action—a brief and costly engagement with the Red Army near Frankfurt-on-Oder in April 1945. Most of the turncoat Russians were seized by Soviet troops or repatriated by the American military authorities. Vlasov and eleven of his subordinates were hanged on or about August 1, 1946.

Neither Germany nor the Soviet Union effectively utilized the political and psychological techniques for waging war that were available. As long as Hitler held the initiative, he scorned anything but a crushing military victory. After Stalingrad, when the Germans began to give consideration to their lost opportunities, it was already too late. The Russians, in turn, began to think almost exclusively in terms of a decision by military means, and it was in their power to summon up the necessary armed strength.

There was nothing inevitable about Germany's defeat following Stalingrad—as it now seems in retrospect. Had Hitler allowed his generals a free hand without continually forcing on them a policy of static defense, it is just possible they could have created a stalemate leading to a separate peace before the Anglo-American forces were prepared to invade the Continent. The German troops in northern Caucasia—a far more exposed position than Stalingrad— managed to extricate themselves in good order during the winter. The Wehrmacht still clung to a front hundreds of miles long with no substantial reserves to bolster its overextended lines. In adversity, Hitler's intuitive strategy worked poorly. An attempt to hold every advance position was suicidal in the face of the mounting potential of the Red Army in men and matériel.

Stalingrad—coupled with less sensational victories by the British in Egypt and Libya and by the Americans in Morocco and Algeria— alleviated some of the ill-feeling that had accumulated because of the absence of a second front. There were long weeks of silence from Stalin in the fall of 1942, relieved only by a cryptic and perhaps ironic "thank you" on October 13 in answer to a lengthy message from Churchill explaining the difficulties in sending convoys because of "Torch." Stalin also declined in December to attend a Big Three meeting, though his tone was gracious and his plea of "front business" was undoubtedly well-founded. He was subsequently informed of the decisions made at the Casablanca Conference (January 1943) between Roosevelt and Churchill. The major military effort by the Western allies in 1943 was to be a cross-channel invasion in August or September.

Stalin keenly resented the fact that his troops continued to face the overwhelming portion of Germany's armed might. Russian suspicions that their allies planned to bleed them white before launching a frontal attack in Europe were never far below the surface. Stalin had expected action in the spring. But his protests at this new postponement were now more dignified than in 1942, for they reflected the self-confidence won at Stalingrad. "I must give a most emphatic warning, in the interest of our common cause," he wrote Churchill on March 15, 1943, "of the grave danger with which further delay in opening a second front in France is fraught."[9]

The gross inequality of sacrifice among the United Nations—as the anti-Axis coalition was now called—gave all the more offense to the Russians when the American ambassador in Moscow, Admiral William H. Standley, complained to newspaper correspondents on March 8 that the Kremlin was deliberately concealing from the Russian people the extent of lend-lease aid from the United States. While the ambassador's statement was substantially true, it was not in the best of taste to remind the Soviet authorities of their lack of gratitude: by any accounting, no amount of material aid could compensate for the flesh and blood that the Russians were expending so lavishly. The Soviet leaders nevertheless responded to the criticism with outward good grace. The press devoted considerable space to the subject of American aid, and a detailed report on the lend-lease program by Edward R. Stettinius, the lend-lease administrator, was published in full.

The "Standley incident" passed off more smoothly than most observers in Washington had been inclined to think. The next major incident had more serious implications. On April 13, 1943, the German radio announced the discovery of a mass grave containing the bodies of more than 10,000 Polish officers in the Katyn Forest near Smolensk. (Later investigation established the number at about 4,500.) It was alleged that the massacre had been perpetrated by the Russians—a typical example of "Jewish-Bolshevik bestiality"—in the spring of 1940 when the area was under Soviet control. Both Washington and London were prepared to dismiss the matter as a Nazi propaganda stunt. But the Polish government-in-exile, headed by General Wladyslaw Sikorski and with headquarters in London, had already accumulated evidence implicating the Soviet Union, and it called for an investigation by the International Red Cross. Moscow promptly charged that the Poles had "dealt a treacherous blow" to the Soviet Union "by making use of the slanderous Hitlerite fake" and that it had decided to sever diplomatic relations.[10] This action was followed in May by the creation of a Polish Kosciusko Division within the Red Army; and the Union of Polish Patriots, organized in March by Polish Communists and other pro-Soviet Poles, began a propaganda compaign against the London government.

In the light of previous Soviet-Polish relations, it is likely that a rupture between Moscow and the London Poles would have occurred sooner or later without the Katyn Forest affair, for Stalin was entirely out of sympathy with their aims and probably welcomed an opportunity to push forward his own pawns on the Polish chessboard. Although Sikorski himself was a man of moderate views, many of his colleagues were passionately anti-Russian as well as anti-Communist; and they were determined that Poland should reclaim her 1939 frontiers. As host, the British government was frequently embarrassed by the anti-Soviet proclivities of its Polish guests, but until the April incident it managed to forestall any acts that might impair the wartime alliance.

A pact between Moscow and the Polish government-in-exile had been signed by Sikorski and Maisky on July 30, 1941. The negotiations were acrimonious, and the Poles acquiesced—though three ministers resigned in protest—in large part because of the British "recommendation." The vital territorial issue was left open, but normal diplomatic relations were resumed, an amnesty was promised for all Polish prisoners, and a Polish army was to be established on Soviet soil. A Polish military mission immediately set out for Moscow, and an agreement was signed on August 8, 1941, in which General Wladyslaw Anders, recently released from a Soviet prison, was named to command the new army. Hundreds of thousands of Polish civilians deported to the Soviet Union were freed from various conditions of confinement. But the effect of the amnesty was marred by tales of hardship and suffering, particularly among those sent to forced labor camps in the frozen wastes of the Arctic region. Nor did the evasive response of Soviet officials to inquiries about the disappearance of some 15,000 Polish officers interned since 1939 lend confidence to an uneasy relationship.

Early in December 1941 Sikorski conferred with Stalin at the Kremlin while the battle for Moscow was raging a few miles away. The Polish premier was received as an honored guest, and except for the customary rebuff when the fate of the missing officers was mentioned, a rare note of friendship crept into Polish-Soviet relations at the highest level. Stalin agreed to an increase in the size of the Polish army and that 25,000 men might leave for England via Iran, where supplies and training facilities were more readily available. He even hinted that with some "slight alterations" Poland's pre-war boundaries would be acceptable to the Soviet Union. Sikorski refused to discuss the matter, and Stalin never again betrayed the slightest intention of budging any distance from the 1941 frontier. At the time, the Polish leaders expected a German victory and could scarcely envisage a future Russian state strong enough to impose its own solution of the problem.

The Stalin-Sikorski talks were not productive of lasting good will. Even as they spoke, several Polish leaders were arrested for alleged subversive activities. The most prominent were Victor Alter and Henryk Ehrlich, two Jewish socialists engaged under Soviet auspices in furthering the work of an "International Jewish Anti-Fascist Committee." Their execution aroused widespread indignation among labor and socialist groups in the West when it became known in 1943.

Early in 1942 Moscow requested the use of a few Polish divisions at the front. Anders' refusal—his men were in no condition for combat duty—was taken as evidence that the Poles intended to stand aside while hoping for a Russo-German war of mutual exhaustion. In March the demand for a cut in the ration strength of the Polish army (then about 75,000 men) to 26,000 was explained by Stalin as necessary in order to give priority to fighting divisions—a slap at the non-combatant status of the Poles. Anders finally gained Stalin's consent to a raise in rations to 44,000 and to the evacuation of the remainder of the Polish forces to Iran. The first contingent of about 40,000—one-third of them civilian refugees—left in the spring. During the summer the Soviet government decided, upon Anders' request, to eliminate the Polish military establishment on Russian soil altogether. Approximately 114,000 soldiers and refugees crossed the border into Iran in August. Many of these troops later fought in the Italian campaign.

Prior to the Katyn Forest incident the only further contact between the Russians and the London Poles was an exchange of surly notes, chiefly in reference to the boundary conflict. As for the Katyn massacre itself, later evidence, most of it unavailable until several years after the war, pointed fairly conclusively to Soviet guilt. Since no similar crime has been ascribed to the Russians—the secret police even during the Great Purge of the thirties did not indulge in mass executions of this type—a plausible (and more charitable) explanation has been advanced that Stalin issued an order to "liquidate" the camps but that an N.K.V.D. officer misunderstood and liquidated the inmates instead.[11] If such was the case, the Soviet government might have gained more through a frank admission that a tragic blunder had been made than by a clumsy campaign to pin responsibility on the Germans. The affair became a *cause célèbre* to the Poles in exile, who were apparently more incensed by the Katyn murders than by the Nazi genocide policy that accounted for millions of Polish victims.

The London Poles suffered a fresh blow on July 4, 1943, when Sikorski was killed in an airplane crash at Gibraltar after returning from an inspection tour of the Polish army in the Middle East. He was succeeded by Vice Premier Stanislaw Mikolajczyk, a leader of the Peasant party and a moderate in the Sikorski tradition. But in the cabinet shuffle several extremists of the Right were given posts, a reorganization that added to the political instability of the regime. The most important new minister was General Kasimir Sosnkowski, a former supporter of Pilsudski, who became the commander of the Polish armed forces. Against the opposition of the Sosnkowski faction, Mikolajczyk attempted to re-establish diplomatic relations with Moscow. In October 1943 Molotov bluntly informed Eden, who acted as go-between, that there was no possibility of healing the breach until there was a Polish government "favorably disposed towards the Soviet Union."[12] Molotov complained, moreover, that the Home Army—the Polish underground behind the German lines—was becoming increasingly inactive as the Red Army approached the Polish frontier.

The Mikolajczyk government continued to pressure its Anglo-American allies for support with undiminished vigor, but it was a forlorn though not entirely forsaken cause. Since winning the war was the chief objective, Roosevelt and Churchill were unwilling to risk disrupting the coalition for the sake of placating the Poles; and as long as the Red Army remained the vital ingredient for ultimate victory, Stalin's moodiness in the absence of a second front was of more immediate importance than finding a solution to scores of secondary issues.

Roosevelt had a well-placed confidence in his ability to break through the hardest shell in a personal encounter, and he conceived the idea of sending a special representative to the Kremlin with an invitation for a conference between the two heads of state during the summer of 1943. Former ambassador to Moscow Joseph E. Davies, well known for his sympathetic appraisal of Soviet policy, accepted the assignment but refused to take over the embassy again because of ill health. Standley, a doubtful choice from the beginning, was not in the best of favor in Washington because of his indiscretion in March and had already sent a letter of resignation to the President. Davies visited the Kremlin on May 20 and had difficulty at first in convincing

Stalin that he had made the long journey simply to deliver the invitation and that the United States had no ulterior motives in mind. Stalin tentatively agreed to meet Roosevelt on July 15.

Early in June the Russians were informed of the results of the Trident Conference—the code name for the Washington meeting in May between Roosevelt and Churchill. There was to be no cross-channel operation until 1944; and in pursuance of Churchill's "soft underbelly" strategy, an invasion of Sicily was planned for 1943. Stalin reacted with predictable indignation and accused his allies of what amounted to deliberate bad faith. Churchill discarded his usual tact in approaching Stalin, and without consulting Roosevelt, as he had customarily done, he replied with considerable heat. For the balance of the summer relations were so strained that some official observers were reminded of the ominous interlude preceding the Nazi-Soviet Pact of August 1939. There was no lack of separate peace rumors, and on two occasions (June 18 and July 17) the Soviet press felt obliged to deny that secret Soviet-German negotiations were in progress. In actuality, contact had been established in Stockholm as early as December 1942 between Soviet and German agents, though neither side seriously contemplated a separate peace. Moscow, after its victorious offensive in 1943, was less attracted by the idea and looked upon the Stockholm feelers, which leaked or were leaked to Western intelligence sources, as an additional means of prodding her reluctant allies into opening a second front.

Soviet displeasure was manifested more directly when the Roosevelt-Stalin meeting was postponed indefinitely; and in mid-August it was revealed that Maisky was being recalled from London for "consultation" and that Litvinov, who had left Washington in May, would not be returning and was to be replaced by the embassy counselor, Andrei Gromyko. As was to be expected in wartime, hardly more than a few hints of the serious division in the ranks of the United Nations were allowed to reach the general public. After more than two decades of incessant anti-Soviet propaganda, the Western public was now confronted by an equally naïve wave of pro-Sovietism based on a common war effort and the astonishing performance of the Red Army. Anglo-American Communism was able to thrive again in an atmosphere infinitely more friendly than the Popular Front days of the thirties; and in their refurbished status of respectability, the party leaders were in the vanguard of a considerable body of responsible opinion campaigning for a second front without further delay.

During the summer of 1943, unlike the previous two years, it became obvious that with or without an invasion of France the Russians would be able to take care of themselves. The Wehrmacht had swept forward on July 5 in its last major offensive on the eastern front. Hitler committed almost all his armored reserve in the hope of eliminating the Soviet salient west of Kursk. This time the defense was prepared in depth, with broad minefields, anti-tank traps, and the main body of troops poised in readiness well back of the front. When the German drive had spent itself, a well coordinated counterattack forced a retreat in the central sector; and the Russians began a general offensive that was not halted for any sustained period until Berlin itself was stormed in the spring of 1945. Hitler's continued insistence upon a static defense allowed the Red Army to probe the weak spots and to keep the Wehrmacht constantly off balance as it tried to shift its dwindling reserves to parry each new thrust.

Stalin's dawning realization that he might be able to win the war without a second front gave him confidence; and increased confidence permitted him to discard his attitude of peevish irritation toward his allies and to seek an accommodation on the political problems of postwar Europe. Having previously avoided a meeting with Roosevelt and Churchill, Stalin now signified his interest. But his first proposal, made in a message to Churchill on August 9, advocated a preliminary conference of "responsible representatives" who would draw up an agenda and draft prospective agreements.[13] The two Western leaders, then at a conference in Quebec, hastened to extend an invitation for a personal meeting in Alaska; or failing that, a parley of foreign ministers. Stalin seized upon the latter suggestion, and in deference to his wishes Moscow was accepted as the conference site.

Eden and Hull, accompanied by their political and military advisers, flew separately to the Soviet capital. Harriman, appointed to replace Standley, joined Hull at Teheran for the journey. Regular daily sessions were held with Molotov and his delegation (October 19–30, 1943). Military questions occupied most of the first two days. The Russians showed marked restraint by raising no objection to the plans for Overlord (the projected invasion of northern France), especially when Stalin was informed in the course of a discussion with Eden that a delay of a month or two might be necessary because of stiff German resistance in Italy.

On political subjects, the conference hardly passed the stage of general principles. Molotov spoke as if it were understood that Soviet interests would be paramount in Eastern Europe after the war, though he disclaimed any desire for a sphere of influence. The British would probably have been willing to bargain along such lines—as indeed they later did. But American diplomacy was traditionally based to a considerable extent on abstract moral principles: to the State Department the idea of a balance of power arrangement in Europe smacked of power politics at its worst. Hull considered it a signal achievement that the Russians agreed to cooperate in the "organization and maintenance of peace and security" in the post-war world. The promise was made in a four-power declaration signed on October 30, the initiating document in the establishment of the United Nations organization as the successor to the ill-fated League of Nations. That China became a signatory—and was thereby acknowledged a great power—was due to the insistence of the United States, for Britain was lukewarm and the Soviet Union had been definitely opposed.

The conference closed with a lavish Kremlin banquet and mutual expressions of satisfaction and good will. Negotiations meanwhile continued among the Big Three regarding a convenient site for their prospective meeting. Stalin held out for Teheran against Roosevelt's desire for Cairo, and at length the Iranian capital was accepted when it became evident that "Uncle Joe"—as Roosevelt and Churchill dubbed him in their personal correspondence—would otherwise refuse to attend. The President's suggestion that Chiang Kai-shek be invited was emphatically vetoed by Stalin, who was anxious to avoid provoking the Japanese. Chiang attended instead the Roosevelt-Churchill meeting at Cairo (November 22–26, 1943), where plans for the Pacific war were the chief topic of discussion.

The American and British delegations flew on to Teheran immediately after the Cairo Conference. Roosevelt accepted Stalin's invitation to stay in the spacious and well-guarded Soviet embassy compound, and shortly after he had installed himself in his new quarters Stalin paid a courtesy call. The two were alone, except for their interpreters, for three-quarters of an hour. Their conversation ranged beyond the amenities to political topics, but nothing of great import was said. When Churchill arrived, the first of four plenary sessions was convened on the afternoon of November 28. Eden, Molotov, and Hopkins attended, as did leading military and naval officers. The military situation took precedence. Churchill argued with his usual persuasive eloquence about possible further operations in Italy and the Mediterranean that would delay Overlord no more than a few weeks. He was quick to back Roosevelt's surprising suggestion—apparently made without previous consultation with his advisers—that an invasion of the Balkans through Yugoslavia might be feasible. Stalin, who chain-smoked and doodled through most of the meetings, would have none of it. Quietly and forcefully he insisted on the original plan. Churchill, finding no further support from Roosevelt, conceded defeat—but not before two more days of argument.

The military talks were confined to questions of strategy. Yet it must have occurred to most of the participants that the duel between Stalin and Churchill was inseparably linked to the political configuration of post-war Europe. Stalin had already begun to look upon the Balkans as a Russian preserve, and he resented any scheme which would challenge that position and at the same time fritter away Anglo-American military strength from a direct assault on Germany. Since Roosevelt was bent upon winning the war as quickly as possible and was wary in principle of Churchill's concern for Britain's imperial ties, a circumscribed but very real Soviet-American community of interest was obtained.

The President did his utmost at Teheran to carry this relationship forward to the future peace settlement. At first he found Stalin "correct, stiff, solemn, not smiling": there was "nothing human to get hold of."[14] In an effort to penetrate the "icy surface," Roosevelt teased Churchill unmercifully and succeeded in raising some hearty chuckles from Stalin. Roosevelt felt that he had obtained some basis of camaraderie—and he may well have been correct. However, he unquestionably overestimated the efficacy of personal diplomacy. Despite Stalin's reputation for inscrutability, he could at times be as emotional as the next man. When on the second day of the conference Churchill presented him with a specially designed and wrought "sword of honor" to commemorate the victory at Stalingrad, he was deeply moved and bowed to kiss it with tears in his eyes.

That the Soviet dictator was a shrewd and ruthless bargainer in matters involving his conception of the Russian national interest—and that he never allowed sentiment to interfere with politics—was to be amply demonstrated in time. But only a beginning was made at Teheran. The Polish question was allowed to dangle, although there was general agreement that the Curzon line[15] would provide an equitable eastern frontier and that the Oder River would provide a suitable boundary in the west (thus slicing off much German territory). Stalin was adamant in his refusal to resume relations with the Polish government-in-exile. The future status of Germany was even more vaguely defined. After some inconclusive talk, in which partition plans were broached, it was decided to turn the problem over to the European Advisory Commission organized during the October foreign ministers' conference in Moscow. Stalin made one significant concession: the Soviet Union would enter the war against Japan once Germany had been beaten. While he had informally said as much to Harriman in

1942 and to Hull on his recent trip, his statement could now be considered a definite commitment, and the American delegation was particularly pleased by it.

Stalin had mellowed once he learned of the Overlord decision, and the last two days of the conference were marked by a conviviality that had been previously lacking. The three leaders parted in a friendly spirit after a final banquet on December 1. The public was informed of the proceedings chiefly through a conventional declaration exuding confidence in ultimate victory and in an enduring peace to come. The press responded enthusiastically to the promise of future cooperation among the United Nations, but even the most astute readers could not have guessed that the really difficult issues were left unsettled at Teheran.

A comparatively minor conference decision, yet one that loomed conspicuously larger when Germany's defeat permitted the revival of political recrimination, concerned Yugoslav guerrilla warfare against the Axis occupation forces. It was agreed that aid should be given to the Communist-led Partisan forces of Josip Broz—better known as Tito—rather than to the Chetnik army of Drazha Mihailovich, a Serbian patriot backed by the Yugoslav government-in-exile in London. The decision was based purely on military considerations. The British, influenced by the exiled royalist government, had originally supported Mihailovich with the few supplies that could be dropped by air. By the summer of 1943, when they had established contact with the Partisans, it was clear that the Chetniks had adopted a passive attitude toward the Axis troops and were often collaborating to stamp out Tito's increasingly popular guerrilla movement. Britain's aid to Mihailovich ceased in late February 1944; the United States maintained contact, partly for intelligence reasons, until November 1944.

Since Tito was a Moscow-trained Communist, it was assumed in the West that he had received the Kremlin's full approval. Ironically, the Russians had been much slower than their allies to discredit Mihailovich and to sing Tito's praises. As in Spain during the civil war, they favored a broad united front against the Axis powers and were fearful that Washington and London would accuse them of plotting to set up a Communist regime in Yugoslavia. Stalin repeatedly refused even token assistance to the Partisans, and he was furious when at the close of 1943 Tito was formally installed as the head of a provisional government that barred King Peter and his London associates from returning to Yugoslavia after the war. Perceiving no outcry from his capitalist partners, Stalin then shifted ground, and the Soviet press began to lavish praise on Tito and to denounce Mihailovich. A Soviet military mission reached Partisan headquarters in February 1944; and in the spring a regular air drop was established to supply Tito's National Liberation Army, as his forces were then called. But Moscow still showed no disposition to recognize his government.

Later in 1944 Tito had conferences with both Churchill and Stalin. The meeting with Churchill, with whom he had been in correspondence since the winter, took place in Naples on August 12. It was amicable but without issue as far as reconciling Tito to the royal government. On September 21, as the Red Army neared the Yugoslav border, Tito flew secretly to Moscow to discuss with Stalin the disposition of their respective forces in the liberation of Yugoslavia. It was his first meeting with the Soviet dictator, and his independent attitude toward "the boss" left Stalin's colleagues aghast. Tito reported that their initial conversation was "very cool," probably, he surmised, because of his telegrams to Moscow during the earlier phase of the war, one of which had read: "If you cannot send us assistance, then at least do not hamper us." Tito was shocked and offended when Stalin spoke of the need to reinstate King Peter. Answering his protest, Stalin said laconically: "You need not restore him forever. Take him back temporarily, and then you can slip a knife into his back at a suitable moment."[16] Tito was not informed of the real reason for Stalin's solicitous attitude toward the Yugoslav government in London: the tentative Anglo-Soviet agreement on the Balkans arranged earlier in the summer assigned Yugoslavia to the British sphere of influence.[17]

Whatever their political differences, Tito received Stalin's cooperation on military matters. Red Army and Partisan units took Belgrade against stiff German opposition in October 1944. The Soviet forces then withdrew for the attack on Hungary, leaving Tito's government in *de facto* control. The Yugoslav army, 800,000 strong by the following spring, completed the final mopping up operations, and the last German resistance in Yugoslavia ceased on May 15, 1945.

III

The unbroken succession of Russian victories in 1944 raised in an ever more imperative fashion the political problems that had been postponed at Teheran. Always more concerned than Roosevelt with the nuances of *Realpolitik*, Churchill hoped to arrive at a mutually agreeable solution to the approaching power vacuum in Eastern Europe by driving a bargain with Stalin. By erecting governments friendly to the Soviet Union but with a democratic and capitalist base, it seemed possible to offer the Russians post-war security against a revival of German strength while avoiding the extremes of either forced Communization or a new anti-Soviet *cordon sanitaire*.

Stalin was in no mood for revolutionary adventurism. His whole career, in fact, demonstrated an erratic but steady retreat from the original goals of international Communism toward the verities of Russian nationalism. When his soldiers crossed the pre-war frontiers of the Soviet Union, they did so as Tsar Alexander I's troops had once invaded Napoleonic Europe, not as revolutionary zealots bent upon propagating a new faith. The only eager Communist missionaries were outside the Soviet orbit: Mao Tse-tung in China, Tito in Yugoslavia, and the anonymous guerrillas of the French and Italian resistance. Stalin either underestimated Communist opportunities—as in China— or sought to direct them into safe channels—as in Yugoslavia. It was not simply the act of a clever dissembler when he assured Mikolajczyk in October 1944 that Poland would remain a capitalist state because "Communism does not fit the Poles" or when he commented on another occasion that "Communism on a German is like a saddle on a cow."[18] In the West his profoundly conservative role between 1944 and 1946 was blurred and finally forgotten—if indeed it was ever really known —in the aftermath of the cold war.

The Polish question was the first order of political business in 1944, for the Red Army crossed Poland's 1939 frontier on January 4. The London Poles promptly claimed the right to administer the liberated territories. Stalin still held the door open by sending a new offer through Eduard Beneš, president of the Czechoslovak government-in-exile, who had visited Moscow at the end of 1943. Some concessions were made in Poland's favor relative to the Curzon line, and it was as generous a settlement as the Poles could have expected to get. Relying on the diplomatic weight of the Atlantic coalition, the Poles stubbornly refused it. On January 17 Moscow excoriated the London Poles, thereby abruptly terminating the possibility of direct negotiations; and as Soviet military power thrust more deeply into Poland, the prospect of a compromise receded still further.

Churchill undertook the disagreeable task of telling the Poles the facts of political life in an interview with Mikolajczyk on January 20. It was to no avail. Roosevelt was less forthright, and the vagueness of his language encouraged the Poles to hope that the United States would try to extract better terms from the Russians. Stalin was angered by the reluctance with which his allies dragged their feet. On March 23, 1944, he sent a blistering cable to Churchill, who had interceded for the Poles, accusing him of defaulting on the agreement made at Teheran. Stalin may have been all the more incensed at Churchill, for

Moscow had recognized the British-backed Italian government of Marshal Pietro Badoglio on March 13. Whether or not Stalin intended his move as a political deal—support for each other's position in Italy and Poland—the Soviet government continued to play a conservative role in Italian affairs. The Italian Communist party underwent a remarkable transformation after the return from Moscow in April 1944 of its leader, Palmiro Togliatti. The party hastily scuttled its anti-Badoglio policy and even warmed to the discredited monarchy that it had so strenuously opposed.

The British prime minister was sharply reminded of the state of flux in the Balkans when Russian forces crossed the River Pruth at the end of March and occupied a portion of Rumania. Molotov declared that his government had no territorial demands (except, obviously, Bessarabia and northern Bukovina) and that there would be no change in the "existing social order of Rumania."[19] Churchill wanted something more specific than verbal assurances, however, and he began to consider an over-all settlement in the Balkans. On May 5 Eden broached the subject through the Soviet ambassador in London, suggesting only that Greece be allotted to the British sphere and Rumania to the Russian. Moscow's acceptance was conditioned upon the approval of the United States. When Churchill approached Roosevelt on May 31, the response was cool. "Spheres of influence" was an obscene phrase to the State Department, and Churchill's adroit effort to disguise the proposal as a temporary wartime expedient failed to obliterate the taint. Without Hull's knowledge Roosevelt was persuaded to withdraw his objections for a trial period of three months. By this time—June 12—it was understood by the parties concerned that Bulgaria was to be within the Soviet domain and Yugoslavia within the British.

Separate negotiations in Washington through Ambassador Gromyko emphasized the reluctance of the United States to endorse the arrangement. No permanent spheres were to be carved out of the Balkans, and the Anglo-Soviet scheme was not to invalidate American interests in the area. Such a demurrer robbed the agreement of its binding qualities, but both powers tried to pretend that nothing was amiss; and until October 1944, when a definite tripartite accord was reached, Moscow and London were markedly deferential in observing each other's Balkan interests.

One problem was at last laid to rest in 1944—the second front. The months and years of recrimination came to an end with the Anglo-American invasion of the Normandy coast on June 6. The rapid development of the original beachhead and the supporting Soviet offensive on the eastern front all but guaranteed a United Nations victory. Stalin was generous in his praise: "One cannot but recognize that the history of warfare knows no other similar undertaking in the breadth of its conception, in its giant dimensions, and in the mastery of its performance."[20]

The achievement of military coordination and its afterglow of good feeling was of short duration. Political realities inevitably intruded, but the clash of divergent policies was dimly perceived, if at all, by the general public. Russo-Polish relations never ceased to be the chief source of irritation. As the Red Army drove into indisputably Polish territory late in June, the issue became more acute. Both Roosevelt and Churchill urged Stalin to see Mikolajczyk. At length an invitation was tendered, and on July 27 the Polish premier left London for Moscow. At Teheran en route he learned that the Kremlin had concluded an agreement with the pro-Soviet Polish Committee of National Liberation, now centered in the Polish city of Lublin as successor to the Union of Polish Patriots. Discouraged at this "betrayal," Mikolajczyk considered turning back. But his morale was bolstered by encouraging messages from Roosevelt and Churchill, and he continued his journey.

The Red Army was then poised within striking distance of Warsaw, and the Kosciusko station in Moscow broadcast an appeal for an insurrection. On August 1 the Polish Home Army rose within the city, hoping to liberate it from the Germans before Soviet troops arrived. The decision was thus largely political, for the Russians had already indicated that the so-called Lublin committee would administer Polish territory conquered from the Nazis. Although the rising had been authorized by the London government, the Warsaw commander, General Bor (Tadeusz Komorowski), was responsible for the timing. The Germans, who had been in the process of evacuating the city, resolved to stamp out the insurgents. The Home Army, constituting nearly 40,000 men and over 4,000 women auxiliaries, had supplies for only a week or ten days and were soon forced to appeal for outside aid. With the greatest difficulty the Royal Air Force, using bases in Italy, was able to drop ammunition and other equipment to the beleaguered Poles. The expected Russian offensive showed no signs of materializing. Stalin turned a deaf ear to pleas for assistance, and in a message to Churchill on August 16 he termed the insurrection a "reckless and fearful gamble" from which the "Soviet command . . . must dissociate itself."[21] Nor would he allow American air crews to land on Soviet airfields previously used for shuttle bombing raids on Germany.

In Moscow, Mikolajczyk was no more successful in his appeals for aid. He found that Stalin had also hardened his political demands: the

London Poles would now have to reach an agreement with the Lublin committee. With great distaste Mikolajczyk met some of the Lublin Poles—"a motley bunch"—on August 6 in a fruitless and none too friendly exchange of views. His mission a failure, but proudly defiant, he left the Soviet capital on the 9th.

As the plight of the Poles in Warsaw grew increasingly desperate, Stalin grudgingly yielded to insistent requests from London and Washington. But he continued to look upon the "Warsaw adventure" as a hopeless enterprise launched by a "handful of power-seeking criminals." American aircraft were permitted to land at Soviet bases, and the Red Air Force made nightly drops beginning on September 14. Soviet artillery bombarded the eastern outskirts of the city, the prelude to an attack in which units of the Red Army seized the suburb of Praga and detachments of the Kosciusko Division temporarily forged across the Vistula. But the Russian advance went no farther. With no hope of succor, the remnants of the Home Army surrendered to the Germans on October 2 after sixty-three days of the heroic but unequal struggle.

The disaster of the Warsaw uprising was a cruel blow to the Polish government-in-exile—the tragic climax to a losing fight with Russian power. Polish nationalism had dug its own grave by spurning the Curzon line while time remained. The insurrection itself, badly timed and without proper coordination with Soviet military plans, was an understandable blunder. Yet Stalin's indifference to the fate of the Home Army and his willingness to allow the Wehrmacht to crush the Polish opposition for him was an act of callous cynicism that shocked informed Western opinion and augured ill for the future harmony of Europe.

Churchill observed the Warsaw tragedy in an agony of spirit. His indignation was restrained by Roosevelt's wish to avoid endangering the common cause. American policy was almost exclusively subordinated to the military struggle, and the value placed upon future Soviet participation in the war against Japan sufficed in itself to avoid any unnecessary provocation. British policy, on the contrary, became more politically oriented as the Red Army and Communism—the two were inseparable in Churchill's mind—pushed more deeply into Central and Southeastern Europe. Rumania and Bulgaria, the countries of immediate concern to Moscow, were tacitly acknowledged to be within the Soviet sphere; and Churchill felt that Britain's relations with them in the past did not call for "special sacrifices."

Rumania asked for terms late in August 1944 after a swift *coup* led by King Michael ousted the pro-Axis leadership. An armistice was signed on September 12, and while the authority of the Soviet military command was unchallenged and several Communists entered the cabinet, the Kremlin's actions gave the Western powers no cause for alarm.

Bulgaria also sued for peace, but under entirely different circumstances. She had never declared war on the Soviet Union, only against the Western powers. The Russians, naturally preferring to deal with the Bulgarians themselves, suddenly declared war on September 5. The expected capitulation followed in short order, and like Rumania, Bulgaria entered the war against Germany. On September 9 a *coup* in Sofia placed the "Fatherland Front" in power. It was a coalition government in which the Communist party was strongly represented but far from dominant.

Finland was Germany's third ally to abandon the struggle: on September 5, 1944, a cease-fire went into effect. After Stalingrad the Finnish leaders had been only too aware that they had chosen the losing side in their desire to avenge the Winter War. Yet numerous peace feelers, and finally direct Soviet-Finnish negotiations in the first quarter of 1944, came to nothing. Military defeat was the only convincing argument, and during the summer the Red Army so pulverized Finnish defenses that Helsinki was obliged to give in. By the formal armistice of September 19 Finland returned to her 1940 boundaries (except for retrocession of the Petsamo district in the north) and agreed to pay an indemnity in kind of $300,000,000 over a six-year period. The terms were mild considering the circumstances. But peace still eluded the Finns, for 200,000 German troops in the northern part of the country had to be dislodged by force; and the senseless vandalism of these erstwhile comrades heaped fresh disaster upon the stricken land.

As Germany's satellite empire collapsed in ruins about her, Churchill hastened to implement his entente with Stalin on the Balkans. A meeting was arranged in Moscow, and Churchill arrived on October 9, 1944. In the presence of Eden and Molotov, the two war leaders plunged directly into the central issue during the first evening. Within a matter of minutes Churchill jotted down and Stalin approved a "percentage plan": the Soviet Union to receive 90 per cent predominance in Rumania and 75 per cent in Bulgaria; Britain to have 90 per cent predominance in Greece; and a fifty-fifty arrangement for Yugoslavia and Hungary. Such a precise delineation of their respective spheres was a rather academic exercise since it was not intended as a guide to proportionate representation in future governments. But the political implications were clear enough in outline. Both Churchill and Stalin were quite satisfied not to probe too deeply into the other's interpretation of the agreement—"to let well alone," as the former later expressed it.[22] Had the United States, instead of viewing the plan with aloof repugnance, indicated approval and worked in harmony with Britain to achieve a solution in Eastern Europe based on political realities, the "Iron Curtain" might not have descended so swiftly and with such finality.

As for the perennial Polish question, no significant progress was made. Stalin was prevailed upon to receive Mikolajczyk again, and a second trip to Moscow was arranged. Churchill openly sided with Stalin on the Curzon line, and the Polish premier was for the first time told of the Teheran decision on his country's future. After a stormy session with Churchill, at which both men lost their temper, Mikolajczyk weakened and seemed disposed to accept the stipulated frontier if the Poles were permitted to retain the Lvov area. Stalin promptly interposed his veto. Nor did he accept Churchill's proposal that Mikolajczyk become the head of a new government in which the London and Lublin Poles would be equally represented.

The Moscow Conference closed on October 19. Churchill was optimistic about a Polish settlement and felt that his relations with Stalin had reached a new peak of amity. No discord had arisen on the many other issues, both political and military, that were discussed. But the one major achievement—the agreement on the Balkans—diminished in importance as the scope of American objections became apparent. In the interim, however, the Churchill-Stalin deal paid one big dividend to the West: Greece was firmly established as a British preserve and as a bastion for Britain's interests in the eastern Mediterranean and the Middle East.

As in Yugoslavia, the Axis occupation of Greece in the spring of 1941 and the subsequent invasion of Russia brought a Communist-led popular resistance movement into being—the E.A.M. or National Liberation Front. By the summer of 1944, when the Germans began to evacuate Greece, the E.A.M. controlled about two-thirds of the country. The British had given some military aid to the guerrilla forces, including several minor groups to the Right of the E.A.M., but as the war drew to a close Churchill looked to the exiled government of King George II for political leadership in Greece. In October 1944, with the Germans in full retreat, British units landed on the coast and paratroopers occupied Athens. The royal government followed in their wake. George Papandreou became premier and the E.A.M. was allotted six cabinet posts.

The British were given an enthusiastic welcome by all factions, although the motive for their "liberation" of Greece was manifestly political rather than military. Since "grass roots" power was held by the E.A.M. and legal authority by the British-backed Papandreou government, the situation was a ticklish one demanding the utmost in tact. Unfortunately, this vital ingredient of successful diplomacy was nowhere in evidence. The E.L.A.S.—the fighting arm of the E.A.M.— rejected as unfair the conditions under which they were to disband their resistance forces. On December 1 the six E.A.M. ministers resigned, and two days later civil war broke out in Athens after police fired upon an unarmed group of E.A.M. demonstrators. Heavy British reinforcements were flown in. On January 15, 1945, a truce was arranged following an E.L.A.S. withdrawal from the city.

Churchill's strong-arm policy was subjected to a barrage of criticism in Britain and the United States as reactionary and imperialist, a judgment that was, of course, drastically revised as Communism later engulfed the other countries of Eastern Europe. Churchill's silent partner and fellow-conservative, Joseph Stalin, behaved with such impeccable restraint at the time that the British statesman paid him a grateful tribute in his memoirs: "Stalin . . . adhered strictly and faithfully to our agreement of October, and during all the long weeks of fighting the Communists in the streets of Athens not one word of reproach came from *Pravda* or *Isvestia*."[23]

Stalin was less tractable about Poland, and Churchill discovered that his hopes after the Moscow Conference were misplaced. Mikolajczyk, upon his return to London, was unable to extract any compromise proposals from his colleagues, and he resigned on November 24, 1944. Disgusted with the intransigence of the London Poles, Stalin decided to proceed unilaterally. On December 31 the Lublin committee formally proclaimed itself the provisional government of Poland. On January 5, 1945, Moscow granted recognition and appointed an ambassador. A week later the Russians launched a new offensive that drove the Germans from Warsaw. The two Atlantic powers, perturbed and irritated, continued to recognize the *émigré* government in London.

Roosevelt and Churchill were by then looking forward with some confidence to a Big Three meeting at which the interplay of personal discussion might resolve the Polish dilemma within the larger framework of a post-war settlement. In February 1945 the three great war leaders met for the second and last time at Yalta in the Crimea.

NOTES

1. Winston S. Churchill, *The Grand Alliance* (Boston, 1950), pp. 370–71 and 381.

2. Robert E. Sherwood, *Roosevelt and Hopkins* (New York, 1948), p. 343.

3. Alan Bullock, *Hitler: A Study in Tyranny* (New York, 1952), p. 600.

4. Sherwood, *Roosevelt and Hopkins*, p. 394.

5. Churchill, *The Grand Alliance*, p. 473.

6. Joseph Stalin, *The Great Patriotic War of the Soviet Union* (New York, 1945), p. 44.

7. Winston S. Churchill, *The Hinge of Fate* (Boston, 1950), p. 341.

8. *Ibid.*, p. 475.

9. Ministry of Foreign Affairs of the U.S.S.R., *Correspondence Between the Chairman of the Council of Ministers of the U.S.S.R. and the Presidents of the U.S.A. and the Prime Ministers of Great Britain During the Great Patriotic War of 1941–1945* (Moscow, 1957), I, 106.

10. Text in Stanislaw Mikolajczyk, *The Rape of Poland* (New York, 1948), p. 263.

11. *Ibid.*, p. 38; Joseph Czapski, *The Inhuman Land* (New York, 1952), p. 163; Samuel L. Sharp, *Poland: White Eagle on a Red Field* (Cambridge, Mass., 1953), p. 293.

12. T. Bor-Komorowski, *The Secret Army* (New York, 1951), p. 179.

13. Winston S. Churchill, *Closing the Ring* (Boston, 1951), p. 278; Ministry of Foreign Affairs of the U.S.S.R., *Correspondence*, I, 142.

14. Frances Perkins, *The Roosevelt I Knew* (New York, 1947), p. 83.

15. See above, p. 87.

16. Vladimir Dedijer, *Tito* (New York, 1953), p. 233.

17. See below, p. 288.

18. Mikolajczyk, *Rape of Poland*, pp. 79 and 100.

19. *Soviet Foreign Policy During the Patriotic War* (London, n.d.), II, 66.

20. *Ibid.*, p. 25.

21. Ministry of Foreign Affairs of the U.S.S.R., *Correspondence*, I, 254; Winston S. Churchill, *Triumph and Tragedy* (Boston, 1953), p. 134.

22. Churchill, *Triumph and Tragedy*, p. 231.

23. *Ibid.*, p. 293.

CHAPTER TEN

THE ABORTIVE PEACE:
YALTA, POTSDAM, AND AFTER

Like Teheran, the Yalta Conference had a lengthy gestation period. A meeting was in the discussion stage as early as July 1944. Postponed by the American presidential campaign in the fall, negotiations were resumed, only to run afoul of Stalin's customary objection to a conference site at any great distance from Moscow. Pleading his doctors' advice against long journeys, he insisted on the Black Sea region. Roosevelt and Churchill, both sensitive to prestige considerations, yielded with reluctance, and Yalta was designated informally before the end of the year.

The two Western leaders arranged for a preliminary meeting on the island of Malta. When Roosevelt and his party arrived aboard the *U.S.S. Quincy* on the morning of February 2, 1945, the combined chiefs of staff had been engaged for three days in debating—sometimes quite heatedly—the problem of delivering a knockout blow to Germany. Churchill, who had arrived by plane on January 30, had lunch and dinner on board the *Quincy*. In the evening the military situation was reviewed, and the report of the chiefs of staff, which embodied the American viewpoint in the main, was discussed and accepted. Eden and Stettinius—the latter had been recently appointed secretary of state to succeed the ailing Hull—were also present and reviewed their conversation of the preceding day on political questions.

Later that evening a mass exodus to Yalta began. As Roosevelt jocularly remarked, it would probably look like a minor invasion to the Russians, for the combined missions numbered some seven hundred persons. Transport planes took off at ten-minute intervals all night to ferry the enormous delegation to "Argonaut" (the code name for the conference). Yalta itself was a small seaport city in the Crimean Peninsula and had once been a favorite vacation resort for Russian royalty. Livadia Palace, the most lavish of the summer residences in the area, became Roosevelt's headquarters and the site of the plenary meetings. As hosts, the Russians spared no trouble or expense in accommodating their guests, and the progress made in renovating the town after the destructive German occupation was impressive.

There were daily plenary sessions during the conference (February 4–11), usually convening at 4 P.M. In addition, extended luncheon and dinner meetings and separate conferences of the foreign ministers and military advisers were arranged. Tête-a-têtes also took place at irregular intervals among the Big Three. It was an exhausting routine, and Roosevelt's increasing weariness was responsible for the exclusion of some topics from the agenda that Churchill and Stalin wished to discuss.

The first formal meeting was devoted to military matters. On the second day the future status of Germany was the sole topic. Since the Red Army was poised at the Oder in readiness for a drive on Berlin and Anglo-American forces were gathering on the Rhine, it was an issue of some urgency. There was no agreement on a plan to dismember Germany, though a special committee was established to make a recommendation. That Germany was to be divided into three zones of occupation had already been decided by the European Advisory Commission, a body set up as a result of the Moscow conference of foreign ministers in the fall of 1943. The Commission's plan was accepted, but the problem of whether France should be given a zone and a place on the Allied Control Council to administer German affairs was not definitely settled until February 10, when Stalin withdrew his objections. France was to be given portions of the British and American zone in western Germany.

The Russians presented a reparations plan obliging Germany to pay $20,000,000,000 over a ten-year period, half of it to the Soviet Union. Churchill was vigorously opposed; Roosevelt took no decisive stand. After the foreign ministers had considered the subject in a separate session, it was revived on February 10 and caused a heated discussion between Churchill and Stalin. The Russian leader evidently suspected the prime minister of desiring a strong Germany after the war as a make-weight against Soviet power. Although Roosevelt's position remained ambiguous, he approved a final protocol accepting the Soviet figure as a "basis of discussion" when the reparations commission met later in Moscow. British disagreement was also recorded.[1]

At the third plenary session on February 6 the question of the future world organization—later to be named the United Nations— was the first item on the agenda. Protracted negotiations at the Dumbarton Oaks Conference in Washington (August 21-October 9, 1944), with Andrei Gromyko at the head of the Soviet delegation, had formulated the basic structure of the new organization. There was to be a General Assembly representing all member nations and a Security Council in which only the great powers would be entitled to permanent seats. The delegates had failed to agree on the voting procedure in the Council; nor had the Russian proposal that all sixteen Soviet republics become Assembly members—designed to offset the voting strength of the Latin American republics and the British Commonwealth—found favor with the Atlantic powers. These were the two points of difference that were referred to Yalta.

The Russians accepted a compromise formula on voting procedure proposed by the United States. It preserved in principle the veto right of the great powers in the Security Council. Stalin also retreated in asking for only three Assembly seats. Roosevelt and Churchill ultimately agreed, and the organization's founding conference was set for San Francisco on April 25, 1945. There was great optimism engendered by the successful outcome of these negotiations, for it augured well for the continuation of Allied unity after the war. That the United Nations organization would founder in the treacherous shoals of the international power struggle was not foreseen at Yalta.

The nagging issue of Poland was also raised on February 6 and occupied a disproportionate amount of time. Neither Roosevelt nor Churchill objected to the Curzon line except in their pleas for a magnanimous gesture in ceding the Lvov area to Poland. Stalin refused to hear of it and reminded his listeners that it was Britain and France, not Russia, which had proposed the line in 1919. "Should we then be less Russian than Curzon and Clemenceau?" he asked.[2] His suggestion that the Poles receive their compensation at Germany's expense by moving the western frontier to the Oder and Neisse rivers was met by Churchill's tart comment that it "would be a pity to stuff the Polish goose so full of German food that it got indigestion."[3] In a formal protocol it was finally agreed that the Curzon line would be followed in the east "with digressions from it in some regions of five to eight kilometres in favour of Poland" and that the western boundary remain temporarily undefined, save that Poland should receive "substantial accessions of territory in the North and West."[4]

The nature of the future Polish government was of much greater moment than its borders—as all three arbiters of her fate acknowledged by the intricacy of their verbal fencing. The polite fiction that the government would ultimately express the will of the Polish people concealed a divergence of aims for which there could be no effective compromise in the long run. In Stalin's view, Soviet security could be obtained only by a subordinate Poland. Whether it was Communist or "democratic" probably did not greatly matter to him at the time. Yet the Western view that Soviet interests would be secure in a freely elected regime took no account of the anti-Russian national bias of the majority of Poles. Stalin was willing to accept a limited number of the London Poles into the Lublin (or provisional) government, while Roosevelt and Churchill strove to create an entirely new government comprising individuals from both factions. Without openly admitting their disunity there was no other course, considering the realities of Soviet power, than to grasp the equivocal formula that Stalin held out to them.

The final declaration on Poland therefore called for a reorganization of the provisional government on a "broader democratic basis with the inclusion of democratic leaders from Poland itself and from Poles abroad." The resulting "Provisional Government of National Unity" should hold "free and unfettered elections as soon as possible on the basis of universal suffrage and secret ballot."[5] Since the crux of the matter—the role of the Polish Communists in the new government—was carefully avoided, the Soviet position was scarcely breached by the promise of Western-style elections.

The three heads of state devoted only brief attention to the other problems concerning Europe and its periphery. No direct reference was made to the Stalin-Churchill "percentage partition" of the Balkans. But on the principle that silence means consent, the agreement was given implicit adherence. The three powers endeavored to preserve the precarious political equilibrium in Yugoslavia by urging that Tito and Ivan Shubashich, the premier-in-exile of King Peter's government, implement their promise to establish a coalition regime. As in the case of Poland, this was a compromise in form but not in content. When on March 7, 1945, the new Yugoslav government took office with Tito as prime minister and Shubashich as foreign minister, it was obvious that effective power lay in Communist hands.

No important decisions were reached concerning the other Balkan states. The Greek situation was barely mentioned, and Stalin assured Churchill that he had "no intention of intervening there in any way."[6] In Rumania and Bulgaria, where the Soviet high command was in full control, the Anglo-American members of the Allied Control Commission were virtually ignored. But the pressure of other business prevented the issue from going beyond the foreign ministers. As a kind of weak substitute for realistic negotiations on the political fate of Eastern Europe, the United States produced a "Declaration on Liberated

Europe," a high-minded collection of platitudes designed to encourage "democratic elements." It is difficult to believe that either Stalin or Churchill took the document seriously; to soothe American sensibilities, however, the declaration was duly signed.

Two Near Eastern questions were touched upon: the Straits and Iran. Stalin expressed a desire that the Montreux convention[7] be revised in Russia's favor, and his suggestion that the foreign ministers, who were to meet every two or three months in the future, consider the subject was adopted. Nothing was decided about the withdrawal of Allied troops from Iran, originally set for six months after the close of hostilities. Soviet interest in Iranian oil concessions was apparent, and one means of pressure—revived in a virulent form a year later—involved the encouragement of agitation for the autonomy of Azerbaijan, the Iranian province adjacent to the Soviet frontier. Because Molotov maintained that Iranian affairs were not a matter of urgency, a rational plan to exploit her oil resources died at the foreign ministers' level.

The most controversial of the Yalta agreements was the secret pact insuring Soviet entry into the war against Japan. In a conversation with Ambassador Harriman on December 14, 1944, Stalin had outlined his price for Soviet intervention. With some exceptions, these claims amounted to a restoration of Russia's position in the Far East at the time of the Russo-Japanese War of 1904: the recovery of the southern half of Sakhalin Island and a leasehold on the Manchurian railways and the cities of Dairen and Port Arthur at the tip of the Liaotung Peninsula. He asked also for recognition of the status of the Mongolian People's Republic as a Soviet preserve and for the cession by Tokyo of the Kuriles, a sparsely inhabited chain of volcanic islands to the north of Japan. The status of Korea, the strategic peninsula once coveted by Tsarist Russia, was not mentioned.

Roosevelt was thus already briefed on the Soviet demands; even before Yalta he felt compelled to meet them in substance. At the conference itself the most recent military intelligence foresaw prolonged resistance, perhaps until 1947, and the loss of a million American lives in invading the Japanese home islands without Russian help. The Kwantung Army in Manchuria was said to be particularly formidable, though it had in fact been seriously weakened by inferior replacements during the course of the war. The details of the accord were worked out in two brief discussions between Roosevelt and Stalin. The Soviet Union promised to enter the war against Japan "two or three months" after the German surrender in return for the concessions that Stalin had asked of Harriman and which he reviewed again for the

President. There was some bargaining, however, and Stalin yielded on several points. Dairen was to be "internationalized," and the Manchurian railways were to be jointly operated with China rather than to become Russian leaseholds. But the effect of this bounty was largely vitiated by a phrase guaranteeing that the "pre-eminent interests of the Soviet Union" in the port and railways would be "safeguarded." Stalin also promised to obtain Chiang's "concurrence" in the agreement, insofar as it related to China and to seek a Soviet-Chinese treaty of friendship and alliance. Churchill, while not a party to the negotiations, signed the completed document.[8]

After the war, when Yalta became a term of reproach and a political football in American party strife, the concessions to Stalin in the Far East were singled out as the most reprehensible of all because Roosevelt was said to have "sold out" China. The attacks were all the more extreme because Soviet intervention had proved to be unnecessary and because the ultimate victory of the Chinese Communists in their civil war with the Nationalist government was a major blow to American foreign policy. But the myths after Yalta bore no relationship to the reality. With the exception of the Kurile Islands, it is unlikely that Stalin's ambition to claim the Tsarist legacy in the Far East could have been thwarted whatever the attitude of the United States and China. Roosevelt probably reasoned that in addition to extracting the Soviet military assistance deemed essential by the joint chiefs of staff, China as well as the United States stood to benefit by acquiescing in the inevitable. In the first place, Soviet good will would be obtained, and to Roosevelt this was an essential precondition for any successful peace settlement. Secondly, by his assurance that the Soviet government was ready to conclude a pact with China, Stalin implied support for Chiang's regime as against the flourishing cohorts of Mao Tse-tung. Subsequent developments demonstrated that he regarded China as an Asiatic Greece in which the Communist opposition was to be discouraged. Whether his attitude was molded by Yalta and its aftermath or by an underestimation of Communist strength—possibly a combination of both—cannot be ascertained.

As for the Chungking government, which neither Roosevelt nor Stalin trusted to keep the secret, the pact was disclosed to its representatives in June 1945 and formed the basis of the Sino-Soviet treaty signed in Moscow shortly thereafter.[9] Only much later did Nationalist spokesmen blame Yalta for their downfall. Yet the record is clear that two decades of political blundering rather than anything which happened at Yalta led Chiang to an ignominious Formosan exile.

II

In the sober light of post-war disillusionment it appeared to Western opinion that Yalta was the incubus of Communist expansion and Soviet imperialism. At the time, however, the results were hailed with hardly a dissenting voice as a harbinger of an enduring peace; and even if one assumes that the chorus of praise would have been sharply muted had the secret protocols also been published, only the acuity of hindsight permits an assault on the viability of the arrangements made. Stalin, too, made concessions and displayed a flexibility that was not to be duplicated by Soviet diplomacy during the aging dictator's remaining years. But however painstakingly the Yalta literature is scrutinized for further clues to the motives, personalities, and aspirations of the participants, the conclusion is inescapable that the roots of Allied disunity lay elsewhere: in the rapid erosion of military necessity—always the best cement for unstable alliances—as victory approached in Europe; in the hidden rivalry to fill the political vacuum left by a collapsing Germany; and in the "normal" resurgence of ideological hostility between two disparate systems.

Within two weeks of the Yalta decisions Stalin moved to bring Rumania more closely into the Soviet fold. Following civil disorders and a sharp attack on the Communists (February 24) by the Rumanian premier, General Nicolae Radescu, Vyshinsky was sent to Bucharest. He pressured King Michael into appointing the Soviet candidate, the pro-Communist leader Petru Groza, to head a new coalition government. Communists also held the key ministries of Interior and Justice. The Anglo-American members of the Allied Control Commission had not been consulted, and the United States took the lead in registering ineffective protests in Moscow. Informed of the painful impression that his bare-faced interference had made in the Western capitals, Vyshinsky's only comment was, "Let the sparrows twitter."[10] Churchill, though no less upset by the Rumanian *coup,* hung back from strong diplomatic representations, conscious of Stalin's circumspect attitude toward Greece. Furthermore, he sought to avoid jeopardizing a prospective Polish settlement.

Following the procedure worked out at Yalta, Molotov and the two Western ambassadors in Moscow met on numerous occasions beginning on February 23, 1945, to consider means by which a representative Polish government might be organized. The Soviet foreign minister was at his most obstinate in insisting that the "Lublin Poles" should form the nucleus of the new government and that they should approve any other Polish leaders called in for consultation. The deadlock depressed Churchill, who feared "an utter breakdown of what was settled at Yalta."¹¹ He urged Roosevelt to join him in an appeal to Stalin in order to prevent a dangerous drift toward open disunity. The President professed some optimism despite his anxiety at the turn of events since the Crimean meeting. But by the end of March he agreed that a direct approach to Stalin should be made. On April 1 he dispatched a firm but courteous message expressing "concern" at recent developments and an inability to understand the "apparent indifferent attitude" of the Soviet government toward the "discouraging lack of progress" in carrying out the decisions made at the conference. He ascribed the impasse to an incorrect interpretation of the Polish agreement by the Russians and frankly stated that "a thinly disguised continuance of the present Warsaw regime would be unacceptable."¹²

Churchill added his own complaints in a separate message. He referred to the "veil of secrecy" that was being drawn over the Polish scene by the Soviet refusal to allow Western observers in the country; and he expressed regret that Molotov was not to attend the forthcoming San Francisco Conference on the United Nations. Stalin replied to both notes on April 7. He blamed the British and American ambassadors for leading "the Polish affair into a blind alley" but offered only slender hope of a compromise. The existing regime should be broadened, not liquidated, and any London Poles invited for consultation would have to accept the Yalta accord and be "friendly" toward the Soviet government.

Meanwhile a more heated controversy had broken out, illustrating Stalin's profound distrust of his allies' motives. He suspected a secret understanding with Germany because of tenacious resistance encountered by the Red Army compared to the slight obstacles in the way of the rapid Anglo-American advance. In reality, German fear of Communism, of Slavic "barbarism," and of the probable severity of the Russians in exacting revenge for the devastation of their homeland was responsible for the difference. His suspicions were deepened by the exclusion of Soviet representatives from the projected surrender negotiations with the German command in Italy. Although talks took place in Locarno, Switzerland, on March 19 and were unproductive, Soviet fears of a secret deal found expression in a shrill protest by Molotov to Harriman and an accusation by Stalin in a letter to Roosevelt that the Germans had used the armistice negotiations as a smokescreen to transfer three divisions to the eastern front.

Stalin refused to accept the President's reassurance. On April 3 he gratuitously charged that the latter had not been fully informed and that his military colleagues, who were "close to the truth," believed that an agreement had been reached to open the western front to the Anglo-American forces in return for more lenient peace terms. Roosevelt was angered by the allegation; and his reply, drafted by General Marshall and Admiral William D. Leahy, ended with a caustic retort: "Frankly, I cannot avoid a feeling of bitter resentment toward your informers, whoever they are, for such vile misrepresentations of my actions or those of my trusted subordinates."[13] Churchill also answered at some length: his previous silence, which Stalin interpreted as a guilty conscience, was dictated solely by his decision to ignore "this most wounding and unfounded charge." The incident blew over when the Western representatives were recalled from Switzerland and Stalin sent less peremptory messages implying regret that his frankness had been considered offensive. As the prime minister wrote to his American colleague, "This is about the best we are going to get out of them and . . . as near as they can get to an apology." It was then, on the threshold of military victory and amidst the perils of post-war readjustment, that President Roosevelt was fatally stricken by a cerebal hemorrhage on April 12, 1945. A profound sense of personal loss engulfed the Allied world. Stalin appeared deeply moved, and as an expression of his desire to cooperate with the United States he accepted Harriman's suggestion that Molotov attend the San Francisco Conference.

Because Roosevelt's death came at a time when the increasing tension of Soviet-American relations was still held in check by the exigencies of military necessity, his successor, Vice President Harry S. Truman, bore much of the blame for the swift disintegration of Allied solidarity. While the new President lacked many of the genial traits by which his predecessor had helped to weld the coalition into a working partnership, it would be straining the bounds of credulity to suppose that even a statesman of Roosevelt's gifts could have resolved the divergent conceptions of the national interest held in Moscow and Washington. The legend of Rooseveltian infallibility persisted nonetheless, and though its cautious acceptance in the Soviet Union during the late forties was pervaded by the base alloy of cold war propaganda, the affection of the Russian people for the memory of this great "capitalist" leader has been genuine and abiding. Like Lincoln, Lenin, and Sun Yat-sen, Roosevelt was fortunate in the timing of his death, for the tasks of reconstruction permit far greater damage to a popular image than the more exciting drama of war or revolution.

German resistance ceased less than a month after Roosevelt's death. Russian and American troops had met on the Elbe south of Berlin on

April 25. A race for the German capital was forestalled by the decision of the supreme commander of the Anglo-American forces, General Dwight D. Eisenhower, to concentrate on the Erfurt-Leipzig-Dresden area. He had communicated his plans to Stalin through the Soviet general staff on March 28. His action distressed Churchill, who for political reasons wished to occupy both Berlin and Vienna before the Russians. He felt that Eisenhower had exceeded the authority given him at Yalta to establish direct liaison with the Soviet high command. But the American chiefs of staff gave priority to military considerations, and President Truman later approved Eisenhower's arrangements for a line of demarcation between the Allied armies centering upon the Elbe.

At the end of April Churchill urged an advance to Prague and was again rebuffed. This concentration upon military rather than political objectives has since been criticized by Western commentators for the presumed advantage it gave the Soviet Union. But it is most questionable that the political configuration of post-war Europe would have been altered in the slightest had American strategy concentrated upon an unabashed effort to meet the Russians as far to the east as possible; nor is it likely that Anglo-American opinion, in the face of such a direct challenge to the Russians—still regarded as heroic comrades-in-arms—would have countenanced more than a temporary occupation of western Czechoslovakia. The Allied zones in Germany had, of course, been marked out in 1944 by the European Advisory Commission.[14] The delineation of the Austrian zones was more difficult, and final agreement on all particulars was not reached until July 1945.

The Red Army cautiously delayed its assault upon Berlin until a broad front had been secured. Vienna was taken on April 13, and four days later Zhukov launched his forces across the Oder for a drive to the Nazi capital. Hitler and the German high command hoped in vain that the Western fear of Communism would yet work a miracle and save the Reich. After Hitler's suicide in his underground bunker in Berlin on April 30, Admiral Karl Doenitz, his designated successor, sought to arrange a surrender solely to the Anglo-American armies. The Doenitz maneuver was spurned, and on May 7, at Eisenhower's headquarters in the French city of Rheims, the terms of unconditional surrender were signed in the presence of Soviet representatives. The Russians were not content with a secondary role; distrustful, too, of German intentions, they arranged a second capitulation ceremony in Berlin on May 9 which followed the fall of the city by a full week. On the same day Soviet troops entered Prague to complete the liberation of Czechoslovakia.

III

In the first flush of victory the Allied press and public were inclined to ignore or to minimize the difficulties of a smooth transition to peace, although in the United States there was a restraint that reflected a sober estimate of Japanese capabilities rather than pessimism about the future course of the Grand Alliance. The end of the war in Europe only accelerated the growing friction between Russia and the West. The controversy over Poland showed no signs of abating. If anything, the situation deteriorated because of Stalin's apparent determination to end the matter with a *fait accompli*. On April 21, 1945, a twenty-year treaty of alliance was signed in Moscow with the existing Warsaw government.

In the course of the next two days Molotov conferred with Truman in Washington and received a severe "dressing down" because of the Soviet stand on Poland. Moving on to the United Nations conference in San Francisco, the Soviet foreign minister revealed that sixteen Polish underground leaders, invited to Moscow for negotiations, had been arrested for what the Soviet press termed "diversionary acts in the rear of the Red Army." Operation of illegal radio transmitters and the concealment of arms and ammunition was the chief evidence cited against them. While the charges may have been technically accurate, they had little to do with the political purpose of the arrests. In June, after a trial in which all but one confessed to charges of terrorism and espionage, twelve were sentenced to terms ranging from four months to ten years and three were acquitted. Another was not tried because of illness. An amnesty in 1946 released those still imprisoned. Stalin's ruthless determination to secure a compliant Polish government, of which the first public manifestation had appeared with his refusal to aid the Warsaw insurrection, was now revealed more fully. The incident dramatized the struggle over Poland in moral terms that could be more easily understood by Western opinion.

At San Francisco, Molotov's conversations with Stettinius and Eden failed to break the Polish log-jam. As a last resort, Harriman persuaded Truman to send Harry Hopkins to Moscow. The veteran "trouble-shooter," in poor health and ostensibly retired from government service, responded to the call with his old-time enthusiasm and held six meetings with Stalin from May 26 to June 6. The talks covered virtually every aspect of Soviet-American relations, though Poland was the kernel of the discussions. Stalin registered a number of complaints about American policy and was particularly incensed by the "unfortunate and even brutal" manner in which lend-lease had been curtailed: if it was "designed as pressure on the Russians in order to soften them up then it was a fundamental mistake."[15] He appeared to be satisfied with Hopkins' denial that lend-lease was being used as a political weapon and in his visitor's explanation that under the law it could be used only to prosecute the war.

Hopkins stressed the importance of Poland as a symbol of future harmony; Stalin vigorously defended the Soviet Union's desire for security, recalling the role of Poland as a bulwark of the *cordon sanitaire* between the wars. He nevertheless showed a disposition to negotiate and once more denied any intention of Communizing Poland: "The Soviet system was not exportable." He proposed that of the eighteen to twenty cabinet posts in the existing Polish government four should be filled from a list submitted by Britain and the United States. Mikolajczyk, hitherto taboo, was declared an acceptable candidate because he had recently announced—under British pressure—his acceptance of the Yalta decisions. It was ultimately decided that twelve Poles should be invited to consult with the Moscow Commission on Poland: three *émigré* leaders, including Mikolajczyk; five non-Communist leaders from Poland; and four representatives of the existing Warsaw regime.

The delegates assembled in Moscow for their first meeting on June 17, 1945. Agreement was reached in a surprisingly short time despite the misgivings of Mikolajczyk and some of his anti-Communist colleagues. As officially announced on June 28, the Provisional Government of National Unity was composed of fourteen "Lublin" Poles and seven "outsiders." The London government was shut out entirely and immediately repudiated the new regime. The United States and Britain, convinced that this was the best that could be done to implement the Yalta formula, granted recognition on July 5.

The Stalin-Hopkins talks also resolved another dilemma that had threatened to disrupt the San Francisco Conference. The Russians stoutly maintained that the veto right in the Security Council should apply even to the *discussion* of a particular dispute. Truman asked Hopkins to intercede with Stalin, and the latter almost perfunctorily conceded the point on June 6. The Soviet delegation also objected to the unlimited powers of discussion granted the General Assembly on problems of international relations. Again Truman felt it necessary to step in. Stettinius was authorized to take up the issue with Molotov—then back in Moscow—and a compromise formula was arranged on June 21 which in substance represented an abandonment by the Russians of their previous position. The United Nations Charter was signed on June 26 with appropriate ceremony. The press was cautiously optimistic; and with the simultaneous easing of the tensions over Poland, it was still possible to believe in a satisfactory perpetuation of the victorious coalition.

It was thus with mixed expectations that the last of the wartime Big Three meetings convened—the Potsdam Conference. Early in May Churchill had suggested such a meeting to Truman and had invited him to a preliminary discussion in London. But the new President, like Roosevelt before him, wished to avoid the appearance of "ganging up" on Stalin. The final arrangements were made during the Hopkins mission, and the date was set for July 15, 1945, despite Churchill's plea for an earlier meeting. Truman and Secretary of State James F. Byrnes, who succeeded Stettinius on July 3, were inexperienced in top-level diplomatic negotiations and diligently labored to inform themselves on every foreseeable contingency. They were determined to take a firm but reasonable attitude toward the Russians and to stand by the Yalta agreements, especially the provision for democratic governments in Eastern Europe. Churchill was thoroughly disillusioned by Soviet conduct, and in his correspondence with Truman he had already referred to the "iron curtain"—a phrase that he was to make famous the following year. As a conservative spokesman of British imperial interests, his anti-Communist instincts, semi-dormant during the war, were now in full working order. He was greatly concerned about the future status of Europe when, presumably, the Anglo-American armies would be withdrawn from the Continent and only a weakened France would fill the power vacuum left by a vanquished Germany.

Stalin's aspirations may only be surmised. That they then included a Communist Eastern Europe may be doubted—not because his frequent protestations to the contrary should necessarily be taken at face value, but because of his actions. His insistence that the "Polish goose" be stuffed with German territory and that the Curzon line become Poland's eastern frontier; his demand for heavy reparations from Germany and her satellites; and his willingness to divide the Balkans with Churchill all bespoke the language of nationalism, not of revolution. The hobbling of a capitalist Germany to insure against future aggression was the key to his strategy in Europe—a far cry from the days of Lenin when Germany had seemed the lodestar of world Communism. The Communist parties of the West were still on good behavior; in France, Italy, and Belgium they participated in their respective governments with no thought of pursuing a revolutionary course. Stalin appeared to expect eventual Anglo-American recognition of Russia's developing "security zone" in the East and to have been deeply chagrined by his allies' refusal to accept what he considered just recompense for the sacrifices his people had made—sacrifices that most authorities have reckoned at between sixteen and twenty million dead.

At Potsdam, in one of the former Hohenzollern palaces near Berlin, these conflicting aims clashed more resoundingly than at Teheran or Yalta. Stalin was delayed for a day by a slight heart attack, and his tardy arrival gave Truman and Churchill an opportunity to feel each other out and to take separate sightseeing tours through the ruins of Berlin. The first of thirteen plenary sessions, which convened in the late afternoon of July 17, was largely devoted to organizing an agenda. Churchill was unusually ill-prepared, perhaps because of the recent election campaign in Britain, and submitted his proposals later in writing.

The first decision, made on July 18, was to create a Council of Foreign Ministers—not to be confused with the periodic meetings arranged at Yalta—to draft separate peace treaties with the defeated countries. Stalin would have preferred limiting the Council to the three great powers, but he acknowledged without discussion the principle that China should be permitted a role in making peace with Japan and that France was entitled to a similar right in relation to Germany and Italy. London was later chosen as the permanent site of the Council, which was scheduled to meet for the first time on September 1, 1945. The creation of the Council, largely the brainchild of Secretary of State Byrnes, thus registered the viewpoint of the United States that the settlement of world problems should be diffused among the great and small powers as widely as possible.

Most of the second day and much time during subsequent sessions was devoted to various facets of the German question. There was unanimity on general policy: complete disarmament and de-Nazification preparatory to a revival of democratic institutions. As to frontiers and reparations, there was serious disagreement. The Russians had already begun their own informal reparations program by seizing materials and industrial facilities for shipment to the Soviet Union as "war booty." The issue was not settled until July 31, by which time Clement Attlee and Ernest Bevin had replaced Churchill and Eden as a result of the Labor party's victory in the British general election. Stalin strove vainly for the $20,000,000,000 figure that Roosevelt accepted at Yalta as a basis for discussion, and he was forced to yield to the Anglo-American plan to take reparations in the form of industrial equipment. The four powers concerned were to make good their claims in their own occupation zones. Russia was to receive as additional compensation a quarter of the "surplus" capital facilities in the Western zones in exchange for 15 per cent of its value in food, coal, timber, and other products. The German fleet and merchant marine was to be split equally among the three allies.

To offset the Western victory on reparations, the Soviet position on the German-Polish boundary—that it should be the line formed by the Oder and Western Neisse rivers—won out. Churchill inveighed against the idea of handing over to Poland an area inhabited before the war by nine million Germans. Stalin maintained that the population had already fled, though in fact some two million people were still there. Since Poland was already in administrative control of the territory, the expedient adopted of recognizing the existing situation while withholding a final decision until the peace treaty hardly concealed the true nature of the transaction. The Russians were also allowed to annex a portion of East Prussia—the rest to go to Poland—to give them Königsberg (renamed Kaliningrad) as an ice-free port on the Baltic.

Little else was achieved at Potsdam except for a free-wheeling exchange of charges and opinions on subjects that time limitations or inappropriateness had not permitted at Teheran or Yalta. Stalin had a host of demands that remained unsatisfied. His proposal that the great powers break relations with Spain, which had dispatched a "volunteer" division to fight against Russia, was tabled when Truman and Churchill expressed disagreement. His bid for a trusteeship over one of Italy's African colonies was consigned to the foreign ministers, who acted as a kind of catch-basin for the unsolved problems of their superiors.

Less frivolous was his claim, already broached at Yalta, for a revision of the Straits convention. The Soviet press had been waging an increasingly clamorous propaganda campaign against Turkey, not only about the Straits but also for the return of Kars and Ardahan, the two provinces lost at Brest-Litovsk and formally ceded to the Turks in 1921. The 1925 treaty with Turkey had been denounced on March 19, 1945, and Moscow was seeking a renewal that would incorporate its territorial demands and allow a naval base in the Bosporus or Dardanelles. Churchill deplored the Soviet pressure on Turkey but again expressed his willingness to modify the Montreux convention. The matter was dropped altogether when Truman espoused a plan to guarantee freedom of navigation for the major European waterways. But an article of the final protocol did call for a revised Straits agreement.

The Western powers, too, registered their complaints, most of them involving Soviet conduct in Central and Eastern Europe. The United States took the lead in challenging Russian policy, although Churchill chimed in with an occasional sally. He referred, for example, to the experience of the British mission in Bucharest, which had been "penned up with a closeness approaching internment." ("All fairy tales," exclaimed Stalin.)[16] He also reproached the Soviet dictator for the failure of the Yalta agreement on Yugoslavia, and in private he protested that their fifty-fifty arrangement was not being kept. Stalin replied that even the Soviet government often did not know what Tito was up to—a statement that was probably received with skepticism but clearly foreshadowed the sensational Soviet-Yugoslav rupture in 1948. He added that "he had been hurt by the American demand for a change of Government in Rumania and Bulgaria" and regarded it as "unjust" because "he was not meddling in Greek affairs."[17] Molotov fanned the blaze by presenting the other foreign ministers with a document denouncing the situation in Greece—without, however, specifically naming Great Britain.

In the end nothing was done to alter the political complexion of the developing Russian satellite empire. Indeed, the possibilities for effective action were severely limited. Stalin was not a man to be swayed by moral exhortation, and a show of force was neither politically nor militarily feasible. The only real alternative lay in exploring the opportunities presented by the Stalin-Churchill pact on the Balkans. Precisely the opposite course was pursued. It became clear at Potsdam, if it had not been before, that the United States would never countenance spheres of influence in Europe. To Stalin it must have seemed that Britain was drawing closer to the American position; certainly Churchill was beginning to have his doubts about the scheme, as his remarks on Yugoslavia revealed. Because the agreement had been, moreover, an informal and personal transaction, the advent of the Attlee government could only arouse concern as to the continuity of its policy. While neither power specifically disavowed the sphere arrangement, Potsdam was an important way-station on the road from *Realpolitik* and secret diplomacy to open negotiations and hollow propaganda triumphs.

Weary but not entirely dispirited, the delegates dispersed on August 2 after spending the last two days in preparing the conference protocol and the official communiqué to be released to the press. There were no secret agreements made except those under the heading of military security. The capitulation of Japan so soon after the close of the Potsdam meeting would have seemed incredible only a few weeks before. The United States still expected a long and bloody campaign to reduce the Japanese home islands, and the "target date" for Japan's defeat was set for November 15, 1946. Stalin had enlivened the plenary session on July 28, however, by revealing that he had received two peace feelers from Tokyo, one on July 18 and the other that very morning, requesting Soviet mediation.

The weapon that was to cut short the Pacific war so unexpectedly —the atomic bomb—had been successfully tested in the New Mexico desert on July 16. A cryptic message, "Babies satisfactorily born," imparted this fateful information to the President at Potsdam. Churchill was informed the next day; Stalin, told after a week's delay, did not appear to grasp the significance of the event. Without consulting the Russians, an Anglo-American-Chinese ultimatum outlining terms— nominally "unconditional"—for the surrender of Japan was promulgated on July 26. Soviet intervention was now regarded by many of Truman's advisers as unnecessary and even detrimental to future American interests in the Far East. But Stalin was determined to claim his rightful share of the spoils of victory. His armies were prepared to strike in the latter part of August, and negotiations for a treaty with China were rushed to a conclusion after his return to Moscow.

Soviet-Japanese relations during the war had been based on the mutual interest of self-preservation. Had Germany been able to achieve the final decision over Russia that eluded her in 1941 and 1942, there is no reason to suppose that Japan would have hesitated in seizing the Far Eastern crumbs from the conqueror's table. In July 1941 her leaders had prudently refrained from occupying Vladivostok at Germany's invitation, and no further opportunity arose after Pearl Harbor. As the balance of military power turned inexorably against her, it was Japan rather than the Soviet Union that had cause to fear the violation of their neutrality pact of 1941. After Tokyo had procrastinated for three years in fulfilling its pledge to give up its concessions in northern Sakhalin,[18] an agreement was concluded in Moscow on March 30, 1944. Because of the increasingly unfriendly tone of the Soviet press thereafter, it could have been no great surprise to the Japanese when Molotov gave formal notice on April 5, 1945, of his government's decision not to renew the neutrality pact when it expired in April 1946. But Tokyo did not anticipate a Russian attack. Through Soviet Ambassador Jacob Malik in Tokyo and the Japanese envoy in Moscow, discreet soundings were taken in May and June to gauge the prospect of a settlement. On June 29 a Japanese spokesman finally made a definite offer of a non-aggression pact in return for the evacuation and neutralization of Manchuria. He also hinted broadly that the sky was the limit for further concessions if the Soviet government was interested in pursuing the subject.

By this time Japan was too weak to bargain effectively. She was "angling in waters where no fish lived," as a Japanese diplomat wryly admits.[19] The offer was left to dangle, and the requests for Soviet mediation—more frequent and insistent than Stalin had indicated at Potsdam—were also turned aside. Moscow demonstrated an unwonted zeal for the niceties of international law when Molotov proposed on July 29 that the United States, Britain, and China prepare a formal petition asking the Soviet government to join the war against Japan. Washington was reluctant to go on record now that Russian participation was deemed less vital, but a suitable formula was found for the projected violation of the Soviet-Japanese treaty in an article in the United Nations Charter requiring member states to forego other international obligations in case of a conflict of interest. Truman wrote Stalin in this vein, and the letter undoubtedly helped to reassure the Kremlin that the United States would not default on Roosevelt's promises at Yalta.

Nippon's war leaders temporized while clutching at the chimera of Soviet mediation. The press and radio were allowed to disseminate the views of the military oligarchy, and the Western powers assumed that the Potsdam declaration had been summarily rejected. The momentous and tragic decision was made to unleash the atomic weapon. On August 6, 1945, the heart of Hiroshima was vaporized by the new bomb.

Orders had already gone out from Moscow to its military commanders in the field to accelerate preparations for the attack. The Russians were concerned lest the war end before the Red Army had an opportunity to collect the political plums held out at Yalta. On August 8 Molotov read a formal declaration of war to the Japanese ambassador, who had sought an audience in another attempt to solicit Soviet good offices in making peace. Stalin thereby fulfilled his Yalta commitment to the letter, for it was exactly three months to the day since the official proclamation of V-E Day. A few hours later three army groups crossed the Manchurian border and began a lightning campaign that swiftly pulverized the once formidable Kwantung Army. All resistance ceased on August 20, and the surrender to the Soviet commander took place two days later. Moscow reported its losses at 8,219 dead and 22,264 wounded, Japan's at 80,000 dead and wounded and almost 600,000 prisoners. Soviet historians were later to magnify the victory beyond all proportion as the decisive blow in winning the war against Japan.

The second atomic bomb had been dropped on Nagasaki on August 9. This fresh disaster, coupled with the Soviet declaration of war, helped turn the tide in favor of peace. On August 14 Tokyo accepted the Potsdam terms. Molotov's suggestion that a Russian general share the duties of the Allied command in the occupation of Japan outraged Harriman, and the Kremlin hastily agreed to the choice of General Douglas MacArthur as the Allied supreme commander. The United States made it clear from the beginning that she intended to follow a unilateral course in Japan similar to Soviet policy in Eastern Europe. As a sop to her allies, a Far Eastern Advisory Commission was to be established in Washington with representatives from the ten nations that had actively participated in the Pacific war. Britain balked temporarily, but the Soviet Union and China promptly accepted.

By MacArthur's General Order Number 1, to be relayed to the Japanese commanders by the Emperor, Soviet forces were to receive the surrender in Manchuria, South Sakhalin, and North Korea. Stalin asked Truman to include the Kuriles and northern Hokkaido in the Soviet zone. The President readily consented to the former, since they had been promised to Russia at Yalta; but to Stalin's annoyance, he refused the Red Army a toehold on the main Japanese islands. The formal surrender ceremonies took place on the *U.S.S. Missouri* in Tokyo Bay on September 2, with General Kuzma Derevyanko representing the Soviet Union. In a proclamation to the Russian people, whose conspicuous lack of enthusiasm for the Far Eastern venture was evident, Stalin hailed the Soviet victory as a revenge for the defeat at Japanese hands in 1904–1905, a struggle that had "left bitter memories upon the people's conscience."[20] He failed to point out, of course, that the bitterness had been directed against the Tsarist regime and not against Japan.

IV

The sudden collapse of Japan automatically ended China's grueling eight-year struggle. That liberation came from the outside was not a source of pride to the Chinese themselves. Unavoidably, China had been pushed to the wings while the great powers occupied the center of the stage. That she was allowed to participate at all in the larger diplomatic and military issues that occupied her more powerful allies was due to the policy of the United States in grooming her to fill the vacuum in the Far East created by the defeat of Japan. Neither Churchill nor Stalin sympathized with Roosevelt's attempts to fob China off upon them as an equal partner, but both had permitted the President some leeway for the sake of unity. Unfortunately for American strategy, the Chungking government, floundering in a cesspool of apathy, corruption, and incompetence, was incapable of fulfilling the rosy expectations of Roosevelt and the State Department.

Chiang Kai-shek had been reluctant to commit his troops against the Japanese while his Communist rivals remained a potential threat; and except for a campaign in Burma under an American commander, General Joseph E. Stilwell, Chungking's army fought poorly when it fought at all. Chiang's elite units still maintained the cordon around Communist territory in the northwest that had been reimposed in 1939 following the partial disintegration of the united front. Kuomintang-Communist tension persisted following the New Fourth Army incident in January 1941.[21] Less serious armed clashes occurred sporadically despite inconclusive talks beginning in the summer of 1943 and continuing intermittently for another two years. The mediation efforts of the American ambassador to Chungking in 1944–1945, General Patrick J. Hurley, was chiefly responsible for keeping the talks alive. Both sides, suspicious and wary, prepared for what seemed an inevitable clash once the Japanese threat had been removed.

Neutral observers, mainly American, were invariably impressed by the orderly and efficient manner in which the Communists sustained a guerrilla war against the Japanese while carrying through a program of reform to win over the peasant population. They could not fail to contrast it with the conditions prevailing under Kuomintang rule and to wonder why such lavish quantities of American aid could not be put to better use. Struck by the non-revolutionary façade of the Communists and unused to the notion that Communism could ever be a constructive force, some of them spread the illusion that these were not "real" Communists. Stalin himself used the term "margarine Communists" and other belittling phrases in conversation with Western visitors, most likely because of past differences with Mao Tse-tung, the chairman of the Chinese Soviet Republic.[22] The United States, though somewhat soured on Chiang by the war's end, continued to give his government official support and prepared to intervene directly to make sure that his troops reached the Japanese-occupied areas before the Communists.

Sino-Soviet relations had been largely uneventful following the German attack in 1941. The Russian press adopted a stiffer tone toward Chungking beginning in the spring of 1944; but it did not presage a shift in Moscow's united front policy nor in Stalin's conviction that the Chinese Communists were too weak to retain their independence after the war. Since he expected no basic change in the Chinese government, the concessions he extracted at Yalta were in the conventional mold of Russian nationalism. Chiang was anxious to obtain an accommodation with Moscow as insurance against its support of the Chinese Communists after the war; and he tried to obtain American participation in any agreement that might be arranged with the Soviet Union. While refusing to be a guarantor of a Sino-Soviet treaty, Washington followed with interested attention the course of the negotiations that began in Moscow on June 30, 1945.

The Chinese representative, Premier and Foreign Minister T. V. Soong, conferred with Stalin and Molotov and also frequently consulted Harriman. The essence of the Soviet proposal was a treaty of friendship and alliance that Chungking would repay by accepting the Kremlin's interpretation of the secret Yalta protocol. Encouraged by the attitude of the United States that the Soviet terms went beyond the Yalta accord, Soong broke off the negotiations on July 14 in order to consult Chiang. The talks resumed after the Potsdam Conference. Soong returned to Moscow with reluctance, for he recognized that he might be held personally responsible for an agreement which would inevitably reflect China's inferior bargaining position. It was probably for this reason that while in Chungking Soong resigned as foreign minister in favor of Wang Shih-chieh, another Kuomintang liberal, who accompanied him back to the Soviet capital as the nominal head of the Chinese delegation.

Time pressed heavily upon Soong in the final stages of the conference: Soviet troops might turn over Manchuria to the Chinese Communists. He therefore made more compromises than Washington thought proper. The completed treaty, an elaborate document consisting of nine different instrumentalities, was signed on August 14, 1945, as Japan capitulated to the Allied coalition.[23] The first two articles of the separate treaty of friendship and alliance, which concerned the common war effort, were thus already outmoded at the time of signature. The most important remaining article provided for a thirty-year defensive alliance against future Japanese aggression. Of greater significance was the appended exchange of notes between Molotov and Wang in which the Soviet government promised to give China its "moral support and aid in military supplies and other material resources, such support and aid to be entirely given to the Nationalist Government as the central government of China." Moscow also recognized China's "full sovereignty" over Manchuria and renounced any intention of interfering in Sinkiang, where a rebellion had broken out against Chungking's authority. The other agreements related to the status of Outer Mongolia, Dairen, Port Arthur, and the Manchurian railways. The Soviet hold over Manchuria was less secure legally than the Tsarist government's on the eve of the Russo-Japanese War, but the ensuing collapse of Chiang's regime rendered the whole treaty obsolete within four years.

Both the Soviet and Chinese governments expressed satisfaction with the results of the deliberations. The United States, contrary to the uncritical praise of the American press, assumed an aloof attitude delicately poised between skepticism and approval. Washington was still uneasy about the sanctity of the Open Door principle. Although Harriman had received Stalin's verbal assurances, he was instructed on August 22 to secure something in writing. Stalin offered a public statement upholding the Open Door in China in conjunction with a similar pronouncement from Chungking. The Chinese declaration was delayed, and the State Department, for reasons not revealed, allowed the matter to lapse.

The Sino-Soviet Pact, like the Yalta agreement, was not a diplomatic necessity for Moscow: the Red Army was in the process of wresting Manchuria from Japanese control as it was being signed. Nor was the status of the Mongolian People's Republic as a Soviet protectorate in any way altered. Yet the Kremlin preferred to legalize its relations with the Nationaliast regime, for the dazzling vision of a Communist China, so natural to the Bolshevik elite in the mid-twenties, was a utopian pipe dream to the hard-bitten leaders of the mid-forties. As in Europe, Stalin was concerned with the traditional by-play of diplomacy and power politics—too much the "realist" to perceive the revolutionary currents which more than two decades of disappointment had taught him were mere figments of overwrought Marxist imaginations. It was left to Western commentators to enshrine the undeserving Stalin as a super-Machiavelli who could simultaneously aggrandize the Soviet state and nurture a revolution on the dimensions of the Chinese upheaval.

Moscow gave no encouragement to either side as the Chinese civil war showed signs of erupting once more after the fall of Japan. To Stalin Manchuria was simply a province conquered from the enemy; and as East Germany had been plundered of its industrial assets, so Japan's continental empire was stripped of raw materials, equipment, and machinery under the guise of "war booty." Much more of value was either damaged or deliberately destroyed; other installations were dismembered by Japanese technicians in a hunt for spare parts toward the end of the war or destroyed in the course of the Communist-Kuomintang struggle for Manchuria in 1946. Soviet policy was bent upon seriously impairing the industrio-military potential of the area before it could again come into Nationalist China's hands. When the

extent of these "reparations" became known, the United States registered vain but vigorous protests at Moscow's unilateral action.

During one of his conferences with Soong in July 1945, Stalin
stated that the evacuation of Soviet troops from Manchuria would be
completed not more than three months after the date of the Japanese
surrender—that is, by December 3, 1945, reckoning from the time of
the official ceremony aboard the *Missouri*. This was of vital concern
to both Chungking and Yenan, since the future control of China
might very well rest upon which army was able to occupy the territory left by the withdrawing Russians. The Chinese Communists had
placed great faith in their mighty Soviet ally as the means of final
victory over the Kuomintang. The Sino-Soviet Pact therefore came as a
stunning rebuff, and it was with difficulty that they managed in their
public pronouncements to put a good face on what must have seemed
a betrayal of the revolutionary heritage of the Soviet state.

The Yenan authorities nevertheless persevered in the race to control
the areas of China proper so recently held by the Japanese. Greatly
outnumbered by the Nationalist troops and altogether lacking in the
heavy equipment shipped by the United States to Chungking during
the war, the Chinese Red Army possessed a distinct geographical advantage—gained by wartime guerrilla campaigns—in its proximity
to the northern and eastern provinces of occupied China. Left to their
own devices, Chiang's forces could not have taken the major cities of
the area; but with American assistance, ostensibly for the purpose of
facilitating the surrender of Japanese troops, Chungking was able to
secure its rule in the chief centers of population. In what has been
called the "greatest aerial troop movement in history,"[24] three Kuomintang armies—approximately 100,000 men—were ferried in September–October 1945 to Peking, Shanghai, and Nanking in American planes. Up to half a million soldiers were also transported to the
coastal cities in American vessels. Further aid came from the Japanese
puppet army of some 700,000 men—and not infrequently from the
"disarmed" Japanese themselves. Joined by 55,000 United States marines, who guarded the key rail lines in North China, it was a bizarre
coalition that preserved the authority of Chiang's regime.

Even against this formidable array, the Communists were able to
occupy much of the rural area of the north and the strategic provinces
forming the gateway to Manchuria. They established contact with
Soviet forces in the border region, and some units were reported in
Mukden as early as September 10. Yet Stalin continued to insist that
Yenan seek a reconciliation with Chiang.[25] The Chinese Communist
leaders had been willing to resume the negotiations that had broken

down the previous March; and as both factions exchanged insults through the press and radio, and while their armies skirmished and fought with one another, Mao spent the month of September and part of October in Chungking for talks with Chiang. Ambassador Hurley was again the mediator. The generalissimo was inflexibly of the opinion that his Communist opponents were simply Soviet agents. Perhaps for this reason he took heart from his pact with the Russians, expecting Mao and his colleagues to obey Moscow's orders. If so, he must have found them singularly obstinate and tough-minded negotiators.

When the Communist delegation returned to Yenan on an American plane on October 11, only superficial progress had been made. The basic distrust remained; no agreement was reached on the liberated areas under Communist control; and Chiang felt no necessity to make concessions. He correctly inferred that while Washington talked compromise, outright military and economic support for his government spoke a different language. The Communists could not fail to resent this contradiction between neutral words and unneutral deeds: the groundwork had been laid for the unrelenting animosity that was to prevail between the United States and Red China.

Moscow had behaved with impeccable restraint immediately following the Sino-Soviet Pact. But there was dissatisfaction in the Kremlin when the United States intervened directly in Chinese domestic affairs. While Stalin was not prepared to involve the Red Army in a similar venture, he decided to prolong the occupation of Manchuria after it was announced on September 30 that the evacuation had already begun. Obstacles were also found to impede Nationalist troop movements into southern Manchuria—obstacles that did not materialize when Communist "civilians" sought to occupy the area. Nor did the Russian commanders object when their ideological compatriots appropriated the arms and munitions that the Japanese had been forced to abandon.

Stalin was likewise offended by Russia's virtual exclusion from Japanese affairs. Truman's curt rejection of his request for an occupation zone in northern Hokkaido still rankled; and he complained to Harriman on October 25, 1945, that the Russian representative in Tokyo, General Derevyanko, had been recalled because he was treated "like a piece of furniture." The Soviet Union, he charged, was being relegated to the role of an American satellite in the Pacific.[26] To lend emphasis to these protests, the Russians boycotted the inaugural meeting of the Far Eastern Advisory Commission held in Washington five days later.

Faced also with dissatisfaction on the part of Britain and Australia, the United States proposed at the Moscow conference of foreign ministers in December 1945 that an eleven-member Far Eastern Commission (to replace the advisory body) be created in Washington empowered to make broad policy decisions and that an Allied Council (the United States, the U.S.S.R., the British Commonwealth, and China) be established in Tokyo with advisory and consultative functions. Molotov raised several objections but finally accepted the American formulation. Subsequent meetings of these two bodies revealed their futility in trying to influence the occupation policies of General MacArthur, whose imperious nature and paternalistic outlook was given a free rein by Washington.

The Russians had more bargaining leverage at the Moscow Conference on the question of China, and Molotov proceeded to make the most of it by barring from the agenda any discussion of the transfer of Manchuria to Chinese Nationalist control. He challenged Byrnes on the presence of American troops in China and proposed a simultaneous withdrawal by both powers not later than January 15, 1946. In refusing, Byrnes offered the disingenuous explanation that the marines were merely assisting in the demobilization and repatriation of the Japanese. Molotov pursued his quarry with such implacable zeal that the secretary of state, wearied of the same dialogue, stated with tart finality: "Mr. Molotov, you must be asking these questions because you like the sound of my voice. I can only give you the answer I have given you every time you have asked the question. For your advance information, when you ask the question tomorrow, you will get the same answer."[27]

Byrnes was received by Stalin later the same day—December 23. Where the servant had been obstinate, the master was benign and even affable. He professed no objection to the United States leaving its forces in China and reiterated his support of the Nationalist regime. But, he slyly suggested, would not Chiang lose his influence if the Chinese people became convinced that the Kuomintang was dependent on foreign troops? Byrnes was reassured by the talk, and Molotov adopted a more moderate attitude the next day. It was agreed, with appropriate ambiguity, that the withdrawal of Soviet and American forces was desirable "at the earliest practicable moment consistent with the discharge of their obligations and responsibilities"; and the three powers reaffirmed the need for a "unified and democratic" China under the Nationalist government.

The Soviet claim that Chungking had twice requested a delay in the departure of the Red Army was only technically correct. The Chinese government was reluctant to press the issue for fear of offending the Russians and because it expected—or at least hoped—that Moscow would cooperate in restoring Manchuria to its jurisdiction. Chiang accordingly agreed to a postponement to January 3, 1946, and once again to February 1. As February waned and no action was taken, anti-Soviet demonstrations erupted in a number of Chinese cities which, if one accepts Moscow's probably accurate claim, were organized by Kuomintang officials. In March the withdrawal began, and though the Soviet government declared that the process would be completed by the end of April, it was not until May 31 that the evacuation of Manchuria (excluding Dairen and Port Arthur) was fully carried out.

On January 10, 1946, a cease-fire was arranged by General Marshall, whom Truman had appointed as his special representative with ambassadorial rank following the resignation of Hurley in November 1945. But the agreement did not apply to Manchuria; and the truce was converted into an empty farce as both sides attempted to consolidate their position upon the heels of the departing Russians. Heedless of the recommendation of his American military advisers, Chiang poured his crack troops into Manchuria. His 1,000-mile-long supply line was logistically untenable, particularly since the Communists had not been dislodged from their holdings in North China and clung grimly to some two-thirds of Manchuria. Impressive geographical gains by the Nationalists did not conceal the weakness of a static position and overextended lines. Years of guerrilla operations against the Japanese and Kuomintang armies had prepared the Communists for a mobile war of attrition. Only the government's still overwhelming superiority in men and matériel and the resumption of American mediation efforts put off the final reckoning.

V

In the year following V-J Day, Soviet relations with the West deteriorated rapidly. The development was all the more unsettling to popular opinion because the slow erosion of good will preceding it, largely confined to the top levels of government, was not subjected to the merciless glare of world-wide publicity. As the legacy of wartime amity gradually dissipated and the most pressing need for secrecy disappeared altogether, diplomats and officials formed the habit of mobilizing public sentiment in their own countries and attempting to influence neutral opinion by self-righteous speeches and statements that could only exacerbate international tension. Obviously this was not a new phenomenon in diplomatic history. But it was soon to become a flagrant and universal practice—made inevitable, perhaps, by modern technology and the attendant growth of propaganda media, by the enormous accretion of governmental functions, and by the difficulty in an atomic age of settling controversies in the old-fashioned manner of force or the threat of force.

The press in Western Europe, and especially that of the United States, approached but never attained the status of a government mouthpiece, a condition normal to the Soviet Union even in the more liberal regime of Lenin's day. Soviet newspapers, ordinarily the most accurate litmus test available on the Kremlin's attitude, retained a respectful tone toward the Western powers much longer than did a goodly share of the Anglo-American press. Not until 1947 did the major organs of opinion of both East and West openly acknowledge that the "cold war"—as it came to be called—had arrived and was likely to stay. Eventually the hackneyed vituperation of Soviet propaganda reached a monotonous consistency unequalled save by the most irresponsible segments of Western journalism.

The approach of what some observers freely predicted would be World War III was heralded by a series of incidents that a case-hardened generation soon learned to take in its stride. The incidents were not atypical of the kind of diplomatic crises that had portended imminent hostilities in the past, but the international community in the post-war world bore only a faint resemblance to what it had been in 1939. Aside from the manifest disappearance of Germany and Japan as great powers, the most striking feature of the new political spectrum was the emergence of the United States and the Soviet Union as "super-powers"—a situation without parallel since the development of the modern nation-state in the fifteenth century. And unfortunately, this extreme polarity in global politics coincided with a renewed conflict of ideologies more acute than any since the schism in the Christian church in the sixteenth century.

Hardly less shattering to the historic state system was the decline of Britain and France as great powers and as world empires. While it was not immediately apparent, neither singly nor in combination could they offset the political and diplomatic dynamism of Communist Russia and build a new balance of power in Europe on the ruins of the old. The United States was by 1947 called in to redress the balance, and for the first time in its history it began to play a role in world affairs that its government—and still more its people—would have viewed with incredulity two years before. Most Americans thought of World War II as they had of World War I—a kind of historical accident that had drawn their country into a gigantic military effort to punish the wicked and uphold the just. With the triumph of good over evil, there seemed no reason to become permanently involved in distant quarrels, although in 1945 the national mood was receptive to the United Nations and far less insular than it had been in the twenties and thirties.

If any trend in popular thinking, as distinct from official opinion, was discernible in the Soviet Union, it was one of profound war weariness and an expectation that the heavy sacrifices of the past would find some reward in an easier and better life in the future. It was certainly not a mood that would encourage the leadership of a democratic country to demand more belt tightening and to pursue a bold and adventurous foreign policy. Yet Stalin and his associates did so, probably in the firm conviction that they had no real alternative. Even leaving out of account the human losses in terms of the killed and permanently maimed, the cost of the war to Russia was greater than that of any other "victorious" power in modern history. Up to a quarter of her pre-war physical assets were destroyed and possibly as much as two-thirds of her total wealth in the occupied areas was lost. The stripping of East Germany and Manchuria of their industrial equipment, which the West regarded as ruthless looting, was a measure of the serious if not desperate straits of the Soviet economy. On August 19, 1945, preparations for a new Five Year Plan—the fourth—were announced; and during the following March it went into effect, with a continuing emphasis on the development of heavy industry. The strict wartime labor discipline was not relaxed, nor was the forty-eight hour work week, introduced in 1940, reduced.

The abrupt termination of lend-lease assistance, which had supplied arms, munitions, food, and equipment to the value of some $11,000,-000,000,[28] was a further economic strain that Moscow hoped to replace by American credits. In January 1945 Stalin had suggested a loan of $6,000,000,000 for post-war reconstruction. Washington equivocated, maintaining that such a huge sum was not readily available. The State Department wanted strings attached that would, as Harriman put it, "protect American vital interests in the formative period immediately following the war."[29] When Moscow pared its request to the relatively lean figure of $1,000,000,000 in August 1945, the pertinent documents were "lost" in the confusion of transferring the records of the abolished Foreign Economic Administration to the State Department and only "rediscovered" in February 1946. Washington's belated reply and explanation could only have grated upon Russian ears, especially since a loan was conditioned upon a settlement of the lend-lease account and a discussion of Soviet foreign trade policy. Moscow rejected these terms, and as time went on the growing estrangement of the two countries precluded even an agreement to negotiate their differences.

Stalin's unwillingness to ease the wartime pace in any significant measure necessitated a new ideological offensive to strengthen discipline and to recall to public consciousness the ideals of Marxism that had been allowed to lapse during the war. The return to revolutionary orthodoxy was fairly mild, however, until the latter part of 1946 when relations with the West had obviously worsened. The Soviet leaders themselves were cautious at first in spelling out the implications of the new propaganda line in the realm of foreign policy. Kalinin, in a speech to a Moscow party conference in August 1945, was perhaps the first to take up the pre-war refrain that the Soviet Union was the "one socialist state in the world" and to imply that the perils of capitalist encirclement had not disappeared with Hitlerite Germany. Molotov amplified the theme on November 6, 1945, when he told a meeting of the Moscow Soviet that the "roots of fascism and imperialist aggression" had not been "finally extirpated." On February 9, 1946, Stalin signaled the return to Marxist first principles by speaking of the "capitalist system of world economy" as concealing within itself the "elements of general crisis and military clashes." He also called for a gigantic increase in steel, coal, and oil production to safeguard the country against "any accidents."

Stalin's remarks, widely publicized abroad, were received as an ominous portent by many Anglo-American leaders. The impression was reinforced later in the month when George F. Kennan, then chargé d'affaires in Moscow and soon to become the chief ideological architect of American policy toward Russia, alerted his superiors in Washington with a shrewd analysis of Soviet policy in which the shift in the party line was traced to internal stresses: "At the bottom of the Kremlin's neurotic view of world affairs is the traditional and instinctive Russian sense of insecurity." He urged a campaign to educate the American people to the "utter ruthlessness and complete unscrupulousness of [the] Soviet ruling clique." His recommendation was eventually overfulfilled in the distorted form of a "Red scare" that dwarfed the similar phenomenon after the First World War and mocked his implied warning against "hysterical anti-Sovietism."[30]

At the time when Stalin publicly avowed the Kremlin's "neurosis" and the little-known American diplomat prepared to diagnose the condition, only the beginning phase of the Iranian affair[31] had occurred to dramatize to either of the future cold war protagonists the perilous but still outwardly friendly relationship between them. The first post-war conference, a meeting of the Council of Foreign Ministers (September 11-October 2, 1945, in London) as provided at Potsdam, had gone off badly. In spite of Molotov's desire to bring in the Japanese question, the agenda was confined to a discussion of five European peace treaties. The Italian treaty was considered first, with the British draft used as a working outline. The Soviet proposals were unacceptable to the Western powers: an Italo-Yugoslav boundary agreement, including the disposition of the city of Trieste, that favored Tito; a reparations settlement of $600,000,000, one-sixth of which would go to Moscow; and a United Nations trusteeship for the Italian colonies that would place Tripolitania under Russian administration.

Unable to dispose of the Italian treaty, the foreign ministers passed on to Rumania. No better results were obtained, and some preliminary skirmishing on the Hungarian and Bulgarian treaties was likewise fruitless. The underlying issue was the West's refusal to acknowledge Soviet preponderance in Eastern Europe. In private conversation, Byrnes, with Bevin's adherence, insisted on the letter of the Yalta declaration on liberated Europe and clung to the ritualistic formula of governments "both friendly to the Soviet Union and representative of all the democratic elements of the country."[32] Byrnes knew, or should have known, that his statement was a contradiction in terms. No democratic government in the Western sense, except perhaps in Bulgaria (and in Finland as it turned out), could have satisfied the Soviet or any reasonable definition of "friendly." Nor did the prospects for democracy in an underdeveloped area whose people had never become familiar with civil liberties, an effective parliament, or a fluid social order seem to trouble the Anglo-American representatives. The Russians were hardly prepared to admit their own unpopularity either as Communists or as would-be imperialists, although Stalin had posed the issue bluntly enough at Potsdam when he remarked that "a freely elected government in any of these countries would be anti-Soviet, and that we cannot allow."[33] But they could—and did—suspect with good reason that it was not so much the state of democracy in Eastern Europe that was the matrix of the dispute as the expansion of Russian power into a region where the tsars had been unable to penetrate save for brief and transitory interludes.

Disgruntled at repeated setbacks and exasperated by the frequency with which the French and Chinese foreign ministers sided with the Byrnes-Bevin position, Molotov advanced a proposal on September 22 destined to abort the Council proceedings. He maintained that the decision made on the opening day to allow discussion (but not a vote) by the French and Chinese delegations on the treaties with Rumania, Hungary, and Bulgaria should be revoked. Stalin backed his subordinate when Truman and Attlee interceded with him, and Molotov declined Byrnes' compromise solution. Nothing was left but to declare the conference a failure. Not even a communiqué for the press could be agreed upon.

Both Moscow and Washington recoiled from an open break and made conciliatory gestures. The United States recognized the provisional governments of Austria (October 20) and Hungary (November 2), and in return the Soviet authorities cooperated by arranging for free elections in both countries. Hungary had been governed by a coalition regime similar to that in Rumania before the Vyshinsky-Groza *coup* of March 1945.[34] Only two days after recognition, probably in the freest election in Hungarian history, an unexpectedly small Communist vote of 17 per cent was returned. The Smallholders party, which won an absolute majority of 57 per cent, took over the premiership and nine cabinet portfolios, but the Communists held the disproportionate number of four ministries.

In Austria the polling took place on November 25, 1945, the first general election since 1930. The same freedom to vote was exercised in the Soviet zone as elsewhere. The Communists emerged with only 5 per cent of the total vote and four seats in the national assembly. Shocked by the poor showing of their ideological kinsmen in Austria and Hungary, the Russians were not again to display such generosity in the matter of free elections within the Soviet sphere.

The United States ventured the first move in reopening high-level negotiations by suggesting a meeting of foreign ministers in Moscow. The Soviet government responded with a formal invitation, and the two Western diplomats made their first trip to the Soviet capital for the conference (December 16–26, 1945). Under no necessity to draft peace treaties and in the more intimate atmosphere of a three-power meeting, a variety of issues were handled with some success. The way was cleared for a reconsideration of the European treaties after the substance of the Soviet stand at London was accepted, and the Russians agreed to invite twenty-one nations for a formal peace conference in Paris not later than May 1, 1946.

To balance the American concession on Japan,[35] Moscow granted what proved to be an equally flimsy means of joint control over Rumania and Bulgaria. In the latter country a suspect election on November 18, 1945, had returned the Fatherland Front to power. The Soviet government promised to give Sofia its "friendly advice" that two "suitable" representatives of other parties who would work "loyally" with the government should be added to the cabinet. The project was never carried out because the opposition leaders set up conditions that the government—again with Moscow's "friendly advice"—refused.

For Rumania a somewhat different procedure was adopted. A three-power commission was authorized to go to Bucharest and oversee a broadening of the government on terms similar to those for Bulgaria. On January 7, 1946, two members of the opposition were duly admitted to the cabinet. Although the extent of Communist domination was only slightly less apparent in Rumania than in Bulgaria, Anglo-American recognition was conferred upon the one (February 5) and withheld from the other.

The sole item for which the Moscow conferees could find no solution, however modest, was the problem of Iran. Soviet troops barred the way to northern Iran, where a separatist movement under the leadership of the Tudeh (later Democratic) party—the Iranian Communists—had recently established an autonomous Azerbaijan. The Western powers feared that Soviet pressure tactics would lead to outright territorial aggrandizement. What the Kremlin actually had in mind was a foothold in the Middle East—a government at Teheran sufficiently oriented to Soviet interests to grant oil concessions equivalent to those enjoyed by Britain and the United States. But the clumsy and circumlocutious manner in which the Russians chose to further their cause alienated Western opinion and prompted Iran to draw closer to Washington and London for protection. As the inaugural session of the United Nations convened during the new year, what could have been a localized affair was blown up into a crisis of major proportions and became the harbinger of the cold war.

On January 19, 1946, the Iranian representative lodged a protest with the newly-organized United Nations Security Council against Soviet interference in his country's internal affairs. While the step was taken without an express Anglo-American recommendation, the attitude of these two governments was a foregone conclusion. Moscow, suspecting that Bevin had inspired the Iranian move, retaliated by filing complaints against the presence of British troops in Greece and Indonesia. After an acrimonious debate anticipating the future division of the United Nations into Eastern and Western blocs, the Council referred the dispute on January 30 to the two contending parties for negotiation. A cabinet crisis in Teheran had meanwhile resulted in the appointment of a new premier thought to be more acceptable to the Russians. He headed a mission to Moscow (February 19-March 10) that failed to produce a settlement.

March 2, the deadline for the withdrawal of foreign troops according to the Anglo-Soviet-Iranian treaty of 1942, found the Red Army still strongly in evidence. American forces had withdrawn by January 1 and the British by the stipulated date. Both governments expostulated with Moscow by sending formal notes. When the Security Council reconvened on March 25, Iran renewed its complaint; and Gromyko, the Soviet delegate, walked out of the chamber three days later when the Council refused to delay the discussion until April 10. A Soviet-Iranian agreement was reached on April 4. Moscow undertook to evacuate its troops in May, and Teheran promised to permit the establishment of a jointly controlled oil company. As for Azerbaijan, although it was declared an internal question, Moscow retained an excuse for interference via the Democratic party in the provision that Teheran should carry out "improvements in accordance with existing laws and in a benevolent spirit toward the people of Azerbaijan."

The Western press complained of a Soviet victory; but in truth the Kremlin had sustained a severe trouncing in public relations before the international forum of the United Nations and in the end had nothing to show for it. Teheran's attitude stiffened after the Russian troops withdrew on schedule, and the United States abandoned its remaining inhibitions about offering all-out support. Most of the Communist leaders were rounded up, and the Azerbaijan regime collapsed ignominiously in December 1946 as the Iranian army marched into the province. The final blow to Soviet ambition came in October 1947 when the Iranian parliament rejected the oil agreement after the government had received military assistance from Washington in the form of advisers and a $25,000,000 credit.

During the Iranian imbroglio the serious impasse in Soviet-Western relations was given international emphasis for the first time by Churchill's celebrated "Iron Curtain" speech. On March 5, 1946, at Westminster College in Fulton, Missouri, in the presence of President Truman and other important dignitaries, Churchill the "private citizen" voiced opinions which the responsibilities of public office would otherwise have inhibited. "From Stettin in the Baltic to Trieste in the Adriatic an iron curtain has descended across the Continent," he charged; and he went on to recommend to the Western democracies a policy of "sedate and sober strength" because "there is nothing they [the Russians] admire so much as strength, and there is nothing for which they have less respect than for weakness."

The outspoken frankness of the address startled most Americans, though a few years later its moderation would seem almost quaint beside the commonplaces of abuse to be found in both official and unofficial sources. Neither in the United States nor in Britain had opinion so congealed in an anti-Soviet mold that there was an automatic chorus of praise for the distinguished elder statesman. Washington held aloof from any suspicion that it favored an Anglo-American bloc directed against the Soviet Union; and from Truman on down there was a thundering silence in government circles on the speech and its implications. In private, of course, Churchill's sentiments were fully shared by the President and most of his confidants.

The Russian press and Communist organs throughout the world, which had diplomatically refrained from citing Churchill's anti-Soviet record while hostilities lasted, soon made up for lost time. Stalin himself entered the lists with a choleric denunciation of his wartime colleague: Churchill and his associates "bear a striking resemblance to Hitler and his friends"; and if they should succeed in organizing a "new military expedition against Eastern Europe," then "one can confidently say that they will be beaten, just as they were beaten twenty-six years ago." Stalin's resentment toward Churchill was also expressed to the new American ambassador, General Walter Bedell Smith, when he was received for the first time in the Kremlin. To Smith's query, "Is it possible that you really believe that the United States and Great Britain are united in an alliance to thwart Russia?" the Soviet dictator responded with a curt "Yes."[36]

Always blunt-spoken in private, Stalin drew back from an all-out attack in public upon Anglo-American policy. His lead was naturally followed by other Soviet spokesmen and by the press and radio. Washington and London reciprocated, and for the balance of the year both blocs kept up the pretense that while relations were troubled there were no immutable barriers to a permanent understanding. Only after this prolonged twilight zone of mutual hesitation did the world enter upon a new era of hot words, cold war, and an omnipresent possibility of nuclear annihilation.

NOTES

1. Text in *Foreign Relations of the United States, Diplomatic Papers: The Conferences at Malta and Yalta, 1945* (Washington, 1955), pp. 982–83.

2. *Ibid.*, p. 669.

3. *Ibid.*, p. 717.

4. *Ibid.*, p. 980.

5. *Ibid.*, p. 973.

6. *Ibid.*, p. 791.

7. See above, p. 194.

8. Text in the *Conferences at Yalta and Malta*, p. 984.

9. See below, p. 312.

10. Hamilton Fish Armstrong, *Tito and Goliath* (New York, 1951), p. 259.

11. Churchill, *Triumph and Tragedy*, p. 426.

12. Text *ibid.*, pp. 743–45; Ministry of Foreign Affairs of the U.S.S.R., *Correspondence*, II, 201–04.

13. Churchill, *ibid.*, p. 446–48; *Correspondence, ibid.*, pp. 205–08; William D. Leahy, *I Was There* (New York, 1950), pp. 333–34.

14. See above, p. 293.

15. Sherwood, *Roosevelt and Hopkins,* p. 894; *Foreign Relations of the United States, Diplomatic Papers: The Conference of Berlin (The Potsdam Conference), 1945* (Washington, 1960), I, 33.

16. James F. Byrnes, *Speaking Frankly* (New York, 1947), p. 74; *The Conference of Berlin,* II, 362.

17. Churchill, *Triumph and Tragedy,* p. 636.

18. See above, p. 256.

19. Toshikazu Kasu, *Journey to the "Missouri"* (New Haven, Conn., 1950), p. 188.

20. *Bolshevik,* No. 16 (August 1945), p. 2.

21. See above, p. 255.

22. Herbert Feis, *The China Tangle* (Princeton, N.J., 1953), p. 140; Conrad Brandt, *Stalin's Failure in China, 1924–1927* (Cambridge, Mass., 1958), p. 174, n. 52.

23. Text in *United States Relations with China* (Washington, 1949), pp. 585–96.

24. Theodore H. White and Annalee Jacoby, *Thunder Out of China* (New York, 1946), p. 282.

25. Dedijer, *Tito,* p. 322; *New York Herald Tribune,* July 25, 1951, cited in Max Beloff, *Soviet Policy in the Far East, 1944–1951* (New York, 1953), p. 44, n. 5.

26. Byrnes, *Speaking Frankly,* p. 217; Feis, *China Tangle,* p. 393.

27. Byrnes, *Speaking Frankly,* p. 227.

28. *Twenty-Second Report to Congress on Lend-Lease Operations* (Washington, 1946), p. 17.

29. Walter Millis (ed.), *The Forrestal Diaries* (New York, 1951), p. 41.

30. *Ibid.,* pp. 136–40.

31. See below, pp. 323–24.

32. Byrnes, *Speaking Frankly,* p. 98.

33. Philip E. Mosely, *Face to Face with Russia* (Foreign Policy Association, Headline Series No. 70, July-August, 1948), p. 23.

34. See above, p. 298.

35. See above, p. 310.

36. Walter Bedell Smith, *My Three Years in Moscow* (Philadelphia, 1950), p. 53.

CHAPTER ELEVEN

COLD WAR: STANDOFF IN EUROPE

During the winter and spring of 1946, while events in Iran and China occupied the headlines, the foreign ministers' deputies worked in comparative obscurity in London on the five peace treaties. It was soon apparent that the differences which had disrupted the Council meeting in September had not disappeared with the passage of time and a change in personnel. The subordinate negotiators were bound by the instructions of their superiors; and in the case of the Russian delegate there was little or no flexibility permissible even in trivial matters—diplomatic procedure that was routine for the Soviet Union.

The deadline of May 1, 1946, set for the European peace conference was already unattainable when Byrnes suggested a second meeting of the Council of Foreign Ministers in Paris to try to speed up the treaty-drafting process. The proposal was accepted, and the initial session took place on April 25. Molotov surprised his colleagues at the outset by agreeing to the French proposition that all four delegations consider the five treaties. His concession was not prompted by a new-found spirit of conciliation but came in response to a change in the press rules, instigated by the United States, giving full publicity to the proceedings. Molotov had no wish to wound France's vanity in her own capital. The propaganda content of the debates skyrocketed under the altered procedure: open quarrels, openly arrived at, henceforth became the fashion in great power negotiations as well as in the United Nations.

After his initial gesture, Molotov reverted to his usual truculent habits. The American attitude had also hardened in the past few months. The President had kept a tighter rein on his free-wheeling secretary of state following the Moscow Conference in December, and he informed Byrnes that he was "tired of babying the Soviets."[1] Under these circumstances, the Council's inability to achieve what it had failed to do seven months before was to be expected. Only a few insignificant details were settled before a month's recess was called on May 16. When the meetings were resumed on June 15, the same weary routine was in order. On June 27, however, Molotov off-handedly agreed to the cession of the Dodecanese Islands to Greece, and he accepted some minor clauses in the Italian, Rumanian, and Bulgarian treaties.

Thus encouraged, the foreign ministers tackled the major problems: Trieste, reparations, and the Italian colonies. The latter was disposed of by postponing the question for a year, at which time the U.N. General Assembly was authorized to settle it if no decision had been reached. This represented an important Russian concession, for the Western powers commanded a large majority in the Assembly, and one of the colonies—Italian Somaliland—was eventually placed under a temporary British trusteeship. The Soviet demand for $100,000,000 in Italian reparations was finally met after Molotov consented to holding the peace conference on July 29. The Trieste area was to be internationalized under the authority of the U.N. Security Council; and the Italo-Yugoslav frontier was drawn according to the recommendation of the French experts, which was slightly to the west of the American and British lines and well to the east of the Russian line.

The Council disbanded on July 12 after a barren three-day discussion of the German treaty. The peace conference to consider the five draft treaties followed on schedule (July 29-October 15, 1946). The Soviet argument that the great powers had won the war and should make the peace was unaltered. The smaller states possessed only advisory rights, but the United States, hoping to salvage something for the principle of a broad and free discussion by all the nations that had fought against the Axis, announced that it would support in future meetings of the Council of Foreign Ministers any proposal adopted by a two-thirds vote of the delegates. The action gave some meaning to the conference; otherwise it would have become merely a large and unwieldy debating society. Of the twenty-one nations represented, five (the Ukraine, Byelo-Russia, Poland, Yugoslavia, and Czechoslovakia) almost invariably voted with the Soviet Union, while the remainder, with less consistency and sometimes with reluctance, formed a Western bloc that was able to outvote its Eastern counterpart with ease. The speakers frequently strayed well beyond the diplomatic proprieties—and of good taste also. But such tactics were becoming the accepted routine for international conclaves. In all, more than three hundred amendments were suggested, some of them on inconsequential details. Of these, fifty-three passed by a two-thirds vote or better, and forty-one were adopted by a simple majority.

Notwithstanding this impressive statistical achievement—a feat of endurance occupying two months of talk and two weeks of balloting—it was not with any great sense of accomplishment that the conference concluded. Peace, as Molotov had said, would not be made by playing with votes.

The scene then shifted to New York where the third Council of Foreign Ministers convened (November 4-December 12, 1946) for final action on the treaties. Molotov's obduracy in refusing to accept any peace conference recommendations that had passed without the approval of the Soviet bloc exasperated Byrnes and Bevin; and Washington's avowed policy of "firmness and patience" was severely strained. After several weeks of ineffectual haggling, Byrnes threatened to abandon the treaties and to adjourn the Council. His gambit brought quick results, for the Russians had more to gain by yielding to the West on all the disputed points than by standing fast and thereby risking what they had. With an abrupt change of pace, Molotov agreed within a matter of days to forty-seven of the amendments that had passed by at least a two-thirds majority and twenty-four of the remainder.

The Council closed its long ordeal by considering the more difficult task of drafting treaties for Germany and Austria. The preparatory work was delegated to the deputies in London, and a new Council meeting was scheduled in Moscow. The completed treaties were signed in Paris on February 10, 1947. They did not materially affect the balance of power in Europe, though the legality of Russia's hold on her developing satellite empire was considerably enhanced. The stubbornness of the Soviet bargaining technique wrung a few minor concessions from the Western powers; but it cost the Russians far more in the long run by the continued diminution of the Anglo-American good will that had built up during the war.

That the reservoir of good will had all but dried up in Washington was illustrated by the forced resignation of Secretary of Commerce Henry A. Wallace on September 20, 1946, after his speech publicly criticizing the "get tough" policy toward Russia. Wallace represented a fast-diminishing body of New Deal sentiment which clung to a policy of conciliation—soon to be labelled "appeasement" by Republican critics—and focused attention upon the American monopoly of the atomic bomb, the drive for strategic overseas air bases, and the reluctance to grant Moscow economic aid as determining factors in bringing on the unhappy state of relations.

At the beginning of 1947 it still seemed possible, on the strength of the modest achievement in finally hammering out the minor peace treaties, that there was some hope of a *modus vivendi* between the two super-powers. The events of the year were to crush that dwindling optimism. Among the casualties was the peace treaty with Germany. In the failure to dispose of this complex issue, the power struggle over Central Europe was clearly exposed, and the restoration of a unified German state was postponed to the indefinite future.

Until November 1945 the Soviet zone of Germany was under the military authority of Marshal Zhukov. The savior of Moscow and the conqueror of Berlin, he was by all odds the most famous and popular of the Russian generals. Since Stalin could brook no rival to his own prestige as the master war strategist, Zhukov was recalled and eventually relegated to a routine post in Odessa. The marshal was replaced by his deputy, General Vasily Sokolovsky. Both military governor and head of the Russian occupation forces, he was also the Soviet representative on the four-power Allied Control Council. Meetings of this body, nominally the supreme authority for Germany as a whole, were held in Berlin three times a month, with unanimous consent required for decisions. Most of the actual work devolved upon the Coordinating Committee of the four deputy commanders, who were in turn responsible for the proper functioning of twelve directorates in charge of different aspects of occupation affairs. Since each directorate found it necessary to establish committees and sub-committees—over 175 were in operation during the winter of 1945–1946—the machinery of government was often cumbersome, particularly due to the necessity of conducting business at these quadripartite meetings in three languages. As top-level disagreements filtered down the chain of command in Germany, many of the committee sessions took on some of the polemical flavor of a foreign ministers' meeting. Time-consuming trivialities were also a regular feature, of which the most glaring instance recorded is that of the Soviet committee member who persisted in discussing for nearly an hour the "question of whether rabbit meat, nuts, and berries should be included in the food resources of Germany, even while admitting that no figures on them were available."[2]

Soviet policy in Germany, aside from the immediate aim of securing reparations and the less pressing goal of rendering the late enemy incapable of future aggression, reflected the Marxist penchant for economic rather than political reform. Indifferent to the favorite Western remedy for political ills—civil liberties and free elections—the Russian occupation authorities carried through by fiat a radical change in the social order which the "revolutions" of 1918 and 1933 had preserved almost intact from the Kaiser's day. Bank accounts were frozen, key industries nationalized, and land reform introduced. It was in no sense a Communist program. As a Red Army officer so forcefully put it: "Give Communism to such swine? . . . We certainly don't intend to bring a noble ideal like Communism to such a people."[3] The redistribution of land, the most important Soviet measure, wiped out the great estates of the Junkers, strengthened the small farmers, and provided a means of livelihood for the German refugees expelled from Eastern Europe. Edwin Hörnle, a German Communist *émigré*, was flown to Berlin in July 1945 to carry out the reform.

The eradication of Nazism was pursued vigilantly throughout Germany, but in the east it became a kind of political crusade without the judicial restraints found in the Western zones. Yet the Russians did not hesitate to employ "bourgeois reactionaries" and even well-known former Nazis if their knowledge or skills were of special use. No obstacles were placed in the way of a political revival except for a ban on Nazis and a certain amount of favoritism to the Communists, who were naturally considered the least tainted by ideological impurities. Communism had been virtually exterminated as an organized movement. Of those party members who had escaped to the Soviet Union during the Nazi era, not many had survived the purge of foreign Communists in the thirties. Wilhelm Pieck was one of the few "old guard" leaders to do so, and with Moscow's blessing he assumed the party chieftainship upon his return to Germany after the war.

The Social Democrats also flourished, and in the summer of 1945 permission was granted the Christian Democratic Union and the Democratic Liberals, two middle-class parties prospering in the West, to organize in the Soviet zone. In April 1946, after secret negotiations encouraged by the Russians, a merger of the Communists and Social Democrats was announced in the form of the Socialist Unity party. The head of the Berlin Socialists, Otto Grotewohl, shared the party leadership with Pieck. The Socialists in western Germany declined similar fusion offers and later broke off relations with their "comrades" in the east.

By 1947 the Socialist Unity party was completely dominated by the Communists, and the Russians gave it semi-official support by means of various special privileges. Wholly subordinate to Moscow's will, it lacked even the vestige of independence that some of the Communist parties of Eastern Europe still enjoyed. What popular following the party had gradually dissipated as the exploitative policy of the Soviet conquerors became more obvious and as the repressive tendencies of the East German regime tightened with the onset of the cold war.

Originally intended as the apex to the structure of Allied military government, the Control Council assumed the status of a four-power conference board as the dividing line between the Soviet and Western zones took on the aspect of a stable political frontier. The peak of Allied cooperation on Germany came on March 26, 1946, when the Control Council accepted a "level of industry" agreement outlining the kind and amount of production permitted. This rationalization of the economy was thought to be the initial step whereby the Russians would receive the reparations from West Germany promised at Potsdam while the British and Americans would be provided with foodstuffs and raw materials from the Soviet zone to ease the financial burden of feeding the population in their zones. But Moscow was absorbed with its own economic problems, and the plight of the German people was a matter of indifference. The Russians continued to seize much of the current output of East German industry as their just due, declining to cooperate either by accounting for the value of the materials already taken or by placing exports in a common pool to help pay for essential imports. The Western powers, quite understandably, took exception to paying what they considered an indirect subsidy to Moscow. On May 3, 1946, General Lucius Clay, the deputy American military governor, precipitated an open break on the German question by informing his Soviet counterpart on the Coordinating Committee that all further reparations from the American zone would be halted. As a pressure device to "soften up" the Kremlin, the action failed completely. It was regarded as a flagrant violation of the Potsdam terms and a deliberate provocation by American "capital."

Soviet intransigence on Germany had been voiced only a few days previously at the Paris session of the Council of Foreign Ministers when Molotov had capriciously objected to the twenty-five year draft treaty on the disarmament and demilitarization of Germany submitted by Byrnes. That the United States was to be one of the four guarantors of the pact was an unprecedented departure from its traditional aloofness toward "entangling alliances." Since Stalin had just four months before declared that he would support such a treaty, Byrnes naïvely ascribed the new Soviet stand to Molotov's personal opposition. Stalin's change of mind was very likely caused by his irritation at the slackened pace of deliveries from the Western zones and his realization that a long occupation would be necessary to fulfill the Soviet requirements for both reparations and political security. He evidently suspected that the treaty was designed to unify the zones and to roll back Russian power before Germany could be forced to disgorge her economic assets; and the Clay statement of May 3 must have seemed conclusive proof.

When the Paris meeting of the Council of Foreign Ministers resumed during the summer of 1946, Molotov took the offensive. He reverted to the Soviet demand at Yalta for ten billion in reparations and called for a four-power agreement to control the Ruhr industrial area. He managed to place the Western occupation authorities in an awkward position before the German public by advocating on July 10 a higher level of industrial production (which Moscow had previously opposed) and the re-establishment of a central government. In an address at Stuttgart on September 6, 1946, Byrnes vied with Molotov in the incipient popularity contest for Germany's favor by abandoning any further notion of a harsh peace; and at the cost of affronting Polish nationalism, he went the Soviet foreign minister one better by casting doubt on the permanency of the Oder-Neisse frontier. His warning that it was "not in the interest of the German people nor in the interest of world peace that Germany should become a pawn or a partner in the struggle for power between the East and the West" was fraught with unintended irony: the struggle over Germany had already begun.

The United States and Britain continued negotiations begun in July for an economic merger of their occupation zones. Final arrangements were not completed until December 2, 1946, and on January 1 of the new year "Bizonia" (the official name of the combined Western sector) went into effect. France held aloof for the time being. The door was held open through the Control Council for Soviet and French adhesion to the Anglo-American economic plan. Moscow may have been induced by the West's *fait accompli* to explore the prospects for a German peace treaty. Whatever the reason, Molotov consented to try at the New York gathering of the Council of Foreign Ministers.[4]

The Moscow sessions of the fourth Council meeting (March 10-April 24, 1947) assembled with one new face: General Marshall had replaced Byrnes as secretary of state at the beginning of the year. The alteration of the American delegation did not improve the situation, for the conference was torpedoed in spirit only two days after it opened by the proclamation of the "Truman Doctrine" in Washington.[5] But the four ministers lingered in corporeal form and belabored the issues with a certain dogged persistence, if not always with patience and tact. The soft-spoken Marshall allowed his fiery-tongued British colleague to take over much of the polemical chore. On de-Nazification and demilitarization policy, Bevin and Molotov exchanged acrid sallies, each accusing the other of pursuing a course that subverted the Potsdam decisions. There was no Soviet retreat on reparations or on the Ruhr, and the Anglo-American entente held firm in rejecting both items. The deadlock was equally rigid on political matters. The formation of a unified German government had become an unattainable goal by this time, and Marshall's suggestion that a commission be set up to examine the German-Polish boundary was considered by Molotov an impertinent attempt to undo the "final" settlement reached at Potsdam. The ministers parted with an agreement to try again in the fall. Only Bevin professed optimism, although Marshall reported that in a private interview Stalin told him that the discussions were "only the first skirmishes and brushes of reconnaissance forces" and that compromise would be possible when the parties had "exhausted themselves in dispute."[6]

The fifth Council of Foreign Ministers met in London (November 25-December 15, 1947) at a time when world tension made a successful outcome even more improbable than in the spring. Relations within the Control Council had also retrogressed, and Moscow moved nearer to the amalgamation of East Germany into its "security system." The propaganda war had begun in earnest; in Germany the information division of American military government was authorized in October to attack Communism as such in retaliation for the campaign against American capitalism and its "agents" in the Soviet-controlled press. On the eve of the London meeting, Sokolovsky, normally an urbane and even witty representative of the Russian cause, delivered a full-bodied indictment of Western policy in Germany before the Control Council.

The foreign ministers probably felt their efforts to be doomed at the start. Yet none was willing to assume the initiative in calling off the conference. The solidarity of the three Western powers was now more uncompromising, for France, a maverick on German questions, rallied to her powerful friends as the scope of Soviet objections to French ambitions was more clearly revealed. Beyond the acceptance of an agenda, the negotiators could find no common denominator. Beneath Molotov's vitriolic charges of capitalist imperialism in West Germany, which his listeners dismissed as vulgar abuse (as indeed it was), lay the very real resentment that his government was being squeezed out of an equitable share of the German pie; and to add insult to injury, Russia's former allies were now, it seemed, ready to combine with the common foe against her. That Soviet actions in East Germany bore the same ominous connotation to the West was incomprehensible to the Kremlin hierarchy, steeped as it was in the logic of inflexible—and often fallacious—Marxist premises. If the United States, Britain, and France, all indubitably capitalist in their social systems, ranged themselves against the one socialist country in the world and thwarted that country in its attempts to rebuild its shattered economy, then Q.E.D., a capitalist plot to crush socialism had been hatched.

A bedrock of reason lay beneath this proliferation of xenophobic fantasy. The pre-war experiences of the Soviet Union were not such as to inspire confidence in the Western democracies; and during the war itself the bitterness engendered by the prolonged delay in opening the second front was not wholly a product of the inequality of bloodshed. It also stemmed from the unspoken realization that while the material wealth of the homeland—created at such a heavy cost to the living standards of the Russian people—was being wantonly pillaged, the United States and to a lesser extent Britain were privileged sanctuaries where capitalists of the Wall Street image waxed fat and sleek on the blood of the Soviet worker and soldier. That this was chiefly an accident of geography rather than a calculated conspiracy was perhaps emotionally indigestible; but the Marxist axiom that war is the health of the capitalist order was a commentary of considerable validity as far as the United States was concerned. The Great Depression had been transformed into general prosperity by the clash of arms, not solely by the natural workings of a free economy. Ironically, the post-war crisis in the capitalist West that Moscow had reason to expect from its theoretical extrapolations was postponed into the indefinite future, mitigated at first by the pent up demand for consumer goods and then by a rearmament program designed to counter the threat of Soviet aggression.

To the non-believer, an analysis of the classic Marxist texts provided increasingly far-fetched explanations for the troubled state of international relations. Moscow perversely became more fundamentalist than ever, though the distinction between propagandist rationale and sincere convictions was difficult, perhaps impossible, to make. The failure to achieve a peace treaty with Germany, for example, was ascribed by Molotov, in a post-mortem examination of the London conference, to the expansionist aims of monopoly capitalism. More specifically, West Germany had become a strategic base for the "adventurist, aggressive plans of American imperialism."[7]

The cancerous tissue of Germany continued to poison the stability of Central Europe. In comparison, Austria was a minor lesion; yet it was one that resisted the scalpels of the great powers until 1955. As Germany's first victim, Austria was not technically an enemy nation. But her territory, resources, and manpower had been an integral component of the Nazi war effort, and it was decided that a formal treaty would be desirable. At the behest of the Russians, the Austrian treaty was put off at successive foreign minister meetings. Aside from Moscow's disinclination to give up an advance base in Central Europe, two major impediments frustrated an agreement: a definition of German assets that would permit the Soviet government a more generous share of reparations from Austria, and the Yugoslav claim to a slice of southern Austria. The powers were on the verge of success in 1949—the frontier question had been solved automatically with the expulsion of Yugoslavia from the Cominform—when the Soviet representatives unaccountably adopted delaying tactics which spun out the negotiations indefinitely. Obliged to endure military occupation for another six years, the Austrians at least had their own central government in Vienna subject only to the nominal supervision of the Allied Control Council.

II

Before the spring of 1947 both Russia and the United States were reluctant to admit that mutual antagonism had reached a point of no return. With the proclamation of the Truman Doctrine on March 12, however, American foreign policy underwent a historic revision. The issue of facing up to Soviet power was squarely joined. What the Russians took as a direct challenge was flung back in a series of moves that outraged Western opinion and all but choked off the remaining channels of compromise. The jockeying for advantage in the cold war was henceforth conducted in grim earnest, with the tacit understanding that a shooting war was to be avoided—a limitation of uncertain proportions since the ground rules were subject to change without notice.

The Truman Doctrine was a bold venture into uncharted terrain, for Greece and Turkey had never before entered the purview of American diplomacy in more than casual fashion. Securely within the British sphere of influence at the end of the war, Greece was ruled by a succession of Right wing governments that mismanaged the national economy and condoned political terror against leftists and moderates alike. Under these conditions, sporadic guerrilla warfare against the Athens regime broke out in 1946 under Communist leadership. Stalin no longer felt obliged to keep his hands off Greece, for he correctly assumed that his Balkan pact with Churchill had lapsed by default.[8] He accordingly encouraged—or at least did not object to—the assistance which the guerrillas of northern Greece received from the neighboring states of Yugoslavia, Albania, and Bulgaria. The British Labor government had not departed from Churchill's policy in Greece; but straitened financial circumstances and mounting criticism from within the Labor party made it imperative by early 1947 that British troops and advisers be removed. The United States prepared to take over the wavering British overlordship in order to plug the dike against Communist encroachment.

The Turkish problem presented fewer complications, involving as it did a historically familiar power struggle rather than civil war. Soviet press attacks on Turkey had become more strident in 1946 as the Turks stoutly resisted Moscow's demands.[9] As in Greece and Iran, the United States at first hesitated to throw its weight into the Near Eastern power vacuum. Britain's strategic interests were much greater, and the Kremlin regarded Turkey as something of a British pawn. The Soviet viewpoint on the Straits question was aptly expressed by the London *Daily Worker* in referring to one of Churchill's speeches: British control of the Mediterranean appeared to be "part of the order of nature, whereas a Soviet fortress on the Straits means that the sun of Christian civilization is setting."[10]

Washington had gone on record in November 1945 with a proposal that would leave the Straits under Turkish sovereignty but placate the Russians by a substantial modification of the Montreux convention. London professed agreement, maintaining that no immediate action was necessary; Ankara was willing to proceed with the American scheme. Moscow did not despair of direct negotiations with the Turks as a means of excluding the Atlantic nations from a Straits settlement. On August 7, 1946, a Soviet note to Ankara urged joint action to safeguard the interests of the Black Sea powers. Simultaneously, the charge that Turkey had failed to keep the Straits closed to Axis vessels during the war was renewed, and a selection of captured German documents was published to prove the allegation. In its unrelenting war of nerves, the Soviet government stationed troops along Turkey's Transcaucasian and Bulgarian frontiers, reportedly with attendant border violations; and the Black Sea fleet conducted maneuvers during the summer months.

The United States demonstrated its support of the Turks by sending an aircraft carrier and other warships to the eastern Mediterranean and by an indirect loan of $25,000,000. In September and October the Turkish army quietly mobilized under the guise of holding maneuvers. Beginning in November an indiscriminate drive against "subversion" in Turkey resulted in the suppression of several radical organizations and the closing of a number of leftist publications. Many suspects were arrested, and forty-five presumed Communists were later sentenced to prison. The brief flirtation of the Turkish Republic with political liberalism in 1945–1946 thus came to an early end.

The imminent retrenchment in Britain's imperial commitments

forced the United States to act sooner than the readjustment in post-war power realities would have made inevitable in any case. Washington was already moving toward a policy later popularized as that of "containment"—a formula to thwart Russian expansion by diplomatic, economic, and military means until a breakdown or significant mellowing altered the nature of Soviet power. Its intellectual basis was the work of George F. Kennan, a career official in charge of a special policy planning staff in the State Department who anonymously published a subsequently famous article expressing his views.[11] Truman and his closest advisers chose to emphasize the purely military aspects of "containing" the Russians, and the President's historic address to a joint session of Congress on March 12, 1947, sounded the tocsin for what Moscow considered a crusade against Soviet Communism.

In effect, Washington prepared to head off World War III with tactics more suitable for preventing World War II. The Russian threat to the "free world," as Western spokesmen preferred to call the anti-Communist portion of humanity, was overwhelmingly political; military aggression in the classic manner of a Napoleon or a Hitler was entirely alien to the Kremlin's strategy, for Soviet faith in the collapse of capitalism and the ultimate triumph of Communism did not rest upon a doctrine of conquest by force of arms. Yet the moral degeneration of Stalin's brand of Communism—the police state features of the 1930's were still an ugly reality—made the prospect of further Soviet expansion a grim problem indeed for the democratic powers.

Truman asked for $400,000,000 to assist Greece and Turkey in the period ending June 30, 1948. Specific mention of the Soviet Union was avoided, but the enemy was unmistakable: "lasting freedom and independence" in the world was unattainable unless Americans were "willing to help free peoples to maintain their free institutions and their national integrity against aggressive movements that seek to impose upon them totalitarian regimes." Put in these terms, the doubts of conservative isolationists, who objected to "global handouts" on principle, and of liberals, who deplored the measure as unnecessarily provocative to Russia and a backhanded slap at the United Nations, were overridden. With some delay Congress passed the appropriation requested, and the President signed the bill on May 22, 1947.

The Truman Doctrine was far more significant as a foreign policy declaration than as a means of providing stop-gap aid to Greece and Turkey. Carried to its logical extreme, it would mean a constant drain on American financial resources to bolster any regime thought to be endangered by Communism, whether by internal threat (*e.g.*, Greece) or external threat (*e.g.*, Turkey). To remove some of the taint of political and military expediency from the doctrine and to supplement it with a more humanitarian project for economic recovery was the State Department's next task. Under-Secretary of State Dean Acheson laid the groundwork in a speech (May 8, 1947) pointing out that the security and prosperity of the United States was tied to the reconstruction of war-torn Europe. His superior, General Marshall, then proposed a long range program of economic aid in an address at Harvard University on June 5. Russia was not specifically excluded, though he conveyed a sharp warning that "any government which maneuvers to block the recovery of other countries cannot expect help from us" and that the United States would oppose "governments, political parties, or groups which seek to perpetuate human misery in order to profit therefrom politically or otherwise." The occasion marked the genesis of the European Recovery Program, a scheme that went into effect the following year and is usually referred to as the Marshall Plan.

Moscow's response to Marshall's speech was almost friendly compared to the scathing remarks that had greeted Truman's. Whereas the Truman Doctrine was "imperialist expansion under the guise of charity," the Marshall offer was treated with a respect that implied some good might be accomplished provided "zealous American reactionaries" did not interfere by attaching conditions "copied after the Greek-Turkish example."[12] Wary of capitalist trickery, the Russians decided to explore the possibilities of the plan by sending Molotov and eighty-nine economic experts and clerical workers to Paris for a conference with British and French representatives (June 27–July 3, 1947). Molotov spurned the establishment of an investigating committee for a survey of Europe's economic needs. He feared an excuse for interference in Eastern Europe and proposed instead that each country submit its own "shopping list" to Washington. It seemed to the British and French participants that Molotov's attitude was fairly cooperative until on the third day of the conference he received a telegram from Moscow, presumably with instructions to break off the negotiations.[13] Whether such was the case or not, the Soviet foreign minister delivered a parting shot as he prepared to leave Paris indicating that the Kremlin's line had changed.

Soviet propaganda rode the theme of American economic imperialism, with a subsidiary refrain that the Marshall Plan was designed to forestall a new depression in the United States. Sixteen nations met in Paris on July 12, 1947, without representation from Eastern Europe. Poland had been eager to attend, and Czechoslovakia had accepted an invitation that was withdrawn after a journey to Moscow by Premier Klement Gottwald and Foreign Minister Jan Masaryk. The latter confessed bitterly to a friend after his return: "I went to Moscow as the Foreign Minister of an independent sovereign state; I returned as a lackey of the Soviet Government."[14] The satellite countries, direly in need of economic assistance that the Russians were unable to provide, had to be content with a series of trade agreements signed in Moscow on July 12. Soon dubbed the "Molotov Plan" in the West, these arrangements constituted an attempt at self-sufficiency within the Soviet orbit.

The Soviet decision to boycott the Marshall Plan added a further chill to an international atmosphere already made perceptibly cooler by the Truman Doctrine and Moscow's vehement reaction. Had the Kremlin been able to inject some finesse into its diplomacy it could have placed the United States on the defensive before European public opinion by accepting—or pretending to accept—American largesse and then waiting for the inevitable reaction of an outraged Congress called upon to stop Communism with one hand and to subsidize it with the other. Even as it was, an initial installment of $5,300,-000,000 for the European Recovery Program was authorized in April 1948 only after much Congressional soul-searching and the assumption that economic aid was the best means of saving Western Europe from Communist domination.

Convinced of the hostile intent of the United States, the Soviet government began to consolidate its power in Eastern Europe. Communist control, effective but partly concealed, of the seven states within Moscow's sphere and the ambiguous status of another—Czechoslovakia—no longer sufficed; Stalin wanted no weak links in the chains that bound them to the socialist fatherland. Each of the satellites was purged of political dissent, and "Muscovites"—Moscow trained Communists—were given preference over the wartime resistance leaders. Before the rigorous Stalinization process of 1947–1948 set in, the Iron Curtain of Churchillian fame had shut out the West from political interference but had not excluded the possibility of "different roads to socialism." Nor had the imposition of Soviet-inspired revolutions been without some benefit to the masses. Social welfare legislation, greater educational and employment opportunities, and land reform, if it failed to gain enthusiastic support for the "peoples' democracies," at least won popular approval.

Poland was perhaps the first to succumb to the Stalinist mold, but concurrent events in other East European countries prevent the assignment of exact priorities. The subordination of Poland by shameless methods of internal pressure, which instead of violent revolution became the Communist trademark in Eastern Europe, was particularly galling to the West because of the strenuous and prolonged struggle with Stalin to erect a genuine coalition regime. The government that had been granted Anglo-American recognition on July 5, 1945,[15] nominally represented five parties. But Deputy Premier Mikolajczyk's Peasant party was the only genuine rallying point for the anti-Communist opposition. As a result it acquired a heterogeneous group of followers whose loyalty to Mikolajczyk's program was problematical. It was even accused, possibly with some justice, of contact with the guerrilla remnants of the Home Army. Whatever the truth of the matter, these allegations served as an excellent pretext for repressive measures. Mikolajczyk chose to contest the government's popularity in a referendum held on June 30, 1946, in which the electorate was asked to approve the abolition of an upper chamber in the legislature, the program of land reform and nationalization of industry, and the frontier changes in the west. The Peasant party instructed its followers to vote "No" on the first question solely as a demonstration of its strength. The government resorted to falsifying the returns and reported that 68 per cent had voted "Yes" on the legislative question. Mikolajczyk claimed an 83.5 per cent majority in the districts where the ballot boxes had been saved.

As the parliamentary elections scheduled for January 1947 approached, violence was more frequently employed to combat the Peasant party's influence. Mikolajczyk was caricatured as a reactionary lackey of Western imperialism in the government-controlled press. He refused to join the government bloc, and in December 1946 he presented the American, British, and Soviet embassies with a 138-page dossier on the reign of terror to which his party was being subjected. Washington sent identical notes to London and Moscow (January 5, 1947) reviewing the situation as one in which there was "little likelihood that elections [could] be held in accordance with the terms of the Potsdam Agreement" unless the Polish government mended its ways. A three-power approach to Warsaw was requested. The Soviet reply raised a formidable smoke screen of "bandit attacks on electoral districts," of "criminal activities of fascist *émigré* circles," and of Peasant party connections with underground organizations. In short, Moscow declined to interfere in the "internal affairs of Poland." Nor did an American note to Warsaw obtain a more satisfactory response.[16]

The elections of January 19 were as much a travesty as Western observers had feared. The government's "Democratic bloc" gained 394 seats to the Peasant party's 28. Both the United States and Great

Britain registered displeasure that the will of the Polish people had not been freely expressed. The American ambassador resigned in protest, and Truman gave a frigid reception to the new Polish ambassador when he presented his credentials at the White House on February 4. Mikolajczyk, who maintained that his party had actually won a 74 per cent majority, resigned his office but continued to fight the regime from his seat in the Sejm. In October 1947 he fled the country to avoid arrest. The Peasant party, purged of its dissident leadership, was brought into the government coalition in February 1948. With the forced merger of the Social Democrats and the Communists the following December, the last shred of legal political opposition was expunged.

Hungary, a "kingdom without a king" since 1918, had officially become a republic in January 1946. The Smallholders-Communist coalition, a result of the November 1945 election,[17] held office for more than a year without a serious crisis. But the Smallholders party had been subjected to a "smear campaign" in the Communist press: it was supposedly a refuge for fascists and middle-class reactionaries without being truly representative of the peasantry. There was just enough truth in these accusations to lend an air of plausibility to the charges of a "conspiracy" that attended the arrest of six of the party's parliamentary deputies in January 1947. On February 26 the secretary-general of the party, Bela Kovacs, was arrested for alleged espionage activity and was later reported to have died in prison. Anglo-American protests on the Kovacs affair were unavailing. The government was reorganized on March 11 in a move to strengthen the Communist position.

A second crisis arose in the latter part of May 1947 while Premier Ferenc Nagy was in Switzerland on a holiday. Kovacs' "confession" had implicated Nagy, and he was forced to resign *in absentia*. His replacement was another member of the Smallholders party but a Communist puppet. Further Western protests made no impression on Moscow. Washington suspended the $15,000,000 credit granted Hungary, and Truman pronounced the events in Budapest an "outrage." While he asserted that the United States "would not stand idly by," this was precisely what did happen. A show of force was not contemplated in an area where the Russians had long since erected "no trespassing" signs.

New elections were held on August 31, 1947, in which franchise restrictions and intimidation prevented a full expression of public sentiment. Yet the three major opposition parties managed to obtain 35 per cent of the vote. The Communists, not unexpectedly, emerged with a plurality—22 per cent—and the three parties allied with them received 38 per cent. In the months that followed the opposition parties were eliminated one by one. The Social Democrats, the last important holdout, were absorbed by the Communists in June 1948 and the hybrid result renamed the Hungarian Workers' party. The final act in the establishment of the Soviet system in Hungary came on May 15, 1949, when the voters recorded a 95.6 per cent victory for the Independent People's Front, the single-ticket distillation of the remaining parties. A new legislative body accepted the Soviet-style constitution of the Hungarian People's Republic.

The pattern in neighboring Rumania varied only slightly. Communist tactics in 1947 were somewhat less blatant, for the coalition government of January 1946[18] was already securely in power and fewer means of "discouragement" were therefore necessary to cow the other parties. Rigged elections on November 19, 1946, produced a huge majority for the pro-Communist government bloc. The National Peasants and the Liberals, the chief opposition parties, boycotted the assembly but were powerless to register a more effective protest. In July 1947 the National Peasant leaders were arrested and the party banned. Nineteen defendants were tried in November on charges of conspiring with American intelligence officers to overthrow the regime. That an inept "plot" had indeed been hatched was clearly revealed at the trial; that it also endangered the security of the state was manifestly absurd. Iuliu Maniu and Ion Mihalache, the party chieftains, were imprisoned for life and the others sentenced to terms ranging from one to twenty-five years.

On November 6, 1947, the Liberal foreign minister, Gheorghe Tatarescu, was forced out of the cabinet, together with his colleagues. Ana Pauker replaced him, and two other "Muscovites" joined the government. Communist domination had now proceeded so far that the monarchy had become a useless anachronism. Upon King Michael's return to Bucharest after a trip abroad, he was forced to abdicate (December 30, 1947). Allowed to leave the country, he claimed in exile that his renunciation of the throne was invalid, and the Rumanian press sought in retaliation to blacken Michael's name by an "exposé" of his wealth and the reactionary role of his dynasty. Another election in March 1948 returned government bloc candidates to all but nine of the 414 seats in the assembly. On April 13 the Rumanian People's Republic was created when the new constitution was approved.

In Bulgaria the traditionally pro-Russian orientation of public opinion eased the Communist road to total power. The failure to broaden the coalition regime after the November 1945 election[19] sounded the death knell for the opposition. The Fatherland Front showed the first signs of cracking when the non-Communist war minister was forced out in June 1946. The unpopular monarchy was abolished in September of the same year when the public voted overwhelmingly against it. A new election on October 27 to create a larger assembly resulted in a 78 per cent majority for the government candidates. Considering the normal procedure of intimidation and fraud, the dissenting Agrarians and Socialists did well. The Communists broadened their control over the cabinet, and Georgi Dimitrov, the famous Comintern leader of the thirties, assumed the premiership.

In June 1947 the chief thorn in Communist flesh, Nikola Petkov, who had openly taunted Dimitrov on the floor of the assembly, was arrested. He was tried in August on a trumped-up charge of plotting against the state and condemned to death. Repeated protests to Moscow by the American and British governments were turned aside: it was "purely an internal Bulgarian matter." This interference from the West was bitterly resented and probably insured that the sentence would be carried out. Petkov was hanged on September 23. Washington pronounced the affair a "travesty of justice" and London used the phrase "judicial murder" in an indignant note to Sofia.[20]

After the official dissolution of Petkov's Agrarian party, only the Socialists under Kosta Lulchev presented any problem to the government. In July 1948 Lulchev and six of his nine fellow deputies were arrested and sentenced to fifteen years' imprisonment. The Fatherland Front then became the unchallenged agency of Communist authority. The customary "Stalin constitution" had been accepted in December 1947.

The capitulation of Poland, Hungary, Rumania, and Bulgaria to Communist rule further solidified public opinion in the West against the Soviet Union. But the political transformation had come about without the dramatic impact of a sudden *coup d'état*, and many had been inclined to write off Eastern Europe as already within the Russian fold. Such was not the case with Czechoslovakia, which by 1947 was regarded as a neutral bridge between the hostile worlds of monolithic Communism and democratic capitalism. A majority of the Czech people took pride in their government's unique status. Still devoted in the main to democratic principles, they had not recovered from the traumatic shock of the Western betrayal at Munich, and even anti-Communists were inclined to sympathize with the Soviet Union as the means of their liberation from the Nazi yoke. The Czech government-in-exile in London had maintained excellent relations with Moscow after the German attack on Russia. A twenty-year treaty of alliance and friendship between the two governments was signed in December 1943. President Beneš and his provisional government was established in Prague in May 1945. Communists held four cabinet posts—one the Ministry of the Interior—in the National Front coalition. The government's first important act was the cession to the Soviet Union of Sub-Carpathian Ruthenia, the eastern appendage of the pre-war Czech state containing a Ukrainian-speaking population. The territory was absorbed by the Ukrainian Soviet Socialist Republic in June. In December 1945 Soviet and American occupation forces were withdrawn from the country.

Parliamentary elections were held on May 26, 1946. The voting was both free and secret, and the Communists won a surprising 38 per cent of the total, a full 20 per cent more than the next highest party. Communist leader Klement Gottwald became the new premier, and his party's cabinet representation was increased to nine. Until the summer of 1947, when Stalin intervened to block Prague's participation in the Paris conference on Marshall Plan aid,[21] Moscow seemed content with the political *status quo* in Czechoslovakia. The Communists, who had played the parliamentary game with circumspection, now began to flex their political muscles. A mysterious "conspiracy" against the Prague government was uncovered in Slovakia in the autumn, and many Catholic members of the Slovak Democratic party were arrested. In January 1948 Minister of the Interior Vaclav Nosek began appointing Communists to leading positions on the police force. With Gottwald's support, he ignored a cabinet decision of February 13 instructing him to reinstate eight police chiefs who had been dismissed in the capital.

Valerian Zorin, a Soviet deputy foreign minister and the former ambassador to Czechoslovakia, arrived in Prague on February 19. Ostensibly his presence was required to supervise Russian grain deliveries —certainly an unusual task for so prominent a diplomat. In fact, he represented Moscow's interest in the developing political crisis, a crisis that the Soviet press was already portraying as a struggle of Czech Communism against "domestic and international reaction." The next day twelve non-Communist ministers resigned from the cabinet. It was a precipitate act, and because of the failure of the Social Democrats to join them it was the protest of a minority. Nor did the twelve take into account the likelihood that the Communists would spurn the accepted rules of parliamentary procedure. The government, now purged by the self-immolation of the dissenters, moved "loyal" police into the capital and ordered all public officials to cooperate with pro-Communist "action committees" secretly organized through-out the country. Parliament was adjourned as armed workers paraded in the streets of Prague under Communist leadership. Headquarters of the leading opposition parties were seized and "subversives" rounded up. Anti-Communist student demonstrations, one of the few signs of popular resentment, were broken up by the police. The army was an uncertain factor which the government preferred to neutralize. As commander-in-chief, President Beneš could have ordered mobiliza-tion and declared martial law. But such a step would have meant al-most certain civil war, a result he was determined to avoid at all costs.

Beneš bowed to the Communists on February 25. He accepted a new "coalition" cabinet that gave four posts to the Social Democrats—now under pro-Communist leadership—and token representation to the other minority parties. The surface features of democracy were retained, and the continuation in office of Beneš and Foreign Minister Jan Masaryk added ornamental prestige to the regime. On March 10, however, Masaryk's dead body was discovered in the courtyard below the windows of his apartment. An apparent suicide, there was fevered speculation in the West that he had been the victim of foul play. Beneš resigned on June 7 without signing the new constitution proclaimed on May 8. Gottwald succeeded him, and Antonin Zapotocky became premier. Beneš' death three months later symbolized the end of an era that had begun with Czechoslovakia's great "president-liberator," Thomas G. Masaryk, in 1918.

The February *coup* was a numbing shock to Western opinion; and though the Russians were to be content with their Berlin-Prague-Vienna picketline, Communist strength in France and Italy—not to mention its influence in Asia—brought renewed fears of Soviet sorties beyond the Iron Curtain. The United States, Britain, and France re-leased a brief joint declaration on February 26 condemning the Com-munist seizure of power for jeopardizing the "very existence of the principles of liberty to which all democratic nations are attached." Unofficial statements were far more harsh. No single event up until that time so aroused the Atlantic community of nations against the Soviet Union as the destruction of Czech democracy.

III

Although the Communist takeover in Czechoslovakia was a flagrant case of concealed aggression and a direct challenge to the West, the Soviet government appeared to conceive of its action as one of defen-sive strategy: the salient that had thrust like a dagger into the heart of its Central European "shelter belt" was eliminated. But in the callous process of manipulating their puppet empire through local votaries, the Russians met serious resistance from within the Communist faith which for the first time they were unable to dispel either by excommunication or by intimidation. The unique phenomenon of "national Communism" was born, and its shaman was Marshal Tito of Yugoslavia. The secession of the Yugoslav heretics from the Stalinist fold in the summer of 1948 more than balanced the acquisition of Czechoslovakia. In political and military terms the two countries were perhaps a fair exchange; in the ideological realm there was no basis for comparison. An unpunished and unrepentant group of schismatics centered at Belgrade was a greater threat to the mother church of Communism than if they had embraced capitalist democracy.

Before the rupture between Stalin and Tito, Yugoslavia had been accorded a position of honor in the Communist hierarchy. Its party was first below that of the Soviet Union, an implied tribute to the prowess that had enabled the Partisans, alone among the Communists of German-occupied Europe, to achieve their own liberation and to establish a Communist government without a helping hand from Moscow.

Yugoslav primacy was conceded until the latter part of 1947, and it was most conspicuously demonstrated by the selection of Belgrade as headquarters for the Communist Information Bureau (Cominform), an association of Communist parties secretly organized in Poland in September 1947. The founding conference was composed of representatives of the Iron Curtain countries (excluding East Germany and Albania) and of France and Italy. In the West the Cominform was immediately designated a revived Comintern when the Soviet press announced its formation on October 5. That Moscow so regarded it is doubtful. The avowed purpose of the Cominform was informational and propagandist—to publish a multi-lingual journal and to act as a kind of clearing house for ideas and problems of mutual interest. Presumably the Kremlin had more important functions in mind. One was to act as a transmission belt for Soviet directives in the realm of Communist policy and ideology, particularly to insure the proper state of conformity in the "people's democracies." The timing involved in creating the organization strongly suggested that it was also conceived as a counter-weapon to disrupt the effects of Marshall Plan aid. Communist-led strikes in France and Italy in November 1947 was evidence of Cominform militancy in this respect. But there was still no reason to think that the Comintern had been reborn in a different guise. Moscow's relationship to world Communism had not altered in the absence of a revolutionary priesthood bearing an official label; and there was no desire to invest the Cominform with duties and responsibilities which the Soviet government had, even in the thirties, accomplished by other means.

Tito had submitted the idea of a Cominform to Stalin in 1945 and again in June 1946. On the latter occasion Stalin proposed that the Yugoslavs take the initiative. But Tito cautiously suggested the French instead. No further action was taken until Stalin deemed the time propitious. Zhdanov, who had emerged since the war as the Kremlin's chief spokesman on matters of intellectual orthodoxy, was given the leading role at the secret Polish meeting and became the secretary-general of the Cominform. The appointment may have been Stalin's method of "kicking upstairs" a man regarded abroad as the number two figure in the Politburo and the aging dictator's heir-apparent. In any case, Zhdanov's new duties were somewhat peripheral to major policy determination in the Soviet power structure. The Cominform's biweekly (later weekly) propaganda organ, cumbrously titled *For a Lasting Peace, for a People's Democracy!*, came under his supervision though it was published in Belgrade under the nominal direction of an editorial board representing the nine member parties. The managing editor was Paul Yudin, a Soviet ideologue of whom anonymous humorists were reported to have said that he was "the best philosopher among the N.K.V.D.-men and the best N.K.V.D.-man among the philosophers."[22] He was a servile tool of the Politburo, and Stalin himself took an active interest in censoring and otherwise altering the paper's contents.

Tito was offended by the Cominform's too obvious subservience to Moscow, and after his falling-out with Stalin he professed to believe that it had been designed from the beginning as a device to knit together the major European parties in a united front against Yugoslavia. The possibility cannot be ruled out that this was among Stalin's motives because the Soviet leaders had not been oblivious to Tito's departures from orthodoxy. Yet the charge has too much the appearance of an after-the-fact construction to be convincing; and to center the Cominform in Belgrade, knowing that the Yugoslavs were soon to be expelled, would certainly have been a strange procedure.

The roots of Tito's defection are to be found in the independent and indigenous development of Yugoslav Communism during the war. In contrast to the other Communist leaders of East Europe, Tito was given extraordinary leeway. But Moscow's unaccustomed deference to Yugoslavia's special status had definite limits, and in the drive for uniformity within the Soviet orbit beginning in 1947 the first fissures of the coming crisis appeared. The Western world remained in ignorance of this incipient eruption. There was little or no intimation that all was not serene, for it was assumed that Belgrade's docility was neither greater nor less than the Kremlin's other dependencies. The twenty-year treaty of friendship and mutual assistance that Tito signed in Moscow (April 1945) was in reality the peak of Soviet-Yugoslav harmony. Yet even this occasion had been marred by the complaints of Milovan Djilas, one of Tito's closest associates, about the Red Army's conduct in Yugoslavia—complaints that Stalin was to recall later in a sinister light.

In internal affairs there was little to distinguish Yugoslav Communism from its Balkan counterparts except that the pretense of coalition government was discarded before the end of 1945. The opposition parties had no real chance to organize, and many anti-Communists were unfairly disfranchised by an electoral law depriving "collaborators" of the right to vote. Deputy Premier Milan Grol, leader of the Serbian Democratic party, resigned in August 1945, and Foreign Minister Shubashich, placed under house arrest in September, gave up his post on October 8. In an election on November 11, 90.5 per cent of the voters were declared to have marked their ballots for the government candidates. While negative votes were permitted and there were no open irregularities, fear of reprisal and the pre-election atmosphere inhibited a true expression of popular sentiment. Yugoslavia was officially proclaimed a republic on November 29, and the assembly formally approved the new constitution on January 30, 1946.

Soviet military and technical experts were provided in considerable numbers to train the Yugoslav army and to rehabilitate the economy. These advisers, while of unquestionable assistance, did not always serve the cause of friendship. Some of the Russians doubled as intelligence agents and recruited Yugoslav citizens into espionage activity. Others were inclined to be arrogant in their manner, rigid in their methods, and contemptuous of Yugoslav culture and mores. But these were minor pinpricks that would have been forgotten in time. More serious, and to the Yugoslav leaders the fundamental reason for the conflict, was the Soviet master plan for the "economic enslavement" of Eastern Europe.[23] Yugoslavia was to remain at least temporarily an under-industrialized country and a producer of raw materials. Tito had other ideas, and in April 1947 he launched an ambitious five-year plan of economic development.

Foreign policy differences caused further estrangement. Belgrade was affronted by Molotov's capitulation to the Western powers on the Italian frontier dispute[24] but made no open complaint. The Kremlin in turn concealed its annoyance when Tito pursued the idea of a federation with Bulgaria and when treaties of alliance were arranged with other Communist nations in 1946–1947. Tito's attitude of independence, though softened by appropriate genuflections toward Moscow, was a constant source of irritation. Nor did the enthusiastic crowds that turned out *en masse* to greet the Yugoslav dictator on the occasion of state visits to the satellite capitals endear him to Stalin. No rivals to the latter's role of Communist patron saint were welcome.

In January 1948 Dimitrov was interviewed in Bucharest to the effect that there might be a future federation of East European nations. This unauthorized statement provoked Moscow's anger, and to air its accumulated grievances the Bulgarian and Yugoslav governments were ordered to send delegations for a conference. In the presence of Molotov and Zhdanov, Stalin proceeded to lay down the law to his two unruly minions in a stormy meeting at the Kremlin on February 10. It was inadmissible that the Soviet government had learned about the Yugoslav-Bulgarian alliance (November 1947) from the newspapers; Moscow had not been sufficiently consulted about military agreements between Yugoslavia and Albania; and the proposed Eastern federation was out of the question. Stalin advanced a plan for three federations: Poland and Czechoslovakia, Rumania and Hungary, Bulgaria and Yugoslavia. Albania should be annexed by the latter pair. The Soviet dictator was outwardly placated by a properly submissive attitude, though the Yugoslavs were not as accustomed to such treatment as the Bulgarians. Before leaving Moscow, Edvard Kardelj, who headed the Yugoslav mission, signed what he considered a humiliating agreement to consult the Russians henceforth on all questions of foreign policy.

Belgrade observed disturbing signs that Stalin's ire had not yet been appeased. At a petty level, it involved the removal, at Moscow's behest, of Tito's portraits from public display in Rumania, where the Yugoslav dictator's popular reception in 1947 had been particularly demonstrative. Less symbolic and of much graver consequence was the rebuff given the Yugoslav trade delegation in Moscow—treatment tantamount to a suspension of commercial intercourse. On March 1, 1948, Tito convened the party's Central Committee, and it was decided to take a firm stand against further Soviet pressure. The prospective union with Bulgaria was abandoned in the belief that Stalin's sudden interest in promoting it was a "Trojan horse" tactic to insure Soviet predominance through a compliant Bulgarian party.

One of the committee members, Sretan Zhuyovich-Tsrni, reported details of the secret meeting to the Soviet ambassador in Belgrade. The Kremlin then sought to bring the Yugoslavs to heel by more pointed measures. On March 19 Belgrade was informed that Soviet military advisers and civilian specialists were being withdrawn at once. Tito wrote to Molotov on March 20, and for the first time the quarrel was brought into the open. His letter was polite but lacked the tone of servility that Moscow had come to expect from its outlying satrapies. He inquired about the nature of the Soviet government's complaints— "that it point out everything which it feels is inconsistent with good relations between our two countries."[25] The reply, signed by Stalin and Molotov, was not encouraging. A crude and haughty document, it was filled with innuendoes and accusations. The Yugoslavs had indulged in underhanded and slanderous anti-Soviet criticism; Djilas had insulted the Red Army by comparing its officers unfavorably with British officers; "capitalist elements" were encroaching upon the Yugoslav socialist system; the assistant minister of foreign affairs was a British spy; the Yugoslav party was undemocratic and suffering from Trotskyist and Menshevist tendencies. This was a witches' brew that seems to have been concocted on the spur of the moment for lack of more convincing fare.

Tito immediately set about drafting an answer which he submitted to the twenty-six members of the Central Committee on April 12–13. After some revisions, the letter was approved by everyone but Zhuyovich. It maintained a respectful tone and diplomatically assumed that Moscow's attitude was based on "insufficient knowledge" furnished by persons whose information was "inaccurate and tendentious." The Soviet aspersions were nevertheless rebutted so meticulously and with such obstinate tenacity that the Yugoslavs could have left no doubt that they were not prepared to make an abject apology for imaginary misdeeds. In one passage, Tito went so far as to accuse the Soviet intelligence service of improper activities: it would no longer be allowed "to spread its net in our country." In closing, the Russians were invited to send representatives to investigate the truth of their charges.

Had Stalin been accustomed to a certain amount of give and take in his relations with non-Soviet Communist leaders, Tito's second message would have given him pause. But he had grown used to blind obedience on the part of these "honest fools," as he sometimes called them, and plunged recklessly onward. "I will shake my little finger— and there will be no more Tito," he assured one of his Politburo associates.[26] On May 4 a letter of some 8,000 words was dispatched to Belgrade. It was even more offensive than its predecessor, and in deprecating the value of the Partisan effort during the war and giving credit to the Red Army for liberating Yugoslavia, Stalin added a touch which he knew would infuriate Tito and his colleagues. The original charges were repeated and embellished; new ones (*e.g.*, that the Yugoslav ambassador in London was also a British spy) were appended. The Yugoslav leaders were pronounced "arrogant" and "still intoxicated with their successes"; they did not "accept criticism in a Marxist manner, but in a bourgeois manner." Moscow claimed that the dispute was a matter of principle, not of "verifying individual facts," and proposed to refer it to the next session of the Cominform rather than send a mission to Yugoslavia.

In Belgrade, Zhuyovich and Andriya Hebrang, another member of the Central Committee suspected of being a Soviet agent, were expelled from the party on May 9. A few days later they were arrested, a move that allegedly forestalled a Soviet attempt to rescue Zhuyovich by airplane. Moscow had to be satisfied with a telegraphic protest threatening dire consequences. Hebrang was later reported to have committed suicide in prison, and Zhuyovich was freed in November 1950 after confessing his treasonable connections with Moscow and writing a recantation.

Tito's response to the Russian document was a brief and dignified note (May 17) declining to prolong the argument and rejecting the Cominform's authority, for the organization had already become an anti-Yugoslav mouthpiece. That the Cominform countries would simply parrot the Kremlin's view was to be expected. Sympathy for the Yugoslavs was *lèse majesté*, though Dimitrov had privately advised Djilas to be firm with Moscow. On May 19 a special invitation arrived by courier urging Tito to attend the forthcoming Cominform meeting in person. Stalin's methods of dealing with political dissenters was precedent enough to discourage the Yugoslavs from sending any representatives—Tito least of all. A round trip passage could not be guaranteed. The Russians, in a letter on May 22, asserted that the Yugoslavs had tacitly admitted their guilt by refusing to appear before their "fraternal" Communist colleagues. The Cominform proceedings were postponed for a month, probably because Stalin still expected to browbeat Tito into submission.

During the latter part of June 1948 the Cominform secretly convened in Bucharest, henceforth the site of its new headquarters. The Yugoslavs sent formal notice of their non-participation on June 20. Zhdanov, who headed the Soviet delegation, encountered difficulty in persuading several of the participants to accept his resolution excommunicating the Yugoslavs. He resorted to a *reductio ad absurdum* —that the Russians possessed information implicating Tito as an "imperialist spy"—which seems to have been sufficient to bring the recalcitrants into line. The Cominform declaration was published on June 28, and for the first time the news of the internal convulsion within the Communist camp was publicly revealed. It was no less a surprise to ordinary Yugoslavs and Russians than to the non-Communist world. Stalin was badly mistaken in his expectation that the Yugoslav people would desert their leaders now that Moscow had pronounced its interdict. Political differences were temporarily forgotten as the masses rallied behind their government in an access of patriotic indignation. The Cominform hope that "healthy elements" in the Yugoslav party would "compel their present leaders" to recognize and rectify their errors—that is, to oust Tito and his clique from power—had slight chance of success. But to make doubly certain that a pro-Soviet *coup* would not take place, several thousand "unreliable" Yugoslav Communists were purged and sentenced to some form of penal servitude.

Yugoslavia's position was by no means enviable however. The possibility of a military attack could not be discounted despite a comparatively advantageous geographical location. Nor, in the absence of good relations with the West, could slow strangulation by economic and political pressure be ruled out. These were precisely the tactics that the Kremlin pursued, and they might have prevailed had the Western democracies not altered their anti-Yugoslav policy. Trade agreements, loans, and direct aid—all without political strings—partially nullified the economic blockade by the Soviet bloc; and if Yugoslav relations with the United States and Britain never achieved real cordiality—the opportunistic basis of the new friendship was too evident for that—Tito and his government were treated with respect and even sympathy.

For some time after the final break Belgrade kept up the pretense that Stalin could somehow be dissociated from the acts of his government; and a few party members sincerely believed that Zhdanov and Molotov were the real culprits. Although the Soviet press and radio set the pace for the Cominform countries by spewing forth an uninterrupted stream of abuse upon the Yugoslav leadership, Tito made no attempt to reciprocate. Judging by propaganda tactics, only late in 1949 did the Yugoslavs become reconciled to the notion that their plight was not simply an accident that the passage of time would set aright. Stalin's name ceased to be invoked as a normal feature of Communist liturgy, and the party theoreticians at length concluded that the Kremlin had perverted the true heritage of Marxism-Leninism. Like Luther after 1517, Tito was swept along by historical forces that he but imperfectly understood; and he ended by founding a new sect within the Communist church.

IV

Among the indirect results of the Communist schism was an end to the Greek civil war. Yugoslavia had been the chief source of material aid to the Greek guerrillas, and in November 1948 Tito cut off the main supply routes. The Greek Communists had obediently accepted the Cominform mandate on Yugoslavia—but not without misgivings. Stalin had never been more than lukewarm toward the Greek party, for indigenous Communism—as in China and Yugoslavia—was not easily disciplined; and he had reportedly turned decisions on Greece over to Andrei Zhdanov. Moscow had even refused to recognize the rebel government set up late in 1947. To check any outbreaks of Greek Titoism, General Markos Vaphiades, the Communist premier and army commander, was deposed in January 1949. In July Tito announced that Greek guerrilla forces would be denied sanctuary in Yugoslavia. Not long afterward Athens flung its army of almost 200,-000 men, now fully equipped with the latest American weapons, into an all-out offensive against the 17,000 insurgents. This time their mountain strongholds were forced, and though a large proportion of the rebels managed to escape to Albania and Bulgaria, the civil war was not renewed. Having preserved Greek "democracy" by diplomacy in 1944–1945, the Western powers were fortunate in saving it again through Moscow's Yugoslav blunder.

The Kremlin's fear of Titoism led to purges in most of the Cominform states, sometimes accomplished in relative secrecy, sometimes with great public fanfare. In most cases those guilty of "nationalist deviationism" were replaced by trusted "Muscovites." The first notable victim—periodic purging of the rank and file was of course normal procedure—was the Rumanian minister of justice, Lucretiu Patrascanu A "premature Titoist," he fell from power in February 1948. The disgrace of Wladyslaw Gomulka, the titular leader of the Polish Communists, in August of the same year was an event of greater moment He recanted his nationalist errors but was dislodged as the party's secretary-general. In January 1949 he was deprived of his position as deputy premier, and the following November he lost his membership in the Central Committee of the United Workers' (Communist) party

Gomulka, though arrested in 1951, resisted confession and thereby avoided the hangman's noose, a fate that was freely predicted in the West. Other satellite leaders were less fortunate. In September 1948 Koci Xoxe, the Albanian minister of the interior, was demoted to a lesser post. He had been closely identified with Tito—indeed, the whole leadership of the tiny mountain republic was somewhat contaminated, having risen to power under Yugoslav tutelage. The Russians had been content to leave Albania in the Yugoslav sphere of influence until the quarrel with Tito. Xoxe's chief rival, Premier Enver Hoxha, was then able to gain Stalin's backing; and after a visit to Moscow in April 1949, where he was presumably given a green light, he jailed the Xoxe faction. Following a secret trial in May, in which the accused were charged with treasonable dealings with Tito—only a technically correct indictment—Xoxe was executed and five others were given prison terms. Blocked from direct access to the Soviet Union by Yugoslavia and Greece, Albania nevertheless became the most thoroughly subjugated of Moscow's Communist appendages during Stalin's last years.

In Bulgaria and Hungary the "cleansing" process was accompanied by public trials. The Bulgarian "traitor," Deputy Premier Traicho Kostov, proved a more stubborn heretic than his Hungarian counterpart, Laszlo Rajk. While not a "Muscovite," Kostov was a devoted Communist of long standing and had been regarded as the logical successor to the ill and aging Dimitrov. But as the economic boss of Bulgaria, he revealed certain independent tendencies disturbing to the Kremlin. Dimitrov, too, was under a shadow. Possibly he was considered too venerable a leader to be publicly rebuked. His death in Moscow on July 2, 1949, was so conveniently timed that it aroused suspicion that his demise was not entirely natural.[27]

Kostov was denounced in March 1949 and divested of his Politburo membership as well as his government offices. In June he was expelled from the party and imprisoned. A wave of dismissals and arrests of prominent party and government officials followed during the autumn. On December 8 Kostov and ten others were tried for various offenses, including espionage, sabotage, Titoism, and Trotskyism. Kostov confounded his captors by refusing to confess his "crimes"—he would admit only to a "national deviation in relation to the Soviet Union" and to opposing Dimitrov—and was hanged on December 16. A fake confession was published the next day. The other defendants dutifully admitted their guilt and were rewarded by prison sentences, five of them to life terms.

The concurrent fall of Rajk, Hungary's former minister of the interior, proceeded more smoothly because of the victim's cooperation. Occupied with underground activities before and during the war, he too had neglected to obtain Stalin's seal of approval by a period of exile in Moscow. Reputedly he had objected at first to the Cominform treatment of Yugoslavia and was sent to Moscow for "overhaul." He was transferred to head the Ministry of Foreign Affairs in August

1948 upon his return. His omission from the cabinet after its re-organization in June 1949 was an unmistakable portent soon realized by his arrest and imprisonment. His trial, together with seven other defendants, opened on September 16, and all admitted a fantastic assortment of treasonable acts. Rajk dispassionately recited his eight-een-year career as a "spy," first for Admiral Horthy's regime and then for the Gestapo and the American and Yugoslav intelligence services. The Soviet press significantly handled the trial as if Tito him-self were in the dock. Rajk and three others were hanged; the rest were given long prison terms.

The purge in Czechoslovakia was late in coming, although more than a quarter of the 2,400,000 Communist party members were ex-pelled or disciplined as early as the winter of 1948–1949. Between the Rajk and Kostov trials many arrests were made which outsiders esti-mated in the thousands but which spared the top ruling group. Titoist tendencies were continually uncovered nonetheless, and Foreign Minister Vlado Clementis was dropped from the cabinet in March 1950. Almost a year later he was jailed as an "imperialist agent." Later arrests culminated in the most spectacular of the post-war "show trials" in November 1952, by which time preoccupation with Titoism had given way to other concerns.[28]

Compared to the sensational developments in the East European Communist parties, the two Cominform members of the West—France and Italy—were scarcely affected. The ruthless methods that had become Moscow's trademark within its own political sphere were naturally impossible to duplicate (and largely unnecessary) in coun-tries where Communism had no immediate prospect of gaining power. In the Western world only the French and Italian parties were serious political movements, which did not, of course, dampen the ardor of Right wing extremists, ever ready—as before the war—to exploit the opportunities presented by a blown-up Red menace.

The French Communists, by their pre-eminent position in the anti-Nazi resistance, had all but wiped out the popular memory of their defeatist tactics in 1939–1940 before the involvement of the Soviet Union abruptly converted the "imperialist" war into a patriotic en-deavor. They had loyally cooperated with the interim regime of Gen-eral Charles de Gaulle after liberation and were the beneficiaries of the pro-Russian attitude of the French people that had led to the sign-ing in Moscow (December 10, 1944) of a twenty-year Franco-Soviet alliance replacing the ill-fated instrument of 1935. In the Assembly elections of October 21, 1945, and again on November 10, 1946, the Communists emerged as the strongest party in France. Denied the key cabinet posts, they were nevertheless granted a responsible share in successive coalition governments. A Communist-Socialist fusion was forestalled in 1945 only by the personal authority and prestige of Leon Blum. Growing Communist intransigence by the spring of 1947 mirrored Moscow's decision to abandon its Popular Front policy because of increased international tension.

An instructive prologue to the uncompromising line that world Communism was to follow after the summer of 1947 was furnished in the United States as early as 1945. Atypical because of its diminutive size but important because of its location, the American party had gone so far during the war in the direction of "American exceptionalism" and "people's capitalism" under its leader, Earl Browder, that the Kremlin chose to step in with a sharp but concealed reprimand. Jacques Duclos, second in command to Thorez of the French party, delivered the blow after a trip to Moscow. It came in the form of an article in the April 1945 issue of his party's theoretical organ, *Cahiers du Communisme,* and lashed out at Browder's abandonment of Marxism-Leninism *à la* Stalin and the decision of May 1944 to dissolve the American party in favor of a "Communist Political Association." The article was translated and reprinted in many Communist publications, especially in the Western Hemisphere. Formally denounced at a party convention in July 1945 and replaced by his former lieutenant, William Z. Foster, Browder was expelled in February 1946 as a "social imperialist." "Browderism" was extravagantly condemned by American Communists—it was a heresy just short of Trotskyism—in an effort to demonstrate their ideological zeal. That Moscow had intended only to curb Browder's "opportunism," not to end his political career, was suggested by his friendly conference with Molotov in the Soviet capital later in the year and his return to the United States as representative of the Soviet state publishing house.

The effects of the Browder affair were confined to the United States, with propagandist overtones in several Latin American countries. The Western European parties had never crawled so far out on the limb of "Right deviationism," perhaps because of the Kremlin's closer supervision. Thorez had spent the war years in Moscow, as had Togliatti, the Italian party chieftain. The French Communists theoretically favored the Popular Front coalition until their propaganda and obstructive tactics in the Assembly caused Socialist Premier Paul Ramadier to oust the five Communist cabinet ministers early in May 1947. The party could then boast a million members and a voting strength of nearly 30 per cent of the electorate. Its later decline may be ascribed to the self-isolating militancy that again demonstrated Communist subservience to Soviet foreign policy. The hardening of the party line was greatly intensified after the formation of the Cominform, but the failure of the November 1947 strike movement did not add to the popularity of the new dispensation. Titoism also made inroads—less upon the mass membership, however, than upon the "fringe" intellectuals who had never considered themselves *bona fide* Communists. The problem was more serious in the smaller parties of Western Europe, and in Norway the Communist movement was split asunder.

In broad outline, the post-war history of Italian Communism paralleled that of France. It, too, had won its spurs during the resistance and shared the burdens of government until May 1947. But though the Italian party was more than twice the size of the French and the largest outside the Soviet Union, its leaders could not duplicate the electoral feats of their French comrades. They were more successful than the French in achieving unity with the socialists, who in January 1947 formed two opposing groups—an anti-Communist Socialist Workers' party and a pro-Communist Socialist majority under Pietro Nenni. The strength of the combined party remained stable as the Cominform's doctrinal rigidity cast its blight upon Togliatti's relatively flexible tactics. As a movement capable of attaining power by democratic means, the Communists temporarily exhausted their potentialities in the decisive election of April 18, 1948. Soundly beaten, they yet constituted a formidable source of internal disaffection as the Christian Democratic government of Premier Alcide de Gasperi aligned Italy with the other Western powers in the political and diplomatic struggle with the Soviet bloc. The Titoist infection took hold in southern Italy, and the Nenni Socialists proved unusually susceptible. But as a predominantly working class movement, the Italian party was not unduly disrupted by the ideological disputes agitating the intelligentsia.

The purification and sterilization of Communist theory in preparation for a renewed onslaught on the capitalist heathen and the eventual extermination of the Titoist apostates necessarily stepped up the Kremlin's own drive for domestic conformity in the realm of ideas. The nascent tone of belligerency that had alarmed Western statesmen in 1945–1946 and the faint stirrings heralding a return to revolutionary Marxism[29] were as nothing compared to the bold trumpetings of the late forties and beyond. The opening round in the Soviet cultural purge was fired by Zhdanov in a series of speeches in August and September 1946. He flayed the "truckling" attitude of Soviet writers toward the decadent bourgeois culture of the West and exhorted them to surpass "philistine foreign literature" with a superior socialist product. The two-year period that followed, ending with Zhdanov's death on August 31, 1948, was a time of recurrent disciplinary action and searching re-examination in almost every field of scholarly and artistic endeavor. Musicians were rebuked for their "formalist" compositions, historians for their deficient appreciation of the heroic Russian past, biologists for their failure to follow the quaint theories on the inheritance of acquired characteristics advocated by the self-taught court favorite, Trofim Lysenko; and Eugene Varga, perhaps the leading Soviet economist, was denounced for daring to suggest in print that the expected post-war crisis of capitalism might be delayed.

The *Zhdanovshchina* by no means ceased with the demise of its foremost proponent. Attacks in 1949 upon "homeless cosmopolitans" in the literary world suggested a veiled assault upon Jewish intellectuals as a group; and even astronomers, hitherto spared like most physical scientists from the indignities of party supervision, were told to fight against "bourgeois cosmology" as a manifestation of the "reactionary science" of the West.[30] Notwithstanding the crudity with which this perversion of Marxism was foisted upon the creative elite of Soviet society, the Kremlin was paradoxically engaged in undermining its edifice of cultural chauvinism by expanding its mass educational program. The legacy of economic and technological backwardness that Russia had inherited from its Tsarist past was fast disappearing; and the pall of peasant illiteracy that had once enveloped the Soviet experiment in a sea of sloth was no longer a grave problem. Stalinist obscurantism, nourished by the passions of the cold war, was breached by the internal pressures of a changing social order, just as its American variant—McCarthyism—wilted in an altered climate of opinion.

V

By the early summer of 1948 no single event among the welter of international incidents and political maneuvers had yet occurred to cause general alarm about the immediate possibility of another world war. That attitude was rudely shaken by the circumstances attending Moscow's decision in June to cut off Berlin, a four-power island in the Soviet zone, from outside contact. The attempt to force the Western powers from the German capital was a risky but not illogical riposte to the intended creation of a West German state without consultation with the Soviet government.

At a conference in London (February 23–March 6, 1948) representatives of the United States, Britain, and France, together with the Benelux nations (Belgium, the Netherlands, and Luxemburg), had disregarded a Soviet protest to discuss the German question. On March 20 Sokolovsky walked out of the Control Council meeting when the Western members declined to provide information on the results of the conference. The Council was not reconvened, and with it disappeared any semblance of quadripartite government in Germany. The London meetings were resumed on April 20 and lasted until June 1. The Western powers decided to internationalize the Ruhr but to exclude the Soviet bloc from the control body; and a West German assembly was to be convened to draw up a constitution. On June 23 the foreign ministers of the eight Communist countries met in Warsaw and issued a lengthy communiqué the next day accusing the West of violating the Yalta and Potsdam agreements. The London decisions, it was claimed, were designed to rebuild Germany's war potential as a means of furthering Anglo-American strategic aims and monopoly interests. The Russians knew that protests and declarations would change no minds in Washington and London, but it was important to mobilize the satellites by forming a common front and to woo German opinion by placing the blame for dismemberment upon the West.

Moscow had already recorded by non-verbal means its objection to being excluded from the councils of its former allies on so vital a matter as Germany. As early as January 1948 Soviet inspectors were harassing military trains between Berlin and the Western zones. This interference had become more than a nuisance problem by late February, and on March 30 the Russian authorities in Berlin announced new restrictions on road and rail transportation. More drastic moves followed as an Anglo-American protest was dismissed, and a small airlift operation began to supply administrative and military personnel. The Russians made no effort to block shipments destined for the use of the Berlin population.

On June 16, 1948, the Soviet delegation walked out of a stormy meeting of the four-power Berlin Kommandatura, using as a pretext the "hooligan action" of the tired and disgusted American representative, Colonel Frank Howley, who had quit the session and left his subordinate to carry on.[31] For all practical purposes the incident ended Allied unity in the German capital, for no subsequent meetings were held. Only two days later a currency reform was announced in the Western zones, a financial measure long overdue because of previous disagreement with Soviet representatives. That same evening railroad passenger service in and out of Berlin was suspended because of "technical difficulties." On June 23 the Russians introduced their own currency into the Eastern zone, declaring it applicable to the whole of Berlin. The Western authorities retaliated by extending their currency into the American, British, and French sectors of the city. Freight traffic was then added to the Russian ban, and the piecemeal closing of the alternate water and highway routes completed the blockade on August 4.

Since more than two million people in West Berlin were in danger of starvation when available food stocks became exhausted, the United States began a gigantic airlift on June 26. For both sides Berlin became a symbol of political prestige in Central Europe, with Moscow and Washington equally fearful of an incident that might provoke serious hostilities. Armed convoys could have broken through the blockade at some peril of precipitating the unwanted conflict, and Soviet planes could have disrupted the airlift by running the same risk. Neither power made the attempt. If Stalin and Truman could not achieve peace, at least they strove to avoid war.

The three Western governments presented formal notes of protest on July 6 demanding that the blockade be lifted as a prerequisite to negotiations on the Berlin question. The Soviet reply refused to define prospective discussions so narrowly. On July 20 the Russians tried to raise the level of their popularity in Germany by offering to feed the whole of Berlin. The Soviet gambit was curtly declined. At the end of the month a counter-blockade of the Soviet zone was imposed, a not ineffective means of retaliation because of weaknesses in the East German economy.

Moscow still held the whip hand, and though the United States, as the core of Western resistance, was resolved to stand firm, a direct approach was made to Stalin. He received the American and French ambassadors and a special British envoy on August 2. As was often the case, he was more conciliatory than his subordinates and offered to call off the blockade provided Russian zone currency was used throughout Berlin. He also expressed a desire that the "insistent wish" of the Soviet government be recorded in favor of deferring the establishment of a West German regime. These terms seemed so promising that the Western powers went ahead with the discussions despite their previous decision not to negotiate under "duress"—that is, while the blockade remained in effect. In trying to work out the details at a subordinate level, the canny Molotov raised several points that diverged from a strict construction of Stalin's proposals. He insisted upon Soviet rather than quadripartite currency control in Berlin and declared that only those transportation restrictions imposed after June 18 (the date of the Western currency reform) would be withdrawn.

Again the three Western diplomats sought out Stalin, who received them on August 23. His good humor had not abated, and he waived substantially all that his foreign minister had so hotly contested. But Stalin's persistence in asking for a paragraph in the proposed communiqué implying that the formation of the West German government had been delayed by mutual agreement was greeted with suspicion. Moscow's eagerness for another round of negotiations was incompatible with Anglo-American political strategy: a West German constituent assembly was due to meet in Bonn a week hence. Washington and London would not budge, and the delegation of plenipotentiary power to the four military governors in Berlin only created a fresh deadlock. The Russians had lost interest in an immediate settlement, content to let the perils of winter deal with the airlift during the coming months. In the contested former capital, Communist-fomented disorders on September 6 broke up a meeting of the city assembly in the Soviet sector, and the non-Communist deputies set up their own government in the British sector a few days later.

Washington took the initiative in referring the dispute to the U.N. Security Council late in September 1948. Vyshinsky argued that it lacked jurisdiction but did not boycott the proceedings when he was faced with an adverse vote. The neutrals bestirred themselves and submitted a formula on October 15 designed to solve the difficulties by successive stages. Reverting to the "duress" argument of the summer, the Western bloc rejected the proposal. A resolution urging that the blockade be withdrawn as the first step toward a settlement was vetoed by Vyshinsky on October 25. Further efforts at mediation proved futile. Neither Moscow nor Washington showed any inclination toward a strategic withdrawal; and as the months passed with no discernible letup in the proficiency of the airlift, the bargaining strength of the Russians began to seep away.

At the end of January 1949 Stalin put out a feeler for a personal meeting with Truman through his answers to several questions submitted by an American journalist. He had frequently used the "interview" method to signal a policy change, and the State Department was encouraged by his omission of the currency controversy from his comment on the Berlin affair. But Dean Acheson, who had succeeded Marshall as secretary of state earlier in the year, promptly quashed the idea of a Stalin-Truman meeting at a press conference on February 2. Western hopes were rekindled after the announcement on March 4 in Moscow that Vyshinsky had replaced Molotov as foreign minister. The analogy between Litvinov and Molotov in 1939 was too tempting to be resisted, although the notion that the scabrous Vyshinsky (whom one wit called a "matador among cows" for his U.N. exploits) was another Litvinov was far-fetched indeed. The move turned out to be more tactical than fundamental, for Molotov was not downgraded and as a member of the Politburo he remained Vyshinsky's superior.

On March 15, 1949, Soviet U.N. representative Jacob Malik informally told the American delegate, Philip C. Jessup, who had inquired a month before upon Washington's instructions, that Stalin's failure to mention the currency problem in his January statement was "not accidental." Confidential talks between Malik and Jessup continued, and on April 26 Moscow and Washington revealed in separate declarations that a tentative agreement had been reached. After a four-power conference in New York on May 4, a communiqué announced that the blockade and counter-blockade would be lifted on May 12 and that other issues relating to Germany would be considered at a meeting of the Council of Foreign Ministers to begin in Paris on May 23. Berlin's long siege ended on the appointed date, and the Russians thereby acknowledged the defeat of their plans to impede the integration of a West German state into the Atlantic bloc.

The threat of a formal Western alliance, foreshadowed by the Treaty of Brussels (a fifty-year defensive pact signed by Britain, France, and the Benelux nations on March 17, 1948), had become a reality on April 4, 1949, with the conclusion of the North Atlantic Treaty. This twenty-year "regional security arrangement," a euphemism for a military alliance directed against the Russian bloc, was signed by the United States, the Brussels treaty nations, Italy, Canada, Norway, Denmark, Iceland, and Portugal. Greece and Turkey were admitted in 1951 and West Germany in 1955. Soviet propaganda, and in the case of Norway diplomatic intervention, had not forestalled the treaty. Avowedly defensive, like every such device to maximize security for one combination of powers, it intensified the apprehension of the other. No funds had been appropriated to put teeth into the document, but the armament race to come may fairly be said to have begun with the final ratification ceremony in Washington on August 24, 1949. The Anglo-Soviet and Franco-Soviet pacts became dead letters, though the three signatories took no immediate steps toward formal abrogation. At the sixth session of the Council of Foreign Ministers (May 23–June 20, 1949), Bevin was the sole diplomatic survivor of the quartet that had attended the London meeting eighteen months before. Yet fresh blood in the persons of Vyshinsky and Acheson, necessarily the two major adversaries, brought little in the way of novelty to the discussions. The settlement of the Berlin dispute and the absence of the cantankerous Molotov produced no new Soviet approach. Vyshinsky's suggestion that the Control Council and the

Berlin Kommandatura be revived was countered by the Western plan to unify Germany by extending to the Soviet zone the Basic Law (or provisional constitution) that had been signed in Bonn on the opening day of the Council meeting. Such a procedure would have relinquished the whole of Germany to the Western sphere of influence: Moscow was under no delusion about the strength of German Communism in a parliamentary regime. Unable to make headway on unification, the ministers passed on to the problem of Berlin. Again the Soviet proposals were found wanting, and the Western formula of free elections for a city government were pronounced unacceptable by Vyshinsky. A communiqué released by the parting diplomats adopted a positive tone in agreeing to another Council session (the date to be determined later) and in authorizing consultation by the military governors in Berlin.

That the foreign ministers at least tried to put a good face on their frustrated endeavors was feeble consolation for the ugly realities of the German situation. Only four years after Hitler's crushing defeat there were in fact two Germanies, one arrayed against the other by the hopeless disintegration of the conquering coalition. The Western allies completed their political handiwork when the Federal Republic of West Germany, officially born on May 23, held elections to the Bundestag on August 14, 1949. The Christian Democrats and Social Democrats shared a convincing majority; the Communists mustered only 5.7 per cent of the total vote. On September 15 the Bundestag narrowly approved as chancellor the Christian Democratic leader Konrad Adenauer, already well known as an adherent of the West.

The Russians had never ceased to inveigh against the Anglo-American policy of "splitting and dismembering Germany," of "restoring the dominant position of reactionary, militaristic, and revanchist elements" in order that "certain imperialist circles" might utilize West Germany as a bridgehead for their "aggressive plans."[32] With the Bonn regime a going concern, they reluctantly concluded that East Germany must also have a government. The decision once made, the legalistic window-dressing was finished off with dispatch. After its leaders had been summoned to a conference with the Soviet occupation authorities, the Socialist Unity party proclaimed on October 4, 1949, the desirability of a German Democratic Republic. Three days later the "People's Council," an unrepresentative body of 330 members, was summoned to meet in Berlin and transformed itself into a provisional parliament. A constitution previously approved by a "People's Congress" was formally adopted. Grotewohl became prime minister and Pieck president. Real power lay in the hands of Walter

Ulbricht, a "Muscovite" whose nominal inferiority to Pieck in the party structure concealed his true status as the Kremlin's favorite.

During the course of the next year the East German republic went through the meat-grinder of political conformity that Moscow's other tributary states had endured. The Christian Democratic Union and the Democratic Liberal party still cherished notions of free electoral activity, but most of their leaders fled to West Germany when that illusion was shattered. The Socialist Unity party, already subjected to a prolonged purge in 1948–1949, was further emasculated after Ulbricht became secretary-general in July 1950. A "democratic" gloss was spread over the hard surface of authoritarianism by parliamentary elections on October 15, 1950. A single list of candidates appeared on a National Front ticket, and an incredible 99.7 per cent affirmative majority was reported by the government. As they had been careful to announce beforehand, neither the Western powers nor the German Federal Republic recognized the validity of the elections; and the German Democratic Republic was officially ignored except by the Communist nations. The anomaly of a divided Germany began to seem less strange and to assume an almost peaceful aspect as the Far East temporarily replaced Europe as the breeding ground of new wars.

NOTES

1. Harry S. Truman, *Memoirs* (Garden City, N.Y., 1955–56), I, 552.
2. B. U. Ratchford and William D. Ross, *Berlin Reparation Assignment* (Chapel Hill, N.C., 1947), p. 159.
3. Saul K. Padover, *Experiment in Germany* (New York, 1946), p. 388.
4. See above, p. 329.
5. See below, p. 336.
6. *Department of State Bulletin*, XVI (May 11, 1947), 924.
7. Margaret Carlyle (ed.), *Documents on International Affairs, 1947–1948* (London, 1952), p. 553.
8. See above, p. 288.
9. See above, p. 306.
10. *Daily Worker*, March 19, 1946, as quoted in George Kirk, *The Middle East, 1945–1950* (London, 1954), p. 27.
11. X, "The Sources of Soviet Conduct," *Foreign Affairs*, XXV (July 1947), 566–82.
12. *Pravda*, March 15 and June 25, 1947.
13. Harry Bayard Price, *The Marshall Plan and Its Meaning* (Ithaca, N.Y., 1955), pp. 27–28; W. B. Smith, *My Three Years in Moscow*, p. 198.
14. Sir Robert Bruce Lockhart, *My Europe* (London, 1952), p. 125.
15. See above, p. 303.
16. Text of the four notes in Arthur Bliss Lane, *I Saw Poland Betrayed* (New York, 1948), pp. 322–27.
17. See above, p. 322.
18. See above, p. 323.

19. See above, p. 322.

20. Text of correspondence in *Documents on International Affairs, 1947–1948,* pp. 302–08.

21. See above, p. 340.

22. Dedijer, *Tito,* p. 297.

23. *Ibid.,* pp. 267–68.

24. See above, p. 328.

25. Royal Institute of International Affairs, *The Soviet-Yugoslav Dispute: Text of the Published Correspondence* (London, 1948), p. 10.

26. Bertram D. Wolfe, *Khrushchev and Stalin's Ghost* (New York, 1957), p. 200.

27. Borkenau, *European Communism,* p. 541; Louis Fischer, *Russia Revisited* (Garden City, N.Y., 1957), p. 154.

28. See below, p. 413.

29. See above, p. 320.

30. *New York Times,* July 14, 1949.

31. Frank Howley, *Berlin Command* (New York, 1950), p. 181.

32. Note to Washington, London, and Paris, October 1, 1949, *USSR Information Bulletin,* October 21, 1949, p. 623.

CHAPTER TWELVE

COLD WAR: THE SOVIET CHALLENGE IN ASIA

The Soviet challenge to traditional Western supremacy in Asia proved more formidable than that of Tsarist Russia or Imperial Japan. It was foreshadowed by the Red Army's conquest of Manchuria in 1945 and apparently confirmed by the Communist revolution in China. In Washington, though not always in London and Paris, the nature of the Muscovite thrust—as in Europe—was seen predominantly in terms of military strategy: proxy armies had enlisted under the banner of Communism to carry Soviet imperialism into Eastern Asia. If that was indeed the case in Korea, where the evidence was not wholly conclusive,[1] it was quite misleading when applied to China or Viet Nam.

The forces of nationalism and revolution in the Far East were not unleashed by the Kremlin. A century and more of Western imperialism dredged the channel that Communism sought to fill—not because Communism was a conspiracy hatched in Moscow to conquer Asia but because it furnished a doctrine and provided the leadership for millions who had known little but poverty, hardship, and oppression. Unlike European Communism, whose hollow triumphs were secured at the cost of popular indifference or outright antipathy, the Asiatic variety was characterized by a revolutionary *élan* that took the politically ossified Stalinist bureaucracy by surprise. In China the Russians were able to avoid a repetition of their Yugoslav mistakes —but only by the narrowest of margins and with the grating knowledge that their Chinese comrades considered themselves junior partners in a joint enterprise, not wage slaves in a monopoly run for the benefit of the Soviet state.

Mao Tse-tung and his colleagues had reason to be self-confident and somewhat disdainful of the Kremlin's counsel: repeatedly advised to abandon their futile civil war, each time they had plunged ahead. It was thus with considerable pride that they could contemplate a victory won without the effective aid of their strongest ally and against a regime receiving the open support of the United States. Washington's intervention in favor of the Chinese Nationalists had not prevented assiduous mediation efforts by General Marshall and Ambassador J. Leighton Stuart. The breakdown of the truce agreement of January 1946[2] was not repaired until the following June when a temporary cease-fire went into effect. But the negotiations between Yenan and Nanking (once more the site of the Nationalist capital) were suspended over the problem of administering areas to be evacuated by the Communists. Chiang was inclined to heed the Right wing of the Kuomintang, now clamoring for a full-scale military offensive. In July the Communists began a concerted attack upon American policy, charging that Nanking's attitude had only been stiffened by military and financial assistance.

For its part, after the withdrawal of Soviet troops from Manchuria in May 1946, Moscow observed neutrality in deed, if not always in thought. Nationalist accusations that their foes were receiving Russian aid were vehemently denied by the Chinese Communists, and they were dismissed by the Soviet press as "provocative propaganda." Since no independent confirmation of Nanking's charges was ever brought forward, the probability is strong that they were manufactured for American consumption. The Russian press and radio was still polite in referring to the Chinese government during the latter half of 1946 —Chiang himself was never criticized—but they showed no such compunction in decrying the involvement of the United States in the internal affairs of China. In September 1946 Stalin conveyed an oblique warning to Washington by returning an affirmative answer to a correspondent's written query: "Do you believe that the earliest withdrawal of all American troops from China is vital to future peace?"

His personal integrity unquestioned (though even this was to be impugned in time), but badly compromised in Communist eyes by the actions of his government, Marshall was recalled at his own request in January 1947 after nearly a year of conscientious labor in a thankless cause. He ascribed the failure of mediation to mutual suspicion ("complete, almost overwhelming") and to unwillingness on the part of either the "dominant group of reactionaries" in the Kuomintang or the "dyed-in-the-wool Communists" to come to an equitable settlement.[3] The Nationalists were not disturbed by an end to the negotiations, for their military successes, capped by the seizure of the abandoned Communist capital of Yenan in March 1947, stimulated their certainty of ultimate triumph. But these were costly Pyrrhic victories, as Communist operations later in the year revealed.

During the Moscow conference of foreign ministers in March 1947 Molotov proposed that the problem of China be placed on the agenda. Marshall objected, and he also declined Bevin's suggestion of an informal discussion away from the conference table. The Nationalists sent a strong note protesting the Soviet move; the Communists countered by backing Molotov and asking for representation. The procedure finally adopted was an exchange of written information on the implementation of the Moscow agreement made in December 1945.[4] In a letter of March 31 Marshall reported that the withdrawal of American troops would be completed about June 1 and that some 6,000 would remain at Nanking's request. Molotov's reply on April 7 expressed dissatisfaction and pointed out that Soviet troops had left China almost a year before. Moscow did not pursue the subject at an official level, though its propaganda organs were less considerate.

By the close of 1947 the Nationalist government verged upon a state of paralysis. The dry rot of defeatism corroded the morale of its army. If not desertion or mass surrender, then token resistance was the most that could be expected of all but the best units. In Manchuria the Kuomintang's " 'carpet-bag' regime of unbridled exploitation," to use the blunt words of an American consular official,[5] had outraged the population; and in "liberated" Formosa (Taiwan) a revolt against the extortionate rule of the military governor was suppressed with a wholesale massacre. Inflation reached disastrous proportions. The official exchange rate between the Chinese and American dollar, one to 45,000 in August 1947, accelerated to one to 6,000,000 in less than a year. Nanking's peace feelers were ignored or denounced as "insincere" by the Communists. One of Chiang's leading generals went so far as to approach the Soviet embassy with a request for mediation in December 1947. The Russians were friendly and offered their good offices to no avail: the Chinese Communists, sensing victory, were in no mood to compromise. In an exultant report to the party's Central Committee on December 27, Mao gloried in the "people's war of liberation" and denounced the "reactionary troops of Chiang Kai-shek, running dog of American imperialism."[6]

Washington was in a quandary as to whether to throw good money after bad. Up to two billion dollars in credits and matériel had been poured into the Chinese sinkhole since V-J Day, and the public was becoming skeptical about the value of additional aid. But once mounted on the tiger of anti-Communism, the Truman administration felt obliged to ride on. Early in 1948 the President asked Congress for $570,000,000 to be spread over fifteen months, and about three-quarters of the sum was appropriated during the year. By summer it was clear, if it had not been before, that no amount of money could salvage Chiang's regime. After a strategy conference held in southern Hopei in July, in which the Soviet view that the Communists should confine their campaign to guerrilla operations was disregarded, a frontal assault was mounted against the major Manchurian and North Chinese cities. Tsinan in Shantung was captured in September after a brief fight; Mukden fell in October when the garrison defected to the enemy. Now well supplied with American arms taken over from government forces, the Communists pressed on to Tientsin and Peking and occupied them in January 1949.

A plea for mediation made by the Chinese foreign minister on January 8 to Moscow, Washington, London, and Paris revealed the government's desperate straits. When all four powers declined, Chiang beat a strategic retreat and resigned the presidency on January 21 without, however, impairing his position at the head of the party and the army. His successor, General Li Tsung-jen, was already the rallying point for Kuomintang liberals dissatisfied with Chiang's leadership. During the previous summer Li had conducted secret negotiations with the Communists that were abandoned when the story leaked into the Peking press. He resumed his contacts but had little left to bargain with, since the enemy controlled the whole of China north of the Yangtze with every prospect of gaining the rest in due course. He also sounded out the Soviet ambassador, who was still under the assumption that China would remain under Kuomintang control, for a Sino-Russian agreement was discussed that would freeze out American influence.

In April 1949 Li spurned the Communist terms, now little better than unconditional surrender. Red troops then crossed the Yangtze for the final conquest. The government fled to Canton, and Nanking and Shanghai were seized without opposition. The local authorities deserted the collapsing regime as the Communist armies consolidated their hold in the south and west by the end of the year. Formosa became the catchbasin for the Nationalist debacle.

China entered upon the most profound revolution in her long history, comparable in significance to that other great revolution of the twentieth century—the Russian. If the precise nature of Red China's relationship to Moscow eluded the outside world, no perspicuity was needed to assess the fact that Western power and prestige in the political struggle with the Soviet Union had suffered a severe reverse. A vast Eurasian "heartland" comprising more than 900,000,000 individuals from Prague to Peking, all of them officially committed to the Communist way of life, was not a vista to be viewed with complacency. China herself, war ravaged though she was, loomed as the new colossus of the Far East. The "sleeping giant" had often stirred in the past half-century, only to confound the prophets of its imminent resurrection by relapsing into a deep coma. Awake at last, China as a great power—still less as a Communist power—did not conform to the stereotypes of either uninformed Westerners or "old China hands."

In some ways the Russians were faced with more difficulties than the West in adjusting to the radical alteration of East Asian politics. They were, of course, flattered beyond their just due by the reaction of conservative American opinion, which in a neurotic search for domestic scapegoats to blame for the Nationalist fiasco, took it for granted that the Chinese Communists were puppets of the Kremlin. And there was no gainsaying the enormous benefits that automatically accrued to the Soviet position. Yet the old contradiction between Russian nationalism and Soviet Communism had to be resolved once more. It was manifestly no accident that the Chinese revolution had caught Stalin unaware. A skilled performer in the game of *Realpolitik,* he had never grasped except by rote the revolutionary possibilities that still inhered in world Communism after twenty years of debasement in the service of the Soviet state. When confronted by a genuinely popular revolutionary movement, as in the resistance forces of France, Italy, Yugoslavia, and Greece, his instinctive reaction was to minimize its importance and to divert it into the well trodden path of Soviet opportunism. The French Communists had been bidden to back de Gaulle's regime, the Italians to support Badoglio, and the Yugoslavs and Greeks to make common cause with their respective royal governments-in-exile.

It was not to be supposed that the Chinese Communists would be considered in a different light. They too had their role to play in supporting Chiang, with whose government Stalin had signed a treaty regaining the Russian sphere in Manchuria. Just as Tito had been strong enough to make his own revolution—thereby innocently disrupting the Stalin-Churchill Balkan pact—so Mao had gone his own way in China without consciously absorbing any ideological impurities. But the germs of heresy were present, and Tito's defection may have been a blessing in disguise to Moscow. The Yugoslavs furnished a needed lesson in humility without which an arrogant Stalin might have driven the Chinese into open rebellion. But the Russian national interest demanded consideration, and it was probably not without pain that he made concessions to Red China which no mere satellite would have been granted.

Only in April 1949 did the Kremlin begin to take the Chinese Communists seriously. For the first time the Soviet press mentioned the Kuomintang in disparaging terms, and its frequent references to the "New China" indicated that the revolution was considered a foregone conclusion. Yet Russian representatives were negotiating with the Nationalist regime about Sinkiang as late as May, and elaborate diplomatic punctiliousness was observed in closing or transferring Soviet consular offices as the Communists approached. Ambassador Nikolai Roshchin accompanied the government to Canton—the only foreign envoy to do so—but was recalled in May for consultation. Moscow recognized the Chinese People's Republic on October 2, only a day after its formal establishment in Peking. Roshchin continued as ambassador. The other Communist states soon followed the Soviet lead, an action which, except in the case of Yugoslavia, was greeted with much fanfare by the new regime. Peking's silence on Yugoslavia was mute testimony that it was determined not to fall afoul of the Kremlin on doctrinal grounds. In this area China's new rulers were content to echo Soviet pronouncements.

The "neutralist" nations also recognized Peking, while Britain irritated American opinion by becoming the only important Western country to do so. Representing only the island of Formosa, the Nationalist regime retained China's permanent seat in the U.N. Security Council; and Foreign Minister Chou En-lai formally protested the incongruity in a note to the secretary-general on November 15, 1949. On January 10, 1950, the Russians announced a boycott of future meetings of the Security Council unless the Kuomintang delegation was expelled. The boycott was extended when their representatives were withdrawn from various U.N. bodies in which the Nationalist Chinese participated. In spite of the apparent deadlock, the United States intimated in May that it was disposed to abide by the decision if a majority voted to admit Communist China to the U.N. The outbreak of the Korean War buried the issue as far as Washington was concerned. Peking's inevitable admission was delayed indefinitely because of the vagaries of American political strife. Outwardly incensed by this shabby treatment of her ally—the disfranchisement of 600,000,000 Chinese could not but cripple the U.N.'s prestige—the Soviet Union was not entirely displeased by the exclusion of Red China. Moscow's undisputed leadership of the Communist world was thus rendered more secure.

To draw up a blueprint systematizing relations between the two most powerful Communist states was the complex task of the Chinese delegation that arrived in Moscow on December 16, 1949. It was headed by Mao Tse-tung himself in what purported to be his first visit to the Russian capital. His protracted stay (until February 17, 1950), in which he negotiated directly—and secretly—with Stalin, pointed to hard-headed bargaining by both parties. Yet the outcome was not encouraging to Western hopes that Soviet tactlessness and a clash of interests over Manchuria, Mongolia, and Sinkiang would create a rift between the two partners.

The new Sino-Soviet Pact was signed by Vyshinsky and Chou En-lai on February 14, 1950. They also exchanged notes annulling the 1945 treaty between Moscow and Chungking but reaffirming the "independence" of the Mongolian People's Republic. A thirty-year "treaty of friendship, alliance, and mutual assistance" obligated the signatories to "render military and other assistance" in case one of them should be "attacked by Japan or States allied with it." The United States was, of course, the power the Communist leaders had in mind.

The agreement on Manchuria substantially improved China's position over that of 1945. The railway system was to be transferred to Peking's authority "not later than the end of 1952," a provision which Moscow honored on December 31 of that year in a formal ceremony at Harbin attended by Chou and the new Soviet ambassador, Alexander Panyushkin. Dairen, whose status was to be determined upon the conclusion of a peace treaty with Japan, remained under Soviet control. Port Arthur, to be returned to China by the end of 1952, was retained by the Soviet government beyond that date as a result of a supplementary agreement signed on September 15, 1952. On May 25, 1955, both countries announced that Soviet forces had withdrawn from the port and that all installations had been turned over to the Chinese government.

Another agreement provided for a $300,000,000 loan prorated over five years at one per cent interest per annum. To be used to purchase Soviet materials and industrial equipment, the credit was absurdly small in view of China's needs, but large scale technical assistance and further financial aid of an undetermined amount compensated for Moscow's initial miserliness. It was probably no coincidence that the new period of generosity set in after Stalin's death in 1953.

The treaty of 1950 was the fulcrum of the Moscow-Peking axis, and nothing of an official nature was allowed to mar the outward serenity of the friendship. What slight opportunities the Western powers had of luring China away from the Soviet Union were dissipated with the coming of the Korean War and the establishment of Formosa as an unsinkable American "aircraft carrier" adjacent to the Chinese main-land. Washington's lavish aid in refurbishing Chiang's tattered military prestige and fostering the delusion—widespread in the United States —that he would someday "liberate" his homeland helped to add a fresh layer of peril to the perpetual war scares of the 1950's.

II

With the major exception of China and Korea, where Soviet interests were obvious, the Asiatic nations fell into two broad categories in their attitude toward Moscow at the mid-century point. The neutrals —India, Burma, and Indonesia—having cast off their colonial bonds, nourished a strong anti-Western tradition, but it was combined with parliamentary systems alien to Communist "democracy." Cold warriors in both the United States and the U.S.S.R. were quick to accuse them of alignment with the enemy, but all three steadfastly pursued their course. Indian Prime Minister Jawaharlal Nehru symbolized the thank-less role of the uncommitted in the global power struggle and became a kind of unofficial spokesman for the neutral "bloc." Japan, South Korea, the Philippines, Indo-China, Thailand, Malaya, and Pakistan formed an unwieldly and often unsteady combination in support of the Western powers.

The unsteadiness was to a large extent caused by the internal threat of Communism, which was frequently an outlet for nationalist fervor and peasant discontent in Southeast Asia. In Japan, too, Communism emerged for the first time as a movement of consequence, though not as a serious competitor for ultimate power. A Japanese Communist party had been founded in 1922, its influence negligible and its mem-bers subject to constant harassment and arrest. During the war years it ceased to exist as a political force. In October 1945 the release of political prisoners and the return of Sanzo Nozaka from a sixteen-year exile in Moscow and Yenan provided the leadership for a revived party which acquired legal status for the first time. The party secured a commanding position in the labor unions despite a registered mem-bership probably not in excess of 100,000 in the peak year of 1949. Communist-led strikes in 1946 further burdened an economy already hard hit by inflation and food shortages. On January 31, 1947, General MacArthur forbade a threatened general strike in the state-operated transportation and communication industries; and following his re-quest in July 1948 for restrictive labor legislation, the government passed an ordinance prohibiting strikes or collective bargaining by public employees. The Soviet representatives in the Allied Council and in the Far Eastern Commission interposed strenuous objections to this and other anti-labor measures without result.

Communist political fortunes reached their zenith in the election of January 1949. The party acquired nearly three million votes—almost 10 per cent of the total—and increased the number of its deputies in the lower house of the Diet from 5 to 35. But these gains were more than offset in 1950 when it fell upon evil days as a result of Soviet and American intervention. The blow from Moscow came in January with an attack in the Cominform organ upon the Nozaka policy of creating what he had termed a "lovable Communist party" engaged in a "peaceful revolution." That the Kremlin, after tacitly accepting a "soft" line two years beyond the changeover in the West, chose to infuse the Japanese party with a spirit of militancy at this particular time suggests that the Chinese Communist success was the spur to a more revolutionary course in Asia. The party had received no forewarning of Moscow's disfavor, and the first report that reached Tokyo was branded by a Communist spokesman as "an attempt by the enemy to disrupt Party unity."[7] Nozaka was slow to recant even after proper authentication had been received. But at length he confessed his errors and apologized for his "rightist opportunist tendencies." A new statement of party goals couched in aggressive terms was released in May.

The party extremists (later identified as "Internationalists" and expelled *en masse* during the summer) organized numerous demonstrations in the late spring of 1950; and in the most publicized incident several American soldiers were attacked. MacArthur had broadly hinted a few weeks before that the government would be well advised to crack down on the Communists, and he chose to take a grave view of the affair. The prime minister was directed to bar twenty-four members of the party Central Committee and seventeen staff members of its daily newspaper from political activity of any kind. Following the outbreak of the Korean conflict the Communists were forced underground by police raids and a political ban that fell just short of legal outlawry. Shorn of parliamentary strength in the election of October 1952, the party became a ghost of its former robust self.

The Russians, witness to the precipitous decline of their Japanese disciples, were reduced to the role of impotent bystanders as far as official relations were concerned. However, American policy underwent a continuous strafing barrage from the Soviet representatives in both the Council and the Commission. MacArthur had attended only the inaugural Council meeting in Tokyo on April 3, 1946, at which he made it clear that he expected the members to become submissive instruments of his occupation policy. At the second meeting, where substantive questions were raised for the first time, MacArthur's deputy behaved so contemptuously in reply to a Soviet request for information that the Australian delegate (representing the British Commonwealth) later pronounced his conduct a "gross and ill-mannered affront to every member of the Council."[8]

In subsequent sessions Japanese problems were subordinated to the growing Soviet-American rivalry. Russian complaints about such matters as land reform and the Zaibatsu, the great financial-industrial monopoly of Japan's leading families, had changed by 1948 to concern over remilitarization. By November 1949 the Soviet indictment was broad enough to include a charge of permitting a return of pre-war fascism, moving the American Council representative to reply with the unedifying comment: "Unadulterated twaddle."

These futile propaganda battles within the Council were repeated at the Commission meetings in Washington. On January 19, 1950, the Soviet delegate walked out because the Chinese Nationalists were not excluded from membership. The boycott ended on October 19 of the same year but not without repeated demands that China should be represented by the Peking regime.

Beginning with the session on December 21, 1949, walkout tactics were also used in the Council whenever the United States tried to raise the question of Japanese war prisoners in Soviet custody. According to Japanese figures, approximately 1,300,000 nationals, including civilians, had been incarcerated by the Russians after the Manchurian campaign. They were to have been repatriated at a rate of 50,000 a month by an agreement signed in December 1946. But the program lagged badly and was suspended altogether for months at a time, supposedly because of "icing and climatic conditions." There were two reasons for Soviet procastination—one economic, the other political. The former involved the use of the prisoners in various construction projects in the Russian Far East, just as the labor of German war prisoners was utilized in lieu of a more satisfactory reparations settlement. Because the high mortality rate in the detention camps—a Japanese estimate placed the number of dead as high as 300,000—reflected the callous attitude of the Soviet authorities, it must be supposed that the value of this labor supply was placed very low. Moscow's political motive involved an intensive indoctrination program conducted with the assistance of the Japanese Communist party. The effort seems to have yielded rather meager results. The hardships of camp life were not conducive to persuasive propaganda, though conditions were greatly improved after the first eighteen months. Nor were the repatriates allowed back into the country without "processing," a procedure which by 1947 included a full measure of political decontamination.

By May 1949 about 900,000 prisoners had been returned to Japan. Moscow announced that 105,000 were still in custody and that all but 10,000 suspected war criminals would be returned by November. The promise was kept, but repeated American attempts to elicit information about the Japanese as yet unaccounted for were rebuffed. General Derevyanko left the Council meeting of January 3, 1950, when the matter was raised once more and continued to boycott further sessions until he and other members of the Soviet mission were recalled to Moscow late in May. In the interval 8,700 more prisoners were released, and the Soviet government declared that the repatriation program was complete except for nearly 2,500 Japanese held on war crime charges. Both Tokyo and Washington insisted that 370,000 Japanese were still missing. Possibly the trial in December 1949 at Khabarovsk of twelve high-ranking Japanese officers accused of waging bacteriological warfare was a diversionary move to divert attention from the American and Japanese charges. The officers were found guilty and sentenced to terms of imprisonment ranging from three to twenty-five years.

On the question of a peace treaty with Japan, the two super-powers agreed in principle as early as 1948 that a settlement was desirable. Not unexpectedly, a procedural wrangle disguised differing points of view. Moscow urged that the negotiations be conducted through the Council of Foreign Ministers, where the Soviet veto would operate, while the United States proposed that the eleven-nation Far Eastern Commission (with a two-thirds majority vote) be given jurisdiction.

By the spring of 1950 the attitude of the British Commonwealth nations and the Japanese people was such that American policy-makers, who had been reluctant to go ahead with the treaty even on their own terms, were pressed into action. Moreover, the Russians intimated that they, together with Red China, were considering a unilateral approach to Japan. In April John Foster Dulles, who had served with the American delegation to the United Nations, was placed in charge of the Japanese treaty problem and conferred with MacArthur in Tokyo. On September 14, 1950, Truman announced that the State Department had been authorized to initiate informal discussions with the governments represented on the Far Eastern Commission. In October Dulles conferred several times with Malik on the occasion of the fifth session of the U.N. General Assembly and presented a memorandum on the peace treaty that was passed on to Moscow. The Soviet reply on November 20 was a contentious document requesting more precise information on the American proposals. Malik was handed an *aide-mémoire* on December 27 which forthrightly declared that because "irresponsible militarism still existed in the world" American troops might continue to be stationed in Japan. To the Russians, Japan was little more than a satellite of the United States.

In January 1951 Dulles undertook another trip to Tokyo—this time with the rank of ambassador. The Soviet press attacked him without quarter as the spokesman for a new combination of aggressors in the Pacific, seeking to victimize the Soviet Union and China. Upon his return late in February by way of the Philippines, Australia, New Zealand, Britain, and France, he expressed the hope that the Soviet government would take part in the preliminary negotiations and threw out a veiled warning that its sovereignty over the Kuriles might be jeopardized in case of refusal. Moscow held aloof but exchanged a series of notes with Washington during the summer recording its opposition to the draft treaty submitted by the United States on March 29. Undismayed by the Soviet reaction, the two Atlantic powers sent out invitations to forty-nine nations on July 20, 1951, to attend a conference at San Francisco in September on the Japanese peace treaty. Although the formal conclave was designed to be a cut and dried affair in which the guests were expected to do little more than sign on the dotted line, the Russians not only announced their intention of sending a delegation but also made known their determination to submit alternative proposals at the conference itself. In view of the Kremlin's previous attitude, this was something of a surprise. Dulles was mildly exercised about the "Russian wrecking crew," sent perchance to demolish the treaty, but he made it clear that the time for revisions was past.

India and Burma declined to participate, and China was not invited because of Anglo-American disagreement as to whether the Nationalists or the Communists should be represented. Since some of the other powers were not satisfied with the treaty, the hosts awaited the Soviet delegation—bolstered by representatives from Poland and Czechoslovakia—with moderate trepidation. Moscow's spokesman at the conference, Andrei Gromyko, was hardly ingratiating, yet his tone was reasonable compared to the fulminations of the Soviet press. He was allowed an hour during the second day (September 5) and used his opportunity to present a number of amendments to the treaty. Japanese remilitarization was his main concern, and he recommended various safeguards as well as a withdrawal of foreign troops. The Kremlin's objection to an American trusteeship over the Ryuku and

Bonin Islands was registered, and the sovereignty of China over Formosa—by this time an unofficial American protectorate—was to be recognized by Japan (and inferentially by the United States). Gromyko also advocated a separate reparations conference, an item that had a certain appeal to the Pacific nations deprived of what they considered adequate compensation for war damages by the treaty's rather vague reparations clause.

As the Soviet government must have anticipated, the Gromyko program was sidetracked by the conference chairman, Dean Acheson, as unacceptable under the recognized rules of procedure. On September 8, 1951, the peace treaty was signed by all the invited powers except the Soviet Union and its two satellites. The terms were remarkably lenient and would have been inconceivable had not the United States and its allies been dependent upon a revived Japan to help maintain the balance of power in the Pacific.

After two years of intermittent negotiations, Soviet-Japanese relations were finally resumed on October 19, 1956, by a "peace declaration" ending the technical state of war. Japan was to receive Soviet support for United Nations membership, and Moscow agreed to repatriate Japanese nationals and to drop its reparations claims.

III

In Southeast Asia the Soviet Union had no vital strategic interests. Not even after the war, when the colonial powers were in rapid retreat, did Moscow encourage close diplomatic ties with the newly independent states of Indonesia, Burma, and the Philippines. But the spectacular growth of Communism in the area was an unexpected boon, although Stalin was even less equipped to deal with it than he had been with the more familiar movements in China and Europe. The revolution in China added impetus and enormous prestige to the Communist cause throughout East Asia, and Peking exercised more influence, if not authority, than Moscow over the individual parties.

Except during the early period of the Comintern, the Kremlin had displayed only perfunctory interest in the fate of Communism in Southeast Asia. Beginning with the heralded "first congress of the peoples of the East" in Baku (September 1920), there had been a flurry of organizational activity. A Communist University of the Toilers of the East was founded in Moscow in May 1921 to train party workers, a Far Eastern Bureau of the Comintern was set up in Shanghai, and a new journal, *Novy Vostok* ("The New East"), was published to lend encouragement to the revolutionary struggle in Asia. By the mid-twenties, however, and particularly after the apparent collapse of Chinese Communism in 1927, Moscow's enthusiasm faded, and the ties between the Comintern and the Southeast Asian parties were tenuous at best. In these lean years heresy in the form of Trotskyism and nationalism flourished; and repression by the colonial authorities inhibited but never quite stamped out the noxious weed of revolution, of which Communism was only one of many varieties. In certain areas, notably Malaya and Thailand (Siam), the Chinese minority furnished the leadership necessary to keep the movement alive.

Beyond China, Communism's only conquest of power came in Viet Nam, the eastern portion of Indo-China comprising the states of Tonkin, Annam, and Cochin-China. Viet Nam's "liberator" and the Lenin of Southeast Asia was Ho Chi-Minh, a veteran Annamese revolutionary and one of the charter members of the French Communist party. In Paris he had acquired a reputation in radical circles as a spokesman for Vietnamese independence, and in 1923 he left for Moscow where he was reputedly trained as a Comintern agent. Later, as one of Borodin's assistants in Canton, Ho founded the Association of Revolutionary Vietnamese Youth in 1925 among his countrymen residing in South China. This group was the nucleus of the Indochinese Communist party, formally organized under Ho's guidance in Hong Kong in 1930. Within another year the party was outlawed in Viet Nam and many of its leaders were arrested or killed. Ho himself was jailed in Hong Kong for two years, and his movements upon his release in 1933 are shrouded in obscurity.

The party was revived by the mid-thirties, and though troubled by Trotskyist disaffection it achieved a measure of respectability in the beneficent climate of the Popular Front. Once more in disfavor following the Nazi-Soviet Pact, the Communists went underground, and by the fall of 1940 they were prepared to strike at the colonial administration of the Vichy French. The revolt misfired and some of the leaders escaped to China. There, in the spring of 1941, Ho organized his Communist followers in the Viet Nam Independence League (Viet Minh for short). Radicalism was submerged in the name of nationalism, and the League acquired many non-Communist members. During the next year a coalition of Viet Nam nationalist groups was formed, and the Viet Minh later emerged as the driving force.

In March 1945 the Japanese, who had ruled through the French, took over direct control and promised "independence" to the various states of Indo-China. This move was the final blow to French authority; and when the troops of the de Gaulle regime finally arrived in the fall of 1945 after Japan's defeat, they found the Democratic Republic of Viet Nam established at Hanoi, Tonkin, with Ho as president. The Communist party, with a membership of perhaps 100,000 at the time, was officially dissolved in November 1945. But the essential features of the organization, including liaison with Moscow and the French Communist party, were presumably maintained in a newly formed "Marxist study group." The coalition government had a genuinely popular basis: Ho was not disposed to model his regime along Soviet lines.

The French had recovered Cochin-China—or more accurately its capital Saigon—and were determined to retain some form of sovereignty over the whole of Indo-China. On March 6, 1946, they reached an agreement with Ho in which the Democratic Republic of Viet Nam was recognized as a "free state, having its own government, parliament, army, and treasury, belonging to the Indo-Chinese Federation and to the French Union."[9] A referendum was to decide the status of Cochin-China, and French troops were to occupy Tonkin and northern Annam.

Neither side was satisfied with the compromise, though the French emerged as the real victors. They were able to re-establish their military position without opposition; and the Vietnamese leaders were hard put to justify their policy to the people, most of whom craved immediate independence. Guerrilla fighting soon broke out again in the south, for France, pending the promised referendum, treated Cochin-China as if it were still a colony. In June Ho flew to Paris for negotiations. The parley fared poorly and was broken off in August by the Vietnamese delegation because the French high commissioner had called together an unrepresentative conference at Dalat in southern Annam in an attempt to weaken the authority of Ho's government.

In November 1946 hostilities flared up in Tonkin. More than 10,000 Vietnamese were killed in a French naval bombardment of Haiphong, and on December 19 the Viet Nam militia attacked the French in Hanoi. After that date the war began in earnest. The national resistance movement against the French incorporated the whole spectrum of Vietnamese politics, and Ho gave greater recognition to the nonpartisan nature of the struggle by dropping several prominent Communists from his cabinet in 1947. The Viet Minh forces, estimated at some 100,000 men, conducted the war as a guerrilla operation and held the rural areas, while a somewhat larger body of French troops controlled the cities and the main lines of communication.

In an attempt to bolster their political stature in Viet Nam, France sponsored a rival regime that was eventually (July 1949) headed by Bao Dai, the former emperor of Annam. By 1950 Viet Nam had become another pawn in the cold war. Communist China furnished assistance to Ho's government, and the United States, particularly following the outbreak of the Korean War, performed a similar service for the French. Moscow had assumed a relatively aloof attitude toward the Vietnamese war of independence. At the London meeting of the U.N. General Assembly in 1946 Soviet delegate Dmitri Manuilsky told a visiting Vietnamese nationalist that his government was not directly interested in the Indochinese political situation.[10] Until 1950 Soviet press coverage was scanty, though the United States was condemned as early as 1948 for its role in suppressing national liberation movements in East Asia. In January 1950 Communist China and the Soviet Union recognized the Republic of Viet Nam, and in February the United States and Britain conferred the same distinction upon Bao Dai's government. The French Communists, having taken a moderate stand in the immediate post-war years, became more militant in 1949. They demanded negotiations with Ho and an end to the "filthy war." By the close of the year Communist-inspired strikes and sabotage were temporarily effective in delaying the shipment of supplies to Indo-China.

During the latter part of 1949 Ho reversed his 1947 policy of minimizing the Communist element in the Viet Minh. Aside from internal changes that alienated leading conservatives, the zealous attempt to follow the Moscow-Peking line on international questions played into French hands by casting doubt on the genuineness of Vietnamese nationalism and estranging sympathizers around the world who were prepared to support a colonial revolt if accomplished under a non-Communist label. Political indoctrination of the population was given increasing attention, and in March 1951 the revived Indochinese Communist party was reconstitued under the name Viet Nam Lao Dong (Workers) party.

By this time the guerrilla nature of the war had altered. As a result of frontal assaults by Viet Minh troops in Tonkin, the French fell back upon the Red River delta near Hanoi. Chinese aid—much of it undoubtedly supplied by the Soviet Union—was substantially increased in 1951, and the possibility that Peking might intervene with "volunteers" as they had in Korea haunted Franco-American deliberations. China's assistance declined considerably in 1952. It was reported that her leaders had agreed to send troops only if the Viet Minh suffered a decisive defeat.[11]

Early in 1953 a Viet Minh offensive against Laos alarmed the West. But after a successful penetration, virtually without opposition, a retreat was ordered that puzzled outside observers. Some ascribed the sudden withdrawal to Moscow's then current "peace offensive." If so, the Kremlin had no similar power—or desire—to influence events in Viet Nam. The French position continued to deteriorate; and in May 1954, with the fall of Dienbienphu, a stronghold near the Tonkin-Laotian frontier, the French cause in northern Viet Nam was all but hopeless. A conference of the great powers, then in session at Geneva,[12] managed to salvage a modicum of French prestige by dividing Viet Nam near the 17th parallel, and on July 27 an armistice brought the military phase of the eight-year conflict to a halt. As a launching site for a global war, Indo-China followed Korea[13] in yielding to the art of diplomacy.

Laos and Cambodia, heretofore considered prime targets for Communist aggression, were preserved to the Western coalition as sovereign states within the French Union. The security of neighboring Thailand, already staunchly anti-Communist in official policy, was thereby enhanced. The feeble Communist movement there had never found wide support in the indigenous population, and in 1952 party membership became a criminal offense. Both Moscow and Peking regarded Thailand as an outpost of American military and commercial aggrandizement in Southeast Asia. But diplomatic relations, instituted for the first time late in 1946 (though a Soviet minister did not take up residence in Bangkok until May 1948), were normal.

Of the former British colonial possessions in East Asia, only Malaya became the cause of real alarm in the West because of a prolonged insurrection led by Communist guerrillas. Both India and Burma maintained good relations with the Soviet Union despite the uncomplimentary nature of Russian propaganda in the late forties. The Kremlin appeared to believe that Anglo-American political and economic influence greatly outweighed the legal fact of Indian and Burmese independence. By 1950 Moscow had come to appreciate the neutral international policy of the two countries far more than the tactics of internal disruption adhered to by the local Communists. In India, Prime Minister Nehru and the Communist party reciprocated an intense dislike, and in 1955 an article in *Pravda* in praise of Nehru was the cause of acute embarrassment to the party leaders. While there was no likelihood of a Communist India in the foreseeable future, the impressive economic progress of Communist China exerted a powerful magnetic attraction—as it did upon the other under-industrialized countries of East Asia.

In Burma the Communists played a leading role in the anti-Japanese resistance movement during the war and in the anti-British nationalist agitation that followed. In 1946 the party split into a radical "Trotskyist" faction (the "Red Flags") and a larger and more orthodox group (the "White Flags"). Moscow was not disposed to heal the schism either by fiat or by more subtle methods. In March 1948, after Burma had been granted its independence early in the year, the White Flags rose in rebellion and were able to dominate much of the countryside between Rangoon and Mandalay. The Red Flags and other rebel groups conducted separate insurrections, and until 1950, when government troops began to make headway, Burma's future looked dark indeed. In October 1953 Communism was legally outlawed in Burma, a move that by no means destroyed its political roots.

The Malayan Communists also revolted in the spring of 1948; and some Westerners theorized on the basis of coincidence that a policy of armed violence, presumably the new Communist strategy in Southeast Asia, had been secretly promulgated at the Calcutta Youth Conference, a meeting called in February 1948 by two international Communist front organizations. Before the war an almost wholly Chinese organization, the Malayan Communist party had led the resistance movement against the Japanese from 1943 to 1945. Some 7,000 guerrillas turned over their weapons to the British authorities after the war, and the party was seemingly content with Malaya's return to colonial rule. A major effort was made to dominate the labor unions, a campaign that was particularly effective in bringing most of the organized workers of Singapore under Communist leadership.

In June 1948, after sporadic acts of violence, police raids were directed against Communist meeting places, and 600 arrests were made. Most of the party leaders had already escaped into the jungle. The "bandits," later officially referred to as "Communist terrorists," were a small minority of the population, probably no more than 6,000 at their peak strength in 1951. In October of that year the party shifted its emphasis from sabotage and assassination to political indoctrination. The resettlement of Chinese squatters, who had fled from the towns and plantations during the Japanese occupation, also cut off the chief source of supply to the guerrillas. By 1953 the worst of the emergency was over, though the Communists had returned to a policy of terrorism and operated underground as an insurrectionary force. Their influence over the Malayan masses had continued to decline, and while the Chinese community was inclined to look favorably upon the achievements of Red China as a matter of patriotic pride, there was no evidence of real devotion to the Malayan party. When the Federation of Malaya became an independent nation within the British Commonwealth in August 1957, Communism was still a formidable political problem. By the early sixties, however, it was only a minor irritant.

The terrorism that characterized the Malayan Communist movement was most closely approximated in the Philippines. But the Filipino Communists (or Hukbalahap, a Tagolog abbreviation for "People's Anti-Japanese Army") were clearly representative of peasant discontent with the landlord system, especially in central Luzon. American rule, though more beneficent toward the native population than the other colonial powers, had shied away from basic social reform in favor of training for democracy and future independence. When Washington cut the political umbilical cord in 1946, the Philippines remained within the American economic and military orbit, and the new government was unprepared to grapple with the array of difficulties soon confronting it.

The "Huks," who had fought bravely against the Japanese during the war, deeply resented the attitude of the American military authorities in supporting former collaborators in their return to political and economic power. In September 1946 President Manuel Roxas, whose friendship with General MacArthur helped to conceal his wartime dalliance with the Japanese, tried to stamp out the Huks with what they termed a "reign of terror." In March 1948 the Huks were declared in league with a foreign power, and while admittedly there was no evidence of direct contact with the Kremlin, they were outlawed by executive decree. Numbering perhaps 30,000 armed activists and up to 2,500,000 passive followers, the Huks were by this time undoubtedly under Communist leadership, but as a rule they were politically unsophisticated. Six months later fighting broke out on a larger scale. Manila itself was threatened in the fall of 1950, and the graft-ridden government seemed incapable of effective resistance.

At this critical juncture Congressman Ramon Magsaysay was appointed secretary of defense and began a thorough reorganization of the army. Aided by a stop-gap fund of $10,000,000 from the United States, the revitalized army conducted a general offensive in 1951 that drastically reduced the Huk menace. Magsaysay, now a national hero, was elected president in November 1953. By a program of land reform and unrelenting military pressure, peasant support for the rebels fell away, and the few bands of Huks still holding out in the jungle were no longer a real danger by 1956. With the emergency past, the Communist party was nevertheless legally proscribed in June 1957.

Of the Communist parties of East Asia not in power, that in Indonesia enjoyed the best outward prospects of ultimate success. Outlawed before the war by the Dutch authorities, the party probably did not exceed 3,000 members—most of them in Java—by mid-1948. This meager number was not at all indicative of Communist strength, for membership was deliberately restricted to an elite group and various front organizations furnished a basis for mass support. In August 1948 a former party leader, Musso, returned to Indonesia from Moscow after an absence of more than twelve years. He proceeded to take charge of the Communist movement, which had been merged with other radical groups earlier in the year into a People's Democratic Front. The coalition, under Communist leadership, assumed a much more hostile attitude toward the Republican government of President Sukarno.

Although Musso was determined to seize power—peacefully if possible, by force if necessary—he was not yet prepared to challenge the government. But he was left with no alternative except armed insurrection when local subordinates launched a premature *coup* on September 18, 1948, at Madiun in eastern Java. Musso called upon the population to overthrow the "traitors" who were subjugating the Republic to Dutch, British, and American imperial interests. The Moscow radio reported a "popular uprising" against the regime of the "Fascist Japanese Quislings," Sukarno and Prime Minister Mohammed Hatta.[14]

The government struck swiftly by arresting prominent Communists, many of whom were unaware of the revolt in Madiun. The bulk of the army was engaged in holding a truce line against the Dutch, and only about 25,000 men were available for action against a slightly smaller number of rebels. These troops eventually proved sufficient, for the masses failed to respond to Musso's appeal, and the insurrection had to be carried on as a guerrilla movement. By the end of October Musso had been killed and the rebellion brought under control. On December 7, 1948, Republican military headquarters announced that all fighting had ceased and that 35,000 persons, most of them guerrillas, had been arrested.

Shortly afterward the Dutch again resorted to a "police action" against the Indonesian Republic. Largely as a result of intervention by the United Nations, negotiations between Dutch and Republican representatives were held at The Hague, and in December 1949 the Netherlands recognized the independence of Indonesia. The Soviet Union had refused to cooperate with the U.N. Security Council and had been severely critical of the Republican regime. In the first half of 1950 the Soviet press became more moderate in its attitude, and an exchange of ambassadors appeared imminent when Moscow launched new propaganda attacks based on the premise of Indonesian subservience to the United States. By 1952 the Kremlin had begun to appreciate more fully Indonesia's association with India and Burma in an East Asian "neutral bloc" in the cold war. Diplomatic representatives were exchanged, and relations became quite cordial after Sukarno visited the Soviet Union in 1956.

The Indonesian Communists took their cue from Moscow in becoming supporters of Sukarno's government. Having led a semi-clandestine existence after the Madiun *coup*—over 15,000 suspects were reportedly arrested during the summer and autumn of 1951—they now prospered to such a degree that the party gained more than 16 per cent of the vote in Indonesia's first parliamentary election in 1955. More than a million members were claimed in 1958 compared to an estimated 7,000 in 1952, a sensational spurt that can be accounted for only by a shift in strategy from elitism to mass participation. Substantial control over organized labor was an even better index to Communist strength.

Further unrest, organized banditry, and separatist tendencies forecast an uncertain future for representative government in Indonesia. In February 1957 Sukarno publicly advocated the "burial" of political parties and the establishment of a "guided democracy" to include Communist participation in the cabinet. The party duly registered enthusiastic approval, but the central government at Jakarta found itself beset by various critics who did not hesitate to resort to arms in expressing opposition. The most alarming of the recurrent rebellions that plagued the Sukarno regime broke out in February 1958 when a rival government was set up at Padang in Sumatra. Representative of the autonomous sentiment of many non-Javanese, the rebels also interjected the Communist issue. As their leader put it, "The problem has become one of a choice between Communism and non-Communism, belief in God and atheism."[15] A vastly oversimplified and demogogic view of Indonesian politics, the statement nonetheless capsulized the sentiments of many, both in and out of Indonesia, who thought of the global ideological struggle in apocalyptic terms of good versus evil. The insurrection was eventually localized, but prospects for democracy—Western style—in Indonesia were poor.

IV

In May 1950 the Korean War burst upon a startled world, and for the first time the uneasy truce of the cold war was shattered by bloodshed: the Communist East and the capitalist West at last confronted each other—but only over the prostrate body of the victim. Until reminded in so unceremonious a fashion, public opinion in Europe and America was barely conscious that a Korean problem existed. To many, Korea had seemed a remote and outlandish place and therefore of little consequence in the larger scheme of international affairs. In the councils of the United Nations and at the official level in Moscow and Washington there had been no complacency about Korea; yet neither had there been any real presentiment that the situation might lead to war.

After its annexation by Japan in 1910, Korea had not come within the purview of the great powers in any significant way until the Cairo Conference (November 1943), where Roosevelt, Churchill, and Chiang agreed that it should "in due course . . . become free and independent." When at Teheran and again at Yalta the subject was broached to Stalin, he concurred in Roosevelt's suggestion of an international trusteeship but made no formal commitment. During his talks with Hopkins in May 1945, Stalin accepted the idea of a trusteeship for Korea consisting of the United States, Britain, the Soviet Union, and China. At the time of the Soviet declaration of war on Japan (August 8, 1945) no understanding had been reached as to the administration or occupation of the country. On August 12 units of the Red Army landed in Korea at its northeastern tip, where a short frontier adjoins Soviet territory about seventy miles southwest of Vladivostok. For purposes of military expediency in receiving the Japanese surrender and insuring that the Russians would not overrun the whole peninsula, the American joint chiefs of staff recommended the 38th degree of north latitude as a demarcation line between Soviet and American occupation forces. The President approved the arrangement, as did Stalin and Churchill. MacArthur made the agreement public on September 2 as a part of his General Order No. 1.[16]

American troops did not land in Korea until September 8. The Russians, who had penetrated as far south as Seoul, then withdrew to the 38th parallel. The line chosen was entirely without political, economic, or geographical justification but quickly assumed a significance—and permanence—that could not have been foreseen at the time. The Soviet command zealously guarded its zone from outside interference and rebuffed the overtures of the American commander. Since most of what little industry Korea had was concentrated in the north and her best farming land was in the south, the complementary economy of the country was arbitrarily sundered. Each portion of the bisected peninsula came to reflect the social system of the occupying power: the Russians concentrated on drastic socio-economic reform within an authoritarian political framework, while the Americans sought to prepare the Korean people for self-rule without an equivalent concern for the economic foundations of a stable democratic society.

The Koreans themselves—or at least their more articulate spokesmen—resented the enforced tutelage that their liberators had brought, for they had interpreted the ambiguous phraseology of the Cairo declaration to mean independence within the shortest possible time. The Korean Communists naturally did not share these sentiments insofar as the Soviet Union was concerned, although a few whose nationalism outweighed their Communism did call for the withdrawal of both powers. Many important party members were released from prison, and others came back from exile in the Soviet Union and in the Communist part of China. The Russian military command exerted its authority from behind a hierarchical organization of Communist-dominated "people's committees." On February 9, 1946, a Provisional People's Committee for North Korea was organized with Kim Il Sung, a veteran Communist, heading an all-Korean coalition cabinet.

At the Moscow conference of foreign ministers (December 1945) it was decided to set up a Joint Commission representing the Soviet and American military commands to assist in the formation of a provisional Korean government. The Commission was to consult "democratic parties and social organizations" and to make recommendations to the four trustee powers—final action to be reserved to the United States and the U.S.S.R. It met at Seoul between March 20 and May 8, 1946, without approaching a solution. The Russians insisted that the political question precede all others, and they proposed to exclude those parties and organizations opposing the trusteeship arrangement and the terms of the Moscow agreement. In effect, this scheme would bar the conservative anti-Soviet leaders of South Korea from the government, an idea that the United States refused to entertain.

The two military commanders, Generals John R. Hodge and Ivan Chistyakov, subsequently narrowed the area of disagreement by an exchange of correspondence. But Moscow was unwilling to resume negotiations for the time being. By the spring of 1947 signs that the United States would sponsor a South Korean government induced the Kremlin to seek a compromise on the basis of the Hodge-Chistyakov formula. In essence, the plan provided that all Korean parties would be consulted if they agreed to the Moscow decisions of December 1945. The Joint Commission reconvened on May 22, 1947, at Seoul, and at first it made progress in the tedious work of sorting applications from the numerous groups seeking a hearing (38 in the North and 425 in the South). In the Soviet zone all organizations were automatically members of the Communist-controlled Democratic Front. In the American zone, where ultra-conservative and nationalist organizations flourished, a preponderance of political influence was held by the parties constituting the Anti-Trusteeship Committee, a body founded in December 1945 to agitate against the Moscow agreement. Virulently anti-Communist, these parties covertly opposed the work of the Commission, and the Russians demanded in July 1947 that they be eliminated from further consideration. The American delegation, apprehensive about overweighting the Communist side, rejected the Soviet condition.

By late summer the negotiations were hopelessly deadlocked once more. The good faith of the United States in the bargaining process was gravely compromised by a reign of terror against "leftists" that broke out in South Korea in July and August. The American authorities, by removing (July 10) the ban on mass demonstrations against the Moscow agreement, were morally responsible for touching off the campaign of violence. Right wing "goon squads" went into action almost immediately, aided and abetted by the police. In Seoul the best known political figure among the moderates, Lyuh Woon Heung, was assassinated on July 19 in broad daylight; and a week later members of the Soviet delegation were attacked. Beatings and arrests proceeded at a high rate, moving the Russians to complain of an American-instigated "pogrom" designed to interrupt the work of the Commission. The Americans retorted that the Russians were abusing their "guest status" by interfering in South Korean affairs.

Washington sought a way out of the impasse on August 26, 1947, by inviting the Soviet, British, and Chinese governments to a conference on September 8. A new approach was envisaged in which elections would be held in the presence of United Nations observers. When Moscow declined participation, the United States declared that it would place the issue before the U.N. General Assembly. The Russians countered with a plan advanced by their Commission representative, General Terenti Shtykov, on September 26: both powers to withdraw their troops by January 1, 1948, to allow the Koreans an opportunity to choose their own government. It was a clever move that embarrassed both the United States and the Korean conservatives. The latter had been clamoring incessantly for an end to the trusteeship arrangements and the evacuation of foreign troops. Abruptly faced with the prospect of their words being transformed into reality, they quailed at the thought. It was claimed—with considerable accuracy, as events turned out—that a North Korean army of 200,000 men had been trained by the Russians and would take over the whole peninsula in the absence of American troops. Already committed to the United Nations appeal, Washington refused the Soviet offer. On the same day—October 18 —the Joint Commission held its final session in Seoul.

After a prolonged debate in the Political Committee of the U.N.

General Assembly, the essence of the American case, presented in the form of a resolution, was accepted by a vote of 43 to 0 in the full Assembly on November 14, 1947. The Soviet bloc abstained. A U.N. Temporary Commission was established to supervise the election of an all-Korean national assembly, and it arrived in Seoul in January 1948. The Russians, who had already indicated their intention of boycotting the Commission, spurned its overtures by silence. The members were sharply divided about proceeding with the election in South Korea alone, but they decided by a small majority to go ahead upon the recommendation of the Interim Committee of the General Assembly. They were fully aware of the danger that Korea might be irrevocably split by their action. So, too, were the moderate and leftist parties in the South, whose leaders strongly opposed an election since it would probably mean victory for the extreme Right wing party of Dr. Syngman Rhee. The American-educated Rhee had been a resident of the United States for most of the past forty years, and his vociferous anti-Communism was a good recommendation to the American authorities even though it was apt to get out of hand. He had once gone so far as to accuse General Hodge and his administration of "trying to build up and foster the Korean Communist Party."[17]

In April 1948 the North Korean political leaders held two successive conferences in Pyongyang that many southerners also attended by invitation. Resolutions were passed upholding the Soviet position, including the withdrawal of occupation forces. An all-Korean election was promised, and it was agreed not to recognize the results of the coming election in the South. General Hodge and the supporters of Rhee denounced the participating southerners as "stooges of Communism." Some of them undoubtedly were, particularly those whose philosophy could be summed up as "better Communism than Rhee"; but others had made the journey to Pyongyang in the sincere conviction that a separate election would only perpetuate the division of their country.

On election day (May 10, 1948) there was little of the overt violence that had marked the past six weeks (official figures later admitted that 589 persons were killed during the period, and it was estimated that perhaps 10,000 "rioters" had been processed in police stations).[18] About 95 per cent of the registrants—72 per cent of the eligible voters—were reported to have cast a ballot. A strongly conservative assembly was chosen, with Rhee's candidates holding a plurality. The American command and the South Korean interim government pronounced the election a great victory for democracy and a repudiation of Communism. Unofficial observers were less sanguine. Widespread bribery and intimidation was reported, and in the Soviet and North Korean press the election was as a matter of course denounced as fraudulent. The U.N. Commission nevertheless declared itself satisfied that the results were a valid expression of the electorate in those parts of Korea accessible to it. Rhee was chosen president by the Assembly, and the new government was formally inaugurated on August 15. Both Rhee and General MacArthur, who was present for the occasion, made speeches containing passages that the Russians could only interpret as warlike threats.

In North Korea the People's Committee adopted a Soviet-style constitution on May 1, 1948, and asserted its validity for the whole country. On August 25 an election was held to choose a "people's assembly," and the Pyongyang radio broadcast the absurd claim that over 8,000,000 South Koreans had also voted. However, over 1,000 delegates purporting to represent the people of South Korea had met on August 22–24 just north of the 38th parallel and selected 360 of their number as deputies in the northern assembly. On September 7 the assembly met and proclaimed the formation of the Democratic People's Republic of Korea with Kim Il Sung as premier. On October 12 Moscow recognized the North Korean regime, and shortly thereafter General Shtykov was appointed ambassador.

The U.N. General Assembly did not take up the Korean question again until December 1948. By a vote of 48 to 6—the dissenters constituted the Soviet bloc—a resolution was passed on the 12th accepting the Temporary Commission's report and recommending that the occupying military forces withdraw "as early as practicable." A new seven-power Commission was to "lend its good offices" toward the unification of Korea and the removal of barriers to economic and social intercourse. Both the Soviet and American governments were already engaged in the evacuation of their troops. Moscow had informed Washington on September 18 that the Russian forces would be withdrawn before the end of the year, and the process was reportedly complete on December 24. Placed on the defensive by the Soviet move, the United States at first temporized and then decided to pull its troops out also. In November the State Department requested a delay—the South Korean leaders were alarmed by the rapidity of the American withdrawal—and a regimental combat team of 7,500 men was allowed to stay until late June of 1949.

By conferring its moral support on Rhee's government, the United Nations succeeded only in making compromise more difficult. Outvoted though it may have been, the Soviet government was all the more determined to adhere to the principles that in its view had been violated by the United States in the summer of 1947. The new U.N. Commission found no change of attitude when it arrived in Korea at the end of January 1949. Moscow ignored a request that it intercede with the northern regime to help the work of the Commission, and Pyongyang bestirred itself to attack the investigators as a "collection of hirelings of American imperialism." Nor did the Seoul government offer to cooperate because of the Commission's desire to negotiate with the leaders of the North. Rhee's attitude was that since the General Assembly had pronounced his regime the only "lawful government" in Korea, its subordinate body should not be encouraged to deal with an "unlawful" government that was no better than a Russian tool. So bitter was his hostility toward the Pyongyang authorities that all trade with the North was banned on April 1, 1949.

In a report to the General Assembly during the summer of 1949, the Commission warned of "much military posturing on both sides of the parallel" and an increase in the intensity of border raids from the North. In October the Assembly approved a resolution expressing concern lest the situation degenerate into open warfare and authorizing the Commission to "observe and report any developments which might lead to . . . military conflict in Korea."[19] At the time of the North Korean attack a plan to station trained observers at critical points along the frontier had not yet gone into full operation.

By the spring of 1950 both the U.S.S.R. and the United States had armed their respective protectorates. After the exodus of the main body of American troops in June 1949, a force of 500 officers and men were left as a training cadre. The South Korean army consisted of some 100,000 men organized into eight infantry divisions. No planes or tanks were permitted as a check on possible aggression. The North Korean army was estimated to be slightly smaller but with heavier equipment. The Soviet military mission was thought to total 3,500 men.

On May 30, 1950, Rhee suffered a sharp political setback when only 48 of the government's supporters were returned to the assembly in South Korea's second election. The U.N. Commission reported that the balloting had been properly conducted, although thirty candidates were held in pre-election "anti-Communist" raids. On June 7 Pyongyang suggested an all-Korean election to be held in August, the assembly so chosen to meet in Seoul. Southern leaders, with the exception of Rhee and a few others, were invited to take part in a conference near the parallel to plan the election. The South Korean government made every effort to suppress the appeal, and whether or not it succeeded, the lack of response was evident. The meeting was abandoned. Pyongyang produced another scheme on June 19: the two legislative assemblies would combine to draw up a constitution, establish a national government, and arrange for a new election. Since Rhee and other "traitors" were to be arrested, the proposal was actually an address to the South Korean people over the heads of their rulers rather than a genuine offer from one government to the other.

The time for verbal provocations, in which both sides had lavishly indulged themselves, came to an abrupt conclusion in the early hours of June 25, 1950, when the North Korean army pushed across the 38th parallel in strength. Pyongyang and Moscow asserted that the South Koreans were the real aggressors and that it had been necessary to counterattack in order to repel an invasion of northern territory. The Western powers unhesitatingly pointed to North Korea as the guilty party but reserved to the Soviet Union the biggest share of moral opprobrium on the assumption—certainly quite likely—that the puppet could perform only at its master's bidding.

Yet there were grounds for supposing that Pyongyang had acted either without the Kremlin's knowledge or without its express approval. Moscow had been boycotting the United Nations to protest the exclusion of Communist China, and it was a reasonable expectation that a forewarned Soviet delegation would have been on hand to veto any action that the Security Council might choose to take against North Korea. Such was not the case: Moscow went on ignoring the U.N., aside from propaganda through the usual media. Furthermore, Stalin had, except in the case of Finland in 1939, consistently displayed a marked distaste for armed aggression as a means of gaining Soviet ends. In the case of the Greek and Chinese civil wars—not dissimilar situations—he had been cautious to the point of timidity. Whatever his reputation in the West, he was not a gambler by nature; and the Korean venture was a gamble of the most dangerous sort. If he did indeed succumb to temptation, the clear indication that the United States considered Korea outside its "defense perimeter" must have played a major role in his calculations. The Soviet failure to make good the losses in equipment suffered by the North Koreans—a circumstance not apparent for some time after the fighting began—was a sign that the Kremlin, if it did not disapprove of the tactics of its Korean subordinates, was at least anxious to localize the conflict.

At the behest of the United States, the Security Council met in a special session on the afternoon of June 25. By a vote of 9 to 0 (Yugoslavia abstaining) a resolution was passed calling for the cessation of hostilities and the withdrawal of the northern forces to the 38th parallel. Taking an extremely broad interpretation of the Security Council's request that all United Nations members "render every assistance" in the execution of its resolution, Truman announced on June 27 that he had ordered American naval and air force units to give "cover and support" to the South Korean troops and that the Seventh Fleet had been sent to prevent any attack on Formosa. The latter measure was an unprovoked challenge to Red China, a fateful first step in bringing Peking into the struggle. Within a few hours of the President's statement the Security Council met again, this time to sanction the action of the United States on Korea by passing a resolution urging U.N. members to "furnish such assistance . . . as may be necessary to repel the armed attack." Yugoslavia voted in the negative, while India and Egypt abstained.

Moscow reacted to the Security Council's flurry of activity by declaring its resolutions illegal in the absence of Soviet and Chinese representatives. On June 27 Washington asked the Soviet government to disavow "responsibility for this unprovoked and unwarranted attack" and to "use its influence with the North Korean authorities to withdraw their invading forces immediately."[20] In reply, the Russians simply reiterated their previous stand that the war had been "provoked" by a South Korean attack. Peking took the same line, and Foreign Minister Chou En-lai released a fiery denunciation of the United States for its "predatory action" in preventing the "liberation" of Formosa. The first full explanation of the official Soviet view was contained in Gromyko's elaborate statement of July 4 that was communicated to the Security Council. He accused the United Nations of allowing itself to be utilized as a tool by the "ruling circles of the United States for unleashing war." A number of historical analogies were recalled, including British intervention in the American Civil War and Allied intervention against Bolshevik Russia.[21]

In the face of the rapid advance of the North Korean army—Seoul was taken on June 27—American ground forces were ordered to Korea on June 30. On July 7 the Security Council carried a resolution in favor of a unified command under American leadership, and Truman designated MacArthur the United Nations commander. Before the end of the year the troops of ten nations were fighting in Korea, though the United States provided the bulk of the combat forces. The demoralized South Korean army had virtually disintegrated in July, but several divisions were salvaged to make a stand with American reinforcements at the "Pusan perimeter" on the tip of the peninsula. In mid-September an American landing at Inchon behind the enemy's lines, combined with a counter-offensive in the south, forced the North Koreans to retreat in confusion. By the end of the month the 38th parallel had been regained, and a lull ensued as Washington pondered the risks involved in invading the Korean Communist domain.

During the summer months, while Moscow's propaganda hewed to the pattern set at the beginning of the conflict, no bellicose words or acts were permitted to mar the Kremlin's determination to avoid direct involvement. On July 15 Stalin replied in a conciliatory fashion to a personal message from Nehru soliciting his cooperation in resolving the crisis. Nehru's idea was to seat Communist China in the Security Council to end the Soviet boycott and then to work out a peaceful settlement among the great powers. An exchange of views along these lines took place in the Russian capital between Gromyko and the British ambassador. But London wished to confine the issue to Korea, and Moscow declined the suggestion that it exert pressure in withdrawing the North Koreans to their own border. Washington found Nehru's proposal untenable as long as "unlawful aggression" subjected the United Nations to "coercion and duress."

Finding that its boycott of the United Nations was a political liability with no compensating assets, the Soviet government announced through Malik on July 27, 1950, that it would return to the Security Council on August 1. The rotating presidency fell vacant on that date, and it was the Russian representative's turn to take the chair. The month was spent in procedural wrangles and choleric debates, with Malik in the role of prosecuting attorney delivering an impassioned indictment of the whole range of American policy in the Far East. On September 6, after the British representative had succeeded Malik as president, a Soviet veto quashed an American resolution condemning the North Koreans for their defiance of the United Nations. The Soviet counter-resolution in favor of withdrawing "foreign troops" from Korea was decisively rejected on the same day.

In September the disposition of Chinese Communist forces in Manchuria near the Korean frontier was noted in the Western press. On the 30th Chou En-lai stated that his government would not "supinely tolerate seeing their neighbors being savagely invaded by imperialists." India, whose ambassador to Peking enjoyed close relations with the top officials, warned that China might intervene if the 38th parallel were crossed. Washington was inclined to treat Peking's attitude as a bluff. MacArthur had already (September 27) been authorized to conduct military operations north of the parallel, and on October 1 units of the South Korean army were allowed to proceed. American troops were restrained temporarily until the U.N. General Assembly could approve the action—already a *fait accompli*. A resolution on October 7, passed by a vote of 47 to 5, did not specifically authorize the advance into North Korea but resorted to the circumlocutious phrase, "All appropriate steps [should] be taken to ensure conditions of stability throughout Korea." Anticipating the vote, American forces had crossed the parallel some hours before.

The war now entered a wholly new phase. Resisting aggression was one thing; "stabilizing" Korea by counter-aggression was still another. At any rate, this was the opinion expressed in most of the neutral countries, and it found a feeble echo in the U.N. Interim Commission for Korea which voted on October 12 to limit Rhee's jurisdiction to South Korea. Peking judged itself directly menaced by the invasion of North Korea. The United States was with good reason considered hostile to Communist China; and the possibility that the Yalu River boundary, including hydroelectric installations vital to Manchurian industry, might fall into American hands was to Peking an alarming prospect. The Chinese press showed no hesitancy in expressing these views, and it also complained of border violations by United Nations aircraft. The truth of these assertions was not confirmed, although Washington later admitted that two American planes had attacked a Soviet airport south of Vladivostok on October 8.

The threat of Chinese intervention was taken lightly in official American circles. MacArthur, who deemed himself a master of "Oriental psychology," was contemptuous of Peking's military prowess and expressed his opinion to Truman during their meeting at Wake Island on October 15, 1950, that the chance of China or Russia becoming involved in the war was extremely remote. On the next day units of the Chinese Red Army crossed the Yalu into Korea but made no attempt to engage the enemy. By early November Chinese "volunteers" were present in such numbers that MacArthur raised the alarm. Still largely inactive, the "phantom army" of some 200,000 Chinese did not strike until November 26 after the beginning of MacArthur's ill-fated "end-the-war" offensive that was to "bring the boys home for Christmas." At the end of the year the United Nations forces were in headlong retreat and the Chinese had forged beyond the 38th parallel.

Peking's intervention presumably received Moscow's blessing, for China was not yet an industrial power of consequence and was forced to rely upon Soviet assistance in arms and equipment. If the Russians made no public intimation that they were prepared to become openly involved in the war—even to the extent that propaganda and over-all strategy would seem to require—there was always the nagging fear among the Western democracies that if the conflict were allowed to spread to Chinese soil the Soviet government would intervene and Korea would become after all the Sarajevo of World War III. The

European allies of the United States were alarmed by the danger of a spreading conflagration. MacArthur, with his flamboyant showmanship and public complaints about China's "privileged sanctuary" in Manchuria, had become a symbol of American irresponsibility. To the Communist nations he was, as Vyshinsky put it, "a maniac, the principal culprit, the evil genius."[22] When Truman acknowledged at a press conference on November 30, 1950, that the atom bomb was among the weapons to be considered in any review of "this military aggression," it triggered a wave of apprehension in Western Europe and was partly responsible for a hurried trip to Washington by Clement Atlee.

Talk of preventive war was heard in some quarters, especially the American military establishment, but the British prime minister found reassurance in his talks with Truman and Acheson that counsels of moderation prevailed. The President was already of the opinion that all-out war with China would be a "gigantic booby trap" from which the Russians would be the chief beneficiaries. A "highly secret report" had also been received from Peking on November 15 that a "top Russian diplomat there had said that if Manchurian airfields were bombed by United Nations planes the Soviet Air Force would strike back in force."[23] The tacit understanding between the Communist and Western powers that the war would be confined to Korea was maintained. Since it was based upon the only sure guarantee of international co-operation—self-interest—the war was successfully localized despite provocative acts later on by both sides.

The United Nations had meanwhile taken up the question of Chinese intervention. Peking was invited to present its views on the Formosa dispute, and on November 28 General Wu Hsiu-chuan reviewed at length his government's grievances against the United States before the Security Council. Two days later a Soviet resolution calling on the United States to recall its forces from Formosa and Korea was easily defeated. Malik, in turn, vetoed a six-power resolution requesting a Chinese withdrawal from Korea. Hamstrung in the Security Council, the Western powers took their case to the General Assembly. There was reluctance to brand China an aggressor, as the United States desired, until the possibilities of mediation had been explored. On December 14 an Asian-Arab proposal for a cease-fire was carried 52 to 5, and a three-man committee endeavored to gain Peking's consent. Because the military situation was then overwhelmingly favorable to China, the committee was sharply rebuffed by Chou En-lai.

On January 17, 1951, Peking rejected a further attempt at mediation but offered to negotiate on terms patently unacceptable to the West.

On February 1 a resolution censuring China for aggression passed the General Assembly by 44 votes to 7 with 9 abstentions. The conspicuous lack of enthusiasm of the Asian-Arab states—India and Burma even voted with the Soviet bloc—deprived the United States of a convincing moral victory in its appeal to world opinion through the United Nations. On February 7 the Soviet charge of American aggression against China, pending since November, was voted down in committee.

In March U.N. forces regained the initiative in Korea; and in April the long overdue dismissal of MacArthur for insubordination brought new hope of compromise. But a fresh Chinese offensive demonstrated that Peking still sought a solution on the battlefield. No significant break-through was achieved, and another offensive in May was driven back with severe losses. On June 23, 1951, as the battle lines were stabilized—in some sectors north of the 38th parallel—the Soviet Union brought forward an unexpected proposal destined to bring peace to Korea after two frustrating years of negotiation. Heretofore content with shadow boxing in the United Nations, Moscow seized the diplomatic initiative for the first time during the Korean War through Malik's suggestion (made at the end of a broadcast series sponsored by the U.N.) that the belligerents arrange a "ceasefire and an armistice providing for the mutual withdrawal of forces from the 38th parallel." The American ambassador in Moscow, seeking clarification of the statement, was informed by Gromyko that his government had in mind a discussion limited strictly to military questions.

Truce talks began on July 10 at Kaesong, a Communist-held town just below the 38th parallel. Suspended by the Chinese-North Korean authorities between August 23 and October 25 because of alleged violations of the conference zone by U.N. aircraft, they were resumed at the nearby town of Panmunjom. The negotiations progressed steadily but at a painfully slow and tedious pace. In December 1951 they became snagged on the prisoner of war issue, and by the following spring the impasse seemed complete. The Communists demanded the return of all prisoners; the U.N. refused repatriation by force. Of the 132,000 prisoners (about 21,000 Chinese, the rest Korean) held by the U.N., some 70,000 were reported willing to return. Washington, without consulting its allies, resorted to military pressure in June 1952 by bombing the hydroelectric installations on the Yalu. The device failed to budge the Communist negotiators and succeeded only in offending the British. The raid was not repeated.

The parley, punctuated by occasional skirmishes between the contending armies, dragged on interminably. The Soviet government was for the most part content to play a bystander's role after Malik's proposal, and no word of its relationship to Peking concerning Korea was allowed to seep into the public domain. Outsiders could only surmise from the available evidence that the Chinese Communists had Moscow's complete backing: Soviet propaganda pursued the expected course toward the prisoner of war issue, as it had every other aspect of the Korean affair; and the excellent Soviet-manufactured equipment of the Communist forces in North Korea, including new jet aircraft, proclaimed that if the Russians were as yet unwilling to salvage the Korean enterprise with direct action, they were prepared to go further than mere salvos of rhetoric.

At the seventh session of the U.N. General Assembly beginning in October 1952, Vyshinsky opposed an American resolution asking for a blanket endorsement of the U.N. command in its conduct of the armistice talks and sponsored one of his own. Vyshinsky's provided for an immediate cease-fire and the establishment of an eleven-power commission to supervise a political settlement by the Koreans themselves and to assist in the repatriation of prisoners on both sides. A majority of the membership urged compromise, and it was supplied by an Indian plan for a neutral repatriation commission. After clarifying amendments had been added, the United States announced its support, and the resolution was carried in the General Assembly on December 3 by 54 to 5. The Soviet bloc furnished the negative votes, and Peking made known its own opposition.

The prospect of an armistice looked as hopeless as ever during the early part of the new year. But in March 1953 the death of Stalin opened up new possibilities; and after Chou En-lai's return from Moscow toward the end of the month, Peking agreed to an exchange of sick and wounded prisoners and proposed that armistice negotiations—virtually suspended since the previous summer—be resumed on terms that approximated those of the Indian resolution of December. On April 26 the full armistice delegations met again at Panmunjom. This time progress was relatively swift, and an agreement was signed on June 8 providing that unrepatriated prisoners be turned over to a neutral commission headed by India. Ten days later President Rhee tried to sabotage the conclusion of a cease-fire by releasing 25,000 anti-Communist prisoners. Moscow and Peking naturally assumed connivance between Rhee and the American authorities: an "indecent farce" was being enacted according to *Soviet News*, the organ of the Russian embassy in London.

In order to teach the Seoul government a lesson, Peking on July 17 launched its biggest offensive in two years and claimed to have pulverized South Korea's finest division and to have routed three others before American reinforcements came to the rescue. Perhaps because they felt that Rhee had been properly chastised, the Chinese did not continue to make an issue of the prisoner incident, and the armistice was signed on July 27, 1953.

After thirty-seven months the fighting had ceased, but Korea remained a significant pawn in the global power struggle. Under these circumstances a solution to the political division of the country seemed a remote eventuality. Collective action had made aggression an unprofitable undertaking; the United Nations had proved something more than an innocuous debaters' forum; and the United States had "contained" Communism in a strategic area. Yet the war had been a frustrating experience for the American people and their government. It had been a stalemate and therefore an affront to patriots; and the real enemy—Soviet Russia—had escaped unscathed, unpunished, and presumably unrepentant. For some there was psychic relief to be found in a domestic heresy hunt and in the knowledge that the Chinese Communists would continue to suffer the humiliation of disbarment from the U.N. and non-recognition by the United States. Peking found this "moral quarantine" offensive enough and the sequestration of Formosa by American arms even more so; but as was the case with the Soviet government in the twenties, Washington's displeasure was scarcely an insuperable obstacle to the stability of the regime. The attitude of the United States was, in fact, a hidden confession of weakness—that American military power had failed to subdue China and that Chinese soldiers, properly trained and with modern weapons, were a match for Western troops. If the revolution in 1949 had not hammered home the lesson that the balance of power in East Asia had irrevocably shifted, the Korean War was the clinching argument.

NOTES

1. See below, p. 394.
2. See above, p. 317.
3. *United States Relations with China,* pp. 686–87.
4. See above, p. 316.
5. *United States Relations with China,* p. 248.
6. Mao Tse-tung, *Turning Point in China* (New York, 1948), pp. 3–4.
7. *Akahata,* January 9, 1950, as quoted in Rodger Swearingen and Paul Langer, *Red Flag in Japan* (Cambridge, Mass., 1952), p. 201.
8. W. Macmahon Ball, *Japan: Enemy or Ally?* (New York, 1949), p. 26.

9. Allen B. Cole (ed.), *Conflict in Indo-China and International Repercussions: A Documentary History, 1945–1955* (Ithaca, N. Y., 1956), p. 40.

10. Ellen J. Hammer, *The Struggle for Indochina* (Stanford, Calif., 1954), p. 201.

11. *Le Monde,* January 28, 1953, cited *ibid.,* p. 253.

12. See below, pp. 424–26.

13. See below, p. 401.

14. George M. Kahin, *Nationalism and Revolution in Indonesia* (Ithaca, N.Y., 1952), p. 294.

15. *New York Times,* February 23, 1958.

16. See above, p. 310.

17. Truman, *Memoirs,* II, 322.

18. George M. McCune, *Korea Today* (Cambridge, Mass., 1950), p. 229.

19. Leland M. Goodrich, *Korea: A Study of U.S. Policy in the United Nations* (New York, 1956), p. 78.

20. Department of State, *U.S. Policy in the Korean Crisis: 1950* (Washington, 1950), pp. 63–64.

21. Text in *The Soviet Union and the Korean Question (Documents)* (London, 1950), pp. 93–99.

22. Richard H. Rovere and Arthur M. Schlesinger, Jr., *The General and the President* (New York, 1951), p. 154.

23. Truman, *Memoirs,* II, 378 and 394.

CHAPTER THIRTEEN

COLD WAR: NUCLEAR STALEMATE

As the breach between East and West widened to a state of unconcealed hostility during the late forties, there was one consoling factor
which the Western powers counted as a solid guarantee of their
supremacy should a general war again break out: American monopoly
of the atomic bomb. It was freely predicted that because of the
backward state of Soviet science and technology the "secret" of atomic
energy could be kept for many years; and there were those who,
knowing little of the realities of Soviet foreign policy except that it
was aggressive, claimed that the only deterrent to a Russian attack
on Western Europe was the threat to the Soviet homeland posed
by the United States Air Force armed with atomic weapons.

American complacency about its superiority in "military physics"
was shattered on September 23, 1949, when President Truman released
a statement to the press revealing that the Soviet Union had exploded
an atomic bomb. Although the United States had a much larger
stockpile of the bombs and was vastly more capable of delivering them
to their target because of its network of strategic overseas airbases,
the sense of immunity from military attack that most Americans had
so long taken for granted was now irretrievably lost. No substantial
information about Soviet progress in the field of atomic energy had
leaked through the Iron Curtain despite Molotov's statement in November 1947, which had received almost no credence in the West,
that the atomic bomb was no longer a secret. It was subsequently
revealed that the Soviet nuclear explosion had occurred between
August 26 and 29, 1949.

The unexpected Russian success induced neither of the cold war
rivals to shift their stand on the international control of atomic energy.
Negotiations on control measures had been deadlocked since 1946,
and they were to remain so even when the development of the hydrogen bomb in the early fifties made the problem of radioactive

fallout from test explosions of acute concern to all nations. The United States had taken the position from the beginning that it should act as trustee for the military and industrial application of atomic energy until such time as proper international safeguards were set up. But the Soviet leaders were suspicious of American "atomic diplomacy," and they looked upon Truman's statement that the bomb was a "sacred trust" as rank hypocrisy.

In January 1946 the United Nations created an Atomic Energy Commission to implement the decision reached by the foreign ministers at their conference in Moscow during the preceding month. At its first meeting in June 1946 the American delegate to the Commission, businessman and "elder statesman" Bernard M. Baruch, submitted a comprehensive plan calling for the establishment of an International Atomic Development Authority to control the production of fissionable materials, to promote the peaceful application of atomic energy, and to inspect all facilities concerned with atomic research and development. A violation of the Authority's rules would constitute an international crime and bring "immediate, swift, and sure punishment," with no possibility of a veto, as in the U.N. Security Council. Only when such a system was in full working order would the United States cease manufacturing atomic bombs and dispose of its existing stock.

Given the premise upon which the Baruch proposals rested—American superiority in the military application of atomic energy—the plan was a fair-minded and even generous attempt to solve an issue as unprecedented as it was difficult. The Russians, then well behind in the race for nuclear weapons, were naturally less than satisfied as to the purity of American motives. The Western powers would unquestionably have a majority in any future Authority and could prevent the Soviet government from upholding a minority point of view, since the veto would be inoperative. Ever suspicious of a capitalist plot against socialism, the Russians also objected to the extensive control and inspection powers to be conferred upon the Authority. Not only would their military installations be subjected to outside scrutiny—at a time when there could be no possibility of retaliation in case of an American attack—but further Soviet industrial development might well be related to the peaceful use of atomic energy and thus come within the scope of the Authority's jurisdiction.

Gromyko, the Soviet spokesman before the Commission, was unable to bring forward any counter-proposals that offered much hope of a compromise. He ignored the problem of inspection and enforcement to concentrate upon the idea of an international convention to prohibit the manufacture and use of atomic weapons. Once the agreement had been ratified, the United States would then be called upon to destroy its bombs. Obviously the United States would not be willing to sacrifice its advantage—however temporary—in the nuclear arms race for only a paper guarantee of Soviet good faith.

Stalin's statement in October 1946 in support of a strong system of control and punishment for violators pointed to a shift in the Kremlin's attitude; and Molotov, in his speeches before the General Assembly, agreed to the principle of international inspection and even to the suspension of the veto in routine matters of supervision. Nevertheless, the crucial disagreement on the use of the veto in case of punitive measures against violators was unresolved. On the last day of the year the report of the Atomic Energy Commission, in effect accepting the American plan, was submitted to the Security Council. After a number of sessions had been devoted to the report, it was turned back to the subordinate body on March 10, 1947, with a request for continued study and for a draft convention embodying the Commission's final recommendations.

Gromyko elaborated new Soviet proposals before a special session convened at his request on June 11. They spelled out in detail the general remarks that Molotov had made the previous autumn but again failed to meet the American objection to the use of the veto should a serious violation of the projected regulations occur. On August 15 the Commission voted unanimously—the Soviet Union and Poland abstaining—to postpone further discussion of the Russian plan. Work proceeded on the draft convention and resulted in proposals that Gromyko maintained were "vicious in their foundation" and incompatible with the fundamental principles of the United Nations. The Commission's second report, presented to the Security Council on September 11, 1947, recommended the strengthening of the control agency's powers to include not only the management but also the ownership of materials and facilities involved in the production of nuclear fuels.

No means were found to break the great power deadlock on the control of atomic energy in the ensuing months, and in May 1948 the Commission issued a discouraging report admitting that negotiations at the subordinate level could serve "no useful purpose." Nor did the Commission for Conventional Armaments, which had been organized in February 1947, view its prospects with greater equanimity. In August 1948 it still awaited "an atmosphere of international confidence and security" without which a system of regulation and reduction of armaments could not be put into effect.[1] The possibility of disarmament of any kind by the latter part of 1948 was exceedingly remote, and in fact global tension had reached such a state that rearmament was already in progress. Western opinion greeted with skepticism Vyshinsky's speech before the General Assembly on September 25 reiterating the Soviet proposals on atomic energy and calling for a one-third reduction in the armed forces of the five permanent members of the Security Council. The Assembly went through the motions of considering the Soviet plan through its committee system; and though the Russians dropped their demand that a convention banning atomic weapons must precede the establishment of the control authority, the Soviet scheme was rejected by a heavy majority.

The Atomic Energy Commission resumed its meetings in February 1949, and by July it had come to the conclusion that additional study of the control problem was pointless. The Commission adjourned against Soviet opposition, a decision that was confirmed by the Security Council in September. But ten private talks among the permanent Council members (August 9–October 24) kept the issue alive without in the slightest degree bringing a settlement nearer. The concurrent debates at the fourth session of the General Assembly in the fall of 1949 produced no new statements of policy, although the announcement of an atomic explosion in the Soviet Union, and reports that the United States had developed a hydrogen bomb, furnished an ominous backdrop for the meeting. Vyshinsky made the extravagant assertion that his government was using atomic energy for peaceful purposes, such as razing mountains and irrigating deserts, but *Pravda* deflated the claim by reporting that this was what Moscow wished to do, not what it was already doing.

The Atomic Energy Commission reconvened in 1950, a futile gesture made more conspicuous by the outbreak of the Korean War. A move to consolidate the functions of the Atomic Energy and Conventional Armaments commissions in a single body finally received the approval of the General Assembly in January 1952. The new Disarmament Commission busied itself in numerous meetings but failed to sway the opposing power blocs on any decisive issue within its jurisdiction. As the decade wore on, the arms race was accepted as one of the inevitable facts of international life; and while there was no cessation of activity in the United Nations in seeking a way out, it was apparent that there could be no effective treatment of symptoms as long as the basic malaise—the cold war—remained uncured.

The Soviet stand on the international control of atomic energy, though not as rigid as the Western public was led to believe, was insufficiently constructive to win much sympathy among non-Communists. It was but one strand of a foreign policy that betrayed an excessive devotion to the national interest as conceived by the Kremlin and an obtuse lack of concern for the decent respect of mankind. Yet, in contradiction to the actual operation of its foreign policy, Moscow displayed unusual zeal in posing before the world as the champion of peace against the "advocates of aggression" and the "fomenters of a new war." In purveying this theme on an international scale, the Communist propaganda apparatus was of course handicapped by the cynical "realism" of Soviet diplomacy; but the Comintern had been similarly embarrassed by the precedence that the Soviet national interest came to enjoy over revolutionary activity, and it had nevertheless managed to function with reasonable efficiency.

Since "peace" was a laudable and universal aim, the Kremlin was able to mobilize some non-Communist sentiment behind a series of international "peace congresses" held in various major cities throughout the world beginning in 1948. The most important of these meetings was held in Paris (April 1949) shortly after the signing of the North Atlantic treaty. The proceedings were strongly flavored by anti-Americanism, and because the promoters of the "Partisans of Peace" movement hardly bothered to conceal the fact that it was designed to serve Communist purposes, the number of non-Communist adherents diminished at subsequent meetings. At a congress in Stockholm in March 1950 the famous "Stockholm peace appeal" was launched, "one of the cleverest political documents this century has seen."[2] It was a brief statement demanding the "unconditional prohibition of the atomic weapon as an instrument of aggression and mass extermination of people." The wording itself offered no hint that Moscow considered the appeal a propaganda tool to bolster its foreign policy; and by August the sponsors of the project reported that one-eighth of the human race, including the total adult population of the U.S.S.R., had signed the document—more than 273,000,000 persons in all.

Plans for another congress to be held in England in November 1950 were abandoned when the British government denied visas to the prospective delegates. The meeting was therefore transferred to Warsaw, where the tenor of the speeches and resolutions even more clearly identified the movement as an adjunct of Soviet policy. A World Peace Council of 208 members, elected at the Warsaw congress, met in Berlin in February 1951, and again in Vienna the following November. The principal effort of the Council between the two sessions was a campaign for a "peace pact" to be concluded among the five major powers, including Communist China. According to the claims of the Council, more than 562,000,000 persons had signed an appeal for such a pact on the eve of the Vienna meeting. Another attempt was made to attract wide non-Communist support at a peace congress held in Vienna in December 1952. The distinguished French scientist, Professor Pierre Joliot-Curie, acted as chairman and maintained that the conferees, unlike their predecessors, constituted a real mass movement. But outsiders were skeptical, and the tenor of the proceedings, despite the presence of eminent non-Communists, hardly differed from previous congresses.

One demand that the Partisans of Peace had been making since late 1950—that bacteriological as well as atomic warfare should be condemned as a criminal act—became the point of departure for a new Communist excursion into cold war propaganda in 1952. Allegations had been made in North Korea in May 1951 that the United States was spreading smallpox germs; but not until February 1952 did Moscow and Peking pick up the germ warfare charge and proclaim that American agents and aircraft had spread the bacillus of smallpox, typhoid, and other diseases in North Korea. In March the Chinese declared that Manchuria was also an object of American bacteriological warfare. During the same month Malik brought the matter before the U.N. Disarmament Commission, and after a choleric debate the members voted 11 to 1 to dismiss the charges as beyond their jurisdiction.

Acheson was the chief spokesman for the United States in formally denying the accusations of germ warfare. He proposed that the International Red Cross undertake an investigation, an offer that Moscow rejected on the grounds that the organization was actually Swiss rather than truly international. Instead, the International Association of Democratic Lawyers, a patently pro-Communist group, conducted its own inquiry and reported in April 1952 that the United States was indeed guilty as charged. Soviet vetoes in the Security Council in July blocked a Red Cross investigation and a resolution condemning the dissemination of false charges about bacteriological warfare. The Communist case, as flimsy as it was, undoubtedly swayed some neutral opinion; yet the result could not be considered a significant propaganda victory. In the West the crudity of the campaign was taken as additional evidence that the Kremlin was as intractable and unscrupulous as ever in its conduct of foreign affairs.

II

The peaceful conclusion to the war scare induced by the Berlin blockade in 1949 and the outbreak of the Korean War in 1950 diverted attention from Moscow's enduring concerns in Europe. The preservation of the *status quo* in Eastern Europe was its first and foremost aim. In spite of threatening gestures toward Yugoslavia—and even border incidents that presumably had their inspiration in the Soviet capital —the Russian leaders were as reluctant to risk war to punish Tito's impudence as they were to avoid direct involvement in Korea. Moscow was apprehensive about the inroads of Titoism in the other Communist countries; but the possibility of direct Western intervention, in the absence of a Soviet attack on Yugoslavia, was so remote that it excited little concern.

The European power struggle continued to focus on Germany. In September 1950 the United States, Britain, and France agreed to end the technical state of war with Germany and to allow the Federal Republic greater autonomy. The Soviet government responded with formal notes of protest on October 18. In Prague, Molotov headed a conference of satellite representatives who issued a detailed statement on Germany (October 21) proposing a peace treaty that would provide for unification and the withdrawal of all occupation forces within a year. An equal number of representatives from eastern and western Germany were to prepare a constitution and to assist in the drafting of a peace treaty. The formula aroused no enthusiasm in the West—why, for example, should 18,000,000 East Germans be treated as equal to 47,000,000 West Germans?—yet it formed the basis for Moscow's proposal on November 3 for a conference of foreign ministers. The three Atlantic powers cautiously expressed their willingness to attend an organizational meeting provided it was not confined to Germany alone. After further correspondence a four-power conference was finally convened in Paris (March 5–June 21, 1951), with Gromyko representing the U.S.S.R. and Philip Jessup the United States.

There were seventy-four sessions in all, but in the end the delegates were no more able to agree on an agenda than if they had contented themselves with a less elaborate exchange of views. German remilitarization had been the Kremlin's paramount concern. But it was Gromyko's insistence that the question of NATO and American overseas bases be placed on the agenda—two items the United States categorically refused to consider—that was the conference's undoing. The Western powers proposed a meeting of foreign ministers in Washington without further preliminaries, a suggestion that the Soviet government spurned unless the United States was prepared to modify its stand. The conference closed with each side blaming the other for its failure.

Meanwhile the government of Premier Grotewohl had made overtures to the Bonn regime denoting Soviet readiness to sacrifice its hold over East Germany in return for some assurance that a unified German state would be neutral in the East-West struggle. While Chancellor Adenauer declined to be drawn into direct communication with his Communist rivals, he was prevailed upon by his political associates to express his views on unification. The substance of his desires was a free election to an all-German parliament and the improvement of civil liberties in the East German state to ensure that the popular will would not be thwarted. These proposals were shunted aside until, in the fall of 1951, Grotewohl seemed disposed to accept most of them. Both in Washington and in Bonn there was some consternation and no little embarrassment at such unpredictable tactics. Unification was a popular issue with Germans of every political persuasion, and the alleged insincerity of Grotewohl's conciliatory statements was difficult to demonstrate by adopting a purely negative attitude. Western diplomats, by painful experience, had become so inured to Communist intransigence that it was difficult to adjust to the idea of a *rapprochement*.

On October 13, 1951, the East German president, Wilhelm Pieck, who had recently returned from a trip to Moscow with Walter Ulbricht, proposed all-German talks without naming any preliminary conditions. Adenauer, who desired unification only on terms that would place the new German state within the Western bloc, held aloof and complained that the Communist government had failed to meet standards of political freedom that would permit a free election to take place. Pieck offered to accept a pre-election investigation conducted under the supervision of the four occupying powers, but he balked at interference by the United Nations. The Western powers had already brought the matter of a German election before the General Assembly, and on December 4 the *Ad Hoc* Political Committee, overriding Soviet objections, decided to conduct an investigation by inviting representatives from both German states to express their views. After the two deputations had been heard, the General Assembly voted 45 to 6 to establish a commission of inquiry to be kept in readiness until such time as all parts of Germany were accessible to it. In March 1952 a four-man commission visited West Germany and western Berlin but was prevented from pursuing its investigations in the Democratic Republic by the failure of General Vassily Chuikov, the Soviet military governor, to reply to its requests for permission to enter.

By a combination of persuasion, cajolery, and pressure the United States had brought its reluctant European allies in the spring of 1952 to accept the unsavory reality of German rearmament provided the Bonn government became a partner in a European Defense Community. Long a worried spectator, the Soviet government perceived that its East German auxiliaries had little chance of enticing Adenauer from a Western alliance by a promise of unification. It therefore entered the diplomatic fray in a more direct manner with a series of notes to the three Western powers. The first, dispatched on March 10, 1952, constituted a sharp reversal of policy on German rearmament. Professing to accept the idea of an armed and unified Germany, Moscow insisted that she abstain from the Western alliance.

The note was an adroit maneuver that made a strong appeal to neutralist sentiment. It placed Adenauer, already under fire from the opposition parties, more squarely under the onus of denying the aspirations of the German people for unity in return for the dubious benefits of rearmament under Western tutelage. But the chancellor was not deterred from his course, and the Western governments responded with chilling politeness that a free election must precede any talk of unification or of a peace treaty. A second Soviet note on April 9 went unanswered for five weeks while the East German Communist leaders attempted with indifferent success to foment strikes and demonstrations in western Germany against Adenauer's policy.

On May 26, 1952, the three Atlantic democracies signed a complex body of agreements with the German Federal Republic granting the latter almost complete sovereignty in the conduct of its affairs. The next day a fifty-year European defense treaty authorizing an integrated army was signed in Paris by France, Italy, West Germany, and the Benelux nations. Moscow had sent a third note on May 24, though by this time the Russian leaders were probably resigned to the treaty. But there was always the possibility of obstructing ratification and of sowing dissension in the ranks of the potential enemy. Washington and Bonn were prepared to fend off indefinitely the reiterated Soviet requests for a quadripartite discussion of the German question. London and Paris preferred a more positive approach, and the Western reply on July 10 left the door open for a conference if the purpose was to seek an agreement on an investigatory commission "to determine whether the conditions necessary for free elections [in Germany] exist."[3]

Moscow's fourth note (August 23, 1952), was more sharply phrased and betrayed an attitude of querulous exasperation. The Western formula was nevertheless found acceptable provided the agenda was broadened to include the discussion of a peace treaty and the formation of an all-German government. In the Western view the Soviet government merely evaded once more the chief issue at stake—the task of assuring a genuinely free election throughout Germany. Moscow was so informed on September 23, and the Russians, apparently recognizing the futility of further diplomacy by correspondence, made no attempt to reopen negotiations.

The Kremlin was undoubtedly encouraged by the long delay in ratifying the defense treaty and may have expected its rejection by some of the parliaments concerned. As could be foreseen because of traditional Franco-German hostility, the French National Assembly was the most reluctant to confer its approval, and formal consideration of the treaty was put off indefinitely while the French government sought modifying protocols within the European Defense Community. In the Bundestag or West German parliament, the treaty was accepted on March 19, 1953, by a vote of 224 to 165, an unexpectedly easy victory for the government over the Social Democratic opposition.

In the meantime French opinion had begun to solidify against the treaty. The threat of Soviet aggression appeared to recede as time went on, and the image of a revived Wehrmacht became a more tangible apparition. On August 30, 1954, amid a stormy scene in the Assembly, the European Defense Community was given the *coup de grâce* when the deputies voted 319 to 264 to pass on to other business.

The U.S.S.R. was slow to counter NATO and the projected E.D.C. with any formal military organization among its vassal states. Given the overwhelming preponderance of the Soviet army within any such military system and the absence of any pretense of equality within Moscow's Eastern orbit, there was in fact no necessity for prompt action. Moreover, the political reliability of the satellite armies was not above suspicion—a situation that had already given the Kremlin much concern. Purges and executions in the higher ranks were among the accepted risks of a military career, but they were usually carried through with less sensationalism than was the case with political offenders. Most of the senior officers had been trained in or served with the Russian army, and by 1952 there were few holdovers from the pre-Communist period. Only in the case of Poland did Moscow place one of its own officers at the head of the military establishment: Marshal Konstantin Rokossovsky became commander of the Polish armed forces and minister of defense in November 1949.

During the early fifties Western sources placed the total armed strength of the Soviet dependencies at nearly 1,500,000 men. Poland had by far the largest army, perhaps twenty-two divisions; Bulgaria and Rumania were said to have twelve, Czechoslovakia and Hungary nine apiece. East Germany had no regularly constituted military force, although by 1949 the Western press had begun to speculate about Russian intentions in building up a semi-militarized "people's police."

The Kremlin probably wished only to forge a reliable instrument for keeping the Communist regime in power; but the possibility of an invasion of West Germany *à la* Korea could not be discounted, and the three Western democracies complained to Moscow (May 23, 1950) that a force of almost 50,000 men had received military training and were equipped with heavy weapons, yet performed no normal police functions. The Russians, predictably, denied the charge and reversed the accusation: the Western powers were doing in their zones what the Soviet government was accused of doing in its zone.

The assumption of increasingly heavy armament burdens was partially but not wholly responsible for a decline in living standards in the satellite countries by 1950. Rapid industrialization was the heart of the problem, and Communist planners foresaw a time of plenty once the basic productive capacity was sufficiently enlarged. But even the Soviet economy was far from that utopian stage, though the Russian people were beginning to enjoy some of the consumer goods that Westerners had long taken for granted. Moscow's commercial arrangements with its Communist "colonies" were by no means generous; and despite Russian technical assistance and raw materials, the exploitative nature of the relationship could not be concealed.

Until the 1950's popular dissatisfaction with Soviet hegemony had appeared to be centered on bread and butter grievances. Yet it was political discontent that agitated Stalin and his associates—not that they were seriously concerned by the absence of mass enthusiasm for Communist leadership in Eastern Europe. They had contracted a kind of political anxiety neurosis about the loyalty of their outlying subordinates since the defection of Marshal Tito. While conventional charges of conspiracy, espionage, Trotskyism, and Titoism were continually leveled at political offenders, the newly discovered crime of "Zionism" had by 1952 given an ominous and entirely different complexion to the fresh wave of heresy trials and purges.

Anti-Semitism as a racial theory was still strictly taboo according to Communist doctrine. Beginning early in 1949, however, the two million or more Russian Jews who had survived the Nazi holocaust were subjected to a campaign of intimidation that fell just short of an open proclamation of their undesirability as a group. Jewish intellectuals were singled out as the prime targets, and even Jews who had disavowed their religious and cultural heritage were attacked for "cosmopolitanism" and frequently dismissed from their posts. The motives behind this covert attack upon Jews, while not easy to fathom, were related to the policy of Russian nationalism and cultural chauvinism that had set in with the *Zhdanovshchina*.[4] Jews were supposedly representatives of an alien Western culture, though the Soviet leaders may also have been pandering to popular anti-Semitism. Stalin himself was known to be an anti-Semite, and in any case no action could have been taken without his encouragement.

Anti-Semitic tendencies did not become manifest in the satellites until the early fifties. During a purge of the Czechoslovak Communist party in the winter of 1951–1952 some 80 per cent of those arrested were reported to be Jews. Among them was Rudolf Slansky, former secretary-general of the party. In November 1952 he and thirteen other prominent defendants—eleven of them Jews—were tried on a variety of charges, including Zionism. The prosecution made a point of linking them with "international Jewry," and all fourteen pleaded guilty. Eleven of the accused, including Slansky and ex-Foreign Minister Clementis, were sentenced to death, and three were given life terms.

Anti-Zionist propaganda and the arrest or disgrace of highly placed Jews, none of whom was deemed important enough for a repetition of the Slansky trial, was a feature of Communist East Europe until early 1953. The best known victim was Rumanian Foreign Minister Ana Pauker, the daughter of a Jewish rabbi. But her dismissal was apparently due to political causes, for other government officials of non-Jewish origin suffered a similar fate. Although Moscow did not issue a blanket edict against Jews in positions of political trust— Premier Mathias Rakosi of Hungary was the outstanding example of a Jew who still enjoyed the Kremlin's favor—the Soviet government verged perilously close to an official policy of anti-Semitism. The denouement came suddenly and with terrifying implications in the sensational "doctors' plot" of January 1953.[5]

III

On October 5, 1952, 1,359 delegates to the nineteenth congress of the Communist party of the U.S.S.R., as well as many foreign Communist leaders, assembled in the great hall of the Kremlin Palace in Moscow. As the first such gathering since March 1939—the party statutes requiring a congress at least once every three years had been ignored—it was an historic occasion. The aging Stalin, the "genius-leader and teacher of all progressive mankind" as *Pravda* put it, was then approaching his seventy-third year, and the world press anticipated, if not important policy decisions, at least some portents that would disclose an heir-apparent. Georgi Malenkov, whose star had risen rapidly following Zhdanov's death, was the keynote speaker, and he delivered a five hour report of the party's Central Committee, a privilege that Stalin had always before reserved for himself. Malenkov was quickly installed in the role of prime favorite. Yet there were other aspects of the party congress indicating that Stalin, far from preparing a graceful exit, had deliberately confused the problem of succession. The eleven-member Politburo was abolished, and in its place was erected an unwieldy new body, the Presidium of the Central Committee, with twenty-five members and eleven alternates. In addition, the five-man party Secretariat was doubled in size.

As if these organizational changes were not enough to mask the power struggle within the Kremlin, Stalin chose to muddy the waters still more by publishing an essay, "Economic Problems of Socialism in the U.S.S.R.," on the eve of the congress. It had been written during the previous February as an outgrowth to a discussion held in November 1951 concerning the preparation of a textbook on political economy. Although a mediocre and pedantic excursion into Marxist theory, it was inevitably, considering the source, a major theoretical pronouncement and had the effect of converting the congress into a kind of claque for the purpose of paying tribute to Stalin's intellectual genius. Neither Malenkov nor the other speakers could expect to shine against such formidable competition.

In his essay Stalin reaffirmed the abiding Soviet faith in the internal contradictions of the capitalist order by emphasizing the disintegration of the world market—"the most important economic consequence of the Second World War." He foresaw a clash among the capitalist states. It was to be essentially a rebellion of the underprivileged nations against American imperialism rather than a concerted assault on the "camp of socialism." However fanciful this particular flight into Marxian scholasticism, his denial of an immediate or even of an ultimate conflict involving the U.S.S.R. served as a rebuke to those of his followers who were advocates of a reckless foreign policy.

If Stalin was now signaling the shift to a defensive strategy of caution and conservation—and he had never ventured beyond the prudent realm of the calculated risk since the cold war began—he went out of his way to demonstrate to the party delegates and to the country at large that the Soviet government was vigilant, even aggressive, in protecting its own interests. The incident in question involved the recall of United States Ambassador George F. Kennan, who had been appointed to the Moscow embassy in February 1952 and had arrived to take up his post in May. The Kremlin had no reason to be other than suspiciously hostile toward a man who had been so widely heralded as the brains behind Washington's "containment" policy. It was probably because of his "warmongering" reputation that Kennan, who was convinced that the Stalinist "hard" line would mellow in the reasonably near future, was given a cool reception in his attempts to initiate exploratory talks with Soviet officials. On a trip to Western Europe in September, he conversed with reporters at a stopover in Berlin and dropped an incautious remark comparing conditions in Moscow to the situation he had experienced in the German capital in 1941–1942 when the Nazis were in power. The Soviet press was stung to an angry and uncomplimentary retort, and the Foreign Office, seizing upon the ambassador's indiscretion, declared him *persona non grata* in a note to Washington on October 3.

Kennan never returned to his diplomatic assignment, and the United States was thus deprived of the services of an official envoy during the critical months between the party congress and Stalin's fatal illness. Tangible evidence of some great internal convulsion came on January 13, 1953, when a Tass announcement publicly revealed that a "terrorist group" of nine Kremlin doctors—six of them Jewish—were under arrest and had confessed to murdering former Politburo members Alexander Shcherbakov (1945) and Andrei Zhdanov (1948) by deliberately incorrect diagnosis and treatment of their ailments. The doctors were also accused of attempting to kill a number of Soviet military leaders and to have been in the service of United States and British intelligence as well as the Jewish Joint Distribution Committee, an American charitable organization barred from the U.S.S.R. since 1938. That so macabre and bizarre an affair was simply a manifestation of anti-Semitism seemed unlikely; and in the absence of more accurate information, it was a reasonable assumption that Stalin himself was the prime mover behind the sinister case and that a new blood purge rivaling that of the 1930's was in the offing. As one observer commented, "The old man has reached for the bottle again."

Such an interpretation was confirmed by press reports of various scandals in the provinces involving the arrest or dismissal of hundreds of locally prominent individuals, most of them Jews. But by February the purge had lost some of its anti-Semitic overtones and had spread to party organizations. Because of lax standards (the "idiotic disease of gullibility, carelessness, blundering and complacency"),[6] the party was allegedly responsible for the "corruption." The scene had been set for a direct strike at the top "conspirators" in the Kremlin itself. Molotov and Anastas Mikoyan, as well as other members of the old Politburo, were apparently among the prospective victims. Then, suddenly, an astonishing announcement came on March 4 that Stalin had suffered a cerebral hemorrhage on the night of March 1–2. Later medical bulletins indicated that he was sinking fast, and in the early morning of March 6 it was revealed that he had expired at 9:50 the previous evening.

If Stalin's death was due entirely to natural causes, it came at a most opportune moment for his successors. On the principle that coincidence has its limits, some Western specialists on Soviet affairs theorized that the aged dictator may have been murdered or at least hastened toward his end. But such a conjecture was not likely to be confirmed by later disclosures. The public obsequies were observed with appropriate tributes to the mighty leader who had fallen, though the eulogies were almost perfunctory compared to the unctuous flattery lavished upon him during his last years; and while the popular mood did not register the genuine grief that had marked Lenin's passing, there was a kind of stunned awe that the great Stalin was also but a mortal man.

Aside from conventional expressions of condolence from official sources, Western opinion was not inclined to waste words of sympathy on a deceased tyrant. Yet there were those who were willing to give the devil his due. Whatever his crimes and follies—and a full catalog might sicken the most hardened of stomachs—the Soviet Union had become under his guidance a world colossus beyond the dreams of the most ardent imperialist of Tsarist Russia. He had also carried through a profound social and economic transformation to place him in the revolutionary tradition of Marx and Lenin, as well as the despotic tradition of Ivan the Terrible and Peter the Great. If Stalin's career once again proved the maxim that power tends to corrupt and absolute power tends to corrupt absolutely, few would deny that his achievements placed him on a higher plane of statecraft than his bankrupt contemporaries, Hitler and Mussolini. Stalin had indeed used "barbarous means to drive barbarism out of Russia";[7] and in the closing years of his rule he had become an anachronism—a kind of fossil remain from a vanished culture. But in attempting too quickly to dispose of the outmoded paraphernalia of Stalinism, his disciples were to run into difficulties that the old master in his prime would never have permitted to develop.

"Collective leadership" was the catch-phrase of the oligarchy that now assumed power. Stalin's corpse was hardly cold before an extensive shuffling of top personnel got underway. Malenkov, as the new chairman of the Council of Ministers, was first among equals. Molotov resumed his old post as foreign minister, and Vyshinsky was demoted to first deputy minister. Perhaps the most striking change was the appointment of Marshal Zhukov as first deputy minister of defense after seven years of obscurity. The party Presidium was cut down to a size resembling the old Politburo—ten members and four alternates—and the party Secretariat was reduced to its former five members. By mid-March experienced handicappers in the Kremlin sweepstakes were touting a new "dark horse" in the person of Nikita Khrushchev, onetime boss of the Ukraine, who grasped the reins of the party apparatus when Malenkov "at his own request" relinquished the post of first secretary.

The initial moves of the new regime encouraged Western hopes of a clean break with the Stalinist heritage. A partial amnesty of political prisoners was decreed, and the "doctors' plot" was exposed as a criminal fraud. The anti-Zionist campaign and the anti-Semitic insinuations in the press were summarily halted. No attempt was made to sweep away the accumulated moral and intellectual debris of Stalinism with a single bold stroke; but the little that was done aroused feverish expectations of more significant reforms to come. The result was a climate of opinion that placed Malenkov and his colleagues in the awkward position of trying to run with the hare of popular favor and to hunt with the hounds of Communist orthodoxy.

In foreign policy there was the same cautious effort to cast aside the rigidities of the past without conceding any vital Soviet interest. Russian diplomats were no longer expected to be aloof and even impolite to foreigners as proof of their loyalty and devotion. In various minor ways the Soviet government sought to convey its new attitude of flexibility to the Western powers: an unwonted courtesy in dealing with an incident in the "air corridor" between West Germany and Berlin, an offer to help repatriate British and French civilian prisoners in Korea, and the abandonment of obstructionist tactics in the election of a new secretary-general of the United Nations. And in one major respect Moscow went beyond a mere display of good diplomatic manners: the Chinese and North Koreans were induced to break the deadlock on the prisoner of war issue that had stalled the Korean armistice negotiations for so many months.[8]

Official Washington was outwardly unimpressed by these signs of Soviet good faith and demanded more conclusive evidence of a fundamental change of policy. Chancellor Adenauer, on a state visit to the United States and Canada during the first part of April, echoed these sentiments as they applied to Germany. But in London and Paris where there was usually a greater disposition to seek a *rapprochement* with Moscow, the idea was openly suggested of a top-level conference at which all outstanding issues could be discussed. The portents were unmistakable that a spring thaw in the cold war had set in; whether a new freeze would follow depended to a great extent upon the future course of de-Stalinization in the Soviet Union.

NOTES

1. Resolution of August 12, 1948, U. N. Commission for Conventional Armaments, quoted in John C. Campbell and others, *The United States in World Affairs, 1948–1949* (New York, 1949), p. 411.

2. Donald H. MacLachlan, "The Partisans of Peace," *International Affairs,* XXVII (January 1951), p. 12.

3. Denise Folliot (ed.), *Documents on International Affairs, 1952* (New York, 1955), p. 177.

4. See above, p. 359.

5. See below, p. 416.

6. Quoted in Wolfe, *Khrushchev and Stalin's Ghost* (New York, 1957), p. 3.

7. Isaac Deutscher, *Russia in Transition and Other Essays* (New York, 1957), p. 15.

8. See above, p. 400.

CHAPTER FOURTEEN

AFTER STALIN:
THE UNCERTAIN THAW

The era of Stalin closed at a time when the United States had just completed a change of administration and was psychologically unprepared for conciliatory gestures on the part of its formidable rival. General Eisenhower, who had defeated the Democratic candidate in the presidential election of November 1952 and had assumed office in January 1953, was a man of peace and of fundamentally decent instincts. But his capacity for leadership was severely limited by his narrow conception of the executive office and by his distaste for the hard decisions demanded by the exercise of political power. In short, the new President reigned but did not rule; and in matters of foreign policy his secretary of state, John Foster Dulles, was allowed virtually a free hand.

An experienced diplomat, Dulles brought to his post a sense of lofty moral purpose presumably accentuated by his avocational career as a leading Christian layman. He thus identified the power of the Russian state with the evil of atheistic Communism, and his air of unctuous piety and sanctimonious righteousness was as irritating to West European opinion as it was provocative to the Soviet government. During the election campaign he and other leading Republicans had charged that the Truman-Acheson policy of "containment" was more truly one of appeasement. They promised a more dynamic and less pusillanimous course: a "rollback" of Russian power and the "liberation" of Communist-dominated states. While these pronouncements were in large part campaign oratory that few informed observers of the American political scene took seriously, the belligerent pose of the Dulles regime—though quickly subdued by the responsibilities of power—caused uneasiness and perturbation in Moscow. Anxiety in Western Europe that the State Department would follow the lead of the Right wing Republicans associated with "McCarthyism" was partially allayed by the appointment and Senate confirmation in March of Charles E. Bohlen, chargé d'affaires in the American embassy under the Truman administration, as ambassador to Russia.

In Eisenhower's speech on April 16, 1953, the United States took official cognizance for the first time of the "new look" in Soviet policy since the death of Stalin. The President suggested that the Russians prove their "sincerity of peaceful purpose" by deeds rather than by rhetoric: the conclusion of an Austrian treaty, the release of war prisoners still held in the U.S.S.R., an armistice and free elections in Korea, and an "end to the direct and indirect attacks upon the security of Indo-China and Malaya." However unwise such tactics may have been in winning Moscow over to more tractable ways, Eisenhower's proposals had none of the tone of an ultimatum with which Dulles contrived to invest them in a major policy speech two days later. His skepticism concerning the genuineness of the Soviet "peace offensive" betrayed some apprehension about the solidity of the Western alliance system in the face of the Kremlin's clever stratagems.

The American secretary of state had further cause for concern when Churchill, now back in office as prime minister, advocated in the House of Commons (May 11) a high level conference of the major powers without delay. Nor was his idea of a new Locarno Pact to guarantee the Russians against aggression from the West—that the "terrible events of the Hitler invasion [might] never be repeated"— at all welcome at a time when Washington was straining every effort to organize the military resources of the Atlantic coalition against the Russian menace. Diplomacy had indeed shifted full circle with Churchill, the cold war herald of 1946, now in the role of peacemaker and would-be protector of Soviet security.

The Soviet press, which had become more restrained in its anti-Americanism, was unusually soft-spoken in capitalizing upon this apparent cleavage in the Anglo-American entente. Moscow made other friendly gestures—"leaving off doing things which we have not been doing to them," as Churchill put it—without coming appreciably closer to Eisenhower's list of specific deeds. But there were other deeds that could not be dismissed as inconsequential. Turkey was informed in a note on May 30 that the Soviet government had abandoned its territorial claims to Kars and Ardahan and had dropped its demand for a bilateral remission of the Montreux convention on the Straits. The propaganda campaign against Yugoslavia was toned down, and on June 14 diplomatic relations between Moscow and Belgrade were resumed. Relations with Israel, broken off in February, were also restored. In East Germany a series of concessions to the population raised hopes that a more thorough reform might follow.

It was, however, the sudden relaxation of Communist severity in East Germany that produced unexpected and far-reaching consequences for the Soviet Union. Moscow's unaccustomed leniency was interpreted as a sign of weakness by the masses, and it sowed uncertainty and confusion in the ranks of the Socialist Unity party. The mayor of East Berlin pleaded for discipline on the part of the "good, honest friends who are seized with doubt and grave concern at the new political course."[1] The Grotewohl government was simultaneously attempting to raise work norms—in effect an enforced wage cut—in order to increase productivity and to control mounting inflation.

This was an explosive combination of ingredients that awaited a spark to set it alight. The incendiarists turned out to be the building trade workers of East Berlin, some 300 of whom marched in protest to government headquarters on June 16. Other workers joined the throng, and what had begun as a demonstration against economic exploitation was soon converted into a spontaneous demand for political freedom. A general strike the next day paralyzed most of the industrial concerns of East Berlin. Riots broke out which the police were unable to control. In the afternoon martial law was declared and Soviet tanks and troops were called in to restore order in various parts of the city. Casualties were minimized because the rioters were unarmed, and the Soviet military command, anxious to avoid the unnecessary multiplication of political martyrs, saw to it that most of the gunfire was directed above the heads of the workers. Like a chain reaction, rebellion spread to other cities in the Soviet zone, where the fighting was often considerably more bloody. In Magdeburg at least forty workers were killed, and several policemen were lynched by angered mobs.

As a dramatic manifestation of popular dissatisfaction with Communism, the East German uprising—coupled with less serious disturbances in Czechoslovakia—was a sobering lesson to the Kremlin's new leadership. It was not the prelude to a general revolt of the satellites, as Washington was tempted to believe, but it was a resounding propaganda defeat for the Russians that tended to cast doubt upon the wisdom of de-Stalinization. There was, however, no attempt to turn back the clock to the worst practices of the Stalin era. Further economic concessions were granted the German workers, including the easing of work norms; and a moderate purge in party and government ranks followed, with some gestures in the direction of a milder political regime. The Communist press ascribed the riots to the machinations of Western agents and provocateurs and to "fascist hirelings" of the American intelligence services. To make an example, the Soviet military authorities executed an unemployed West Berlin house painter for acting "on the orders of a foreign intelligence organization." His only apparent crime was his presence in the Soviet sector on the 17th.

The fall from power on June 26, 1953, of Soviet Minister of the Interior Lavrenti Beria was linked by most Western observers to the Berlin riots, though in precisely what manner they were unable to agree. It was conjectured that the party and the army had allied themselves against the political police. Whatever the actual situation, Beria was regarded as a dangerous conspirator by his colleagues in the Presidium, and he was shot in secret following a special meeting called to confront him with his guilt.[2] The customary purge of the political associates and disciples of the fallen one then ensued. Prominent among them were the German Communist leaders Wilhelm Zaisser, minister of state security, and Rudolf Herrnstadt, editor of *Neues Deutschland,* both of whom had allegedly plotted to take over the Socialist Unity party from Ulbricht.

Despite bold talk of "liberation" in Washington, the United States acted with the utmost discretion during Moscow's German travail. Possible diplomatic collaboration by the Western powers was prevented by a recurrence of political crisis in France and by the ill health of Churchill and of Foreign Secretary Anthony Eden. The prime minister's bid for a conference of heads of state was bypassed in favor of a renewed invitation to the Soviet government on July 15 for a foreign ministers' meeting on German unification and the Austrian treaty. Thus began another tedious round of correspondence on the German question in which the old arguments were given a thorough re-airing. On August 8 Moscow pushed forward an impressive counter on the diplomatic bargaining table when Malenkov, in a speech before the Supreme Soviet, stated that the United States no longer had a monopoly of the hydrogen bomb. His review of Soviet foreign policy contained friendly references to Russia's non-Communist neighbors—Finland, Turkey, and Iran—but his attitude of confident reasonableness did not exclude a sharp attack on the American policy of "atomic blackmail."

To counter Eisenhower's letter (July 23) supporting Adenauer in the coming election campaign in the Federal Republic, Grotewohl and Ulbricht were received in Moscow at the head of a large delegation of East German officials. A communiqué issued on August 22 revealed that negotiations had taken place and that a number of concessions had been granted the Democratic Republic: a partial amnesty of

German prisoners in Soviet custody sentenced for war crimes, a cancellation of reparations after January 1, 1954, the reduction of occupation costs in the Soviet zone to 5 per cent of the national revenue, and other economic benefits. Malenkov launched a verbal assault on Adenauer the next day as a "warmonger" who wished to perpetuate the division of Germany and who was responsible for the failure of the powers to conclude a peace treaty. This carrot-and-stick approach had no discernible effect in dislodging *Der Alte*, for the chancellor's Christian Democratic Union won an impressive 45.2 per cent plurality in the Bundestag elections of September 6, 1953. The Communists were all but wiped out, winning only 2.2 per cent of the vote and losing all of the 15 seats acquired in 1949.

The thrust and parry between Russia and the West with respect to a conference on Germany lasted until late December, when it was agreed that a meeting of the Council of Foreign Ministers would be held in Berlin. The chief negotiators—Molotov, Dulles, Eden, and Georges Bidault—met during alternate weeks in the eastern and western sectors of the German capital (January 25–February 18, 1954), the first such attempt to arrive at a settlement with the Russians since June 1949.[3] During months of correspondence in 1952–1953 neither power bloc had altered its basic position, and no fresh approach was revealed as the Council sessions wore on. It was made doubly clear that the Soviet government, with or without Stalin at the helm, was unwilling to sacrifice an area as strategically valuable as East Germany without adequate guarantees that the unified German state would not be aligned with the West. No amount of talk about the advisability of free and secret elections—undoubtedly a just and democratic solution as far as the German people themselves were concerned—could shake this stubborn fact.

Again the delegates had to confess their failure. Molotov's debating manners had been more agreeable and the concluding speeches were laced with courteous phrases, but the only tangible gain was a decision to hold a conference at Geneva in the spring on Korea and Indo-China. Communist China was to be invited—a victory for Bidault and Eden over Dulles rather than a diplomatic triumph for Molotov. There was no more explosive issue in American politics than the recognition of China, and Dulles' disingenuous explanation that Peking would be called "to account [in Geneva] before the bar of world opinion" for its conduct in Korea and Indo-China did not appease his Right wing critics.

The labyrinthine negotiations at Geneva (April 26–July 21, 1954) involved in reality two distinct conferences: a nine-power conference on Indo-China and a nineteen-power conference on Korea. The proceedings of both were of course dominated by the great powers, and to the unconcealed chagrin of the United States, China was included, with Chou En-lai as its chief spokesman. Dulles, who left Geneva on May 3, accounted it a notable achievement that he had never once acknowledged Chou's presence; and it was in the face of almost constant sniping by the American delegation that the Geneva meeting in the end enjoyed the distinction of being the only really successful post-war conference of the major powers.

Korea dominated the first phase of the parley. The foreign ministers of North and South Korea presented conflicting plans for unification, plans that were modified in certain particulars as the U.S.S.R. and China on one side and the three Western democracies on the other sought to narrow the area of disagreement. As in the case of Germany, lip service to the principle of free and secret elections did not conceal a procedural wrangle on the method by which they were to be conducted. Each coalition sought the formula that seemed best suited to winning the whole of Korea as an ally: the West insisted on supervision by the United Nations, and the Communist powers steadfastly maintained that a commission drawn equally from both sides of the Korean border should arrange the elections and presumably select the candidates appearing on the ballot. On this latter point the Communist representatives were inscrutable, and on June 15 the sixteen nations that had contributed troops to the U.N. "police action" broke off the negotiations. The armistice agreement continued by common consent, although President Rhee, an inflexible advocate of unification by force of arms, tried in vain to convince the American government during a trip to Washington in July that preventive war against China was the only way out of the Korean stalemate.

The negotiations on Indo-China had meanwhile shown little promise of yielding more substantial results. The perilous state of the French military position in Viet Nam[4] had not softened Bidault's uncompromising attitude nor his hope that armed intervention by the United States would save the situation. But the trial balloons sent up by the Eisenhower administration to test American public opinion had recorded such overwhelming sentiment against involvement that there was scant prospect of help from this quarter. In mid-June two events served to break the deadlock: the fall of the French government and Eden's threat to quit the conference unless some discernible progress was made. The Communist delegations, anxious to avoid another diplomatic mishap on the order of the Korean failure, proposed that foreign troops be withdrawn from Laos and Cambodia—an oblique offer to guarantee the two states against Viet Minh invasion.

The conference went into partial recess on June 19—subordinate committees continued to meet—and the new French premier and foreign minister, Pierre Mendes-France, met Chou En-lai for private talks in Berne three days later. Mendes-France's previously announced intention of securing an agreement on Indo-China by July 20 or of resigning was considered an unnecessary weakening of his own bargaining strength, but the two men achieved a certain rapport. Dulles was still missing when the foreign ministers reassembled on July 12. Formal sessions were dispensed with during the closing stages of the conference as Molotov, Chou, Eden, and Mendes-France met informally, but with a pressing sense of urgency, to compose their differences before the latter's self-imposed deadline expired. The armistice documents were not in fact signed until the morning of July 21, though no one begrudged the premier the extra few hours. The United States, not a signatory, issued a separate declaration promising to respect the arrangements made and to view any violation of them with "grave concern."

The essence of the Geneva settlement was the partition of Viet Nam at approximately the 17th parallel and the neutralization of Laos and Cambodia. Elections were to be held in July 1956 in both parts of Viet Nam, a provision from which the Western powers backed away when the time for fulfillment neared. Neutral opinion, especially in Asia, could hardly fail to note that the democratic principles so zealously pursued in the case of Germany and Korea were somehow less important when applied to a country where Communism might arrive via the ballot box. Contrary to the frequently expressed American view that the conference had been a Far Eastern Munich, the West won by negotiation what it could reasonably have expected to lose on the battlefield. Had Russia and China chosen to ignore the larger implications of all-out support in matériel for the Viet Minh forces, Ho Chi Minh would probably have become the ruler of Indo-China instead of northern Viet Nam. It appeared that Ho's aspirations had been sacrificed to Moscow's desire for an accommodation with the West.

Although Southeast Asia became relatively tranquil after the peaceful resolution of the Indochinese crisis, the United States indulged its predilection for military alliances by proceeding with plans for a Southeast Asian defense pact. On September 9, 1954, SEATO (an inaccurate but euphonious rendition of Southeast Asian Collective Defense Treaty) was brought into being at a conference in Manila. An eight-power alliance, it had no terminal date and was designed to resist armed aggression and—uniquely—internal subversion. A toothless substitute for Dulles' original concept of a Far Eastern NATO, the treaty was in reality a Western arrangement to which only three Asian states—the Philippines, Thailand, and Pakistan—belonged. SEATO was largely an American diplomatic showpiece, and like the Baghdad Pact,[5] it aroused Soviet resentment and fostered Western illusions of increased security without essentially altering the global balance of military and political power.

II

Moscow's post-Geneva strategy continued to bear those marks of deftness and originality that had characterized it since Stalin's death. The Soviet leaders gave every indication that they were satisfied with the *status quo* in the Far East; and while they very likely counseled patience to their Chinese friends on the Formosa issue, the Moscow-Peking axis seemed one of genuine equality or something very close to it. In Europe the satellites were not elevated to a position remotely approaching autonomy, but living standards showed signs of improvement and the political climate became so mild that various "national Communists," "Titoists," and other culprits were released from prison.

The French rejection of E.D.C.[6] was a liberal bonus for Malenkov's "soft" line, yet Russian efforts to weaken NATO were of no avail. A note to the Western powers on March 31, 1954, suggested that the Soviet government be admitted to NATO membership and that the United States might participate in Moscow's proposed European security treaty. Though Washington considered the move a crude maneuver "to undermine the West's security," the three Atlantic democracies replied formally in more gracious tones conveying their lack of interest in what one writer has called a "polite hint by the wolf of willingness to join the sheepfold."[7] Renewed attempts were made after Geneva to interest the West in a conference on European security, and they culminated in an invitation on November 13 to attend a meeting either in Moscow or in Paris on November 29. The offer was so transparently a means of thwarting ratification of the Paris agreements—concluded on October 23, 1954, and designed in part to replace the lost E.D.C.—that Western rejection was automatic.

The Russians doggedly plunged ahead with plans for a conference. But only their own delegates, those of the satellite countries, and a Chinese observer attended the sessions beginning in Moscow on November 29. In the absence of representation from even the minor non-Communist states of Europe, the meeting inevitably became a forum for the dissemination of Soviet policy objectives. It was strongly implied that an Eastern military alliance on the NATO model would be established if the Paris agreements were ratified and a West German army created. Soviet intentions along these lines were more clearly spelled out in a note to the Western powers on December 9.

The harsh tone of Soviet pronouncements at the year's end tended to clash with the preceding campaign for "peaceful coexistence." Because in Western eyes the partial "thaw" of Russian policy was chiefly associated with Malenkov, his resignation as premier on February 8, 1955, seemed to confirm a retreat toward a Stalinist "hard" line. Furthermore, his emphasis on the production of consumer goods rather than the customary concentration on heavy industry had come under attack at the beginning of the year, and his policy was now reversed. Marshal Nikolai Bulganin stepped into the top governmental post, and his position as defense minister was assumed by Marshal Zhukov, who became the favorite of those who saw in the Soviet army an aspirant for political power. Malenkov kept his seat in the Presidium, a significant improvement over the former practice of vilifying and executing fallen favorites.

The pudgy extrovert Khrushchev, still without an official place in the government, emerged as the chief oligarch on the strength of his commanding position in the party. His ascendancy had been signaled by a number of events in 1954, of which the Khrushchev-Bulganin mission to Peking (September 29–October 12) was the most important. The technical and economic aid promised to China placed Russian industry under an additional strain which, together with the probability of West German rearmament, helped to undermine Malenkov as the leading protagonist of the Soviet consumer.

Western concern about a return to Stalinism proved ill-founded. Khrushchev's ebullient personality lent a new vigor to Soviet foreign policy and was best exemplified by his good will visits to foreign lands —a remarkable campaign of personal diplomacy unprecedented in Soviet history and only faintly comparable to Peter the Great's famous trip to Western Europe late in the seventeenth century. The most productive of his journeys in terms of immediate results was his visit to Belgrade in the late spring of 1955 with Bulganin and other top ranking party members. Tito welcomed his distinguished guests with dignified reserve and received a belated but handsome apology from the Soviet delegation for the ill-treatment to which he had been subjected eight years before. Beria was selected as the whipping-boy for Stalin's mistakes, a bit of historical myth-mongering that was rectified the next year when the dead dictator was unceremoniously deprived of his place in the Communist pantheon. While Khrushchev failed to re-establish the pre-1948 relationship, he did win Yugoslav support for the Soviet diplomatic objectives set forth in a joint declaration. It was Tito, of course, who emerged the real victor in the encounter. His past position was fully vindicated, his prestige enhanced, and Yugoslavia's immunity from Soviet-inspired aggression assured.

In July the Khrushchev-Bulganin team visited East Germany and Switzerland, and later in the year (November 17–December 22) they made a triumphal tour of India, Burma, and Afghanistan. Some of their "off the cuff" anti-Western utterances were embarrassing to their hosts, but the Soviet leaders acquitted themselves skillfully by admiring what they saw and praising the neutral policy of their Asiatic neighbors. The unqualified success of the mission served to underscore the vigorous self-assurance of the Kremlin's "collective leadership" and to highlight the ability of the Soviet government to furnish economic and technical assistance to the uncommitted countries. The modest aid the Russians promised Nehru and Premier U Nu of Burma, though it constituted as yet no serious challenge to the "Point Four" program of the United States, symbolized for many Asians the dynamic energy of a once backward people like themselves who had arrived at greatness by their own unaided efforts.

Khrushchev and Bulganin ventured upon less friendly terrain in April 1956 when they accepted an invitation to visit England. Their public reception was rather cool; nor was anything of note settled in the informal exchange of views with British officials. Khrushchev's role as an apostle of reconciliation—"[we] should stop facing each other like fighting cocks"—was sometimes overshadowed by his verbal indiscretions, notably an argument with Labor party officials on the fate of the socialist opposition in the Communist countries. The sensational treatment given the death of a British "frogman," who had been engaged in spying on the Soviet cruiser that brought the Russian visitors, also dampened the somewhat nebulous good feeling engendered by the trip.

Nothing loath to try his luck in the United States, Khrushchev's hints were politely rebuffed in Washington. The Soviet leaders were eager to practice reciprocity, and Nehru, U Nu, Tito, Adenauer, Sukarno, the Shah of Iran, French Premier Guy Mollet, and a host of lesser dignitaries all paid their respects in Moscow in 1955–1956. If no marked advance toward a global *détente* could be recorded as a result of these numerous visits of state, they did constitute a reassuring sign that the diplomatic austerity of the Stalinist epoch had ended.

The smiling face that Soviet diplomacy presented to the world was good public relations and further evidence that the more extreme xenophobic manifestations of the past decade were wearing away. But there was little disposition on the part of the Western powers to relax their guard—indeed there were constant warnings, especially in the United States, against succumbing to Soviet lures by disarming. The Western alliance was greatly strengthened by the accession of West Germany to NATO on May 6, 1955, after the ratification of the Paris agreements had given the Bonn regime full sovereignty and established the Western European Union. Soviet retaliation was almost instantaneous. On May 7 the Presidium of the Supreme Soviet abrogated the 1942 treaty of alliance with Britain and the similar pact signed with France in 1944. Since the pace of events had long since drained these documents of any meaning, the nullification proceedings were only a formal gesture of protest. The signature in Warsaw on May 14 of a twenty-year treaty of friendship, cooperation, and mutual aid among the Communist nations of Europe was a more effective counter-measure. The Warsaw Pact, the Soviet answer to NATO, provided for a unified military command, and Marshal Ivan Konev was placed in charge.

The juxtaposition of rival military alliance systems did not, paradoxically, plunge Europe into a new siege of nervous tension. The power blocs had long since been well defined, and the balance of military forces was not basically altered by the enlargement of NATO or by the Warsaw Pact. Diplomacy was, moreover, in the process of solving the Austrian question; and with both sides now negotiating from positions of strength, the long delayed "summit" conference of heads of state that Churchill had proposed in 1953 become a possibility.

The Austrian state treaty had been stalled since 1949 because of Moscow's obduracy.[8] In February 1955 Molotov intimated that the most recent Soviet condition—that a German treaty precede the Austrian—might be abandoned, and he invited Austrian Chancellor Julius Raab to Moscow for negotiations. In April he and other Austrian officials arrived in the Russian capital and were given the "red carpet" treatment, usually an infallible sign that the Soviet leaders were anxious to conclude an agreement. A communiqué issued on April 15 revealed that the Russians were willing to accept less than Austria and the Western powers had previously been disposed to grant. Austria was to be neutralized and the occupation forces withdrawn; war prisoners were to be released, and the $150,000,000 in reparations that Moscow had demanded in cash was to be paid in goods. A conference of ambassadors in Vienna (May 2–13, 1955) ironed out the last details of the treaty. The Soviet government again made concessions, and the document was signed on May 15 in the presence of the Big Four foreign ministers. After ratification the treaty became effective on July 27, an event that was enthusiastically celebrated throughout Austria.

The "Austrian solution" might have been applied to Germany, though the difficulties would have been enormous. But having worked so diligently to secure the Federal Republic as an ally, it was not to be supposed that the Atlantic powers—the United States least of all —would forego additional military strength for political stability in Central Europe in the form of a neutral Germany.

The summit conference idea had meanwhile progressed to the stage of serious discussion. In late May the Soviet government formally accepted a Western invitation for a heads of state meeting, though more time elapsed before the powers compromised upon Geneva as a satisfactory conference site. The Russians embarked upon a fresh "crusade of amiability," and even Molotov unbent sufficiently in a journey to San Francisco in honor of the tenth anniversary of the United Nations to convey the impression that he was a genial fellow at heart. (Molotov's smile, Acheson recalled in another context, had all the "spontaneity of a mechanical tiger.") Yet the Soviet press was not so good humored that it turned the other cheek when Dulles suggested that the "activities of international Communism" and the status of the satellites would be proper subjects for discussion at Geneva.

A full decade since the last conference at the summit—Potsdam— the pressure of world opinion made it imperative that the Geneva conferees seek some sort of surface accommodation even if prolonged and confidential bargaining, the usual hallmark of diplomatic achievement, had little chance to come into play. The meetings (July 18–23, 1955) were held in the Palace of Nations, once the headquarters of the old League, with daily plenary sessions and separate parleys of the foreign ministers. Buffet dinners helped to inject a note of informality into the proceedings. Eisenhower's earnest good will impressed the Russians—Khrushchev, Bulganin, and Zhukov—who were themselves on their best behavior; but the delegates understood, if the general public did not, that personal exchanges, no matter how friendly, provided no automatic solution to the problems of international politics. When the six days of speeches and conversations were over, it was agreed that the level of cold war tension had been significantly lowered. The conference was an undoubted psychological success, and for several months the afterglow of the "Geneva spirit" lent a veneer of cordiality to East-West relations.

For those who had hoped for tangible gains, Geneva was a disappointing "exercise in procrastination."[9] The hard questions of European security, German unification, and disarmament—Far Eastern issues were not even on the agenda—had been considered and then postponed to a meeting of the foreign ministers scheduled in October. The only advance over previously enunciated positions was Eisenhower's "open skies" inspection proposal. It involved an exchange of "blueprints" of military installations in the United States and the U.S.S.R. and the facilitation of aerial photography as a means of mutual surveillance. The plan had the merit of novelty and had stolen the headlines from the prosaic but more comprehensive Soviet disarmament "package": gradual reduction of nuclear weapons to a point where existing stocks would be destroyed and a troop limitation of 1,500,000 men for the United States, the U.S.S.R., and China, and 650,000 men for Britain and France. The idea of international inspection, which Moscow accepted in principle, was entirely too nebulous to satisfy the Western powers. On the other hand, the Russians found the Eisenhower scheme to their disadvantage, for the United States had far fewer military and industrial secrets than the Soviet Union.

By reducing its military strength, Moscow made a gesture toward perpetuating the "spirit of Geneva." On August 13 it was declared that by the following December 15 the Soviet armed forces—estimated at more than 5,000,000 men—would be slashed by 640,000; and in May 1956 a further cut of 1,200,000 men to be made during the course of the year was announced. Unfortunately, these projected decreases in troop strength were not accompanied by progress in the more important field of nuclear disarmament. The Eisenhower inspection proposal was all but laid to rest by Bulganin's letter of September 19, 1955, pointing out that American bases overseas were completely omitted from the plan.

The Kremlin also gave notice that it had not relented on the subject of German unification. Adenauer, who had accepted with high hopes an invitation to visit the Soviet capital, emerged from long talks with Bulganin (September 9–13, 1955) under no illusion that West Germany's new status as a sovereign member of NATO enabled her to drive a hard bargain. The German chancellor agreed to the establishment of diplomatic relations between Bonn and Moscow in return for an oral pledge to release some 10,000 German war prisoners still held in the Soviet Union. Washington claimed the Adenauer mission as a victory for the West because Moscow had been forced to abandon its "bankrupt" German policy and to "negotiate over the head of the so-called Democratic Republic." If any refutation of such a fantasy was necessary, it was provided by the arrival in Moscow of an East German delegation close upon Adenauer's heels. The Soviet leaders made a point of publicly emphasizing their determination to resist German unification on Western terms. "NATO is not a sports organization," said Khrushchev caustically, "but a team for war against the Soviet Union." A communiqué released on September 22 revealed that East Germany was to be granted sovereign status, and that Bonn would have to deal with the Communist regime in future negotiations on German unity.

With both coalitions still at loggerheads on the German issue, the prognosis for the conference of foreign ministers was poor. But the diplomats met at Geneva (October 27–November 16, 1955) with traces of the good will generated during the summer still lingering in the conference room. After a week's debate on Germany brought the usual standoff, tempers became a trifle frayed. A three-day recess was declared while Molotov flew back to Moscow for the anniversary celebration of the Bolshevik Revolution and Dulles conferred with Tito at Brioni, the latter's island retreat in the Adriatic. The other two items on the agenda—disarmament and East-West contacts—fared no better, and a parting communiqué conceded failure while offering no prospect of negotiations in the foreseeable future.

The smoldering crisis in the Middle East had passed its shadow over the Geneva meeting without obtruding directly upon the discussions. The Russians had made no threatening gestures toward their southern flank since the abortive diplomatic offensive against Iran in 1946. Yet they were unwilling to allow a vital link in the Soviet defense perimeter and a region of fabulous oil reserves to go by default to the Western powers. The military weakness of the Middle East had been a source of anxiety to Britain and the United States since the beginning of the cold war, and efforts to erect a barrier against possible Soviet encroachments were held up by the spreading passions of Arab nationalism. Egypt led the Arab League in a ceaseless feud with Israel, while the separate Anglo-Egyptian quarrel over the Suez Canal and the Sudan—two notable reminders of nineteenth century Western imperialism—provided a source of common grievance for the Arab masses and an emotional release from their grinding poverty.

By concentrating on the "northern tier" of states (Turkey, Iraq, Iran, and Pakistan) that were less intimately involved in Arabian affairs and whose geographic positions impinged more closely upon the Soviet frontier, Washington and London were able to record some diplomatic gains by 1954. However, a formal alliance system was not established until November 1955 when Britain and the "northern tier" states signed the Baghdad Pact, a defense treaty renewable after five years for further five-year terms. Though not a formal signatory, the United States became the guarantor of the alliance by its promise of military assistance.

The Baghdad Pact completed the military *cordon sanitaire* around the Soviet Union begun with NATO and carried forward with SEATO. But the alliance was a poor substitute for real political and military strength; and it became the unintentional means of precipitating the Soviet Union directly into the Middle Eastern power struggle. Egypt was grossly offended by the major role that the West had assigned to Iraq, her arch-rival for Arab leadership, and had needed no prompting when the Kremlin first made overtures during the summer of 1955 for an arms deal. In September generous financial terms were arranged in which Czechoslovakia undertook to supply Cairo with heavy military equipment, including planes, tanks, and submarines in return for Egyptian cotton and rice. The Russians also promised economic assistance, and a series of barter agreements were concluded with the Communist bloc nations. Egypt's prestige skyrocketed, as did that of her ruler, President Gamal Abdel Nasser, the rising hero of the Arab world.

At a single bound Moscow had leap-frogged the West's "northern tier" defense perimeter before its formal completion and asserted Soviet interests in an area that even Tsarist Russia had been unable to penetrate. By making no political demands upon Egypt and her allies, Moscow had only to ride the tail wind of Arab nationalism to nullify the Baghdad Pact. Henceforth nothing of importance could be settled in the Middle East without Soviet participation, although the Atlantic powers were to make valiant efforts in the coming months to exorcise the Russian menace.

III

By the beginning of 1956 the subtlety and suppleness of Soviet diplomacy under Khrushchev had become a formidable match for the West. Gone were the ham-handed tactics of Stalinism that had so often rescued Western policy-makers from the consequences of their own mistakes. If the bright promise of Geneva had dimmed before the somber realities of German disunity and the Soviet break-through in the Middle East, then at least the undiminished harshness of the cold war had not fully returned. Since they had managed to seize the initiative, the Russians appeared satisfied with a policy of competitive coexistence. Supremely confident that Communism would in the long run assert its "natural" superiority over capitalism, they had not departed in the slightest from their basic ideological commitments. As

Khrushchev had told the East German delegation in September 1955: "We are in favor of a *détente*, but if anybody thinks that for this reason we shall forget about Marx, Engels, and Lenin, he is mistaken. This will happen when shrimps learn to whistle."[10]

It was from strength rather than from weakness that Khrushchev took the final measure of the Stalin cult in a secret speech to the delegates of the twentieth party congress at its closing session (February 25, 1956). The text of his astonishing remarks was not published in the Soviet Union, though summaries were transmitted through the party apparatus so that few politically alert Russians remained ignorant of the disclosures. Some of the foreign Communist parties were eventually given edited versions of the speech, and from this source the United States Department of State obtained a copy and released it to the press on June 4, 1956. The unsavory revelations about Stalin's character and judgment went beyond the most vitriolic anti-Stalinist literature; and aside from the immediate sensation that the speech produced in the non-Communist world, the foreign Communist parties, particularly in the West, were thrown into a paroxysm of doubt and confusion.

The rambling informality of Khrushchev's indictment of Stalin suggested somewhat hasty improvisation. But it was hardly an impromptu performance, for he had obtained the prior approval of the party's Central Committee—a sizable minority of Stalinist die-hards dissenting—and the release of some heretofore secret documents to the delegates demonstrated considerable preparation. Just what domestic pressures led the "collective leadership" to such a radical step defied the divinatory efforts of Western commentators; but whatever the reasons, the political stakes were deemed high enough to override the danger that Communist morale might be completely shattered by the grisly story that Khrushchev unfolded. While it was a harrowing experience for devout Communists both in and out of Russia, in most cases party discipline proved equal to the task of overnight conversion to anti-Stalinism. Togliatti of Italy was the most recalcitrant of the non-Russian party leaders. His extended remarks constituted the first open criticism of the Soviet regime from within the Communist fold since the 1920's. That he was neither censured nor excommunicated was in itself a remarkable commentary on the changing political climate in Moscow.

The moral crisis generated among the Communists of Western Europe by the Khrushchev speech did not produce more than nominal concern in Moscow, but there was annoyance that the recent campaign to interest Western socialists in united front tactics could now be accounted a definite failure. Only the Yugoslav Communists had been psychologically prepared to hear the worst about Stalin. Tito's ultimate vindication came with the posthumous disgrace of his onetime suzerain. Soviet anxiety to win over the Yugoslavs as allies led to the dissolution of the Cominform on April 17; and Molotov's dismissal as foreign minister was timed for the eve of Tito's visit to Moscow and other Russian cities (June 2–20, 1956).

One of the last of the Old Bolsheviks, Molotov had been conspicuously absent from the Khrushchev-Bulganin good will tours and had been gently downgraded for more than a year. Because he was still closely identified with Stalin's Yugoslav fiasco and had become a symbol to the West of Soviet intractability, his further decline served a dual purpose in implementing Khrushchev's "de-Stalinized" foreign policy. The new foreign minister, Dmitri Shepilov, was a veteran party propagandist and the former editor of *Pravda*. A Khrushchev protégé, he had accompanied his superior on the "Canossa visit" to Belgrade in 1955 and became an advocate of the "Yugoslav orientation."

Moscow also took the initiative in quietly demoting some of Tito's enemies in the satellite countries—ardent Stalinists all—and in restoring the reputation of purged "Titoists." Budapest announced late in March 1956 that Laszlo Rajk and his associates had been posthumously cleared of all charges. Even the long dead Bela Kun was rehabilitated. Sofia, too, admitted that Traicho Kostov and his co-defendants had been convicted on faked evidence. But the Yugoslav dictator complained in Moscow that one of the most notorious of the Stalinists and his special *bête noire*, Rakosi of Hungary, had retained his position at the head of the party though ousted as premier in July 1953. Moscow had likewise failed to remove such stalwarts of Stalinism as Hoxha of Albania ("a scoundrel"), and no changes of any kind had been made among the top leaders of Rumania or Czechoslovakia. In Bulgaria, Vulko Chervenkov had been dropped to the rank of deputy premier but allegedly still ran both party and government.

At the conclusion of Tito's triumphal tour—the Russian people had greeted him with wild enthusiasm as a symbol of the political "thaw"— a joint communiqué conferred formal recognition upon the doctrine of "different roads to socialism." In effect, the Kremlin conceded the viability of "national Communism" and disavowed one of Stalin's most cherished articles of faith: that Moscow possessed the only set of blueprints to the Communist utopia envisaged by Marx and Lenin. Yet the Soviet party Presidium was neither unanimous in its anti-Stalinism nor as devoted to rooting out the political legatees of Stalin as Marshal Tito. The anti-Stalin campaign had nevertheless gathered a momentum of its own; and the ruling cadre of Communism learned almost too late the lesson that the Bourbons and Romanovs had never absorbed—that belated reform combined with weakness and hesitation can be more explosive revolutionary ingredients than tyranny and poverty. In 1953 Moscow had damped down the fires of revolt in East Germany with a timely display of force. In 1956 spontaneous combustion in Poland and Hungary presented an entirely new set of fire-fighting problems.

The Poles were far in the vanguard as the "peoples' democracies" stepped up the pace of liberalization in the wake of Moscow's attack on the "cult of personality." The secret police had already been drastically curbed and the press censorship partially lifted. The ferment of the intellectuals—writers, editors, students, and professors—reached a crescendo by the spring of 1956. Journals and newspapers furnished a forum for the repressed grievances of a decade as the masses, still predominantly Roman Catholic and anti-Russian, applauded the apparent recession of the Soviet glacier. The United Workers (Communist) party, riddled with doubt and dissension, was swept along by the tide of public opinion. Its leader, President Boleslaw Bierut, had died in Moscow in March, and for a brief period he became a Polish hero because of unconfirmed rumors that he had met with foul play. His successor, the irresolute and vacillating Edward Ochab, was chosen by the party Central Committee in preference to the candidate whom Khrushchev—ostensibly in Warsaw for Bierut's funeral—had openly backed.

As in East Berlin three years before, the seething tensions within the "camp of socialism" suddenly burst forth. The site was Poznan, an industrial city of some 365,000 inhabitants in western Poland. A hotly contested wage dispute in a heavy manufacturing plant resulted in a strike on the morning of June 28. A protest march to the center of the city attracted thousands of supporters along the way. A false rumor spread that several members of a workers' delegation sent to Warsaw had been arrested; and a crowd gathered before the city prison, forcing the release of its inmates. Later the offices of the Communist party and other public buildings were sacked. In attacking the administrative headquarters of the secret police, a hated symbol of oppression, resistance was offered for the first time. The local garrison was called out, but the Polish army proved itself an uncertain instrument of repression. There was some fraternization and a few cases of outright desertion to the rebel cause. The fighting was confined to Poznan, however, and special Polish security troops were able to quell most of the rioting by the morning of the second day. Official casualty figures gave 53 dead and 300 wounded.

Communist sources, parroting the Soviet press, unhesitatingly attributed the insurrection to "imperialist agents" and "fascist provocateurs." But the Polish Communists, chastened by their experience, were soon hedging that stereotyped verdict: the trouble had been "in no small degree precipitated by the bureaucratic warpings of the proletarian state."[11] Bulganin and Zhukov, sent to Warsaw to appraise the situation, recommended stern measures. Most of the Polish leaders favored political and economic concessions and chose the perilous path of national Communism.

Khrushchev's policy of courting Tito and reviling Stalinism, having led to near-disaster in Poland, was subjected to critical review within the party Presidium. Molotov and Lazar Kaganovich, the leaders of the Stalinist "old guard," rallied sentiment for a toughening of the "soft" line. The decision was to discourage further flirtation with Titoism, and a confidential circular letter to that effect was dispatched early in September 1956 to Moscow's viceroys in the satellite capitals.

On September 19 Khrushchev flew to Yugoslavia, and in a conference at Brioni he sought Tito's cooperation in decelerating the runaway program of de-Stalinization in Eastern Europe. The Stalinists, he explained, might otherwise regain control of the Presidium and nationalist tendencies in Poland and Hungary might get out of hand. In either case Yugoslavia would be the loser. The danger once past, a moderately liberal program could be reinstituted. Tito was slow to be convinced. After eight days of discussion both men—still "on vacation" according to official press releases—departed by airplane for the Black Sea area, where Bulganin, Voroshilov, Shepilov, and Erno Gerö of Hungary joined the parley. Western rumor mills buzzed with uncertainty as these mystifying talks lasted until October 5. It later appeared that Tito was reconciled with Gerö, who was invited to a conference in Belgrade, and that with some reservations on his part the Yugoslav dictator had reached an understanding with Khrushchev.

But events in Poland had already outstripped Khrushchev as he groped for a formula to curb the centrifugal force of independent Communism. Wladyslaw Gomulka, whose credentials as a living martyr to Stalinist oppression were unsurpassed among Polish Communists, had been released from prison in December 1954, and upon his restoration to party membership on August 4, 1956, he automatically became the favorite of the liberal faction. It was proposed that he replace Ochab as the party's first secretary, a move strenuously opposed by the die-hards around Marshal Rokossovsky.

On the morning of October 19, 1956, a meeting of the party's Central Committee was scheduled, the second since the Poznan riots. It was postponed by news that Khrushchev, Molotov, Kaganovich, and Mikoyan, accompanied by an intimidating array of Russian generals, had arrived at an airport near Warsaw. The Soviet delegation, stung by the refusal of the Polish leaders to come to Moscow, was bent upon disciplining their unruly minions lest the Poles succumb to the Yugoslav heresy. To lend authority to their words, the Russians had ordered Soviet army units in Poland and East Germany to converge upon Warsaw; and Rokossovsky's Polish troops had been set in motion preparatory to a *coup d'état* that would place the pro-Soviet Poles in power. But the threat had been countered by prompt action in covering the approaches to the capital with military detachments of the Polish security police. An armed workers' militia was also alerted for duty as a reserve force.

At the airport the Khrushchev party was given a polite but perceptibly chilly reception by the top Polish Communists, including Gomulka. A Russo-Polish conference took place shortly afterward at the Belvedere Palace in Warsaw. Khrushchev laid down his terms in the course of a ninety-minute opening harangue: Rokossovsky and the Polish Stalinists were to stay in the Politburo; Gomulka could not be permitted to head the party, but he might enter the Politburo with several of his sympathizers. When the Poles proved reluctant, Khrushchev was blunt: "I will show you what the way to socialism looks like," he is reported to have shouted. "If you don't obey we will crush you. . . . We will never permit this country to be sold to the American imperialists."[12]

Before noon the meeting was recessed, and the Poles repaired to the nearby Council of Ministers building to debate the Soviet ultimatum. The Stalinists, having lost the support of the moderates, were now outnumbered by the Gomulka faction. The conference with the Russians resumed in the afternoon, and with intermissions it continued far into the night. Moscow's hand, called at last, revealed a bluff. Khrushchev recoiled at the risk of open warfare, for it was clear that Polish troops would not act as proxies for Moscow against their own countrymen. He and his associates returned to the Soviet capital on the morning of the 20th. The Polish Central Committee reconvened, and the next day a new nine-man Politburo was elected which excluded Rokossovsky and his faction. Gomulka was also elected first secretary of the party. Later removed as defense minister, Rokossovsky reacquired his Soviet citizenship and became Zhukov's deputy.

Gomulka and the Polish party had won a stunning victory in leading the nation to a peaceful revolution within a Communist framework. It remained to be seen whether his prestige as a national hero could hold in check massive pressures for radical reform and a decisive break with Moscow. In that event Soviet intervention was a foregone conclusion. The Russians had been outmaneuvered, but they did not propose to stand idly by while the "peoples' democracies" dictated their own terms of independence. That was the grim and tragic lesson the Hungarian people absorbed as they sought to imitate and then to exceed the permissible limits of the Polish experiment during the last week of October 1956.

Hungary, while it lacked the anti-Russian tradition of Poland, was the proud possessor of a revolutionary heritage second to none. The iron grip of Stalinism, somewhat relaxed in 1953, had disintegrated in the wake of Moscow's courtship of Tito and the dramatic Poznan riots. Rakosi was relieved of his post as party chief on July 18 at a meeting of the Central Committee attended by Mikoyan. He was replaced by Gerö, a less gifted Stalinist who tried to swim with the Titoist current by yielding to the "liberals." His most significant concession in the light of future events was the restoration of the Petoefi clubs. Named in honor of Sandor Petoefi, a poet who had lost his life in the Hungarian revolution of 1848–1849, these organizations had become forums for the dissemination of unorthodox political views and had been banned on June 30. They once more became rallying points for the Hungarian intelligentsia, the lightning conductor, as in Poland, of popular discontent.

On October 13, 1956, Imre Nagy, premier during the "Malenkov period" (1953–1955) and later expelled from the party as a "deviationist," was restored to membership and almost at once found himself in the limelight as a Hungarian Gomulka. The next day Gerö and other party leaders left for Belgrade to cement friendly relations with Tito. In their absence Gomulka's stirring triumph over the Russians fired the enthusiasm of the Hungarian masses. Radio Budapest and *Szabad Nep,* the chief party newspaper, fell under the influence of "radical" Communists and expressed open sympathy for the Poles.

On October 22 Budapest university students held several meetings, the most important of which attracted an audience of over 4,000 people and led to the formulation of sweeping political demands in a sixteen-point program. The next morning the capital was seized by a fever of excitement. Work stopped by common consent, and in the afternoon townspeople and students joined in orderly processions to the statues of Petoefi and General Joseph Bem, another hero of 1848–1849. From the Bem statue most of the crowd crossed the

Danube to the Parliament building, where by early evening more than 200,000 persons had massed in the square and in adjoining streets. At 8:00 P.M. Gerö, who had returned from Belgrade that morning, lectured the population in strident tones over Radio Budapest. His speech struck a raw spot in the public psyche, and a false report spread that he had referred to the people as "fascist rabble."[13] About an hour later the first acts of violence were recorded when the A.V.H. (secret police), firing on a crowd attempting to storm the radio station, left a number of dead and dying upon the street. Fighting broke out in various parts of the city and continued all night as the rioters acquired weapons from military barracks, an arms factory, and sympathetic police and soldiers.

Early the following morning (October 24) Radio Budapest announced that Nagy had been appointed premier and a member of the party Politburo. The news had no discernible effect in pacifying the rebels. Although it was unknown at the time, Nagy was premier in name only: he was held virtually incommunicado at party headquarters until October 26, when Gerö fled to Moscow. On the previous day, Janos Kadar, a devoted Communist who had suffered imprisonment and torture under the Rakosi regime, had replaced Gerö as party secretary. The Hungarian army had already melted away; most of the soldiers who joined the insurrection did so in a civilian capacity. Soviet troops, equipped with a full complement of heavy tanks, had entered Budapest in force on the 24th and were more reliable agents of suppression despite poor morale and some instances of disaffection. Yet the "freedom fighters" held their own in an amazing demonstration of courage and endurance as the revolution gradually spread over the rest of the country. No similar rising of a whole population had taken place since the Russian people, with comparatively little bloodshed, had overthrown the Tsar almost forty years before.

On October 27 Nagy organized a new cabinet that included several non-Communists and eliminated most of the "Stalinists." Major political concessions—notably the abolition of the secret police and the restoration of a multiple party system—were announced during the next few days. The pretense that "fascist reactionary elements" and "counter-revolutionary gangs" were responsible for the violence was abandoned, and Nagy spoke of a "great national and democratic movement" which had exploded with "elemental force" because of the "grave crimes" committed by the old party leadership.[14]

An armed truce was arranged on October 28 after the Soviet government agreed to withdraw its troops from Budapest. While the Russians were in the process of evacuation, fresh units, uncontaminated by garrison duty in Hungary, were massing on the frontier and in some cases crossing it. Moscow was preparing to act if the necessity arose: another Gomulka might be tolerated, but Nagy's veneer of national Communism had worn thin under the stress of revolutionary events. The forces of compromise prevailed nonetheless, and the Soviet government issued a declaration on October 30 admitting past mistakes with the countries of the "great commonwealth of socialist nations" and offering to apply the "Leninist principles of equality of peoples" in the future. Mikoyan and Mikhail Suslov, Moscow's Hungarian specialists, negotiated in Budapest with the Nagy government and offered the withdrawal of all Soviet troops except those stationed in Hungary on the basis of the Warsaw Pact.

Nagy could not have remained in office had he accepted the Soviet terms; and on November 1 he cast his lot with the revolutionaries by publicly repudiating the Warsaw treaty. A "declaration of neutrality" (*i.e.*, independence) was proclaimed, and an appeal was sent to the United Nations asking for assistance in maintaining Hungary's new status. Two days later a coalition government was organized with only four Communists in a twelve-man cabinet.

The capital was by this time ringed with Soviet troops, for Moscow had decided to act without further equivocation. Shortly after midnight on November 4 the Hungarian delegation negotiating for the withdrawal of the Russian forces was arrested at Soviet military headquarters in Budapest. The Soviet attack came at daybreak and was so annihilating that prolonged resistance was impossible. The back of the revolution was broken before nightfall, but guerrilla fighters harried the Russians for several weeks in the countryside. The members of Nagy's government dispersed, and the premier found sanctuary in the Yugoslav embassy. Janos Kadar was induced to form a pro-Russian "shadow cabinet" on the 4th, though he was reportedly in Moscow at the time and did not appear in Budapest until the 6th or 7th.

The Western world, simultaneously involved in the Anglo-French-Israeli invasion of Egypt, could offer only sympathy and moral support to the Hungarian rebels. A U.N. Security Council resolution to censure the Russians was defeated by a Soviet veto. Yugoslavia abstained, a decision reflecting Tito's opinion that while the initial Soviet intervention was unjustified, "reactionary elements" had threatened to seize control of Hungary; and to avert the catastrophe of civil war or of a new world war, the "lesser evil" of military intervention was necessary. No matter how far he had strayed from Moscow's fold, Tito was still a Communist, and he had viewed with dismay the sudden appearance of a "bourgeois" revolution on the Yugoslav doorstep.

The Hungarian tragedy, aside from thousands of casualties and the disrupted lives of nearly 180,000 patriots who chose a life of exile, conferred a new legacy of bitterness upon the global struggle. Revulsion against Communist methods and indignation at the scope of Soviet aggrandizement, feelings that had softened in the West under the impact of the "Khrushchev thaw," was now aroused once more. Khrushchev's own political future was jeopardized, and in self-defense he was obliged to conduct a partial retreat along the Stalinist terrain that he had traversed so blithely earlier in the year.

IV

That Khrushchev not only managed to salvage his political career but emerged less than a year later as the sole major survivor of the ten-man Presidium installed at Stalin's death seemed less than likely in the closing weeks of 1956. Had the Hungarian revolution succeeded or had the other satellites seized the opportunity for an "adventurist" policy, his fall from power would probably have been foreordained. But the blood bath in Hungary, though it cost Moscow dearly in international good will, prevented the collapse of Communism in Eastern Europe; and by a combination of political firmness and economic concessions, Khrushchev was able to ride out the storm.

Russia suffered less opprobrium among the Afro-Asian nations than Westerners were prepared to admit, for the Hungarian affair was regarded not so much a noble bid for freedom as a civil war within the Communist orbit. Moscow's feat of legerdemain in snatching Egypt from the maw of Anglo-French imperialism—or so it was considered in the Arab world, if not beyond—more than offset the passing ill will engendered by the brutal intervention in Hungary; and it bolstered Khrushchev's prestige at a most propitious moment.

Israel had launched her preventive war against Egypt on October 29, 1956. The plan of campaign was brilliantly conceived, and within a few days most of the Sinai Peninsula was occupied by Israeli troops. In unacknowledged complicity with Israel, Britain and France prepared to occupy the Suez Canal, the vital link to the Middle Eastern oil supply that Nasser had taken over in July. After a preliminary aerial bombardment of military objectives, paratroops were dropped on November 5 at the north end of the waterway, and the next morning British and French infantry scrambled ashore to support the action.

A crushing defeat for Egypt and the political eclipse of her leader, the "Hitler of the Nile," appeared imminent. But Moscow reacted promptly and forcefully. On November 5 stiff warnings amounting almost to ultimatums were dispatched to London, Paris, and Tel Aviv. Israel's "very existence . . . as a state" was declared in jeopardy; and the note to Britain, considered the ringleader, referred to the existence of "rocket weapons"—presumably available if necessary—and contained the ominous sentence: "We are fully determined to crush the aggressors and restore peace in the [Middle] East through the use of force." As the Left wing British Labor leader, Aneurin Bevan, so aptly put it: if the government wished to "reimpose the law of the jungle," it should "remember that Britain and France are not the most powerful animals in it. There are much more dangerous creatures prowling around."[15] Some hours later a Russian spokesman tempered the threat by explaining that the "we" in the message referred to the U.S.S.R. in conjunction with the United Nations. On the same day a note to Washington proposed joint Soviet-American intervention to halt the invasion, a suggestion that Eisenhower termed "unthinkable." The United States was nevertheless embarrassed by the undisguised aggression of its allies and exerted every effort for a cease-fire.

In London and Paris the Soviet threat, accompanied by hints that Soviet troops would be sent to Egypt, was viewed with grave concern. Coupled with growing pressure from Washington, the diplomatic buffeting from the two super-powers was too much to withstand. The invasion was halted with victory in sight, and fighting officially ceased at midnight on November 6. A resolution of the U.N. General Assembly called on the three occupying powers to withdraw their troops from Egypt, a move endorsed by Moscow in a formal injunction that "volunteers" would be sent to help its beleaguered ally should the directive be disregarded. With great reluctance, Egyptian territory was evacuated by the end of December (except that Israel retained the Gaza Strip and a portion of the Sinai Peninsula several months longer as a guarantee of Egyptian good faith).

The Suez War was a fiasco for the Western powers even though the United States was not directly tarred with the brush of imperialism. Balanced against the partial destruction of Egypt's new military equipment imported from behind the Iron Curtain and the salutary lesson that Israel taught her Arab neighbors was a formidable list of liabilities: the temporary blockade of the canal by Egyptian sabotage; the rift in the Atlantic alliance; the spread of Arab nationalism in the pernicious mold of "Nasserism"; the boost to Soviet influence in the Middle East as the guardian of Arab independence; and the blunting of the moral issue involved in Moscow's repressive role in Hungary. Washington found little solace in the knowledge that the Russians had made no inroads upon the "northern tier" states and that the other Arab nations by no means constituted a uniform bloc breathing defiance—Nasser style—of Western machinations.

The Russians kept the Middle Eastern cauldron boiling by sending Egypt enough arms to make good her recent losses and by accusing Britain, France, and Israel of plotting aggression against Syria, Lebanon, and Jordan. The pro-Nasser government of Syria, also a beneficiary of the Kremlin's arms program, went so far as to appeal to the United Nations on December 1, 1956, to look into the alleged threat to her security. Nothing came of the protest, and Moscow allowed the artificially inflated war scare to die a natural death.

Early in the new year the United States attempted to paper over the unseemly cracks in its Middle Eastern policy by a solemn preachment which the press promptly labeled the "Eisenhower Doctrine." Essentially the new scheme was an extension of the Truman Doctrine to cover the Middle East—a program enunciated by the President before a joint session of Congress on January 5, 1957, asking for authorization to give military and economic assistance to those countries requesting it and for permission to employ the armed forces of the United States to repel Communist aggression in the area should the need arise. Dutifully and without much enthusiasm the necessary resolution passed both houses of Congress in February. To a greater extent than the Baghdad Pact, the Eisenhower Doctrine represented a political maneuver that failed to confront the real problems of the Middle East—one that was calculated to increase rather than to decrease Soviet influence. A Russian attack was wholly unnecessary— and hardly likely except in answer to armed intervention by the West —at a time when the tide of Arab nationalism was running heavily in Moscow's favor.

The Soviet propaganda apparatus opened a saturation barrage on the new American doctrine that scored heavily in the Middle East and with neutral opinion everywhere. Khrushchev predicted that the doctrine would end on the "garbage heap of history," thus expropriating without credit one of Trotsky's favorite phrases. Moscow's rejoinder on the diplomatic front came on February 12 when Shepilov delivered identical notes to the three Western ambassadors proposing a six-point plan for the neutralization of the Arab world. Since the terms included the "liquidation of foreign [*i.e.*, Western] bases and the withdrawal of foreign troops," the proposition met a cool reception. On the same day the Russian delegation at the United Nations asked the General Assembly to consider its charges that the United States was guilty of "aggressive acts" (the Eisenhower Doctrine, new atomic bases abroad, increased arms expenditures, and the like) "constituting a threat to peace and security." As the Soviet government had no doubt anticipated, the request was killed at the committee stage; but the Russians had made their point before the forum of world opinion.

With the Eisenhower Doctrine and the attendant vehemence of the Soviet reaction, East-West relations reached a new low in the gradual descent from the high resolve and lofty purpose of the summit conference of 1955. This subtle shift in Moscow's mood, though it was not a return to the intransigence of former days, was signaled on February 15, 1957, by a change in foreign ministers. Shepilov's appointment had marked the most balmy days of Soviet "Titoism," and his replacement by Gromyko, who had served a long apprenticeship under Molotov, presaged a return to the "business as usual" professionalism of the Chicherin-Litvinov era rather than a reversion to Stalinist methods.

By this time Khrushchev had regained the confidence of at least a majority of his colleagues—or at any rate their acquiescence—and had managed a satisfactory compromise with Stalin's ghost. At a Kremlin New Year's Eve party he had praised the late dictator as a "great Marxist" and "fighter against imperialism." "The imperialists call us Stalinists," he went on to say. "Well, when it comes to fighting imperialists, we are all Stalinists."[16] On January 19, 1957, the Soviet press recognized Stalin's partial rehabilitation by printing the text of Khrushchev's remarks at a reception for Chou En-lai at the Chinese embassy two days before. For those who had devoted their lives to the revolutionary movement, he said, "Stalin's name was inseparable from Marxism-Leninism."

The "internal contradictions" in the "socialist camp" still worried the Soviet leaders. Having drawn an intangible line between the barely permissible (Poland) and the wholly unacceptable (Hungary), they were forced to make numerous adjustments while maintaining constant vigilance lest further disturbances mar the hard-won outward serenity of Eastern Europe. There was no repetition of the rebellious turbulence of 1956, and judged by this pragmatic test Moscow's policy of strength tempered by appropriate measures of moderation and economic reform worked well. Some of the major decisions were made at a conference in Budapest (January 1–4, 1957) which Khrushchev, seconded by Malenkov, attended with the party and government chiefs of Hungary, Czechoslovakia, Rumania, and Bulgaria. The absence of representatives from Warsaw signified that an important place on the agenda was reserved for the Polish problem.

If there was any departure from previous policy decisions, the course of events did not reveal them. In mid-November Gomulka had obtained a limited declaration of Polish independence during his consultation with the Soviet leaders in Moscow; and on January 20, 1957, he received a popular mandate from the Polish voters that reassured the Russians and forestalled any overt moves toward intervention. Even the most anti-Soviet Poles, heeding the advice of the Roman Catholic hierarchy, had recognized the danger and turned out at the polls to endorse the Communist-dominated National Front ticket. Gomulka, his political career better secured, was frank to admit Poland's pressing economic difficulties. The Russians made a number of concessions, and a Polish mission to Washington in February eventually obtained a $141,000,000 loan, chiefly in the form of surplus wheat and cotton, from the somewhat suspicious American government.

Hungary, still under the heel of the Soviet occupation, was passive but sullenly defiant as the last vestiges of the revolutionary spirit—the workers' councils and the strike movement—succumbed to political repression and economic hardship. Thousands of political prisoners were reportedly sent to Soviet labor camps as Moscow and Budapest ignored repeated resolutions by the U.N. General Assembly seeking a Russian withdrawal and permission to send in observers. Among the arrested was Imre Nagy, who had left his refuge in the Yugoslav embassy under a promise of safe conduct.

Moscow and Belgrade had resumed their ideological sparring while avoiding any telling blows that would end the possibility of reconciliation. The Russians seriously contemplated the restoration of the Cominform as a means of isolating the virus of Titoism and reasserting Moscow's primacy among the Communist nations. But the Chinese interposed their veto and were supported by the Poles and Italians. Togliatti, like other Communist leaders in the West, had been dismayed by the disruptive effect of the Hungarian revolution upon his party's fortunes and was determined that Muscovite discipline should not be reimposed.

By his criticism of Soviet policy in the satellites as a form of "great power chauvinism," Mao Tse-tung had as early as 1954 (at the time of Khrushchev's visit to Peking) aligned himself with the Kremlin "liberals." He and his colleagues had little cause to remember Stalin with affection, and they considered themselves the equals of his successors. Yet they sided with Moscow in the revived dispute with Tito; and with even more surprising orthodoxy, they lent encouragement to the upgrading of Stalin. The Peking government was faced with domestic problems similar to those of Russia in the 1920's—a backward industrial economy and a semi-literate peasant population—and it depended, despite occasional flirtations with "liberalism," upon the ruthless but tried techniques of Stalinism to modernize China before the "imperialists" of the West would presumably strike. The Chinese party chiefs were therefore in no mood for the kind of relaxation that had led to near disaster for Communism in Hungary; nor did they propose to risk weakening their economic and diplomatic ties with the Soviet Union as long as their independence was respected. In conjunction with his visit to Moscow in January, Chou En-lai conferred with Gomulka in Warsaw and Kadar in Budapest, and his efforts as a mediator and interpreter of "neo-Stalinism" were apparently well received.

By the spring of 1957 the Russians had made a safe recovery from their attack of nerves on the occasion of the Hungarian uprising and the Western assault on Egypt. Khrushchev again became the affable salesman of peaceful coexistence. British Prime Minister Harold Macmillan was pressed to visit Moscow; the Soviet government curtailed its series of notes to the West European nations threatening dire consequences should they permit the establishment of bases for nuclear missiles; the London disarmament conference, meeting under United Nations auspices, made some progress when the Soviet delegate presented a modified variation of Eisenhower's "open skies" plan; and the Kremlin threw out some feelers about the desirability of another top-level conference. But the Western powers did not respond readily to Moscow's return to a friendlier posture. Macmillan declined the Russian invitation, and the United States held conspicuously aloof.

On June 20, 1957, the special U.N. Committee on Hungary issued a documented report contradicting Moscow's version of the Hungarian revolt as the work of counter-revolutionaries and foreign agents. The United States urged the recall of the General Assembly to consider the report, and American officials, including the President, annoyed the Russians with references to the ultimate "liberation" of Eastern Europe. Relations were further irritated by Dulles' curt refusal to welcome a visit to Washington by Marshal Zhukov, a visit that Eisenhower had encouraged by an impromptu remark at a press conference on July 17. Khrushchev was resentful: "We are a proud nation and we do not want to go down on our knees to arrange these things."[17]

The Presidium "Stalinists," whose power appeared to wax during the closing weeks of 1956 and to wane in the spring, made an unexpected comeback on June 17–18 by combining with the "liberals" to demand Khrushchev's resignation following his nine-day good will tour of Finland. He was able to transfer the issue to the party's Central Committee, where a prolonged debate (June 22–29, 1957) resulted in a crushing defeat for the "desiccated pettifoggers," as Khrushchev referred to his opponents. The ensuing purge of the "anti-party" group in the Presidium—Molotov, Kaganovich, Malenkov, and Shepilov—was spectacular but bloodless. All were assigned relatively minor positions in the Soviet hinterlands, Molotov as ambassador to the Mongolian People's Republic. Zhukov, elevated to full membership in the new fifteen-man Presidium as a reward for rallying the armed forces to the "correct" side, was Khrushchev's only serious rival; and he was eliminated from the power struggle during the fall when he was replaced as defense minister by Marshal Rodion Malinovsky and dropped from the Presidium and Central Committee.

Despite his semi-dictatorial status, roughly akin to that of Stalin's in the late twenties, Khrushchev was careful to preserve the outward forms—and perhaps also the inward substance—of "collective leadership." Having vanquished the opposition with more finesse and considerably less bloodshed than Stalin, Khrushchev's avowed policy of relaxing international tensions was not consistently pursued—at least in a manner that the Western world could regard with any degree of equanimity. Insofar as his policy contributed to easing tension, the effects were almost entirely confined to Moscow's Eastern orbit.

In July Khrushchev and Bulganin paid an eight-day visit to Czechoslovakia. A communiqué released in Prague proclaimed agreement on the need to fight "revisionism" (Titoism) and "conservatism" (Stalinism) as well as "bourgeois ideology." Many of the leaders of world Communism converged upon Moscow at Khrushchev's return. Edvard Kardelj and Alexander Rankovich, the two Yugoslav vice presidents, were among them, ostensibly to discuss the $250,000,000 aid program the Russians had cancelled after their new quarrel with Tito. Khrushchev was self-confident and even pugnacious as he outlined his "centrist" position on Communist unity. He was careful to leave the door open for Tito's return to the fold but warned Poland and Yugoslavia: "Socialism that gets help from Dulles smells bad." It was decided several days later to resume economic aid to Yugoslavia. The move prepared the way for a friendly meeting between Khrushchev and Tito in Rumania early in August that appeared to restore Soviet-Yugoslav relations to their former harmonious state.

Khrushchev continued his travels with a week's visit to East Germany (August 7–14, 1957), in which Mikoyan replaced Bulganin as his right hand man. The Soviet party secretary roundly denounced Adenauer, charging that he was preparing the German people for a new war, and the trip confirmed Moscow's determination not to yield to Western terms on the question of German unity. A new flareup of the perpetual Middle East crisis and the failure of the London disarmament conference further served to convince Washington that the Kremlin's policy had toughened. The disappointing result of the London meeting, the most promising discussion on arms limitation since the war, did in fact coincide with Moscow's terse announcement on August 26 that a successful test of an intercontinental ballistic missile had taken place in the Soviet Union. Zorin, the Russian delegate, had immediately assumed a more belligerent stance by rejecting the elaborate Western proposals *in toto*. Although a new dimension had been added to the global "balance of terror," American opinion was inclined to minimize the importance of the Soviet achievement—and there were confirmed skeptics prepared to dismiss the whole matter as Communist propaganda—until in early October Russian progress in the race for long range missiles was demonstrated so convincingly that the "natural" superiority of Western science and technology could never again be taken for granted.

NOTES

1. Alistair Horne, *Return to Power: A Report on the New Germany* (New York, 1956), p. 196.

2. Wolfe, *Khrushchev and Stalin's Ghost*, pp. 316–17.

3. See above, p. 363.

4. See above, p. 383.

5. See below, pp. 433–34.

6. See above, p. 412.

7. Cora Bell, *Survey of International Affairs, 1954* (New York, 1957), p. 157.

8. See above, pp. 335–36.

9. Richard H. Rovere, *Affairs of State: The Eisenhower Years* (New York, 1956), p. 283.

10. Hollis W. Barber and others, *The United States in World Affairs, 1955* (New York, 1957), p. 68.

11. *Trybuna Luda* (Warsaw), July 6, 1956, quoted in Fischer, *Russia Revisited*, pp. 176–77.

12. *New York Times*, October 21, 1956.

13. United Nations, General Assembly, *Report of the Special Committee on the Problem of Hungary* (New York, 1957), p. 81.

14. Paul E. Zinner (ed.), *National Communism and Popular Revolt in Eastern Europe* (New York, 1956), p. 429.

15. Paul Johnson, *The Suez War* (New York, 1957), p. 116.

16. *New York Times*, January 2, 1957.

17. *Ibid.*, October 9, 1957.

CHAPTER FIFTEEN

ENTERING THE SPACE AGE

On October 4, 1957, Soviet scientists achieved a spectacular break-through in the race for technological supremacy by placing a 184 pound artificial satellite (*sputnik* in Russian) in orbit around the earth. As mankind's first triumph in the conquest of outer space, the date was a scientific milestone comparable to the dawn of aviation. Both the Soviet Union and the United States had previously announced their intention of launching earth satellites in conjunction with the International Geophysical Year (July 1957-December 1958), but only a few Western scientists—unheeded by the general public—acknowl-edged the possibility of Soviet priority in the field. The impressiveness of Moscow's achievement was at once generously conceded in the West, particularly by those in a position to appreciate the enormous technical difficulties that had been overcome.

Within a few days, however, the military implications of the Soviet accomplishment had received so much publicity that its scientific purpose was all but lost to view. If the Russians possessed a launching mechanism capable of propelling such a heavy object into orbit, their priority in the field of long-range missiles was evident. Rendered complacent and even lethargic by their traditional pre-eminence in industry and applied science, the American people were soon involved in a rather undignified display of self-criticism and recrimination which the launching on November 3 of a second sputnik—six times as large as the first—aided materially.

Having so often reaped a propaganda harvest from a meager plant-ing, Moscow was not slow to extract the maximum psychological advantage from its spectacular feat. The Western powers had long been under the delusion that time was on their side, that once they had established an overwhelming preponderance of military strength the Soviet government would bow to superior force and withdraw from its overextended periphery to more traditional political frontiers.

The policy had been bankrupt for some time, but Washington had stubbornly insisted upon pursuing it: the negotiation of a mutual withdrawal—as in Germany—would be "appeasement" and a betrayal of the "free world." Democratic statesmen and Communist oligarchs used a different set of clichés to cloak the realities of power in the more fitting raiment of moral imperative.

With the balance of military power now shifted at least temporarily in Moscow's favor, the Kremlin did not hesitate to employ "sputnik diplomacy" as it had once accused the United States of using "atomic diplomacy." Khrushchev was alternately sober and jubilant in assessing the gains that had accrued to the Communist side. While asserting that bombers had been rendered "obsolete," he was nevertheless aware that American planes carrying nuclear weapons were still fully capable of decimating the Soviet Union's major cities. In probing the Western position in the Middle East, Moscow revived on a more menacing scale the mild Syrian war scare of the previous year. Turkey was accused of plotting an attack on her southern neighbor to gratify the United States, which had become incensed by the August 1957 *coup* placing a pro-Soviet clique in command of the Syrian army. The United States had rushed arms to Jordan, Saudi Arabia, and Lebanon and added to the supply which Iraq and Turkey, as Baghdad Pact members, had already received. The Arab world, even the nominally pro-Western states, reacted unfavorably to American interference, and Egypt began dispatching troops to Syria in late September to protect its ally.

Gromyko warned Washington on October 16 that his government was prepared to intervene should an invasion of Syria take place, and Dulles promptly countered by declaring that a Russian attack on Turkey "would not mean a purely defensive operation by the United States, with the Soviet Union a privileged sanctuary."[1] At Syria's request the U.N. General Assembly opened a full-scale debate on the crisis. The American delegate raked the Soviet Union as the "arsonist" in the affair, "trying his best to start another fire and demanding the right to lead the fire brigade." As the target date for the alleged invasion passed without incident—October 27 according to Moscow— the "threat" to Syria was played down. By greatly magnifying its alarm at the possibility of Western-inspired aggression the Kremlin had again successfully posed as an Arab "big brother" and checkmated Washington's clumsy attempt to "quarantine" Syria.

The Middle Eastern turbulence had all but subsided by the time of Moscow's mammoth celebration of the fortieth anniversary of the Bolshevik Revolution. Virtually the whole galaxy of the Communist world—Mao Tse-tung, Ho Chi Minh, Kim Il Sung, Togliatti, Thorez, Ulbricht, Gomulka, Kadar, and many others—were on hand to honor the occasion and to demonstrate by their presence the solidarity of a common purpose. Only the absence of Marshal Tito, who pleaded an attack of acute lumbago—apparently a diplomatic illness—struck a note of discord and implied that the new-found serenity of Soviet-Yugoslav relations was again to be short-lived.

In a speech before a special session of the Supreme Soviet on November 6, 1957, Khrushchev re-emphasized the notion of peaceful coexistence and urged socialist-capitalist competition in the economic realm. He put in a bid for another summit conference with the proviso that it should take into account the recent "change in the relationship of forces in the international arena"—an oblique suggestion that the West would do well to accept the Soviet position of strength in the post-sputnik era. Reluctant to negotiate the frozen issues of the cold war even in the relatively favorable climate of the preceding two years, the United States would hardly grasp at the offer while Moscow's self-assurance verged upon arrogance. On December 3 Dulles firmly discouraged the idea.

Following the social and ceremonial aspects of the anniversary celebration, the Communist leaders met for formal discussions—the closest approximation to a Comintern meeting since the seventh and last congress in 1935. The results were couched in two communiqués, one a declaration of "basic laws" and "unity of aims," the other a "peace manifesto" endorsing the objectives of Soviet foreign policy and signed by the representatives of sixty-four Communist parties. The declaration, by far the more significant document, recommended the revival of "popular fronts" in the non-Communist world "to win power without civil war." But the main theme was Communist unity—"the invincible camp of socialism headed by the Soviet Union." Khrushchev, Mao, and Gomulka signed, as did nine other Communist leaders whose parties enjoyed political power. Kardelj, the Yugoslav delegate, declined to affix his signature, and the Khrushchev-Tito quarrel was resumed thereafter in muted tones. Gomulka, too, was unhappy about the declaration, though he was not tempted to imitate Kardelj. Poland retained its unique status in the Communist world, but it was plain that her leaders were prudently bent upon curbing the "radicals" in the party who would follow the Yugoslav lead.

The major preoccupation of Soviet diplomacy during the first months of 1958 was a renewed drive for a top-level international conference. In the prolonged East-West debate accompanying the persistent overtures from Moscow, only one Soviet proposal—the so-called Rapacki

Plan—broke away from the rigid stance that both power blocs had so long maintained. Originally suggested by Polish Foreign Minister Adam Rapacki, it was a scheme to create a nuclear-free zone in Central Europe to be followed by a mutual withdrawal of armed forces. While some segments of Western opinion greeted the idea as a promising area for future negotiations, official Washington condemned it as another variation of the Kremlin's design for a neutral Germany and the eventual evacuation of American troops from Europe. The United States, while willing to be pushed toward a conference by its allies, preferred a preliminary meeting at the ambassadorial or foreign minister level to gauge Russian sincerity. The reluctance of the Atlantic powers to heed the Soviet call to the summit placed them at a disadvantage before neutral opinion; and some Westerners were inclined to agree with the harsh verdict rendered by British Labor party leader Hugh Gaitskell that the Anglo-American notes to Moscow had been "confused, clumsy and inadequate" and that both governments had acted with "continual prevarication" in their efforts to ward off the Soviet conference proposals.[2]

Gromyko's announcement before the Supreme Soviet on March 31, 1958, that the U.S.S.R. was voluntarily suspending tests of "all forms of atomic and hydrogen weapons" was clearly a political and propaganda victory for the Russians. Although Eisenhower referred to the action as a "gimmick" and Dulles called it "nothing but propaganda," it was not an effective answer to Khrushchev's gibe made at a public address in Budapest: "If Eisenhower really thinks that we have stopped . . . bomb tests for propaganda reasons, then why don't he and other Western statesmen conduct the same propaganda and stop the tests?" Moscow's move was timed with exquisite precision, for the Russians had just completed a series of nuclear tests and the United States was preparing to launch a series of its own.

During the spring Gromyko conferred individually and at length with the Big Three ambassadors in Moscow in an attempt to prepare the ground for their superiors. As these confidential negotiations inched forward, the Soviet government's previous ardor for a conference appeared to have diminished considerably. A charge that American aircraft were making "provocative" flights toward Russia over the Arctic region—certainly not a new development—was pressed in the United Nations, and Washington's proposal for an Arctic inspection system was vetoed in the Security Council. These unnecessary affronts to Western opinion were coupled with a renewed ideological onslaught upon Yugoslavia; and the fact that it was joined—indeed led—by Communist China served not only to highlight the resurgence of

"Stalinist" tendencies in Peking but to demonstrate as well the increasingly significant role that Mao and his colleagues were playing in the council tables of international Communism. Peking could scarcely fail to resent its intended exclusion from summit talks. Whether or not China's attitude was responsible for Khrushchev's shifting tactics, the Soviet premier was faced with domestic opposition that persistently cleaved to a "hard" line in matters of Communist orthodoxy and in the realm of foreign policy.

These internal pressures may have been conclusive in the decision to execute Imre Nagy, General Pal Maleter, and two other leaders of the Hungarian revolution in spite of the injury it would surely inflict upon the Soviet Union's international position. The news was released on June 17 after a secret trial in Budapest, and the wave of revulsion that swept the democratic world at this brutal act of political vengeance made meaningful diplomatic negotiations temporarily impossible. The bitterness of the Western reaction was undoubtedly a revelation to the Kremlin; but Communist propaganda obstinately contended that Nagy and his associates had been traitors, and in Moscow "popular" demonstrations were organized before the Danish, West German, and American embassies in retaliation for similar demonstrations in the West.

Recriminations over the Nagy affair had not yet quieted before the flames of another crisis in the Middle East began to lick at the precarious stability of East-West relations. A pro-Nasser, anti-American rebellion had broken out in the tiny pro-Western state of Lebanon on May 10 and could not be quelled by the half-hearted efforts of the regular army. President Camille Chamoun complained of a "massive infiltration" of men and arms across the Syrian border to aid the rebels —a charge later pronounced "not warranted" by a United Nations observation team—and called upon the United States for armed assistance. Washington seemed indisposed to intervene until the news of a successful anti-Western revolution in Iraq on July 14 caused great alarm in official circles that the whole of the Middle East might succumb to Nasser's brand of Arab nationalism and thus lower the flood gates to Soviet penetration on a major scale. The next day some 2,500 American marines were landed in Lebanon, followed by a somewhat larger number of British paratroopers who were flown to Jordan and to various points along the Persian Gulf as a precautionary measure. Again the Western powers—and this time the United States was regarded as the chief culprit—were arraigned before Communist, Arab, and neutral opinion as aggressors. It was an unexpected windfall for Moscow that somewhat obliterated the repellant odor of the Nagy case.

On July 19 Khrushchev seized the diplomatic initiative by proposing a heads-of-government meeting to begin in Geneva in three days. The United States, fearful of a propaganda circus with the effervescent Soviet premier as the star performer, favored a flatly negative answer but was prevailed upon by its allies to suggest as an alternative a summit conference within the framework of the U.N. Security Council. It was thought that the Russians would most certainly decline to attend so circumscribed a meeting, but Khrushchev's quick acceptance aroused consternation in Washington. However, the ensuing argument on procedural details, which in turn concealed the divergent strategies of the two super-powers, effectively blocked any immediate prospect of a meeting. China had been consistently ignored throughout the crisis, and its importance in the Communist world was given fresh emphasis when Khrushchev turned up in Peking for talks with Mao (July 31–August 3, 1958). Possibly to avoid the impression that his Chinese colleagues had vetoed a United Nations conference, Khrushchev waited until August 5 to dispatch a tart rejoinder to the latest Western proposals in which the Security Council was designated an "auxiliary organ" of the State Department. The General Assembly was called into emergency session when it became clear that there was to be no dramatic Khrushchev-Eisenhower confrontation in the Security Council. The inevitable deadlock was almost miraculously dissolved on August 21 when an Arab resolution was accepted without dissent: members of the Arab League were to avoid interference in one another's internal affairs, and foreign troops were to be withdrawn from Lebanon and Jordan.

As the tension abated in the Middle East, the world once more found itself "on the brink" as Communist China began an intensive artillery bombardment of the Nationalist-held Quemoy Islands a few miles off the coast. While not legally committed by its pact with Chiang to defend the numerous offshore islands along the Chinese mainland, the United States had since 1950 followed a policy dedicated to the "moral quarantine" of Peking and was unwilling to be exposed as a "paper tiger" by conceding that the islands were an integral part of China. Moscow stood by its ally in unequivocal terms, and Washington took the extreme measure of rejecting one of Khrushchev's letters to Eisenhower on the subject because of "false accusations" and "abusive and intemperate language."[3]

By late September the adamant American position began to weaken in the face of opposition at home and the openly critical attitude of the nations comprising the Western bloc. Peking responded with a cease-fire on October 6; and although the artillery barrage was temporarily renewed later in the month as a political demonstration, a tacit armistice was achieved early in November assuring a substantial reduction in the Nationalist garrison on Quemoy. The Chinese Communists were primarily interested in gaining Formosa rather than the offshore islands: the issue was only one of many capable of lighting the fuse for World War III.

The Western powers were granted no time for a breathing space. The Soviet government abruptly began a diplomatic offensive designed to maneuver them out of Berlin. The Russians disguised their aim by claiming that the Potsdam agreement was "out of date" because of Western violations and that it was time to end the four-power occupation. Presumably the solution favored by the Kremlin would involve handing over the traditional German capital to the East German regime, but a formal note from Khrushchev on November 27, 1958, contained a proposal that was reasonable enough on the surface: Berlin should become a demilitarized "free city." If negotiations had not progressed to this point within six months, he warned, Soviet forces would retire in favor of the German Democratic Republic. While there was no suggestion that the Berlin blockade would be reimposed, the threat was implied by the very nature of the situation. In any case, the Western allies refused to consider a withdrawal that would place West Berlin at the mercy of a Soviet puppet state.

Moscow maintained diplomatic pressure with a stream of press comment and impromptu declarations by Khrushchev. Russian strategy envisaged a Western retreat from Berlin as a first step toward neutralizing Germany, for the United States appeared determined to include West Germany in its plans for arming the NATO powers with nuclear weapons; and this eventuality the Soviet government was equally determined to prevent at any cost short of precipitating a shooting war. The other participants in the Atlantic coalition hung back from such a fateful move. They obviously preferred, in deference to a considerable groundswell of popular support, to negotiate some kind of agreement for military disengagement in Europe. Germany, of course, was the area of chief concern. Yet in an age of jet planes and intercontinental missiles the possibilities of reducing tension in such a manner were limited. Disarmament—or at least a halting beginning in the realm of nuclear test suspension—provided a more basic approach, but a three-power conference in Geneva (October 31–December 19, 1958) failed to dissolve the old differences on the problem of inspection and control before an end-of-the-year recess. Moscow had resumed its testing program on November 1, resolved to match the forty or more nuclear explosions that the United States and Britain had set off between them since the Gromyko declaration of March 31.

As the feints and alarms of the cold war continued to focus on Berlin in 1959, the Kremlin exerted its efforts in the direction of personal diplomacy by dispatching Mikoyan, now second only to Khrushchev in the party hierarchy, on an extended "unofficial" visit to the United States in January. The highest Soviet official ever to visit American soil, Mikoyan was an adroit and reasonably effective ambassador of good will. Yet he was unable to make significant headway against ingrained public skepticism of Russian motives and intentions. Prime Minister Macmillan's visit to the Soviet Union in February in response to a long-standing invitation was somewhat more productive as a diplomatic mission. His talks with the temperamental Khrushchev were not uniformly friendly—the Soviet leader became so annoyed on one occasion that he refused to accompany his guest on a scheduled trip to Kiev because of a "toothache"—but the total result was encouraging to the proponents of negotiation. Moscow seemed willing to postpone its tentative May 27 deadline for a Berlin settlement, and in March both power blocs agreed to a meeting of foreign ministers. Khrushchev's remark at a press conference—"Let's put in the heavyweights"—epitomized, however, the Soviet preference for a top-level parley.

The meeting of the foreign ministers in Geneva (May 11–June 20, July 13–August 5, 1959) disclosed the usual disagreements on Germany and Berlin. If possible, Gromyko was more unyielding than in the past, though his conduct off the rostrum was one of amiable good fellowship. The rigidity of his instructions from Moscow allowed no leeway for true negotiations. The peripatetic Soviet premier frequently sniped at the Western position from vantage points in the Communist capitals. An exchange of visits between Soviet Deputy Premier Frol Kozlov and Vice President Richard M. Nixon during the summer months offered more lively press copy than the interminable round of diplomatic charades at Geneva. The foreign ministers parted with a less pronounced sense of failure than they had in 1955. After so many disappointments, one more was only routine. And in talking instead of threatening imminent moves against the Western enclave in Berlin, the Russians at least assumed a more agreeable posture than could have been expected six months before. Moreover, the delegates were apprised that Khrushchev had accepted an invitation to visit the

United States in September and that Eisenhower would reciprocate later in the fall.

Washington's retreat on the sore question of receiving the effervescent "Mr. K." (to use the shorthand of American headline writers) predated the death of Secretary Dulles in May. But the actual decision was not reached until July, and final arrangements were not completed until late August. Two days before Khrushchev's scheduled arrival in Washington the Soviet Union successfully launched a "lunik"—a rocket to the moon. In the words of Sir Bernard Lovell, a prominent British astronomer, it was "a brilliant demonstration of the advanced state of Russian technology." The feat was a well-timed piece of political showmanship and underscored the Soviet leader's sensitivity to issues of national prestige, especially in the field of scientific and economic competition with the United States.

Khrushchev's stay (September 15–27) involved a coast-to-coast tour and furnished such vignettes of American life as a Hollywood movie production and an Iowa corn farm. Curiosity was the predominant mood of the general public. Khrushchev was quick to note it: pointing to his nearly bald pate, he quipped that he had scarcely enough hair to conceal a pair of horns. His salty proverbs and ready wit alternated with moods of petulance and anger, a baffling combination of personality traits that few were prepared to unravel. But it was generally agreed that as a tough, shrewd, and agile politician he had no superior either in the Communist or the democratic world.

The most productive feature of Khrushchev's visit from the diplomatic standpoint was an informal meeting with Eisenhower at the presidential retreat in Camp David, Maryland. In return for a withdrawal of the Soviet "ultimatum" on Berlin, Eisenhower agreed to a summit conference in Paris the following spring. His journey to the Soviet Union was thus postponed, partly to help prevent any untoward incident from disrupting the "spirit of Camp David."

The dramatic and highly publicized program for complete and universal disarmament that Khrushchev presented to the United Nations was received with cool skepticism. It was reminiscent of Litvinov's utopian venture in 1927, and as on the earlier occasion the cry of "propaganda" was raised. Although the two situations were basically dissimilar—the Soviet Union of forty years before was incapable of aggressive action against a major power—an attempt to highlight the "peace loving" nature of the Soviet regime and the "warlike" propensities of the capitalist nations was a common ingredient of both performances. The Russia of 1959 had already been on trial in so many ineffectual disarmament conferences that the circumstances under which Khrushchev chose to present his scheme could not be other than suspicious. The proposal was eventually shunted to the new ten-nation disarmament committee scheduled to meet in 1960.

After stopping briefly in Moscow, the Soviet premier went on to Peking for secret talks with the Chinese leaders in connection with the tenth anniversary of the Chinese People's Republic. China's "great leap forward" in building an industrial society was accompanied by an increasingly aggressive foreign policy. For the time being an apostle of the *status quo*, Khrushchev gently chided his hosts by reminding them that it was wrong to "test the stability of the capitalist system by force." Marxists, he observed, "recognize only wars of liberation" and condemn those that are "predatory and imperialistic." The Chinese displayed no open resentment, but they also showed no disposition to relax their unbending stand against the United States.

Moscow spoke softly on the major cold war issues during the fall and early winter as the Western leaders debated among themselves about a common policy at the forthcoming summit conference. Yet the firm tone of Soviet pronouncements in the new year, particularly the Warsaw Pact communiqué on Germany (February 4, 1960), revealed no concessions to the Western view on Berlin. Khrushchev visited India, Burma, Indonesia, and Afghanistan (February 11–March 5), his first journey to South Asia since 1955. His speeches constantly compared the vigorous growth of the Soviet economy with the "decadent bourgeois" capitalism of the West. In late March, seeking to influence French opinion before the meeting with Eisenhower in Paris, the Soviet premier embarked on a tour of France. He sought to break up the incipient Franco-German *rapprochement* inaugurated by President Charles de Gaulle, and in one intemperate outburst he accused Adenauer of Hitlerite tendencies. His warnings about a revival of German militarism were skillfully designed to arouse the dormant anxieties of French patriots.

As the May 16 summit deadline approached, there was no relaxation of the Soviet "hard line" on Berlin. But neither was there any advance warning that the comparative serenity of cold war politics was to be shattered once more. On May 1, 1960, an American photo-reconnaissance plane, a single-engine U-2 jet, was shot down at an altitude of 68,000 feet some 1,300 miles inside the Russian border. This was the version released in Moscow in successive installments beginning on May 5, and its essence was subsequently confirmed by the captured pilot and by "espionage equipment" found in the wrecked aircraft.

Washington's embarrassment was compounded by blundering prevarication: the missing plane was at first declared to have been lost on a routine weather research flight, and when this explanation proved untenable, it was announced that no deliberate attempt had been made to violate Soviet air space. On May 9 an official statement admitted that for several years "extensive aerial surveillance" had been conducted over Soviet territory.

No better propaganda bonanza could have been arranged for the Soviet Union had Khrushchev himself directed the enterprise from start to finish. It was useless to point out that Soviet espionage of a less obtrusive kind was normal procedure and that geographical disadvantages combined with a lack of foreign bases deterred the Russians from similar flights. Khrushchev adopted the tone of an injured martyr and seemed willing to absolve Eisenhower from personal responsibility. But the President, following the somewhat archaic tradition of the commander-in-chief who automatically assumes either credit or censure for the acts of subordinates, shouldered the blame and refused to apologize for what, after all, was a flagrant breach of international law. "Overflights" were in fact justified by Secretary of State Christian A. Herter as necessary to protect the American people and "free peoples everywhere" from the danger of a surprise attack, and he implied that they would continue. Mindful of his own domestic position, Khrushchev denounced the statement as both "outrageous" and "impudent."

The Soviet premier arrived in Paris sooner than expected—May 14. After conferring informally with de Gaulle the next day, he demanded that the United States express its regrets, cancel further flights, and punish those responsible before he would attend the conference. Although he had already ordered the suspension of aerial espionage, Eisenhower refused to accept the humiliation of a Soviet ultimatum. The summit meeting therefore expired on this note of mutual frustration and injured national pride. On May 18 Khrushchev held an extraordinary press conference in Paris in which he put his case in such scurrilous language that it repelled most of his listeners and confirmed the Western impression that he had intentionally wrecked the parley. His mounting indignation after May 1 suggests, however, less a desire to torpedo the Paris negotiations out of pure spite than an effort to prove to his critics—both at home and in China—that Soviet policy had not grown pusillanimous under his care. The U-2 affair was simply not an issue about which Khrushchev could afford to be accommodating, especially when the United States tried to gloss over its action with fumbling denials and self-serving explanations.

II

Despite the summit fiasco, the Russians permitted the Berlin question to lie relatively quiescent for a time. But on other diplomatic fronts they pursued an obstreperous course that offered no prospect of a *détente*. Among several new international trouble spots, the anarchic situation in the Republic of the Congo gave Moscow a temporary foothold in African affairs. The Congolese, though wholly unprepared for self-government, were precipitously granted independence by Belgium in June 1960. The United Nations, invited to intervene in July by the central government at Leopoldville, sent in troops to maintain order. Premier Patrice Lumumba was less anxious to protect lives and property than to expel Belgian forces and to secure control over the separatist provinces—notably Katanga—that had broken away from Leopoldville. Failing United Nations support for these aims, he threatened to call in Soviet troops. Moscow, fulfilling its self-assigned role as guardian of "colonial" nations against "Western imperialism," expressed its willingness to dispatch "volunteers" while subjecting U.N. Secretary-General Dag Hammarskjold to unwarranted abuse for an arduous and thankless task. In August the U.S.S.R. and Czechoslovakia began sending aircraft and military supplies to Lumumba for use against his internal enemies.

In September 1960 the tangled politics of the Congo were enmeshed in a fresh crisis when President Joseph Kasavubu, acting without parliamentary sanction, dismissed the demagogic Lumumba. The latter refused to abide by what he considered an illegal seizure of power, but he was placed under house arrest by Congolese troops commanded by Colonel Joseph Mobutu. The swollen Soviet and Czech embassy staffs, ordered to leave Leopoldville, departed by air on September 17. Blocked in the U.N. and ousted from the Congo, the Russians were reduced to the status of boorish spectators. The imprisoned Lumumba remained a Soviet hero, while Mobutu was denounced as an "ignoramus Napoleon" and Kasavubu was derided as a *"putschist* in the hire of American imperialists."

Moscow's sense of grievance was redoubled in February 1961 when Lumumba was murdered, apparently while in custody. An angry mob stoned the Belgian embassy in the Russian capital, and meetings of protest were held throughout the Soviet Union. Lumumba's deputy premier, the pro-Communist Antoine Gizenga, had meanwhile organized a government in Stanleyville, and he received Soviet recognition as the legitimate ruler of the Congo. But the colorless and timid Gizenga rallied few supporters, and as the Congo achieved a modicum of political stability in 1962 a real lever for Soviet influence was lacking. "Of all our African friends," complained one Communist bloc leader, "Gizenga is the real pigmy."

A more successful foray of international Communism—or so it was regarded in Washington—was the establishment of Fidel Castro's revolutionary regime in Cuba. As successor in 1959 to the degenerate and brutal dictatorship of Fulgencio Batista, "Fidelismo" won the cautious approval of American liberals and struck political sparks everywhere in Latin America. Castro's repressive single-party rule, his insistence on radical economic and social reforms, and his flirtation with Moscow all combined to wipe out this favorable first impression. Official relations between Washington and Havana became strained in 1960 after the nationalization of American property in Cuba and a near embargo on the importation of Cuban sugar into the United States. In a speech on July 9 Khrushchev promised Soviet help in resisting the "economic blockade" by the United States and warned of possible military aid "should the aggressive forces in the Pentagon dare to start intervention in Cuba." Trade and assistance agreements with China and other Communist nations so alarmed Washington that its politicians and diplomats openly talked as if Cuba had become a Russian satellite in the Caribbean.

Under the auspices of the Central Intelligence Agency, the United States began the clandestine training of anti-Castro *émigrés* in Florida and Guatemala. On April 17, 1961, a force of some 1,400 men landed before dawn on a swampy Cuban beach. Relying on a popular revolt which never materialized, the invaders—all Cubans—were cut down or taken prisoner. Before the extent of the debacle became known, Khrushchev sent a heated protest to President John F. Kennedy. Citing the fact that the aggressors had been "trained, equipped, and armed in the United States," he pledged the Castro regime "all necessary assistance." Thousands of demonstrators converged on the American embassy in Moscow and had to be fought off by Soviet police and militia.

The invasion was an admitted fiasco. Cynical French journalists, veterans of Hungary and Algeria, lampooned it as "Budapest managed by choir boys." It was a minor political trauma and an educational catharsis for the American people and their leaders. The Kennedy administration comprehended that the yeast of social revolution was in ferment throughout Latin America, and it had the wisdom to initiate a bold program of economic aid—the Alliance for Progress—in the hope of raising living standards and making Fidelismo less appealing to the impoverished masses. Castro eventually acknowledged that he was a "Marxist-Leninist"; his well-wishers deplored his erratic leadership and his enemies denounced him as a Communist stooge.

Washington's anxiety about Cuba, which had moderated during the first part of 1962, flared up again when Soviet military assistance to Castro's regime became a reality. On October 24, 1962, the United States instituted an arms blockade of Cuba, charging that missile bases had been constructed and manned by Russian personnel. With this bold challenge to the Soviet Union, the world was plunged into the most acute crisis since the onset of the cold war. Khrushchev reacted with comparative restraint and admitted the substance of the American charges by offering to give up Soviet bases if the United States reciprocated by removing its missiles from Turkey. Kennedy brushed off the proposal as the United States threatened air attacks on the Cuban installations if the missile sites were not abandoned. Khrushchev then accepted the American position by promising to dismantle the Soviet rockets. In return, the United States pledged that the blockade would be lifted and that Cuba would not be invaded. The immediate crisis passed quickly, but the propensity of great powers to "coordinate" small and obnoxious neighbors—a point that the United States had made with telling effect in the case of the Soviet Union—did not augur well for the future of Fidelist Cuba.

A third area of Communist penetration was Southeast Asia, where the North Vietnam regime of Ho Chi Minh was more directly concerned than the Soviet Union. The tiny landlocked kingdom of Laos, created at the Geneva Conference in 1954 as a neutral buffer state, was disrupted by periodic *coups* and sporadic civil war. A Communist-led guerrilla movement—the Pathet Lao ("Land of Lao")— had gained control over two northeastern provinces during the Indochinese conflict and sought a share in the government coalition of Prince Souvanna Phouma. A Right wing clique seized power in 1958, and as the recipient of indiscriminate American largess it soon acquired an unsavory but well-deserved reputation for waste and corruption. The Pathet Lao, drawing upon adjacent North Vietnam for supplies and equipment, began to harass government forces in the summer of 1959. Guerrilla activity became less menacing when a United Nations investigating team was sent to Laos in the fall. But it flared up again in the latter part of 1960 as factional strife ended any immediate hope of installing a neutralist regime that would satisfy the great powers. Soviet planes based in North Vietnam sent aid to the rebels, and the United States assisted the "legal" government based in Vientiane. The Pathet Lao controlled about half the country when a cease-fire went into effect on May 3, 1961, prior to a fourteen-nation conference on

os in Geneva. Pressure was placed on the principal Laotian politi-
ns to form a coalition cabinet under Souvanna Phouma, a scheme
at was stalled for many months by the obstructionist tactics of the
nerican-backed Prince Boun Oum. On July 23, 1962, agreement was
ally reached by the Geneva representatives. A neutralist government
as established, and the independence and territorial integrity of the
untry was guaranteed by the participating powers.

As a semblance of peace was restored to Laos in 1961, South
etnam erupted into violence. Some 12,000 Viet Cong (Communist)
errillas, their jungle supply line from the north intact, fought the
0,000-man army of President Ngo Dinh Diem. Trained by some 8,000
nited States troops and equipped with the latest American weapons,
e forces of the Vietnamese Republic were unable in 1962 to make
nificant headway. Ngo's authoritarian and scandal-ridden govern-
ent was the prototype of others that sought to extirpate Com-
unism solely by military repression. Moscow and Peking, though at
ds on other issues, charged Washington with incendiary moves
at might endanger world peace.

The addition of France in 1960 to the heretofore exclusive "nuclear
ub" of the United States, the Soviet Union, and Great Britain pointed
the dangers of an accelerating arms race. On June 27, 1960, alleging
estern bad faith, the Communist delegates abruptly quit the ten-
tion disarmament conference in Geneva. The Russians suggested
rther negotiations at the regular autumn session of the U.N. General
ssembly. To highlight the importance of the occasion, Khrushchev
mself proposed to attend, and he urged the leaders of the other
ember states to do likewise. This novel approach to United Nations
plomacy naturally commended itself to the Communist nations. The
utrals were also attracted, and even Eisenhower was induced to
ake a formal address. The President, who declared beforehand that
did not intend to debase the U.N. by being a party to a "battle of
vective and propaganda," carefully avoided a personal meeting with
hrushchev. As an assemblage of notables it was by far the most
ectacular gathering in the history of the United Nations.

The regular business of the Assembly was deferred until after the
atform summitry had been completed. Khrushchev's blistering as-
ults on Western policy, coupled with his rowdy antics—heckling,
sk-pounding, and shoe-waving—stole the publicity spotlight. His
peal to "mount the final offensive against colonialism" was warmly
ceived by the Asian and African representatives, yet his renewed
tack on Hammarskjold and his proposal to replace the office of the
cretariat by a three-man executive committee aroused little favorable

sentiment outside the Communist entourage. The Soviet premier' departure from New York on October 13 left the basic pattern of th cold war unchanged.

The election of a new American president in November encourage(Moscow to sponsor a brief honeymoon with the incoming administra tion. The steady propaganda drumbeat about Berlin was muffled, an(the supposed iniquities of West Germany were less fully and offen sively catalogued. Khrushchev even offered to forget the U-2 affai as Soviet diplomats dropped hints that another try at the summit coul(be arranged. President Kennedy responded cautiously and indicate(through his ambassador in Moscow, who had been recalled for cor sultation, that he preferred normal channels of diplomacy. By Marc 1961 the Soviet press had adopted a more caustic tone, and *Izvesti* lodged a waspish complaint that Kennedy had not yet cleaned out th "Augean stables" left by the Eisenhower administration and was pe haps getting "used to the stench."

On April 12 the Soviet Union won another victory in the race int outer space by launching a five-ton manned rocket into orbit aroun the earth. The historic achievement confirmed Russia's leadership i rocketry and spurred recurrent but unfounded Western fears that th United States was lagging behind in the missile field. Khrushchev foreign policy, already too recalcitrant for Washington, could not b(derive strength from this fresh technological break-through. The d(terioration of Soviet-American relations to a point approximating th of Eisenhower's final months in office so bothered Kennedy that l arranged an informal meeting with Khrushchev in Vienna on Ju 3–4. It was announced that "frank, courteous, and wide-ranging" e changes had taken place, a rather euphemistic description of wh were in fact "somber talks" (Kennedy's phrase) that revealed no d position to back down on either side.

Berlin was the perpetual "bone" stuck in Khrushchev's throat, an he renewed his threat to sign a separate peace treaty with Ea Germany. Kennedy countered with a buildup of American milita strength. The West Berlin garrison was reinforced as Moscow order(the East Berlin authorities to seal off the border from the Weste zone. On September 1 the Soviet Union broke the informal moratoriu on nuclear testing, a voluntary ban in effect (except for the four te: by France) for almost three years. In drawing upon itself the mo: opprobrium of being the first of the Big Three to resume nuclear te: ing, the Soviet government acted under a rigid conception of the r tional interest. The stationary Russian missile bases were high vulnerable to a "pre-emptive" strike by the United States, a:

rushchev presumably deferred to expert military opinion in seeking
ore mobile ballistic missiles.

Apart from further pollution of the atmosphere with radioactivity,
e Soviet violation of the truce aroused fresh tremors of apprehension
out the unstable "balance of terror" and aggravated the already
ave tensions between East and West. "Once again the foul winds
 war are blowing," observed a discouraged Nehru as he arrived in
oscow to reason with Khrushchev. Kennedy ordered a resumption of
derground testing but avoided following the Soviet example until
 seventeen-nation conference, beginning in Geneva in March 1962,
d wrestled anew with the elusive phantom of disarmament.

The internal stresses and strains of the Communist orbit were oc-
sionally, sometimes inadvertently, revealed to outsiders. The mono-
hic unity that Stalin had briefly contrived before the split with Tito
as shattered beyond repair. No one openly challenged Khrushchev
 the leadership of international Communism, but his authority
sted less upon the ruthless exercise of force—always a latent threat
than the traditional primacy of the Soviet party. The word "Comunist," loosely used to describe a variety of individuals and countries
knowledging the principles of Marx and Lenin, had become a
mantic monstrosity by the 1960's. Yugoslavia was Communist by
to's definition but preferred the role of an independent nation aloof
om the quarrels of the great powers; Poland retained the peculiar
mi-autonomy of "Gomulkaism"; Cuba was a "fellow traveler" with
bious credentials as a Communist state; the new African republics
 Ghana, Mali, and Guinea, whether from motives of opportunism or
nuine conviction, were warmly sympathetic to Soviet Communism;
d China, the new enigma among world powers, demonstratively
lled away from Moscow's guidance.

The growing rift between China and the Soviet Union became a
atter of public record in 1960. The presence of a common foe in the
nited States was the chief preservative of the shaky Sino-Soviet
liance. Until 1956, when Khrushchev's impetuous attack on the cult
 Stalin caught Peking by surprise, the Chinese were content to
knowledge Russia's seniority as the political and ideological director
 the Communist camp. They deeply resented the lack of consultation
eforehand, and in later years Khrushchev's unilateral courtship of
e United States was extremely irritating to Mao and his colleagues.
hey were also offended by Soviet interference in the intra-party
ruggle of 1959 when the Chinese defense minister, Marshal Peng
eh-huai, obtained Moscow's backing for his criticism of the Maoist
ne. Nor did the Kremlin's refusal to share nuclear weapons or scien-

tific information and its ostentatious lack of support for China's d
putes with India and Indonesia seem to Peking the proper way
maintain good comradely relations. China, still in a stage of "primiti
socialist accumulation," felt that relative prosperity had weakened t
Russians' moral fiber: the revolutionary zeal expected of sincere Ma
ists was lacking, and the struggle against "capitalist imperialism" h
faltered. It was not, as the West mistakenly assumed, that the Chine
believed in the inevitability of a third world war. But they did affi
the warlike nature of the enemy and the necessity of assisting "natio
liberation movements."

Moscow had at first declined to be drawn into a doctrinal confl
with the Peking dialecticians. Unable to ignore these pinpricks
definitely, yet unwilling to bring the controversy out into the op
the Soviet press resorted to Aesopian language in the summer of 19
and campaigned against "leftists," "dogmatists," and "sectarians." Be
the Russians and the Chinese circularized the other parties in sear
of ideological allies. In November the anniversary of the Bolshe
Revolution was the excuse for a new gathering of the Communist cla
Delegations from eighty-one parties participated in a lengthy co
ference in Moscow to draft a statement of principles to replace t
1957 declaration. An ambiguous compromise in the name of unity w
the chief result. The prolix document issued on December 6 serv
for a time to bind the wounds of international party strife. Liu Sha
chi, the titular head of the Chinese People's Republic, was among t
signatories, and in his subsequent tour of the Soviet Union extolli
Sino-Soviet friendship he politely refrained from hinting at the d
sension behind the scenes.

The two Communist giants clashed publicly less than a year la
over the issue of Albania, China's diminutive Balkan satellite. Env
Hoxha, Albania's vest pocket Stalin, was an ardent foe of Titoism a
had incurred Khrushchev's wrath at the Communist meeting in M
cow. (He had called the Soviet chieftain a traitor to the Commun
idea, and the enraged Khrushchev is said to have shouted: "Comra
Hoxha, you have poured a bucket of dung on me, and you will ha
to wash it off!")[4] At the twenty-second congress of the Soviet Co
munist party in October 1961, Khrushchev denounced Albania for
Stalinist tactics. Chou En-lai, one of the "fraternal" delegates, repli
by questioning the manner in which the Soviet premier had chos
to chastise the Hoxha regime: "If there are quarrels in the social
camp, we consider that they should be settled through bilateral co
tacts." Pleading urgent business in Peking, he left the congress in mi
session.

Another round in the periodic bouts of "de-Stalinization" seized oscow. Such political straw men as Molotov, Voroshilov, Malenkov, d Kaganovich were again set up as targets for Khrushchev and e party elite. A pointed rebuke to Peking was also concealed in e energetic campaign to exorcise Stalin's crimes by casting his name to the memory hole along with those of Trotsky, Zinoviev, Bukharin, d other fallen heroes of the Soviet past. Only a few days after Chou d deposited a floral wreath in the Lenin-Stalin mausoleum—it was scribed "To J. V. Stalin, the great Marxist-Leninist"—Stalin's corpse s removed for burial near the Kremlin wall. Perhaps the ultimate dignity was the renaming of Stalin's city on the Volga: Stalingrad, llowed by the deeds of the Red Army, became Volgagrad.

In December 1961 the Soviet Union broke diplomatic relations with bania. Peking stood by the Tirana government while shying away m an overt offensive against Moscow. Soviet economic and techcal assistance, though parsimonious and grudging, was a valued set in overcoming the calamities of nature that plagued the Chinese anners. And no matter how harshly Moscow and Peking berated ch other in their respective propaganda organs, only the most exeme provocation could have produced a political schism in the face the capitalist adversary. Western "Kremlinologists" habitually igred these uncomfortable realities in their eagerness to expose the scord in Communist ranks. Nevertheless, the history of both political d religious doctrine demonstrates that an ideological fissure, even en papered over with verbal adjustments, widens with a momentum its own. In the long run the cleavage in the Sino-Soviet axis was ely to become a permanent feature of the Communist landscape.

NOTES

1. *New York Times,* October 17, 1957.
2. *Ibid.,* March 30, 1958.
3. *Ibid.,* September 21, 1958.
4. *Ibid.,* March 31, 1961.

CHAPTER SIXTEEN

SOVIET COMMUNISM AND THE GLOBAL STRUGGLE

The Russian Revolution is now far enough in the past to acquire
aura of historical inevitability—even of respectability. Like the Fren
Revolution in the age of optimism before the First World War, it h
been the twentieth century's great catharsis—a symbol of the eleme
tal violence and radical social change that has characterized the pa
half-century. The Revolution was corrupted by Stalinism, just as t
French ideals of "liberty, equality and fraternity" were defaced
Bonapartism. Yet the search for a more just and humane social ord
was never abandoned. Soviet Communism has never deliberate
sought to imitate the savage nihilism of German Nazism, either
the domestic or the international scene, although the unfortuna
victims of Stalin's concentration camps could certainly be pardon
for failing to grasp the distinction.

To say, as Khrushchev has in effect, that Stalinism was a diversi
from the true path of Marxism-Leninism is a facile and overly simp
explanation of an intricate subject. And so, too, is the Western versi
that Marx provided the intellectual tools and Lenin the practi
weapons for the closed society that triumphed in the Soviet Unic
The cross-fertilization of socialist doctrine with economic backwar
ness produced in Russian Bolshevism an apparent mutation from t
"normal" course of civilized development. To the property-minded an
relatively prosperous citizens of the West, the Soviet Union was
unappetizing mélange of rude compulsion and political fanaticism—
caricature of the abject poverty and brutal tyranny that the Bolshev
conspirators of Tsarist times thought they were combating. In spite
the strenuous missionary efforts of international Communism, t
"wage slaves" of industrial capitalism were sluggish and unresponsiv
Only in the under-developed countries of Asia, Africa, and La

erica have the restive masses, seeking an escape from their grinding
and constant penury, proved susceptible to Communist appeals.

he Kremlin's attempt to combine the conventional attributes of a
:ign policy with formal devotion to the revolutionary ideals of
nmunism has been the source of confusion to both friends and
·ersaries. Stalin's imperialist ventures in Eastern Europe, widely
alded as the spearhead of a great Communist offensive, were in
lity carried out in the best tradition of Russian nationalism. The
ive Communist movements received at best only token encourage-
nt. Stalin's disdain for truly revolutionary change, except when
nessed to the interests of the Soviet state, sabotaged the prospects
international Communism, brought on the Yugoslav schism, and
to moral depravity and bureaucratic ossification at home.
rushchev broke out of the cul-de-sac of Stalinism, only to become
neshed in the political and ideological quicksands of national Com-
nism. More flexible than Stalin, he has nevertheless been harried
contradictions within Soviet-style socialism not unlike those fore-
n by Marx in the workings of bourgeois capitalism. The benefits of
nned production, an alluring but distant mirage to the consuming
>lic, are at last within reach; the assault upon illiteracy has yielded
ew generation of comparatively sophisticated technicians, admin-
ators, and specialists; and the phenomenal growth of science and
nnology threatens to surpass Western capabilities in many fields.
t the institutional basis of a free society lags badly. Authority from
)ve and obedience from below remains the unacknowledged premise
party philosophy and governmental practice. While no longer a
ice state, at least in the forbidding image of untrammeled despotism
l pictured in the democratic West, the Soviet Union lingers in the
)crustean bed of totalitarianism. A barrier to domestic progress and
obstacle to the spread of Communism abroad, Soviet totalitarianism
retained some of its most repugnant features even under the "be-
n" aegis of Khrushchev. His successors, heeding the compulsion of
ernal pressure, will undoubtedly make more far-reaching conces-
ns to political and intellectual freedom.

)nly a shooting war or the unbearable tensions associated with
bal brinkmanship are likely to forestall further mellowing trends
5oviet Communism. These possibilities are, of course, always present,
is the very real danger of an accidental triggering of a nuclear
ocaust. The U.S.S.R. is now the conservative power within the
nmunist bloc, and any aggressive moves are apt to be initiated by
Chinese. As the affluent partner in an unstable alliance, Moscow
become a cautious apostle of the *status quo* in those areas where

no vital national interest is at stake. The thriving Communist part
of India and Indonesia are docile supporters of the constituted
thorities; and in the diplomatic crises over Laos and South Vietn
Moscow's disposition to compromise smacked of appeasement
Peking. "Anti-colonialism" is a major theme of Soviet propagan
however, and no opportunity has been lost—the Congo was a flagr
case in point—to pose as the defender of the downtrodden and
champion of the disinherited.

Soviet prerogatives within its own orbit are jealously guarded, a
nothing is so calculated to enrage the Russians as Washington's p
vocative statements about the "captive nations" of Eastern Euro
Berlin is in the anomalous position of a Soviet redoubt and an isla
of Western influence behind the Iron Curtain. Until the city can
neutralized as a minimum precaution against periodic war scares,
problem of Germany—and of European equilibrium—will conti
to disturb East-West relations. The political unification of German
scarcely negotiable, but neutralization of the country as a "free zo
in the escalating arms race presents a more hopeful means of esc
from the German maze. Washington's anxiety about a Soviet milit
takeover in Western Europe, an assumption that was never re
tenable, has so far blocked this approach. To equate the Kreml
churlish manners, dogmatic certainties, and delusions of persecut
with aggressive intentions is not the proper basis for a construct
foreign policy.

The spread of indigenous Communism, not the supposed threat
invading Soviet armies, will increasingly concern the Western pow
Neither hydrogen bombs nor anti-guerrilla combat teams are effect
methods of checking Communism when the alternative is reaction
dictatorship and an archaic social system. However bitterly Mosc
and Peking may clash on the proper response to anti-Communist mo
both are agreed that "national liberation movements" are the inevita
course of history and should be given encouragement and assistan
To suppose that such Communist successes, wherever and un
what conditions they may occur, necessarily pose an automatic th
to Western security is to imbue Communism with diabolical quali
that it does not possess. A few more Yugoslavias might actu
enhance Western security. A conspiratorial view of the historical p
ess corrodes the healthy functioning of a democratic society. Polit
freedom and the sanctity of the human personality are powe
weapons, but they are worthless unless the search for social jus
includes a commitment to the physical well being of the individual.

With the world already deeply mired in a second decade of c

r, it is perfectly apparent that a majority of its three billion inhab-
nts are less concerned with the rights and wrongs of the international
wer struggle than with the means of combating mankind's oldest
l most persistent enemy—hunger. Until more energetic measures
e taken to curb the disastrous rate of population growth, political
ology will be subordinate to the struggle for survival. Largely by
cumstance rather than by design, the two super-powers have ar-
ged a precarious armed truce. "Victory" in the long-range contest
ween two ways of life, assuming that Armageddon is indefinitely
stponed, should logically go to the side that wins over the un-
mmitted masses.

Conventional methods of capital appreciation have elevated the
ndard of living of Americans and West Europeans to unparalleled
ghts. Elsewhere they have been inadequate. India, despite its
tral foreign policy, has symbolized the Western hope that a com-
ation of private enterprise and government assistance would sig-
cantly raise living standards and provide a democratic answer to
challenge of Communism. But the harsh "Stalinist" methods of
ina have brought her more quickly within striking distance of
ustrial greatness; and they furnish an alternative—though its com-
sive features are unattractive—to the perpetual treadmill of over-
pulation, underconsumption, and low levels of production. Whatever
United States may do to pretend that the "real" China is ensconced
the island of Formosa, a Communist giant of 650,000,000 souls is
nly established in East Asia; and it is bound to exert an ever greater
hority in world politics. Soviet leaders have occasionally intimated
"off the record" discussions that they also recognize the dangers
erent in a dynamic revolutionary state with a population approach-
a quarter of the earth's inhabitants.

Western speculation about a future entente with the Soviet Union
ed on mutual concern over a hypothetical "yellow peril" can only
considered fanciful midst the immediate problems of shoring up
leaky bulkheads of peaceful coexistence. By an increasingly effec-
e program of assistance to non-Communist countries and by a
ndiose Seven Year Plan announced at the twenty-first party congress
January 1959, Moscow served notice that an economic dimension
l been added to the global contest. Americans have been especially
ne to assume the inferiority of Communism as an economic system
ause of the notoriously low standard of living that has always
vailed in the Soviet Union. But with a rate of industrial growth
re than twice that of the United States, the decade of the 1960's
uld lend weight to Khrushchev's prediction that his country will

eventually lead the world in both productive capacity and liv standards. Future Soviet leaders will undoubtedly pay a price for t prosperity in a further loss of revolutionary *élan* and in the continu fragmentation of world Communism. The prospect of peaceful e nomic competition is therefore one that the West should encoura whatever the limitations of "free enterprise" as an article of exp

BIBLIOGRAPHY

e following works represent a selection of those used or consulted
the preparation of the present volume. A few recent publications
re added, however, after the manuscript had been completed. With
umber of exceptions, articles and unpublished works have been
itted. Less significant publications cited in the reference notes have
 been omitted. It is understood that a chapter-by-chapter arrange-
nt is somewhat arbitrary, for many books relevant to more than one
apter are listed only once.

GENERAL: FOREIGN RELATIONS

ennan's *Russia and the West* is a brilliant series of essays. Fischer
till standard on the 1920's, as is Beloff on the 1930's, but neither is
table for the general reader. Dallin's two volumes are likewise stand-
 on Far Eastern relations, although first-rate studies of Sino-Soviet
1 Japanese-Soviet relations are lacking. Laqueur, an able survey of
ddle Eastern relations, is chiefly concerned with the 1950's. While
ming is encyclopedic on the cold war, his analysis of Soviet policy
ather uncritical.

ams, Arthur E. (ed.). *Readings in Soviet Foreign Policy*. Boston, 1961.
en, Luther A. "The French Left and Soviet Russia to 1936: Inter-
action Between French Party Alliances and Franco-Soviet Diplo-
nacy." Ph.D. thesis, University of Chicago, 1955.
nstrong, John A. *The Politics of Totalitarianism: The Communist
Party of the Soviet Union from 1934 to the Present*. New York, 1961.
torkhanov, Abdurakhman. *Stalin and the Soviet Communist Party*.
New York, 1959.
iley, Thomas A. *America Faces Russia*. Ithaca, N.Y., 1950.
rghoorn, Frederick C. *The Soviet Image of the United States: A
Study in Distortion*. New York, 1950.
rmine, Alexander. *One Who Survived*. New York, 1945.

Beloff, Max. *The Foreign Policy of Soviet Russia, 1929–1941.* 2 v New York, 1947–49.

Bessedowsky, Grigorij. *Den Klauen der Tscheka entronnen: E nerungen.* Leipzig and Zurich, 1930.

Bilmanis, Alfred. *A History of Latvia.* Princeton, N.J., 1951.

Bishop, Donald G. (ed.). *Soviet Foreign Relations: Documents Readings.* Syracuse, N.Y., 1952.

Buss, Claude A. *War and Diplomacy in Eastern Asia.* New York, 19

Cardwell, Ann Su [Margaret Super]. *Poland and Russia: The L Quarter Century.* New York, 1944.

Carr, Edward Hallett. *German-Soviet Relations Between the T World Wars, 1919–1939.* Baltimore, 1951.

Chase, Thomas G. *The Story of Lithuania.* New York, 1946.

Cheng, Tien-fong. *A History of Sino-Russian Relations.* Washingt 1956.

Chiang Kai-shek. *Soviet Russia in China: A Summing-Up at Seve* New York, 1957.

Coates, W. P. and Zelda K. *A History of Anglo-Soviet Relations.* 2 v London, 1944–58.

———. *Six Centuries of Russo-Polish Relations.* London, 1948.

Conquest, Robert. *Power and Policy in the U.S.S.R.* New York, 1961

Craig, Gordon A., and Gilbert, Felix (eds.). *The Diplomats, 1919–19 Princeton, N.J., 1953.

Creel, George. *Russia's Race for Asia.* Indianapolis, 1949.

Dallin, Alexander (comp.). *Soviet Conduct in World Affairs.* N York, 1960.

Dallin, David J. *The Rise of Russia in Asia.* New Haven, Conn., 194

———. *Soviet Espionage.* New Haven, Conn., 1955.

———. *Soviet Russia and the Far East.* New Haven, Conn., 1948.

Dark, E. P. *The World Against Russia?* Sydney, Australia, 1948.

Davidson-Houston, J. V. *Russia and China.* London, 1960.

Davis, Kathryn W. *The Soviets at Geneva: The U.S.S.R. and League of Nations, 1919–1933.* Geneva, 1934.

Degras, Jane (ed.). *Soviet Documents on Foreign Policy.* 3 vols. N York, 1951–53.

Dennis, Alfred L. P. *The Foreign Policies of Soviet Russia.* New Y 1924.

Dulles, Foster Rhea. *The Road to Teheran: The Story of Russia America, 1781–1943.* Princeton, N.J., 1944.

Duroselle, Jean-Baptiste (ed.). *Les Frontières européennes de l'U. S.S., 1917–1941.* Paris, 1957.

Farr, Philip. *Soviet Russia and the Baltic Republics.* London, 1944.

cher, Louis. *The Soviets in World Affairs.* 2nd ed., 2 vols. Princeton, N.J., 1951.

ming, D. F. *The Cold War and Its Origins, 1917–1960.* 2 vols. Garden City, N.Y., 1961.

tters, Gerard M. *Outer Mongolia and Its International Position.* Baltimore, 1949.

ler, Sterling Hale. "The Foreign Policy of the Soviet Union in the League and United Nations." 2 vols. Ph.D. thesis, University of Texas, 1952.

ver, Dietrich. *Die Sowjetunion und Iran.* Tübingen, 1955.

dwin, Robert A., and Zetterbaum, Marvin (eds.). *Readings in Russian Foreign Policy.* 3 vols. Chicago, 1953.

nes, C. Grove (ed.). *The Threat of Soviet Imperialism.* Baltimore, 954.

tlieb, Wilhelm Walter. *Das politische Vertragssystem der Sowjetnion, 1920–1935.* Liepzig, 1936.

nderson, H. W. *An Outline of Polish-Soviet Relations.* Glasgow, c. 944.

ger, Gustav, and Meyer, Alfred G. *The Incompatible Allies: A Memoir-History of German-Soviet Relations, 1918–1941.* New York, 953.

dus, Maurice. *Russia and Japan.* Garden City, N.Y., 1952.

kson, J. Hampden. *Estonia.* London, 1941.

es, Goronwy J. *From Stalin to Khrushchev.* London, 1960.

nnan, George F. *Russia and the West Under Lenin and Stalin.* Boston, 1961.

——. *Soviet Foreign Policy, 1917–1941.* Princeton, N.J., 1960.

in, Fritz. *Die Diplomatischen Beziehungen Deutschlands zur Sowtunion, 1917–1932.* [East] Berlin, 1953.

uchnikov, Yu. V., and Sabanin, Andrei (eds.). *Mezhdunarodnaya olitika noveishevo vremeni v dogovorakh, notakh i deklaratsiyakh* International Politics of Contemporary Times in Treaties, Notes, nd Declarations]. 3 parts in 2 vols. Moscow, 1925–29.

han, Lionel. *Russia and the Weimar Republic.* Cambridge, England, 1954.

ovalov, S. (ed.). *Russo-Polish Relations.* Princeton, N.J., 1945.

ski, W. W. *Peaceful Co-existence: An Analysis of Soviet Foreign olicy.* Chicago, 1959.

oste, Raymond. *La Russie Soviétique et la question d'Orient.* Paris, 946.

queur, Walter Z. *The Soviet Union and the Middle East.* New York, 959.

478   *Soviet Russia in World Politics*

Lenczowski, George. *The Middle East in World Affairs*. 2nd ed. Itha¶ N.Y., 1958.

———. *Russia and the West in Iran, 1918–1948*. Ithaca, N.Y., 1949.

Levi, Werner. *Modern China's Foreign Policy*. Minneapolis, 1953.

Lobanov-Rostovsky, A. *Russia and Asia*. 2nd ed. Ann Arbor, Mi¶ 1951.

Lukacs, John A. *The Great Powers and Eastern Europe*. New Yo¶ 1953.

———. *A History of the Cold War*. Garden City, N.Y., 1961.

MacNair, Harley F., and Lach, Donald. *Modern Far Eastern Inter¶ tional Relations*. 2nd ed. New York, 1955.

Mahaney, Wilbur Lee, Jr. *The Soviet Union, the League of Nations ¶ Disarmament, 1917–1935*. Philadelphia, 1940.

Manning, Clarence A. *The Forgotten Republics*. New York, 1952.

Marks, Stanley J. *The Bear That Walks Like a Man*. Philadelphia, 19¶

Marriott, Sir J. A. R. *Anglo-Russian Relations, 1689–1943*. 2nd ed. L¶ don, 1944.

Mazour, Anatole G. *Finland Between East and West*. New York, 19¶

Meiksins, Gregory. "The Doctrine of Coexistence in Soviet Diploma¶ Ph.D. thesis, New School for Social Research, 1954.

———. *The Baltic Riddle*. New York, 1943.

Middleton, K. W. B. *Britain and Russia*. London, c. 1947.

Milioukov, P. *La Politique extérieure des Soviets*. 2nd ed. Paris, 19¶

Ministerstvo inostrannikh del SSSR. *Dokumenty vneshnei politiki SS¶ [Documents on the Foreign Policy of the USSR]. 4 vols. Mosc¶ 1957–60.

Moore, Harriet L. *Soviet Far Eastern Policy, 1931–1945*. Princet¶ N.J., 1945.

Moseley, Philip E. *The Kremlin and World Politics*. New York, 196¶

Papouktchieva, Maria. *La Politique de la Russie a l'égard des détro¶ Geneva, 1944.

Phillips, G. D. R. *Russia, Japan, and Mongolia*. London, 1942.

Polish Research Centre. *Poland and the U.S.S.R., 1921–1941*. Lond¶ c. 1942.

Polish-Soviet Relations, 1918–1943: Official Documents. Washington¶ 1943.

Potemkin, V. P. (ed.). *Istoria diplomatii* [The History of Diploma¶ 3 vols. Moscow, 1944–45.

Povolny, Murray. "The Role and Function of the United Nations¶ Soviet Foreign Policy." Ph.D. thesis, University of Chicago, 1954.¶

Preston, Thomas. *Before the Curtain*. London, 1950.

a, Kaarel Robert. *The Soviet Union and the Baltic States.* New
ork, 1942.

erts, Henry L. *Russia and America: Dangers and Prospects.* New
ork, 1956.

instein, Alvin Z (ed.). *The Foreign Policy of the Soviet Union.*
ew York, 1960.

ra, Chattar Singh. *India and Anglo-Soviet Relations (1917-1947).*
ombay, 1959.

piro, Leonard. *The Communist Party of the Soviet Union.* New
ork, 1960.

man, Frederick Lewis. *American Policy Toward Russia Since
17.* New York, 1928.

——. *Russia Since 1917.* New York, 1957.

——. *Soviet Politics at Home and Abroad.* New York, 1946.

n-Watson, R. W. *Britain and the Dictators.* New York, 1938.

iro, Leonard (comp. and ed.). *Soviet Treaty Series: A Collection
Bilateral Treaties, Agreements and Conventions, Etc., Concluded
tween the Soviet Union and Foreign Powers.* 2 vols. Washington,
50–55.

well, James T., and Laserson, Max. *Poland and Russia, 1919-1945.*
ew York, 1945.

well, James T., and Deák, Francis. *Turkey at the Straits.* New York,
40.

ès, H. *La France et l'Union Soviétique.* Paris, 1935.

ser, Robert M., and Triska, Jan F. *A Calendar of Soviet Treaties.*
anford, Calif., 1959.

tor, Ivar. *The Soviet Union and the Muslim World, 1917-1957.*
attle, 1959.

levitch, E. *Les États baltes et la Russie Soviétique.* Paris, c. 1930.

ke, Arnolds. *History of Latvia.* Stockholm, 1951.

rianos, L. S. *The Balkans Since 1453.* New York, 1958.

usz-Hupé, Robert, and others. *Protracted Conflict.* New York, 1959.

g, Peter S. H. *Russian and Soviet Policy in Manchuria and Outer
ongolia, 1911-1931.* Durham, N.C., 1959.

in, M. *10 let vneshnei politiki S.S.S.R.* [Ten Years of the Foreign
olicy of the U.S.S.R.]. Moscow, 1927.

acouzio, T. A. *The Soviet Union and International Law.* New York,
35.

——. *War and Peace in Soviet Diplomacy.* New York, 1940.

ulis, Albert N. *Soviet Policy Toward the Baltic States, 1918-1940.*
otre Dame, Ind., 1959.

Tikhomirov, M. *Vneshnaya politika Sovetskovo Soyuza* [The For(Policy of the Soviet Union]. Moscow, 1940.

Tompkins, Pauline. *American-Russian Relations in the Far East.* N York, 1949.

Treadgold, Donald W. *Twentieth Century Russia.* Chicago, 1959.

Umiastowki, R. *Russia and the Polish Republic, 1918–1941.* Lon(1945.

Uustalu, Evald. *The History of the Estonian People.* London, 1952.

Von Rauch, Georg. *A History of Soviet Russia.* 2nd ed. New York, 1!

Vyshinsky, A. Y., and Lozovsky, S. A. (eds.). *Diplomatichesky sl(* [Diplomatic Dictionary]. 2 vols. Moscow, 1948–50.

Wagner, Wolfgang. *Die Teilung Europas: Geschichte der Sowje ischen Expansion bis zur Spaltung Deutschlands, 1918–1945.* St gart, 1959.

Walters, F. P. *A History of the League of Nations.* 2 vols. New Y 1952.

Wei, Henry. *China and Soviet Russia.* Princeton, N.J., 1956.

Williams, William Appleman. *American Russian Relations, 1781–1* New York, 1952.

Wolff, Robert Lee. *The Balkans in Our Time.* Cambridge, Mass., 1!

Wu, Aitchen K. *China and the Soviet Union.* New York, 1950.

Yakhontoff, Victor A. *Russia and the Soviet Union in the Far East.* N York, 1931.

———. *USSR Foreign Policy.* New York, 1945.

Zhukov, E. H. (ed.). *Mezhdunarodnie otnoshenia na dalnem vos((1840–1949 gg.)* [International Relations in the Far East (18 1949)]. 2nd ed. Moscow, 1956.

GENERAL: INTERNATIONAL COMMUNISM

Seton-Watson is the most satisfactory attempt to combine inte events with the history of international Communism, although i highly compressed and often superficial. Salvadori is a brief intro(tion. A comprehensive history of the Communist International has to be written, but Borkenau's pioneering effort is both controversial stimulating. Nollau presents the basic facts skillfully and concisely.

Alexander, Robert J. *Communism in Latin America.* New Brunsw N.J., 1957.

Bellini, Fulvio, and Galli, Giorgio. *Storia del partito communista i(ano.* Milan, 1953.

Blofeld, John. *Red China in Perspective.* London, 1951.

henski, Joseph M., and Niemeyer, Gerhart (eds.). *Handbuch des 'elt-kommunismus.* Freiburg, 1958.

enau, Franz. *European Communism.* New York, 1953.

——. *World Communism: A History of the Communist Interna-
onal.* New York, 1939.

ndt, Conrad, and others. *A Documentary History of Chinese Com-
unism.* Cambridge, Mass., 1952.

ux, Jean-Jacques. *La Chine du nationalisme au communisme.*
aris, 1950.

rat, Maurice. *La Trahison permanente: Parti communiste et poli-
que russe.* Paris, 1948.

e, G. D. H. *Communism and Social Democracy, 1914–1931* (Vol. IV,
History of Socialist Thought). 2 parts. London, 1958.

——. *Socialism and Fascism, 1931–1939* (Vol. V, *A History of So-
alist Thought*). New York, 1960.

niels, Robert V. (ed). *A Documentary History of Communism.*
ew York, 1960.

ras, Jane (ed.). *The Communist International, 1919–1943.* 2 vols.
in progress). New York, 1956–.

per, Theodore. *American Communism and Soviet Russia: The
ormative Period.* New York, 1960.

——. *The Roots of American Communism.* New York, 1957.

ewanowski, M. K. *The Communist Party of Poland.* Cambridge,
Iass., 1959.

on, Martin. *World Communism Today.* New York, 1948.

cher, Ruth. *Stalin and German Communism.* Cambridge, Mass.,
948.

chtheim, Ossip K. *Die Kommunistische Partei Deutschlands in der
Veimarer Republik.* Offenbach, 1948.

rinsky, Michael T. *World Revolution and the U.S.S.R.* New York,
933.

ter, William Z. *History of the Communist Party of the United
tates.* New York, 1952.

——. *History of the Three Internationals: The World Socialist and
Communist Movements from 1848 to the Present.* New York, 1955.

we, Irving, and Coser, Lewis. *The American Communist Party.*
Boston, 1957.

Chiao-mu. *Thirty Years of the Communist Party of China.* London,
951.

nes, C. L. R. *World Communism, 1917–1936.* New York, 1937.

nnedy, Captain Malcolm. *A History of Communism in East Asia.*
New York, 1957.

Kun, Bela (ed.). *Kommunisticheskii Internatsional v dokumentak*. [The Communist International in Documents]. Moscow, 1933.

Laqueur, Walter Z. *Communism and Nationalism in the Middle Eas*. New York, 1956.

Laurat, Lucien. *Du Komintern au Kominform*. Paris, 1951.

Lazitch, Branko. *Les Partis communistes d'Europe, 1919–1955*. Pari. 1956.

McLane, Charles B. *Soviet Policy and the Chinese Communists, 1931 1946*. New York, 1958.

Miff, P. *Heroic China: Fifteen Years of the Communist Party of Chin*. New York, 1937.

Nollau, Gunther. *International Communism and World Revolution History and Methods*. New York, 1961.

North, Robert C. *Moscow and Chinese Communists*. Stanford, Calif 1953.

Oren, Nissan. "The Bulgarian Communist Party." M.A. thesis, Colun bia University, 1956.

Pelling, Henry. *The British Communist Party*. New York, 1958.

Possony, Stefan. *A Century of Conflict: Communist Techniques World Revolution*. Chicago, 1953.

Rosenberg, Arthur. *A History of Bolshevism*. London, 1934.

Rossi, A. [Angelo Tasca]. *Les Communistes français pendant la dro de guerre*. Paris, 1951.

———. *La Guerre des papillons: Quatre ans de politique communis (1940–1944)*. Paris, 1954.

———. *Physiologie du parti communiste français*. Paris, 1948.

Rothschild, Joseph. *The Communist Party of Bulgaria: Origin and D velopment, 1883–1936*. New York, 1959.

Salvadori, Massimo. *The Rise of Modern Communism*. New York, 195

Schwartz, Benjamin I. *Chinese Communism and the Rise of Mao*. Car bridge, Mass., 1951.

Seton-Watson, Hugh. *From Lenin to Khrushchev: The History World Communism*. New York, 1960.

Shannon, David A. *The Decline of American Communism*. New Yoi 1959.

Simon, Paul. *Le Mouvement communiste en Chine des origines a r jours*. Paris, 1939.

Spartakus. *German Communists*. London, 1944.

Sturmthal, Adolf. *The Tragedy of European Labor, 1918–1939*. N York, 1943.

Walter, Gérard. *Histoire du parti communiste français*. Paris, 1948.

silon [Johann Rindl and Julian Gumperz]. *Pattern for World Revo-*
ution. New York, 1947.

GENERAL: BIOGRAPHY

There are few good biographies of Soviet leaders. Those by Deut-
ier are contemporary classics and contain much relevant material on
viet foreign relations and the Comintern. See Chapter 14 for works
Khrushchev.

sseches, Nicholas. *Stalin.* New York, 1952.
lainkin, George. *Maisky: Ten Years Ambassador.* London, 1944.
omage, Bernard. *Molotov: The Story of an Era.* London, 1956.
lbars, Yves. *Le Vrai Staline.* 2 vols. Paris, 1950–51.
utscher, Isaac. *The Prophet Armed: Trotsky, 1879–1921.* New York,
1954.
——. *The Prophet Unarmed: Trotsky, 1921–1929.* New York, 1959.
——. *Stalin: A Political Biography.* New York, 1949.
iranty, Walter. *Stalin & Co.: The Politburo.* New York, 1949.
rrara, Marcella and Maurizio. *Palmiro Togliatti.* Paris, 1954.
itton, J. Bernard. *Stalin—the Miraculous Georgian.* London, 1961.
rnev, N. *Litvinov.* Moscow, 1936.
pe, Arthur Upham. *Maxim Litvinoff.* New York, 1943.
ub, David. *Lenin: A Biography.* Garden City, N.Y., 1948.
uvarine, Boris. *Stalin: A Critical Survey of Bolshevism.* New York,
1939.
otsky, Leon. *My Life.* New York, 1930.
——. *Stalin: An Appraisal of the Man and His Influence.* New York,
1946.
alter, Gérard. *Lénine.* New York, 1950.

CHAPTER ONE—THE TSARIST LEGACY

No comprehensive work devoted exclusively to a history of pre-Soviet
reign relations exists, but there are numerous histories of Russia con-
ining chapters on Tsarist foreign policy. Probably the best of these
Florinsky, though it may be supplemented on the period of the last
ree Tsars by Seton-Watson. Some of the essays in Lederer are very
od.

lbertini, Luigi. *The Origins of the War of 1914.* 3 vols. New York,
1952–57.

484   Soviet Russia in World Politics

Albrecht-Carrié, René. *A Diplomatic History of Europe Since Congress of Vienna.* New York, 1958.

Bolsover, G. H. "Aspects of Russian Foreign Policy, 1815–1914," A. J. P. Taylor and Richard Pares (eds.), *Essays Presented to Lewis Namier.* London, 1956.

Florinsky, Michael T. *Russia: A History and an Interpretation.* 2 v New York, 1953.

Gottlieb, W. W. *Studies in Secret Diplomacy During the First Wo War.* London, 1957.

Grunwald, Constantin de. *Trois siècles de diplomatie russe.* Paris, 19

Kohn, Hans. *Pan Slavism: Its History and Ideology.* 2nd ed. N York, 1960.

Korff, S. A. *Russia's Foreign Relations During the Last Half Centu* New York, 1922.

Lederer, Ivo J. (ed.). *Russian Foreign Policy: Essays in Historical P spective.* New Haven, Conn., 1962.

Lobanov-Rostovsky, Andrei A. *Russia and Europe, 1789–1825.* D ham, N.C., 1947.

———. *Russia and Europe, 1825–1878.* Ann Arbor, Mich., 1954.

Malozemoff, Andrew. *Russian Far Eastern Policy, 1881–1904.* Berkel Calif., 1958.

Renouvin, Pierre (ed.). *Histoire des relations internationales.* 7 vc Paris, 1953–57.

Romanov, B. A. *Russia in Manchuria (1892–1906): Essays on the H tory of the Foreign Policy of Tsarist Russia in the Epoch of Imperi ism.* Ann Arbor, Mich., 1952.

Seton-Watson, Hugh. *The Decline of Imperial Russia, 1855–1914.* Lc don, 1952.

Smith, C. Jay, Jr. *The Russian Struggle for Power, 1914–1917: A Stu of Russian Foreign Policy During the First World War.* New Yo 1956.

Sumner, B. H. *Russia and the Balkans, 1870–1880.* Oxford, Englan 1937.

———. *Tsardom and Imperialism in the Far East and Middle Ea 1880–1914.* London, 1942.

Tarle, E. V. *Evropa v epokhu imperializma, 1871–1919 gg.* [Europe the Epoch of Imperialism, 1871–1919]. Moscow, 1928.

Taylor, A. J. P. *The Struggle for Mastery in Europe, 1848–1918.* Oxfor England, 1954.

Vernadsky, George. *Political and Diplomatic History of Russia.* Bosto 1936.

CHAPTER TWO—REVOLUTIONARY DIPLOMACY:
BOURGEOIS AND BOLSHEVIK

A lengthy bibliography may be found in Warth, *The Allies and the Russian Revolution.* Only recent publications and a few important secondary works are listed here.

Browder, Robert Paul, and Kerensky, Alexander F. (eds.). *The Russian Provisional Government, 1917: Documents.* 2 vols. Stanford, Calif., 1961.

Chernov, Victor. *The Great Russian Revolution.* New Haven, Conn., 1936.

Fainsod, Merle. *International Socialism and the World War.* Cambridge, Mass., 1935.

Kirchhoff, Raymond L. "The Stalinist Revision of History: The Case of Brest-Litovsk," *World Politics,* V (October 1952), 66–85.

Gorky, M., and others (eds.). *The History of the Civil War in the U.S.S.R.* 2 vols. London, 1937–47.

Kennan, George F. *Russia Leaves the War* (Vol. I, *Soviet-American Relations,* 1917–1920). Princeton, N.J., 1956.

———. "The Sisson Documents," *Journal of Modern History,* XXVIII (June 1956), 130–54.

Mayer, Arno J. *Political Origins of the New Diplomacy, 1917–1918.* New Haven, Conn., 1959.

Moorehead, Alan. *The Russian Revolution.* New York, 1958.

Sukhanov, N. N. *The Russian Revolution, 1917.* New York, 1955.

Trotsky, Leon. *The History of the Russian Revolution.* 3 vols. New York, 1932.

Walter, Gérard. *Histoire de la révolution russe.* Paris, 1953.

Warth, Robert D. *The Allies and the Russian Revolution: From the Fall of the Monarchy to the Peace of Brest-Litovsk.* Durham, N.C., 1954.

Wheeler-Bennett, John W. *The Forgotten Peace: Brest-Litovsk, March 1918.* New York, 1939.

Zeman, Z. A. B. (ed.). *Germany and the Revolution in Russia, 1915–1918: Documents from the Archives of the German Foreign Ministry.* London, 1958.

CHAPTER THREE—A TIME OF TROUBLES

Chamberlin's second volume is still the standard account of the civil war. However, Footman is well written and takes account of more re-

cent scholarship. A comprehensive work on Allied intervention has
to be written, but the events of 1918, emphasizing American poli
are analyzed with artistry and subtlety in Kennan's volume.

Ackerman, Carl W. *Trailing the Bolsheviki: Twelve Thousand M
With the Allies in Siberia*. New York, 1919.

Albertson, Ralph. *Fighting Without a War*. New York, 1920.

Alioshin, Dmitri. *Asian Odyssey*. New York, 1940.

Arenz, Wilhelm. *Grenzmärkische Forschungen: Polen und Russla
1918–1920*. Leipzig, 1939.

Baerlein, Henry. *The March of the Seventy Thousand*. London, 19

Bechhoffer, C. E. *In Denikin's Russia and the Caucasus, 1919–19
London, 1921.

Bečvar, Gustav. *The Lost Legion: A Czechoslovak Epic*. London, 19

Beneš, Dr. Eduard. *My War Memoirs*. Boston, 1928.

Beryozkin, A. *SShA—Aktivny organizator i uchastnik voennoi int
ventsii protiv Sovetskoi Rossi (1918–1920 gg.)* [*The USA—Act
Organizer and Participant in Military Intervention Against Sov
Russia (1918–1920)*]. Moscow, 1952.

Boldur, Alexandre. *La Bessarabie et les relations russo-roumain
Paris, 1927.

Bothmer, Karl von. *Mit Graf Mirbach in Moskau*. Tübingen, 1922.

Brinkley, George A. "The Volunteer Army and General Denikin's
lations with the French." M.A. thesis, Columbia University, c. 19

Buell, Raymond Leslie. *The Washington Conference*. New York, 19

The Bullitt Mission to Russia. New York, 1919.

Bunyan, James. *Intervention, Civil War, and Communism in Russ
April–December 1918: Documents and Materials*. Baltimore, 19

Chamberlin, William Henry. *The Russian Revolution, 1917–1921.
vols. New York, 1935.

Churchill, Winston. *The Aftermath* (Vol. IV, *The World Crisis*). N
York, 1929.

Clark, Charles Upson. *Bessarabia: Russia and Roumania on the Bla
Sea*. New York, 1927.

Coates, W. P. and Zelda K. *Armed Intervention in Russia, 1918–19
London, 1935.

Chronicler, A [John Cudahy]. *Archangel: The American War w
Russia*. Chicago, 1924.

Coffey, Lt. Col. Joseph I. "The Pattern of Soviet Imperialism: A Ca
History (Poland, 1919–1921)." Ph.D. thesis, Georgetown Univ
sity, 1954.

nference on the Limitation of Armament: Washington, November
2, 1921–February 6, 1922. Washington, 1922.

bernon, Viscount. *The Eighteenth Decisive Battle of the World:
Warsaw, 1920.* London, 1931.

nikin, A. I. *Ocherki russkoi smuty* [Sketches of the Russian Tur-
noil]. 5 vols. Paris and Berlin, c. 1921–c. 1926.

———. *The White Army.* London, 1930.

ujina, Gleb. "The History of the North-West Army of General Yudenich." Ph.D. thesis, Stanford University, 1950.

puy, R. Ernest. *Perish By the Sword: The Czechoslovakian Anabasis
and Our Supporting Campaigns in North Russia and Siberia, 1918–
1920.* Harrisburg, Pa., 1939.

her, H. H. *The Famine in Soviet Russia, 1919–1923.* New York, 1927.

otman, David. *Civil War in Russia.* London, 1961.

rdon, Alban. *Russian Civil War.* London, 1937.

rn, Vasily. *Grazhdanskaya voina na severo-zapad Rossi* [The Civil
War in Northwest Russia]. Berlin, 1923.

aves, William S. *America's Siberian Adventure, 1918–1920.* New
York, 1931.

eat Britain, War Office. *Army. The Evacuation of North Russia, 1919.*
London, 1920.

iswold, A. Whitney. *The Far Eastern Policy of the United States.*
New York, 1938.

ondijs, Ludovic-H. *La Guerre en Russie et en Siberie.* Paris, 1922.

kovsky, A. I. *Frantsuzskaya interventsia na yuge Rossi, 1918–1919
gg.* [French Intervention in South Russia, 1918–1919]. Moscow, 1928.

alliday, E. M. *The Ignorant Armies.* New York, 1960.

odgson, John Ernest. *With Denikin's Armies.* London, 1932.

oover, Herbert. *Memoirs.* 3 vols. New York, 1952.

hihashi, Yamoto. *The Washington Conference and After.* Stanford,
Calif., 1928.

onside, Edmund. *Archangel, 1918–1919.* London, 1953.

nin, General [Maurice]. *Ma Mission en Sibérie, 1918–1920.* Paris,
1933.

panese Intervention in the Russian Far East. Washington, 1922.

awakami, K. K. *Japan's Pacific Policy.* New York, 1922.

azemzadeh, Firuz. *The Struggle for Transcaucasia (1917–1921).* New
York, 1951.

edrov, M. S. *Bez bolshevistskovo rukovodstva (iz istorii interventsii
na Murmane)*[Without Bolshevik Leadership (From the History of
Intervention in Murmansk)]. Leningrad, 1930.

———. *Za sovetsky sever* [For a Soviet North]. Leningrad, 1927.

Kennan, George F. *The Decision to Intervene* (Vol. II, *Soviet-Ameri[c]* *Relations, 1917–1920*). Princeton, N.J., 1958.

———. "Soviet Historiography and America's Role in the Interv[en]- tion," *American Historical Review*, LXV (January 1960), 302–22[.]

Kindall, Sylvian G. *American Soldiers in Siberia*. New York, 1945.

Kirkien, L. *Russia, Poland and the Curzon Line*. Duns, Scotland[?] 1944.

Klante, Margarete. *Von der Wolga zum Amur: Die tschechische Leg[.]* *und der russische Bürgerkrieg*. Berlin, 1931.

Komarnicki, Titus. *Rebirth of the Polish Republic: A Study in [a]* *Diplomatic History of Europe, 1914–1920*. London, 1957.

Kunina, A. E. *Proval amerikanskikh planov zavoevania mirov[o]* *gospodstva v 1917–1920 gg.* [The Failure of the American Plans the Achievement of World Domination in 1917–1920]. Moscow, 19[?]

Laserson, Max M. *The Curzon Line*. New York, 1944.

Lloyd George, David. *The Truth About the Peace Treaties*. 2 vols. L[on]- don, 1938.

———. *War Memoirs*. 6 vols. Boston, 1933–37.

Machray, Robert. *Poland, 1914–1931*. London, 1932.

Manning, Clarence A. *The Siberian Fiasco*. New York, 1952.

Mantoux, Paul. *Les Délibérations du Conseil des Quatre (24 mars– juin 1919)*. 2 vols. Paris, 1955.

Martel, Leon C., Jr. "Russian Foreign Policy and the Establishment the Far Eastern Republic." M.A. thesis, Columbia University, 19[?]

Marty, André. *La Révolte de la Mer Noire*. 4th ed. Paris, 1949.

Masaryk, Thomas Garrigue. *The Making of a State*. New York, 1927.

Maynard, Major-General Sir C. *The Murmansk Venture*. London, 1928.

Mints, I. *Angliiskaya interventsia i severnaya kontrrevolyutsia* [E[ng]- lish Intervention and the Northern Counter-Revolution]. Mosco[w] 1931.

——— (ed.). *Yaponskaya interventsia 1918–1922 gg. v dokumenta[kh]* [The Japanese Intervention of 1918–1922 in Documents]. Mosco[w] 1934.

Moore, Captain Joel R., and others (comps. and eds.). *The History the American Expedition Fighting the Bolsheviki*. Detroit, 1920.

Morley, James William. *The Japanese Thrust into Siberia, 1918*. N[ew] York, 1957.

Nansen, Fridtjof. *Russia and Peace*. London, 1923.

Newbolt, Henry. *History of the Great War Based on Official Doc[u]- ments: Naval Operations*, Vol. V. London, 1931.

Nicolson, Harold. *Curzon: The Last Phase, 1919–1925*. London, 19[?]

rton, Henry Kittredge. *The Far Eastern Republic of Siberia*. London, 1923.

ge, Stanley W. *The Formation of the Baltic States*. Cambridge, Mass., 1959.

gès, Émile. *Campagne de misère: Sibérie, 1919*. Paris, 1933.

svolsky, Leo. *Russia in the Far East*. New York, 1922.

vlovsky, Michel N. *Chinese-Russian Relations*. New York, 1949.

sudski, Joseph. *L'Année 1920*. Paris, 1929.

bes, Richard. *The Formation of the Soviet Union: Communism and Nationalism, 1917–1923*. Cambridge, Mass., 1954.

povici, Andrei. *The Political Status of Bessarabia*. Washington, 1931.

iest, Lyman William. "The Cordon Sanitaire, 1918–1922." Ph.D. thesis, Stanford University, 1954.

——. "The French Intervention in South Russia, 1918–1919." M.A. thesis, Stanford University, 1947.

ikhberg, G. *Yaponskaya interventsia na dalnem vostoke* [Japanese Intervention in the Far East]. Moscow, 1935.

shetar, John S., Jr. *The Ukrainian Revolution, 1917–1920*. Princeton, N.J., 1952.

ynolds, E. E. *Nansen*. London, 1932.

S.F.S.R. Commissariat du peuple pour les affairs étrangères. *Livre rouge: Recueil des documents diplomatiques relatifs aux relations entre la Russie et la Pologne, 1918–1920*. Moscow, 1920.

ymour, Charles (ed.). *The Intimate Papers of Colonel House*. 4 vols. Boston, 1926–28.

likhter, A. G. (ed.). *Chornaya kniga* [Black Book]. Ekaterinoslav, 1925.

lyapnikov, A. G., and others (eds.). *Kto dolzhnik?* [Who is the Debtor?]. Moscow, 1926.

tein, B. E. *"Russkii vopros" na Parizhskoi mirnoi konferentsii* [The "Russian Question" at the Paris Peace Conference]. Moscow, 1949.

korski, L. *La Campagne polono-russe de 1920*. Paris, 1928.

iith, C. Jay. *Finland and the Russian Revolution, 1917–1922*. Athens, Ga., 1958.

rensen, Jon. *The Saga of Fridtjof Nansen*. New York, 1932.

itar, Andrew. *With Ironside in North Russia*. London, 1940.

ffens, Lincoln. *Autobiography*. New York, 1931.

wart, George. *The White Armies of Russia*. New York, 1933.

akhovsky, Leonid I. *American Opinion About Russia, 1917–1920*. Toronto, 1961.

——. *Intervention at Archangel*. Princeton, N.J., 1944.

————. _The Origins of American Intervention in North Russia_ (1918 Princeton, N.J., 1937.

Subbotovsky, I. _Soyuzniki, russkie reaktsionery i interventsia_ [The A lies, the Russian Reactionaries, and Intervention]. Leningrad, 192

Takeuchi, Tatsuji. _War and Diplomacy in the Japanese Empire._ Ga den City, N.Y., 1935.

Temperley, H.W.V. (ed.). _A History of the Peace Conference Paris._ 6 vols. London, 1920–24.

Thompson, Charles T. _The Peace Conference Day By Day._ New Yor 1920.

Thompson, John M. "Allied and American Intervention in Russia, 191 1921," in C. E. Black (ed.), _Rewriting Russian History: Soviet Inte pretations of Russia's Past._ New York, 1956.

Ullman, Richard H. _Intervention and the War_ (Vol. I, _Anglo-Soviet R lations, 1917–1921_). Princeton, N.J., 1961.

U.S. Department of State. _Papers Relating to the Foreign Relations the United States, 1919: The Paris Peace Conference._ 13 vols. Was ington, 1942–47.

————. _Papers Relating to the Foreign Relations of the United State 1919: Russia._ Washington, 1937.

Unterberger, Betty Miller. _America's Siberian Expedition, 1918–19_ Durham, N.C., 1956.

Varneck, Elena, and Fisher, H. H. (eds.). _The Testimony of Kolch and Other Siberian Materials._ Stanford, Calif., 1935.

Vondracek, Felix John. _The Foreign Policy of Czechoslovakia, 191 1935._ New York, 1937.

Ward, Colonel John. _With the "Die-Hards" in Siberia._ New York, 19

Weale, Putnam [Bertram Lenox Simpson]. _An Indiscreet Chronic from the Pacific._ New York, 1922.

Weygand, [General Maxime]. _Miracles et réalité._ Paris, 1957.

White, John Albert. _The Siberian Intervention._ Princeton, N.J., 1950.

Wollenberg, Erich. _The Red Army._ London, 1940.

Woodward, E. L., and Butler, Rohan (eds.). _Documents on Briti Foreign Policy, 1919–1939._ First series, Vol. III. London, 1949.

Wrangel, General Baron Peter N. _Always With Honour._ New Yo 1957.

Xydias, Jean. _L'Intervention française en Russie, 1918–1919._ Paris, 19

Yoffe, Ya. _Organizatsia interventsia i blokady Sovetskoi respubli 1918–1920_ [The Organization of the Intervention and Blockade the Soviet Republic, 1918–1920]. Moscow, 1930.

Young, A. Morgan. _Japan in Recent Times, 1912–1926._ New York, 19

Zetkin, Klara. _Reminiscences of Lenin._ London, 1929.

ıltowski, Adam. *Border of Europe: A Study of the Polish Eastern Provinces.* London, 1950.

ıyev, F. *Mezhdunarodny imperializm—organizator napadenie panskoi polshi no Sovetskuyu Rossiyu (1919–1920 gg.)* [International Imperialism—Organizer of the Attack by the Polish Nobles on Soviet Russia (1919–1920)]. Moscow, 1954.

CHAPTER FOUR—COMINTERN VS. NARKOMINDEL

Volume three of Carr's *Bolshevik Revolution* and a portion of his *terregnum* (both parts of *A History of Soviet Russia,* still in ogress) are impressive analytical surveys of Soviet foreign policy. he work presupposes some knowledge of Soviet history. Freund's ex- ıllent monograph is better informed on German policy than Russian.

nderson, Evelyn. *Hammer or Anvil: The Story of the German Working-Class.* London, 1945.

nglo-Sovetskie otnoshenia* [Anglo-Soviet Relations]. Moscow, 1927.

ılabanoff, Angelica. *My Life As a Rebel.* New York, 1938.

ıuer, Otto von. *Die österreichische Revolution.* Vienna, 1923.

erlau, Abraham Joseph. *The German Social Democratic Party, 1914–1921.* New York, 1949.

lücher, Wipert von. *Deutschlands Weg nach Rapallo.* Wiesbaden, 1951.

öhm, Wilhelm. *Im Kreuzfeuer zweier Revolutionen.* Munich, 1924.

arr, Edward Hallett. *The Bolshevik Revolution, 1917–1923.* 3 vols. New York, 1950–53.

———. *The Interregnum, 1923–1924.* New York, 1954.

———. *Studies in Revolution.* London, 1950.

attell, David T. "Soviet Russia and the Hungarian Revolution of 1919." M.A. thesis, Columbia University, 1949.

he Communist International Between the Fifth and the Sixth World Congresses, 1924–8.* London, 1928.

onference at The Hague: Minutes and Documents.* The Hague, 1922.

onference de Moscou pour la limitation des armements.* Moscow, 1923.

oper, Rudolph. *Failure of a Revolution: Germany in 1918–1919.* Cambridge, England, 1955.

owden, Morton H. "The Soviet Union, International Communism, and the British General Strike of May, 1926." M.A. thesis, Columbia University, 1951.

raig, Gordon. *The Politics of the Prussian Army, 1640–1945.* Oxford, England, 1955.

D'Abernon, Viscount. *The Diary of an Ambassador.* 3 vols. Garde City, N.Y., 1929–31.

Daniels, Robert Vincent. *The Conscience of the Revolution: The Con munist Opposition in Soviet Russia.* Cambridge, Mass., 1960.

Dimitrov, G., and others. *The September Uprising.* [Sofia, 1953

Der I. Kongress der Kommunistischen Internationale. Hamburg, 192

Eudin, Xenia Joukoff, and Fisher, Harold H. *Soviet Russia and th West, 1920–1927: A Documentary Survey.* Stanford, Calif., 1957.

Freund, Gerald. *Unholy Alliance: Russian-German Relations from th Treaty of Brest-Litovsk to the Treaty of Berlin.* New York, 1957.

Frölich, Paul. *Rosa Luxemburg.* London, 1940.

Gatzke, Hans W. "Russo-German Military Collaboration During th Weimar Republic," *American Historical Review,* LXVIII (Ap 1958), 565–97.

———. *Stresemann and the Rearmament of Germany.* Baltimore, 195

Gessler, Otto. *Reichswehrpolitik in der Weimarer Zeit.* Stuttgart, 195

Gordon, Harold J., Jr. *The Reichswehr and the German Republic, 191 1926.* Princeton, N.J., 1957.

Goure, Leon. "Soviet Foreign Policy and the March 1921 Crisis Essay, Columbia University, 1949.

Graubard, Stephen Richards. *British Labour and the Russian Revol tion, 1917–1924.* Cambridge, Mass., 1956.

Great Britain, Turkey No. 1 (1923). Cmd. 1814. *Lausanne Conferen on Near Eastern Affairs, 1922–1923.* London, 1923.

Gregory, J. D. *On the Edge of Diplomacy.* London, c. 1928.

Gulick, Charles A. *Austria from Hapsburg to Hitler.* 2 vols. Berkele Calif., 1948.

Halperin, S. William. *Germany Tried Democracy: A Political Histo of the Reich from 1918 to 1933.* New York, 1946.

Helbig, Herbert. "Die Moskauer Mission des Grafen Brockdor Rantzau," *Forschungen zur Osteuropäischen Geschichte,* II (1955 286–344.

Howard, Harry N. *The Partition of Turkey: A Diplomatic Histor 1913–1923.* Norman, Okla., 1931.

Jászi, Oscar. *Revolution and Counter-Revolution in Hungary.* Londo 1924.

Kaas, Baron Albert, and De Lazarovics, Fedor. *Bolshevism in Hungar The Béla Kun Period.* London, 1931.

Karolyi, Michael. *Memoirs: Faith Without Illusion.* London, 1956.

Kessler, Count Harry. *Walther Rathenau.* New York, 1930.

Koblyakov, I. K. *Ot Bresta do Rapallo* [From Brest to Rapallo]. Mc cow, 1954.

asin, L. B. *Voprosy vneshnei torgovli* [Questions of Foreign Trade]. Moscow, 1928.

assin, Lubov. *Leonid Krassin: His Life and Work.* London, 1929.

garde, Ernest. *La Reconnaissance du gouvernment des Soviets.* Paris, 1924.

zitch, Branko. *Lénine et la IIIᵉ International.* Paris, 1951.

vi, Paul. *Unser Weg: Wider den Putschismus.* Berlin, 1921.

berman, Simon. *Building Lenin's Russia.* Chicago, 1945.

man, Richard W. *The First Labour Government, 1924.* London, 1957.

aisky, I. *Vneshnaya politika R.S.F.S.R., 1917–1922* [The Foreign Policy of the R.S.F.S.R., 1917–1922]. Moscow, 1923.

atériaux et documents sur l'intervention, le blocus et les dommages causés par eux à la Russie. Vol. IV, *Les Réclamations de la Russie aux états responsables de l'intervention et du blocus.* Genoa, 1922.

elville, Cecil F. *The Russian Face of Germany.* London, 1932.

erker, Paul. *Deutschland: Sein oder nicht sein?* 2 vols. Mexico, D.F., 1944–45.

eyer, Karl W. *Karl Liebknecht.* Washington, 1957.

ills, J. Saxon. *The Genoa Conference.* London, 1922.

inistere des Affaires Étrangères. *Documents diplomatiques: Conférence economique internationale de Gènes, 9 Avril–19 Mai 1922.* Paris, 1922.

euberg, A. [Heinz Neumann]. *L'Insurrection armée.* Paris, 1931.

elssner, Fred. *Rosa Luxemburg.* Berlin, 1951.

ge, Stanley W. *Lenin and World Revolution.* New York, 1959.

pers Relating to International Economic Conference, Genoa, April–May, 1922. Cmd. 1667. London, 1922.

svolsky, Leo, and Moulton, Harold G. *Russian Debts and Russian Reconstruction.* New York, 1924.

otokoll des III. Kongresses der Kommunistischen Internationale. Hamburg, 1921.

otokoll des Vierten Kongresses der Kommunistischen Internationale. Hamburg, 1923.

aty vsemirny kongress kommunisticheskovo internatsionale [Fifth All-World Congress of the Communist International.]. 2 vols. Moscow, 1925.

benau, General Friedrich von. *Seeckt: Aus seinen Leben, 1918–1936.* Leipzig, 1940.

dek, Karl. *Vneshnaya politika Sovetskoi Rossi* [The Foreign Policy of Soviet Russia]. Moscow, 1923.

Rosenfeld, Günter. *Sowjetrussland und Deutschland, 1917–1922.* Be
lin, 1960.

Rosmer, Alfred. *Moscou sous Lenine: Les Origines du communism*
Paris, 1953.

Rossi, A. [Angelo Tasca]. *The Rise of Italian Fascism, 1918–1922.* Lo.
don, 1938.

Rotter, Seymour. "Soviet and Comintern Policy Toward German
1919–1923." Ph.D. thesis, Columbia University, 1954.

R.S.F.S.R., Narkomindel. *Materialy Genuezskoi kontferentsii* [M
terials on the Genoa Conference]. Moscow, 1922.

Rubinshstein, N. L. *Sovetskaya Rossiya i kapitalisticheskie gosudarst*
v gody perekhoda ot voiny k miru (*1921–1922 gg.*) [Soviet Russ
and the Capitalist States in the Year of Transition from War
Peace (1921–1922)]. Moscow, 1948.

———. *Vneshnaya politika Sovetskovo gosudarstva v 1921–19.*
godakh [The Foreign Policy of the Soviet State in 1921–1925]. Mc
cow, 1953.

Scheffer, Paul. *Seven Years in Soviet Russia.* New York, 1931.

Scheidemann, Philip. *The Making of New Germany.* 2 vols. New Yor
1929.

Schieder, Theodor. *Die Probleme des Rapallo-Vertrags: Eine Stud*
uber die deutsch-russischen Beziehungen, 1922–1926. Cologne, 195

The Second and Third Internationals and the Vienna Union. *Offic*
Report of the Conference Between the Executives. . . . London, 192

Slocombe, George. *A Mirror to Geneva.* London, 1937.

Snowden, Viscount Philip. *An Autobiography.* 2 vols. London, 1934.

Stern-Rubarth, Edgar. *Graf Brockdorff-Rantzau.* Berlin, 1929.

Stranjakovitch, Branislav. *Lénine et la IIIᵉ Internationale.* Genev
1950.

Swire, J. *Bulgarian Conspiracy.* London, 1939.

Trotsky, Leon. *The First Five Years of the Communist Internation*
2 vols. New York, 1945–53.

Vaks, Boris. *Ot Oktyabrya do Genui* [From October to Genoa]. Mc
cow, 1922.

Valerin, R. *Ot razryva do vosstanovlenia anglo-sovetskikh otnoshei*
[From the Rupture to the Restoration of Anglo-Soviet Relations
Moscow, 1930.

Veridicus. *Suisse et Soviets: Histoire d'un conflict.* Paris, 1926.

Volkov, F. D. *Krakh angliiskoi politiki interventsii i diplomaticheск*
izolyatsii Sovetskovo gosudarstva (*1917–1924 gg.*) [The Failure
the English Policy of Intervention and Diplomatic Isolation of tł
Soviet State (1917–1924)]. Moscow, 1954.

aite, Robert G. L. *Vanguard of Nazism: The Free Corps Movement in Postwar Germany, 1918–1923.* Cambridge, Mass., 1952.

aldman, Eric. *The Spartacist Uprising of 1919 and the Crisis of the German Socialist Movement.* Milwaukee, 1958.

arth, Robert D. "The Arcos Raid and the Anglo-Soviet 'Cold War' of the 1920's," *World Affairs Quarterly,* XXIX (July 1958), 115–51.

——. "The Mystery of the Zinoviev Letter," *South Atlantic Quarterly,* XLIX (October 1950), 441–53.

einberg, Meyer. "The Beginnings of the German Communist Party, 1914–1920." M.A. thesis, University of Chicago, 1945.

heeler-Bennett, John W. *The Nemesis of Power: The German Army in Politics, 1918–1945.* New York, 1954.

noviev, G. *Twelve Days in Germany.* Moscow, 1921.

er zweite Kongress der Kommunist International. Hamburg, 1921.

CHAPTER FIVE—REVOLUTIONARY ADVENTURISM IN CHINA

Isaacs is the ablest history and analysis of the Chinese revolution of e 1920's, although the point of view is Trotskyist. The Brandt and hiting volumes are much narrower in scope but virtually definitive til more sources become available. There is no adequate biography either Sun Yat-sen or Chiang Kai-shek.

kulin, A. V. *Zapiski ob Ukhanskom periode kitaiskoi revolyutsii* [Notes on the Wuhan Period of the Chinese Revolution]. Moscow, 1930.

rkov, Robert. *Strong Man of China: The Story of Chiang Kai-shek.* Boston, 1938.

rg, Dorothy. *American Policy and the Chinese Revolution, 1925–1928.* New York, 1947.

andt, Conrad. *Stalin's Failure in China, 1924–1927.* Cambridge, Mass., 1958.

hao Min-chin. "The Rise of the Chinese Communist Party." M.A. thesis, Columbia University, 1950.

hapman, H. Owen. *The Chinese Revolution, 1926–27.* London, 1928.

hen, Stephen, and Payne, Robert. *Sun Yat-sen.* New York, 1946.

alin, Sergei. *Ocherki revolyutsii v Kitae* [Sketches of the Revolution in China]. Moscow, c. 1928.

udin, Xenia Joukoff, and North, Robert C. *Soviet Russia and the East, 1920–1927: A Documentary Survey.* Stanford, Calif., 1957.

rancis, William Wallace. "The Stalin-Trotsky Controversy Over Soviet Policy in China, 1925–1927." M.A. thesis, Columbia University, 1957.

use, K. *Soviet Policy in the Orient.* East Peking, 1927.

Gannes, Harry. *When China Unites: An Interpretive History of t* *Chinese Revolution*. New York, 1937.

Gould, Randall. *China in the Sun*. Garden City, N.Y., 1946.

Green, O. M. *The Story of China's Revolution*. London, c. 1945.

Hahn, Emily. *Chiang Kai-shek*. Garden City, N.Y., 1955.

Holcombe, Arthur N. *The Chinese Revolution*. Cambridge, Mass., 193

Huston, Jay Calvin. "Sun Yat-sen, the Kuomintang and the Chine Russian Political Economic Alliance." Ms., Hoover Library, Sta ford University, c. 1934.

Isaacs, Harold R. *The Tragedy of the Chinese Revolution*. 2nd e Stanford, Calif., 1951.

Kapitsa, M. S. "Sovetsko-kitaiskie otnoshenia v 1917–1924 godak [Soviet-Chinese Relations in 1917–1924], *Voprosy istorii*, No. (March 1954), 74–90.

Krarup-Nielsen, A. *The Dragon Awakes*. New York, 1928.

Leng, Shao Chuan, and Palmer, Norman D. *Sun Yat-sen and Con munism*. New York, 1960.

Li Chien-nung. *The Political History of Modern China, 1840–192* Princeton, N.J., 1956.

Liu, F. F. *A Military History of Modern China, 1924–1949*. Princeto N.J., 1956.

MacNair, Harley Farnsworth. *China in Revolution*. Chicago, 1931.

Mif, P. *Kitaiskaya revolyutsia* [The Chinese Revolution]. Mosco 1932.

Misselwitz, Henry Francis. *The Dragon Stirs*. New York, 1941.

Oudendyk, William J. *Ways and By-Ways in Diplomacy*. London, 193

Pollard, Robert T. *China's Foreign Relations, 1917–1931*. New Yor 1933.

Powell, John B. *My Twenty-Five Years in China*. New York, 1945.

Ransome, Arthur. *The Chinese Puzzle*. London, 1927.

Roy, M. N. *Revolution and Counter-Revolution in China*. Calcutt 1946.

Saposhnikov, B. G. *Pervaya grazhdanskaya revolyutsionnaya voina Kitae, 1924–1927 gg.* [The First Civil Revolutionary War in Chin 1924–1927]. Moscow, 1954.

Sheean, Vincent. *Personal History*. Garden City, N.Y., 1937.

Smedley, Agnes. *The Great Road: The Life and Times of Chu Te* New York, 1956.

Sokolsky, George E. "The Kuomintang," *The China Year Book, 192* Tientsin, 1928?

————. *The Tinder Box of Asia*. Garden City, N.Y., 1932.

teffens, Charles Frederick. "The Canton Uprising, 11–14 December 1927." M.A. thesis, Columbia University, 1957.

trong, Anna Louise. *China's Millions: The Revolutionary Struggle from 1927 to 1935.* New York, 1935.

'ang Leang-li. *The Inner History of the Chinese Revolution.* New York, 1930.

––––––. *Wang Ching-wei.* Peking, 1931.

'ong, Hollington K. *Chiang Kai-Shek: Soldier and Statesman.* 2 vols. Shanghai, 1937.

'ong, Te-kong. "Kuomintang-Communist Relations and the Russian Influence, 1924–1927." M.A. thesis, Columbia University, 1952.

'rotsky, Leon. *Problems of the Chinese Revolution.* New York, 1932.

Veigh, Ken Shen. *Russo-Chinese Diplomacy.* Shanghai, 1928.

Vhiting, Allen S. *Soviet Policies in China, 1917–1924.* New York, 1954.

Vilbur, C. Martin, and How, Julie Lien-ying (eds.). *Documents on Communism, Nationalism and Soviet Advisers in China, 1917–1927.* New York, 1956.

Villoughby, Westel W. *Foreign Rights and Interests in China.* 2 vols. Baltimore, 1927.

Voo, T. C. *The Kuomintang and the Future of the Chinese Revolution.* London, 1928.

Voodhead, H. G. H. (ed.). *The China Year Book.* 3 vols. Tientsin, c. 1924–27.

'urev, M. F. *Rol revolyutsionnoi armii na pervom etape kitaiskoi revolyutsii* [The Role of the Revolutionary Army in the First Stage of the Chinese Revolution]. Moscow, 1952.

CHAPTER SIX—STALIN AND THE RISE OF
SOVIET NATIONALISM

rowder, Robert Paul. *The Origins of Soviet-American Diplomacy.* Princeton, N.J., 1953.

ullock, Alan. "The German Communists and the Rise of Hitler," in Maurice Baumont and others (eds.), *The Third Reich.* New York, 1955.

––––––. *Hitler: A Study in Tyranny.* New York, 1952.

'hang, Tao Shing. *International Controversies Over the Chinese Eastern Railway.* Shanghai, 1936.

'lark, R. T. *The Fall of the German Republic.* London, 1935.

'onolly, Violet. *Soviet Trade from the Pacific to the Levant.* London, 1935.

Current, Richard N. *Secretary Stimson: A Study in Statecraft.* New Brunswick, N.J., 1954.

Dirksen, Herbert von. *Moscow-Tokyo-London: Twenty Years of German Foreign Policy.* Norman, Okla., 1952.

Documents With Reference to the Sino-Russian Dispute, 1929. Nanking, 1929?

Der Faschismus in Deutschland. Moscow, 1934.

Ferrell, Robert H. *American Diplomacy in the Great Depression.* New Haven, Conn., 1957.

————. *Peace in Their Time: The Origins of the Kellogg-Briand Pact.* New Haven, Conn., 1952.

Graham, Malbone W., Jr., "The Soviet Security System," *International Conciliation,* No. 252 (September 1929), 345–425.

Heiden, Konrad. *Der Fuehrer.* Boston, 1944.

Herbette, Jean. *Un diplomate français parle du péril bolcheviste.* Paris, 1943.

Hoover, Calvin B. *The Economic Life of Soviet Russia.* New York, 1931.

Knickerbocker, H. R. *Fighting the Red Trade Menace.* New York, 1931.

League of Nations. *Appeal By the Chinese Government: Report of the Commission of Enquiry.* Geneva, 1932.

Litvinov, M. *Vneshnaya politika SSSR: rechi i zayavlenia, 1927–1937.* [The Foreign Policy of the USSR: Speeches and Statements, 1927–1937]. 2nd ed. Moscow, 1937.

Oberstein, Alvin I. "The Communist Party and the Comintern in Germany, 1931–1933." M.A. thesis, Columbia University, 1952.

Protokoll sechster Weltkongress der Kommunistischen Internationale. 4 vols. Hamburg-Berlin, 1928.

The Sino-Russian Crisis. Nanking, 1929?

Smith, Sara R. *The Manchurian Crisis, 1931–1932.* New York, 1948.

Spielman, Herbert. "Henry L. Stimson and American Policy Toward the Chinese Eastern Railway Dispute." Ph.D. thesis, University of Chicago, 1949.

Tong, Hollington K. *Facts About the Chinese Eastern Railway Situation.* Harbin? 1929.

Trotsky, Leon. *The Third International After Lenin.* 2nd ed. New York, 1957.

Tsao Lien-en. *The Chinese Eastern Railway.* Shanghai, 1930?

U.S. Department of State. *Foreign Relations of the United States, Diplomatic Papers: The Soviet Union, 1933–1939.* Washington, 1952.

Valtin, Jan [Richard Krebs]. *Out of the Night.* New York, 1940.

Wheeler-Bennett, John W. *Disarmament and Security Since Locarno, 1925–1931*. London, 1932.

——. *The Pipe Dream of Peace: The Story of the Collapse of Disarmament*. New York, 1935.

——. *Wooden Titan: Hindenburg in Twenty Years of German History*. New York, 1936.

Willoughby, Westel W. *The Sino-Japanese Controversy and the League of Nations*. Baltimore, 1935.

CHAPTER SEVEN—COLLECTIVE SECURITY AND THE
POPULAR FRONT

Thomas is a superb history of the Spanish Civil War. Cattell's two monographs supplement it well. The appeasement era as a whole has yet to find its historian, and there is no single work specifically devoted to Soviet diplomacy in the Litvinov era. Snow's *Red Star Over China* is a journalistic classic on the Chinese Communists in the 1930's.

Abend, Hallett. *My Life in China, 1926–1941*. New York, 1943.

Against Aggression: Speeches By Maxim Litvinov. New York, 1939.

Allen, David Edwards, Jr. "The Soviet Union and the Spanish Civil War, 1936–1939." Ph.D. thesis, Stanford University, 1952.

Alvarez del Vayo, Julio. *Freedom's Battle*. New York, 1940.

——. *The Last Optimist*. New York, 1950.

Beck, Colonel Jozef. *Final Report*. New York, 1957.

Beloff, Max. "Soviet Foreign Policy, 1929–1941: Some Notes," *Soviet Studies*, II (July 1950), 123–37.

Bertram, James M. *First Act in China: The Story of the Sian Mutiny*. New York, 1938.

Bisson, T. A. *Japan in China*. New York, 1938.

Bolloten, Burnett. *The Grand Camouflage: The Communist Conspiracy in the Spanish Civil War*. New York, 1961.

Bonnet, Georges. *Défense de la paix*. 2 vols. Geneva, 1946–48.

Borkenau, Franz. *The Spanish Cockpit*. London, 1937.

Brenan, Gerald. *The Spanish Labyrinth*. 2nd ed. Cambridge, England, 1950.

Broad, Lewis. *Sir Anthony Eden*. London, 1955.

Brockway, Fenner. *The Truth About Barcelona*. London, 1937.

Brogan, D. W. *France Under the Republic*. New York, c. 1940.

Buber, Margarete. *Under Two Dictators*. London, 1949.

Cameron, Elizabeth R. *Prologue to Appeasement: A Study in French Foreign Policy*. Washington, 1942.

Campbell-Johnson, Alan. *Sir Anthony Eden.* 2nd ed. London, 1955.

Casado, Colonel S. *The Last Days of Madrid.* London, 1939.

The Case of N. P. Vitvitsky [*et al.*] ... *Charged with Wrecking Activities at Power Stations in the Soviet Union.* ... 3 vols. in 1. Moscow 1933.

Cattell, David T. *Communism and the Spanish Civil War.* Berkeley Calif., 1955.

———. *Soviet Diplomacy and the Spanish Civil War.* Berkeley, Calif. 1957.

Celovsky, Boris *Das Münchener Abkommen, 1938.* Stuttgart, 1958.

Chennault, Claire Lee. *Way of a Fighter.* New York, 1949.

Chiang Kai-shek, General and Madam. *General Chiang Kai-shek: Th Account of the Fortnight in Sian When the Fate of China Hung i the Balance.* Garden City, N.Y., 1937.

Coates, W. P. and Zelda. *World Affairs and the U.S.S.R.* London, 193£

Colodny, Robert Garland. *The Struggle for Madrid.* New York, 1958.

Cot, Pierre. *Triumph of Treason.* Chicago, 1944.

Davies, Joseph E. *Mission to Moscow.* New York, 1941.

Dimitroff, Georgi. *The United Front: The Struggle Against Fascisn and War.* New York, 1938.

Dingle, Reginald J. *Russia's Work in France.* London, 1938.

Documents on British Foreign Policy, 1919–1939. Second Series, Vol VII; Third Series, Vols. VI and VII. London, 1953–58.

Duroselle, Jean-Baptiste (ed.). *Les Relations germano-soviétiques d 1933 à 1939.* Paris, 1954.

Dzelepy, E.-N., and Mounereau, Guy. *Moscou rempart de Versailles* Paris, 1935.

Fabry, Jean. *De la place de la Concorde au cours de l'Intendance* Paris, 1942.

Feiling, Keith. *The Life of Neville Chamberlain.* London, 1946.

Fischer, Louis. *Men and Politics.* New York, 1941.

Flandin, Pierre-Étienne. *Politique français.* Paris, 1947.

François-Poncet, André. *The Fateful Years: Memoirs of a French Am bassador in Berlin, 1931–1938.* New York, 1949.

Furnia, Arthur H. *The Diplomacy of Appeasement: Anglo-French Re lations and the Prelude to World War II, 1931–1938.* Washington 1960.

Gafencu, Grigore. *Last Days of Europe: A Diplomatic Journey in 1939* New Haven, Conn., 1948.

Gonzalez, Valentin, and Gorkin, Julian. *El Campesino: Life and Death in Soviet Russia.* New York, 1952.

Great Britain, Foreign Office. Russia No. 1 (1933). Cmd. 4286. *Correspondence Relating to the Arrest of Employees of the Metropolitan-Vickers Company at Moscow.* London, 1933 .

Grew, Joseph C. *Turbulent Era: A Diplomatic Record of Forty Years, 1904–1945.* 2 vols. Boston, 1952.

Halifax, Earl of. *Fulness of Days.* London, 1957.

Hernandez, Jesus. *Yo fuí un ministro de Stalin.* Mexico, D.F., 1953.

Herriot, Edouard. *Jadis.* 2 vols. Paris, 1948–52.

Iidaka, Noboru (comp.). *Manchoukuo-Soviet Border Issues.* Hsinking? 1938.

Isaacs, Harold R. (ed.). *Five Years of Kuomintang Reaction.* Shanghai, 1932.

Jellinek, Frank. *Civil War in Spain.* London, 1938.

Johanson, J., and Taube, O. (introd.). *Räte-China: Dokumente der chinesischen Revolution.* Moscow, 1934.

Jones, F. C. *Japan's New Order in East Asia: Its Rise and Fall, 1937–1945.* New York, 1954.

Garcia, Khose [José]. "Internatsionalny brigady v Ispanii (1936–1938 gg.)" [The International Brigades in Spain, 1936–1938], *Voprosi istorii,* No. 7 (July 1956), 33–48.

Krivitsky, W. G. *In Stalin's Secret Service.* New York, 1939.

Langer, William L., and Gleason, S. Everett. *The Challenge to Isolation, 1937–1940* (Vol. I, *The World Crisis and American Foreign Policy*). New York, 1952.

Last, Jef. *The Spanish Tragedy.* London, 1939.

Mackiewicz, Stanislaw. *Colonel Beck and His Policy.* London, 1944.

Mao Tse-tung. *Selected Works.* 4 vols. London, 1954–56.

Martin Blázquez, José. *I Helped to Build an Army.* London, 1939.

Marty, André. *Heroic Spain.* New York, 1937.

Matthews, Herbert L. *Two Wars and More to Come.* New York, 1938.

———. *The Yoke and the Arrows: A Report on Spain.* New York, 1957.

Monkhouse, Allan. *Moscow, 1911–1933.* London, 1933.

Morrow, Felix [Joaquin Maurin]. *Revolution and Counter-Revolution in Spain.* New York, 1938.

Namier, L. B. *Diplomatic Prelude, 1938–1939.* London, 1948.

———. *Europe in Decay: A Study in Disintegration, 1936–1940.* London, 1950.

———. *In the Nazi Era.* London, 1952.

Noël, Léon. *L'Agression allemande contre la Pologne.* Paris, 1946.

Orwell, George. *Homage to Catalonia.* New York, 1952.

Paul-Boncour, J. *Entre deux guerres.* 3 vols. Paris, 1945–46.

Ravines, Eudocio. *The Yenan Way.* New York, 1951.

Reed, Douglas. *Insanity Fair*. London, 1938.

Reynaud, Paul. *Au coeur de la mêlée, 1930–1945*. Paris, 1951.

Richards, V. *Lessons of the Spanish Revolution*. London, 1953.

Ripka, Dr. Hubert. *Munich: Before and After*. London, 1939.

Rosinger, Lawrence K. *China's Crisis*. New York, 1945.

———. *China's Wartime Politics, 1937–1944*. Princeton, N.J., 1944.

Rothstein, Andrew. *The Munich Conspiracy*. London, 1958.

Routh, D. A. "The Montreux Convention . . ." in Arnold J. Toynbee *Survey of International Affairs, 1936*. London, 1937.

Schuman, Frederick L. *Europe on the Eve*. New York, 1939.

Selle, Earl Albert. *Donald of China*. New York, 1948.

VII Congress of the Communist International: Abridged Stenographic Report of the Proceedings. Moscow, 1939.

Smedley, Agnes. *Battle Hymn of China*. New York, 1943.

Snow, Edgar. *Journey to the Beginning*. New York, 1958.

———. *Random Notes on Red China (1936–1945)*, Cambridge, Mass. 1957.

———. *Red Star Over China*. 2nd ed. New York, 1944.

Soria, Georges. *Trotskyism in the Service of Franco*. New York, 1938.

Souchy, Augustin. *The Tragic Week in Barcelona*. Barcelona, 1937.

SSSR i fashistskaya agressia v Ispanii: sbornik dokumentov [The USSR and Fascist Aggression in Spain: A Collection of Documents]. Moscow, 1937.

[T'ang Leang-li]. *Suppressing Communist-Banditry in China*. Shanghai 1934.

Taylor, A. J. P. *The Origins of the Second World War*. London, 1961.

Templewood, Viscount [Sir Samuel Hoare]. *Nine Troubled Years*. London, 1954.

Thomson, S. Harrison. *Czechoslovakia in European History*. 2nd ed. Princeton, N.J., 1953.

Van der Esch, P. A. M. *Prelude to War: The International Repercussions of the Spanish Civil War*. The Hague, 1951.

Wales, Nym. *Inside Red China*. New York, 1939.

Werth, Alexander. *France and Munich*. New York, 1939.

———. *France in Ferment*. New York, c. 1935.

———. *Which Way France?* New York, 1937.

Wheeler-Bennett, John W. *Munich: Prologue to Tragedy*. New York 1948.

Wolfe, Bertram D. *Civil War in Spain*. New York, 1937.

Wolfers, Arnold. *Britain and France Between Two Wars*. New York 1940.

Yakhontoff, Victor A. *The Chinese Soviets*. New York, 1934.

CHAPTER EIGHT—THE NAZI-SOVIET MISALLIANCE

While overly technical, Weinberg is the most reliable survey of German-Soviet relations for this period. Rossi is more readable but less objective. Lundin contains an admirably judicious account of the Winter War, and Jakobson presents the diplomatic side in great detail.

alossini, Cajo Enrico. *Le Declin de la Société des Nations.* Geneva, 1945.

ennett, Thomas Hanley. *The Soviets and Europe, 1938–1941.* Geneva, 1951.

erzinsh, Alfreds. *I Saw Vishinsky Bolshevize Latvia.* Washington, 1948.

ilmanis, Dr. Alfred. *Latvia Between the Anvil and the Hammer.* Washington, 1945.

ouvier, J., and Gacon, J. *La Vérité sur 1939: La Politique extérieure de l'U.R.S.S. d'octobre 1938 à juin 1941.* Paris, 1953.

hambon, Henry de. *La Tragédie des nations baltiques.* Paris, 1946.

oates, W. P. and Zelda K. *Russia, Finland and the Baltic.* London, 1940.

———. *The Soviet-Finnish Campaign.* London, c. 1942.

oulondre, Robert. *De Staline à Hitler: Souvenirs de deux ambassades, 1936–1939.* Paris, 1950.

ox, Geoffrey. *The Red Army Moves.* London, 1941.

allin, David J. *Soviet Russia's Foreign Policy, 1939–1942.* New Haven, Conn., 1942.

lliston, H. B. *Finland Fights.* Boston, 1940.

storick, Eric. *Stafford Cripps.* New York, 1949.

eis, Herbert. *The Road to Pearl Harbor.* Princeton, N.J., 1950.

he Finnish Blue Book. Philadelphia, 1940.

inland Reveals Her Secret Documents on Soviet Policy, March 1940–June 1941. New York, 1941.

afencu, Grigore. *Prelude to the Russian Campaign.* London, 1945.

amelin, Général [Maurice]. *Servir.* 3 vols. Paris, 1946–47.

allancz, Victor (ed.). *The Betrayal of the Left.* London, 1941.

Iarrison, E. J. *Lithuania's Fight for Freedom.* New York, 1952.

Ioptner, J. B. *Yugoslavia in Crisis, 1934–1941.* New York, 1962.

akobson, Max. *The Diplomacy of the Winter War.* Cambridge, Mass., 1961.

Kolarz, Walter. *Russia and Her Colonies.* London, 1952.

Kordt, Erich. *Wahn und Wirklichkeit.* 2nd ed. Stuttgart, 1948.

angdon-Davies, John. *Invasion in the Snow.* Boston, 1941.

Langer, William L., and Gleason, S. Everett. *The Undeclared Wa 1940–1941* (Vol. II, *The World Crisis and American Foreign Policy* New York, 1953.

Lundin, C. Leonard. *Finland and the Second World War*. Bloomington Ind., 1957.

Mannerheim, Marshal. *Memoirs*. New York, 1954.

Meissner, Boris. *Die Sowjetunion, die baltischen Staaten, und da Völkerrecht*. Cologne, 1956.

Oras, Ants. *Baltic Eclipse*. London, 1948.

Pakštas, K. *The Lithuanian Situation*. Chicago, 1941.

Republic of Poland, Ministry for Foreign Affairs. *The Polish Whit Book: Official Documents Concerning Polish-German and Polish Soviet Relations, 1933–1939*. London, 1940?

Rossi, A. [Angelo Tasca]. *The Russo-German Alliance*. Boston, 195

Schmidt, Dr. Paul. *Statist auf diplomatischer Büne, 1923–45*. Bonn 1949.

Schuman, Frederick L. *Night Over Europe*. New York, 1941.

Schwartz, Andrew J. *America and the Russo-Finnish War*. Washington 1960.

Scott, John. *Duel for Europe: Stalin Versus Hitler*. Boston, 1942.

Swettenham, John Alexander. *The Tragedy of the Baltic States*. Lon don, 1952.

Tanner, Väinö. *The Winter War: Finland Against Russia, 1939–194* Stanford, Calif., 1957.

Toynbee, Arnold and Veronica M. (eds.). *The Initial Triumph of th Axis* (*Survey of International Affairs, 1939–1946*). New York, 195

U.S. Department of State. *Nazi-Soviet Relations, 1939–1941: Docu ments from the Archives of the German Foreign Office*. Washington 1948.

The U.S.S.R. and Finland: Outstanding Facts and Documents. Mos cow, 1939.

Weinberg, Gerhard L. *Germany and the Soviet Union, 1939–194* Leiden, 1954.

Weizsäcker, Ernst von. *Memoirs*. Chicago, 1951.

Wolfe, Henry C. *The Imperial Soviets*. New York, 1940.

Wuorinen, John H. (ed.). *Finland and World War II, 1939–194* New York, 1948.

CHAPTER NINE—INTO THE MAELSTROM

There is as yet no satisfactory account of the Russo-German conflic Both Feis and McNeill are excellent diplomatic histories of the Allie

war effort. Churchill, Sherwood, and Dedijer contain indispensable
primary source material.

Adamic, Louis. *My Native Land*. New York, 1943.

Allen, W. E. D., and Muratoff, Paul. *The Russian Campaigns of 1941–43*. Harmonsworth, England, 1944.

———. *The Russian Campaigns of 1944–45*. Harmondsworth, England, 1946.

Amtliches Material zum Massenmord von Katyn. Berlin, 1943.

Anders, Lt.-General W. *An Army in Exile: The Story of the Second Polish Corps*. London, 1949.

———. *Hitler's Defeat in Russia*. Chicago, 1953.

———. *Katyn*. Paris, c. 1949.

Atholl, Duchess of. *The Tragedy of Warsaw and Its Documentation*. London, 1945.

Bilainkin, George, *Tito*. London, 1949.

Bor-Komorowski, T. *The Secret Army*. New York, 1951.

Bryant, Arthur. *The Turn of the Tide*. Garden City, N.Y., 1957.

Butler, J. R. M., and others. *Grand Strategy* (*History of the Second World War: United Kingdom Military Series*). 3 vols. London, 1956–57.

Byford-Jones, W. *The Greek Trilogy*. London, c. 1945.

Churchill, Winston S. *The Second World War*. 6 vols. Boston, 1948–53.

Ciechanowski, Jan. *Defeat in Victory*. Garden City, N.Y., 1947.

Clissold, Stephen. *Whirlwind: An Account of Marshal Tito's Rise to Power*. New York, 1949.

Czapski, Joseph. *The Inhuman Land*. New York, 1952.

Dallin, Alexander. *German Rule in Russia, 1941–1945*. New York, 1957.

Dangerfield, Elma. *Beyond the Urals*. London, 1946.

The Dark Side of the Moon. New York, 1947.

Dawson, Raymond H. *The Decision to Aid Russia, 1941*. Chapel Hill, N.C., 1959.

Deane, John R. *The Strange Alliance*. New York, 1947.

Deborin, G. A., and others. *Istoria velikoi otechestvennoi voiny Sovetskovo Soyuza, 1941–45*. [The History of the Great Patriotic War of the Soviet Union, 1941–45]. Vol. I (in progress). Moscow, 1961–

Dedijer, Vladimir. *Tito*. New York, 1953.

Dzelepy, E. N. *Le Drame de la résistance grecque*. Paris, 1946.

Einsiedel, Heinrich von. *I Joined the Russians*. New Haven, Conn., 1953.

Falls, Cyril. *The Second World War*. 2nd ed. London, 1948.

Feis, Herbert. *Churchill-Roosevelt-Stalin: The War They Waged and the Peace They Sought.* Princeton, N.J., 1957.

Fischer, George. *Soviet Opposition to Stalin.* Cambridge, Mass., 1952.

Fischer, Louis. *The Great Challenge.* New York, 1946.

Fotich, Constantine. *The War We Lost.* New York, 1948.

Freidin, Seymour, and Richardson, William (eds.). *The Fatal Decisions.* New York, 1956.

Fuller, Major-General J. F. C. *The Second World War, 1939–45.* London, 1948.

Guderian, General Heinz. *Panzer Leader.* London, 1952.

Guillaume, Général A. *La Guerre germano-soviétique, 1941–1945.* Paris, 1949.

Higgins, Trumbull. *Winston Churchill and the Second Front, 1940–1943.* New York, 1957.

Hull, Cordell. *Memoirs.* 2 vols. New York, 1948.

Institute of History, Academy of Science of the USSR. *Ocherki istori velikoi otechestvennoi voiny, 1941–1945* [An Outline History of the Great Patriotic War, 1941–1945]. Moscow, 1955.

The Katyn Forest Massacre: Hearings Before a Select Committee to Conduct an Investigation of the Facts, Evidence, and Circumstance of the Katyn Forest Massacre. 82nd Congress, 2nd session. 6 parts in 3 vols. Washington, 1952.

King, Ernest J., and Whitehill, Walter Muir. *Fleet Admiral King.* New York, 1952.

Kleist, Dr. Peter. *Zwischen Hitler und Stalin, 1939–1945.* Bonn, 1950.

Knezevich, Lt. Col. Zivan L. *Why the Allies Abandoned the Yugoslav Army of General Mihailovich.* Washington? 1945.

Korbonski, Stefan. *Fighting Warsaw: The Story of the Polish Underground State, 1939–1945.* New York, 1956.

Kousoulas, Dimitrios G. *The Price of Freedom: Greece in World Affairs, 1939–1953.* Syracuse, N.Y., 1953.

Krylov, Ivan. *Soviet Staff Officer.* London, 1951.

Kusnierz, Dr. Bronislaw. *Stalin and the Poles.* London, 1949.

Kuusinen, Otto. *Finland Unmasked.* London, 1944.

Lazitch, Branko. *La Tragédie du général Draja Mihailovitch.* Paris, 1946.

Leahy, Fleet Admiral William D. *I Was There.* New York, 1950.

Léderrey, Colonel [Ernest]. *La Défaite allemande a l'Est.* Paris, 1951.

Leeper, Sir Reginald. *When Greek Meets Greek.* London, 1950.

Leonhard, Wolfgang. *Child of the Revolution.* Chicago, 1958.

Liddell Hart, B.H. *The German Generals Talk.* New York, 1948.

—— (ed.). *The Red Army.* New York, 1956.

Mackiewicz, Joseph. *The Katyn Wood Murders*. London, 1951.

Maclean, Fitzroy. *Escape to Adventure*. Boston, 1950.

——. *The Heretic: The Life and Times of Josip Broz-Tito*. New York, 1957.

Manstein, Field-Marshal Erich von. *Lost Victories*. Chicago, 1958.

Martel, Lt.-Gen. Sir Gifford. *The Russian Outlook*. London, 1947.

Martin, David. *Ally Betrayed: The Uncensored Story of Tito and Mihailovich*. New York, 1946.

McNeill, William Hardy. *America, Britain, and Russia: Their Cooperation and Conflict, 1941–1946* (*Survey of International Affairs, 1939–1946*). New York, 1953.

——. *The Greek Dilemma: War and Aftermath*. Philadelphia, 1947.

Mikolajczyk, Stanislaw. *The Rape of Poland*. New York, 1948.

Ministry of Foreign Affairs of the U.S.S.R. *Correspondence Between the Chairman of the Council of Ministers of the U.S.S.R. and the Presidents of the U.S.A. and the Prime Ministers of Great Britain During the Great Patriotic War of 1941–1945*. 2 vols. Moscow, 1957.

National Liberation Front (E.A.M.). *White Book, May 1944–March 1945*. New York, 1945.

Neumann, William L. *Making the Peace, 1941–1945*. Washington, 1950.

Padev, Michael. *Marshal Tito*. London, 1944.

Perkins, Frances. *The Roosevelt I Knew*. New York, 1947.

Peter II, King of Yugoslavia. *A King's Heritage*. New York, 1954.

Piyade, Mosha. *About the Legend That the Yugoslav Uprising Owed Its Existence to Soviet Assistance*. London, 1950.

Pogue, Forrest C. *The Supreme Command*, Washington, 1954.

Pridonoff, Eric L. *Tito's Yugoslavia*. Washington, 1955.

Reitlinger, Gerald. *The House Built on Sand: The Conflicts of German Policy in Russia, 1939–1945*. New York, 1960.

Roosevelt, Elliott. *As He Saw It*. New York, 1946.

Rozek, Edward J. *Allied Wartime Diplomacy: A Pattern in Poland*. New York, 1958.

Sarafis, General Stefanos. *Greek Resistance Army: The Story of ELAS*. London, 1951.

Scaevola. *A Study in Forgery*. London, 1945.

Schröter, Heinz. *Stalingrad*. New York, 1958.

Seth, Ronald. *Stalingrad: Point of Return*. New York, 1959.

Sharp, Samuel L. *Poland: White Eagle on a Red Field*. Cambridge, Mass., 1953.

Sherwood, Robert E. *Roosevelt and Hopkins*. New York, 1948.

Shirer, William L. *The Rise and Fall of the Third Reich*. New York, 1960.

Snyder, Louis L. *The War: A Concise History, 1939–1945.* New Yor
    1961.
Soviet Foreign Policy During the Patriotic War: Documents and M
    terials. 2 vols. London, 1946.
Stalin, Joseph. *The Great Patriotic War of the Soviet Union.* Ne
    York, 1945.
Standley, William A., and Ageton, Arthur A. *Admiral Ambassador t*
    Russia. Chicago, 1955.
"Statement of the Special Commission . . . [on] the Shooting of th
    Polish Officers . . . in the Katyn Forest by the German Fascist I
    vaders," *VOKS Bulletin,* No. 1 (1944), 15–29.
Stavrianos, L. S. *Greece: American Dilemma and Opportunity.* Ch
    cago, 1952.
Stern, H. Peter. *The Struggle for Poland.* Washington, 1953.
Stettinius, Edward R., Jr. *Lend-Lease: Weapon for Victory.* New Yor
    1944.
Tansill, Charles Callan. *Back Door to War: The Roosevelt Foreig*
    Policy, 1933–1941. Chicago, 1952.
Thorwald, Jürgen. *Wen sie Verderben wollen: Bericht des grosse*
    Verrats. Stuttgart, 1952.
Umiastowski, R. *Poland, Russia and Great Britain, 1941–1945.* Londo
    1946.
U.S. Department of State. *Foreign Relations of the United State*
    Diplomatic Papers: The Conferences at Cairo and Tehran. Wash
    ington, 1961.
Vail Motter, T. H. *The Persian Corridor and Aid to Russia.* Washing
    ton, 1952.
Vneshnaya politika Sovetskovo Soyuza v period otechestvennoi voin
    [The Foreign Policy of the Soviet Union in the Period of the Patriot
    War]. 3 vols. Moscow, 1944–47.
Wagner, Stanley P. "The Diplomacy of the Polish Government in Exil
    . . ." Ph.D. thesis, University of Pittsburgh, 1953.
Werth, Alexander. *The Year of Stalingrad.* New York, 1947.
Woodhouse, C. M. *Apple of Discord.* London, 1948.
Yakemtchouk, Romain. *La Ligne Curzon et la IIe guerre mondial*
    Paris, 1957.

CHAPTER TEN—THE ABORTIVE PEACE:
YALTA, POTSDAM, AND AFTER

Snell presents a balanced analysis of the Yalta Conference and in
cludes a useful bibliographical essay. Feis is the best and most detaile

ccount of the Potsdam Conference. Crocker is an interesting specimen f the historical myth-mongering favored by the extreme Right.

ttlee, C. R. *As It Happened.* New York, 1954.
elden, Jack. *China Shakes the World.* New York, 1949.
lond, Georges. *The Death of Hitler's Germany.* New York, 1954.
utow, Robert J. C. *Japan's Decision to Surrender.* Stanford, Calif., 1954.
yrnes, James F. *All in One Lifetime.* New York, 1958.
———. *Speaking Frankly.* New York, 1947.
lark, Mark W. *Calculated Risk.* New York, 1950.
rocker, George N. *Roosevelt's Road to Russia.* Chicago, 1959.
isenhower, Dwight D. *Crusade in Europe.* Garden City, N.Y., 1948.
pstein, Israel. *The Unfinished Revolution in China.* Boston, 1947.
eis, Herbert. *Between War and Peace: The Potsdam Conference.* Princeton, N.J., 1960.
———. *The China Tangle: The American Effort in China from Pearl Harbor to the Marshall Mission.* Princeton, N.J., 1953.
———. *Japan Subdued: The Atomic Bomb and the End of the War in the Pacific.* Princeton, N.J., 1961.
rabski, Stanislaw. *The Polish-Soviet Frontier.* New York, c. 1944.
amzavi, A. H. *Persia and the Powers: An Account of Diplomatic Relations, 1941–1946.* London, 1946.
urewitz, J. C. *Middle East Dilemmas.* New York, 1953.
nes, F. C. *The Far East, 1942–1946* (*Survey of International Affairs, 1939–1946*). London, 1955.
———. *Manchuria Since 1931.* London, 1949.
rdan, Z. *Oder Neisse Line: A Study of the Political, Economic and European Significance of Poland's Western Frontier.* London, 1952.
ase, Toshikazu. *Journey to the "Missouri."* New Haven, Conn., 1950.
ato, Masuo. *The Lost War: A Japanese Reporter's Inside Story.* New York, 1946.
uter, Laurence S. *Airman at Yalta.* New York, 1955.
ohbeck, Don. *Patrick J. Hurley.* Chicago, 1956.
oorad, George. *Lost Peace in China.* New York, 1949.
orrell, Sydney. *Spheres of Influences.* New York, 1946.
emec, František, and Mondry, Vladimir. *The Soviet Seizure of Subcarpathian Ruthenia.* Toronto, 1955.
uley, Edwin W. *Report on Japanese Reparations to the President of the United States, November 1945 to April 1946.* [Washington, 1946].
igemitsu, Mamoru. *Japan and Her Destiny.* London, 1958.

Shwadran, Benjamin. *The Middle East, Oil and the Great Powers.* New York, 1955.

Snell, John L. (ed.). *The Meaning of Yalta.* Baton Rouge, La., 1956.

——. *Wartime Origins of the East-West Dilemma Over Germany.* New Orleans, 1959.

Stettinius, Edward R., Jr. *Roosevelt and the Russians: The Yalta Conference.* Garden City, N.Y., 1949.

Stimson, Henry L., and Bundy, McGeorge. *On Active Service in Peace and War.* New York, 1948.

Strauss, Harold. *The Division and Dismemberment of Germany.* Ambilly, France, 1952.

Stypulkowski, Z. *Invitation to Moscow.* London, 1951.

Thomas, Lewis V., and Frye, Richard N. *The United States and Turkey and Iran.* Cambridge, Mass., 1952.

Tōgō, Shigenori. *The Cause of Japan.* New York, 1956.

Trial of the Organizers, Leaders and Members of the Polish Diversionist Organizations in the Rear of the Red Army . . . : Verbatim Report. London, 1945?

Truman, Harry S. *Memoirs.* 2 vols. Garden City, N.Y., 1955–56.

U.S. Department of State. *Foreign Relations of the United States. Diplomatic Papers: The Conference of Berlin (The Potsdam Conference), 1945.* 2 vols. Washington, 1960.

——. *Foreign Relations of the United States, Diplomatic Papers, The Conferences at Malta and Yalta, 1945.* Washington, 1955.

——. *United States Relations with China with Special Reference to the Period 1944–1949.* Washington, 1949.

Wagner, Wolfgang. *The Genesis of the Oder-Neisse Line.* Stuttgart, 1957.

Wedemeyer, General Albert C. *Wedemeyer Reports!* New York, 1958.

White, Theodore, and Jacoby, Annalee. *Thunder Out of China.* New York, 1946.

Wilmot, Chester. *The Struggle for Europe.* New York, 1952.

CHAPTER ELEVEN—COLD WAR: STANDOFF IN EUROPE

The literature on the Soviet takeover in Eastern Europe is huge but perhaps the ablest summary is Seton-Watson's *East European Revolution.* Korbel is a perceptive account of Czechoslovakia and the events leading to the Communist *coup* in 1948. Different aspects of Titoism are skillfully analyzed in Armstrong and in Ulam. Ingram's history of the first decade of the cold war is readable and objective but places a rather generous construction on Soviet aims and policies.

cheson, Dean. *Sketches From Life of Men I Have Known*. New York, 1961.

damic, Louis. *The Eagle and the Roots*. Garden City, N.Y., 1952.

rmstrong, Hamilton Fish. *Tito and Goliath*. New York, 1951.

rnold, G. L. *The Pattern of World Conflict*. New York, 1955.

alfour, Michael, and Mair, John. *Four Power Control in Germany and Austria, 1945–1946 (Survey of International Affairs, 1939–1946)*. New York, 1956.

arghoorn, Frederick C. *Soviet Russian Nationalism*. New York, 1956.

artlett, Vernon. *East of the Iron Curtain*. New York, 1950.

arton, Paul. *Prague à l'heure de Moscou*. Paris, 1954.

ass, Robert, and Marbury, Elizabeth (eds.). *The Soviet Yugoslav Controversy, 1948–58: A Documentary Record*. New York, 1959.

eamish, Major Tufton. *Must Night Fall?* London, 1950.

eneš, Dr. Eduard. *Memoirs: From Munich to New War and New Victory*. London, 1954.

etts, R. R. (ed.). *Central and South East Europe, 1945–1948*. London, 1950.

ishop, Robert, and Crayfield, E. S. *Russia Astride the Balkans*. New York, 1948.

lack, C. E. (ed.). *Challenge in Eastern Europe*. New Brunswick, N.J., 1954.

randt, Willy (as told to Leo Lania). *My Road to Berlin*. New York, 1960.

regman, A. (ed.). *Faked Elections in Poland*. London, 1947?

rown, John. *Who's Next? The Lesson of Czechoslovakia*. London, 1951.

urchett, Wilfred. *Cold War in Germany*. Melbourne? 1950.

arman, E. Day. *Soviet Imperialism*. Washington, 1950.

arr, Albert Z. *Truman, Stalin and Peace*. Garden City, N.Y., 1950.

arton de Wiart, [Henry]. *Chronique de la guerre froide*. Brussels, 1950.

atroux, General [Georges]. *J'ai vu tomber le rideau de fer: Moscou, 1945–1948*. Paris, 1952.

enter for International Studies, Massachusetts Institute of Technology. *The Soviet Takeover of Eastern Europe*. Cambridge, Mass., 1954.

lay, Lucius D. *Decision in Germany*. Garden City, N.Y., 1950.

onnally, Senator Tom (as told to Alfred Steinberg). *My Name is Tom Connally*. New York, 1954.

ounts, George S., and Lodge, Nucia. *The Country of the Blind*. Boston, 1949.

retzianu, Alexandre (ed.). *Captive Rumania*. New York, 1956.

Dalmas, Louis. *Le Communisme yougoslave depuis la rupture ave* *Moscou.* Paris, 1950.

Davidson, Basil. *Germany: What Now?* London, 1950.

Davison, W. Philips. *The Berlin Blockade: A Study in Cold Wa* *Politics.* Princeton, N.J., 1958.

Deborin, G. A. (ed.). *Mezhdunarodnie otnoshenie i vneshnaya politik* *Sovetskovo Soyuza, 1945–1949* [*International Relations and th* *Foreign Policy of the Soviet Union, 1945–1949*]. Moscow, 1958.

A Decade of American Foreign Policy: Basic Documents, 1941–4 (Senate Document No. 123, 81st Congress, 1st session). Washingto* 1950.

Dennett, Raymond, and Johnson, Joseph E. (eds.). *Negotiating Wit* *the Russians.* Boston, 1951.

Dewar, Hugo. *The Modern Inquisition.* London, 1953.

Diamond, William. *Czechoslovakia Between East and West.* Londo* 1947.

Djilas, Milovan. *Conversations With Stalin.* New York, 1962.

Dokumente zur Deutschlandpolitik der Sowjetunion. Berlin, 1957.

Dragnich, Alex N. *Tito's Promised Land: Yugoslavia.* New Brunswicl N.J., 1954.

Duchacek, Ivo. "The February Coup in Czechoslovakia," *World Po* *itics*, II (July 1950), 511–32.

Duhnke, Horst. *Stalinismus in Deutschland: Die Geschichte der sou* *jetischen Besatzungzone.* Cologne, 1955?

Einaudi, Mario, and others. *Communism in Western Europe.* Ithac* N.Y., 1951.

Farrell, R. Barry. *Jugoslavia and the Soviet Union, 1948–1956.* Hamde* Conn., 1956.

Fejtö, François. *Histoire des démocraties populaires.* Paris, 1952.

Friedman, Otto. *The Break-Up of Czech Democracy.* London, 1950.

Friedmann, W. *The Allied Military Government of Germany.* Londo* 1947.

Gluckstein, Ygael. *Stalin's Satellites in Europe.* Boston, 1952.

Gottlieb, Manuel. *The German Peace Settlement and the Berlin Crisi* New York, 1960.

Grayson, Cary Travers, Jr. *Austria's International Position, 1938–195* Geneva, 1953.

Griffis, Stanton. *Lying in State.* Garden City, N.Y., 1952.

Gruber, Karl. *Between Liberation and Liberty: Austria in the Post-W* *World.* London, 1955.

Guiton, R. J. *Paris-Moskau: Die Sowjetunion in der auswärtigen Polit* *Frankreichs seit dem Zweiten Weltkrieg.* Stuttgart, 1956.

nther, John. *Behind the Curtain*. New York, 1949.

alasz, Nicholas. *In the Shadow of Russia: Eastern Europe in the Postwar World*. New York, 1959.

alperin, Ernest. *The Triumphant Heretic: Tito's Struggle Against Stalin*. London, 1958.

ill, Russell. *Struggle for Germany*. New York, 1947.

iscocks, Richard. *The Rebirth of Austria*. London, 1953.

odgkinson, Harry. *Challenge to the Kremlin*. New York, 1952.

owley, Brigadier General Frank. *Berlin Command*. New York, 1950.

gram, Kenneth. *History of the Cold War*. New York, 1955.

nes, Joseph M. *The Fifteen Weeks (February 21–June 5, 1947)*. New York, 1955.

sten, Josef. *Oh My Country*. London, 1949.

ertesz, Stephen D. *Diplomacy in a Whirlpool: Hungary Between Nazi Germany and Soviet Russia*. Notre Dame, Ind., 1953.

—— (ed.). *The Fate of East Central Europe*. Notre Dame, Ind., 1956.

limov, Gregory. *The Terror Machine: The Inside Story of the Soviet Administration in Germany*. New York, 1953.

orbel, Josef. *The Communist Subversion of Czechoslovakia, 1938–1948*. Princeton, N.J., 1959.

——. *Tito's Communism*. Denver, 1951.

ane, Arthur Bliss. *I Saw Poland Betrayed*. New York, 1948.

ászló Rajk and His Accomplices Before the People's Court. Budapest, 1949.

azitch, Branko. *Tito et la révolution yougoslave, 1937–1956*. Paris, 1957.

ee, Arthur Gould. *Crown Against Sickle: The Story of King Michael of Rumania*. London, 1950.

——. *Special Duties*. London, 1946?

eiss, Amelia C. (ed.). *European Peace Treaties After World War II*. Boston, 1954.

ie, Trygve. *In the Cause of Peace: Seven Years with the United Nations*. New York, 1954.

ippmann, Walter. *The Cold War*. New York, 1947.

öwenthal, Fritz. *News from Soviet Germany*. London, 1950.

alara, Jean, and Rey, Lucienne. *La Pologne d'une occupation à l'autre (1944–1952)*. Paris, 1952.

arkham, Reuben H. *Rumania Under the Soviet Yoke*. Boston, 1949.

——. *Tito's Imperial Communism*. Chapel Hill, N.C., 1947.

atthews, Ronald. *The Death of the Fourth Republic*. New York, 1954.

McVicker, Charles P. *Titoism: Pattern for International Communism* New York, 1957.

Meissner, Boris (ed.). *Das Ostpakt-System.* Frankfurt-on-Main, 195
———. *Russland, die Westmächte und Deutschland: Die sowjetisch Deutschlandpolitik, 1943–1953.* Hamburg, 1953.

Middleton, Drew. *The Struggle for Germany.* Indianapolis, 1949.

Millis, Walter, and Duffield, E. S. (eds.). *The Forrestal Diaries.* Ne York, 1951.

Ministry of Foreign Affairs of the U.S.S.R. *The Soviet Union an the Question of the Unity of Germany and of the German Peac Treaty.* Moscow, 1952.

Molotov, V. M. *Problems of Foreign Policy: Speeches and Statement April 1945–November 1948.* Moscow, 1949.

Nagy, Ferenc. *The Struggle Behind the Iron Curtain.* New York, 194

Neal, Fred Warner. *Titoism in Action: The Reforms in Yugoslavia Aft 1948.* Berkeley, Calif., 1958.

Nettl, J. P. *The Eastern Zone and Soviet Policy in Germany, 1945–5 New York, 1951.

Padev, Michael. *Dimitrov Wastes No Bullets: Nikola Petkov, The Te Case.* London, 1948.

Peterson, Maurice. *Both Sides of the Curtain.* London, 1950.

Pickles, Dorothy. *French Politics: The First Years of the Fourth Re public.* London, 1953.

Price, Harry Bayard. *The Marshall Plan and Its Meaning.* Ithaca, N.Y 1955.

Pridonoff, Eric L. *Tito's Yugoslavia.* Washington, 1955.

Radulovic, Monty. *Tito's Republic.* London, 1948.

Reale, Eugenio. *Nascita del Cominform.* Milan, 1958.

Reitzel, William, and others. *United States Foreign Policy, 1945–195 Washington, 1956.

Rieber, Alfred J. *Stalin and the French Communist Party, 1941–194 New York, 1962.

Riess, Curt. *The Berlin Story.* New York, 1952.

Ripka, Hubert. *Czechoslovakia Enslaved.* London, 1950.
———. *East and West.* London, 1944.

Roberts, Henry L. *Rumania: Political Problems of an Agrarian Stat New Haven, Conn., 1951.

Ruhm von Oppen, Beate (ed.). *Documents on Germany Under Oc cupation, 1945–1954.* London, 1955.

Schaffer, Gordon. *Russian Zone.* London, 1947.

Schmidt, Dana Adams. *Anatomy of a Satellite.* Boston, 1952.

:ton-Watson, Hugh. *The East European Revolution*. 3rd ed. New York, 1957.

——. *Neither War Nor Peace: The Struggle for Power in the Postwar World*. New York, 1960.

:ttel, Arthur (ed.). *This is Germany*. New York, 1950.

\epherd, Gordon. *The Austrian Odyssey*. New York, 1957.

——. *Russia's Danubian Empire*. London, 1954.

\e *Soviet-Yugoslav Dispute: Text of the Published Correspondence*. London, 1948.

\anier, John W. *American Foreign Policy Since World War II*. New York, 1960.

\owe, Leland. *Conquest By Terror: The Story of Satellite Europe*. New York, 1952.

:rang, Lord. *Home and Abroad*. London, 1956.

:ransky, Jan. *East Wind Over Prague*. London, 1950.

Student of Affairs. *How Did the Satellites Happen?* London, 1952.

\aborsky, Edward. *Communism in Czechoslovakia, 1948–1960*. Princeton, N.J., 1961.

\hompson, Elizabeth M. "Yugoslavia and the Soviet Union, 1941–1948." M.A. thesis, Columbia University, 1950.

\omasic, D. A. *National Communism and Soviet Strategy*. Washington, 1957.

rial of the Former National Peasant Party Leaders Maniu, Mihalache . . . and Others. Bucharest, 1947.

\he *Trial of Traïcho Kostov and His Group*. Sofia, 1949.

\lam, Adam B. *Titoism and the Cominform*. Cambridge, Mass., 1952.

.S. Department of State. *American Foreign Policy, 1950–1955: Basic Documents*. 2 vols. Washington, 1957.

——. *Paris Peace Conference, 1946: Selected Documents*. Washington, 1946?

——. *The Problem of the Turkish Straits*. Washington, 1947.

\.S. House of Representatives, 83rd Congress, 2nd Session, Select Committee on Communist Aggression. *House Report No. 2684*. 16 parts. Washington, 1954–55.

\andenburg, Arthur H., Jr. (with the collaboration of Joe Alex Morris) (eds.). *The Private Papers of Senator Vandenburg*. Boston, 1952.

\oigt, F. A. *The Greek Sedition*. London, 1949.

——. *Pax Britannica*. London, 1949.

\/arriner, Doreen. *Revolution in Eastern Europe*. London, 1950.

\/erth, Alexander. *France, 1940–1955*. London, 1956.

\/hat Happened in Czechoslovakia? *An Account of the Government Crisis in February 1948*. Prague, 1948.

White, John Baker. *Pattern for Conquest.* London, 1956.

White, Leigh. *Balkan Caesar: Tito Versus Stalin.* New York, 1951.

White Book on Aggressive Activities By the Governments of t *U.S.S.R., Poland, Czechoslovakia, Hungary, Rumania, Bulgaria an* *Albania Towards Yugoslavia.* Belgrade, 1951.

Winterton, Paul. *Inquest on an Ally.* London, 1948.

Wolfe, Bertram D. *Six Keys to the Soviet System.* Boston, 1956.

Yindrich, Jan. *Tito v. Stalin: The Battle of the Marshals.* London, 195

Zacharias, Ellis M. (in collaboration with Ladislas Farago). *Behir* *Closed Doors: The Secret History of the Cold War.* New York, 195

Zink, Harold. *The United States in Germany, 1944–1955.* Princeto N.J., 1957.

CHAPTER TWELVE—COLD WAR: THE SOVIET CHALLENGE IN ASIA

Beloff is reliable and objective, virtually the only work in the fiel Trager and Brimmell are scholarly studies of Southeast Asian Cor munism, somewhat difficult for the uninitiated. Japanese Communis is ably covered in Swearingen and Langer. Lancaster is the outstan ing work on Indochina. Comparable studies of China and Korea are u fortunately very few, primarily because of the scarcity of reliable firs hand material.

Abaya, Hernando J. *Betrayal in the Philippines.* New York, 1946.

Allen, Richard C. *Korea's Syngman Rhee.* Rutland, Vt., and Toky 1960.

Astafyev, G. V. *Interventsia SShA v Kitae i eyo porazhenie (194 1949 gg.)* [The Intervention of the USA in China and Its Defe (1945–1949)]. Moscow, 1958.

Ball, W. Macmahon. *Japan: Enemy or Ally?* New York, 1949.

———. *Nationalism and Communism in East Asia.* 2nd ed. Carlto Australia, 1956.

Beloff, Max. *Soviet Policy in the Far East, 1944–1951.* New York, 195

Berger, Carl. *The Korea Knot: A Military-Political History.* Philade phia, 1957.

Bernstein, David. *The Philippine Story.* New York, 1947.

Boorman, Howard L., and others. *Moscow-Peking Axis: Strengths an* *Strains.* New York, 1957.

Borton, Hugh, and others. *Japan Between East and West.* New Yor 1957.

Brimmell, J. H. *Communism in South East Asia: A Political Analysi* London, 1959.

rines, Russell, *MacArthur's Japan*. Philadelphia, 1948.

ady, John F. *A History of Modern Burma*. Ithaca, N.Y., 1958.

hang, Carsun. *The Third Force in China*. New York, 1952.

hassin, Général L.-M. *La Conquête de la Chine par Mao Tse-tung (1945–1949)*. Paris, 1952.

hung, Henry. *The Russians Came to Korea*. Seoul and Washington, 1947.

ohen, Bernard C. *The Political Process and Foreign Policy: The Making of the Japanese Peace Settlement*. Princeton, N.J., 1957.

olbert, Evelyn S. *The Left Wing in Japanese Politics*. New York, 1952.

ole, Allan B. (ed.). *Conflict in Indo-China and International Repercussions: A Documentary History, 1945–1955*. Ithaca, N.Y., 1956.

everall, Richard L-G. *Red Star Over Japan*. Calcutta, 1952.

evillers, Philippe. *Histoire du Viêt-Nam de 1940 à 1952*. 3rd ed. Paris, 1952.

ruhe, David N. *Soviet Russia and Indian Communism, 1917–1947*. New York, 1959.

airbank, John King. *The United States and China*. 2nd ed. Cambridge, Mass., 1958.

all, Bernard B. *The Viet-Minh Regime: Government and Administration in the Democratic Republic of Vietnam*. 2nd ed. New York, 1956.

earey, Robert A. *The Occupation of Japan: Second Phase, 1948–50*. New York, 1950.

ifield, Russell H. *The Diplomacy of Southeast Asia, 1945–1958*. New York, 1958.

ischer, Ruth. *Von Lenin zu Mao: Kommunismus in der Bandung-Ara*. Düsseldorf, 1956.

itzgerald, Charles Patrick. *Revolution in China*. New York, 1952.

orman, Harrison. *Blunder in Asia*. New York, 1950.

ayn, Mark. *Japan Diary*. New York, 1949.

luckstein, Ygael. *Mao's China: Economic and Political Survey*. Boston, 1957.

oodrich, Leland M. *Korea: A Study of U.S. Policy in the United Nations*. New York, 1956.

ammer, Ellen J. *The Struggle for Indochina*. Stanford, Calif., 1954.

——. *The Struggle for Indochina Continues*. Stanford, Calif., 1955.

anrahan, Gene Z. *The Communist Struggle in Malaya*. New York, 1954.

ahin, George McTurnan. *Nationalism and Revolution in Indonesia*. Ithaca, N.Y., 1952.

Kautsky, John H. *Moscow and the Communist Party of India*. New York, 1956.

Kawai, Kazuo. *Japan's American Interlude*. Chicago, 1960.

Lacouture, Jean, and Devillers, Philippe. *La Fin d'une guerre: Indochinie, 1954*. Paris, 1960.

Lancaster, Donald. *The Emancipation of French Indochina*. London, 1961.

Latourette, Kenneth Scott. *The American Record in the Far East 1945–1951*. New York, 1952.

Lauterbach, Richard E. *Danger From the East*. New York, 1947.

Leckie, Robert Hugh. *Conflict: The History of the Korean War*. New York, 1962.

Lewe van Aduard, Baron E. J. *Japan from Surrender to Peace*. New York, 1954.

Lindsay, Michael. *China and the Cold War*. Carlton, Australia, 1955.

MacGregor-Hastie, Roy. *The Red Barbarians: The Life and Times of Mao Tse-tung*. Philadelphia, 1962.

Mao Tse-tung. *Turning Point in China*. New York, 1948.

Martin, Edwin M. *The Allied Occupation of Japan*. Stanford, Calif., 1948.

Masani, M. R. *The Communist Party of India*. New York, 1954.

McCune, George M. (with the collaboration of Arthur L. Grey, Jr.) *Korea Today*. Cambridge, Mass., 1950.

McVey, Ruth. *The Calcutta Conference and the Southeast Asian Uprising*. Ithaca, N.Y., 1958.

———. *The Development of the Indonesian Communist Party and Its Relations with the Soviet Union and the Chinese People's Republic*. Cambridge, Mass., 1954.

Meade, E. Grant. *American Military Government in Korea*. New York, 1951.

Miller, Harry. *The Communist Menace in Malaya*. New York, 1954.

Napier, J. P. *A Survey of the Japan Communist Party*. Tokyo, 1952?

Oliver, Robert T. *Syngman Rhee*. New York, 1954.

———. *Verdict in Korea*. State College, Pa., 1952.

———. *Why War Came in Korea*. New York, 1950.

Overstreet, Gene D., and Windmiller, Marshall. *Communism in India*. Berkeley, Calif., 1959.

Payne, Robert. *Portrait of a Revolutionary: Mao Tse-tung*. 2nd ed. New York, 1962.

Purcell, Victor. *Malaya: Communist or Free?* Stanford, Calif., 1954.

Pye, Lucian W. *Guerrilla Communism in Malaya*. Princeton, N.J., 1956.

Romulo, Carlos P. *Crusade in Asia: Philippine Victory*. New York, 1955.

Rovere, Richard H., and Schlesinger, Arthur M., Jr. *The General and the President and the Future of American Foreign Policy.* New York, 1951.

Rudolph, Philip. "North Korea, 1945–1958: A Case Study in Communist Development." M.A. thesis, Columbia University, 1959.

Scaff, Alvin H. *The Philippine Answer to Communism.* Stanford, Calif., 1955.

Smith, Robert Aura. *Philippine Freedom, 1946–1958.* New York, 1958.

The Soviet Union and the Korean Question (Documents). London, 1950.

Spanier, John W. *The Truman-MacArthur Controversy and the Korean War.* Cambridge, Mass., 1959.

Stone, I. F. *The Hidden History of the Korean War.* New York, 1952.

Swearingen, Rodger, and Langer, Paul. *Red Flag in Japan: International Communism in Action, 1919–1951.* Cambridge, Mass., 1952.

Tang, Peter S. H. *Communist China Today: Domestic and Foreign Policies.* 2nd ed. Washington, 1961.

Taruc, Luis. *Born of the People.* New York, 1953.

Thompson, Virginia, and Adloff, Richard. *The Left Wing in Southeast Asia.* New York, 1950.

Tinker, Hugh. *The Union of Burma: A Study of the First Years of Independence.* New York, 1957.

Trager, Frank N. (ed.). *Marxism in Southeast Asia.* Stanford, Calif., 1959.

Tsukahira, Toshio G. *The Postwar Evolution of Communist Strategy in Japan.* Cambridge, Mass., 1954.

Utley, Freda. *The China Story.* Chicago, 1951.

Vandenbosch, Amry, and Butwell, Richard A. *Southeast Asia Among the World Powers.* Lexington, Ky., 1957.

Vinacke, Harold M. *Far Eastern Politics in the Postwar Period.* New York, 1956.

——. *The United States and the Far East, 1945–1951.* New York, 1952.

Walker, Richard L. *China Under Communism.* New Haven, Conn., 1955.

Whiting, Allen S. *China Crosses the Yalu: The Decision to Enter the Korean War.* New York, 1960.

Whitney, Major General Courtney. *MacArthur: His Rendezvous with History.* New York, 1956.

Wildes, Harry Emerson. *Typhoon in Tokyo: The Occupation and Its Aftermath.* New York, 1954.

Shils is a cogent and penetrating essay, undeservedly neglected Blackett's works are provocative and highly critical of Western policy

Biorklund, Admiral Elis. *International Atomic Policy During a Decade* Princeton, N.J., 1956.

Blackett, P. M. S. *Atomic Weapons and East-West Relations.* Cam bridge, England, 1956.

———. *Fear, War, and the Bomb: Military and Political Consequence* *of Atomic Energy.* New York, 1949.

Cohen, Elliot E. (ed.). *The New Red Anti-Semitism.* Boston, 1953.

Coit, Margaret. *Mr. Baruch.* Boston, 1957.

Dewhurst, Brigadier C. H. *Close Contact.* Boston, 1954.

Goldberg, B. Z. *The Jewish Problem in the Soviet Union.* New York 1961.

Gruliow, Leo (ed.). *Current Soviet Policies: The Documentary Recor* *of the 19th Communist Party Congress and the Reorganization Afte: Stalin's Death.* New York, 1953.

Morray, Joseph P. *From Yalta to Disarmament: Cold War Debate.* New York, 1961.

Nogee, Joseph L. *Soviet Policy Towards International Control o Atomic Energy.* Notre Dame, Ind., 1961.

Salisbury, Harrison E. *American in Russia.* New York, 1955.

———. *Moscow Journal: The End of Stalin.* Chicago, 1961.

Schwartz, Solomon M. *The Jews in the Soviet Union.* Syracuse, N.Y. 1951.

Shils, Edward A. *The Atomic Bomb in World Politics.* London, 1951

Teller, Judd L. *The Kremlin, the Jews, and the Middle East.* New York 1957.

Tugwell, Rexford G. *A Chronicle of Jeopardy, 1945–55.* Chicago, 1955

White Book on the Bonn War Treaty. [East] Berlin, 1952.

CHAPTER FOURTEEN—AFTER STALIN: THE UNCERTAIN THAW

Dallin is a comprehensive survey, anti-Soviet in tendency and likely to be standard on the period for many years. Ripka is a popular bu well-informed history stressing events in the 1950's. Brzezinski is a original and perceptive study of the satellites but hard going for the novice. Váli is the most thorough and objective study of the Hungarian revolution. The semi-revolution in Poland is recounted in Lewis and in Syrop, both of them first-class works of journalism.

Adams, Michael. *Suez and After: Year of Crisis*. Boston, 1958.

Alexander, Edgar. *Adenauer and the New Germany*. New York, 1957.

Aptheker, Herbert. *The Truth About Hungary*. New York, 1957.

Bain, Leslie B. *The Reluctant Satellites*. New York, 1960.

Beal, John Robinson. *John Foster Dulles*. New York, 1957.

Berliner, Joseph S. *Soviet Economic Aid*. New York, 1958.

Brant, Stefan. *The East German Rising: 17th June 1953*. New York, 1957.

Brzezinski, Zbigniew K. *The Soviet Bloc: Unity and Conflict*. 2nd ed. New York, 1961.

Bulganin, N. A., and Khrushchov, N. S. *Visit of Friendship to India, Burma and Afghanistan: Speeches and Official Documents, November-December 1955*. Moscow, 1956.

Campbell, John C. *Defense of the Middle East*. New York, 1960.

Childs, Marquis. *The Ragged Edge: The Diary of a Crisis*. Garden City, N.Y., 1955.

Dallin, David J. *Soviet Foreign Policy After Stalin*. Philadelphia, 1961.

Deutscher, Isaac. *Russia: What Next?* New York, 1953.

Donovan, Robert J. *Eisenhower: The Inside Story*. New York, 1956.

Drummond, Roscoe, and Coblentz, Gaston. *Duel at the Brink: John Foster Dulles' Command of American Power*. New York, 1960.

Eden, Anthony, *Full Circle*. Boston, 1960.

Ellis, Harry B. *Challenge in the Middle East*. New York, 1960.

Embree, G. D. *The Soviet Union Between the 19th and 20th Party Congresses, 1952–1956*. The Hague, 1959.

Fejtö, François. *Behind the Rape of Hungary*. New York, 1957.

Fischer, Louis. *Russia Revisited: A New Look at Russia and Her Satellites*. Garden City, N.Y., 1957.

Free Europe Committee. *The Revolt in Hungary: A Documentary Chronology of Events*. New York, 1956.

Free Europe University in Exile (College de l'Europe Libre). *La Révolution hongroise vue par les partis communistes de l'Europe*. [Paris, 1957].

Garrison, Mark Joseph. "The Courtship of Tito By Stalin's Successors." M.A. thesis, Columbia University, 1955.

Gibney, Frank. *The Frozen Revolution: Poland, A Study in Communist Decay*. New York, 1959.

————. *The Khrushchev Pattern*. New York, 1960.

Goold-Adams, Richard. *The Time of Power: A Reappraisal of John Foster Dulles*. London, 1962.

Great Britain, Foreign Office, Miscellaneous No. 5 (1954). Cmd. 9080. *Documents Relating to the Meeting of Foreign Ministers of France,*

the United Kingdom, the Soviet Union and the United States o
America: Berlin, January 25–February 18, 1954. London, 1954.

Gruliow, Leo (ed.). *Current Soviet Policies—II: The Documentar*
Record of the 20th Communist Party Congress and Its Aftermath
New York, 1957.

Hildebrandt, Rainer. *The Explosion: The Uprising Behind the Iror*
Curtain. New York, 1955.

Humbaraci, Arslan. *Middle East Indictment: From the Truman Doc*
trine, the Soviet Penetration and Britain's Downfall to the Eisen
hower Doctrine. London, 1958.

Johnson, Paul. *The Suez War.* New York, 1957.

Kellen, Konrad. *Khrushchev: A Political Portrait.* New York, 1961.

Kennan, George F. *Russia, the Atom and the West.* New York, 1958.

Kertesz, Stephen D. (ed.). *East Central Europe and the World: De-*
velopments in the Post-Stalin Era. Notre Dame, Ind., 1962.

Laqueur, Walter Z. (ed.). *The Middle East in Transition.* New York,
1958.

Lasky, Melvin J. (ed.). *The Hungarian Revolution.* New York, 1957.

Leonov, V. *The Events in Hungary.* Moscow, 1957.

Lewis, Flora. *A Case History of Hope: The Story of Poland's Peaceful*
Revolutions. Garden City, N.Y., 1958.

McClellan, Grant S. (ed.). *The Middle East in the Cold War.* New
York, 1956.

Mende, Tibor. *China and Her Shadow.* London, 1961.

Meray, Tibor. *Thirteen Days That Shook the Kremlin.* New York, 1959.

Mikes, George. *The Hungarian Revolution.* London, 1957.

Neal, Fred Warner. *War and Peace and Germany.* New York, 1962.

Newman, Bernard. *The Three Germanies.* London, 1957.

Paloczi-Horvath, George. *Khrushchev: The Making of a Dictator.* Boston, 1960.

Pistrak, Lazar. *The Grand Tactician: Khrushchev's Rise to Power.* New
York, 1961.

Prittie, Terence. *Germany Divided: The Legacy of the Nazi Era.* London, 1961.

Pusey, Merlo J. *Eisenhower the President.* New York, 1956.

La Révolution hongroise vue par les partis communistes de l'Europe de
l'Est. Paris, 1957?

Riess, Curt. *Der 17. Juni.* Berlin, 1954.

Ripka, Hubert. *Eastern Europe in the Post-War World.* London, 1961.

Rovere, Richard H. *Affairs of State: The Eisenhower Years.* New York,
1956.

Rush, Myron. *The Rise of Khrushchev.* Washington, 1958.

ussian Institute, Columbia University. *The Anti-Stalin Campaign and International Communism: A Selection of Documents.* New York, 1956.

chmitt, Walther E. *Krieg in Deutschland: Strategie und Taktik der Sowjetrussischen Deutschlandpolitik Seit 1945.* Düsseldorf, 1961.

ethe, Paul. *Zwischen Bonn und Moskau.* Frankfurt-on-Main, 1956.

herman, George. "The Russians and the East German Party (Prelude to June 17th 1953)," *Soviet Affairs,* No. 1. London, 1956.

ulzberger, C. L. *The Big Thaw.* New York, 1956.

yrop, Konrad. *Spring in October: The Polish Revolution of 1956.* London, 1957.

he *Truth About Hungary: Facts and Eyewitness Accounts.* Moscow, 1957.

nited Nations, General Assembly. *Report of the Special Committee on the Problem of Hungary.* New York, 1957.

J.S. Department of State. *The Suez Canal Problem, July 26–September 22, 1956.* Washington, 1956.

áli, Ferenc A. *Rift and Revolt in Hungary.* Cambridge, Mass., 1961.

Veymar, Paul. *Adenauer: His Authorized Biography.* New York, 1957.

Volfe, Bertram D. *Khrushchev and Stalin's Ghost: Text, Background and Meaning of Khrushchev's Secret Report to the Twentieth Congress on the Night of February 24–25, 1956.* New York, 1957.

illiacus, Konni. *A New Birth of Freedom? World Communism After Stalin.* London, 1957.

inner, Paul E. (ed.). *National Communism and Popular Revolt in Eastern Europe: A Selection of Documents on Events in Poland and Hungary, February–November, 1956.* New York, 1956.

———. *Revolution in Hungary.* New York, 1962.

CHAPTER FIFTEEN—ENTERING THE SPACE AGE

Deutscher is a brilliant essay on the Soviet Union and the cold war een in historical perspective. Neal is a penetrating criticism of American policy toward Russia intended for the general public. On he arms race, Nutting and Barnet are good capsule surveys, while Bechhoefer is the most detailed. Zagoria covers the public record of the Soviet-Chinese dispute with painstaking thoroughness.

Barnet, Richard J. *Who Wants Disarmament?* Boston, 1960.

Bechhoefer, Bernhard G. *Postwar Negotiations for Arms Control.* Washington, 1961.

Benes, Vaclav L., and others (eds.). *The Second Soviet-Yugoslav Dispute: Full Text of Main Documents, April–June, 1958.* Bloomingto Ind., 1959.

Boyd, R. G. *Communist China's Foreign Policy.* New York, 1962.

Champassak, Sisouk Na. *Storm Over Laos: A Contemporary Histor* New York, 1961.

Dallin, Alexander. *The Soviet Union at the United Nations.* New Yor 1962.

Deutscher, Isaac. *The Great Contest: Russia and the West.* New Yor 1960.

Draper, Theodore. *Castro's Revolution: Myths and Realities.* Ne York, 1962.

Fischer, Louis. *Russia, America, and the World.* New York, 1961.

Gunther, John. *Inside Europe Today.* New York, 1961.

Hamm, Harry. *Rebellion gegen Moskau.* Cologne, 1962.

Howard, Michael. *Disengagement in Europe.* Baltimore, 1958.

Hudson, G. F., and others. *The Sino-Soviet Dispute.* New York, 196

Kalb, Marvin L. *Dragon in the Kremlin: A Report on the Russia Chinese Alliance.* New York, 1961.

Karol, K. S. *Khrouchtchev et l'Occident.* Paris, 1960.

Khrushchev in New York: A Documentary Record . . . September 19 to October 13th, 1960. New York, 1960.

Kovner, Milton. *The Challenge of Coexistence: A Study of Soviet Ec nomic Diplomacy.* Washington, 1961.

Lash, Joseph P. *Dag Hammarskjold.* New York, 1961.

Leonhard, Wolfgang. *The Kremlin Since Stalin.* New York, 1962.

Lippmann, Walter. *The Communist World and Ours.* Boston, 1959.

London, Kurt (ed.). *Unity and Contradiction: Major Aspects of Sin Soviet Relations.* New York, 1962.

Mackintosh, J. M. *Strategy and Tactics of Soviet Foreign Policy.* Ne York, 1962.

Mander, John. *Berlin: Hostage of the West.* Baltimore, 1962.

Matthews, Herbert L. *The Cuban Story.* New York, 1961.

Meissner, Boris. *Russland unter Chruschtschow.* Munich, 1960.

Metaxas, Alexandre. *Moscow or Peking?* London, 1961.

Miller, Richard I. *Dag Hammarskjold and Crisis Diplomacy.* Ne York, 1961.

Neal, Fred Warner. *U.S. Foreign Policy and the Soviet Union.* San Barbara, Calif., 1961.

Noel-Baker, Philip. *The Arms Race.* New York, 1960.

Nutting, Anthony. *Disarmament: An Outline of Negotiations.* Londo 1959.

ɔunds, Norman J. G. *Divided Germany and Berlin*. Princeton, N.J., 1962.

:hlamm, William S. *Germany and the East-West Crisis*. New York, 1959.

:human, Frederick L. *The Cold War: Retrospect and Prospect*. Baton Rouge, La., 1962.

:hwartz, Harry (ed.). *Russia Enters the 1960's: A Documentary Report on the 22nd Congress of the Communist Party of the Soviet Union*. Philadelphia, 1962.

ɔeier, Hans. *Divided Berlin: The Anatomy of Soviet Political Blackmail*. New York, 1961.

:ulc, Tad, and Meyer, Karl E. *The Cuban Invasion*. New York, 1962.

ɪnham, George K. *Communist Revolutionary Warfare: The Vietminh in Indochina*. New York, 1961.

ʹarburg, James P. *Disarmament: The Challenge of the Nineteen Sixties*. Garden City, N.Y., 1961.

ʹise, David, and Ross, Thomas B. *The U-2 Affair*. New York, 1962.

ɪgoria, Donald S. *The Sino-Soviet Conflict, 1956–1961*. Princeton, N.J., 1962.

INDEX

Acheson, Dean, 339, 362, 363, 379, 398, 420, 431; germ warfare, 408
Adenauer, Konrad, 364, 410, 411, 449, 460; in the U.S., 418, 423; Malenkov, 424; in Moscow, 429; German unification, 432
Afghanistan, 107, 173, 195, 460
Afrika Korps, 270
Agrarian party (Bulgaria), 344
Alaska, 279
Albania, 204, 436; aid to Greece, 336; Yugoslavia, 355; USSR, 468–469
Alexander I, 15, 16, 284
Alexander II, 18
Alexander, King, 186
Alexandra, Empress, 23
Alexis, Tsar, 12
Alexis, son of Nicholas II, 23
Algeria, 273, 463
Allied Control Council, 293, 295, 298, 330, 331, 332, 333, 334, 336, 360, 363, 374, 375–76
Allied Council, 316
Allied Supreme Council, 77, 78
Allies, 32; mission to Russia, 33–34; Kornilov, 36; war aims, 37, 47; representatives, 40, 44, 53, 64; Trotsky, 41 51; intervention in Russia, 53, 55–61, 63, 65–66, 67–68, 77, 79–81; economic blockade, 63, 83
Alter, Victor, 276
American Relief Administration, 75, 81, 123
Amsterdam International, 131
Anarchists (Spain), 200, 201, 202
Anders, Wladyslaw, 275, 276
Anglo-Russian Trades-Union Unity Committee, 131, 132
Annam, 380, 381

Anti-Comintern Pact, 214, 235, 250; signed, 195
anti-Semitism, 413, 414, 416, 418
Antonov-Ovseyenko, Vladimir, 203
Arab League, 433, 456
Archangel, Intervention at, 61, 80, 81
Arcos raid, 133–34
Ardahan, 90, 91, 306, 421
Armed Forces of South Russia, 82
Armenia, 56
Armistice, 66, 67, 79
Astakhov, Georgi, 230, 231, 232
Atlantic Charter, 267
Atlantic Conference, 263, 264
Atomic bomb, 308, 398, 403
Atomic Energy Commission (U.N.), 404, 405, 406
Attlee, Clement, 305, 321, 398
Austerlitz, Battle of, 15
Australia, 315
Austria, 13, 21, 22, 24, 43, 59, 123; Tsarist Russia, 14, 15, 16, 17, 18, 19; *Anschluss*, 207–8, 227; zones, 301; election, 322
Austrian State Treaty, 335–36, 421, 430
Autumn Harvest Uprisings, 156
A.V.H. (Polish secret police), 441
Azerbaijan, 296, 324

Babarin, Eugene, 231
Badoglio, Pietro, 285, 371
Baghdad Pact, 427, 433–34, 445, 452
Balabanov, Angelica, 101
Baldwin, Stanley, 126, 133, 134, 134, 198, 207
Balfour, Arthur, 59
Balkan League, 21
Balkans: Tsarist policy in, 18, 21, 254; German occupation, 258; as Russian preserve, 281; Stalin-Churchill

DATE DUE

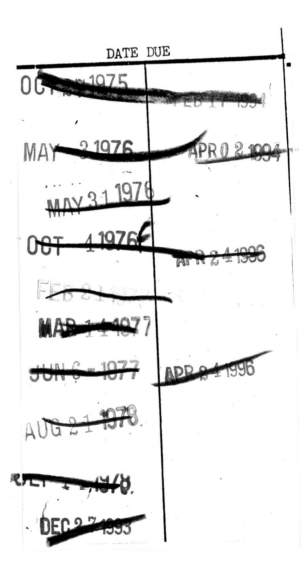

OCT   1975   FEB 17 1994

MAY   3 1976   APR 0 2 1994

MAY 31 1976

OCT   4 1976   APR 2 4 1996

FEB 2 1 1977

MAR 1 4 1977

JUN 6 1977   APR 2 4 1996

AUG 2 1 1978

OCT 1 2 1978

DEC 2 7 1993